J. P. Mahaffy

The Greek World Under Roman Sway

From Polybius to Plutarch

J. P. Mahaffy

The Greek World Under Roman Sway
From Polybius to Plutarch

ISBN/EAN: 9783337008901

Printed in Europe, USA, Canada, Australia, Japan

Cover: Foto ©ninafisch / pixelio.de

More available books at **www.hansebooks.com**

THE GREEK WORLD
UNDER ROMAN SWAY

FROM POLYBIUS TO PLUTARCH

BY

J. P. MAHAFFY

FELLOW, ETC. OF TRINITY COLLEGE, DUBLIN; HON. FELLOW OF
QUEEN'S COLLEGE, OXFORD; KNIGHT OF THE ORDER OF THE REDEEMER;
AUTHOR OF
'PROLEGOMENA TO ANCIENT HISTORY'; 'KANT'S PHILOSOPHY FOR ENGLISH READERS';
'SOCIAL LIFE IN GREECE'; 'RAMBLES AND STUDIES IN GREECE';
'GREEK LIFE AND THOUGHT';
'A HISTORY OF GREEK LITERATURE,' ETC.

London
MACMILLAN AND CO.
AND NEW YORK
1890

All rights reserved

ARTHURO JACOBO BALFOUR
QUEM NON
IMPROBI CONVICIIS
STULTI CONSILIIS
ADVERSARII INSIDIIS
AB INSTITUTIS, LITTERIS, LUDIS SUIS
DETURBARE POTUERUNT
D D D
AMICUS SCRIPTOR

PREFACE

THIS volume completes another stage in the social life and the civilisation of the Greeks, and pursues my subject from the subjugation of Hellenic lands by Rome down to the accession of Hadrian, when we may fairly say that Greece recovered her ascendancy. For from that day onward there was no distinction in honour between Greek and Latin ; in fact almost all our later histories of Roman affairs are in the Greek tongue. This then is one valid reason for halting about the year 120 A.D. Moreover the *Sophistical Revival* is set down by all the historians of later Greek literature as commencing with Hadrian, and with the state endowment of professional teaching which he systematised, though he did not originate it.

But more important than all these reasons for adopting my present limit is the fact that so far we may treat of Greek life without taking into account the new religion which presently invades all the Hellenistic world. Christianity had indeed been born, and was being preached; but on the great Greek teachers of the first century it leaves hardly a trace, and so far we may discuss Hellenism without it. From the days of Hadrian onward, such abstraction is impossible; and indeed, if I resume the subject in a subsequent volume, it will be my duty to begin by overlapping the present book, and tracing the obscure beginnings of the new faith which, though alive, is of no import in the society here described. This seems to me the most orderly, and therefore profitable way of unravelling the complicated phenomena of the first century.

In deference to serious and friendly critics of my *Greek Life and Thought* (which may be regarded as the forerunner of the present work), I have given many more references to authorities than was my previous custom. This change is not made from any desire to justify myself against those who accused me of not knowing the newer sources, because I did not parade them; but in addition to the advice of competent friends, it seemed to me that the evidence for the facts brought together in this volume was so scattered, so fragmentary, so dependent on inscriptions and on little known texts, that fuller references were due to the reader. He will find the abbreviations in my references fully explained in the Index. These materials have not been gathered or systematised by any previous historian; Hertzberg, for example, confines himself strictly to Greece proper under the Romans—a mere fraction of the history of later Hellenism, and Boissier, in his interesting book on Cicero and his friends, has never once considered the point of view taken in my Sixth Chapter on the same subject.

Indeed, since I wrote the opening of this Preface I have encountered a practical illustration of the difficulty there is in including all the evidence in such a history, and of the strong probability that the increased activity of antiquarians and travellers will furnish us constantly with new facts, or with corrections of our former deductions.

Mr. Flinders Petrie, in searching a small and insignificant necropolis at Kurob some six hours' ride from Medinet-el-Fayoum, found a number of mummies of the Ptolemaic epoch in cases of the usual appearance. They were all (he tells me) distinctly anterior in style to those of the Roman period. On examining these cases with care, he found that they were made of layers of papyrus glued together, in some cases only laid together, and varnished within and without. Perceiving that much of this papyrus showed traces of writing, he took several cases to pieces, and thus gathered a large quantity of fragments, covered with Greek and demotic writing: the Greek fragments he kindly sent to Mr. Sayce, with whom I examined them in August 1890. We have identified fragments of the *Phædo* of Plato, written in a beautiful hand, and not posterior to 250 B.C., also a considerable passage from the lost *Antiope* of Euripides, and a passage on the duties of the comrade (φιλέταιρος), by some rhetor earlier than Alexander's time. These texts, which we shall presently publish in *Hermathena*, and which I need not now discuss, show that even under the second Ptolemy Greeks had settled in the country parts of Egypt, and had with them such plenty of books that some of them were used as waste paper. A large number of letters, dated in the reigns of the second and third Ptolemies (284-224 B.C.), and written in good Greek, but in a very difficult cursive script, attest the same conclusion perhaps even more strongly. Lastly, there were used among the waste paper what seem to be the records of the Græco-Egyptian Probate Court at Crocodilopolis, the capital of the nome or district called Arsinoe—drafts of wills, with the date, the name and description of the testator, and the names and descriptions of the witnesses. In two of three cases the details of the bequests are to be made out, though in lacerated fragments. This series of documents, in good Greek, and written in all sorts of hands, presents us with formulæ constantly recurring, but still varied both in their place and even in their expression, so proving that they were not the work of lawyers composing them for ignorant people, but the dictation of educated men. Pending my publication of these texts, in the *Bulletin de Correspondance Hellénique* I cannot enter into further detail; but this I must say, that they modify considerably the estimate I had formed of the depth and breadth of Greek influences in Egypt. As the reader will see in the note to p. 202, I was already beginning to doubt the ancient view which confines Greek life (outside Alexandria) to Ptolemais and Arsinoe; now that view seems to me completely exploded. Indeed *Arsinoe*, which is commonly understood to mean a town, was used as the name of a district.

As I am writing these words there comes to me the just published exhaustive monograph of M. Th. Reinach on Mithridates, which I should have gladly used in discussing that king.

These sudden additions to our evidence and to the sifting of it are the delight and the despair of historians—the delight of those who are ready to abandon accepted views and popular prejudices, the despair of those who cling to them, who pretend to give a final judgment on things but partially known, regarding a correction as merely a demonstration that they were wrong, not as the means of escape from a cherished error, and an enlargement of our common knowledge. The present scholarship both of Germany and of England has been positively vitiated by the fashion among its Professors of taking criticism as an act of hostility, and pursuing the critic with such rancour, that no quiet man thinks it worth his while to set his neighbour right, or expose, however gently, a piece of literary imposture, at the cost of being annoyed and maligned for the rest of his life.

As I have now acknowledged my obligations to Mr. Petrie and his important discovery, so I trust I have nowhere omitted to acknowledge my conscious obligations to previous authors; it is impossible to do so adequately to those colleagues—Mr. Louis Purser and Mr. Bury—who have helped me with advice and correction all through the book. To appropriate the work of a colleague, or to utilise it with that scanty acknowledgment which amounts to deliberate reticence, is a form of vice not the less odious, because the culprit generally escapes with impunity.

My friend Mr. Sayce has also corrected the sheets, and has made many important suggestions.

OXFORD, *October* 1890.

CONTENTS

CHAP.		PAGE
I.	The Immediate Effects of the Roman Conquest upon Hellenism	1
II.	Hellenism in the Far East	18
III.	Hellenism in Syria and in Egypt	38
IV.	The Acclimatisation of Greek Philosophy in Roman Society	61
V.	The General Reaction of Hellenism upon Rome	80
VI.	The Hellenism of Cicero and his Friends	113
VII.	The Period of the Civil War—From Cicero to Augustus	151
VIII.	Ascetic Religion in the First Century	179
IX.	Western Hellenism under the Early Roman Emperors—Colonisation	189
X.	The Remaining Hellenism of Italy (chiefly Magna Græcia)	207
XI.	Eastern Hellenism under the Early Roman Empire	223
XII.	The Condition of Greece from Augustus to Vespasian—the Hellenism of the Early Emperors	249
XIII.	Plutarch and his Times—Public Life	291
XIV.	Plutarch and his Times—Private Life	323
XV.	Eastern Hellenism under the Flavian House	351
XVI.	The Literature of the First Century	369
Appendix		399
Index		407

CHAPTER I

INTRODUCTION

THE IMMEDIATE EFFECTS OF THE ROMAN CONQUEST
UPON HELLENISM

POLYBIUS and the thoughtful Greeks who talked with him after the fall of Carthage and of Corinth must have felt that they had lived to see one of the great turning-points in the world's history. There was now no longer any doubt that all the civilised nations hitherto at variance, in opposition, distracted by reason of contrasts in population, in government, in language, in traditions, would now be directed by the will of one people, by the influence of one system of law, by the predominance of a common language.

It was not the first time that this grand prospect had been held forth to the world. When Alexander was yet a young man, returning from his conquests in the far East, men must have anticipated, as very near, an empire not unlike that of Rome; for the conquest of the West would have been no difficult matter to Alexander, with all the resources of Asia under his hand. The successes of Pyrrhus, with his small army, against the adult Rome of the third century, fresh from her Samnite conquests, show what would have been the successes of Alexander, with his giant genius and armaments, against the younger and feebler Republic. And if the realisation of the conqueror's dreams was hindered by his early death, most of the early Diadochi had each for many hard-fought years aspired to be his sole successor, completing his work and regenerating the distracted world by the potent influence of Hellenistic culture.

A world-empire, including all the lands and nations about the Mediterranean Sea, reaching to the frozen North and the torrid South as its natural limits, exchanging the virgin ores of Spain for the long-sought spices of Araby the blest, was therefore no real novelty in imagination. But while those who had conceived it and striven for it consciously had failed, who could have imagined that it should drop almost suddenly, unexpectedly, by the force, not of genius, but of circumstances, into the hands of a people who attained it not by the direction of an Alexander or a Napoleon, or even by the successes of a Clive, but by those national qualities which had gained for Sparta precedence and respect, coupled with those aggressive wars under the guise of securing ever-widening frontiers which mark the rapid strides of Macedonia?

Any political thinker who witnessed this mighty outcome of half a century might indeed feel uneasy at the result, if he were not, like most of the Stoics, a religious fatalist. There was no doubt the manifest gain of a great peace throughout the world, of the real settlement of disputes by the arbitration of an umpire with power to enforce his will, of the consequent development of wide commerce over the world, with its diffusion not only of wealth but of enlightenment. These material gains were indisputable, even though a dangerous monopoly was being established not merely through the enormous advantages inseparable from Roman influence, but by the jealous destruction of all those commercial centres, which might have rivalled Rome by reason of favoured situation or old traditions of trade.

But far more serious was the patent fact, that neither the Roman people nor their rulers had received any education to fit them for an imperial policy. Administrative ability there was in plenty, just as there had been tactical knowledge to win battles without any strategy to plan campaigns. Higher education was confined to the 'Scipionic circle.' Hence it resulted that not only did the common people degenerate rapidly into a vulgar mob, pursuing solely its material pleasures, but the dominant classes, when vast opportunities of wealth and power were thrown into their hands, did not resist even for a generation the seductions of the world and the flesh, and became steeped in such luxury and vice as the Greeks had not reached in a decadence of centuries. Polybius and Diodorus[1] speak of these things in terms almost identical. They mention the rapid rise in the prices of luxuries at Rome, how a jar of wine came to cost 100 drachmæ, a jar of Euxine sardines 400, a good slave-cook 4 talents,[2] and worse ministrants to worse pleasures higher still. Both authors do not indeed omit to point out, that the great traditions of Roman dignity and virtue still survived. Diodorus quotes a number of instances of righteous Roman governors, and Polybius in an earlier generation speaks of the Scipios as the recognised models of civic excellence. But we feel that these good men were rare exceptions, and that the apparent peace of the Roman

[1] *Frag.* lib. xxxvi.
[2] Nearly £1000. Drachmæ may be counted as modern francs for convenience' sake, though slightly less in silver weight.

world was a delusive calm, to be interrupted, if not from without, at least by violent eruptions from within. For injustice and oppression have never yet failed to bring upon themselves their due rewards.

So it was that the completed conquest which Polybius saw,[1] and which appeared to be a final settlement of the world, brought no contentment into the hearts of men. For while the position of the few, of the dominant class at Rome, was magnified beyond their wildest expectations, the condition of the many was not only made worse, but even became wholly intolerable. This is the key to those disturbances in the Roman world, which could not indeed shake off the yoke, but which showed the internal sores with which the mighty commonwealth was affected.

The first symptom was the slave war which broke out in Sicily very few years after the so-called pacification of the world by the ruin of Carthage and of Corinth in 146 B.C. I have endeavoured in a special monograph to explain the causes and character of this outbreak,[2] and will therefore content myself with here giving the results.

It was always remarked, whenever an invasion discloses to us the condition of the territory of Carthage, that nothing was more wonderful than the fertility of the farms and homesteads in that favoured land. Its natural gifts were so enhanced by intelligent cultivation that the Italians at once saw and confessed their inferiority, and upon the fall of Carthage we hear that the Senate, probably after some delay, ordered the translation of the received handbook on agri-

---

[1] I have given his evidence in detail in the last chapter of my *Greek Life and Thought*, which brings the subject up to the period treated in this book.
[2] In *Hermathena* for 1890.

culture long current in that state, which referred all the wisdom and experience of centuries to the authorship of the ancient Mago, the reputed founder of Punic greatness, not only in the arts of war, but also in those of peace.[1] Of this treatise we possess only stray quotations, in Varro's handbook and elsewhere,[2] mostly on the management of cattle and the farmyard, though we know from Cicero that it was a very voluminous work, as indeed is proved by the publication of two separate compendiums in later days. But there is one sentence, with which the book opened, that shows how far different was the spirit of the Punic farmer from his Roman imitator, and how useless the attempt to graft the African figs, which excited Cato's envy, upon the Italian thistles. 'A man who wants to farm,' said Mago, 'has no business with a town house. If he has one, let him sell it; if he be more attached to town life, what does he want with a country seat.'[3] What advice to give to a Roman patrician, even such as Cato, with his thrifty husbandry! To abandon Rome was to abandon the world, and to retire into the disgrace and the oblivion of exile.

A further attempt was made, apparently in connection with the colonising efforts of Caius Gracchus, to instruct

---

[1] See the personality of this Mago discussed in *Hermathena*, No. xvi. Our evidence for this act of the Senate is Pliny, *H. N.* xviii. 5, the opening chapters of Columella and Varro (*de Re Rustica*, i. 1, 10), whom I will quote: 'All the [Greek] writers hitherto cited are surpassed in reputation by Mago the Carthaginian, who wrote in Punic, and embraced the scattered subjects of agriculture in twenty-eight books [translated into Latin, adds Pliny, by D. Silanus, and others skilled in Punic], which Cassius Dionysius of Utica translated in twenty books, and sent to the praetor Sextius, in which he inserted many things from Greek authors, and omitted eight books of Mago. Diophanes of Bithynia contracted these twenty into six, and dedicated them to king Dejotarus.'

[2] I have transcribed the list of fragments, *op. cit.* p. 30.

[3] Columella, i. 1, 18.

the more cultivated settlers—for Gracchus did not send out the mere refuse of the people—by a Greek compendium, which contracted the twenty-eight books of the original into twenty.[1] The third version, in still briefer form, was made for the use of that king Dejotarus whom Cicero mentions[2] as a most diligent farmer and grower of cattle, and shows that even in the long-civilised Asia Minor the Punic prescriptions were valued.

But quite apart from this fruitless theoretical measure to reform and improve the farming of the ever-increasing Roman domains was the practical imitation of the Punic habit of growing great tracts of wheat with the aid of slave labour. In the climate of North Africa nothing paid a higher interest; but in the absence of all modern machinery the cultivation of wheat required many hands, and, therefore, capital with a command of many slaves. This was the enterprise which the Romans sought to transfer to Sicily, where the land and climate permitted some hope of rivalling the waving crops of Africa. The capture of Carthage, like all such conquests in ancient days, threw an enormous number of slaves into the market, or rather there was an immense market of them immediately after the storming of the place. Not only all the slaves of the Carthaginians but the masters themselves were bought in gangs by Roman and Sicilian speculators, and carried off to till the plains of Sicily. Thus the great slave population of Carthage, mostly kidnapped or captured in eastern lands, and speaking the Greek tongue, was transferred to new masters, another soil, perhaps harsher conditions, and with no hope of liberty.

This was the vast multitude which revolted about the

---

[1] See the arguments for this theory in my article, *op. cit.* p. 164.
[2] *Pro rege Deiot.* § 27—*diligentissimus agricola et pecuarius.*

year 140 B.C., assumed the style and title of a Syrian state, made one of their number, who professed miraculous prophetic powers, their king, and met the Roman power in the open field.[1] If they had been assisted by the pirates, who began to infest all the seas in consequence of the Roman conquest, the result would have been very serious. But, as I have elsewhere shown, the pirates were themselves great slave dealers, and were the last people to spoil their own trade by playing the Romans false in this particular.[2] What is specially to be noted about the insurrection is its Hellenistic character. The majority of these people had been subjects of the Seleucids, and this was the type of society and of government which they naturally endeavoured to set up. The state assumed by the insurgent king was a Hellenistic state. He had his peers and his household, his jester and his cook, his baker and his shampooer.[3]

Though the second slave war came a generation later (103-99 B.C.), it may be well to treat it in connection with the first, so far as it serves to illustrate how the Greek elements are now being absorbed into the Roman world. After the struggle with Jugurtha had shown how corrupt the Roman oligarchy had already become, there supervened the desperate crisis of the

---

[1] Our authority for these disturbances is the thirty-fourth book of Diodorus, preserved in copious excerpts by Photius. The first leader was Eunus, a Syrian of Apamea, whose wife was of the same city. He took the royal name of Antiochus, called his wife *queen*, and his followers Syrians. The other prominent leaders were Achæus (called by Diodorus an Achæan, but perhaps taking his name from Achæus's royal house in Asia Minor) and Cleon, a Cilician. Cf. the details in *Hermathena*, xvi. 169.

[2] *Hermathena*, xvi. 178.

[3] Diod. *frag.* xxxiv. *sub. fin.*—ἐξειλκύσθη ἅμα τεττάρων, μαγείρου καὶ ἀρτοποιοῦ καὶ τοῦ τρίβοντος αὐτὸν ἐν τῷ λουτρῷ καὶ τετάρτου τοῦ παρὰ τοὺς πότους εἰωθότος ψυχαγωγεῖν αὐτόν. It is curious that Diodorus does not give the official titles; or is it Photius that paraphrases them?

Cimbric invasion. When several hosts had been swallowed up by the flood of the advancing hordes, just as the splendid army of Bajazet disappeared before the wave of the Tartars, the Senate sent to ask for auxiliaries from the Hellenistic kings in alliance, as it was called, with Rome. Nicomedes of Bithynia replied that he had no men left to send, seeing that the body of his population had been sold into slavery to satisfy the extortions of the Roman tax-gatherers.[1] The reply was probably exaggerated, since it was so admirable an opportunity of making a protest against the terrible oppression of the *publicani;* but it awoke the Senate to the injustice and the danger of such a policy, and they set about correcting it by a new and still more obvious blunder. An order was issued forbidding any free citizen of an allied state to be kept in bondage for such debts; and this order, which seems to have been issued for Sicily, the province whither all these eastern slaves were, as a matter of course, drafted, was the occasion of the outbreak.

Crowds of slaves had come in and claimed their liberty, so much so that the terrified owners hurried to the Roman prætor, and persuaded him to suspend the order. No doubt the danger was great; it was not likely that these long-oppressed and degraded strangers would make any good use of their liberty. But the mischief was done. Finding their one hope of liberty at the hands of the Roman Senate baulked, these unfortunate creatures were driven by fury and despair into another dreadful insurrection. There were of course many horrors—awful revenge taken upon cruel masters in their isolated villas, wholesale crucifixions of prisoners as criminals, and, after a hard struggle, a riveting of the old bonds upon the

---

[1] The history of this affair and of the second slave war is in the excerpts from Diodorus, lib. xxxvi., by Photius.

wretched remnant left from the ravages of fire and sword.

In this war too, we find that the names of the leaders[1] point to Hellenistic origin, and that the body of the slaves were of that kind, though it is to be noted that the style assumed by the leader Tryphon is not Syrian but Roman, and that he has a senate and lictors instead of peers and a royal household.[2] But the use of miracle and prophecy is there; there is a strange expectation of some coming Saviour, who shall redeem the poor and the afflicted from their tormentors; there is a combination of the free poor with the slaves, all of which symptoms indicate a widespread feeling that injustice and oppression had attained such a height that the world's Providence must bring some relief. And this, as I pointed out, is the common feature of the second slave war with the war of Aristonicus, the illegitimate representative of the Attalids, who called his nation to arms when a will, suborned or extorted, of Attalus III, left Pergamum to the Roman people. The coast cities and the dynasts opposed him vigorously; the slaves and the poor people in the interior supported him, and he dreamed of founding a new City of the Sun, in which his Heliopolitans would escape the oppressions of the new and terrible masters of the Hellenistic world.[3]

There were other outbreaks in Italy, but neither important nor, so far as we know, Hellenistic in character. The shepherds and neatherds of the Italian pastures were sparse and rude, unable to plan or carry out a dangerous revolt. The only droves of slaves who could thus combine

---

[1] At least of Athenio. But the other, Salvius, assumed a Syrian royal name, Tryphon. Cf. *Hermathena*, xvi. 175.

[2] This appears from Diodorus, xxxvi. 535.

[3] Cf. the details in my article, *op. cit.* p. 181 *sq.*

did in due course of time combine, and produce a desperate war. They were the gladiators under Spartacus. But though joined by a good many shepherds, their numbers were never very great; they won battles by the high training of their bloody profession, and it is clear that this class was least of all recruited among the Greek-speaking population, which had neither the muscle nor the physical courage of the Thracian or the Spanish mountaineers.[1]

These wild and hopeless contests are, however, the earliest protests against the Republican conquest of the world, and indicate that here lie the forces which will overthrow it. They are, moreover, protests of the gentler, more cultivated Hellenic spirit against the iron despotism which treats enslaved men, without regard to their original rank or education, as mere beasts of burden. There were, no doubt, dark spots on the humanity of Hellenism in this respect. The slaves in the silver mines of Laurium, in the quarries on the islands, or in the gold mines of the Ptolemies in Nubia, were treated as horribly as ever human beings were treated, and were selected, we may hope, from the criminal classes. The Egyptian tradition had certainly been to make this work a direct penal servitude, and so we find it in Pliny's letters to Trajan.[2] But still there was something hard,

---

[1] The same causes which produced these wars also produced the prevalence of highway robbery in the wilds of Italy and Greece, and still more the extraordinary prevalence of piracy, upon which we shall have much to say in the succeeding chapters.

[2] The mines alluded to by Pliny were probably those in Pontus, for Strabo describes the mountain Sandaracurgion near Pompeiopolis in Pontus thus (xii. 3, § 40): 'The mountain is hollowed out with mining, the workmen entering it by great shafts: it is managed by *publicani*, who use as workmen slaves sold by reason of their crimes: for in addition to the hard labour the air is said to be deadly and unbearable on account of the odour of the soil, so that nobody lasts long there. And indeed this mining has often been intermitted because it does not pay, there

relentless, cruel, in Roman ways, which must always have filled Greek servants and subjects with horror and dismay. Not only what was done, but the way in which it was done, was harsh and cold, and so I imagine the Romans to have held the place in European disfavour which the middle class Englishman now holds, who knows no foreign tongue, respects no foreign habit, recognises no foreign virtue, but walks through the world assuming the English respectability, just as the Roman assumed his *gravitas*, to be the stamp of a superior race.

Hellenism, under the immediate grip of Rome, in Sicily, in Pergamum, found at once that anything was better than submission—hence the slave wars and the war of Aristonicus. The states in looser dependence were not so unfortunate, and were able to tolerate their servitude somewhat longer; yet even they, when they found a leader, as in Mithradates, or an escape into the high seas, took up arms eagerly against their new masters. Such then was the miserable state of Hellenism, from which a gradual reaction, together with the dissensions of the Romans, only produced a slow and partial recovery.

A little more than a century elapsed from the destruction of Corinth to the establishment of the Empire. There is probably no epoch of ancient history for which we have more ample and curious materials; yet they are all concerned with the Roman side of the world, and only mention

---

being more than 200 workmen required, who are constantly consumed by disease and death.'

The Nubian gold mines will recur again in connection with the evidence of Agatharchides.

No doubt all these were old-established tortures, used by Pontic dynasts, and Athenian speculators, and Egyptian kings for their selfish ends, making light of human life and suffering, as slave owners only will dare to do.

Greeks and Asiatics in relation to their conquerors. Agitated also and eventful as these years were, we cannot say that any great new principle of government was discovered, or any but material advantages gained for the world. It was perfectly manifest 140 years before Christ that the Romans would remain masters of the Mediterranean countries, so far as force could keep them so. The only chance of escape from their sway must arise from their internal dissension, and it very soon appeared that no internal dissension was likely to produce a separation of the Roman power into parts or provinces. In fact, Rome was so distinctly the capital, that no insurgent thought himself of any account till he made good his claims there. No life was thought worth living by Roman magnates except that at Rome. I suppose that the Latin and Samnite subjects, had they conquered in the great social war at the opening of the first century B.C., would simply have demanded their share, greater or less, in the spoils of the rest of the world, and continued the same kind of empire which the Romans had established at their cost, and with their blood.

To escape then from the military power of Italy seemed hopeless, even when her soldiers became debauched and her generals corrupt.

But the internal dissensions which began to rend the great commonwealth must have given intelligent Greeks an early prospect that the abominable oligarchy which ravaged the provinces in the guise of governors and commanders must soon be overthrown. It was impossible that such plundering should continue with impunity from the gods, or at least from those Romans who felt excluded from the privilege. And whenever a very lucrative privilege can be assailed on the score of justice and mercy, it will very soon be abolished by those who can combine the zeal of private interest with the dignity of sound arguments. Any wise political philosopher might have foretold that the oligarchy would fall at the hands of the masses. He might also have known, both from reading Aristotle and from observing the mob of Rome, that this new democracy must inevitably fall into the net of despotism. The first leader who could combine military genius with political insight was sure to command the situation.

A very strange phenomenon delayed for a generation the fulfilment of this inevitable cycle in the life of ancient —perhaps of all—states. The first man who overthrew all his foes and made himself master of Rome was an aristocrat and an oligarch, Sylla. He undertook to restore the old domination of the Senate, and turn back the course of history one hundred years. He massacred or outlawed all his opponents; no scruples restrained him; he was one of those rare examples in history of an unselfish despot, who swept away his enemies for a principle, and who restored the old order of things in the interest of the aristocracy rather than his own. When his work was done he even resigned, and was able to contemplate the establishment of all his political ideas.

It is one of the most instructive lessons in all history that this restored aristocracy, this realisation of the wildest of Tory dreams, fell to pieces in a few years, in spite of all its author's safeguards and protections, in spite of the massacre of all his adversaries, in spite also of the fact that no great genius started up at once to destroy it. The Syllan constitution fell to pieces of itself, because it contradicted the spirit of the times, and when the natural overthrower of the republic—the Liberal politician, Cæsar— came into the arena, it was practically gone, though it had been established but twenty years.

It was only with the advent of an intelligent despot that the Greek-speaking provinces might fairly anticipate some relief from the systematic rapacity and injustice of the nobles, whom he would subdue and keep in check.

The political side of this period of Hellenism (up to the establishment of Cæsar) must therefore have been unutterably sad and dreary. The only alternative the subject states saw before them was whether a Licinius or a Cornelius was to plunder them, not to speak of the occasions when a civil war among the possessors of the world imposed upon the wretched provinces requisitions from both sides. Thus the Hellenic peninsula was made the theatre of three vast and devastating conflicts, two of which were civil wars among Romans, in which Greece had no concern.

Far more interesting to the historian than the actual provinces, with their uniformity of management under Roman prætors, and their small contrasts of so-called free cities and actual subjects, are the outlying fragments of Hellenism which had not yet fallen under Rome at the close of the century before us, and were only gradually absorbed by the conquests of Lucullus and Pompey, or by the rise of the Parthian power. I say fragments of Hellenism, because not only were the Hellenistic empires either shattered or decayed, but there had been growing for some time a distinct reaction of oriental or separate nationalities against the adventitious culture imported by the conquests of Alexander. The enormous area then to be civilised, and the indelible type of old Greek culture, made it necessary that the *form* of spreading Hellenism should be by planting cities (strictly speaking city-polities) in the midst of the foreign populations, cities more or less densely or sparsely sown over a large area, but always separate *loci* of Greek culture, surrounded by a rural population excluded from the city privileges, or at least possessing none of their own.[1] In Syria, for example, these cities were very numerous, in Egypt very few, and so in India and the far East. But everywhere beyond the immediate coasts of the Ægean they were marked by their language, which remained foreign to the country people, and which, though learned by vast numbers of Semites, never became the native tongue or vernacular of any tract of country not long since peopled by Hellenes. Subsequently, the Arab conquest of the East, like the Roman of the West, imposed not only its culture but its language upon the vanquished; it is plain, then, that Hellenism did not lay the same hold upon the nations which it subdued and occupied.

One reason of this difference was undoubtedly the isolation of Hellenistic towns by special privileges, which their country neighbours could not freely obtain; another may have been the generic difference between Greek and Semitic languages, while both Romans and Arabs imposed their speech mainly upon cognate tongues. Still the Arabs did far more than that. But both these races of conquerors had more time than the Greeks to produce their full effects upon the world. Hellenism as a dominant power

---

[1] The country people lived κωμηδόν in contrast to the city, which was technically called πόλις οἰκουμένη, a *constituted city*, *e.g.* by Xenophon (*Anabasis*, i. 2) several times, and Strabo says (iii. 4, § 13), ἄγριοι γὰρ οἱ κατὰ κώμας οἰκοῦντες. To reduce the population to village life was to destroy the city, ἀνάστατον ποιεῖν τὴν πόλιν, or ἀοίκητον, which does not imply the massacre of the population any more than the Roman *capitis diminutio* implies execution. It is characteristic of this form of civilisation that Cicero tells us the distinctive inferiority and barbarism of Sardinia was shown by its not possessing a single *free city* (*pro Scauro*, § 44), for this is what he means by *amica pop. Rom. et libera civitas.*

did not last more than two centuries. Would the Romans or Arabs have imposed their languages permanently in that space of time? It is more than doubtful. How soon, for example, Britain lost her acquired Latin when other conquerors intervened?

According, therefore, as the eastern nationalities became stronger, the Hellenistic towns became more and more isolated, more and more foreign, settled in a strange country, and most of them would have gradually reverted to, or been absorbed by, their non-Hellenic surroundings, had not the Romans maintained them everywhere as Greek cities in their settlement of the East. Thus arose a new phase, which I may call *Roman Hellenism*, and which, like the Corinthian order so universally adopted by Roman builders, produced some splendid results. But this Roman Hellenism is not yet before us. What we have to consider is the decaying life of the cities of the Diadochi founded all over the empire of Alexander.

For the close of the second century B.C. is marked in the East by a strong and widespread reaction of national feeling against Hellenistic domination. It is shown clearest in the breaking away of whole provinces under national leaders, who brought back the national religion and language as symbols of their patriotism, in Parthia and India; it is shown also in the gradual estrangement of the provinces left under indigenous princes, such as Cappadocia and Armenia; in the growing importance of Arab chiefs, such as Aretas and Sampsiceramus: it is further shown by the many obstinate insurrections in Egypt, the revival of old Egyptian cults, the disappearance of Greeks from court, and the substitution of Jews as the advisers of the Ptolemies; we may perhaps see an echo of this great oriental reaction in the *character* of the slave wars just described—I mean the prominence of Syrian wonder-working and Syrian religion even in the Greek-speaking slave population of Sicily.¹ This is the great field over which we must range to find the action and reaction of the Greek spirit upon the other nationalities of the ancient world.

¹ Cf. on these points B. Stark's *Gaza*, p. 480.

CHAPTER II

HELLENISM IN THE FAR EAST

PERHAPS the period after the collapse of Hellenism, as a political system, under the rising power of Rome, is the most favourable for considering the remote and obscure provinces of its influence. While Greece and Macedonia were reduced to the absolute silence resulting from a sanguinary military conquest and a reorganisation as Roman provinces—while the kingdoms of the nearer East were lapsing into the anarchy of disputed successions or the decay of an effete culture—there were still able and ambitious rulers holding aloft the torch of Hellenistic civilisation in the far East, and extending their influence far beyond the limits attained even by Alexander the Great.

We know that the first Seleucus attempted to penetrate beyond the Indus, but during the confusion of the wars which followed the death of Alexander, his loyal satrap, the Indian Porus, had been murdered by the Macedonian Eudemus, and then a revolt of the Indian natives had brought to the surface an able adventurer, Chandragupta (in Greek Sandracottus), who not only conquered all the Indian province of Alexander, but even extended his sway to the valley of the Ganges, and founded the greatest empire which had yet been known beyond the Indus. It was with this king that Seleucus waged war, as soon as he had established himself firmly in the possession of the Syrian and Persian provinces. We do not know whether Seleucus found his adversary too strong to attack, or whether he was actually defeated in battle, or whether (what I think most likely) he found the complications of the West, and the threatening power of Antigonus and his son Demetrius, so urgent a danger, that he was ready to conclude his Indian campaign upon easy terms. Certain it is, that he not only made peace and a marriage alliance with Sandracottus, but ceded to him the lands immediately west of the Indus, so making the Hindukush and the great Persian desert the new boundaries which separated the Hellenistic world from the farther East. But Sandracottus, on the other hand, seems to have paid him for the provinces not only with treasure but with those 500 elephants which turned the scale at Ipsus,[1] and made Seleucus master of the world.

Sandracottus's friendly relations, moreover, with Seleucus were maintained, and so it was that a Greek envoy, Megasthenes, was sent to the Indian court at Palimbothra, the Indian Pataliputra, a great city on the Ganges near the site of the present Patna, but all swept away in the course of centuries by the changing floods of the great river. It was from the work composed by Megasthenes, his *Indica*, that the Hellenistic world first obtained a distinct account of the wealth and wonders of this land of fable. Not that Megasthenes, any more than Marco Polo or Sir John Mandeville, escaped the snare of credulousness as to monstrous animals and strange phenomena. But in spite of this the large extracts quoted in Strabo's geography, which are worked together into an able sketch in Lassen's

[1] Cf. *Greek Life and Thought*, p. 37.

great work,[1] show us that the *Indica* were genuine studies, which are corroborated by our other evidences of old Indian life and habits, and that we have lost in them an inestimable source of information.

Sandracottus, after a prosperous reign of some twenty-five years, bequeathed his great kingdom to his son Vindusara, known to the Greeks by one of his titles as Amitrochates. We hear that this king also kept up friendly relations with the West, and that the second Ptolemy sent an ambassador called Dionysius to his court, probably to promote trade relations from the Indus by coasting to the Red Sea. The next king, Vindusara's youngest son—known to us commonly as Açoka—though he came to the throne by the oriental method of murdering his brethren, and began life with cruelty and violence, not only extended his kingdom to the mouth of the Ganges as well as of the Indus, and over a large part of the Deccan, but, owing to his conversion to Buddhism and his great missionary efforts, introduced the most splendid epoch in all Indian history. The monuments and inscriptions which still survive from his long and brilliant reign exceed in interest anything else in the archæology of the country.

Before we proceed to question these remains for the traces they show of Hellenistic influence, we must revert to the history of those eastern provinces which were still claimed by the Syrian kings. The reign of the second Antiochus (Theos), whose accession (261 B.C) followed shortly upon that of Açoka, marks the moment when these outlying provinces began to revolt and assert their independence. The great satrapy of Bactria led the way, together with Sogdiana, which Alexander had found so difficult to subdue, and where he had established many

---

[1] *Indische Alterthumskunde*, vol. ii.

Greek cities as outposts for protection and for trade. Diodotus, the satrap of that country, declared himself an independent sovran.

The reader must not take his notions of Bactria from modern maps, which represent Balkh and Samarcand as lying on the border of the steppes, a land of sand and of barrenness, only fit for nomad shepherds. Bactria was, and indeed still is, a province of great natural wealth, once fertile in all the produce, except olives, valued by civilised men—cattle, corn, and wine, and, moreover, the natural centre-point in which the caravans from China and from India met on their way by the Caspian and Caucasus into Europe. When Darius was defeated, it was the satrap of this province, then Spitamenes of Sogdiana, who took the lead, and the country possessed a wealthy aristocracy dwelling in strong castles, and going out to war with their retainers—an aristocracy proud enough to furnish a suitable queen to the great conqueror himself. Here then, somewhere about 250 B.C., Diodotus established himself as king of Bactria. His example was followed by the satrap of Areia, the next province to the south, and indeed by other satraps, whose exact dominions within Bactria, Sogdiana, and Areia we cannot distinguish.

It seems quite certain that the great synod of Buddhists which Açoka held in the thirteenth year of his reign, and in which the doctrines of the faith were revived and purified, took place before the revolt of these provinces from Antiochus Theos. For Açoka mentions in the inscriptions which he ordered to be inscribed in stone, and set up all through his kingdom in both full and abbreviated texts, that he sent out his missionaries with cures of herbs for men and beasts as far as Antiyaka (Antiochus II), Turamaya (Ptolemy II), Maga (of Cyrene), and Alissandra (of Epirus), and that they also listened favourably to the preaching of the Buddhist gospel.[1] He therefore had friendly relations so far with the kings of the West, though it is highly improbable that his envoys reached Cyrene and Epirus—nay, even that the two kings mentioned, who died about 258 B.C., were alive at the time of his mission, which took place about that very year. If, therefore, Diodotus had been established as king at Bactria, it seems certain that Açoka would have mentioned him, seeing that he enumerates all the neighbouring states and nations as having received his missionaries.

Nevertheless this great and brilliant reign of Açoka, and the extraordinary spread of the Buddhist religion, did more than anything else to stop the eastward progress of Hellenism. Though Açoka boasts that in accordance with his faith he was tolerant of all other creeds, and only sought the moral and spiritual regeneration of mankind, it is quite certain that the dogma, the miracles, the monasticism, the relic-worship, the abnegation of the new gospel, were not only quite strange to Hellenistic feeling, but established a strong national Indian feeling, which could resist all encroachment of foreign fashions. This, I think, accounts for the fact that though all the extant remains of antiquity in North-Western India begin with Açoka,—there is nothing earlier known,—and though we have from his day various monuments, there is no trace of Hellenistic influence at that date.

The rise of Diodotus in Bactria was followed by the revolt of Arsaces in Parthia (to the west of Bactria), and the establishment of that kingdom, afterwards so famous, as a

[1] He was commonly supposed to have asserted their conversion, but the recent careful analysis of Senart—in the *Journal asiatique* for 1885, p. 290 *sq*.—tends to show that the king speaks positively only of his remedies being accepted, and quite generally of the courteous receptions of his religion, without asserting any further consequences.

distinct protest of the native population against the Macedonian sway. The Arsacids were for a long time weaker than their Bactrian neighbours. The Parthian was only able to withstand Seleucus Callinicus, but fled away when Antiochus the Great made his victorious campaign into the East.[1] The Bactrian house of Diodotus had been already displaced by another line, but the opponent whom Antiochus found there, with whom he made peace and a treaty, was Euthydemus, whose kingdom seems to have spread from Areia northward into Bactria. Presently the Parthians grew stronger and seized most of Bactria, so making a great barrier between the eastern and western Hellenism of Asia. But the new Greek kingdom extended itself to the South and East. After the death of Açoka and his son their great kingdom began to decay, and Strabo tells us that the Indo-Greek king Menander owned 1000 cities in India. 'So popular,' says Plutarch (*reip. ger. præc.* 28), 'was this king, that when during a campaign he died in his camp his obsequies were celebrated by all his cities in common, and there ensued a quarrel for the possession of his remains, which they with difficulty settled by dividing his ashes, of which each carrying home its share set up in every city a monument to the king.' This reminds us of the contest over the remains of Alexander, which Ptolemy secured for Egypt.[2] We know too of a Eucrates, who in truly Hellenistic fashion founded a new capital, Eucratideia. This Græco-Indian kingdom, which lasted through the second century B.C., was the kingdom which seems to have influenced India far more than the earlier Græco-Bactrian monarchy. The existence of both, asserted by Strabo and Justin, has of recent years been further established by the discovery of a vast number of

[1] *Greek Life and Thought*, p. 398.   [2] *Ibid.* p. 197.

coins, purely Greek in the case of Diodotus, Euthydemus, and the earlier sovrans, and of the best workmanship, then gradually debased in artistic value, adopting Indian script beside the Greek, and finally lapsing back again into purely oriental work.

These coins have excited the liveliest interest, and able numismatists have sought to reconstitute the proper series and the relations of the many kings—at least twelve are known —from the workmanship and the titles on these medals. I am loth to say one word against these acute and patient inquirers, who have certainly taught us a great deal; but still I cannot accept many of their hypotheses, which seem to me wanting in a sound perception of the nature of evidence. Thus when Lassen argues, as he often does, that a certain king must have reigned a short time, because his now extant coins are very few, he surely argues from what may be the mere accident of non-discovery as if it were a positive fact. It seems to me also that the beautiful coinage of these kings has been too readily taken as evidence of general Hellenistic culture in their dominions.[1] It *may* have been an almost isolated Hellenistic feature. We know that the Arsacids for a long time to come had their coinage struck by the Greek cities which they tolerated as Hellenistic islands in their thoroughly oriental constitution. Seleucia on the Tigris, for example, which entitles one of them Philhellene on account of his favours, was no specimen of the rest of Parthia, nor could these kings have laid claim to much else than their coinage as a proof that they were influenced by Alexander's conquests.

Had we no further evidence than coins, the case of Euthydemus and Eucrates might not be much stronger.

[1] The history of these Greeks and the Arsacid reaction will be found in Strabo, xi. 9.

But the summary of Strabo from Apollodorus of Artemita, in addition to the collections of coins just mentioned, and the distinct traces of Hellenistic influence in architectural remains throughout the Punjab, make the existence of a Græco-Indian culture indisputable.

According to the English antiquarians, who have spent years in studying these remains, Alexander's conquest produced a perfect revolution in Indian architecture, for till that day the people on the Indus and the Ganges had not known the use of stone in building! This theory seems to me to have been established on the authority of the architect Fergusson, who maintained it not only in his general History but in a special work on Indian building. It is the sudden appearance of stone pillars carved with Açoka's inscriptions in many parts of India, together with the total absence of any earlier dated building or carving in stone, which has determined Fergusson and his school. On the other hand, Rajendralala Mitra,[1] in contesting this view, has asserted the far greater antiquity of some of the cave-dwellings, in which the natural features are much modified both by cutting and by ornament, and has urged the great improbability that any old and advanced culture, such as that of India, should exist without this obvious discovery.

The author also extracts from early Indian books, such as the Mâhabhârata, allusions to stone-building and sculpture. But whether this epic is indeed from the sixth century B.C., and not posterior to Açoka, is a matter of dispute. It is, indeed, true that the early stone-buildings found and described by Fergusson showed clear imitations of wooden structure, such as we might expect from the earliest attempts in stone; but Rajendralala shows that quite recent buildings in Mohammedan times, even down to our fifteenth and

[1] In his work on the antiquities of Orissa.

sixteenth centuries, show the same close imitation of woodwork, so that this feature is no proof, in India, of the novelty of the art.

Let me add that the argument from the absence of evidence is very weak when applied to a far-gone time, for we can show astonishing gaps of tradition in even recent centuries; and there are nations who consider the destruction of earlier work not only natural, but even a proper assertion of a new faith and a new civilisation. The spreading of Buddhism by Açoka, the grandson of the Sandracottus (Chandragupta) whom Megasthenes visited, was no doubt a great epoch in Indian history, and the multiplication of his stone records quite a novelty; but to postulate that this ready and apparently familiar use of a very hard material was a foreign importation seems hardly reasonable.

The advocates on either side seem not to have thought of examining the evidence of Megasthenes, where both might have found curious support. For in the first place his statement that the walls of Palimbothra were made of wood, with apertures for shooting at the enemy,[1] seems to imply that stone walls were not used. But the valley of the Ganges about Patna is very devoid of stone, and it is quite possible that the floods of the river, which seem to have carried away every trace of this ancient capital, made it desirable to have some light and pervious or even removable fortification.

On the other hand Megasthenes notes[2] the *philotechnia* or mechanical talent of the race in imitating what they found novel among the invading Macedonians—how they manufactured imitation sponges, and adopted the strigil and oil-flask of the Greeks. Is it likely that when mentioning such

---
[1] ξύλινον περίβολον ἔχουσαν. Meg. in Strabo, xv. 1, § 36.
[2] Strabo, xv. 1, § 67.

facts he would have omitted noticing the adoption of so all-important a novelty as the use of stone-building? I can hardly think so, and, though unable to bring any further light to bear upon the question, incline to agree with the patriotic view of the Indian scholar, who naturally desires to ascribe to his country the most complete early civilisation.

If, however, there was, as Cunningham asserts, a sudden development of stone architecture about the middle of the third century B.C., which degenerated rapidly in about 300 years into oriental barbarism, what are the evidences of this decadence? It is likely enough that many designs are set down as Hellenistic which are really indigenous in conception. Thus there are festive scenes set down as Dionysiac which need have no other origin than the delight in revelry and its connection with religion which we find in many diverse races.[1] Thus again when we are told[2] that the figures of Surya (the sun) with four horses point to a Greek original, I should like to see it proven that the Indians never drove four horses abreast, and could not have originated that design.[3] The Tritons and spearmen to be seen on Açoka's railings at Buddha Gaya are interpreted by Cunningham in the same way,[4] but I will allow only this much to his argument, that a multiplication of these analogies gradually produces the conviction of their value as evidence.

Far more definite, however, than argument from sculptural

---

[1] Cf. on this point F. S. Growse, in *Journal of Asiatic Soc. of Bengal* for 1875, p. 213.
[2] Cunningham's *Archæological Survey*, iii. 97.
[3] He quotes the Vedas to show that seven was the Indian number of these horses. But when carving in stone the artists may have been content to give four, as the representation of seven would offer great technical difficulties as well as difficulties of design.
[4] *Op. cit.* p. 100.

types are the lessons to be learned from the use of Greek forms in the bases and capitals of pillars. Unfortunately the extant specimens are not very early; they belong not to the first days of Hellenism, but to the epoch treated in the present volume, their dates ranging from about 40 B.C. to 100 A.D—that is to say, after the splendours of Menander and Eucrates were gone by, and the national reaction was reducing everything to its oriental level. We have, however, specimens of Greek capitals during this epoch, which Cunningham classifies[1] as Indo-Doric (in Kashmir); Indo-Ionic (at Taxila); Indo-Corinthian (in the Kabul valley). Of these the first is represented by some specimens so late and so barbarous as to have little weight in the discussion. The very simple form of the Doric pillar and capital is easily developed from the mere practical conditions of making a stone support, and as I do not think the well-known examples at Beni-Hassan (in Egypt) of such primitive pillars prove any connection with the Greek Doric, so I think in these examples from Kashmir that the resemblances may be merely accidental.[2]

It is not so with the Ionic capital discovered at Taxila (Shah-dheri, north of Lahore), and now preserved in the Museum of Lahore. This no doubt belongs to the temple described in the very mendacious life of Apollonius of Tyana as being of great size with a complete peristyle, but having the walls covered with metal reliefs in gold, silver, orichalcum, bronze, and iron, representing the wars of

---

[1] Cf. *Arch. Survey*, iii. preface, p.v.; v. 69, 85, and Appendix A, with the plates of illustration—a most interesting collection of materials.

[2] The example given in the plates at the end of the volume I am now citing is indeed very suggestive of a Greek origin, especially in its fluting, with sharp *arrises*. The capital is considerably modified, but on the whole some far-off echo of Greek style is probable.

Alexander with Porus.[1] But if the temple had indeed been a rich Hellenistic temple covered with ornament, how can we account for the extremely simple and archaic character of the capital in question, which might indeed be fairly used to prove that the Ionic order originated in the far East, and was derived by the Ionians from oriental models? I can only argue from the careful description and illustration of this temple by Cunningham,[2] for neither a photograph nor any illustrated catalogue of the objects in the Museum at Lahore is to be obtained in Europe.[3] What is still more puzzling concerning this temple is its late date, for under the foundation was discovered a formal deposit of coins of king Azas, dating from about 80 B.C. So then these apparently Hellenistic influences were surviving long after the acknowledged decay of all Greek domination in the East.

This is eminently the case with the beautiful specimens of Corinthian pillars and pilasters given in the same volume.[4] These, while showing a masterly application of the acanthus leaf ornament, introduce figures in the capital, a perfectly free and original treatment of the feature derived from Greek architecture.[5] But these also date from the first century, and may possibly have been the work of artists who had visited the Græco-Roman world. It is more likely, however, that they are directly due to the influence of the older Indo-Greek civilisation, and so we can trace with

---

[1] Philostratus, *Vita Apoll.* ii. 20.
[2] *Arch. Survey*, v. 69 *sq*.
[3] Even the kind solicitations made by high officials on my behalf have failed to procure me this catalogue.
[4] Cf. *op. cit.* Appendix A.
[5] These highly ornamental pillars, with their very wide-spreading capitals, seem to have stood alone, with a figure or figures set up upon them. This too is a Greek, or a Græco-Roman fashion.

considerable evidence a collateral action of western culture corroborating the inferences from the coins.

We are told by the geographers that in far later days the old Indo-Greek coins were still current in commerce with nations at the mouth of the Indus,[1] and Strabo preserves for us from Nicolaus Damascenus (a very respectable authority) the following remarkable proof of the persistence even of the Greek language as the organ of diplomacy up to the Christian era. 'He said that at Antioch he had met with the Indian ambassadors who had been sent to Cæsar Augustus. Most of them had been killed or laid up by the length of the journey, three only had reached Antioch, with a missive written in Greek on a leather skin' (parchment) 'containing polite messages from Porus' (as the Indian king was entitled), 'with sundry presents, among which was a creature called Hermas, from his resemblance to the pillars of that name, his arms having been taken off at the shoulder.' This person Strabo himself saw at Rome.

Thus then as regards material civilisation the Greeks had done not a little in the far East. They had founded kingdoms, built cities, coined money, dedicated temples, and showed to the natives of the Indus and Upper Ganges a culture widely different from that of the eastern Aryans. But the genius of these nations was too different in kind from that of Europe for any permanent assimilation. Superficial imitations were possible, and they were many; we cannot point to a single spiritual legacy left by the successors of Alexander to these remote conquests, unless it be the drama. And here we come upon a most interesting, but a very difficult literary problem.

[1] The author of the *Periplus* (probably in the second century A.D.) says:—ἀφ᾿ οὗ μέχρι νῦν ἐν Βαρυγάζοις παλαιαὶ προχωροῦσι δραχμαὶ γράμμασιν Ἑλληνικοῖς ἐγκεχαραγμέναι ἐπίσημα τῶν μετ᾿ Ἀλέξανδρον βεβασιλευκότων Ἀπολλοδότου καὶ Μενάνδρου.

The principal plays in Indian literature have been translated by the late Professor H. H. Wilson,[1] with a very instructive preface upon the rules and precedents of this peculiar drama. Their *Poetics* had been elaborated with the usual love of intricacy shown by oriental scholars, so that there is a luxury of directions quite grotesque to the European reader. Thus the types of the chief character, according to the emotions he is to portray, are divided and subdivided till they reach 144 varieties![2] Tragedy and comedy are not very clearly distinguished, as a happy ending is prescribed even to the most serious pieces, so that the modern melodrama is our nearest parallel. Indeed, as Wilson has shown clearly enough,[3] there are analogies to be found both to the Greek, the French, and the English drama, and he very naturally ascribes these to the uniformity of the conditions required by any stage, and the certainty that all civilised men will endeavour to solve similar problems by similar devices. The wide divergences, therefore, of the Indian drama from the Greek, in many details, combined with its close resemblances to the modern European plays which owe least to classic sources, have persuaded Wilson that he has before him a perfectly original and independent development. Christian Lassen also, a far higher authority, pointing to the fact that the habit of attending plays is implied in the oldest Buddhistic writings, evidently attributes the origin of the Indian drama to an age prior to all Hellenistic influences, which he formally rejects.[4] He

[1] *Select Specimens of the Theatre of the Hindus*, 2 vols., 2d ed., London, 1835.
[2] *Op. cit.* introduction, p. lxiv.
[3] *Op. cit.* preface.
[4] *Ind. Alterthumskunde*, ii. 507.

considers it to have arisen out of dances and songs to the gods, quite in the manner of the Greek drama.

I know not how much either author may have known of the Hellenistic drama and its diffusion through the East; how much either may have underrated the importance and long persistence of Indo-Greek culture in the kingdoms of Euthydemus and of Eucrates. But to us who have recovered many more traces of this culture than were known in Wilson's day, the filiation of these plays from Greek patterns will appear almost certain.

We have indeed a gap between the decay of Greek civilisation in the second century and the composition of the extant Indian plays, which may not be of earlier date than what we should call the Middle Ages. The particular examples which Wilson cites, though he evidently believes their antiquity exaggerated, do not profess to be older than the first century B.C., and very few even of that age. It is much more likely that none of them arose till the habit of hearing Greek plays had died out, which could hardly have been the case till the second century A.D.[1] But the majority are probably far more recent. While this long interval makes it quite reasonable to expect wide variations and new developments from any Greek original, we must note, on the other hand, that the whole tone of the Indian drama is archaic; the language of the principal characters being Sanskrit, the speaking of which was long since extinct among men; the language even of the inferior parts being a Prakrit or vulgar dialect far removed from ordinary life, and highly artificial.[2] Thus these plays can never have been easily understood, and required much commentary,

---

[1] This is the date assigned to the oldest of them, the Mrikkakatika, by Lassen, *Ind. Alt.* ii. 512.

[2] Wilson, *op. cit.* p. lxiii. *sqq.*

which was added by way of prologue to the performance, even for those grandees and their households before whom they were produced.

This use of a non-vernacular language either points to an origin of vast antiquity, which no Indian scholar ever suggests, or else—and I think very distinctly—to the copying of those Greek plays which were long in vogue at the Indian courts by strolling companies of Dionysiac players for the amusement of princes, who were, or posed as, Greeks, while the majority of their retinue must have found the dialogue quite incomprehensible. In the well known case of Euripides's *Bacchæ*, acted at the Parthian court, when the head of Crassus was brought in, we have an example of the model which native poets would emulate. It was the fashion to hear plays, in a foreign language, and a time came when that language was an archaic foreign language, which those of the former generation had understood better than those of to-day. There were no Greek theatres built in India, but an extempore stage was constructed in the court of a palace by these strolling companies. At the same time they were not like the strolling players of modern times, often mountebanks or paupers, trying to earn a miserable livelihood, and treated with contempt, but guilds in the service of Dionysus, of much wealth and importance, and a necessary adjunct to every Hellenistic feast, or founding of a city. All these features are carefully reproduced in the Indian drama,[1] and what could be more

---

[1] 'Companies of actors in India must have been common at an early date [Wilson appears to know nothing of the Greek strolling companies], and must have been reputable, for the "inductions" often refer to the poets as their personal friends, and a poet of tolerable merit in India, under the ancient *régime*, was the friend and associate of sages and kings.

'The Hindu actors were apparently never classed with vagabonds or

natural than to compose plays in a purely literary form of Indian speech, when the habit of hearing Greek plays died out for want of either players to act them or princes to patronise them? The number of extant Indian plays is only about sixty, and no author is credited with more than three—another evidence that this drama is neither very old nor really national. It appears to me nothing more than an attempt to keep alive a foreign drama by means of indigenous talent, successful to a certain extent, and giving rise to much theory and commentary, as might be expected in a very subtle metaphysical society of scholars, but in reality the last echo of the Hellenistic kingdoms, which once had promised to subdue the regions of the East to western language and western civilisation.

This view of the question has been adopted by eminent recent Indianists, Weber, Brandes, and Windisch, the last of whom has given an excellent summary of the arguments in a special tract.[1] These scholars do not indeed maintain that the Indian drama owes its *origin* to the Greek, but rather that some rude mimic representations of earlier days were transformed by Hellenistic contact into the sort of play now extant. It appears that the worship of Çiva was near enough in character to that of Dionysus to allow of a transference, and that the Indian plays were produced at the

menials. . . . As to theatrical edifices, the manners of the people and the nature of the climate were adverse to their existence, and the spacious open courts of the dwellings of persons of consequence were adapted to the purposes of dramatic representation. We should never forget that the Hindu drama was not exhibited as an ordinary occurrence, or an amusement of the people, but that it was part of an occasional celebration of some solemn or religious festival' (Wilson, *op. cit.* p. lxvi.) One might use these very words to describe the performances of the Hellenistic Dionysiac troupes in the East.

[1] *Der griech. Einfluss im Indischen Drama.* Berlin, 1882.

spring feasts of that Indian god. Windisch has gone *seriatim* through the characters of the Greek drama, and has shown that in the earliest extant Indian play, which he takes to be the *Toy-cart* (translated in Wilson's first volume), the stock figures of the new Attic comedy, reproduced in the Roman comedy, are distinctly to be traced. He notes that the whole idea of representing ordinary life, with courtesans, parasites, etc. is so opposed to what we know of old Indian literature as to point strongly to a foreign influence. The number and arrangement of the actors, the disposition of acts and scenes, are all analogous to those in Plautus and Terence, though not without many changes required by Indian life and habits. It can surely be no accident that the curtain which concealed the green room behind the scene, and so formed the background, is called *yavanikâ*, the Greek curtain. In the *Toy-cart* the raising of the virtuous courtesan to a rank of respectability by her marriage in the end of the play, is a feature foreign to old Indian life.[1] The device of recognition by toys or amulets is also Greek. I must refer the reader for many further details to the tract in question.

The author shows with great ability that the later specimens of this drama drift away from the Greek traditions, and become more and more purely Indian, even in their religion. The special worship of Çiva is replaced by that of Vishnu. But, I think, he does not appreciate the very great importance of the manager or impresario (who was often the leading actor) in a company of *strolling* players, who had to carry with them, or find their 'properties,' and construct their own stage for each performance. This is the meaning of the manager in Indian drama being called by a name which

[1] *Op. cit.* p. 30.

also means *architect;* this is the cause of the importance of the prologue. The religious address or prayer (Nândi) seems to have been spoken by a special personage, perhaps no Greek layman.

This drama then, the beautiful Corinthian decorations of some temples, and the adoption of Greek ornament in Indian building, together with the wealth of Hellenistic coins, are the total result now remaining of the influences of Greek culture upon the far East.[1] It does not seem necessary to refer these effects to the pre-Roman period of this influence, for neither the date of the greatest diffusion, nor the character of what remains, points to anything distinct from that Hellenism which pervaded the Roman East. It is therefore not improbable that Roman power and Roman influence had something to say to the respect with which these things were adopted and copied by people of purely oriental origin.

The brilliancy and gradual decay into barbarism of the Greek kingdoms of Bactria and of India are similar, on a large scale, to the history of those isolated settlements about the Crimea and the Sea of Asov, which we shall meet in the wars of Mithradates, and in the travels of Dion Chrysostom. Here too we shall find old Greek colonies separated from their mother-cities, maintaining themselves with marvellous vigour, and preserving an affecting attachment to the traditions and memories of their long lost Hellas. But here, too, we cannot but see that the force of surrounding barbarism was too much for them; the constant struggle for existence

---

[1] Lassen, *Ind. Alterthums.* ii. 359, though he elsewhere admits some influences in architecture, sums up the whole Greek influence upon Bactria and India as amounting merely to a revolution in the art of coining; all the rest is not provable, or was merely transitory. I have said nothing of Hindu astronomy, but learn from experts that this too shows traces of Greek influence.

led to weariness, to concessions which contaminated their purity and dissipated their energy, and so without any Mithradates, and without any Romans, these outlying cities, like Posidonia in the land of the Samnites, would have been ultimately barbarised out and out. It was the greatest of Rome's missions to protect Hellenism from this fate, even where this mission was performed with contempt, with injustice, and with the oppression of those whom she professed to make free and independent.

CHAPTER III

HELLENISM IN SYRIA AND IN EGYPT

I HAVE already alluded to the cities which remained Greek under the Parthian Empire. We know little about them, either as to their number or their importance, except indeed that Seleucia on the Tigris was comparable in size with Antioch or Alexandria. This city certainly enjoyed considerable privileges from the Parthian kings, and this not the least, that they did not quarter their household troops—chiefly Scythian cavalry—upon the citizens, or even within the walls of the town, but at Ctesiphon, the Royal Residence, some twelve miles from Seleucia. This residence, which by the way is also designated a Greek city, stood in some such relation to Seleucia as Versailles to Paris. Nevertheless the Greek cities felt the yoke, for Josephus tells us [1] that it was at their invitation that Deme-

---

[1] xiv. 5, § 11, καὶ γὰρ οἱ ταύτῃ (Mesopotamia and the upper provinces) Ἕλληνες καὶ Μακεδόνες συνεχῶς ἐπρεσβεύοντο πρὸς αὐτόν, εἰ πρὸς αὐτοὺς ἀφίκοιτο, παραδώσειν μὲν αὐτοὺς ὑπισχνούμενοι, συγκαταπολεμήσειν δὲ Ἀρσάκην τὸν Πάρθων βασιλέα. This resulted in his captivity. We hear that one Parthian king, Phraates, appointed a favourite, Himerus, governor of Babylon, and that this man was tyrant of both Babylon and Seleucia, where he committed many violences (Posidonius in Müller, *FHG* iii. 258, 259).

trius Soter went into the East, hoping from thence to recover his kingdom. The same inducements may have enticed Antiochus Eusebes to make the same attempt, and with similar but more fatal failure. For while Demetrius was taken captive, and sent back again after some years as a claimant to the throne from which a new assailant threatened Parthia, Antiochus Eusebes killed himself when thoroughly defeated, though after some initial successes. The Greek cities, therefore, in Upper Asia enjoyed privileges from, and had complaints against, their Parthian lords.

The same was the case with the many Hellenistic cities of Syria and Palestine, and we are here, fortunately, better informed. In the period now before us (146 to 67 B.C.), which closes with the Roman settlement of Syria by Pompey, Palestine as well as Cœle-Syria was recognised to belong to the lord of Antioch, as had been the case, nominally at least, ever since these lands had been wrested from Egypt by Antiochus the Great. The sixth Ptolemy (Philometor) had indeed for a moment conquered Syria, and was actually crowned with the double diadem of Syria and Egypt at Antioch, but his death in battle in that very campaign (147 B.C.) had caused the retreat of his army, and his brother, Ptolemy VII (Physcon), had never essayed the reconquest of Palestine. But Syria, from the date just mentioned, and Egypt from the death of Physcon (117 B.C.), fell under the misfortune of perpetually having rival claimants, two brothers, or a queen-mother in conflict with one and allied to the other—a state of things which repeats itself with such a weariness of intricacy that the history of both kingdoms during their decadence is justly abandoned to a few specialists.

If the memoirs of this time were preserved to us, no doubt all these complications of dynastic struggles would regain a lasting interest. For example Athenæus tells of Alexander Bala, how he had at his court a man of Seleucia called Diogenes, who posed as an Epicurean philosopher, though the king usually favoured the Stoics. The king humoured him, in spite of his mean qualities, his jealousy and his backbiting, for the fun of the thing, and even granted his very unphilosophic request to let him wear a purple tunic and a gold crown with a figure of Virtue set in its front, and call himself her priest. These ornaments Diogenes gave away to a singing woman of whom he was enamoured. Whereupon the king, hearing of this, gave a feast to philosophers and distinguished men, and when Diogenes appeared, asked him where his dress and crown were. Upon his giving an evasive answer, the king ordered the musicians to come before him, when the singing woman appeared in the philosopher's dress.

This Alexander was of gentle disposition and fond of letters. But Antiochus Sidetes, a much abler man, when he attained the throne, put Diogenes to death, on account of his abusive tongue. Here the contrast of the gentle and laughter-loving Alexander both to the harsh and unpopular Demetrius and to the downright Antiochus Sidetes is made clear. It seems that Antiochus did not content himself with silencing Diogenes, but that he expelled all professed philosophers from Syria, as we read in Athenæus.[1] The king's rescript to Phanias (probably his commander-in-chief or prime minister) is quoted verbatim: 'We have already directed you that no philosopher shall stay in the city or district, yet we hear there are not a few, and that they debauch the young, owing to my orders not being carried out. Upon receipt therefore of this letter, issue a decree to expel all philosophers, threatening any

[1] v. p. 211 ; xiii. p. 547.

youths found in their company with hanging, and their parents with the gravest censure. Let there be no mistake about this.' Athenæus is probably right in inferring a great diffusion of Epicurean teaching as the probable cause of such a decree.

The point of interest to us in the complicated and bloody struggles for the Syrian and the Egyptian succession which we have just mentioned is that the intermediate and lesser powers, the Jews, and the free Greek cities on the Philistine coast, or in the valleys of the Jordan and the Orontes, were petted and honoured by the rival princes, who were constantly outbidding each other by granting privileges and remitting imposts. It is this condition of the Syrian power which explains the rise and consolidation of the Maccabees, till with John Hyrcanus and Alexander Jannæus they became strong enough to make conquests and secure for themselves a considerable part of Cœle-Syria. It is this condition of things also which accounts for the importance in population, trade and wealth of the Greek cities, especially those on the coast, like Ptolemais and Gaza, which obtained from the Syrian kings autonomy, and marked it by dating from an era [1]—most of these local city eras start about 120 B.C.—by a coinage of their own, and by other regular Greek phenomena, such as even the frequent occurrence of tyrants.[2] These cities always paid some tax, levied by themselves upon their citizens, and were probably obliged to contribute soldiers to their suzerain. But war was now a lucrative trade, so much so that mercenary service was considered an honour and not a burden by the non-Hellenic population

[1] Cf. Stark's *Gaza*, p. 474, for details.
[2] Cf. Stark (*op. cit.* p. 478), who mentions nine of them. He thinks the example of tribal chiefs among the surrounding nomads had some effect on the cities, in addition to the ordinary political causes operating in every small Greek autonomy of the kind.

of these lands. And it must have been a safety-valve even for the Hellenistic towns to provide the young and turbulent with foreign service. The weaknesses, therefore, of the great Hellenistic empires were on the whole a source of strength and of prosperity to those frequent but isolated cities, which represented Greek city culture all through Palestine, Phœnicia and Syria.[1]

But a great danger arose from the action of the same causes upon the nation of the Jews. For as the Jews grew in power they developed the notion of a far stricter sovranty over the lands which they incorporated in their empire. Not that the dynasty of the Maccabees was free from Hellenistic influences, or averse to adopting Hellenistic culture. Judas and his brothers were at first little more than Jewish insurgents, who took to the mountains, and maintained themselves as patriot bandits have often done since. When they came gradually to be recognised, and treated by the Seleucids as allies, or provincial governors, according to the needs of the moment, their views expanded, and they developed into Hellenistic princes.

The interesting thirteenth book of Josephus's *Antiquities*[2] gives ample proof of both policies in the Maccabees— on the one hand their fierce Semitism in subduing their neighbours and compelling them to adopt Jewish customs, on the other hand their constant intercourse with Hellenism. The first formal ruler, Simon, who declares

---

[1] The condition of the Roman colonies, when the Imperial power waned, is not without strong analogies to the present case. These outlying cities were permitted, or compelled by circumstances, to assert themselves, and ultimately formed the nuclei of new political systems. Had the Roman power not intervened in Syria, and had the Seleucids left no equally vigorous successor, some such results as happened in the later Roman Empire would have ensued.

[2] Especially cap. viii. *sq.*

Jewish independence in 143 B.C. is indeed called by Josephus *ethnarch* and *Euergetes* (xiii. 6, § 7). But this may be the translation of a Jewish title into the most current Greek. His successor Hyrcanus was defeated by Antiochus Sidetes, but the conquest only resulted in a closer alliance with the Syrian king. Hyrcanus opened (says Josephus, xiii. 8, § 4) the tomb of David, and took out 3000 talents of silver, with which he, first of the Maccabees, raised a mercenary army. He moreover accompanied Antiochus with his forces in the campaign against the Parthians. Upon the death of Antiochus he forthwith, like a true Hellenistic king, set upon the cities of his ally, as well as upon the Idumeans, and made all those he conquered conform to Jewish rites. But while he was a stern nationalist in this respect, he takes pains to send an embassy to Rome, to obtain the support of the Senate against Syria,[1] and the very names of the ambassadors—Simon, son of Dositheus; Apollonius, son of Alexander; and Diodorus, son of Jason, cultivated men, (ἄνδρες καλοὶ καὶ ἀγαθοί), who doubtless spoke Greek perfectly at Rome—show the worldly side of John Hyrcanus. They were treated with distinction by the Senate, and their expenses for the home journey defrayed.

The death of Antiochus Sidetes, and the succeeding conflict between two new Antiochuses (Cyzicenus and Grypus) and Alexander Zebinas gave Hyrcanus rare opportunities. 'For after the death of Antiochus he revolted from the Macedonians, and was neither their subject nor their friend, but greatly strengthened his own power and wealth, while they were engaged in mutual conflicts.' This was the time he chose to destroy Samaria,

---

[1] The date appears to be 129 B.C., in which year C. Sempr. Tuditanus and M'. Aquillius were consuls. The text of Josephus has L. Mannius L. f. (xiii. 9, § 2).

a centre not only for the opposing worship of Mount Gerizim, but also for Hellenic religion and manners. Yet the sons whom he sent to perform this national undertaking were called *Antigonus* and *Aristobulus*.

The struggles of Hyrcanus with the Sadducees and Pharisees do not concern us here, interesting as they are,[1] and we pass on to Aristobulus, who turns his high priesthood into a regular Hellenistic royalty, and assumes the diadem of the Hellenistic kings.

But I will pause for a moment to comment upon another feature in these days of decline and death-struggle among the fragments of Alexander's empire. In Syria, in Judæa, in Egypt, we have queen-mothers left in command, and controlling their sons, the rightful kings, with both force and fraud. Aristobulus began by putting to death his mother (whom Hyrcanus had left in sole control)[2] as well as his brother; the remorse of these crimes brought on him a disease of which he died in a year. He was in policy a Hellenist (χρηματίσας μὲν φιλέλλην), but in his conquest of Ituræa compelled all the inhabitants either to migrate or adopt Jewish rites. Upon his death the widow Salome, called by the Greeks Alexandra, takes as usual a prominent part, and sets up as king Jannæus Alexander, who completes the policy of the dynasty by subduing the strong Greek cities of the coast.

The long war about the coast fortress Ptolemais, in which Ptolemy Lathyrus of Egypt, his regent mother Cleopatra (Cocce), with her Jewish generals Chalcias and Ananias, and others, took part, ended in the complete

---

[1] Josephus, *Antiqq.* x. 6, 7.
[2] ἐκείνην γὰρ Ὑρκανὸς τῶν ὅλων κυρίαν κατελελοίπει, Josephus, xi. 1. See also Jos. xiii. 16, § 6, on the character of Alexandra. He speaks similarly of Tryphæna, Selene, and others.

devastation of the coast. The destruction of Gaza, a regular Greek city of very considerable importance, was a deathblow to Hellenistic civilisation in that part of the world.[1] The inhabitants became bandits, mercenaries, and pirates, and the trade of the Eastern Mediterranean must have suffered terribly till Pompey pacified the East. 'For then, since there were so many and continuous simultaneous wars, and many cities were cleared of their inhabitants, and even those who had escaped from them were outlaws, so that they were nowhere safe, many men turned to a life of rapine. Now robbery on land, as it was within the observation of settled societies, and left its traces manifest, was sure to be stopped. But piracy became rampant. For the Romans being otherwise engaged, it had time to spread widely over the seas, and become organised.'[2] The list of the cities which Hyrcanus conquered is given by Josephus;[3] it includes many of the Greek cities of the interior, such as Scythopolis and Pella, which he destroyed because they absolutely refused to adopt Jewish customs. This then was a great and serious blow to Hellenism, perhaps more lasting than was dealt anywhere else in the world, for after all in other anti-Hellenic conquests the Hellenistic sentiment was dominant, whereas in Judæa it was overruled in the kings by the narrow and zealous sect of the Pharisees.

It was owing to this wholesale subjugation and even destruction of the Syrian Hellenistic cities that not only the Arabs or Bedouin, who have always infested the inner country, appear now as an important military power in-

[1] Ascalon saved itself by timely and complete submission. Ptolemais, the stronghold of the queen Selene, was not taken by Tigranes till just before the advent of Lucullus.
[2] Dion Cassius, xxxvi. 3.
[3] *Antiqq.* xiii. 15, § 4.

vading Syria and Palestine, but also that Tigranes and the Parthians were actually able to subdue and hold Syria. It was, in fact, the advent of the Romans and the reconstitution of these cities by Pompey, and afterwards by Herod, as free Greek cities, which reintroduced a certain spurious kind of Hellenism—Roman Hellenism—into the once well cultivated and civilised regions of Cœle-Syria, Sidon, and Philistia.[1]

We may judge from the fragments of Posidonius[2] that there had been not only great wealth but great luxury in these cities. 'On account of the fertility of the country, and the absence of any necessity for toil, they had frequent meetings at which they feasted, using their gymnasia as baths, anointing themselves with rich oil and unguents, and dwelling in their schools' (so they called their public dining-halls) 'as if in houses, surfeiting themselves there with meats and wines, and even carrying away much; listening to the music of the loud lyre, so that whole cities re-

[1] The accurate determination of the Hellenistic and Aramaic cities respectively is not easy, and has been attempted by B. Stark in his learned and careful book on *Gaza and the Philistine Coast*, p. 447 *sq.*, as well as by Schürer in his more recent *History of Israel about the Christian Era*. The first point of interest is to separate the Egyptian from the Syrian foundations. Names ending with πόλις point to a usual formation in Græco-Egyptian foundations, and of course the Egyptians would naturally establish cities on the coast, while the lords of Antioch would occupy Cœle-Syria and the inner country. The Seleucidæ also adopted old Greek names, such as Anthedon, Arethusa, instead of the composite Egyptian formations or adaptations of Ptolemaic names. The several cities, or rather the principal men chosen in each for that purpose, arranged the imposts and duties of the town with the royal officers, called ἔπαρχοι or τόπαρχοι, who raised from the country people and non-Greek inhabitants not only taxes on crops (the third part) and fruit trees (half the produce), but a capitation tax never levied on the *Greeks*.

[2] Müller, *FHG* iii. 256 *sq.* The tone of the epigrams composed in these cities, to which I shall revert hereafter, points to the same conclusion.

echoed with these sounds.' We might imagine that it was from Tyre and Sidon, as Ezekiel describes them, that these habits were derived; possibly even the famous prophecy against Tyre may have come to the knowledge of the Stoic historian : 'They shall make a spoil of thy riches, and make a prey of thy merchandise ; and they shall break down thy walls, and destroy thy pleasant houses ; and they shall lay thy stones, and thy timber, and thy dust, in the midst of the water. And I will cause the noise of thy songs to cease ; and the sound of thy harps shall be no more heard. And I will make thee a bare rock : thou shalt be a place for the spreading of nets.'[1] The whole description which follows of the trade of Tyre may be fairly applied to the coast cities which succeeded to her mercantile position after her destruction by Alexander. We may also imagine their morals and manners as not better, being largely affected by the troops of rich and pampered mercenaries from Crete, Rhodes, Spain, Galatia, as well as from Greece, a motley crowd in their streets, who spent their ill-gotten wealth in luxury and wantonness.

If we turn to the Egypt of this period we find the same confusion in the royal succession, the same interminable conflicts between mother and son, between rival brothers ; and at Alexandria we observe a distinct decay of Greek together with a rise of Jewish influence, especially since two Jews, Chalcias and Ananias, undertook to manage the affairs of Queen Cleopatra Cocce, and refused to attack Palestine when she desired it. The Museum was therefore languishing, and Ammonius, who had succeeded to Aristarchus, was far from sustaining a reputation equal to that of his great predecessor.

The chief interest which appears in the literature, or

[1] Ezek. xxvi. 12 *sq*.

fragments of literature of this period, is the interest in geography, both as science and as exploration. The scientific side belongs to another kind of history,[1] but the adventurous may here occupy us for a short time. The remains of Posidonius show with what interest a Stoic of that day could view the outskirts of the world. It is to this period that I am also disposed to attribute many of the geographical vagaries in the *Life of Alexander*, which became in fact the Alexandrian popular fairy book, like the mediæval Cairene collection known as the *Arabian Nights*.

But the account of Eudoxus, the explorer, given us at some length by Strabo, is too instructive not to be related in full. Luckily Strabo has thought fit to tell us the whole story in spite of his unbelief.

Posidonius related that in the days of the second Euergetes (Physcon) there came a certain Eudoxus from Cyzicus to Egypt on an embassy concerning a treaty, and to attend the festival of Persephone, and that he discoursed with the king and his court, particularly about the ascent of the Nile, as he was curious concerning peculiarities of climate, and was an educated man. Now it happened that at this time there was sent up to the king by those that guarded the mouth of the Red Sea an Indian, who was found half-dead in a boat alone, and they could not tell who or whence he was, as they did not understand his speech; so the king ordered him to be taught Greek. When the Indian had

---

[1] The great name of Hipparchus, the foremost astronomer in antiquity, marks the period now before us, as he died towards the end of the second century B.C. To treat of his discoveries would be to enter upon the history of Greek science—a formidable study, seeing that we have a very large quantity of Greek mathematics surviving, written in technical language. Cf. the catalogue of the many authors and their writings in Munk, *Gesch. der Griech. Literatur*, ii. 501 *sqq.*, and Mr. Gow's *History of Mathematics in Alexandria*.

learned it he told them that, sailing from India, he had been driven out of his course, and had lost all his comrades by starvation ; he also undertook to show the way to the Indies to those appointed by the king, among whom was Eudoxus. They set out provided with presents, and brought back as an exchange-cargo spices and precious stones—some of which come down the rivers with pebbles, some are dug out of the ground, apparently solidified from moisture, like our crystals.

But Eudoxus was cheated of his expectations, for the king took away from him the whole of the cargo. The king's death supervening, his widow Cleopatra assumed the power, and by her Eudoxus was again sent out with ampler means. On his way he was carried by winds beyond Ethiopia, and conciliated the natives whom he reached with gifts of corn and wine and sweet cakes, which they did not possess, and they allowed him in return a supply of water, and directed his course for him ; he also wrote down some words of their language. Moreover, finding on the shore a wooden figure-head with a horse carved on it, he learned that it was the wreck of a ship with people who had come from the west, and he brought this figure-head home with him. When he got back to Egypt it was no longer Cleopatra but her son who reigned, and again his whole cargo was seized ; for he was convicted of having abstracted a great deal after his former voyage. The figure-head he brought down to the merchant harbour in Alexandria, where it was at once recognised as belonging to Gades, where the greater merchants fit out large ships, the poorer small ones, which they call *horses*, from the form of the figure-head ; and these sail as far as the river Lixus to fish on the coast of Mauretania. Some of the skippers at Alexandria pronounced this figure-head to belong to one of these ships, which had gone too far along the coast, and had never returned.

When Eudoxus drew from this the conclusion that Libya must be circumnavigable, he went home, and realised all his property to stake it upon this venture. And first he went to Dicæarchia (Puteoli), then to Massilia (Marseilles), and then along the coast as far as Gades (Cadiz), making careful inquiries everywhere, and at last succeeded in fitting out one large vessel and two smaller of the nature of piratical barks, in which he embarked slaves trained in music, and physicians and other artists, and set sail for the Indies across the high seas with a steady west wind. But when his crews were weary with voyaging he was obliged to put in to the shore, which he greatly feared on account of the flux and reflux of the tides. And the very thing he anticipated really occurred. His big ship grounded, but quietly, so that it did not go to pieces until all the cargo and most of the timber were carried on shore. Out of the latter they constructed a new boat in the shape of a penteconter, and then sailed onward till he came to people speaking the same tongue of which he had already (as has been told) written down words. Accordingly he discovered that these people were akin to the former Ethiopians he had met, and that they were neighbours to the kingdom of Bogos. He then abandoned the journey to the Indies and turned homeward, and as he went along noted an island, well watered and wooded, that was not inhabited. When he got back to Maurusia (Western Mauretania), getting rid of his ships he crossed by land to Bogos, and advised the king to take up the enterprise, but the king's counsellors prevailed against the traveller by showing the danger of attacks from any outside people, upon the kingdom, when the way was discovered. So when Eudoxus found out that they were going to send him out nominally in command of the proposed expedition, but that the real design was to leave him on some desert island, he escaped into the Roman province, and thence crossed to Iberia. Having again provided himself with a merchant ship and a long pinnace, so that he could keep at sea in the one and make expeditions along the shore with the other, he set out on the same journey, carrying with him farming utensils, and seeds, and masons, with this intention, that if delayed on the voyage he could winter on the island he had already observed, and having taken out a crop could use this supply to complete the expedition on which he was determined.

So far, said Posidonius, I can go in the narrative about Eudoxus, but what happened afterwards, I suppose the people of Gades and from Iberia would know.

This whole narrative, so profoundly interesting in disclosing to us a character with the boundless resource and ambition of a Columbus, and like him misled by underrating the size of the earth, strikes Strabo as a mere string of lies, either invented by Posidonius, or told him by the inventor. As regards Posidonius himself, he was a man of high character, a Stoic philosopher, and as worthy of credit as Strabo himself; nor is it likely that, being a good traveller, and a much experienced man, he would be taken in by any such stories. We may therefore be sure that there was considerable foundation for the whole account, however inaccurately the details may have been reported.

Here are the main points of Strabo's criticism. How could any Indian be cast upon the shore of the Red Sea, for this sea is very narrow at the mouth, and therefore landing would be easy outside? How could a single survivor manage a considerable ship? How did he learn Greek so quickly as to persuade the king to carry out his plan? How could Euergetes want information from such a guide, seeing that the road to India was already well known? How was it that a stranger from Cyzicus should first be entrusted with such an expedition, then deprived of all he brought back, and then again trusted with another command? Why was he surprised at the figure-head, seeing he himself must have come from the coast? How could he return home, for nobody was allowed to leave Alexandria without a passport, and this man had appropriated royal property? 'Nor could he sail out secretly, the harbour and all other exits being carefully guarded by custom-house officers, who even now remain, as I know from having lived some time at Alexandria, though things are much relaxed since the Roman sway; then the royal guards were far more strict,' etc. etc. He concludes by saying that if each of these details is not in itself impossible, their combined occurrence is out of the question.

So far as the first part of the critique goes, it is simply upset by supposing that the solitary 'Indian' was driven not from the East, but from the South, and that he really belonged to the African coast, or to Madagascar. The rest of Strabo's objections seem to me so foolish as not to require any answer. The account of Eudoxus's difficulties, and especially of his turning about when he had got a long way on his first journey, is no doubt incomplete; but either want of provisions or a mutiny among his crew is a natural and adequate cause for such a failure, even in an enthusiast, as he seems to have been. The date of these adventures is very well defined by the death of Ptolemy VII and the regency of his widow, with whom her son was associated shortly after; they must lie within 120-112 B.C.

Even the enthusiasm of remarkable individuals arises out of the circumstances of their generation, and we have ample evidence remaining to show that in this case an educated man might find plenty of books to excite his imagination and fire his ambition for discovery. The unity of the Roman sway must have tended to increase the knowledge of, and stimulate the interest in, outlying countries. For the same armies now fought with Spaniards on the far coast of Spain, with the wild tribes of Africa beyond the bounds of Numidia, with the savage Cimbri and Teutones of the north, with the Illyrians of the Balkan peninsula; while the southern regions of the Red Sea,—the Nubians, Abyssinians, and Troglodytes had been long since a subject of interest to the Ptolemies. The great geographical stimulus given to the world by Alexander seems now in some sense renewed, for from the authors of the day we can select no inconsiderable number who devoted themselves to descriptive geography, especially noting the *paradoxa* or strange phenomena, which the traveller ought to witness in each province of the world.

The first man who got the title of Περιηγητής (which may be best translated as *guide*) was Polemo, early in the second century B.C., and he wrote tracts on all the special art-centres of Greece, as well as on *marvels*—apparently a series of handbooks which were the earliest forerunners of our Murrays and Bædekers. Long before his time there had been local *cicerones*, who explained to such travellers as Herodotus or the elder Scylax the curiosities of their respective native towns. But now, with the increased solidarity of the world, and the great growth of travelling, both for trade and for amusement, educated people wanted some safer and more cultivated director, especially on the antiquities of historic cities. In the last quarter of the second century B.C. we have Mnaseas of Patræ, Agatharchides of Cnidos, Metrodorus of Scepsis, Artemidorus of Ephesus, Demetrius Callatianus, Diophantus, Basilis,[1] and within the next twenty years Alexander Polyhistor and the so-called Scymnus of Chios, all composing this sort of book. It is remarkable also that most of them made *epitomes* from their own, as well as from earlier works, showing that they lived not only in an age of reading but an age of hurry, when men wanted knowledge packed together in the smallest compass.

Of two of these authors enough has survived to give us a good idea of the kind of work popular at the epoch which is now before us. The five books of Agatharchides on the Red Sea, under which he includes all the seas washing Arabia, were used by Diodorus so freely in his third book, and excerpted so copiously by Photius, that we seem to possess them almost complete. The author speaks of himself as an old man placed in the onerous and responsible position of tutor to a young king of Egypt, whom most critics take to be Ptolemy VIII (called Soter II and Lathyrus).[2]

The most striking passage in the book, as we have it, is the description of the terrible slavery endured in the Nubian gold-mines, where a whole population of condemned people, with women and children, laboured night and day under the lash to hack out quartz rock in veins deep under the earth, to bring this quartz to the surface, and then to crush it and extract the gold. The details of the 'hewers' with their lamps tied round their heads, the 'shifters,' the 'underviewers' superintending, the children used for carrying,— all this reminds one strongly of the process to be seen any

---

[1] Cf. Müller's *Geog. Graeci.* i. p. lviii.

[2] There are not wanting reasons which induced Niebuhr, and since his day Droysen and Hiller (*Jahn's Jahrbüch.* 1867, p. 597), to ascribe this passage to Aristomenes, the well-known tutor and regent of Ptolemy V (Epiphanes). Even if this be the case, it is probably an extract from Aristomenes quoted by Agatharchides.

day in the English coal-mines.[1] This mining with convict labour, now carried out so diligently by the Ptolemies, was a mere inheritance from the Pharaohs, whose despotism had been exercised for many centuries upon their subjects in many terrible ways, but in none more awful than this sustained cruelty in the sleepless search for gold within the bowels of the earth.

The African shore of the Red Sea was studded all the way down to its mouth with stations established by the earlier Ptolemies, for they had soon discovered that it was far easier to bring up the treasures of the South, especially elephants, by coasting vessels than by the Nile, where the cataracts made unshipping necessary, and where in any case the Nile voyage was long and did not admit of large ships. The names of these stations, which were almost all called after Egyptian captains and explorers,—we know some thirty of them,[2]—show us that such voyages were at first voyages of discovery, where the names given are naturally derived from the circumstances of the moment. The peculiarities of the Troglodytes are given with considerable detail, and so are the varieties of the customs in different tribes. Thus those that kill elephants—they used huge bows and arrows, which were worked by three men together, two holding the bow planted in the ground, and the

---

[1] C. Müller, *Geog. Græci.* i. 124 *sq.*, who gives both Diodorus's (iii. 12, 13) and Photius's excerpts from Agatharchides. The evidence on these hardships is quite uniform. From the *Digest* (viii. 19, 28) Mr. L. C. Purser quotes to me: *proxima morti pœna metalli coercitio*, which agrees perfectly with the words of Diodorus: 'There is no pity of remission of labour whatever for the feeble, or the maimed, or the aged, or for the weaker sex ; all are forced with stripes to slave at their work, till they die of their hardships. Wherefore these wretched people look to the coming day as worse than the present, by reason of the exceeding greatness of their punishment, and accept death as a blessed escape from life.'

[2] Cf. Müller, *Geog. Græci.* i. p. lx.

third drawing the string—would not desist from their stupid waste of these precious animals, which they massacred (as the American Red Indians did the buffaloes), though Ptolemy[1] king of Egypt offered them all kinds of wonderful inducements to desist. On the other hand, there were savages who risked their lives and lost some men in capturing a huge snake for Ptolemy Philadelphus, as they knew the king's desire to have such things in his Zoological Gardens. They ultimately drove it into an enormous wicker trap (lobster pot) prepared for the purpose, and this snake was tamed, and was for a long time on show at Alexandria.[2] The navigation of the Red Sea is very carefully described, with all its dangers, which the Ptolemies sought to diminish by leaving wrecked ships where they had stranded by way of warning. This was a royal πρόσταγμα.

The result of all this was to turn the once peaceful inhabitants of the Arabian coast into pirates,[3] who became as bad as the Tauric people in the Euxine, and had to be checked by the severest punishments, being apparently drowned whenever they were caught on the sea. The wealth of the Sabæans on account of their spices is described as most extraordinary, and on the coast adjoining their territory were to be seen at anchor ships from the farthest East as well as from Greek Egypt, all trafficking for this unique luxury. I have given these details, culled from a vast array of facts, in order to show what sort of knowledge had become interesting to the Hellenistic world of that day.

The metrical geography, commonly entitled the περιήγησις of Scymnus of Chios, is a specimen of another kind of

---

[1] Probably Ptolemy II, according to the 'stone of Pithom,' recently discovered and explained by Mr. Flinders Petrie and Mr. Naville.
[2] *Op. cit.* pp. 162-164.   [3] *Op. cit.* p. 179.

popular book in these after-days of culture. It was a metrical handbook, giving a compendium of the accredited researches of older authors on geography, and professing no originality. It belongs, therefore, to that large class of abbreviated books, which were at this time brought out to suit the hurry and the superficiality of the age. Such, for example, was the abridgment of Mago's twenty-eight books on husbandry, reduced to six, and dedicated to king Dejotarus, probably within the same generation as the work before us.[1] What remains to us is about 1000 verses, in iambic metre, but with the licenses of comic iambics. The existing portion refers altogether to Europe, including the shores of the Euxine, and is valuable to us now in giving the dates of a good many early Greek colonies, such as Massilia, which we should not otherwise have known. The author begins with a sort of dedicatory epistle (135 lines), which is so characteristic and so unknown among ordinary scholars that I shall here give a free translation of it.

May it please your sacred majesty, Nicomedes. Comedy has this most desirable virtue, that it tells everything tersely and clearly, and delights every sane critic. Wherefore, having proved the persuasiveness of its diction, I formed the ambition to approach you through it in a brief discourse, and to offer you this handy and useful compendium, as through you I shall make it of public service to all those who seek information. As I desire therefore at the outset to expound to you the method of the whole treatise, I beg you will allow me a few words by way of preface; I am resolved to speak laconically —very little upon very large subjects. Here is what I have to say.

For the use of the kings of Pergamum, whose glory, though they are gone, yet lives on amongst us for ever, one of the genuine Attic philologers (Apollodorus) having been a hearer

---
[1] Above, p. 6.

of Diogenes the Stoic, and a long time at school with Aristarchus, composed a *chronography* reaching from the capture of Troy to the present day. He expounded a period of 1040 years, recounting the taking of cities, the expeditions of armies, the wanderings of nations, the incursions of barbarians, the course of naval operations, public games, treaties, battles, the acts of kings and other celebrated men, the removal of tyrants —an epitome of all that is told diffusely; and he preferred to set it forth in metre, and chose the comic,[1] for the sake of clearness, and seeing that it would thus be most easily committed to memory. He takes an illustration from life. If a man wants to carry a number of logs, he could not do it unless he tied them together, so a metrical story has its advantage over prose. He then having gathered the chronicle of time into this summary, paid the compliment of dedicating it to king Philadelphus, which becoming known all over the world conferred immortal glory on that Attalus whose name appeared in the dedication.

But I, hearing that you alone of present kings show royal graciousness, thought I would make trial of it myself, and present myself to see what a king is like, that I might have it to tell to others. Wherefore I chose for a supporter of my project him who both established your father in his kingdom, as we hear, and who is truly in all respects honoured by you also—I mean Apollo the Didymæan, the prophet and leader of the Muses. Trusting in him I come to your hearth, which is well-nigh free to all literary men, and may he help my undertaking! For from the scattered materials in various histories I have written for you in epitome the colonisations and foundings of cities, and the ways by sea and land over all the earth. Passing over the obvious things briefly, I have dwelt upon the less known, so that you may have, O king, a short description of the whole habitable earth, the peculiarities of great rivers, and the situation of the two continents; also what are the Greek cities in each, who founded them, and when, who the surrounding barbarians are—nomadic, or tame, and of their manners and customs, which of them are the most inhospitable and savage; the amount of populations, and their various laws and habits, and the richest trading marts,

---

[1] So Strabo says, p. 677

as also the islands, [and so on]; so that he who hears [it read] will not only be diverted, but will get, if nothing else, this useful information, to know where he is, and where his own country lies, and from what mother city it received its inhabitants. To sum it all up, without undertaking the wanderings of Ulysses told in story, but remaining comfortably at home, he may learn not only the life of foreign races, but the cities and the laws of all nations. But my book receiving you as its illustrious sponsor and benevolent patron, will pass through the labour of its birth into life, and will herald your glory, O king, to all, carrying your good report from place to place even to the ends of the world.

And now at the outset I will enumerate the authors on whose authority I have made my statements. I place most reliance in Eratosthenes, the most eminent of geographers, as to climate and configuration of lands, in Ephorus and Dionysius of Chalcis on the founding of cities, in Demetrius Callatianus, the Sicilian Cleon and Timosthenes [then the MS. is mutilated and illegible for some lines] Timæus, and what Herodotus has said. In other cases I have brought my own diligent inquiry and personal observation to bear, having seen not only the cities in Greece and Asia, but knowing the regions of Adria and the Ionian Sea, and having travelled as far as Tyrrhenia and Sicily to the west, as well as through most of Libya and Carthage.

He then proceeds at once to his description of Europe. A scrap of the following part (on Asia) is also preserved.

The very curious and instructive passage above translated shows us that we are dealing with a society more like that of the last century than any that went before. Literary men were seeking out noble patrons, and carefully informing them that their patronage was not only profitable to the recipient, but honourable to themselves. Under these circumstances we may be sure that the flattery of the Hellenistic authors did not fall short of the exhibitions to be seen in the dedications of the eighteenth century. Nevertheless in the present instance commentators justly, I think, refuse to believe that our author would have addressed Nicomedes II in these terms, seeing that this Nicomedes had put to death his father Prusias, a monster of iniquity.[1] This parricide, however palliated by the circumstances of the case, would have afforded a curious commentary on the poet's allusions to Apollo as the patron of both father and son.

It is indeed novel, nay, positively comical, to find the authors of 'handy guide-books' dedicating them to kings, and speaking of the celebrity which this would confer. In our day the compiler is neither so ambitious nor so self-important. But we must imagine Scymnus writing not for an old and settled society, like that of Athens or Argos, but for those new and outlying kingdoms, where many Syrians, Gauls, Armenians, Jews, entered Greek cities, got civic rights, and desired to acquire Greek civilisation in a hurry. To these people compendious short-cuts to knowledge would be as important as they now are to the Americans who make rapid fortunes in new western cities of the States. These rough-and-ready business people find themselves suddenly with wealth enough to live cultivated lives, but no antecedents to enable them to do it. And so they must strive to attain by the shortest route manners and ideas foreign to their birth and breeding.[2] Here then compendiums are in high favour, and many a millionaire would be very proud to accept such a dedication as that which I have just transcribed.

I have been so long studying the outskirts of Hellenism and the surface of its culture, that it is high time to turn back to its centres, old and new, and to the deeper aspects of its thinking, and consider what progress was made both in Greece and in Rome by the philosophy of the age.

[1] See the whole story of his revolt (aided by Aristomenes) told in Appian, *Mith*. 3 *sq*. Mommsen decides in favour of Nicomedes III.

[2] The reader to whom this most interesting phase of modern society is not familiar may study it in Mr. Howell's *Rise of Silas Lapham*.

CHAPTER IV

THE ACCLIMATISATION OF GREEK PHILOSOPHY IN ROMAN SOCIETY

NOTHING is more remarkable in the history of Greek philosophy than its diffusion and vitality in the period before us, in spite of the insignificance of the men who were then the recognised leaders of the schools. The succession of the various scholarchs has been a subject of curiosity ever since the Christian era, and has given rise to many tracts, down to the famous essay of Zumpt.[1] But in almost every case we now find a mere name sustaining the responsibility or at least occupying the place of a Chrysippus or an Epicurus. Perhaps the first thing that strikes us when we scan the list of these names in Diogenes, in the columns of Clinton, or in the labyrinthine footnotes of Zeller, is that they hail from all parts of the Hellenistic world. It is hard to say that any portion of Alexander's empire was more prolific in philosophers than the rest. My impression is that perhaps Greece proper was somewhat poorer and Syria somewhat richer than the average, but I will not venture to assert this positively. The coast of Cilicia was perhaps more likely to produce Stoics, owing to

[1] *Uber den Bestand der philos. Schulen, etc.* Berlin, 1843 (*Trans. of the Berlin Academy*).

the causes adduced in a previous volume of this social history;[1] but certain it is that Babylon, Seleucia on the Tigris, Tyre, Sidon, Gadara, Apamea, Antioch, Soli, Alexandria, Tarsus, Cyzicus, Heraclea, and a hundred other cities, sent philosophers into the world, who, while they settled at Rome or Athens or Rhodes, nevertheless did not belie their origin, and were known as the glory of their native cities. But though these men were acute or laborious enough to gain reputation by their books, or even to rise to the position of head of an Athenian school, we cannot find that they made any permanent advance in real thinking, with one notable exception.

The fact is that most of the scholarchs mentioned are remarkable for the number of their years, so that the schools must have been usually presided over by old men. The natural tendency of this condition of things is, first, to make the teaching conservative, clinging to the traditions of former days and revolving round the ideas acquired in the professor's youth; second, to make it timid, not daring to face new problems, or even to defend the startling paradoxes, the extreme views, which had been boldly asserted in the rejuvenescence of Greek philosophy. This timidity often took the form of contracting the outworks, and sacrificing the points most liable to attack—nay, even of conceding to the opponents that they were in some respects right, or to the sceptics that, after all, nothing was certain. It may, therefore, be said of the second century B.C. that it was the period when the schools were very strictly preserved, but when the sceptical school of Pyrrho, which had been blown

---

[1] *Greek Life and Thought*, p. 142. If the edict referred to above (p. 40) was really issued by Antiochus Sidetes against young men learning philosophy, this may be another reason why so many Syrians appear as philosophers at Athens and in the West in this and the next generation.

to the winds in the days of great original thinkers and of profound convictions, saw its seed taking root in other schools, and producing not only a general distrust of all dogmatic philosophy, but a distinct development of negative and destructive thinking.

Hence we find this sceptical tendency showing itself in Arcesilaus, who belongs to the earlier years of the second century, but patent in the one man whom I have already called a brilliant exception—Carneades, the founder of what was called the *New Academy*, which was in reality no development of Plato's doctrine, but rather a sceptical onslaught on the only system which still put forward any bold claims to preaching absolute truth—I mean of course the Stoic.

We know a great deal about the personality of Carneades, though he left no writings, as he was the founder of the only new school of note since the third century, and as we have in Cicero a full account of the doctrines of his successor, Antiochus. The scepticism of Carneades was very keen and brilliant, but he had no great trouble in overthrowing the physical and logical positions of the dogmatists of those days—in fact, the means of attack, both in arms and in argument, were then far stronger than the means of defence. But Carneades was not content with merely refuting the Stoics; he was perhaps the first to elaborate a *doctrine of probability*, which to a sceptic like him was the only guide of life, and which he applied specially to ethics, as the practical side of philosophy immediately concerned with human happiness and misery.

The logical outcome of this systematic refutation of all absolute dogmas and the substitution in their place of probable truths was clearly *eclecticism*—the selecting from various systems their strongest and most practical conclusions, and making this selection the guide of life. This accordingly, as we shall see, became the prevalent fashion of the schools in the commencement of the first century B.C. But in addition to the home forces which urged philosophy in this direction, there was an important external factor—the influence of Roman life and the demands of Roman society. This is, therefore, what we must trace through the second century before we can speak of the eclecticism which took possession of Greek thinkers, till deeper wants brought out the deeper convictions of Neo-Platonism.

The first essays at introducing Greek wisdom to Rome—I mean abstract wisdom—are so spasmodic that they are rather interesting than instructive. We have no information about the motives of Ennius in reproducing the impious fables of Euemerus in Latin. The work had been long discredited in the Greek world as a conglomerate of lies and blasphemy, having some loose connection with the Epicurean notions of religion, in that it asserted the gods to be mere glorified men who had done good to the human race in old times. But not even the shabbiest Epicurean would have accepted it in the second century as an exposition of his views. Seeing, therefore, that Ennius was attached to particular Roman nobles, such as the Fulvius whom he accompanied to Ætolia in 189 B.C., I suppose it was merely to please some individual that the poet transcribed the Messenian's rude assault upon faith and credibility into Latin. It does not appear to have had much success, though it is likely that the Epicurean system, from its simplicity and vulgarity, would most easily attract the Romans who were first let loose upon the East.

It must have been within a few years of Ennius's performance—for we are now to speak of the year 181 B.C.—that a bold attempt was made to pass off Greek dogmas under the ægis of Numa's name. The story is told by

Livy (xl. 29) as follows : 'In that year the labourers on the farm of L. Petilius the scribe, under the Janiculum, digging somewhat deeper than usual, found two stone chests, about eight feet by four each, their lids being fastened down with lead. The chests were inscribed with Latin and Greek letters [respectively], to the effect that in the one Numa Pompilius, son of Pomponius, king of Rome, was buried, in the other were contained the books of Numa. When after consulting with his friends the owner of the farm had opened these chests, that which had the title of the buried king was found empty, without trace of human remains or anything else, all being gone with the decay of centuries. In the other were two bundles containing seven books each, not only undamaged but perfectly new in appearance. The seven Latin were on pontifical law, the seven Greek on the theory of wisdom, which might have belonged to that age. Valerius Antias [the historian] adds that these latter were Pythagorean books, the vulgar belief that Numa was a disciple of Pythagoras having evidently suggested this plausible fiction. The books were first read by the friends who were there when they were opened ; presently when they were becoming common property according as more people got access to them, Q. Petilius, then *prætor urbanus*, borrowed them from L. Petilius in order to read them ; and this was a common practice of his, as when quæstor he had chosen Lucius as secretary into his decuria. When a cursory study had shown him that most of the contents would tend to upset existing religious services, he told Lucius that he was going to throw the books into the fire, but that before he did so, he would let Lucius try whether by action at law or in any other way he could make good his claim to recover them ; and that if he did so the prætor would regard it merely as a friendly suit. The scribe appealed to the tribunes of the plebs, who referred it to the Senate. The prætor offered to take an oath that in his opinion these books should not be read or preserved. The Senate decreed that it was satisfied with the prætor's oath, that the books should be burned in the comitium as soon as possible; that damages should be paid for them to the owners, according to a price fixed by the prætor and the majority of the tribunes. This money the scribe refused to accept. The books were accordingly publicly burned in the comitium, in a fire made by the victimarii.'

That some deliberate fraud was here at work is almost certain. But in whose interest was it attempted? The alarm of the prætor and Senate is easily to be accounted for when we remember that only five years before there had been literally a state panic about the *Bacchanalia*, which were forbidden by law and numerous adherents punished with death.[1] We may even suppose that the documents were in some way connected with this superstition, and hidden away under ground, when the searching and bloody inquiry of the year 186 was going on. This is far more likely than the suggestion that sober Greek doctrines were promoted by such sensational tricks.

But we have no facts left to help us, except the clear evidence that novelties in religion and philosophy attracted the Roman public, and alarmed the Roman government. If so, we are not surprised that in 173 B.C. they expelled from Rome two obscure Epicurean teachers, Alcius and Philiscus, because they were corrupting the Roman youth.[2]

The next step of the Senate was taken in 161 B.C., and

---

[1] Livy, xxxix. 8 *sqq*.

[2] Our authority is here Athen. xii. 547, who mentions L. Postumius as consul. This gives us our choice between 173 and 155 B.C., but I prefer the former, for had this interference with the Epicureans taken

affected both Greek philosophers and rhetors; I believe it to have been mainly directed against the rhetors, who undertook to teach the Roman youth the art of persuasion, and were accordingly expelled from the city.[1]

It is quite possible that this decree is to be brought into connection with the importation of all the Greek and Macedonian exiles after the victory of 168 B.C. I have elsewhere observed[2] how completely these educated exiles disappear from notice when once interned in Italy, and I therefore disagree with Zeller,[3] who assumes that many of them lived, like Polybius, in daily intercourse with great Roman nobles. I consider Polybius to have been quite an exception, and that the tribe of Greeks flooding Rome, which he himself mentions contemptuously to young Scipio,[4] were people of a totally different rank of life and character. But still the enormous number of Greek-speaking and Greek-educated men reduced to misery in Italy must have contained many anxious to earn their bread even by the humblest kind of teaching, and it was plainly the policy of the Senate to have them interned in obscure towns of Italy, not at Rome, where they might do mischief.

But as in the case of Scipio, so the story went that Æmilius Paullus had already, after his victory over Perseus, asked the

place in 155 B.C., the very year after the embassy of the three philosophers from Athens to Rome, we may be sure that Cato would have been mentioned as a mover in the matter, and it would also have been mentioned in connection with that embassy.

[1] These expulsions of philosophers were not, as we have seen, confined to Rome. The decree of Antiochus Sidetes (above, p. 40), which I have quoted from Athenæus, might have been penned by Cato himself. It refers, too, specially to the young. We hear of the Epicureans being expelled from Messene, at what time we know not (Suidas, *sub. voc.* 'Επίκουρος).   [2] *Greek Life and Thought*, p. 562.
[3] *Gesch. der Phil.* iii. 1, 532, *note*.   [4] Polyb. xxxii. 10.

Athenians for a good painter and a sound philosopher, and that they sent him Metrodorus, who excelled in both.[1]

There may have been other isolated cases. But when Cicero[2] argues that there must have been many leading Romans devoted to Greek philosophy at this time, for otherwise the Athenians would not have rooted out from their scholastic seclusion three philosophers to plead their cause in Rome, he is clearly wrong. For more than 150

[1] This story, told by Pliny (*H. N.* xxxv. 135), seems to me inconsistent with the famous narrative of Polybius (xxxii. 9, 10), which implies distinctly that there was no rival Greek educator in the house. The latter says in fact expressly that if Scipio wants mere instruction, there is a whole tribe of such Greeks pouring into Rome, whom he can easily employ. This either means that there was no Metrodorus in the house, or that Polybius chose deliberately to ignore him as an impostor. For the alleged invitation of Paullus and the settlement of Polybius in his mansion must be proximate in date, both having happened shortly after the battle of Pydna. The general statement of Plutarch (*Aem. Paullus*, 6) that not only grammarians and sophists and rhetors, but also sculptors and painters and dog- and horse-trainers and teachers of hunting—all Greeks—were kept about his children, seems to me also vague, and not consistent with Polybius. It is a question, and perhaps a grave one, whether the Greek historian has not exaggerated his own influence in the education of Scipio Æmilianus. This suspicion is greatly strengthened in my mind by the utter silence of Polybius concerning Panætius, who was certainly another Greek friend and adviser of Scipio. It is hardly possible that Panætius did not come into the house till Polybius had returned to Greece after 146 B.C. But this *may* be the explanation. Yet Cicero (*de Repub.* i. 21) speaks of Panætius and Polybius being together with Scipio. Had he any further evidence than we have?

[2] *Tusc. Quæst.* iv. 3.—*Sapientiæ studium vetus id quidem in nostris; sed tamen ante Lælii ætatem et Scipionis non reperio, quos appellare possim nominatim. Quibus adolescentibus, Stoicum Diogenem et Academicum Carneadem video ad senatum ab Atheniensibus missos esse legatos, qui quum reipublicæ nullam unquam partem attigissent, essetque eorum alter Cyrenæus, alter Babylonius, nunquam profecto scholis essent excitati, neque ad illud munus electi, nisi in quibusdam principibus temporibus illis fuissent studia doctrinæ.* He might as well argue that Alexander's regent Antipater studied philosophy because Xenocrates was selected to go before him at a critical moment.

years it had been the fashion in any grave crisis to ask the scholarchs, the grave and solemn philosophers, who took no direct part in politics, to represent states on embassies, just as the bishops in the early Middle Ages did, or as the heads of colleges now go on a deputation of importance to the Prime Minister in London.[1]

This mission, however, of the three heads of the principal schools of Athens—Critolaus the Peripatetic, Diogenes the Stoic, and Carneades the Academic—marks an epoch, slightly earlier indeed than the period we are discussing, but still convenient as the new starting-point, when Greek philosophy began to assert itself openly at Rome. The mission in question took place in 156-155 B.C., and the case to be argued by the three envoys was a very bad one. They wished to obtain the remission of a fine of 500 talents imposed by arbitration on the Athenians for violating the territory and plundering the property of the people of Oropus.

It turned out that their official mission was the least important side of the visit. After their first audience with the Senate, at which C. Acilius acted as interpreter, there appears to have been intentional delay, in order that the famous teachers might give some public lectures at Rome. This they did, with considerable effect. But doubtless the results would have been much greater had not two of the ambassadors, Critolaus and Diogenes, been very old men, and evidently past doing this kind of work effectively. I have above commented on this weakness in the Greek schools and its results at home. Critolaus is indeed left out in many of our accounts,[2] simply I fancy for this reason.

---

[1] I have already commented on this practice, *Greek Life and Thought*, p. 132.

[2] Cf. the passage from Cicero quoted above.

Nor did Diogenes make anything like the impression produced, in spite of a less popular doctrine, by Carneades. Even he too was not young, probably not less than fifty-five years old, but from the fact that he lived twenty-seven years longer, and taught during most of them, we may infer that his vigour was not yet decayed. He entertained the Roman youth with brilliant sceptical discourses, especially with a refutation of the current arguments for political justice, and with an implied vindication of all the Roman foreign conquests.[1] It was in fact the new Anaxarchus preaching to the new Alexander.[2] We are not therefore surprised to hear from Plutarch[3] that old Cato, the personification of the Roman *gravitas*, urged the decision of the Senate concerning Oropus, with the object of dismissing the three professors as soon, and as politely as possible, from the the city. Of course our old friend, Aulus Postumius,[4] and his rivals were disappointed at this. They now had a grand opportunity of airing their Greek, and displaying their *humanities* while showing the philosophers the curiosities of the city.[5] Yet we cannot but be amused at the want of

---

[1] Cicero (*de Repub.* iii. 5-8) says he discoursed one day before Galba, Cato, and other dignitaries in a conservative spirit, rehearsing and enforcing all the old Platonic arguments for justice ; the next day he proceeded to refute them all from his own sceptical point of view.

[2] *Greek Life and Thought*, p. 132. [3] *Cato maj.* 22.

[4] *Greek Life and Thought*, p. 567.

[5] Cic. *Acad. prior.* ii. 45, for an anecdote. It is very probable that numbers pretended to enjoy the discourses of Carneades whose knowledge of Greek was quite inadequate to follow his impetuous delivery, just as numbers of people would go in London to M. Renan's *Hibbert Lectures* who could not understand the greater part of them. But we must remember in mitigation of this carping conjecture that Greek was not taught at Rome by Romans, who could not speak it, out of grammars, but always by Greek-speaking masters, just as English is taught to the Russian nobility. Hence any knowledge there was of

thoroughness in old Cato, and his zeal for strict Roman morals, when we reflect that in these days, while he was railing against the occasional visits of the philosophers, the comedies of Diphilus and Menander, now ten years old at Rome in Terence's versions, were spreading not Greek theories of speculative ethics, but Greek pictures of the lowest practical morals, through Roman society. And this Menandrian comedy was but a fresh outburst, somewhat more refined, of the flagrant immoralities of the Plautine stage.[1]

Here was a philosophy being taught openly, and in Latin, which the Athenians would not have ventured to put forward in their embassy. For Epicureanism, though a very popular religion, and represented by a fixed school with fixed traditions, was at this time never recognised by states in the Hellenistic world as of the same respectability and condition as the rest. The scholarch of this sect at Athens was now Apollodorus, surnamed the *Tyrant of the Garden* (κηποτύραννος), and he was certainly as eminent a man as either Critolaus or Diogenes, but no one thought of including him in the embassy, though possibly his teaching would have been far easier and more practical to many of the Roman youth.

But while the Epicureans steadily declined all political duties, and never, so far as we know, were induced to depart from that principle, such abstention as this made them suspected and disliked in many cities, and there are statements abroad (derived, it must be added, from their enemies) that they were expelled from many Greek cities as well as from Rome.

Greek at Rome was so far real that it was colloquial, and not mere linguistic anatomy.

[1] Cf. *Greek Life and Thought*, p. 119 sqq.

The facts of this famous embassy show us that the heads of the other great schools had agreed to differ, but were otherwise very good friends. Carneades had spent most of his life in refuting Diogenes, and yet they travelled together to Rome, went about together, with Critolaus, to see the sights, and did not apparently indulge in mutual controversy during their visit. I fancy this would not have been the case had the Tyrant of the Garden been added to their number. To suggest modern parallels: the various divisions of Protestant clergy might unite on a solemn deputation, but they would not admit a Roman Catholic priest among their number. An English clerical deputation might perhaps consent to the support of Cardinal Manning and Dr. Martineau, but they would pause and object were a Positivist preacher requested to accompany them. And I know that in America many sects agree to co-operate, who would not tolerate a Mormon elder to sit among them as a colleague.[1]

The savage bitterness of the charges made against Epicurus himself, and against his school, reminds us of the attacks made on Des Cartes and on Spinoza by the clerical party of the seventeenth century. No other scholarch, no other accredited sect, ever received such rude treatment from rivals or opponents.[2] But to this intolerance the uncompromising attitude of the other schools was confined.

Gradually, then, at this period, not only from the influence of Rome, which required practical lessons without subtlety, but from internal causes, from the decay of earnest

---

[1] I once addressed a great congregation at Chautauqua, made up of at least nineteen (non-Romanist) sects, joining heartily in a service mainly culled from our *Book of Common Prayer*, and quite ready to hear any broad Christian views expounded.

[2] Cf., for example, the details given in Diogenes L. x. § 6 *sq.*, and in Suidas, *sub. voc.* ἐπίκουρος.

faith in speculation, of earnest faith in the aims of practical life, *eclecticism*, the creed of weary minds, laid hold of the Hellenistic world. Carneades had not only shattered all the remaining dogmatism by his brilliant polemic, but he had laid down as his highest principle *mere probability*, so that there was no reason why the researches of any set of men might not contain some approximate truth. And as the doctrines might be culled from any school, so the men who taught them might hail from any country. Hellenism had been wide enough in former generations; we now seem to approach an even wider cosmopolitanism. The successor of Carneades, Clitomachus, was born in no part of the Hellenistic world, but at Carthage, where he had taught philosophy in his own tongue.[1] He became a pupil of Carneades, whose spoken teaching he committed to writing. But Diogenes L. also makes this characteristic remark, that Clitomachus was a man distinguished in the three philosophies—the Academic, the Stoic, and the Peripatetic.[2] Both he and the many obscurer followers of the new Academy are said to have added nothing to its tenets, save that they laid more stress than Carneades on the positive side, on the necessity of some guide of life, while the rival schools were compelled to abate their pretensions, to surrender some of their positions, and reduce themselves to what might reasonably be accepted without any enthusiasm. In this condition the schools no longer excited suspicion at Rome. We hear of no further objections there to Greek philosophy, for a bridge of mutual concessions was being made, which would

[1] Diog. L. iv. 67.
[2] He dedicated two of his writings to Romans—the poet Lucilius and the consular Censorinus. He addressed his Carthaginian fellow-countrymen in a philosophical consolation for the loss of their fatherland. He died in 110 B.C. This is, therefore, essentially a figure belonging to the epoch now under our consideration.

unite the once widely severed societies of dominant Rome and literary Greece.

We may pursue for a few more pages the growth and development of the eclectic spirit before we revert to other subjects.

It may be assumed as certain, that to the Romans neither the minute erudition of the Peripatetic, nor the minute controversy of the Academic, would afford any great attraction. This practical people would rather turn to those schools of life—the Epicurean and the Stoic, which had always put practice before speculation, and now, as we shall see, were quite prepared to lay aside this lesser but harder side of theory, and announce themselves as mere rules of life for men of the world. As might be expected, the better schools were attractive to the highest and most cultivated Romans, who possessed or were willing to acquire some knowledge of Greek; while, according to Cicero, the Epicurean disciples at Rome did not delay to bring out in Latin an account of their tenets, and this book, prepared by one C. Amafinius, obtained great circulation, and converted the lower herd of the semi-educated to the lower theory.[1]

The historians of philosophy assert that no school was less affected by eclectic tendencies than this Epicurean school. Yet these early Latin books, which converted the multitude, and which we must ascribe to the second century B.C., were surely very narrow and inadequate accounts of a

---

[1] Cic. *Tusc. Disp.* iv. 3.—*Itaque illius verae elegantisque philosophiae, quae ducta a Socrate—nulla fere sunt aut pauca monumenta—quum interim, illis silentibus, C. Amafinius exstitit dicens: cujus libris editis commota multitudo contulit se ad eandem potissimum disciplinam, sive quod erat cognitu facillimum, sive quod invitabantur illecebris blandae voluptatis, sive etiam, quia nihil prolatum erat melius, illud, quod erat, tenebant. Post Amafinium autem multi ejusdem aemuli rationis multa quum scripsissent, Italiam totam occubaverunt,* etc.

system which is as difficult and abstract as metaphysic can well be, both in the tenth book of Diogenes Laertius and in the great poem of Lucretius, who by the way boasts that he is the first to expound these principles in Latin poetry. These books, no doubt, omitted all the physical and cosmological speculations, and were satisfied with the ordinary stuff which was current among the Greek idlers of the market-place. It is possible that they contained something about friendship being a pleasure in itself, but the researches of Zeller and others have proved clearly, that whatever omissions they may have permitted, none of them ever belied the theory of their great master. In fact, that school, like no other Greek school, never had a second master, never had a second independent thinker, who could assert himself by developing further consequences, or asserting new principles. It remained once and for all the school of Epicurus, and of Epicurus alone.

The case was very different with the Stoics, who from the moment of Chrysippus's death, began to question some of the physical theories till then received, and gradually to approximate in their views to the Peripatetics. This is specially recorded of his immediate successor Zeno of Tarsus, then more positively of Boethus of Sidon, the pupil and contemporary of the Diogenes of the embassy. We hear that most of them rejected the theory that the world would ultimately perish by fire, and maintained, with Aristotle's school, its eternity.

But these men do not here interest us except as links in the chain which leads to Panætius, who not only adopted their views, but went much further in his disagreement, and, though distinctly a Stoic, was nevertheless the founder of almost a new school—of that Roman Stoicism which plays so prominent a part in the history of the Empire. He came from Rhodes, and was a pupil of Diogenes at Athens. The most important part of his life was, however, spent at Rome, in the house of Scipio Æmilianus,[1] the centre of the Scipionic circle, where he trained up a number of Roman nobles to understand and to adopt his views. He seems to have taken the place of Polybius, and to have accompanied Scipio in his tour to the East (143 B.C.) He died as head of the Stoic school in Athens about 110 B.C.

This was the man who, under the influence of the age, really modified the rigid tenets of his sect to make it the practical rule of life for statesmen, politicians, magnates, who had no time to sit all day and dispute, but who required something better than effete polytheism to give them dignity in their leisure, and steadfastness in the day of trial. He denied, indeed, with his teachers the eternity of the world, but also with the Epicureans the immortality of the soul, as we know from Cicero's refutation. His main work, however, was the teaching of practical duties,—those perfections falling short of the Stoic perfection,—which Cicero reproduces in his treatise *de officiis*. In theology he, like Polybius, regarded the traditional gods as a mere political convenience, and he ridiculed the divines, in the style of Carneades.

With the pupils of Panætius begins the long roll of Roman Stoics—Lælius; his son-in-law Q. Mucius Scævola; Q. Tubero, the nephew of Scipio, to whom Panætius dedicated his work on *Duties;* Rutilius Rufus, the just administrator of Asia, whom the publicani exiled for his protection of the Asiatic province from their extortions; and many others to whom Cicero refers. But as yet I do not wish to cross the threshold of the first century B.C., so I forbear.

---

[1] Cp. above, p. 67.

Here then, after all the dissolute and disintegrating influences of Hellenism,—its *comœdia palliata*, its parasites, its panders, its minions, its chicanery, its mendacity—had produced their terrible effect, came an antidote which, above all the human influences we know, purified and ennobled the world. It affected, unfortunately, only the higher classes[1] at Rome; and even among them, as among any of the lower classes that speculated at all, it had as a dangerous rival that cheap and vulgar Epicureanism, which puffs up common natures with the belief that their trivial and coarse reflections have some philosophic basis, and can be defended with subtle arguments.

But among the best of the Romans Hellenism produced a type seldom excelled in the world's history, a type as superior to the old Roman model as the nobleman is to the burgher in most countries—a type we see in Rutilius Rufus, as compared with the elder Cato. Whoever reads Plutarch's *Life* of this latter person will see that he was in many senses a worthy man, an able man, an educated man, but he was no gentleman. Rutilius conducted his life, and performed his public duties, as Cato had done, with a purity exceptional in any society; but when sentenced to exile by a decision so flagrant that it convulsed the public mind with disgust, he bore his misfortune not only with refined calmness and cheerfulness, but spent a happy and honoured

[1] And when I say higher classes, I do not confine the word to the conservative patricians. Tiberius Gracchus, whose whole education had been entrusted to Greeks (as Cicero tells us), was advised and probably incited in his radical schemes by Blossius of Cumæ, no doubt a very inferior teacher to Panætius, but a far more dangerous enthusiast. This man left Rome after Tiberius's death, and joined Aristonicus in his war against Rome for the kingdom of Pergamum. When the pretender was defeated, Blossius committed suicide. There may have been a deep anti-Roman feeling stimulating this philosopher's theories of political reform.

retirement at Smyrna, where Cato would have been miserable, and offensive to the provincials. Everything we hear of Rutilius shows not only his high principle, but his perfect temper and his large culture. It is, indeed, to be regretted that his *Memoirs* are not preserved. We know him through the many allusions of Cicero, Seneca, and others.[1] It was in this way that Hellenistic philosophy made itself a home in Italy, and acquired pupils who in the next generation became masters in their way, and showed in Cicero and Lucretius no mean rivals of the contemporary Greek.

Lucretius is so essentially a Roman figure, and his poem so Roman a poem, that I will not turn aside to criticise it at any length. But as the author himself tells us, his philosophical masters were Democritus and Epicurus, his poetical masters Empedocles and Ennius, so that he only claims originality for having been the first to treat this Greek system of philosophy in Latin—perhaps in Latin poetry. Even here his claim is made doubtful by what Cicero says of Amafinius, and the vulgar herd who reproduced Epicurus in Latin prose. Yet, still, there is far more originality in Lucretius than he claims for himself. In the first place he recasts the ostentatiously slipshod writing of Epicurus into a noble poem, and for his model he selects not the fashionable Alexandrian poets, as his contemporary Catullus did, but a famous old master, of real Hellenic purity.[2] And to reproduce the effect of this old Epic speech, he goes back to the archaic Ennius, and resuscitates forms which were antiquated and forgotten by the fashionable literati of his day. This bold attempt, executed with undoubted genius, was perhaps too original to meet with general favour

[1] Cf. Zeller, *op. cit.* p. 536.
[2] Cf. on Empedocles my *Class. Greek Lit.* i. 124 *sq.*

from the advocates of the new school, though it influenced the best of them, Catullus and Virgil, very considerably. But however little he may have been appreciated by his compeers, posterity has recognised the first great success in reproducing Greek thought and Greek artistic style in a Roman dress. The poem of Lucretius stands beside the prose of Epicurus as superior in literary form as the poetry of Virgil beside that of Apollonius Rhodius, or the English Bible beside the Greek. The Romans were indeed imitators and pupils; but what pupils![1]

[1] The attempt of Pub. Nigidius Figulus, whom Mommsen rates so extraordinarily (*R. G.* iii. 573), chiefly on the authority, too, of that Cicero whom he derides and despises, I shall consider in connection with the new Pythagoreanism of Alexandria and the East at this period—the most curious of all the philosophic developments of the century before Augustus.

CHAPTER V

THE GENERAL REACTION OF HELLENISM UPON ROME

I HAVE chosen for our first and most serious consideration the settlement of Greek philosophy at Rome, because there was no purer or more distinctly Greek product, and one which kept its individual character and language so long. Till the poem of Lucretius and the works of Cicero, we may say nothing in Latin worth reading existed on the subject. Whoever wanted to study philosophy, therefore, down to that time (60 B.C.) studied it in Greek. Nearly the same thing may be said of the arts of architecture, painting, and sculpture. There were indeed distinctly Roman features in architecture, but they were mere matters of building, and whatever was done in the way of design, in the way of adding beauty to strength, was done wholly under the advice and direction of Greeks.

The subservience to Hellenism in the way of internal household ornament was even more complete. No painting or sculpture from native artists would now be tolerated at Rome. Extravagant prices were paid for statues and pictures from Greece, also for silver plate and for Greek marbles, though there were precious quarries lying idle in Italy. The prices then paid for old silver—twenty to thirty times the price of the metal—rival those lavished in our own day on 'Queen Anne' plate. And with the ornaments of the house, the proper serving of the house, especially the more delicate departments—the cooking of state dinners, the attendance upon guests, the care of the great man's intimate comforts—could only be done fashionably by Greek slaves. The outburst of Hellenistic fashions of this sort at Rome must have far exceeded the outburst of French fashions in England after the peace of 1815, when England with all her great wealth and European prestige had been practically excluded from the progress of material civilisation in France for a whole generation, and suddenly awoke to the fact that in many respects she was still rude and barbarous.

But of course these lower sides of Hellenism had no more potent effect in civilising Rome than the employing of French cooks and valets and the purchase of French ornaments and furniture had in improving our grandfathers. Much more serious was the acknowledged supremacy of the Greeks in literature of all kinds, and still more their insistence that this superiority depended mainly upon a careful system of intellectual education. A self-taught man—*autodidaktos*—or even the man who learned late—*opsimathes*—was in the Greek world always considered a man of imperfect breeding, and wanting in real refinement. This is the point where Polybius, after his seventeen years' experience of Roman life, finds the capital flaw in the conduct of public affairs. In every Hellenistic state, he says, nothing engrosses the attention of legislators more than the question of education, whereas at Rome a most moral and serious government leaves the training of the young to the mistakes and hazards of private enterprise.

That this was a grave blunder as regards the lower classes is probably true. The Roman mob during the next few generations showed all the vices and violences of an ignorant populace entrusted with the affairs of a mighty empire. If, therefore, the almost universal assumption be really true, that the mob of any nation can be educated out of passion and folly into a reasonable crowd, then the Senate is liable to a crime of omission which brought upon the government terrible punishment. But as regards the upper classes, whose education the Senate did no doubt carefully consider, the Roman theory held that home education was the only education worth having, and that the unpaid interest taken in the young by parents and parents' friends was the proper influence to be brought upon the rising generation. So long as the requirements of the day were small, and consisted chiefly of practical good sense in the management of household affairs or civic duties, this theory did not show its weakness. But when Rome grew from a city controlling Italy to an empire directing the world, such men as Æmilius Paullus saw plainly that they must do something more to fit their children for the splendid position they had themselves attained, and so they were obliged to keep foreign teachers of literature and art in their houses as private tutors.

The highest class of these private tutors was that of the philosophers, whom we have considered, and while the State set itself against their public establishments, great men in the State openly encouraged them and kept them in their houses. Cicero says that he treated his literary slave Dionysius better than Scipio treated Panætius; and the jibe of Lucilius, that his horse and groom were worth more to him than his philosopher, seems to corroborate this.[1] But still, so far as philosophy was concerned, the Romans could hardly say anything reasonable to depreciate the Greeks. No Roman of that day could produce anything beyond the

[1] Cf. Mommsen, *R. G.* ii. 425.

obscure and probably contemptible Latin Epicureanism of Ennius and Amafinius.

As regards literature, however, in the close of the second century B.C. a change was visible, which announced the new and marvellous results of the first. The Romans had begun with translating as best they could Greek masterpieces, then had attempted national poems like those of Nævius. But according as the best judges began to appreciate the Greek originals and use them with greater ease, these early versions became ridiculous and were despised. We have before us only one large example of this change in critical taste—the versions of Greek comedy we find in Plautus and Terence respectively. The refined diction of Terence shows us what was the taste of the younger Scipio and Lælius, and what they required in a translation as compared with the rude attempts of the older days. Still more remarkable is it that this brilliant success was not popular with the masses, and that it led to no further attempts in the same direction. Terence, far the most perfect, is also the last in the long series of early Roman translations from the Greek.

Nor are the causes far to seek. In the first place, this clearer and deeper comprehension of the great originals led to two conclusions—that the grace and beauty of Greek poetry were unattainable in Latin, and that they were in any case far above the enjoyment of the masses. In the second, the refinement attained in the style of Terence suggested that the Latin tongue had after all a future of its own, and was destined to pursue an independent course in literature. This latter expectation was realised by the rise of Lucilius, the first original Latin poet, whose medleys on life and manners were not only popular within the circle which patronised and supported Terence, but among that far larger public which could not or would not appreciate the refined vices of Menander in Roman speech. The attempt of Nævius to create a national poetry had failed, for the time was not ripe. The attempt of Lucilius succeeded, as the long line of Roman satirists abundantly proves.

But the reaction in prose literature is still more remarkable. There were circulated during these days at least two specimens of Latin prose writing which were essentially Roman, and yet in no wise lacking either force or purity. These were the speeches of Caius Gracchus—of which fragments remain—and the letters of his mother Cornelia. Such books showed that Latin eloquence had powers of its own, and need not build entirely upon Greek rhetoric. Accordingly Crassus and Antonius, the famous orators at the end of this century, whom Cicero has glorified in his treatise *de Oratore*, though far from ignorant in Greek lore, were distinctly national, and founded the great school of Latin eloquence suggested by, but not derived from, its Greek sister. There is even abroad a spirit of antagonism to Greek rhetoric, as a school of subtlety and of unpractical discussion, a spirit manifested not only in the traditions of these early orators, but in the edict against the Latin pedants who imitated the Greek professors (92 B.C.)

Accordingly even in grammar, which Dionysius Thrax had been teaching at his school in Rome since 107 B.C., there arose a Latin school, of which the founder was L. Ælius Stilo, who taught Roman youths gratuitously, as the great jurisconsults did, by way of advice as a friend, and who based his lessons on Latin grammar and style upon a study of the older Latin models. The fashion of writing for posterity in Greek began to wane, and a Roman literature, solid and founded upon rational study, supplanted the exotic growths so long fashionable.

Thus even in letters Roman culture began to take

its place beside Greek, and the whole civilised world was divided into those who knew Greek letters and those who knew Roman only. There was no antagonism in spirit between them, for the Romans never ceased to venerate Greek letters or to prize a knowledge of that language. But of course there were great domains in the West beyond the influence of the most western Greeks, even of Massilia, where the first higher civilisation introduced was with the Roman legions and traders, and where culture assumed permanently a Latin form. In the East, though the Romans asserted themselves as conquerors, they always condescended to use Greek, and there were prætors proud to give their decisions at Roman assize courts in that language. Hence there might have been fairly anticipated a peaceful development of both under the Roman sway, and a long period of prosperity for Hellenism of the material and moral, though not of the political kind. The injustice of governors and traders who presumed on Roman domination was indeed a pressing evil. Yet the development of higher culture at Rome, the spread of Stoic philosophy, the occurrence of men like the Gracchi, the Scipios, and Rutilius point to an improvement not only in the rulers but in public opinion, and a growing disposition to hear the complaints of provincials and in time to redress them.

But the great internal troubles of Rome supervened and cast into the shade all this higher development. While the select few were really advancing on the higher paths, the bulk of the nobility and the populace were involved not only in the Gracchan troubles, and by and by in the shocking violences of Cinna and Marius, but also in the Jugurthan war, in the great Cimbric tumult, and then in the revolt of the Italian subjects. So it is that wars and rumours of wars fill the pages of the historian to the exclusion of social and spiritual life. And so it is with the Greek world now under the domination of Rome. Here too the days of reform in provincial administration were too long delayed, and the great catastrophe of a new unsuccessful revolt came upon the larger and better portion of Hellenism. When Mithradates, an oriental despot merely varnished with culture, created his kingdom round the shores of the Euxine, and came into collision with the Romans, the cruelties and oppressions of the publicani and prætors had been such, that the great body of Greeks in Asia and Hellas rose with him against their tormentors.

The nations which are our special study thus suddenly move again into the foreground of history, and the events in Greece and Asia Minor become suddenly as important as the annals of the capital. This prominence was, however, purchased at a terrible cost; the reprisals and confiscations of the conquerors exhausted the Hellenistic world for generations. Far worse, too, than even this was the renewed estrangement between Greek and Roman, which the events of the last fifty years had been tending to efface. The friends of the 100,000 Italians massacred in Asia and at Delos must have made up their minds that after all there was a national antipathy which nothing could allay; they must have felt that henceforth the only safe policy was to cripple completely an empire of subjects who, after all the public favour bestowed in the way of internal liberty and public respect, were ready to join any barbarian invader against the Republic of the West.

The wars of Mithradates with Sylla and then with Lucullus are a matter of ordinary Roman history, here again profoundly interesting because we have, besides Appian, the inestimable Plutarch, whose lives of Sylla, Sertorius, and Lucullus lead up to those of Pompey and Cæsar. What we have to do is to search the events of this momentous epoch for evidences of the progress or decay of Hellenism in the world.

And first of all let me turn to a very outlying province, which might easily be mistaken for a province of Hellenism in the technical sense, but which is really of quite a different type—I mean the civilisation which the generals of Mithradates found and protected on the north of the Euxine, in the Crimean kingdom.

This outlying portion of the Greek world had been planted centuries before by the Milesians and Megarians for the purpose of trade, and a number of cities had been built along the strait which forms the outlet of the Sea of Asov. The country on the east side of that sea was productive in corn and cattle. The shallow sea was peculiarly rich in fish, and with the gradual rise of population in Greece, and of luxury in Greek cities, this Cimmerian Bosphorus obtained an unlimited market for wheat, salt-fish, and hides. So its wealth and importance increased, and though always threatened by the nomad hordes of the North, the Greeks managed, either by building strong cities and walls across the isthmus, or by treaties and intermarriages with barbarians, to maintain themselves in wealth and culture. There were important free cities, and there were despots[1] ruling over the inner country. One of these despots, Leucon, is mentioned by Demosthenes[2] as having obtained for himself and his heirs the freedom of the city of Athens, in requital for the gifts of corn he had bestowed on the Athenians in a time of scarcity. The tombs of these despots, which were still unrifled in our time, have yielded treasures to the Museum of Kertch (sacked in the Crimean war by the French and English) and to that

---

[1] ἐκαλοῦντο δὲ τύραννοι καίπερ οἱ πλείους ἐπιεικεῖς γεγονότες (Strabo, vii. 4, 4). [2] In *Leptinem*, §§ 30-40.

of S. Petersburg, which have been reproduced in splendid coloured plates by the Russian government.[1] These ornaments not only show that large quantities of gold must have been brought to these Greek cities from the Ural, but that they possessed artists of the highest quality there to work it into beautiful and rich designs.

The Macedonian conquest seriously affected the prosperity of the Crimean Greeks. The decay of Greece, not to speak of the rival wealth of Egypt, spoiled their long-established market. When the political centre of gravity moved westward Africa and outer Spain could supply both wheat and salt-fish better and cheaper than the Sea of Asov, for the Mediterranean is not comparable to the Atlantic fish, and how could the climate of Scythia compete with Sicily and Africa—a climate where it was possible indeed to grow vines, but necessary to cover them completely with earth every winter;[2] a climate, moreover, where a great battle could be fought and won upon the ice, a feat which one of Mithradates's generals actually performed.[3]

The whole progress of Alexander's conquest neglected the Cimmerian Bosphorus and its Chersonese as of no importance, and this decay of prominence meant of course decay of power, and hence growing inability to meet or resist the demands of the nomads, who expected the southerners to cultivate the land, but to pay a heavy tax or black-mail for this privilege. And this tax was determined by the strength and rapacity of those who demanded it. So there was repeated a history like that of Byzantium which I have already told in my *Greek Life and Thought*.[4]

---

[1] *Antiquités du Bosphore cimmérien*, giving the remains found in the tumulus of Koul-Oba, near Kertch.

[2] Strabo, ii. 1, § 16. The practice still exists in Hungary, and I suppose elsewhere in those parts of Europe which have a severe winter.

[3] *Ibid.*   [4] P. 348 *sq*.

The details of this Crimean history, and the results in the time of Mithradates, which were till recently only known from Strabo's summary,[1] are now confirmed and enlarged by the long inscription in honour of Diophantus,[2] which tells us that he was a Sinopean, solicited by the king to undertake this command, and that he repeatedly won victories for the king over the Scythians hitherto deemed invincible.[3]

The generals of Mithradates brought a small army of disciplined troops to the aid of the distressed Greeks, whose last king, Parisades, consented to pay a tribute of 200 talents and a vast amount of wheat to the Pontic sovran on condition of being saved from the Scythian marauders. The battles which took place were famous as demonstrating again the absolute superiority of discipline and of better arms over any numerical majority of savages. Diophantus with 6000 men defeated and almost annihilated a host alleged to be 50,000 strong. I am always suspicious of the numbers in ancient histories; but the general statement is to be accepted, and is all the more interesting as we now attribute our superiority to Zulus and Arabs wholly to our arms of precision, which are generally different *in kind* from those of savages, and not, as the arms of Diophantus's army, merely better

---

[1] vii. 4, § 17, probably taken from Posidonius.

[2] Which may be most easily read in Dittenberger's *Sylloge*, No. 252.

[3] τοὺς ἀνυποστάτους δοκοῦντας εἶμεν Σκύθας τρεψάμενος πρῶτον ἐπ' αὐτῶν ἐπόησε βασιλέα Μιθ. Εὔπατ. τροπαῖον ἀναστᾶσαι κτλ. The titles of the city authorities at Chersonesus, where the inscription was set up, also inform us that in spite of titular *kings*, who were no more real kings than the *rex sacrificulus* at Rome, the constitution was democratic, and manifestly modelled from the old arrangements of Megara, which had founded Heraclea, the immediate mother-city of Chersonesus. Even the *kings* as religious officers, chosen by lot, occur in old inscriptions of Megara, as well as at Chios; and the eponymous officer at Calymnæ was called μόναρχος down to the first century A.D. (cf. *Bull. de corresp. hell.* viii. 30; ix. 286).

swords, shields, and spears. No doubt the field artillery must have been even more important then than it is now, and must have astonished the Scythians as it did the Thracians when attacked by Alexander.[1]

The protection of Mithradates lasted but a short time, and was exchanged for that of the Romans, who during all the century before us were occupied with domestic struggles, and were in any case culpably lax and careless about their outlying subjects. So then the overthrow of the Pontic power was probably a heavy blow to these cities.[2] But the point to be noticed is this, that they never had formed part of any Hellenistic kingdom, nor had they been directly affected by any of the new influences which so deeply modified Hellenedom. Hence we shall find them under the Roman Empire a curious remnant of old-world culture, differing *toto cælo* from the newer settlements of Syria and inner Asia; but we must leave our further consideration of them till they again emerge in the pages of Dion Chrysostom.[3]

As regards the real regions of Hellenism, Egypt was altogether unconcerned in the Mithradatic struggles, and firmly but politely refused to aid Sylla when he sent his lieutenant, the famous Lucullus, to beg for ships. The young king (Ptolemy Alexander) entertained the Roman with great splendour, but sent him away without help. The Syrian cities were now under Tigranes, whom they hated; but Tigranes was not implicated in the first war of his brother-in-law. It was in fact only Asia Minor and Greece (apart

---

[1] Cf. my *Alexander's Empire*, chap. i.

[2] There is a Latin inscription as late as the reign of Domitian lauding Ti. Plaut. Silv. Ælianus, legate *pro praetore*, of Mœsia (58-69 A.D.), for saving the town of Cherson from a siege by a Scythian king, and so enabling a large quantity of corn to be sent to Rome (cf. *CIL* iii. 781, and *Bulletin de corresp. hell.* (*BCH*) ix. 275).

[3] Below, chap. xi. Note there Pliny's letter on the subject.

from the Crimean (Greeks) which appeared in the struggle with Sylla.

Here we may note first of all the greater predominance and importance of Asia. The primacy seems reversed, and whereas of old Ionia had been long insignificant as compared with the European states, now there is hardly any account taken of the latter except Athens, the Asiatic cities showing not only a far larger number of inhabitants, especially foreigners, but also greater independence in their policy. Though the majority join the invader and massacre the hated Italic residents, several isolated members of this great society of towns hold firm in their allegiance to Rome, and even withstand the victorious armies of the Cappadocian. Of course there were many more who turned upon the king as soon as they found the Roman power was likely to overcome him. Of this we have an interesting case in the Ephesians, whose decree of recantation and of loyalty to the Romans may now be read at Oxford.[1] Far more honest was the Carian League, headed by the town of Stratoniceia, which from the first boldly resisted the Pontic invader, and in consequence received great rewards and favours from Sylla. There has been recently found at Lagina, which represents the site of Stratoniceia, a now famous inscription containing a letter from Sylla, and a *senatus consultum*, which the dictator got passed in the year 80 B.C., confirming to the inhabitants all the privileges he had bestowed upon them—remission of taxes, increase of territory, right of priority in consulting the Senate, and, above all, the right of asylum for their famous temple of Hecate, which had been acknowledged generally by the Greek world.[2]

[1] Cf. Hicks, *Man. of Inscrips.* p. 352.
[2] *BCH* ix. 437 *sq.* To this document I shall revert.

We can easily understand this philo-Romanism, even apart from long-sighted policy, such as we might have anticipated in the Rhodians. For oppressive as were the Italians, the Pontic king was worse,[1] and was distinctly a barbarian, in spite of his knowledge of Greek, his Greek mercenary generals, and his fine promises to the Greek world. Appian, in describing his character,[2] says he studied Greek culture, honoured Greek temples, and was fond of Greek music. He was also a collector of antique works of art;[3] but his harem, and his utter dependence on eunuchs, which indeed was the main cause of his final overthrow, show his oriental side plainly enough. His armies, too, though commanded by Greeks, were distinctly armies of barbarians. If the Romans had indeed been expelled from the East, the cause of Hellenism would certainly have suffered more even than it did from their exactions. For the best Romans were already, or were daily becoming, real members of the Hellenistic world, and we can see from the policy of Sylla, Lucullus, and Pompey how even the manifest dislike and treachery of the Greeks, and their enthusiastic reception of the murderer of 100,000 Italians, had not unsettled the fixed idea that Greeks were one thing, and all the rest of the East another; that Greeks had the

[1] His *anoekism* of the Chians—a ruthless piece of cruelty—is to be paralleled by the proceeding of Tigranes mentioned by Strabo (xi. 14, 15), when he was founding his new capital, Tigranocerta, from twelve Greek cities emptied for the purpose. This policy was frustrated in time by the conquest of Lucullus.

[2] *Mith.* 112.

[3] *Ibid.* 115, *sub. fin.* Strabo also (x. 4, 10), in a digression upon his own ancestors and their relations to Cnossus in Crete, speaks of the intimacy of both Mithradates Energetes and his son Eupator with the Greek family of Dorylaos, professor of military tactics. The younger Dorylaos (nephew of the elder) was brought up as an intimate with the great Pontic king.

monopoly of culture, and that the rest were only fit to serve them and the Romans.

The gross ingratitude of the Greeks of Asia, who, in spite of this profoundly sentimental, theoretical admiration, took practical extortion and cruelty so much to heart as to massacre their admirers wholesale, was not indeed forgotten by the Romans;[1] but in the moment of victory the cynical and relentless Sylla only punished them with an immense war indemnity, and his successor, Lucullus, sought to save them from the financial ruin which threatened them in consequence. The wealth of the free cities in Asia Minor seems to have been so great, that not even the levying of five years' taxes in advance would have ruined them, had they not been induced or constrained to borrow from the Roman speculators, who treated them in the same way as Verres afterwards treated the Sicilians. The usurers took care to make all escape from their clutches impossible.

We hear of no parallel exactions from Greece, though the resistance of Athens and the Piræus was to Sylla a far more serious offence than the mere massacre of Italian traders. Indeed, Sylla specially gives up, in his argument with Mithradates,[2] the defence of M. Aquillius's character, and concedes that his greed for gold and dishonesty in selling provinces had been an important factor in the war. This admission would of course apply also to the inferior extortioners who infested the province of Asia.

But Athens and the Piræus really blocked the way, and made Sylla run imminent risk of losing everything; and

[1] What was even worse, the massacre and loss of property caused a financial crisis at Rome, an important fact omitted in the modern histories (cf. Cic. *pro lege Man.* § 19). *Nam tum, quum in Asia res magnas permulti amiserant, scimus Romæ, solutione impedita, fidem concidisse.*

[2] Appian, *Mith.* 156, 157, no doubt taken from Sylla's own *Memoirs*.

though the latter was held by a foreign army under a foreign general, Archelaus, Athens had put itself under the direction of a mere impostor, and permitted him, while bringing the city into great misery by his selfish cruelty, to insult and delay Sylla.

The story of this Aristion is very interesting, as it shows us a prominent example of the curious class so widespread in that age—I mean the impostor in philosophy. The story is copied by Athenæus from Posidonius, who was a contemporary authority, and there is no reason to question the main facts.[1] This Aristion was son, by an Egyptian slave mother, to an Athenian who was a long time a pupil in the Peripatetic school of Erymneus (scholarch about 110 B.C.) He succeeded to the goods of his father, who had apparently no legitimate son, and so he got himself enrolled as an Athenian citizen. We may imagine that in these decayed times any man with some money, who could show an Athenian father, found little

[1] Athen. v. 48 sq., 212. Appian (*Mith.* 28) differs in many details. Athenæus calls him Athenion, but is wrong, as is proved not only by other writers, but by the existence of a coin of Athens, with the names of Mithradates and Aristion on it. It is reproduced in Duruy's *Hist. of Rome*, ii. 660, 661. Plutarch has the name right, *reip. gub. præc.* 14. On a set of coins found in 1881 at Athens, which had evidently been buried at the moment of Sylla's invasion, we find a gold coin (which is unusual, as only military conquerors seem to have made them) not only with Μιθραδάτης Βασιλεύς, and under it Aristion (as his satrap), but even with Mithradates's 'cognisance,' a winged Pegasus drinking at a fountain (cf. *Revue des études grecques*, ii. 145). In an able article on Athens and Mithradates suggested by this evidence, R. Weil (*Mittheilungen des deutsch. Inst. in Athen*, vi. 314 sq.) argues that the story in the text, being derived from the Stoic Posidonius, is coloured by the strong prejudices of scholastic rivalry. Indeed the schools now took opposite sides, the Academics and Stoics holding with the Romans, the Peripatetics with the Pontic king. It may have been that Posidonius calls the man Athenion to assert his illegitimacy, by which name he would have been known but for his success in foisting himself on an Athenian tribe. The details must, therefore, be accepted with caution.

difficulty in accomplishing this. He then married a pretty slave girl, and adopted the profession of sophist, touting for youths who wanted education.[1] So having practised both at Messene and at Larissa in Thessaly, and having made a good deal of money, he came to Athens. Such wandering sophists were to be found all over the world. Thus a few years later, during the war of Lucullus with Tigranes, we hear of one, Amphicrates, who, flying from Athens arrived at Seleucia on the Tigris, where the people besought him, as being an Athenian, to establish himself as a sophist. But he said he would not be a triton among minnows,[2] and went off to the queen of Tigranes, Mithradates's sister, where he obtained enough influence to be suspected of cabals with the Greeks of Parthia, and was put to death.

In the same way Aristion was ambitious of figuring at court, and got himself nominated as ambassador from Athens to Mithradates. Pontus and Cappadocia had old relations with Athens. Sinope and Amisus especially, close to Eupatoria, the royal residence, were full of old Attic settlers since the days of Perikles, and both religious rites and names record this connection. It seems, however, that the moving force which drove Athens to take this disastrous step was anger and jealousy at the Roman and Phœnician traders, who had settled in crowds at Delos, and had ousted the Athenian citizens, to whom the island now formally belonged, from all their business. No doubt the Italians were not only overreaching but self-asserting, and rode roughshod over the rights of the Delian merchants. 'Aristion was sent out to Pontus, and here he was eminently suc-

[1] γήμας τε παιδισκάριον εὔμορφον πρὸς τὸ σοφιστεύειν ὥρμησε μειράκια σχολαστικὰ θηρεύων.
[2] Plutarch, *Lucullus*, 22. His joke was really much more insolent, seeing how great a city this Seleucia was—ὡς οὐδὲ λεκάνη δελφῖνα χωροίη.

cessful, so that he sent letters to Athens telling of his great influence with the king, and that he would not only obtain remission of their encumbrances and a reconciliation of parties, but that they would recover their democracy, and receive great presents both as individuals and for their state. So the Athenians were greatly excited at this hope, and at the chance of getting rid of the Roman supremacy.'

'No sooner had Mithradates overrun Asia than Aristion set out for Athens, and was sent for to Carystos by the people with warships and great pomp. The whole city came out to meet him, like a new Alcibiades, and so this side-wind citizen excited the astonishment of all that beheld him, entering Athens in a gorgeous litter with purple hangings—a creature who had never seen such a thing at Athens in his life before, for not even a Roman would assume such airs in Attica. Every man, woman, and child ran together to witness his arrival, and naturally expected great things from Mithradates, seeing that this pauper, Aristion, who had made his living by 'subscription lectures,' was now set up by him in lavish luxury. The Dionysiac artists[1] also came out to meet him, inviting him as the envoy of the new Dionysus—so the Pontic king was called by Asiatic flatterers—to all their feasts and privileges. So the man who had gone out from a hired lodging was led back to the mansion of the rich Diaeus (who owned revenues at Delos), which was adorned with carpets, paintings, statues, and silver plate. From this he issued forth in splendid robes, wearing a ring with the head of Mithradates, preceded and followed by a numerous escort. In the *temenos* of the artists sacrifices and libations were offered in honour of his advent. People waited in crowds next day to see him pass, and all went to the public assembly

[1] Cf. *Greek Life and Thought*, p. 383.

without summons in the hope of hearing him. At last he appeared with a volunteer guard about him, every one being anxious even to touch the hem of his garment.' He then ascended the rostra prepared for the Roman governors, and made a pompous speech, of which Posidonius gives us his own version.[1]

He represents him as having painted the king's power in glowing language, how all hither Asia obeyed him, how the Roman generals, even Manius Aquillius, the conqueror of Sicily (in the Slave war), was following him in chains, and the rest of the so-called Romans in Asia either were embracing the knees of the gods as suppliants, or had got rid of their togas and were now proclaiming their former nationalities— a very graphic feature, and no doubt in accordance with the facts.[2] So Thrace and Macedonia are sending him troops, and both the Italian insurgents and Carthage (!) are asking him to join in destroying Rome. 'Let us then no longer tolerate the anarchy inflicted upon us by the Roman Senate, while they deliberate how we are to be governed, and let us not bear to see the temples shut up, the gymnasia unkept, the theatre without assemblies, the courts silent, the Pnyx taken from the people, the solemn processions disused, and the schools of the philosophers deserted.'

If this language was used, it was surely intended to be understood in a loose sense. Athens had upon the whole been better treated by the Romans than any other Greek city. She apparently alone retained the privilege of coining silver, and received the proconsul attended by one lictor only. But we can see some colour in Aristion's statement

[1] Athenæus, p. 213.
[2] οἱ δὲ λοιποὶ μεταμφιεσάμενοι τετράγωνα ἱμάτια τὰς ἐξ ἀρχῆς πατρίδας πάλιν ὀνομάζουσι. Even the famous Rutilius Rufus, an ostentatious Stoic, was glad to drop his toga and assume a Greek dress for a disguise. He was living in exile at Smyrna.

when we consider that the franchise had been restricted; the Eleusinia interfered with, and a supervision over the schools exercised.[1] However, the sham philosopher gained his object, was forthwith declared *military strategus*,[2] and thereupon began a systematic persecution of all the wealthier people, who naturally adhered to the Roman interest. Then were re-enacted such scenes as have already been noticed in my former volume in connection with the revolt of the Achæan league.[3] The property of the suspects was seized; they were imprisoned and put to death without fair trial; the gates were guarded, and no citizen permitted to escape; even the country was scoured for stray fugitives, and a strict 'curfew' established in the city. Aristion sent his lieutenant, Apellicon of Teos, to seize the riches of Delos, where this other Peripatetic was defeated by the Roman guard and most of his men killed.[4] Here, as in the province of Asia, the Pontic king ordered a great massacre of Italians, and 20,000 are said to have lost their lives.

So the wretched Athenians were implicated in the great war; they were compelled to stand a disastrous siege; all their fair suburbs were devastated by Sylla in his search for siege materials and provisions; the Piræus was ultimately

[1] Cf. R. Weil in *MDI* vi. 315.

[2] In these later times it appears that, in imitation of the Roman consuls, the chief power at Athens had been vested in two *strategi*, one ἐπὶ τὰ ὅπλα, the other ἐπὶ τὴν διοίκησιν. The name of Philo appears beside that of Aristion on one of the coins. Ultimately the former strategus gave the name to the year, and becomes the sole chief magistrate (cf. Th. Reinach in the *Revue des études grecques*, i. 169 *sq.*) We have his marble arm-chair remaining in the theatre at Athens.

[3] *Greek Life and Thought*, p. 452.

[4] Our information concerning the contact of Greeks and Romans at Delos is so new, and so instructive, that I shall revert to it more fully at the end of this chapter.

dismantled and reduced to an open fishing village,[1] and the city itself sacked with great slaughter and rapine. The descriptions given of these events would make us believe that Athens was almost destroyed, and only recovered some dignity under the patronage of Hadrian. But this language is exaggerated, as we may infer from the allusions of Cicero a few years later. Thus Fimbria is said to have destroyed Ilium more completely than Agamemnon did, because the Ilians wanted to side with Sylla. But this too is beyond the truth. Still we may be sure that Sylla's terrible war in Attica and his two campaigns in Bœotia inflicted irreparable harm on continental Greece. The temples were plundered;[2] the inhabitants conscribed; the country ruthlessly taxed; and though the carrying away of statues to Rome was not yet practised on a large scale, many valuable collections were taken as booty. Sylla seized as his private share the library of Apellicon of Teos, a collector of old documents and early copies of authors, who had (it was said) brought the original MSS. of Aristotle and Theophrastus[3] from Scepsis, where they had long mouldered in a cellar. The transference of this important collection to Rome is noted as a special moment in the higher education of that city.

[1] The celebrated arsenal of Philo, of which the remains have lately been excavated and the plan recovered, was burnt down by Sylla. Its site has been recently excavated, and the whole plan restored with admirable sagacity by W. Dörpfeld, with plans and drawings (cf. *MDI* vol. vi.)

[2] Plutarch, *Sylla*, 12.

[3] This story, told by Strabo (xiii. 1, § 54), has excited much controversy. Apellicon was also accused by Posidonius of borrowing old state documents, and sending back copies, for which he was threatened with prosecution at Athens (Athen. v. § 53, pp. 214, 215). For my own part, I believe what Strabo tells us about these adventures of Aristotle's books.

As regards the rest of Greece we hear nothing, save that there had been at Dyme (in Achæa) a democratic revolution of the usual kind against the people of property, to whom the Romans entrusted the management of affairs. This and the other disturbances in Greece were put down by Sylla, or whoever the Roman governor was, on fixed principles. They executed ringleaders, and took care to exclude from the franchise all the people who had no property. Sylla was a cynic in the modern sense, and in spite of all the trouble the Greeks gave him kept them about him constantly to amuse him. It may be said of almost all the other eminent Romans of these days—Lucullus, Pompey, Crassus—that they regarded it as a sort of indispensable luxury to have a Greek philosopher in their retinue and an inmate of their house. And in this they were probably imitating the Hellenistic kings, who had adopted the same fashion, especially in new and outlying portions of the Hellenistic world.

The campaigns of Lucullus and Pompey were rather beyond the bounds of Hellenism, but not beyond the regions where many isolated cities were settled among orientals or barbarians. We have already taken notice of the violences done to these cities both by Mithradates and Tigranes. The latter insisted upon the inhabitants of many well-established towns leaving their homes to settle in his new capital, Tigranocerta. The conduct of Mithradates to the Chians was another specimen of the same kind of tyranny.[1] We have also noticed the harsh treatment the Greek towns received from the later Maccabee sovrans.[2]

All these separate cities through Asia Minor, Syria, and

---

[1] Cf. Plut. *Lucullus*, 14, 21, 26, 29, 32.
[2] Above, p. 42 *sq*.

Palestine received a new life, and many dated a new era, from the victory of the Romans. Sylla, Lucullus, and Pompey all carried out the old policy of favouring the isolated cities, and of securing their communal privileges in the midst of the territories of the various dynasts still left in control of native affairs. They would willingly have abolished all or most of these regents, but, to their astonishment, the Asiatic populations, even in contact with Greek culture, were known to refuse the proffered boon, and to beg for monarchical rule.[1] These native princes were, however, only inferior governors under Roman rule, just as many native princes in India govern under the supervision of the English, and they were not allowed to interfere with the free cities known as Greek.

But this Hellenism established by Rome was distinctly a communal affair, and the isolated cities through Asia never hoped for or pretended to any empire over neighbours, such as was still claimed by the Tauric settlements about the Sea of Asov. The cities of Asia Minor and the coast, with the exception of Rhodes, had not done so for centuries, and therefore easily fell into the groove marked out for them. So that all the exactions of the Romans, the losses by earthquakes, the contributions levied by warring powers, were unable to crush the prosperity of the cities of Asia. The cities of Greece proper, and of the Crimea, with their very different traditions, found the change hard, and rebelled against it both in open war and by stubborn discontent. The result was, that except Athens, whose primacy not even the sack and devastation of Sylla could destroy, the cities of Greece proper languished; their streets became empty; their business decayed. The exactions of war, the pressure

[1] *E.g.* the Cappadocians, when Pompey, on the extinction of their royal family, offered them liberty (Strabo, xii. 2, § 11).

of occasional famine and disease, were fatal to such decaying societies, and we can show from the attempts at union or even fusion among these very separatist societies how much they had come to feel their weakness.

We now have a case of the positive amalgamation of two towns, Medeon and Stiris in Phocis, which seems to me unique.[1] But what other meaning can the many κοινά have, which the Romans permitted, as soon as Greece had calmed after the destruction of Corinth, and which meet us at every turn in the inscriptions down to the days of the Empire. Not only had Ætolia, Bœotia and Phocis, the great islands of Rhodes and Crete, each united into κοινά embracing the whole districts or islands, but we find smaller local combinations under the same title meeting at Demetrias (Magnesians), Anticyra (Oeteans), Larissa (Thessalians), and even a κοινὸν τῶν ’Αθαμάνων dedicating a statue to the legate Q. Brut. Sura. These local gatherings of cities, now villages (though to be called κῶμαι would have been an insult, and would have been politically and socially false), had their embassies, their diplomacies, their festivals, as if Greece were yet politically alive. But this subject will recur more naturally in connection with Plutarch's times.

I have already noted the habit usual with Roman magnates of bringing Greek philosophers in their train. Thus Antiochus of the Academy was the constant companion of Lucullus, Theophanes the Mytilenæan of Pompey, as Panætius had been of the younger Scipio.[2] But in Sylla we have a partial

---

[1] Cf. Beaudouin in *BCH* v. 43 *sq*. on this curious document, equalising the rights of all the citizens of both places, and enacting that such of the Medeonians as have held office already are not to be required to do so at Stiris, unless they volunteer. This view of public offices as burdens is characteristic of the times. I put the date later than M. Beaudouin does, and would refer it to the times now before us.

[2] Cf. also the remarks of Strabo (xi. 1, 6) upon the relations of

exception. He seems to have preferred less serious companions, and to have rather consorted with those Greek artists whose character is so reprehended in Aristotle's *Problems*,[1] actors, singers, etc., and still more those soothsayers and prophets who were rife among the sanctuaries of Asia. This religion of emotion, this fear of occult influences, this worship of fortune as compared with reasonable forecast, were phenomena really more oriental than Greek, and were always at home in the eastern domain of Hellenism, while philosophy and with it scepticism dominated Greece.

But the long residence of Roman troops in Asia and the special temper of Sylla seem to have made this worship of wonder, and belief in miracles, the fashion in what I may call the school of Sylla. In the *Lives* of Lucullus and Pompey, as well as in the *Life* of the Dictator, there are strange stories told which would have been ridiculed by the circle of Scipio, or by the rational school of Cicero and Cæsar, who learned from the philosophers of Athens and of Rhodes.[2] Though we may note this retrogression, there can be no doubt that the many aristocrats in Sylla's staff and in his army acquired a familiarity with Greek quite different from that acquired by their elders from teachers in Rome.

Posidonius to Pompey. 'How can we trust him about obscure matters, where he had no probable evidence to quote, when he says such extraordinary things about what is well known, and this too when he was Pompey's companion on his expedition to the Caucasus, between the Caspian and Colchian seas. For when Pompey set out for the pirate war he chanced to meet Posidonius at Rhodes, and to have a discourse with him, and asked as he was departing, whether the philosopher had any advice to give. Whereupon he answered in the words of Homer, " Ever be brave and superior to the rest." Add to this that he wrote the history of Pompey's deeds.'

[1] Cf. my *Greek Life and Thought*, p. 384.

[2] Cf. the anecdotes in Plutarch's *Sylla*, 27 ; *Lucullus*, 23 ; where Sylla's remark is quoted, that no forecast is so trustworthy as what is foretold in dreams.

So Lucullus was always studying Greek culture, and Pompey, after settling the East, came back to Mytilene, Rhodes, and Athens to enjoy a literary and artistic holiday.[1] When there were daily dealings with Greek populations, and billeting in Greek towns, and leisurely winter quarters in historic places like Ephesus and Smyrna, the young generation of Romans must have acquired a ready and practical knowledge of Greek language and Greek ways. Plutarch, at the opening of his *Life of Marius*, notices that general's absolute ignorance and contempt of Greek letters as something exceptional, and yet even Marius was obliged to give a Greek representation on the stage, which he attended only for a moment. But he was, perhaps, the last of the narrow and vigorous Roman boors.

The very same causes, especially the winter campaign of Sylla in Asia Minor, are set down by the historians of Greek art as fixing the moment when the Roman taste for that splendid adornment of cities passed from a public into a private and individual feature. It had indeed long been the habit of the conquerors to bring the spoils of conquered cities to Rome, and this habit has remained in fashion through later days, as the arch of Titus manifests, down to the days of Napoleon, and even our own, when relics of King Koffee or Cetwayo or Theodore are still treasured as interesting records of British victories. The results of the early victories of Rome over Greek cities were of course far more important, for the streets and public places were becoming crowded with statues famous in their homes, and therefore prized without further discrimination by the victors. Even so educated a man as Cicero, brought up in the midst of these exhibited masterpieces, specially disclaims (in his Verrine orations) the title of connoisseur. Yet in his day the

[1] Plut. *Pomp.* 42.

art treasures of great Greek cities had surely been long enough in Rome to educate any people of even moderate capacities. Marcellus had carried away from Syracuse in 212 B.C. the finest statues and pictures of that splendid art-centre, and they were exhibited in the temple of Honos and Virtus at the Porta Capena. The ruin of Capua brought additions to this booty, but trifling compared with the spoil of Tarentum, brought home in 209 B.C. by Fabius, of which Lysippus's colossal statue of Heracles was long famous on the Capitol.

A few years later (197 B.C.) the triumph of Flamininus gained for Rome all the treasures which Philip V of Macedon had either inherited or plundered—the first contribution from eastern Greeks to the growing capital of the world. Even this acquisition was cast into the shade by the treasures paraded in his triumphs over the Ætolians by M. Fulvius Nobilior in 187 B.C. These comprised not only the wealth of Thermus, of which I have spoken elsewhere,[1] but that of Ambracia, the brilliant capital of Pyrrhus and his successors. We hear of 285 bronze and 230 marble statues in this collection, for which the victor built the temple of Hercules Musarum. I need not do more than mention the names of Mummius and Corinth (145 B.C.)

This long series[2] shows how fully Rome had been equipped with materials and museums—the special temples above-named were in fact museums—for a thorough art education. Yet up to this point, and indeed for a generation following, there is hardly any sign of a development of Roman taste. We know that Metellus Macedonicus brought from Greece a company of architects and other artists to build

[1] *Greek Life and Thought*, p. 417.
[2] A very convenient list of all the named statues thus set up in Rome is given by Saalfeld (*Hellenismus in Latium*, p. 84 *sq.*)

his famous portico; but had even this specimen of Greek superiority remained isolated, his company of Greeks would have produced no further effect than the famous Italian stucco-workers did who came to Dublin in the last century, and filled all the old mansions of that city with their delicate art, and whose departure can be fixed almost to a year by the shocking contrast of the home work done while their beautiful designs were still fresh upon the walls, and before the eyes of the Irish workmen. And yet over and over again Irish workmen have shown that they possess a talent for decoration of the highest kind, when a sufficient stimulus has been given.

In the Roman case this stimulus is usually referred, not to the great exhibitions of art treasures which we have enumerated, but to the acquisition of the royal treasures of Pergamum through the bequest (genuine or forged) of the last Attalid. For then Romans first began to dwell in Greek Asia, and the most brilliant part of it, as administrators and curators of these things; their value as property came to be discussed, and no doubt many offers of money were made by rich Asiatic Greeks for art objects which the Romans had overlooked as mere furniture. The campaigns of Sylla, implying winter quarters in Greece and Asia, enforced and extended this new knowledge in no ordinary degree, as the text of Plutarch tells us, so that this is really the epoch when the Romans began to turn from mere collectors of spoil into individual amateurs and *dilettanti*, at first on the average gross and vulgar like Verres, then refined and educated like Lucullus. For of course the two types existed from the first, but the relative numbers of the former kept diminishing while the latter increased.

The recent researches of the French school at Delos have, however, shown us that other permanent influences must have contributed to the result, and that Pergamum cannot be credited with so complete a monopoly in Roman education.

These scholars have discovered a wealth of inscriptions both unexpected and unparalleled, except it be that of the Athenian Acropolis or the temple of Delphi; nor do I suppose that either of these great repositories of state-documents equalled Delos, the latter in importance, the former in the catholicity of its records, for Greeks from all parts of the world sought permission from the Delians, more even than from the Delphians, to set up copies of important treaties in their famous sanctuaries, both for publicity and for security in days to come. The result has been that upon the site of the temple of Apollo, and in other holy places at Delos, M. Homolle has already recovered sixty slabs, with at least 400 multifarious inscriptions, many of more than a hundred lines, some even several hundred lines long. One of them, an inventory of the treasures of the temples, which was required when a new committee of curators (ἱεροποιοί) took over the charge from their predecessors, occupies forty-eight large pages of close printing.[1] From this and the other documents quite a new light has been thrown upon the history of the island, and especially upon its relations to the Romans, which have been treated by M. Homolle in special monograph.[2]

Delos, as a sacred island, enjoyed from the earliest times the respect of all Greece, so that it was nominally free and inviolate, though its weakness made it really subject to the dominant power for the time being in the Ægean. Under

---

[1] *BCH* vi. 1 *sq.*, with M. Homolle's commentary.

[2] *Les Romains à Délos*, *BCH* viii. 75 *sq.* These articles supersede all previous work upon the subject, even that of serious excavators like M. Lebègue, who began the work.

the Athenian supremacy the treasures were administered by *amphictions*, afterwards by ἱεροποιοί. Even the Spartans, during their brief naval supremacy (404-394 B.C.), show by the offerings they made, and still more by their declaration to respect the rights and liberties of the island,[1] that they really controlled it. Under the renewed supremacy of Athens, when her reins were not drawn so tightly, and during the days of Philip and Alexander, we hear but little of Delos. The conflict for supremacy was not at that epoch a naval question.

In the troubles which supervened upon the death of Alexander the islanders of the Ægean either formed or formulated more definitely a confederation, known in the inscriptions as κοινὸν τῶν νησιωτῶν, probably for mutual defence against pirates. Several inscriptions thank certain individuals and give them general civic rights in all the islands for benefits conferred upon the *islanders*, and direct that they shall be crowned at the *Ptolemœa*, when the tragedies are being performed.[2] This feast indicates to us once more the able and far-seeing policy of the first Ptolemy, which I have shown in its proper light elsewhere ;[3] for he took under his protection this League, and was probably declared its formal president. Indeed all the leading Diadochi, beginning with Peucestas and Craterus, sent offerings to Delos, but the struggle for political power was between the Ptolemies and the Antigonids, one of whom (Gonatas) after his great victory at Cos controlled the League, as the *Antigoneia* celebrated there for some years prove.[4] He lost this control again after his defeat at Andros,

---

[1] Cf. M. Homolle on the restoration of this text, *BCH* iii. 13.
[2] *BCH* iii. 321 ; iv. 320 ; vii. 5.
[3] *Greek Life and Thought*, p. 161 sq.
[4] *BCH* x. 105.

and the Ptolemies, who apparently celebrated this victory by the founding of the *Euergesia*, maintained themselves till the slothful Philopator abandoned all foreign policy. Under all these competing sovrans, with their many bounties, commemorated in formal votes of thanks, the Delians, nicknamed the *parasites of Apollo*, and their league of islanders, which perhaps met at Tenos as well as Delos, lived on in at least material comfort, and were probably under the protection of Macedon when the interference of the Romans and the declaration of independence made by Flamininus left them without a strong hand to preside over them.

This duty was undertaken by the Rhodians, who from 200 to 167 B.C. kept the seas with their guardships (φυλακίδες), and protected both trade and island property.[1]

But even now there begins the long series of inscriptions either bilingual or relating to Italians, which make us feel that here, above all, the Romans were determined to effect a permanent lodgment on Greek soil. Accordingly Delos begins suddenly to rise in importance, when the settlement of Greece after the battle of Pydna (168 B.C.) took place, and the Rhodians were to be punished for their independence or their secret sympathies with Macedon.

It was clearly in the interest of Roman traders that Delos was selected for the free port of the Ægean, and therefore the great centre of all the trade of the N.E. Mediterranean. But the island was nominally handed over to the Athenians, who proceeded to expel the Delians, and occupy it in company with Romans. Inscriptions now speak not of the *demos of the Delians*, but of the *demos of the Athenians, and of the Romans dwelling in Delos*. We know that it became a great slave market: we know that in addition to the

[1] Cf. *BCH* x. 123, 199, where Epicrates, an ἄρχων ἐπὶ τῶν νήσων, ἀποσταλεὶς ὑπὸ τοῦ δήμου τῶν Ῥοδίων, is thanked for his services.

Jews, Phœnicians, and Egyptians who had gradually settled there with their gods, Roman traders came in crowds; the destruction of Corinth in 146 was probably suggested by the strong commercial jealousies of Roman Delos; and though the government and its civil service were conducted by Athens, which sent there a High Commissioner (ἐπιμελήτης), as we once did to Corfu, and though the titles of many officials show that sundry Athenians derived their income from this source, it is plain that to the Romans fell the lion's share of the profits.

It was from this stepping-stone that the Roman businessmen passed over to the province of Asia, which fell to them by the will of Attalus in 133, and which added greatly to the importance and the population of Delos. This is indeed the most brilliant epoch of its later history. Now it is that we find great Corporations or Companies of Merchants settled there with splendid buildings, porticoes, temples of their own, and commemorating in many inscriptions their prosperity and their thanks to the gods. Of these the Hermaists were the most Roman, and the most important, with a sort of public place, like an Exchange, within their porticoes. Most of their dedications are from Romans, and the whole island is tinged with Italian influences. The Athenians and Romans jointly built quays, marts and temples, and even Puteoli is called a little Delos! For besides the Hermaists were Apolloniasts, and Poseidoniasts, who were not only Hellenic Greeks, but Syrian Greeks from the coast of Palestine, Jews, and even freed men. We find the worship of the *Lares*, the *Compitalia*, and an altar to *Bona Fides* commemorated in inscriptions about the year 100 B.C., as well as temples to Sarapis, Isis, the Syrian Aphrodite, Adad and Atargatis, even before that date. Delos was bidding fair to rival Alexandria, and collect all the wares of Asia Minor and of the Black Sea in her mart.

If the Athenians had been allowed to levy port dues, what a mine of wealth their possession of the island would have brought them! But the Romans insisted upon its freedom; the rich merchants even maintained a military guard, and we can imagine the Athenians jealous and bitter at these limitations, perhaps for that very reason hailing Mithradates as a naval power which would rid them of the Romans, whereas the population of the island was strongly Roman in policy, as it was mainly Roman in blood. Hence the impostor Aristion strove to seize it, and presently, when the Pontic fleet swept the Ægean, the Romans were massacred, and Mithradates ruled the island, not without solemn offerings, which are commemorated in the inscriptions.[1] After about three years (86-84 B.C.) he was expelled by the Romans, and now the *demos of the Delians* reappears. But Sylla was so forgiving and so conservative that he gave back the island to the Athenians. In 84 B.C. the Hermaist Corporation was revived, in 79 the other two above mentioned, and a new course of prosperity seemed at hand. But though Cicero in his speech for the Manilian Law[2] speaks of it as quite safe from the inroads of the pirates, that awful scourge fell upon Delos. The pirate Athenodorus, not twenty years after the massacre by Theophanes, made a systematic attack upon Delos, and not only slew or enslaved the whole population, but deliberately destroyed the splendid buildings and temples which were the evidence of Roman life.

From this second disaster the island never recovered, though some inscriptions, and the founding of a sodality called the Pompeiasts, show that in the pacified Ægean

[1] *BCH* vi. 343.   [2] 18, 55.

the merchants tried to reconstruct their shattered homes. But whether, as M. Homolle thinks,[1] Puteoli carried off the trade, or whether, as I would suggest, the resurrection of Corinth, and its rapid rise, made Delos unnecessary, the island lost both its wealth and its population, and sank gradually into silence and decay. There only remained the ruins of its former splendour, and among them countless records of laudation, of dedication, of supplication to the gods, from all nationalities and countries, from Massanassa of Numidia to Mithradates of Pontus (*BCH* xi. 255), as well as catalogues of treasure, treaties of alliance, lists of membership in societies of which the name is often effaced. In these laudations, which form the larger part of the inscriptions everywhere during this epoch, and in which the preamble is the important part, for it often recites historical facts, men are praised not only for their public conduct but for their sentiments, for their good manners, for their modesty as well as for their eloquence or poetic taste employed in the exaltation of Delos.[2]

Such are the materials from which the sagacity of M. Homolle has recovered a connected and rational story. Here we have in its focus the concentration of Roman-Hellenistic commercial life.

[1] *Op. cit.* viii. 153.
[2] Here are some specimens from Nysa, in the valley of the Mæander:
—ἡ βουλὴ καὶ ἡ γερουσία καὶ οἱ νέοι ἐτείμησαν Κ. νεανίαν ἐπιφανῆ, γένους τε ἕνεκεν, καὶ τῆς ἐν τοῖς ἤθεσι σεμνότητος, etc.; the next, διὰ τὴν ἰδίαν αὐτοῦ κοσμιότητα καὶ διὰ τὰς τῶν προγόνων εὐεργεσίας (*BCH* xi. 347). Another to a physician, because no one suffered from his hauteur (*op. cit.* xii. 328). Another to a poet, ἐπειδὴ Δημοτέλης Αἰσχύλου ῎Ανδριος, ποιητὴς ὤν, πεπραγμάτευται περί τε τὸ ἱερὸν καὶ τὴν πόλιν τῶν Δηλίων, καὶ τοὺς μύθους τοὺς ἐπιχωρίους γέγραφε, he is to be crowned with bay, etc. Cf. also *BCH* xiii. 245.

CHAPTER VI

THE HELLENISM OF CICERO AND HIS FRIENDS

THE Hellenism of Cicero and his circle are quite worth a separate chapter, for not only does the career of this celebrated man form an epoch in the history of Greek letters at Rome, but he has given us such copious and reiterated explanations of what he intended, and what he performed, that we are in no doubt or hesitation as to his peculiar title to literary fame.

We are not concerned here with Cicero as a politician, unless it be to show that his character in this relation corresponds with its literary aspects. He aspired, like most men of great intellect and of weak character, to act as mediator between extreme men on both sides; he earned, as usual, what many such men have not deserved, the character of a trimmer. But in his case the general verdict is justified by his own statements. Any one who will take an Index of Cicero and look up what he has said to and of Cæsar before his supremacy, during his supremacy, and after his murder, will require no further evidence. The retort of the displaced knight Laberius sums it all up. He was looking for a seat in the theatre, when Cicero, who did not want his company, but desired to retain his goodwill, said: 'I should gladly have made place for you beside me, were I not squeezed for room.' 'It is odd that you should be squeezed,' was the retort, 'seeing you generally sit upon two stools.'

Yet it is a curious reflection that what was in politics his disgrace was in letters his greatest title to honour. He was a mediator; he was distinctly the first Roman able to appreciate and translate Greek thought of the highest kind, while he also produced solid and splendid Latin work of his own. With Cicero Latin prose became distinctly a rival of the best Greek prose, and no critic who has honestly studied the great roll of Latin writers down to the Middle Ages, can deny that here the Romans have produced a literature as first-rate, and as independent, as ever was produced by a people coming late in history, and therefore necessarily starting with great models before them.

This, then, is the keynote which Cicero perpetually strikes, and with reasonable pride. He boasts that in his day the highest species of Greek prose, which had hitherto defied the efforts of the Roman writers—philosophy—had been mastered by him, and reproduced in a clear and elegant Roman form. Whatever metaphysical critics may say as to the substance, and yet even here Cicero is by no means contemptible, there is no doubt as to the form. Any one who has had metaphysical ideas to propound, ever since, has found Latin an adequate medium, from Seneca to Descartes. There were other departments of prose in which he had great forerunners, as we have already mentioned (above, p. 84). In poetry, where he tried to naturalise Epic hexameters, he distinctly failed. He met the fate of most great prose writers who have attempted poetry. Lucretius, his greatest literary contemporary, of whom he hardly speaks, would probably have been as poor in prose as Cicero was in poetry. But the concurrent appearance of Lucretius and Catullus as poets, and of Cæsar as a historian, with Cicero as an orator and philosophic essayist, shows that his genius, like every other great and successful genius, expressed the spirit and the temper of its age.

Let us now turn from generalities to the details which he gives us concerning the education which produced these splendid results.

We may start from a curious passage which will lead us to many important inferences. In the speech *pro Rabirio*, among other very flimsy arguments which the orator is called upon to refute, is the following:[1] 'Object if you please, that he went about in a [Greek] pallium [not a Roman toga], that he wore the insignia of a non-Roman man; all that this means is merely that he was rash in trusting his money, his fame, his fortunes to the caprice of a king [of Egypt]. He was foolish, I confess; but the facts remain; either he must wear a pallium at Alexandria, if he was ever to resume his toga at Rome, or he must lose all his fortune if he stuck to his toga. We have often seen not merely Roman citizens, but noble youths, and even some senators of the highest families, not too in their private gardens or suburban villas, but in the town of Naples, wearing a Greek head-dress—mitella, *deliciarum caussa et voluptatis*.[2] You see L. Sylla the dictator in a [Greek] chlamys, and the statue of L. Scipio, who conquered Antiochus, in the Capitol, not only in a chlamys, but in

[1] § 25 *sq.*
[2] 'Here, at Naples,' says Strabo, writing two generations later, 'are found the deepest traces of Greek life, gymnasia and ephebies and phratries and Greek proper names, though the people are Roman. Now they have also a five-yearly feast, with musical and gymnastic contests which rival the most famous in Greece. . . . The Greek customs of Naples are kept up by those who have lived by educating,

Greek slippers. And these men did not incur prosecution, or even criticism. We need not cite the case of P. Rutilius, who escaped the massacre of Mithradates at Mytilene by adopting Greek dress. So when Rabirius went to king Auletes, and the king proposed this way of saving the money, that he should become the king's agent [diœcetes], both the name and the dress were odious to him; but there was no help for it. For we know what it is to serve an absolute king.'

We have here a plain statement of the fact that at an earlier stage of the contact between Greece and Rome an imitation of Greek fashions was tolerated, which was unpopular and censured in Cicero's day. Thus, to cite other evidence, T. Flamininus was, no doubt, both proud and envied because he could speak Greek, and join in the deliberations of a Greek assembly, whereas it was made a distinct charge against Cicero by a supporter of Verres, that he had actually attended a Greek Senate (at Syracuse) and spoken in Greek there.[1]

Many natural causes can be assigned for this reaction.

and others who retire hither from Rome by reason of age or sickness and live at their ease. This Greek aspect of society pleases not a few Romans who dwell there from choice' (v. 4, § 7). This kind of refined retirement is quite different from the *pergræcari* of Plautus, a word which passed out of use with the idea it represents, and is noted in the Dictionaries as ante-classical. Nicolaus Damasc. (βίος Καισ. 4) specially insists that Augustus never in his youth wore anything but *Roman* dress, though he lived much in Greek lands.

[1] *Ait indignum facinus esse, quod ego in senatu Græco verba fecissem, quod quidem apud Græcos Græce locutus essem, id ferri nullo modo posse* (*in Verr.* ii. 4, § 66). I suppose the fear that lucrative foreign appointments might be limited to good Greek scholars was one cause of this strong feeling among the vulgar and greedy Roman nobles. There was a regular profession of interpreters in Sicily to explain Greek to the Romans (*in Verr.* ii. 3, § 84). These people were like the Levantines, who do this kind of duty now in Syria and Egypt.

The evils which came in with Hellenism became more and more evident; and if about the very period with which our history in this volume begins (140 B.C.) the greatest families still held fast to the principle that all higher culture must come through Greek, the results were such as to alarm many strict and patriotic Romans. The political views of Scipio Æmilianus, the pupil of Polybius and Panætius, were suspicious enough, and his advocacy of a larger cosmopolitanism so dangerous as to cause his assassination (129 B.C.) The career of the Gracchi, both trained from the outset by Greek philosophers and grammarians, was still more ominous. The practical insignificance of the Greek race in politics made their theories all the more extravagant and reckless, and such a man as Blossius of Cumæ, who first inflamed Tiberius Gracchus and then joined the insurgent or claimant Aristonicus in his war for Pergamum against Rome, must have appeared to respectable Romans, even of a liberal type, peculiarly mischievous.

Cicero accordingly represents the great orators of the generation preceding his own,—Antonius and Crassus,—as distinctly repudiating Greek training in their public utterances, on account of its unpopularity with the Roman public. He adds, no doubt, that in secret they zealously learned what they could from Greek books, and that they knew far more about them than they pretended. But to go to Greece for the purpose of study would have been in their day thought unpatriotic and unpractical. Crassus, indeed, had a confidential Greek slave as his amanuensis and reader,[1] but both he and Antonius are represented by

[1] *Quod enim neque precibus unquam nec insidiando nec speculando assequi potui, ut, quid Crassus ageret meditandi aut dicendi caussa, non modo videre mihi, sed ex ejus scriptore et lectore Diphilo suspicari liceret*, etc. (*de Oratore*, i. § 136).

Cicero in the Dialogue as explaining how they came to Athens *in the course of their Roman official business*, and not for the purpose of study.[1] The whole treatise *de Oratore*, put into the mouths of these famous Romans, is indeed based and built upon the Greek rhetoricians, with such practical modifications as Roman life dictated, but still the statements just quoted are clear evidence of the drift of public opinion at the moment.

At the same time this very Crassus, when censor, issued an edict silencing the new Latin rhetoricians, who had started in imitation of the Greeks, and the reason he assigns[2] is not their introduction of Greek habits, but their gross ignorance as compared with Greek teachers in the same subject. They only professed Greek impudence without Greek learning. We find this strong contempt of Latin professional teaching (I am not speaking of the gratuitous lessons given by noble Romans) lasting up to the time of Cicero, though naturally, as Latin letters rose in importance, Latin schoolmasters improved in position and attainments. The orator tells us in a fragment[3] that he remembered as a boy a certain L. Plotius, the first man who began to teach boys [rhetoric] in Latin ; that Plotius was very popular, and attended by many zealous youths, so much so that Cicero himself wished to join his classes. 'I

---

[1] Cf. for Crassus, *de Oratore*, i. § 45.—*Audivi enim summos homines, quum* quæstor *ex Macedonia Athenas venissem, florenti Academia,* etc. For Antonius, *ibid.* § 82, which is still more explicit : *namque egomet, qui sero ac leviter Græcas litteras attigissem, tamen, quum pro consule in Ciliciam proficiscens Athenas venissem, complures tum ibi dies* propter navigandi difficultatem *commoratus: sed, quum quotidie mecum haberem homines doctissimos,* etc. The combination *homo doctissimus* seems to me to mark the Roman standpoint of respectful contempt very well.

[2] According to Cicero, *de Orat.* iii. § 93.

[3] Fr. 222 (ed. Nobbe), *ad M. Titinium.*

was restrained from doing so,' he adds, 'by the authority of the most learned men, who were of opinion that our talents would be better developed by Greek exercises.' On these, therefore, Cicero had been nurtured, but at Rome; nor did he visit Greece for the purpose of study until he was a mature man, and well known as an advocate in the Forum.

In a most interesting educational autobiography[1] he tells us how eagerly he studied in his youth the foremost Roman orators, and how he grieved at the exile of Cotta, one of the best. 'But about that time, when the chief of the Academy, Philo, together with the leading men of Athens, fled to Rome in the Mithradatic war, I devoted myself altogether to him' and his philosophy, though he denied all certainty in human judgments. In this year and the next, four of the principal Roman orators were put to death. 'At that time I also attended Molo the Rhodian, a consummate pleader and teacher, at Rome.' He then mentions a newer generation of Roman orators. 'All this time I was immersed in every kind of study. I was under the Stoic Diodotus, who lived in my house till his recent death.' With him Cicero chiefly studied dialectic. 'I also practised declamation with one Piso and others, in Latin, and more frequently in Greek, either because Greek offered many means of improving my Latin, or because I could not be corrected or instructed by the highest Greek teachers unless I spoke in Greek.' It was not till he had practised two years at the Roman bar that his friends and physicians made him travel to Asia for his health. He spent six months at Athens with Antiochus of the old Academy and Demetrius, with Menippus and others in Asia. He then went to visit Molo at Rhodes.

He has told us nothing of the impressions produced

[1] *Brutus*, cap. 89 *sq.*

upon him by this voyage, apart from his mere studies. Perhaps we may take it as a solitary trait from his own experience when he makes a speaker in the treatise *de nat. Deorum* say:[1] 'What percentage of men can be called beautiful? When I was at Athens, there was only one here and there to be found in the crowds of ephebi.'

With his son and nephew, the young Ciceros, we advance another step. They are sent to study at Athens in their early youth, and are brought to travel in Asia Minor, by way of good education. They have a Greek tutor at home, and are accompanied by one abroad; but this does not prevent their going on a visit to king Dejotarus in Cappadocia while Cicero was proconsul in Cilicia. We have a letter from the orator's son, written from Athens,[2] in which he gives an account of his studies. The letter is rather a correct and priggish document, and we should greatly have preferred to see what he reported to his young Roman friends from his visit to king Dejotarus, who no doubt provided for him all the amusements of a Hellenistic court. What the policy of Dejotarus in lavishing these civilities was, and what his moral standard, will appear from Plutarch's account of Cato's visit to the same sovran.[3] The barefaced offering of presents and open profusion of bribery so offended Cato the very night of his arrival that he left the king next morning. Even then he found on his journey the king's gifts and money, which had been sent before him to Pessinus, with letters begging him to let his followers take these things even if he refused them. What must have been the ordinary morals of Roman nobles when Dejotarus could hardly credit that Cato was an exception? Nor need we suppose that the king's presents and gratifications to young men excluded what he did not venture to offer the sober Cato. But we

[1] i. § 79.   [2] *Ad Fam.* xvi. 21.   [3] *Cat. minor*, p. 15.

must be content with an epistle intended for his seniors, of which the following is the substance: 'Cicero junior to his dearly-beloved Tiro all hail. I had been anxiously awaiting postmen, who came the forty-sixth day after they had left you. Their arrival delighted me intensely. For the letter of my very kind and beloved father afforded me the greatest pleasure, while the addition of your letters brought it to a climax. Accordingly the interval which has elapsed in our correspondence no longer affords me any annoyance. For I really profited greatly by my silence as it brought out your anxiety about me. I doubt not, dearest Tiro, that you were highly pleased at the reports which reached you about me, and I shall strive my best that this nascent opinion of yours shall grow and strengthen every day. Wherefore I hope you will be thoroughly justified in doing what you promise, in becoming a trumpeter of my fame. For I confess that such pain and anguish come upon me at the errors of my youth, that not only my mind recoils from the facts but my ears from the very mention of them. . . . As therefore you once suffered grief about me, I shall take care that your joy may exceed it.

'Let me tell you that I am great friends with Cratippus, not as a disciple, but as a son. For I not only hear him with pleasure, but appreciate above all his characteristic sweetness. I spend whole days with him, and often a good part of the night. For I beg him to dine with me as often as possible. This having become a practice, he often comes out of his box without our thinking about it, as we dine, and laying aside severe philosophy jokes with us delightfully. So I hope you will soon meet this most excellent and pleasant person. For what shall I say of Bruttius? whom I never allow to leave me; whose life is strict and proper, while his company is charming. For fun is not foreign to love of letters and daily intercourse. I have hired him a lodging close by, and as well as I can, sustain him in his poverty from my limited means. Besides, as I have begun declaiming in Greek at Cassius's house, I wish to practise in Latin with Bruttius. I have intimates with whom I spend my days, whom Cratippus brought with him from Mytilene, learned men and well known to him. Epicrates, chief of the Athenians [ephebi?] is much with me, and Leontides and such others. This is our news. As to what you write about Gorgias, he was very useful to me in my daily declamations, but I thought it paramount to obey my father. For he had written expressly that I should dismiss him at once. I did not like to temporise, lest my exceeding anxiety might cause him some suspicion, and of course it occurred to me that I had no right to question his judgment.' He then goes on to congratulate Tiro on having purchased a farm and turned a rustic Roman. He also promises to help him with capital whenever he shall want it. 'But I beg of you to have a writing slave [librarius] sent to me as soon as possible, for I am losing much time in writing out my notes of lectures.'

Here, then, is the sort of document a young man wrote to his parents from Athens. It is remarkable for its want of any appreciation of the natural beauties and historic interests of the famous city. And we need not make the excuse that he probably had said all this in other letters. For we perceive the very same absence of feeling for the picturesqueness of Greece in Cicero's own letters when he travelled through the East. We have a whole series of them [1] from Athens, Delos, Ephesus, Laodicea, and some of these cities he had not seen before. In none of them do we get

---

[1] *Ad Att.* v. 9 *sqq.* Sulpicius's letter (*ad Fam.* iv. 12) may be an exception.

even a hint as to the curiosities of these famous places. His mind is so full of Rome and politics that he has no time for anything else. What does he tell us of Athens? After a page of politics to Atticus,[1] 'What more have I to say? Nothing but this: Athens delighted me much—that is to say the town, and the decking out of the town (*urbis ornamentum*), and your great popularity and some kindness shown to us. But what about the philosophy? It is all upside down. If there be any, it is in my host Aristos. For I had surrendered our common friend Xeno to be Quintus's host. But we saw him constantly.'

This is all he has to say upon any of the Greek cities. Here is another characteristic passage:[2] 'I hear that Appius is building a propylæa at Eleusis.[3] Would you think it foolish for us to do the same at the Academy [of Plato]? I think you will answer that you would. Well, then, write and say so. I indeed love Athens itself greatly. I wish to be known by some distinct monument. For I hate false inscriptions put on other people's statues in my honour.'[4] Here the love of Athens is shown to mean nothing more than the amount of glory which he expected to gain from some connection with it. There is only one passage in all Cicero—the opening of the fifth book

[1] v. 11.   [2] *Ad Att.* vi. 1, 26.

[3] The remains of this entrance porch still exist, and were found in the recent excavations. Cf. the *Athens* of the *Guides-Joanne*, 1888, p. 200, or the English *Bædeker's Greece*, p. 113 (published Jan. 1889). I quote this as the newest information on the subject.

[4] To this fashion existing at Rhodes we shall revert when considering the evidence of Dion Chrysostom. On the other hand the fashion of Romans building monuments at Athens has left remains to the present day. One of Cicero's most studiously worded letters is to Memmius, dissuading him from erecting a building on part of the original holding of Epicurus at Athens. Patro, the leading disciple of that school, who evidently thought it sacrilege, had entreated Cicero's interference (*ad. Fam.* xiii. 1), and hoped to recover the site for the school.

de Finibus—which shows the smallest sentiment in visiting this famous scene, and then it is merely the suggestion of the great philosophers which rises in his mind—no word about natural beauty, no word about art. The intelligent Romans, therefore, who visited Greece in these days went to talk with philosophers, to hear lectures from rhetoricians, but, so far as we can see, this was all.

This view is confirmed by the whole series of letters of consolation addressed to noble Romans who were living in exile owing to the defeat of Pompey's party. The sixth book *ad Familiares* is full of these consolations, in none of which will be found one word of advice to study Greek art, antiquities, and history, and so relieve the mind of the tedium of separation from Rome. Cicero holds out hopes of restoration; he preaches Stoical resignation; he sympathises; he mourns. But he never thinks of advising his friends to do what any of us would have naturally suggested —to make the best of their enforced residence by entering into all the historic interests clustered about every Greek city. Cicero speaks for himself as being politically an exile at Rome—*non incommodiore loco, quam si me in Rhodum aut Mytilenas contulissem.* He exhorts Trebatius: *tu modo ineptias istas et desideria urbis et urbanitatis depone;* but then Trebatius was in Britain or Northern Gaul. Had he been in Athens Cicero's language would hardly have been different. Thus he says to Curius: 'I remember when I thought you a fool for preferring to live with these people rather than with us; for residence in this city, as it once was, is far more suited to your culture and politeness [*humanitati et suavitati tuæ*] than the whole Peloponnesus, not to say Patras. Now, on the other hand, I see some sense in it,' etc. All this language is perfectly consistent with his attitude in the Verrine oration *de Signis*, where he formally deprecates being thought an art critic, as if it were something undignified and un-Roman.[1]

Nevertheless, educationally, the value of Greece seems to have recovered again in the eyes of the Romans from the disfavour which we have seen expressed in the period 120-100 B.C. It was still the fashion to have a philosopher living in your house at Rome. It was still the fashion to carry with you a Greek historian, or else a Greek poet to the wars, who would celebrate your victories in courtly verse or in eloquent history. Lucullus never went without his Greek to his wars, neither did Pompey.[2] Such was the *war correspondent* of that day. He was in the pay of the general, not of the public. There is also an interesting letter of Cicero to Cæsar[3] recommending a freedman of Crassus, called Apollonius, as a learned man; for he had spent much time with Diodotus the Stoic at Cicero's house: *Nunc autem, incensus studio rerum tuarum, eas litteris Græcis mandare cupit. Posse arbitror: valet ingenio; habet usum.* He had in fact attended Crassus for the same purpose. And he now offers himself as war historian to Cæsar in Spain. For even yet, as Cicero declares in another passage, Greek was the world-language, while Latin was only used by the conquering race. 'He that thinks he will attain less glory from Greek verses than from Latin is totally wrong. Because Greek is read by almost the whole world; Latin is confined to narrow limits.'[4]

This was the history of the poet Archias's success. He came from Antioch at an early age to Italy, and not only

[1] Cf. above, p. 105; and *ad Fam.* vii. 6, 28.
[2] As to Pompey, cf. Cic. *pro Archia* § 24. *Quid? Noster hic Magnus qui cum virtute fortunam adæquavit, nonne Theophanem Mytilenæum scriptorem rerum suarum, in concione militum civitate donavit?* As to Lucullus and his philosopher Antiochus, *Acad. prior.* ii. § 4.
[3] *Ad Fam.* xiii. 16. [4] *Pro Archia*, § 23.

made a reputation throughout Magna Græcia for extempore verses, but celebrated both the Cimbric war for Marius and the Mithradatic for Lucullus. He attained great popularity, says Cicero, not only among those who understood and appreciated him, but among those who pretended to do so. And of the latter there was a large supply. Accordingly there was a very smart demand for Greeks at Rome, not merely for mountebanks and jesters to suit the tastes of Sylla and his society, not merely for musical and artistic people such as accompanied a Clodius and directed the æsthetic judgments of a Verres, but for philosophers and literary men, half-friends, half-dependents, who helped both to educate and to amuse their patrons. We have already seen how Panætius began to accommodate philosophy to Roman wants. He was followed in this path by Cicero's teachers, Antiochus and Molo, and we may be sure that what the heads of the schools did very seriously at Athens was done with facile complaisance by mere amateurs who dwelt at Rome.

It is not very safe to trust Cicero as a witness when he is pleading a cause. But in the following passage he must have known he was depicting a usual and typical case; I therefore quote it here as clearly relevant in the present connection. Cicero is usually very hard on the Epicureans; it is in fact only when writing to Atticus that he makes concessions to his friend's principles. But when he is handling an enemy like Piso there is no limit to his censure of this very demoralising theory. No doubt he found language as violent as any he used in the Stoic and other Greek books against Epicurus, to which I have referred in a former chapter (above, p. 72).

The orator is describing the vulgarity and the vices of his opponent, and proceeds as follows:[1] 'There is a kind

[1] *In Pisonem*, § 67 *sqq.*

of luxury reprehensible indeed and extravagant, but still the luxury of a gentleman.' We may suppose the orator was thinking of such a case as that of Lucullus. 'This man had nothing tasteful, elegant, attractive; there is nothing large about him but his lust. No ornamental plate; huge wine cups, and by way of compliment to his origin, of Placentian ware; his table supplied not with oysters or fish, but with joints of overkept meat. There are shabby slaves in attendance, some even old; the cook answers the door; there is no bread baked in his house, in fact no storeroom; his bread and wine are bought round the corner. His Greek boon companions are packed tight at table, five or more on each couch [made to hold three]. He occupies the head of the table alone, and will drink what is served him from the same jar. When he hears the cock crow he imagines the founder of his race [the crier of Placentia] is come to life again. He then stops the feast.'

'But some may say: How do you know all this? There is a certain Greek who lives with him, a man, as I can truly say from personal knowledge, quite a gentleman (*humanus*) in himself, or when he associates with anybody else than Piso. The Greek meeting this brazen-looking youth, did not scorn his friendship, more especially as he was solicited, and became so intimate with Piso as hardly ever to be seen apart from him. I take it for granted I am now addressing an audience of educated men. No doubt you have heard that the Epicurean philosophers measure all human aims by the resulting pleasure. Whether this be right or wrong is no affair of ours, at least in the present connection, but it is a slippery kind of advice to give to a not very intelligent youth, and is often dangerous. So as soon as this stallion heard pleasure being rated so high by a philosopher, he made no delay about it; he got so excited;

he neighed in assent to the argument so loudly, that the other found himself no teacher of virtue, but an authoriser of vice. The Greek began accordingly to make reservations and distinctions, to explain in what sense the words must be taken. It was all no use. The other stuck to what he had heard, and was ready to take his oath that Epicurus expressly said no human good could be conceived, were all the pleasures of the body taken away. We need go no further. The facile and charming Greek would not persist in contradicting a Roman senator—*Græcus facilis et valde venustus nimis pugnax contra senatorem populi Romani esse noluit.*

'This man is, moreover, versed not only in philosophy, but also in letters, an unusual thing for an Epicurean. He proceeded to make a poem about Piso as graceful, as elegant, as can well be conceived. Let any of you that likes blame him, but in reason, not as an obscene and audacious ruffian, but as a Greekling, a flatterer, a poet. He fell into the snares of Piso, and being a Greek and a stranger was deluded by the same appearances that have deluded the great and wise Roman State into making Piso consul. Once involved in his intimacy, he could not recover himself, and of course he feared the charge of fickleness. Being pressed, incited, compelled, he addressed Piso in a poem expressing in very polished verses all his amours, adulteries, and other lusts.

'I should quote from this mirror of Piso's life, which is widely known, did I not think it unworthy of the present surroundings, and, moreover, I do not want to damage the writer. Had he been more fortunate in his disciple, he might have been more grave and sober; circumstances brought him into this sort of writing, most unworthy of a philosopher; if indeed philosophy, as they say, contains the discipline of duty and virtue, whose professors therefore should sustain a very lofty and responsible position. But the same circumstances which led him to profess philosophy without knowing what philosophy it would turn out, also defiled him with all the grossness of that obscene and abandoned brute.'

By an exceptional good fortune we are not left to judge of this philosopher-companion from Cicero's picture only; there are embedded in the volumes of the *Anthology* many poems of Philodemus of Gadara, one of which is addressed to Piso.[1] There were also embedded in the lava of Herculaneum many rolls of Epicurean philosophy—the library of some citizen who studied or professed this school. Among them have been unrolled the charred fragments of treatises by the same Philodemus, so that we can judge him both in his sportive and his serious moments. So exclusively indeed are the deciphered rolls Epicurean in character, and so many of them, even duplicates, are treatises by Philodemus, that Comparetti and others believe this library to have been that of the southern villa of his patron Piso, and that the philosopher not only lived in it, but probably wrote some of the books with his own hand.[2] However this may be, the epigrams[3] in the *Anthology* attributed to him corroborate but too plainly the verdict of the orator. Polished and often elegant in form, so much so as to be frequently the model of Ovid, sometimes of Horace, in amatory verse, the subjects and tone of these short poems are among the most sensual and gross in the *Anthology*. If, as Kaibel insists, positive obscenity is avoided, it is at least suggested at every turn, nor can we conceive any worse companion of

---

[1] *Anth. Pal.* ix. 44, ed. Kaibel, No. 22.
[2] Cf. Scott, *Frag. Herad.* p. 12.
[3] Edited specially by Kaibel, Program of Greifswald for 1885.

a half-educated Roman youth than this polished discourser upon vice. Serious too he was at times, and cultivated, as his tract on music shows; exceedingly careful in his verse composition, as is shown in a careful analysis by his recent editor, but he was morally as bad as bad could be, and showed in a practical example how easily the Epicurean theory might degenerate into mere sensuality.

As regards his views on music they are contained in the chief treatise extant among the papyri, the tract *de Musica*. Of this the fourth (and last) book is almost complete; and indeed the lacerated condition of the first three is less to be regretted, as the stray sentences show that in them, as in the last book, the author keeps restating the same arguments with tedious iteration. The purport of the work is to explode the current theory of all the older Greek philosophers, and of the Stoics, that music has a direct effect on morals, and is of direct benefit or the reverse to human character, according as it is wisely or foolishly applied. He argues that none of the arts could be assisted by playing music for the artist when at work, that it is impossible to sever the influence of the words from the music, and that whatever effects music may have arise from this and other associations, not from any direct effect of mere sounds upon the mind. He thinks it excusable for a simple and ignorant person to be misled by the authority of the ancients, but for an educated man and a philosopher it is a reproach.[1] His whole attitude is exactly that of ordinary modern thinkers, and opposed to the almost universal doctrine of the older Greeks.

Such being the character of the house-philosopher in this ascertained case, we cannot doubt that Cicero's

---

[1] τὸ δ' ὑπὸ τῶν ἀρχαίων τετιμῆσθαι τὴν μουσικὴν ἰδιώτῃ μὲν καὶ ἀπαιδεύτῳ τεκμήριον ἡγεῖσθαι τῆς εὐχρηστίας συγγνωτόν, πεπαιδευμένῳ δὲ καὶ μᾶλλον ἔτι φιλοσόφῳ μέγ' ἂν ὄνειδος κ.τ.λ. (*de Mus.* iv. 11).

highly coloured picture represents a very frequent occurrence at Rome. Many Greeks, politically annihilated, financially ruined, having lost their national dignity and self-respect, saw no better occupation before them than to become the confidants of a Roman scapegrace.

So frequent indeed had this sort of educator become, that the Roman estimate of the Greeks began gradually to change, and the Romans, who were once ridiculously anxious to pose as a branch of the Hellenic race, now assume a very different tone. They begin to despise the Greeks as such, they begin to assert themselves as a superior race; and whatever archæological sentiment still remained, such as is implied by the legend of Æneas, the real condition of things was now this, that the Greeks counted as one of the conquered nations foreign to Rome (*exteræ nationes*) and inferior to their conqueror. The evidence for this changed attitude is to be found in allusions all through the speeches and letters of Cicero. The reader will desire me to bring before him some of the scattered texts which prove my assertion.

We must remember that we are dealing with the evidence supplied by an inveterate advocate, who always sees men and things in the light of his client's, or his own, interests. But in spite of this, nay, sometimes because of this, as he always speaks to please a Roman audience, we can frame a clear picture of the mutual relations which then subsisted between the Roman victors and their Greek subjects. It is his interest in the Verrine orations to represent the Sicilian Greeks as the most reasonable and respectable of men, whose evidence is unimpeachable, and whose wrongs are without parallel. Yet even here, in introducing this subject,[1] what does he say? After speaking of this province as an

[1] *In Verr.* ii. 2, § 7.

old and valued granary of Rome, and a pleasant place of excursion for Romans, he proceeds: 'In the men too of the province, gentlemen, there is such hard work, worth, and frugality, that they approach nearest to our own antique course of life, not to that which has since come into fashion among us. *There is nothing in them like the rest of the Greeks ;* no laziness ; no luxury ; but the greatest diligence and economy in both public and private affairs.'

Yet, in speaking of certain arbitrators named by Verres, he says,[1] 'there was no Roman citizen among them, but sacrilegious Greeks, inveterate villains, brand-new Cornelii ;' and in these very speeches, when he comes to the case of Verres appointing one of this admirable and honest Sicilian people commander of a fleet, he does not so much inveigh against the character of this particular person, Cleomenes, as against the indignity, the unheard-of insult, of putting a fleet of the Roman people under the command of a Sicilian Greek.[2] Let me add, in correction of the charge just cited of laziness and luxury against all the Greeks, that the orator tells us he himself saw at Sparta bands of youths fighting almost to death, in contempt of pain, and that they still submitted to flogging at the altar of Artemis without a word, till some of them even died.[3] Accordingly, as typical examples of men bearing pain better from hereditary traditions and from training than most philosophers could bear it from principle, he cites not the solid Romans, but the volatile Greeks ! The truth of his statement about the Spartan boys is confirmed twice over by the testimony of Plutarch, who says he saw them die under the lash, and by that of Dion.[4]

[1] ii. 3, § 69.   [2] ii. 5, § 82.
[3] *Tusc. Quæst.* ii. 14 and 20 ; v. 27.
[4] Plut. *Lycurg.* 18 ; *Aristid.* 17 ; Dion Chrys. *Or.* xxv.

The defence of L. Flaccus is an interesting counterpart of the prosecution of Verres. Flaccus had vigorously helped Cicero in the affair of Catiline, and so the orator undertakes to defend him, though the whole of Asia demands his punishment for three years' extortion and malversation when pro-prætor in that province. I will not say that Flaccus was as unvarnished a ruffian as Verres. But this is certain, that if he had been, Cicero would not have scrupled to defend him as he has done; and this is also certain, that if he had not committed the grossest crimes and injustices, the provincials would never have raised a finger to prosecute him. They would have been too grateful even to a moderately unjust and vicious Roman governor. Our interest therefore in this speech fixes on the way in which the orator speaks to Roman prejudices as regards the Greeks of Asia.

He first attacks the witnesses against Flaccus *in globo*. 'What witnesses are they? Greeks. Not that I of all men should derogate from the credit of this nation. If ever there was a Roman of Greek predilections, given to Greek studies, it was I; and when I had more leisure, to a greater extent even than now. There are among them many good, learned, sensible men, but they do not appear before us; many of the reverse kind, who are here. Moreover, this I will say about the whole Greek race; I grant them talent in letters, in teaching many arts; I will not deny their grace in conversation, their acuteness in thinking, their wealth of eloquence; if they claim any additional merits, I concede them. But strictness and truth in giving evidence — *testimoniorum religionem et fidem* — that nation has never practised; they have no idea of the importance, weight, and authority of this matter.' And so there is a Greek phrase known even to those who know no other word in the language : *Lend me your testimony.*[1]

He goes on to cite cases of Romans refraining from giving evidence against their opponents. 'Had these been Greeks, and had not our morals and training been stronger in them than their wrath and bitterness, they would all have sworn they were robbed and ruined. The Greek witness comes forward to injure his opponent; he does not think of his oath, but of the damage he can do. To break down in evidence he regards as most disgraceful; against that he guards himself, he cares for nothing else.' And so he describes them as a people, *quibus jusjurandum jocus est; testimonium ludus; existimatio vestra, tenebræ; laus, merces, gratia, gratulatio proposita est omnis in impudenti mendacio.*

It is difficult not to wonder at the modern complexion of all this. Parallels in our own day and our own empire start up unbidden, however angrily the pedant may threaten us, however loftily he may warn us against illustrating a remote age of civilisation by the clear analogies of modern life. Let it be remembered that most Greeks looked upon the Romans as foreign conquerors, who had taken from them their liberties, whose law was therefore a foreign law, to be evaded or violated, as far as possible, not only without guilt, but with a certain show of patriotism. They were proud 'to defeat, and by defeating to defy this law,' if I may use the words recently addressed to his diocese by an Archbishop of the Roman Church in Ireland.

Cicero goes on to criticise the value of a Greek *psephisma*, or plebiscite, given by show of hands of the assembled cobblers and tinkers of a city, excited with harangues, and

---

[1] A comparison of Plutarch's observations on this point (*de vit. pudore*, 6) will corroborate what Cicero says, as being true, even in later days. ' For nations seem never to change their essential features.

voting without a moment's interval for reflection. The whole of Greek history, he says, not only in its present decadence, but in its best days, was disgraced by the license of its public assemblies, by the random judgments of people gathered together to hear harangues. He contrasts with it the wisdom of the Romans in separating the voting altogether from the *concio*, and so interposing an interval between the discussion and the decision.[1]

But Cicero introduces this famous attack on Greek public honesty (which tallies so well with what Polybius had said two generations earlier [2]) with the remark that he knew many good, true, and cultivated men among them. What evidence have we of any friendship with such Greeks in his writings? I will not speak of the philosophers from whom he learned, and who were not his friends any more than schoolmasters or college tutors are now friends of most of their pupils. But even taking them into account, is it not remarkable that among them all he had not (except his freedman Tiro) a single correspondent, so far as we know from his very numerous epistles? The reader may wander through books of them, many written to and from Hellenistic lands, and yet he will find no Greek or Asiatic friend mentioned as a correspondent. When we come to the thirteenth book *ad Familiares*, which consists of letters of introduction or recommendation, we at last stumble upon a number of letters commending Greek acquaintances to the Roman governors or officers of the provinces. He speaks of these Greeks, indeed, in the highest terms, saying that not only had they been his hosts, but that he lived with them *familiariter*, and that he had been delighted to see them at Rome. But they are clearly not of his rank; he

---

[1] *Pro Flacco*, § 15 *sqq*.
[2] Cf. *Greek Life and Thought*, p. 527.

regards them as a man of rank would now regard a respectable lodging-house keeper.[1] Many of them are freedmen, some of them traders with whom he and his friends had invested money. The real feeling towards all these people comes out in the last of the series, which commends Democritus of Sicyon. 'He is not only my host,' says Cicero, 'but what seldom happens, especially among Greeks, very intimate with me. You will find him the principal man, not only of his city, but perhaps of all Achæa.' It was evidently of the last importance to these Greeks to be well recommended by a Roman of distinction to the incoming prætors or proconsuls, and we may be sure Cicero's letters were anxiously solicited. But though they were requitals for hospitalities received, they were not real or deep expressions of genuine friendship or respect.

The views of Cicero come out in many other places. In writing to his favourite freedman and secretary Tiro, who was ill, and to whom he uses almost extravagant words of affection, he says[2] of the very Lyso whom he had strongly recommended among the people above mentioned: 'I fear our Lyso is rather negligent, *first, because all Greeks are so;* next, because he did not answer my letters.' He says of the boy's tutor Dionysius, who had not shown any loyalty to them when their party was overthrown by Cæsar: 'But I don't expect such qualities in a Greek.'[3] He says the ebullition of public feeling at Naples when Pompey recovered from his illness was *ineptum sane negotium et Græculum*,[4] and he sums up all these judgments in the famous letter to his brother Quintus on the duties of a provincial governor,[5]

---

[1] The special letters in point are *ad Fam.* xiii. 1, 19, 20, 23, 24, 25, 28 b, 32, 34, 36, 37, 48, 52, 53, 54, 67, 70, 78.
[2] *Ad Fam.* xvi. 4.   [3] *Ad. Att.* vii. 18.
[4] *Tusc. Disp.* i. § 86.   [5] *Ad Q. Fratrem*, i. 1, § 16 *sq.*

where he warns him against intimacies with the Greeks, of whom but few are still worthy of ancient Hellas. Most of them are fickle and deceitful, and through long slavery trained to excessive complaisance. They should all be treated liberally, and the best of them even admitted to your house and friendship. But too great intimacy with them is not safe, for they dare not oppose our wishes, and they envy not only us, but one another. . . . Be therefore very cautious and careful in making friendships with provincials and Greeks. He adds in another place [1] a candidly dishonest apology for his own apparent violation of these precepts. 'I now come to answer your letter in which you complain that I strongly recommended to you Zeuxis of Blandus (in Phrygia), an undoubted matricide. Concerning this case, and all others like it, if you should wonder at my courting popularity so strongly among Greeks, pray observe what follows. Perceiving that the complaints of the Greeks have more influence than is right, owing to their natural habit of exaggerating, I soothed in any way I could all such as I heard were complaining about you. First I mollified the people of Dionysopolis, who were strongly against me, whose chief man Hermippus I muzzled not only by talking to him, but by admitting him to my intimacy. Hephaestus of Apamea, Megaristus of Antandrus, a worthless person, Nicias of Smyrna—the most trivial creatures, I compassed with all my affability, even Nympho of Colophon. I did all this, not that such men, or even their whole nation, delight me; I am sick of their want of character (*levitas*), their obsequiousness, their devotion not to principle, but to the profit of the hour.' He then goes into very interesting details concerning these cases.

At last, then, the Romans were beginning to assert them-

[1] *Ad Q*. i. 2, § 4.

selves, not only against Italian provincials, whom they despised as speaking Latin with a bad accent and in rustic phrase,[1] but against all their subjects, barbarian and even Greek. The opening of the *Tusculan Disputations* is a noble and eloquent assertion of this Roman dignity. The deep severance between barbarians—Africans, Spaniards, Gauls—and Greeks is indeed still felt,[2] but the fierce prosecution of Ligarius by Tubero is justly called by the orator a foreign thing. 'No Roman citizen ever did it. *Externi isti sunt mores.* The hatred of either fickle Greeks or savage barbarians is wont to demand blood.'[3] Nor is this remarkable phrase solitary. In the tenth *Philippic* he speaks of *exteræ nationes a prima ora Græciæ usque ad Ægyptum.*

Thus we have the Romans at last repudiating or forgetting their ancient anxiety to pose as an offshoot of the Hellenes, and coming to regard the Greek as only a superior kind of outsider, worse than the Roman in moral principles, worse even in manners owing to his fickleness, and also to his ungovernable excitability, which caused many extra-

[1]. I am not here concerned with the Latin subjects, but call attention to the passage, *de Orat.* iii. § 42, on this question. Just as the commonest Athenian far surpasses the most learned Asiatic in the tone and sweetness of his accent, so the most ignorant Roman speaks better than the most learned of the Latins, though they study literature far more closely than Romans do. He reverts to this subject of accent in his *Brutus* (§ 171 *sqq.*) in discussing the learning and ability of provincials. Even the orator himself turns aside in his speech *pro Sulla* (§ 22 *sq.*), to answer the taunt that he is a *peregrinus* because he came from Arpinum. We have no parallel to this, however an Irishman or Scotchman may be twitted for his provincialism, for Ireland and Scotland are far stronger in regard to England than the Italian provinces were to Rome. All this does not prevent Cicero from recognising even in Roman Latin a vulgar and low way of speaking—*oppidano quodam et incondito genere dicendi*, as opposed to the *urbanum genus*. On the Spanish brogue of Corduba, cf. *pro Arch.* § 26.

[2] *Ad. Q. Fratrem*, i. 1, §§ 28, 33.   [3] *Pro Ligario*, § 11.

.vagances painful to a calm and self-possessed aristocracy. It is quite consistent with this that we should find another mark of the foreign manners in the *over-gesticulation* of the Greeks, which Cicero censured when they were giving evidence in court. They seasoned their replies with raising of eyebrows and shrugging of shoulders. We could imagine him an English critic censuring French or Italian witnesses.[1]

There were perhaps only two points in which the supremacy of the Greeks was still acknowledged—art and philosophy. I have put art first, as we shall dispose of philosophy in very few words. There is a whole speech of Cicero against Verres (*de Signis*) devoted to art questions, for Verres pretended to be an art critic, and many of his worst thefts were of works of art. Hence Cicero can give us much information both on the nature and on the number of the precious objects preserved and valued by the Sicilians and other Greeks in these days. For as Verres's robberies were not confined to Sicily, so we hear stray facts concerning the artistic condition of other provinces. But Cicero almost ostentatiously repeats to the jury that he himself is no art critic, and that what he says on this point is derived from the judgment of the Greeks — paramount masters in this branch of culture, and whom even Verres must keep beside him as advisers upon the value of antiquities. Cicero[2] gives an account of two miscreants who had to fly from their home at Cibyra, where they had been workers in terra cotta, and who took refuge with Verres to perform the duty of revising his judgments on art. But

[1] *Dixerunt hic modo nobiscum ad hæc subsellia, quibus superciliis renuentes huic decem millium crimini? Iam nostis insulsitatem Græcorum ; humeris gestum agebant* (*pro Rabirio*, § 36).
[2] *In Verr.* ii. 4, § 30.

for all that they did not save him from atrocities in taste, as well as in life and morals.

We are astonished, in the first place, that in a province so long subject to Rome, after the devastations of the slave wars, of publicani, and of prætors, so many art treasures should still have survived in Sicily. But such seems really to have been the case. Not only were the temples adorned with statues by the greatest Greek artists—statues which had been carried to Carthage and formally restored by Scipio when he conquered that city, but there were rich private individuals who possessed such treasures, which were the pride of their cities, and were most liberally shown to all Roman visitors by the owners.

The opening case in the speech, that of Heius of Messina, is a case in point. He had in a private chapel four *chefs-d'œuvre*, which Verres plundered under pretence of a sale for the ludicrous sum of 6500 sesterces (£40)—a Cupid of Praxiteles for 1600! whereas, says Cicero, we have often seen 40,000 given at an auction for a small bronze.[1] The only work of art left to Heius by his plunderer was an archaic wooden statue of Fortune, probably because the taste for antiquities, as such, did not yet exist among Romans of this class. Cicero repeatedly declines all responsibility for the judgments pronounced upon these things; he says he has seen many of them, indeed they were the first thing shown to visitors in any Greek town, and that by a special class called *mystagogi*.[2] He mentions in other houses cups of Boethus, chased work of Mentor; gems and medallions which Verres tore from their settings in cups and vases. In fact there was hardly a respectable house in

---

[1] § 14.
[2] How disgusted he would have been had he foreseen that in after ages this profession should be called *Cicerones*!

Sicily which did not retain at least a remnant of old luxury in platters, or censers of old plate, used in the family devotions, and prized above all else.[1]

These were the articles which Verres everywhere sought and carried off from the people. And, indeed, what wonder, when he had robbed the young king Antiochus (son of Selene), who visited him when returning from Rome to Asia, and who was unsuspecting enough to show him his splendid plate. The details of this shameless robbery are well-nigh incredible (§§ 61-72). There were also famous historical paintings, the battles of Agathocles, portraits of the old kings and tyrants; there were splendid double doors wrought of gold and ivory, generally dedicated to temples, just as our treasures of mediæval painting and carving are almost all to be found in old churches. All such things Verres ruthlessly carried off. But what Cicero represents as the worst of all was the rape of the gods themselves from their shrines, and this under the constant pretext that the authorities of each city had sold them.

'Do you think, gentlemen, that this despoiling of their temples affected them with any ordinary grief? Not so, verily, first because all men have religious feelings and think that their paternal gods, handed down from their ancestors, are to be sedulously preserved and honoured; secondly, because these treasures, these works of art, statues, pictures, delight the Greeks beyond measure. And thus from their complaints we can gather that these losses are to them most bitter, which may perhaps seem to us trifling and of little account. Believe me, gentlemen, of all the calamities and injustices suffered during late years by our allies and foreign nations, none have the Greeks felt, or do they feel, worse than this plundering of temples and shrines. Let Verres

[1] § 46.

pretend he bought them as much as he likes; believe me, no polity in the whole of Greece or Asia ever did sell of its own accord to anybody any statue, picture, or public ornament.[1] ... Know then that this alleged sale is far more offensive to the cities than if he had carried away their treasures by force. They deem it the lowest turpitude for a city to be induced by money to part with the public heirlooms handed down to them from their ancestors. For remember that the Greeks delight marvellously in things which we despise. And so our ancestors suffered all these things to remain among their allies, that they might be as prosperous as possible under our empire; and to those whom they made tributary they left them, in order that they who delight in things which we despise, might have them to beguile and solace their servitude. What do you think the people of Rhegium would take for their marble Venus? or the Tarentines, to lose their Europa sitting on the bull, or their Satyr in the temple of Vesta? or the Thespians, for their Cupid, the sole attraction of Thespiæ? or the Cnidians, for their marble, or the Coans for their painted, Venus? What the Ephesians for their Alexander, or they of Cyzicus for their Ajax or their Medea? What the Rhodians, for their Ialysos? What the Athenians, for their marble Iacchus, or painted Paralus, or the bronze cow of Myron? It is tedious and unnecessary for me to

[1] It seems, nevertheless, that the town of Sicyon parted with its famous pictures a very few years later to liquidate a public debt to Cicero's friend, the banker and money-lender Atticus (cf. Pliny, *N. H.* xxxv. 11, 127). Nor do I imagine that this was the only case. I suppose these city heirlooms were not more sacred or more precious than the private heirlooms of great English nobles—pictures, plate, china, books, which we see coming into auction-rooms every year. The mansions of these people will presently resemble the unfortunate and degraded Greek cities, with their empty temples, their deserted senate houses, and their auctioned gods.

enumerate all the treasures which are to be seen in each city of Greece and Asia. I mention them that you may realise the grief which is felt when such things are carried off' (§ 132 *sqq.*)

How deeply significant is all this passage as to the altered relations of Rome to Hellenism! What was true of Sicily was certainly true, in a greater degree perhaps, of Asia. The wealth in art and antiquities was even greater, the excesses of Roman governors—Verres, Piso, Gabinius,[1] Flaccus whom Cicero defended—fully as odious. The love of art in the Greek cities, and its close identification with religion, were actually coming to be despised by serious Romans, who associated this fancy with levity of character.

But there was a lower stratum of Romans who took up the fashion of art, ignorantly and without the smallest *religion*, and these were the most odious scourge of the subject nations. For there appears to have been no improvement since the condition of things described in a former chapter. Nay, rather, since the revolution of C. Gracchus, who had handed over the trials for provincial peculation to juries of Roman knights, from whom the tax-gatherers were also drawn, convictions were usually to be obtained only against such governors as Rutilius Rufus, who protected the provincials. Nothing is more affecting than Cicero's pictures of the misery of these subjects, and yet it is almost a rhetorical commonplace with him.

Here are some characteristic passages. When speaking of Pompey's high qualities,[2] 'consider his temperance! no avarice, no lust, the beauty of no city seduced him to indulgence, its historic fame to sight-seeing; finally, the statues and pictures and the adornments of Greek cities, which others regarded as plunder, he would not even look at.'

[1] Cic. *pro Sestio*, §§ 93, 94.   [2] *Pro lege Man.* § 40.

This was by contrast to such men as Piso, who was called the *Vulture of the Provinces*.[1] Cicero states[2] that as soon as he himself held assize courts in his province of Cilicia, he freed many towns from the most savage tributes, the most oppressive usury, and fictitious debts. His advices to Quintus on provincial government imply the same state of things, and his public letter *to the Senate* as regards the threatened Parthian war[3] sums up the natural results : ' For the auxiliary forces of our allies are either so weak, owing to the severity and injustice of our rule, that they cannot help us much, or so disaffected that nothing can be expected from them, far less entrusted to them. It is hard to express, Quirites, how hated we are among foreign nations, owing to the lust and injustice of those whom we sent to govern them during these years.'[4] At the opening of his oration *de provinciis consularibus*, he draws a picture of the state of the eastern provinces as shocking as that of Sicily under Verres, and recounts the atrocities perpetrated in Macedonia, in the city of Byzantium, in Achæa, and in Syria. I need not quote from the opening chapters details closely analogous to what has already been given. We can, therefore, hardly call his rhetorical outburst in the Verrines[5] exaggerated: *Lugent omnes provinciæ, queruntur omnes liberi populi; regna denique jam omnia de nostris cupiditatibus et injuriis expostulant: locus intra occanum jam nullus est, neque tam longinquus neque tam reconditus, quo non per hæc tempora nostrorum hominum libido iniquitasque pervaserit. Sustinere jam populus Romanus omnium nationum non vim,*

---

[1] *In Pis.* §§ 37, 38. Cf. also *pro Flacco*, § 18.—*Mirandum vero est, homines eos, quibus odio sunt nostræ securcs, nomen acerbitati, scriptura, decumæ, portoria morti, libentes arripere facultatem lædendi, quæcunque detur.*   [2] *Ad Fam.* xv. 4.
[3] *Ibid.* xv. 1.   [4] *Pro lege Man.* § 65.   [5] ii. 3, § 207.

non arma, non bellum, sed luctum, lacrimas, querimonias non potest.

This evidence, so constant, so uniform, cannot but be regarded as proving the proposition laid down early in this work, that the officers of the Roman Republic were the worst tyrants whom the world had yet seen, and that any agent able to overthrow them would be justly hailed as the deliverer of mankind.

I say the officers of the Republic were tyrants, for if nothing remained but the official decrees of the State, we should no more suspect the real state of things than we should from the decisions of the Inquisition, which hand over the victim to the civil power to be punished *citra sanguinis effusionem*.

As the name of the dictator Sylla appears in several recently recovered inscriptions, so the name of *Marcus* (Μααρκος) *Tullius Cicero Cornelia* (of the Cornelian tribe) turns up as one of the senatorial witnesses to a *senatus-consultum* sent to the town of Oropus in Bœotia, and engraved on marble by that grateful polity. This is one of a score of documents of the kind recovered in their Greek version from various parts of the Greek world. I am not concerned with these decrees in their Roman, but in their Greek aspect, and I cite them in the same way as Josephus cites them, as evidence of the consideration in which the dependencies of Rome stood to the ruling powers.

The earliest of these documents which come within the period of this book (there is one as early as 189 B.C.) follows closely upon the Roman pacification of Greece, but I have reserved it till this moment, when the whole group can be conveniently discussed.[1] It is the decision of the Senate in an old dispute concerning

---
[1] Cf. Latichew in *BCH* vi. 364 *sq*.

boundaries between the towns of Narthakion and Melite in Thessaly, which had been decided in favour of Narthakion by Flamininus, in his settlement of northern Greece.[1] Not content with his verdict, the Melitæans had appealed to external Greek arbitrators—a common practice, as numerous inscriptions prove—but the Samians, Colophonians, and Asiatic Magnesians had given it against them. At last they appealed to the Senate, when C. Host. Mancinus is named as prætor, and they received from it a decision confirming the previous adverse sentences. The facts of the case, with a special reference to Flamininus, and the decree, were set up in an inscription at Narthakion, on the site of which it was recently found.

The other two which I shall here specify[2] are those from the days of Cicero, shortly after the conquest of the East by Sylla. One of them confirms all the privileges accorded by the dictator as plenipotentiary-general to Stratoniceia in Caria, which at the head of Carian cities stoutly resisted Mithradates, and incurred great danger and loss. Its date must be 81 B.C.; and in answer to eight petitions of the Carians the Senate (under Sylla's direction) gives eight confirmatory replies.

The third is known as the *senatus consultum* of Oropus, which has been commented on by Mommsen (*Hermes*, xx. 262 *sq.*) It is the answer of the Senate to an appeal from Oropus against the *publicani*, who insisted upon taxing the lands about the temple of Amphiaraus. Sylla had declared that the property of the gods should be exempt. The *publicani* declared that Amphiaraus was not a god. Cicero was

[1] Cf. Livy, xxxvi. 51.
[2] There are at least seventeen now recovered in inscriptions, of which a partial list is given by Cousin and Deschamps, *BCH* xi. 225. Viereck's *sermo graecus*, etc., is the most complete tract on this question (Göttengen, 1888).

present at the discussion, and his name, as I have already told, is appended as a witness. The case remained in his memory, for he alludes plainly to it years after in his tract on the Nature of the Gods.[1] *An Amphiaraus sit deus et Trophonius? Nostri quidem publicani, cum essent agri in Bœotia deorum immortalium excepti lege censoria, negabant esse immortales ullos qui aliquando homines fuissent.* But this scepticism, prompted by greed, the Senate would not accept.

Quite apart from the tenor of these documents, which exhibit the reasonable and just side of Roman rule—I mean the public and responsible acts of the Senate as opposed to the injustices of individuals invested with arbitrary powers— the form of them is interesting as giving not only the order of procedure, but the style and composition of these Greek documents. Foucart was the first to perceive that they were translations from the Latin originals, made at Rome, and sent to the provincials without the Latin text. They are written in the vulgar 'common dialect' of the Greek world, with stock translations, and bad ones, of Latin terms. There are also gross Latinisms, which show that such men as Cicero could hardly have revised them.[2] So careless had the Senate now become of the appearances of culture, which were so studiously put forth in earlier days.

Nevertheless, this contemptuous tyranny, and perhaps still more contemptuous justice towards the Greeks, had not yet eradicated the old Roman weakness of copying their greater refinement. We cited above the habit of wearing Greek costume (p. 115); we hear of many Romans on their travels soliciting the 'freedom' of their cities from

[1] iii. 18, § 49.
[2] Cf. Cousin and Diehl in *BCH* ix. 37 for a list of these defects. *Pro magnanimitate sua* is ὑπὲρ μεγαλοφροσύνης; *Suus* appears as ἴδιος; *extra ordinem* as ἐκτὸς τοῦ στιχοῦ; *integer* is ἁγνός, and so on (cf. Viereck, *op. cit.* 59 *sq.*) This must be the work of some inferior clerk.

the Greeks, though, as Cicero explains,[1] such a privilege was inconsistent with Roman citizenship, which was *exclusive*, in contrast to Greek citizenships, which could be multiplied, and did not exclude any foreign privileges. 'And so we see in the Greek states, *e.g.* at Athens, Rhodians, Lacedæmonians, etc., enrolled, and the same men citizens of many cities. Misled by this, I see some uneducated persons, citizens of ours, enrolled at Athens among the jurymen and Areopagites, named as to tribe and number; whereas they ought to know, that if they obtained that citizenship, they must *ipso facto* have lost ours, unless they recovered it by the process called *postliminium.*' In the case of Roman exiles in Greece, this Greek adoption was almost the rule, but when the punishment was over, the legal fiction Cicero names should have been necessary, strictly speaking, before the Roman could return to his home.

But there were still many Romans who not only affected Greek citizenship; they affected the Greek language; they professed fancies as to Greek prose, some rejecting Demosthenes for the simplicity and antique grace of Lysias, others pretending to admire Thucydides, whom they could not understand, above Xenophon, whom they could.[2] These are the people whom Lucilius ridiculed in the person of Albucius, their coryphæus in this generation, and who coupled this admiration of Greek with contempt of Latin orators and poets.[3]

To turn from art to philosophy, they adopted too, with Epicurean tenets, other Greek practices. Cicero describes to Pætus[4] a dinner party to which he went at the house of a Volumnius called *Eutrapelos*, or 'the *Versatile*' in Greek, where were his friend Atticus and

[1] *Pro L. C. Balbo*, § 28 *sqq.* [2] Cicero, *Orator*, §§ 23, 30.
[3] *De Fin.* i. § 9; *ibid.* § 4 *sq.* [4] *Ad Fam.* ix. 26.

others, and a Greek courtesan (the host's mistress) named Cytheris. He anticipates Pætus's surprise, and says he did not know that she would be present. But he excuses himself with a remark from Aristippus. Possibly this company also condescended to dance, a horrible opprobrium to a Roman gentleman, as Cicero admits when refuting the charge brought by Cato against Murena.[1]

There were again others who actually professed Pythagoreanism, like Nig. Figulus and the wretched Vatinius,[2] and there were the famous Roman Stoics, though in some of them, such as Tubero, we hear of traits which seem a stupid parody of Stoic principles. He served his share in the funeral feast to his uncle, Scipio Africanus, upon the commonest ware, and with the rudest appointments, as if the cynic Diogenes and not the splendid Africanus were to be honoured. The public were justly indignant.[3]

So then, among the Roman nobles, who almost all submitted to the tyrannous fashion of learning something of Greek philosophy, there were all the grades of intelligence, from that of L. Gellius to that of Cicero. 'L. Gellius,[4] when he had come as proconsul after his prætorship into Greece, summoned all the philosophers then at Athens to meet together, and advised them seriously to make an end of their controversies. If they were really minded not

---

[1] *Pro Mur.* § 13.   [2] *In Vat.* § 14.

[3] *Pro Murena*, § 75.—*Fuit eodem ex studio vir eruditus apud patres nostros, et honestus homo et nobilis, Q. Tubero. Is quum epulum Q. Maximus Africani patrui sui nomine populo Rom. daret, rogatus est a Maximo, ut triclinium sterneret, quum esset Tubero ejusdem Africani sororis filius. Atque ille, homo eruditissimus ac Stoicus, stravit pelliculis hædinis lectulos Punicanos et exposuit vasa Samia, quasi vero esset Diogenes Cynicus mortuus, et non divini hominis Africani mors honestaretur. . . . Hujus in morte celebranda graviter tulit populus Rom. hanc perversam sapientiam Tuberonis.*

[4] Cic. *de Legg.* i. § 53.

to spend their lives in disputes, agreement was surely possible, and he promised them his assistance (as umpire) if they would strive to effect it!' Cicero, on the other hand, protests against his teachers, Philo and others, not insisting upon their differences from their rivals, and regards their attempts at any mediation among systems as a sign of weakness.[1] Philosophy had, in fact, become at Athens what it now is in our universities, no longer a rule of life, but a means of education in acuteness and in the practice of logical controversy.

[1] *De Nat. Deor.* i. § 16.

CHAPTER VII

THE PERIOD OF THE CIVIL WAR—FROM CICERO TO AUGUSTUS

PLUTARCH'S *Life of Cimon* opens with a strange story, which will serve us as a text for the cruel days which are the subject of the present chapter. It is a bit of local history, which the biographer tells about his native place.

There was an ancient family descended from the seer Peripoltas, who had come with the first settlers from Thessaly, which had furnished many eminent members who fought and died in the Persian and Galatian wars. The hero of our story was, however, the last scion, an orphan, called Damon Peripoltas (as if he had a family name), excelling the rest of the youth in beauty and vigour; but uneducated, and gloomy in temper. This youth was tempted by a Roman commander, who was wintering with his troops in Chæronea, and who did not disguise that he would use force when he failed with persuasion; our paternal city, adds Plutarch, being then in a bad way, and despised for its smallness and poverty. Damon, therefore, feeling outraged and dreading the results, made a conspiracy against this man with a few of his own fellows. The whole number, amounting to sixteen, blackened their faces with soot one night, and having taken unmixed wine, fell upon the Roman at break of day as he was sacrificing in the agora, and having slain him and a good many of those about him, left the city. In the excitement that supervened the Senate of the Chæroneans came together and condemned the whole party to death, by way of an apology from the city to the Romans. But that evening as the magistrates, according to custom, were dining together, Damon's party rushed into the town-hall and slew them, and fled away again.

Now it happened that about this very time L. Lucullus was passing through with an army on some expedition. As the occurrence was quite fresh he stopped his march, and having made inquiry into the facts, found that the city had rather suffered than done wrong; so he simply withdrew the garrison and took it with him. But when Damon kept plundering their territory by constant raids and robberies, and persecuted the city, the citizens induced him with friendly embassies and public resolutions to return, and made him gymnasiarch; but as he was anointing himself in the bathroom they murdered him. For a long time after, as our fathers tell us, he haunted the place, till they built up the door of the room; and even now the neighbours believe they hear and see him at times. Those of his race that yet remain (particularly about Steiris in Phocis, speaking Æolic dialect) they call the *sooty* (ἀσβολωμένους), on account of Damon having blackened his face with soot when he was going to commit the murder.

But the neighbouring people of Orchomenos, who had a quarrel with the Chæroneans, hired a Roman sycophant, and he, treating the city as a single defendant, brought against it a charge of murdering those slain by Damon. The court was that of the prætor of Macedonia (for at that time there was not yet a prætor of Achaia), at which the counsel for the city appealed to the evidence of Lucullus, who replied to the prætor's letter, telling the whole truth, and thus saving the city from the most serious danger. Accordingly a statue of Lucullus was set up in Chæronea, which suggested to Plutarch this story.

We have here a sort of combination of what happens in Ireland and what has happened in Greece in our own times. Most murders have been committed in Ireland with blackened faces, and under the stimulus of strong drink; the habit of taking to the mountains to escape the law, and appealing to the sympathy of other outlaws, and victims of what is considered tyrannous authority, is hardly yet out of fashion in most parts of southern Europe.

The events we have just related probably took place in 75-74, B.C., when the third Mithradatic war was commencing. It was a period when all the coasts were being devastated by Corsairs, almost under the eyes of the very Lucullus just mentioned, the first Roman commander that attempted with any success to combat this scourge of the civilised world. The long and bloody war in Crete, carried on by Metellus in spite of the objections and resistance of Pompey, ended in the partial depopulation of that island and the subjugation of the last fragment of independent Hellenism. Many of the pirates were indeed settled in the deserted Dyme, and about Patras in Achaia, but no such artificial and sporadic renewals of population could compensate for the heavier losses from war, from emigration, and from increasing poverty, which sapped the life-blood of most Hellenistic lands.

The stray anecdotes preserved to us show that the more vigorous part of the population did not seek to reconquer the land gone out of cultivation, but rather to live by plunder, cursing their fate and regarding the laws which restrained them as made unjustly to oppress the poor and the unfortunate. The details given by Cicero in his oration *for the Manilian Law*, a measure which put all the coasts and islands under the autocratic power of Pompey, show that there was not wanting a feeling of race hatred in these pirates, together with the ordinary love of plunder and lawlessness. In very many cases it was the Greek man revenging the loss of home and property upon his Roman conqueror. This may have been specially the case with the ravaging of Delos, now practically a great Roman mart in the Ægean. For not only was it plundered, but the temples were destroyed and the warehouses razed, although such ravages were no part of a pirate's policy, nay, even inconsistent with it.

We must also remember that great as was the success of Pompey in restoring peace and security upon the seas,[1] every disturbance in the Roman world was followed by a new outburst of piracy. As highwaymen infested the roads, so the lately settled pirates of Dyme abandoned the dulness of an agricultural life, and left the vintage of their hills for the 'unvintagable brine,' as Homer called it, upon which they knew how to reap a plentiful harvest. The many extant allusions make it certain that the Cilicians bore away the palm for daring and adroitness in this traffic of violence and cruelty; and, as has already been explained, the ruin of the Hellenistic cities on the Syrian, and the decline of Rhodes

---

[1] It seems to me that he treated these marauders with too much clemency, probably with the short-sighted policy of obtaining new glory through the astonishing promptness of his great results. His pacification was accordingly complete at the moment, but not thorough; for the peaceable subjects were left without any recognition of their passive virtues, while the pirates were rewarded for abandoning their crimes. Cicero (*de Off.* iii. 11) expresses the cause of public discontent when he says: *Piratas immunes, socios vectigales habemus.*

upon the Carian, coasts, gave the pirates ample recruits from both these seaboards.

Yet it is hard to say that any people have ever been more ingrained pirates than the Greeks proper, whose serrated coast, rocky islands, and unexpected harbours, whose lofty promontories and sea-side fortresses invite every lawless member of the community to try his luck in this adventurous game. From Homer to Byron this natural instinct never died out, not even in the palmy days of the *pax Romana* and the general security of the world. Nor do I believe it would now be extinct, but for the invention of steamers, which are too costly for the pirates to fit out, and which make the capture of their sailing boats a certainty. I believe the Malay Archipelago presents, or presented lately, an aspect of insecurity very like that of the Levant in Græco-Roman days.

Had the settlement of Pompey been followed by a century of calm, it is possible that this deep-seated Greek vice might have been eradicated. But before twenty years had elapsed all the East was in commotion at the tremendous conflict between Cæsarians and Pompeians, and every Greek must declare himself upon one side or other—most of them did so for each party in turn, according as the fortunes of war oscillated. Four times within the century (including the invasion of Mithradates) was the Greek peninsula racked by these colossal conflicts, in which the Greeks were of no moment except to furnish a few soldiers and enormous requisitions, to amuse the victorious leaders with their plentiful wit and wisdom, their gushing laudations, their pompous decrees; to feed them with their scanty provisions, and to work for them like beasts of burden.

It is the business of the historian of wars and of policy to follow out the details of this wretched period, which did more than any other down to mediæval times for the degradation and disintegration of Hellenistic life. Its effects reached not only all the peninsula but the nearer portions of Asia Minor and the islands, where Roman leaders demanded the advance of ten years' taxes, sacked towns, burnt fleets, and carried off sacred treasures. In their interludes these same men enjoyed themselves in the fashionable delights of Greek culture. Athens in particular was the scene of popular demonstrations which remind us of the days of Demetrius *the Thunderbolt*.[1]

In the first Roman struggle, that of Cæsar and Pompey, it is remarkable that Athens was not the residence of either chief. The sympathies of Pompey lay further to the East, and his main support came from Asia. His philosopher-guide, Theophanes, came from Mytilene, and may have been jealous of the possible influence of Athenian rivals, if Pompey came within the fascination of that eternal city. Cæsar on the other hand, though he had spent much of his youth in the East, and like all the Roman leaders knew the Hellenistic world well, is the first of them who dispensed with Greek private chaplains and panegyrists, and trusted to himself both for wisdom to act and literary power to chronicle his deeds. His *Memoirs* seem to me a calm and noble protest from the Roman magnate against the flattery, the tinsel, the unreality of the Greek rhetorician. His philosophy, so far as he professed any, was Epicurean, and that school did not usually afford tutors and counsellors to kings. But his real Roman sense revolted against the Hellenistic sentimentality of his rival, and this probably gave him weight and dignity with many serious Romans— the more so, as he was able to make good with his own pen any supposed deficiency, and compose an account of

[1] Cf. *Greek Life and Thought*, p. 86.

his doings with a simplicity and gravity quite novel to the then world of letters. This contempt for what I will call sentimental Hellenism, combined with the large measures of relief and justice which he accorded to the maltreated Greeks,[1] as soon as his power was assured, is one of the most remarkable, though little noticed, features in the character and policy of the great Dictator.

But if neither Cæsar nor Pompey dallied in Greece, as the eastern invaders had ever been prone to do, it was a very different thing with the sentimental Brutus and the luxurious Antony. Brutus spent the whole winter after the murder of Cæsar at Athens in organising the senatorial party from the remains of the Pompeians left in Macedonia, from the resources of the now loudly anti-Cæsarian Greeks, and from the legions and stores already in transit for the East, when Cæsar's plans had been arrested by his death. But we are told that Brutus's leisure hours were spent in discourse with the philosophers, who no doubt ransacked history to fortify his doubtful conscience with examples of virtuous tyrannicides. They even set up his statue beside those of Harmodius and Aristogiton, the imaginary founders of Athenian liberty.

[1] Thus he included 500 Greeks, probably of those resident in Italy, among the 5000 Roman colonists whom he sent with full citizen rights to his new foundation at Como; cf. Strabo (v. 1, § 6), who says these Greeks were the most distinguished of the townspeople. On the other hand, his foundation of the Roman colony at Corinth settled a Roman public, and not of the best sort, in Greece, and from this town such customs as gladiatorial shows were introduced into Greece. I infer the character of these people from the remark of Strabo (viii. 6, § 23), who tells us that on finding bronzes and ancient pottery in some of the tombs they ransacked every one they could find, and sold both bronzes and pottery (νεκροκορίνθια) for great prices at Rome till the fashion changed. There is also an epigram ascribed to Crinagoras (No. 32, ed. Rubensohn) which complains bitterly of the class of men—twice sold slaves—who now walked upon the ashes of the Bacchiadæ.

Unfortunately, we have very few details of Greek life beyond these generalities, during this agitated period. We hear that when Cæsar's legate, Calenus, stormed Megara, after the battle of Pharsalia, the Pompeians let loose against him the lions which were then on their way to the Roman amphitheatre, and that they attacked both sides indiscriminately. They were in fact as impartial in their emnity as their Greek keepers were in their flattery towards the Romans.[1] We also hear that Dolabella on his way to Asia stopped at Argos to purchase a horse, which was descended from the horses of the Thracian Diomede, for which he paid 100,000 sesterces, but which brought all its successive owners fatal ill-luck.[2]

Far more interesting than these stray trifles is it to pause a moment before the character of Brutus, 'the noblest Roman of them all,' in the judgment of most of his contemporaries, but in that of history a very mischievous doctrinaire, who for the sake of a bug-bear of his own—his artificial horror of tyranny—inflicted perhaps the greatest mischief any one man ever inflicted upon his generation. In exact contrast to the practical directness of Cæsar, Brutus was constitutionally sentimental, as for example when he went to Naples to *persuade* Greek players to come to Rome, and asked his friends to secure for him in the same way a special actor, as it was wrong to coerce any Greek.[3] He constantly saved and pardoned his bitterest enemies in the Civil war, yet he urged Cicero, as we know from the sixth book of the *Letters to Atticus*, to use his pro-consular authority in Cyprus on behalf of a villainous money-lender called Scaptius, who had tried to extract 48 per cent from the Salaminians,

---

[1] These lions had been purchased by Cassius for display at his ædileship. Plutarch (*Brutus*, 8) repeats an absurd story that it was their loss which set Cassius against Cæsar.

[2] Aul. Gell. iii. 9, 1. [3] Plut. *Brut.* 21.

together with compound interest, and had locked up the Senate of Salamis in their council chamber, till five of them died of hunger. This villain was acting with the knowledge of Brutus, and yet he protected and encouraged him, possibly for his own interest.

After the first battle of Philippi, when he found his victorious army encumbered with a crowd of captives, in face of the enemy, he ordered all the slaves among the prisoners to be massacred, while he liberated with polite speeches the free men—a proceeding which Plutarch mentions without comment. But the same biographer relates with indignation that he promised his soldiers the sack of Thessalonica and Sparta if they were victorious. And yet he rode up and down crying and ringing his hands before the town of Xanthus, where the inhabitants, to avoid capture and sacking by his troops, allowed their city to take fire, and committed suicide *en masse*. He offered rewards for the saving of their lives. For he was in theory a humane man, and a philosopher, but distinctly of the Roman Stoic type, always talking philosophy in Greek, but not apparently attached to any Greek sect, not even to the Stoics, who were clearly the people he should have joined. Plutarch specially[1] calls him a follower of Cato, and so far as he was definite, a follower of the older Academy from Plato to Antiochus. He mentions[2] that at Athens he sought the company of Theomnestus the Academic, and Cratippus the Peripatetic, not of the Stoic school. All this points to his Roman eclecticism, even though he knew Greek perhaps better than any of his contemporaries.

Both the philosophy and the Hellenism of Brutus have a close resemblance to those of his model, the younger Cato. A comparison of the lives of both in Plutarch will,

---

[1] Cap. 2.   [2] Cap. 24.

however, show that Cato was by far the stricter and more consistent Stoic, even to the verge of that coarse simplicity which parades meanness or indecency. His appointing of parsley crowns instead of the usual money prizes, when ædile, reminds us of the absurdity of Tubero,[1] and the account of his reception of the Egyptian Ptolemy at Rhodes savours rather of the vulgarest cynic than of a Roman gentleman.[2] He was trained by Antipater of Tyre, and afterwards took great pains to go and seek out Athenodorus at Pergamum and take him into his household.[3] But we must admit that he won his position at Rome by long-tried virtue rather than by one signal crime. While his curiosity in visiting the East shows an educated taste, and his honesty and economy among the provincials were in all respects honourable, the simplicity of his appointments, and his habit of walking when all the rest rode, have a certain theatrical air about them which is even more obtrusive in the circumstances of his suicide. He too, in contrast to Cæsar, had all his nearer intimates Greeks, so had Brutus, and so had Antony, so that these, and not Roman nobles, were the companions of each in his last moments.

Cato made his great mistake in attempting to carry on the politics of this corrupt and violent time on Stoic principles. The tyrannicide idea, which Brutus was always parading with such ostentation, was not prominent in Cato's conversation, because he must have felt very clearly that if Cæsar was assassinated, Pompey would remain actual master of the state—probably a far worse autocrat. But these tyrannicide notions were imported from the writings of Greek aristocrats into the talk of Roman aristocrats, and were really the outcry against the loss of privileges and of license among nobles, rather than the genuine assertion of political liberty among

---

[1] Above, p. 149. [2] *Cat.* 35. [3] *Ibid.* c. x.

the mass of the free population. This latter principle was put forward as a pretence and a cloak; what both Greek and Roman tyrannicides really resented was the rule of one man over the privileged classes, whom he levelled down to the inferior people. Thus when the tyrannicide Cassius, who shared with Brutus all the sentimental horrors of the republican against despotism, came to control and plunder Syria, he quickly forgot his vaunted principles. Josephus tells us of a certain Marion, whom Cassius had left as master over the Syrians; this man divided Syria into distinct tyrannies and so controlled it![1]

But in philosophy Cassius was a declared Epicurean, who (according to Plutarch) aired his notions in opposition to Brutus. His physical explanation of the tragic apparition of Brutus's evil genius is a curious piece of bathos. But the more serious differences of the two philosophical murderers were soothed by a third kind of dilettante, Marcus Favorinus, a passionate follower of Cato, 'who did not philosophise by study so much as by some kind of impulse and mad passion.' Brutus called him a mere Cynic and a sham one.[2]

On one point they all seem to have agreed—on plundering the Greeks for the sake of their own civil war. Cassius especially acted with violence and cruelty. When the Rhodians resisted he stormed their island town after defeating their fleet, and we hear that he robbed them of some £2,000,000 of our money, nearly all of it private property;[3] and this gives us some notion of the comparative wealth of Rhodes and Athens at this period. Athens could only send a fleet of three ships to aid Antony at the battle of

---

[1] xiv. 12.—τυραννίσι γὰρ διαλαβὼν τὴν Συρίαν οὗτος ὁ ἀνὴρ ἐφρούρησε.
[2] Cf. Plut. *Brut.* 34-37 for the details.
[3] 8000 talents from requisition, 500 more from the public funds (Plut. *Brut.* 32).

Actium. The plunder of Asia and the islands was so great that Brutus was able to lavish money on his troops during the final campaign, and it is quite possible that this frightful crisis, followed within ten years by the still more monstrous requisitions of Antony, inflicted a financial blow never recovered by the Greeks of Hellas and the islands.

We have in Antony the old and vulgar style of phil-Hellene, who liked Greek life for its pleasures, and Greek society for the keener imagination of that people in providing entertainments, as well as for the more piquant flattery in which they were acknowledged masters. Plutarch justly brings Antony's *joieuse entrée* into Ephesus[1] and his debauches at Athens into comparison with the extravagances of king Demetrius the Besieger, which we have already noticed in a previous volume. At the same time he did not scruple to use any of them as slaves, to carry burdens like mules, or to perform the most menial work. He stole three colossal statues by Myron from the Samians, of which Augustus restored[2] two. There was little Hellenistic culture in the man, though he liked Hellenistic pleasures.

Plutarch notices that he particularly favoured the Asianic style of rhetoric,[3] at that time very fashionable, and having a great analogy to his own life.[4] It is very interesting to find

[1] *Anton.* cap. xxiv.   [2] Cf. *MDI* ix. 260.

[3] *Ant.* 2. This is corroborated by Suetonius (*Octav.* 86) when speaking of Augustus's purism. '*M. quidem Antonium ut insanum increpat, quasi ea scribentem, quae mirentur potius homines, quam intelligant. Deinde ludens malum et inconstans in eligendo genere dicendi ingenium ejus addit haec:* . . . *an potius Asiaticorum oratorum inanis sententiis verborum volubilitas in nostrum sermonem transferenda?*' This shows that Antony's Greek studies had affected his Latin. Strabo (p. 523) mentions Dellius as the special historiographer of Antonius's Parthian war, therefore probably in Greek.

[4] κομπώδη καὶ φρυαγματίαν ὄντα καὶ κενοῦ γαυριάματος καὶ φιλοτιμίας ἀνωμάλου μεστόν (bombastic and frothy, and full of vain boasting and capricious ambition).

in one of his official letters to the Jews, cited by Josephus,[1] a passage which thoroughly corroborates Plutarch. Antony recites his recent victory at Philippi in these words, the effects of which can hardly be rendered in a translation : ἡμεῖς, ὡς οὐχ ὑπὲρ ἰδίου μόνον ἀγῶνος, ἀλλ' ὑπὲρ ἁπάντων κοινοῦ, τοὺς αἰτίους καὶ τῶν εἰς ἀνθρώπους παρανομιῶν καὶ τῶν εἰς θεοὺς ἀνομημάτων ἠμυνάμεθα δι' ἃ καὶ τὸν ἥλιον ἀπεστράφθαι δοκοῖμεν, ὃς καὶ αὐτὸς ἀηδῶς ἐπεῖδε τὸ ἐπὶ Καίσαρι μῖσος. Ἀλλὰ καὶ τὰς ἐπιβουλὰς αὐτῶν τὰς θεομάχους, ἃς ὑπεδέξατο ἡ Μακεδονία, καθάπερ ἴδιος αὐτοῖς τῶν ἀνοσίων τολμημάτων ἀὴρ, καὶ τὴν σύγχυσιν τῆς ἡμιμάνους κακοήθως γνώμης, ἣν κατὰ Φιλίππους τῆς Μακεδονίας συνεκρότουν, καὶ τόπους εὐφυεῖς καταλαμβανόμενοι μέχρι θαλάττης ἀποτετειχισμένους ὄρεσι, ὡς πύλῃ μιᾷ τὴν πάροδον ταμιεύσασθαι, τῶν θεῶν αὐτοὺς ἐπὶ τοῖς ἀδίκοις ἐγχειρήμασι κατεψηφισμένων, ἐκρατήσαμεν.[2] I need quote no more to show how truly Plutarch has spoken. The companion letters in the same chapter are much tamer, and do not show this peculiarity so strongly. Possibly that quoted may have been written before the excitement of the great victory had worn off, and by himself, while he entrusted to his secretaries the later and mere business letters.

The splendid and eccentric hospitalities of Cleopatra, the Egyptian queen, have made his life notorious. But though the brilliant Cleopatra, whose ancestors had now been thoroughly Hellenised for centuries, whose capital had long been the centre of Greek learning, had turned her great talents exclusively to practise the art of fascination, and was of course ready to take from Greek culture anything that could add grace or refinement to sensuality, though she spoke Greek perfectly, as all her house had done,

[1] *Antiqq.* xiv. 12, § 3.
[2] I apologise for giving so much Greek in the text, but I have tried in vain to reproduce the effect of this rhodomontade in English.

yet the whole spirit of her court was Egyptian and oriental rather than Hellenistic.

It is plain that during this century the great work of Alexander suffered more than in any like period for a long time before or after. The rise of Roman importance turned the whole stream of Greek emigration westward; Antioch and Alexandria were no longer the El Dorado of the Greek fortune-hunter. I have already explained[1] how, ever since the seventh Ptolemy, Greek influence had waned even in Alexandria, and perhaps the only interesting personal story in Diodorus is his account how in this very generation (about 56 B.C.), when the Romans were greatly feared, and it was of the last importance to retain their favour, a Roman accidentally killed a cat; and how the fury of the populace at this crime against Egyptian religion was such that, though the offence was caused by an accident, though the king sent soldiers at once to protect the man from the mob, nothing could save his life. This anecdote seems to indicate that Alexandria was no longer a mainly Greek and Jewish city. The old tough race had been reasserting its ineradicable peculiarities.

This is clearly the case if we compare generally the Egypt of the Ptolemies with the Egypt of the Romans. From the days of Augustus it was no longer the chief of Hellenistic lands, but a foreign and oriental country, full of natural wealth and of curiosities, but foreboding peculiar danger to the Empire from its isolated and defensible position, and from the fact that the strange enthusiasm of the old Egyptians might any day accept some saviour like the modern Mahdis, and rise in dangerous revolt. All this is non-Hellenistic, Oriental, and essentially Egyptian. At Alexandria there was of course a good deal of the Ptolemaic tone left. The court spoke Greek still, and the uniforms and etiquette were the

[1] *Greek Life and Thought*, p. 506.

old Macedonian, long after Macedon had disappeared for ever from the catalogue of nations. Watchwords and commands were no doubt still issued to the household guards in Macedonian, though the later kings had neglected to learn even this hereditary dialect, and had contented themselves with Greek. But it is significant that Cleopatra found it useful to speak Egyptian and Syrian as well as Greek, and this extraordinary accomplishment has been exaggerated into the statement that she could speak the languages of all her subjects, even of Troglodytes.[1]

And yet with all her fascinations the occasional details we hear of her ordinary life show that her high culture had not included really refined manners. If the account of Josephus[2] be true, she offered herself with disgusting facility, whether from mere passion or policy, to other people than Antony, so that Herod could boast that he had rejected her addresses. The whole scene of her visit to Jerusalem, while Antony had gone upon his disastrous expedition against the Parthians, though told with matter-of fact dulness by the historian, is perhaps the most dramatic in the romantic histories of the Jewish king and the Alexandrian queen. They were each in their way the representatives of that Syrian and Egyptian Hellenism which was accommodating itself to the Roman sway. Both were strikingly handsome, and versed in the arts of looking young,[3] both were persuasive and versatile. To these

[1] I notice that our artists, who often take Cleopatra for their subject, always represent her a bronze-coloured Egyptian in the old national costume. We know that she was fair, and may infer with certainty that she lived and dressed as a Greek.

[2] *Antiqq.* xv. 4, § 2.

[3] I need not adduce evidence in the case of Cleopatra, but will quote Josephus (xvi. 8, § 1) on Herod: μελαίνοντα τὰς τρίχας, καὶ κλέπτοντα τὸν ἔλεγχον τῆς ἡλικίας!

qualities both owed their power, created or established for them by the Romans. From Antony especially Herod had received his title of king and his dominion. But from Antony too the more potent Cleopatra had obtained the formal proclamation of her younger son Ptolemy as king of kings in Phœnicia, Syria, and Cilicia, and the boy had been produced to the people of Alexandria in the robes and Macedonian diadem of the Syrian sovranty.[1] Hence her interests and Herod's were opposed, and the problem before each of them was how to preserve authority under Antony, or if Antony fell, under his successor. Herod played the longer game, and won. But the scene at Herod's palace must have been inimitable. The display of counter-fascinations between these two tigers; their voluptuous natures mutually attracted; their hatred giving to each that deep interest in the other which so often turns to mutual passion while it incites to conquest; the grace and finish of their manners, concealing a ruthless ferocity; the splendour of their appointments—what more dramatic picture can we imagine in history?

The prosaic Josephus adds that Herod consulted his council whether he should not put her to death for this attempt upon his virtue. He was dissuaded by them on the ground that Antony would listen to no arguments, not even from the most persuasive of the world's princes, and would take awful vengeance when he heard of her death. So she was escorted with great gifts and politenesses back to Egypt.

Such, then, was the character of this notorious queen. But her violation of temples and even of ancient tombs for the sake of treasure must have been a far more public and odious exhibition of that want of respect for the sentiment

[1] Plutarch, *Antonius*, 54.

of others which is the essence of bad manners. Of the same kind were her violences to her attendants, whom she flew upon, beating them and tearing their hair even in the presence of the noblest Roman visitors.[1] When Octavius was sitting beside her, and she gave him a list of all her treasures, she used this violence to her steward, who said the list was incomplete; Cæsar smiled and restrained her. These details come from the memoirs of his confidential physician, Olympus.[2] This Hellenism then, even in queens, was far below the pure Hellenedom of earlier days or even the teaching of the schools in Athens and Rhodes.

The same kind of outrage upon manners is exhibited in the tragic scene told by Josephus[3] when the condemned Mariamme, going in silence to her death, is assailed by her mother Alexandra, who thought to secure her own safety by reviling her unfortunate daughter. In addition to loud and calumnious accusations, she did not even refrain from tearing her daughter's hair! We cannot but feel that though of royal descent, with a Greek name, and probably screaming out her abuse in Greek, there was here little more of Hellenism than a skin-deep varnish.

To return to Egypt.

The court of this marvellous queen can hardly be called either strictly Hellenistic or Egyptian; for she sought what was fascinating from all quarters, and was probably more cosmopolitan in her tastes than any one who had as yet appeared in the Hellenistic world. Beyond the court, together with the decaying Museum and the Greek trade in the port,

[1] Plut. *Ant.* 83.
[2] Σελεύκου δέ τινος τῶν ἐπιτρόπων ἐλέγχοντος ὡς ἔνια κρύπτουσαν καὶ διακλέπτουσαν ἀναπηδήσασα καὶ τῶν τριχῶν αὐτοῦ λαβομένη πολλὰς ἐνεφόρει τῷ προσώπῳ πληγάς.
[3] *Antiqq.* xv. 7, § 5.

we know of nothing but the reassertion of the old nationality. The revolt and devastation of Thebes which took place under Lathyrus about 85 B.C., and from which that wonderful city never recovered,[1] would at first seem an assertion of Alexandrian ideas against the old traditions and claims of the natives. But the result was probably the very reverse. Whatever cosmopolitan culture—Greek or Roman—might creep into a great Egyptian city far up the Nile by way of trade or garrison would never reach ruined palaces, or the villages which held the remains of the population. The Egyptians became more and more a mere agricultural peasantry with no great centre in Upper Egypt (for Ptolemais was wholly Greek), and so sank gradually into the position of the Indian ryot or other free labourer, who is practically a slave to earn taxes for his rulers.

The peculiar religions and philosophic developments at Alexandria which came just before and with the rise of Christianity will be discussed in due season.

Let us now turn to Syria and Asia Minor. The long quarrels and wars of the wretched Seleucid princes and princesses at last produced in the most loyal of the Syrians a conviction that any foreign rule would be better than this constant and bloody confusion. As Egypt was exactly in the same difficulties, there seemed no possibility of obtaining a proper regent from that quarter, and the Romans had already shown their harsh and grasping character in the East. So it seems that the Armenian and Parthian sovran Tigranes was invited or permitted to occupy the throne peaceably for about eighteen years. Then came his connection with the Mithradatic wars and the conquests of

---

[1] Mr. Sayce informs me that on the *ostraca* he has collected in Egypt, Thebes (Diospolis) is called a μητρόπολις till this time; afterwards it is cited as consisting merely of villages (κῶμαι).

Lucullus, ending in the settlement of Pompey, by which Syria was taken from Tigranes and from the remaining Seleucids and made a Roman province. This settlement rehabilitated all the isolated cities within the limits of Syria. Josephus specially tells us that the coast cities such as Gaza, which Jannæus had destroyed, as well as the inland cities such as Scythopolis, were all declared free of Jewish or Syrian rule; if they were held by tyrants, which was the case with some of them, these tyrants were dispossessed; if they were ruined, they were given to their exiled inhabitants to rebuild. For the isolated Greek city was the form of polity apparently best understood by Rome and most convenient for distant dependencies. Nevertheless the rapacity and tyranny of the Roman governors made this change less beneficial than would at first sight appear.

We have unfortunately no picture of Syrian Hellenistic life at this period. But except that many philosophers, grammarians, and epigrammatists come from the coast cities, there is little sign of any stirring or interesting intellectual and social life from this time to the establishment of the Empire. All the Roman decrees cited in the fourteenth book of Josephus's *Antiquities* were to be engraved and set up in Roman and Greek, not in any local idiom, such as Syriac. It is everywhere assumed in that book that the Jewish people perfectly understand Greek, though very few could write it correctly. The names of almost all their public men are also Greek.

The requisitions of the Roman party leaders were of course here as elsewhere very oppressive. Still worse, the civil wars entailed a neglect of the frontier, and after the great victory over Crassus the Parthians kept invading not only Syria but Asia Minor with impunity. Cæsar was preparing to conquer them when he was assassinated, but in the years immediately succeeding they penetrated through Asia Minor and actually reached the Ægean.[1] The victories of Ventidius, the lieutenant of Antony, were followed by the graver defeat of Antony himself, so that the Roman sway over Syria was often interrupted and always precarious. In these frequent Parthian raids the Greek cities suffered great loss, and doubtless many more Greeks were carried off as slaves into the interior of Asia. A certain varnish of Hellenistic culture extended even to the Parthian court, as the celebrated story of the appearance of the head of Crassus at a Greek play in Parthia implies. But I think the weight of this piece of evidence is overrated; for it may have been fashionable to see the performances of Greek strolling players, who went round the scattered Greek cities of Parthia, without understanding them at all clearly.[2] Even nowadays crowds of people in London go to German, Italian, and French plays for fashion's sake, without being able to follow one sentence of the dialogue. Our whole knowledge of the Arsacid power tells us that it was distinctly oriental and non-Hellenistic, quite different from that of the Seleucids, perhaps even from that of Tigranes.

On the other hand, the really Hellenistic cities of the East were now affected or infected with a Roman element, which seriously altered their complexion in politics, art, and manners. Pompey had already posed as a great founder of cities in the East—cities, indeed, after the Hellenistic model, but with names derived from himself and his conquests, sometimes with a population increased from his own veterans, and probably in every case looking to Rome, and not to Antioch or Alexandria, as the real model of a

---

[1] The inscriptions of Stratoniceia in Caria imply this disastrous invasion, cf. *BCH* xi. 156.   [2] Cf. above, p. 33.

city.[1] Still more was the Italic element strengthened in some of them by the fact that Roman communities were settled in them, a population apart from, and certainly not inferior to, the Greeks. Such was the case with Nicopolis, Sinope, Byzantium, and others.[2] As I have already noted, all the decrees issued by Roman generals at this time in Syria were published in Latin and in Greek, and thus there arose and grew that peculiar fusion which afterwards marked the civilisation of the Empire.[3]

The coryphæus of this movement in the East, the most interesting Hellenistic figure of the day, who stands alone, with Cleopatra, above the vulgar herd of worthless dynasts, in versatility, in daring, and in consequent success, was the Idumæan Herod, whose earlier life, which falls within our period, fills the fascinating fourteenth and fifteenth books of Josephus's *Antiquities*. The wonderful adventures and vicissitudes of this clever upstart, his gradual rise to power upon the ruins of the Asmonæan house, his cruel domination over the Jews, are all matters of well-known history. But beyond the fact of his success, the manner of it is strangely interesting. He must clearly have been the most fascinating of men. Whenever his crimes or the hostility of the conservative party and of the legitimate royal house brought him into imminent danger; whenever his foes expected that his fall at the hands of the Roman governor was certain, his visit to headquarters as an already

---

[1] Cf. on this settlement, and on the new or newly-enlarged cities of the East, Mommsen, *R. G.* iii. 152 *sq.*

[2] Thus in the old piratical forts of the Alpine Isauria, we have in an inscription : 'Ισαυρέων ἡ βουλὴ καὶ ὁ δῆμος οἵ τε συμπολιτευόμενοι 'Ρωμαῖοι (*BCH* xi. 67).

[3] It is in this sense only that the eulogy of Augustus in Philo (*Leg. ad Caium*, 22) is true—ὁ τὴν μὲν 'Ελλάδα 'Ελλάσι πολλοῖς παραυξήσας, τὴν δὲ βάρβαρον ἐν τοῖς ἀναγκαιοτάτοις τμήμασιν ἀφελληνίσας.

condemned criminal turned out the occasion for new extension of his territory, for new privileges, for new favours. He is reported to have bribed Gabinius, Antony, Cleopatra, and others in turn. Of course he did so. But anybody else could adopt this vulgar and obvious means of persuasion. He must have added some singular eloquence of words or of manner, some extraordinary plausibility, to win so many desperate causes. His military career was very similar. Sometimes defeated, often in great difficulties, his unwearied resource, his obstinate courage, his popularity with his mercenaries, made him recover lost battles, and reduce his enemies' victories to successes in unsuccessful campaigns.

But what makes him far more interesting to us than all his wars and his wiles is the story of his love. Married to Mariamme, the most splendid beauty of her day, he seems really to have gained the deep affection of this princess of the house he had dethroned, but the passion that dominated him made her feel secure, and too outspoken in her contempt for his mother and sister, whom she derided as ignoble. The king was so completely devoted to her, that even the irresistible Cleopatra, who tried to seduce him, only met with contempt, and would have lost her life at his hands but for the dictates of prudence, as I have already explained.[1]

Josephus quotes his facts from Herod's own *Memoirs*, which gave a more favourable account of the king than was contained in independent histories.[2] How interesting must these memoirs have been! We wonder what account he gave in them of the tragedy with

---

[1] Above, p. 166.
[2] *Antiqq*. xv. 6, § 3 : ταῦτα δὲ γράφομεν ἡμεῖς, ὡς ἐν τοῖς ὑπομνήμασι τοῖς τοῦ βασιλέως 'Η. περιείχετο.

Mariamme; or did he omit all domestic matters as beneath his dignity? His furious jealousy led him gradually not only to suspect every intimate of his pure and noble wife, but to take the odious precautions of an oriental despot, lest upon his death she should survive and pass into the possession of any other man. Her discovery of these precautions led to bitter recriminations, abject repentance on Herod's side, reconciliations, and new estrangements. The story of the pathetic preludes to her death make the pages of the tame historian glow with lurid splendour. When at last the schemes of her female enemies succeeded, and she was condemned to death at the demand of Herod, her calm dignity and silence left in his heart the indelible conviction of his own injustice, and the stings of a remorse heightened to madness by the unspeakable misery of his self-inflicted bereavement. His great passion for Mariamme returned with such a storm into his soul that his reason as well as his health were shattered. All attempted distractions proved vain, and for months he lay a mere wreck in the hands of his despairing physicians in Samaria.

Let me quote the words of Josephus: 'But after she was executed, the king's passion was inflamed even beyond the condition we have already described. For his love was not calm, or such as arises from companionship, but had begun with enthusiasm, and was not prevented by the outspokenness of married life from growing stronger every day. So then it appeared that he had been set on to destroy her by some Divine retribution, and oft would he call upon her by name, oft fall into unseemly lamentation, though he also devised all possible beguilements for his soul, making convivial nights and entertainments his serious pursuit. But none of these things availed him. He then abandoned the administration of his kingdom to others, and was so overcome with his calamity, as actually to order his attendants to call Mariamne, as if she were alive and could respond. At this time there supervened a pestilence, which carried off both much people and the majority of his most honoured peers, and was interpreted by public opinion as the visitation of Providence for the outrage done upon his queen. This too had a grave effect upon the king, and at last betaking himself to the deserts, and wandering about there distraught, under the pretext of hunting, after some days he fell into a dreadful sickness—fever and inflammation of the neck, with loss of reason, nor were any of the usual remedies of avail, except to intensify the disease and drive his attendants to despair.' At last his doctors, in perplexity, allowed him whatever he desired, leaving his recovery to chance. In this condition he lay sick in Samaria.[1]

It was after this tragic episode of his life had passed that he succeeded in conciliating at Alexandria the final conqueror in the civil wars, and received from Augustus the confirmation and extension of his royal position. Then it was that he undertook to rebuild and adorn Jerusalem, and presently Cæsarea, in accordance with the ideas of the day. The later history of Herod falls under the Empire. But here we have already full blown that new type of which I have spoken—Hellenism coloured with Roman habits, modified by Roman tastes, not from any real admiration, but because it was politic, nay even necessary, to conciliate and flatter the rulers of the earth.

Having slain the last remnants of the legitimate high priest's ruling family, Herod proceeds thus:[2] 'Whereupon he departed yet further from the national customs, and kept corrupting the old order of things with new fashions, because he could not control them; and this did us no

---

[1] *Antt. Jud.* xv. 7, § 7.   [2] *Op. cit.* xv. 8.

small harm even in succeeding times, as those things became neglected which led the common people to religion. For first he established a five years' feast of athletic contests in honour of Cæsar, and built a theatre in Jerusalem, and again on the plain beneath an enormous amphitheatre, both of them remarkable for their splendour, but foreign to Jewish customs; for the use of them, and such exhibitions, are against our traditions. He thereupon celebrated his five years' feast with great splendour, having announced it round about, and invited people of every nation. Athletes and other performers were induced to come from every land by the promise of valuable prizes, and the reputation of so famed a competition, and so the best of all kinds were secured. For very valuable rewards were offered, not only for gymnastics, but for musical skill. He also offered prizes for races with four, two, or single horses; and whatever devices had elsewhere been adopted to exhibit riches and splendour, these he carefully imitated from motives of ambition. Round the theatre were medallions of Cæsar, and trophies of the nations conquered by him, wrought in pure gold and silver. In robes, too, and precious stones, there was nothing too splendid to be expended upon the decoration. There was a large provision of wild beasts—quantities of lions and other animals of exceptional strength or rarity, and these were set to fight with each other, or with condemned criminals.

'The visitors were astonished with this extravagance, and delighted with the excitement of these conflicts, but to the natives they seemed a manifest violation of ancient traditions, for it was clearly impious to cast men to wild beasts for mere amusement, impious too to supplant the Law with strange ordinances. But what vexed them most of all were the trophies, as they regarded the figures surrounded by the arms as images.' The historian goes on to explain how Herod was obliged to take particular pains to get rid of this difficulty! His murders, his espionage, and his exactions seemed to his people far less shocking.

In addition to this readornment of Jerusalem, ultimately condoned by the Jews, owing to his splendid rebuilding and magnifying of the great temple some years later,[1] Herod built two more Hellenistic centres,[2] wherein to show both his architectural fancies and his profound veneration for the emperor, Sebaste (which was the Greek for Augusta), on the site of the old Samaria, and Cæsarea on the coast, where he constructed a large artificial harbour—as it were a seaport for his capital, on a coast singularly devoid of any natural refuge for ships. The details of this great work are minutely described by Josephus; and indeed such enterprises must have gratified the peculiar ambition of Herod to be known as a munificent builder. For he was in the habit, when he visited Asia Minor, of giving large sums to various cities to set up stoas, temples, and other public edifices. He set up again the ruined stoa of Chios,[3] and showered benefits on Ephesus, Samos, and Ilium. He was the mediator with Agrippa for many supplications from these cities, and often obtained for them a remission of burdens.

In all this Hellenistic work he had beside him as his teacher, his *ancient*, his adviser, Nicolaus of Damascus, one of the most prolific authors of that day, who is reported to

[1] By the way, with Corinthian pillars (Jos. xv. 11, § 5).
[2] When the Jews sent an embassy to Rome after his death to protest against the oppressions of Archelaus, his successor, a special complaint against the rule of Herod was that he adorned and favoured outlying Greek towns, to the loss and detriment of his Jewish subjects. Josephus, *Antt. Jud.* xvii. 11, § 2: πόλεις μέν γε τὰς μὲν περιοικίδας, καὶ ὑπ' ἀλλοφύλων οἰκουμένας κοσμοῦντα μὴ παύσασθαι, καταλύσει τε καὶ ἀφανισμῷ τῶν ἐν τῇ ἀρχῇ αὐτοῦ κατῳκημένων.
[3] Jos. xvi. 2, 2.

have done much to whitewash Herod's reputation. In an interesting fragment from the autobiography of Nicolaus[1] he tells how Herod got tired of philosophy, and made him set to work at rhetoric. Presently Herod got weary of rhetoric, and took to history. It was the necessity of working up history with Herod that set Nicolaus to extend his own studies till he composed a great general history, which he says is a labour which would have puzzled Heracles, if Eurystheus had chosen to set it before him. It is specially mentioned of this Nicolaus that he openly boasted of being from Damascus, whereas rival teachers were often anxious to acquire the citizenship of some famous city, and then drop their native place. This by the way.

I will conclude with the significant passage in which Josephus explains the policy of this remarkable philo-Roman sovran:[2] 'By his ambition in doing these good offices, and the constant court which he paid to Cæsar and the most influential Romans, he was compelled to transgress Jewish customs, and to infringe much of the law, building cities through ambition, and setting up temples—not in Judæa, for they would not there have been tolerated as they were erected in honour of images after the Greek fashion. But he did this beyond the boundaries, making as his excuse to the Jews that he did it not of his own accord, but according to command for Cæsar and the Romans, really preferring their favour to that of his own people, and all the while promoting his ambition to leave signal evidences of his own greatness.'

Such is the character of this very remarkable personage, who represents the progress of the new Hellenism among a people above all others stern and uncompromising in their Semitic nationalism. But this brings us already under the

[1] Müller, *FHG* iii. 350.   [2] *Antt. Jud.* xv. 9, 5.

shadow of the Roman Empire, and close to the origin of that great religion which made Greek its expression and its vehicle throughout the civilised world. Thus another epoch in our subject opens before us, and we must pause before entering upon this fresh and no less arduous task.

CHAPTER VIII

ASCETIC RELIGION IN THE FIRST CENTURY

IT will be a proper introduction to the great spiritual regeneration which took place in the next century, as well as an antidote to the worldly, immoral, and superficial Hellenism of Herod, if we consider that development of mystic asceticism which invaded the whole Hellenist-Roman world in the first century before Christ, and showed itself prominently not only in numerous writings but in distinct societies, and in the ordinances of a higher spiritual life. I allude chiefly to the Pythagoreans and their rivals the Essenes.

The habit of turning from the worn-out artificialised systems of latter days to the fresher, vaguer, more poetical guesses of older thinkers had long since been adopted by Hellenistic philosophers. The Stoics and Epicureans turned away from Plato and Aristotle, and went back to the enigmas of Heracleitus and the assumptions of Democritus for their physics. They seemed to have no more ability to frame a new system than modern architects have to design a new style. No field seems to remain for the originality of either profession, save to borrow from some model more obsolete than the rest, or to combine the ideas of various older schools in some novel way. In the century we have been studying, the Stoic, Epicurean, and Academic systems had become as threadbare as were the older rational systems of Plato and Aristotle in the third century B.C. Positive scepticism had been administered plentifully as a cure for both dogmatism and doubt, and, as usual, had proved at first attractive, then tedious, at last disgusting, like some new and piquant food, wherewith one might try to supplant that plain vulgar bread of ordinary life, which lasts through fashions and tastes, and remains the support of man in preference to anything seasoned or sweetened by artifice.

Nothing, therefore, remained but to return to some other ancient system, either of religion or of philosophy, which had satisfied the men of other days and other lands, and see whether sustenance could there be found for the spiritual hunger of mankind. Oriental religions, as we know, came much into fashion, and among the Greeks those orgiastic worships were sought out which savoured most of mystery and of inspiration. The worship of the Phrygian Cybele, with her cymbals and her shawms, her orgies and revivals, replaced the sober offering and quiet prayer to Hera or Athene.

Recent researches into the inscriptions at Delos and at Samothrace, the great homes of Hellenic religion in the Ægean, have put this growth of oriental influences beyond all doubt. I will not set down as certain the theory of M. Foucart, that every private religious association among the Greeks, all those ὀργεῶνες and θίασοι of *Dionysiasts*, and other -*asts* which recur so frequently in the inscriptions, were under the protection of a Deity really imported from the East, even though frequently disguised under a Hellenic name.[1] But from the days when Corinth was destroyed and Delos rose to be a great commercial, as well as religious centre, the number of dedications by Eastern princes, such as those of Pontus, Cappadocia, and even the Parthian Arsaces, as well as allusions to strange oriental gods in offerings and vows, increases so rapidly that we feel ourselves hardly in a Hellenic place of worship. The same change is said to be noticeable in the votive offerings and dedications recovered in Samothrace.[2]

It was the same spirit in the more cultivated minds of the day which led them back to the theological, mystical, suprasensible doctrine of Pythagoras, with its vague conceptions of harmony as a law of the universe, its worship of order, its spirituality in conceiving the Godhead, its asceticism as the highest of earthly conditions. The original teaching of the sage of Samos was indeed almost completely lost; there survived but scanty and vague traditions,[3] which served as sparks to rekindle the flame of this higher light. And, perhaps, such faintness of tradition was even favourable to the preachers of the revived truth, for they were enabled not only to supply from Plato and the Stoics many conceptions undeveloped or unrecognised by the real Pythagoras, —they were also able to produce them under the guise of ancient lore, recovered from oblivion in the fragments of Archytas, Ocellus, and other venerable names.

There was a whole library of such literature, beginning with the first century B.C., from which fragments of some ninety authors are still extant. They preach the unity and pure spirituality of the Highest, who contains within Himself

[1] Cf. Foucart, *Associations religieuses chez les Grecs*, p. 109, a book of great learning and judgment.
[2] Cf. S. Reinach in *BCH* vii. 348; and Foucart, *ibid.* p. 467.
[3] ζώπυρα ἄττα πάνυ ἀμυδρὰ καὶ δυσθήρατα, is the expression of Iamblichus usually quoted (cf. Zeller, *Phil. der Griechen*, iii. 2, 112).

the seeds of the universe, of which the world and the stars are the lesser gods, with a life of their own derived from His substance. The laws of numbers are the principles upon which all the order and beauty of existence are based. Whether the absolute spirituality of God could be reconciled with His diffusion through every element of the universe as its living principle did not trouble them. They taught both doctrines, perhaps, in turn, helping man to form some inadequate notion of His perfections. For this was their main object—to supply the wearied age not with a system more logical and consecutive than those that went before, but rather with nobler emotions, with deeper comfort, with higher aspirations. They maintained the eternity of the world, and consequently of the human species, whose souls were but a lower grade of intelligence, above which the demons or genii, inhabiting the air, formed the link uniting them to the astral gods. To these demons was entrusted the detail of the government of our world.

But far more interesting to us than their physics is their practical philosophy. In direct contrast to the elaborate reasoning, the minute controversy, the subtle distinctions of the other schools, these Pythagoreans and their kindred sects believed first of all in purity and soberness of life, as the proper training for that deeper insight which is the appanage of goodness. It was by doing the will of God that they would learn to know His doctrine. And this knowledge was not a logically reasoned-out conclusion, but a moral insight, a higher intuition, which told them not only the right way, but even attained to a prophetic foresight of future events. Exceptional holiness produced exceptional wisdom, and the demons who governed the world were willing to reveal hidden things to such admirable obedience.

From this came the ascetic aspect of life,—attributed freely to the original Pythagoras in the later documents of this age,—the institution of an almost monastic brotherhood, which refused to take oaths, perhaps also to sacrifice animals or eat them, to drink wine, or in other ways to pander to the lusts of the flesh. It is further to be observed that the main preaching of this doctrine is not in the formal tracts which have been preserved (at least in copious extracts), but in the portraits of the ideal men, Pythagoras, and afterwards Apollonius of Tyana. The official descriptions of the Pythagorean theory contain very little that is original, and are only an eclectic combination of well-known Platonic, Aristotelian, and Stoic views. Even among these Aristotle is at least as prominent as Plato.[1]

To set up for imitation the picture of a perfect life seems to have been the real teaching of this school. Not only the clear separation from the ordinary world, but the high principles of serving God with the spirit, and not with sacrifice; of self-examination, and of justice, positive as well as negative, to our neighbour; of silent contemplation of the perfections of God and His world—these were the attributes of the Pythagorean ideal, which was not, like the Stoic Wise Man, an abstraction, but realised in more than one definite historical figure.

In giving this general description of the doctrine which marks the first century B.C., I have as yet said nothing of the particular part of the world in which it arose, and it may be thought doubtful whether it really belongs to the history of Hellenism. There seem at first sight very un-Greek, very oriental, features about it, and two of its centres, so far as we know them, were on the outskirts of the Greek world. Nevertheless, Pythagoras himself, what-

[1] Cf. the discussion in Zeller, iii. 2, 127 sq.

ever his education may have been, was a Hellene of the Hellenes, and taught Greeks in Greek; and he was truly a more tangible model for the new school than any oriental sage known to us. Moreover, all the evidence we have concerning this school is either in Greek or taken from Greek sources; so that there can be no doubt of the Hellenistic complexion of this new face in the world's thinking.

Our evidence points to two actual homes of the neo-Pythagorean faith—Italy and Judæa, and we know from very good internal evidence that the former, if not the latter, must have learned it from Alexandria, which was still the real centre of the world's deeper thinking. For though Cicero, probably with justice, speaks of his friend P. Nigidius Figulus as the reviver of Pythagoreanism in Italy,[1] we can say with certainty that no new school could have originated at Rome without Greek lessons, and the numerous fragments quoted by Stobæus and others from Greek books of this age show plainly enough whence came the new inspiration. We hear also from Philo of a sect settled on Lake Mareotis, called Therapeutæ, who professed in general the principles of cenobitic life, and we know that they had before them earlier Egyptian practices of the same kind. There is extant a petition to Ptolemy Philometor from a man who had voluntarily confined himself for years in the Serapeum at Memphis—men and women seeking to purify themselves by avoiding the temptations of the world.[2]

We do not hear of any such practical working out of this

---

[1] He used to say that all the successful acts of his consulship were done under the emulation and with the advice of this Pythagorean philosopher (Plut. *an seni*, 27 *sub. fin.*, and also Cicero's letter to him, *ad Fam.* iv. 3). Cf. the account in Zeller, *Phil. der Griech.* iii. 2, 93 *sq.*

[2] Cf. the account given in Delaunay's *Moines et Sibylles*, p. 17 *sq.*

new faith at Rome.¹ Probably it was confined to a few
enthusiasts like Nigidius, who took up the prophetic and
wonder-working side of it; or to sceptics like Varro, who only
learned it as a matter of speculative curiosity. But in the
very different climate and spiritual atmosphere of Judæa
there arose a movement, the Essene, so analgous to the
Egyptian that it still remains a matter of controversy whether
it may not be traced directly to the influence of Greek ideas
on Jewish religion. The information we have is almost exclusively from Josephus, who does not give us any account
of the dawn or growth of this school—that of the Essenes
—but speaks of it as in full development at the end of the
second century B.C. He has turned aside from his narrative
twice to describe pretty fully this remarkable heresy among
his people. I call it a heresy, for the Essenes objected on
principle (like the Pythagoreans) to bloody sacrifices, and
were accordingly excluded by the orthodox Jews from the
temple at Jerusalem. But even this stigma does not seem
to have deterred them from forming a schismatic society
on the inner slopes of the mountains near Hebron, where
they dwelt together to the number of 4000.

The fullest account which we possess is in the *History of
the Jewish War*,² and I cannot but feel that Josephus wrote
this account with the view of magnifying the philosophic
genius of his nation. Though he compares the Essene
belief in a happy elysium for the souls of good men to the
Islands of the Blest in Greek mythology, though he says
that these sectaries were most diligent in searching out the
lore of ancient writings, he implies clearly that these were not
ancient Mosaic books, but others which were carefully kept
from the outer public. These books, in fact, and the names

---

¹ The very limited school of the Sextii may be a qualified exception
(cf. Zeller, *Phil. der Griechen*, iii. 1, 677 *sq.*) ² ii. 8.

of the angels, were among their chief mysteries. His account of their practical life of piety, charity, and community of goods is so closely analogous to the life of the first Christian church at Jerusalem, that we can hardly conceive the two systems to be mutually independent. But the Essene reverence for the sun, before whose rising, which they saluted with some kind of adoration, they would undertake no kind of work, and their concealment of their sacred books, point in my mind clearly to a foreign source. So do the abhorrence of oil, which they regarded as polluting, and the aversion to bloody sacrifices. The latter was, no doubt, to be found in the old Pythagoreanism of Greece, but what shall we say to the hatred of oil?

These, and other points which would require too long a discussion, incline me to take the side of those who in this difficult controversy assume that direct influences from the East produced this remarkable Jewish asceticism. We know that the Buddhists in their early inscriptions claim to have preached their gospel to Antiochus, Antigonus, and Ptolemy.[1] It may, therefore, be assumed as certain that Buddhist missionaries had come as early as the third century into Syria. Whether they founded some sort of school in Galilee or the mountains of Judæa, which gave the tone to the after developments of religion in this home of creeds, will, perhaps, for ever remain a matter of surmise; but surely the probabilities are in its favour. Josephus, of course, desires either to magnify the originality of his people, or to show that they had anticipated the philosophical discoveries of the Greeks. We may, therefore, suspect that the neo-Pythagorean features of Essenism are not given in faint colours, but rather brought out more prominently than the facts warranted. Yet even so, there

[1] Cf. above, p. 21.

is much in his account not easy to reconcile with the
Alexandrian origin, which Zeller inclines to adopt, nor do
I think that national Jewish features can account for the
non-Pythagorean side of the system.

It is not within the province of this book to enter into
the oriental side of these sects. What has been said is
sufficient at least to vindicate for Hellenism at this moment
a deep and striking practical development. In the face of
those who repeat the statement that the Greek mind was
always spiritually superficial and thoughtless, we must insist
upon this : that in these latter days it eagerly took up the
solemn ideas developed by the world's experience ; and that
if the Stoics had indeed received some stimulus from the
East, it was no new or peculiar effect, seeing that Pythagoras
either exhibits an original Greek development of what is
considered the Semitic tone, or else illustrates the suitability
of Eastern to Greek thought even in very ancient times.
Need I add the long roll of serious and noble Greeks—Hellenes of the Hellenes—who were pure without the profession of purity, and lofty without the clouds of mystery,
Anaxagoras, Xenocrates, Cleanthes, *primi inter pares?*

The present age, however, made Roman-Greek men
acquainted with sundry ideas which long afterwards came
to dominate the world. First of all, there is the teaching of
morality by holding up the life and acts of an ideal person
as more effective than repeating precepts and expounding
dogmas. Secondly, the notion of separation from the world,
from the society of average human beings, for the purpose of
living a stricter and holier life, and hence the notion of a
spiritual aristocracy, of which the old Pythagorean brotherhood in Magna Græcia seems to have been the earliest model.
Thirdly, we find the belief coming in that logic, discursive
thinking, debate and controversy, which had long been

thought the only path to higher knowledge, were after all but clumsy methods, which killed the inner life of religion by dissecting its organism. Moral purity, ascetic contemplation, direct spiritual intuition, gave the clearest and highest knowledge of the mysteries of God and of the human soul.

It will, perhaps, be urged that these profound novelties must indeed be foreign to Hellenism, as they took no root at Athens or at Rhodes, the real foci of its culture. Such an inference, however, does not seem to me warranted. Old universities with fixed chairs professing traditional knowledge are the very last to adopt new ideas. Every established church regards novelties of doctrine as dissent and schism from the truth. It seems proved by the researches of Matter[1] that even at Alexandria, the hot-bed of new and semi-Hellenistic creeds, the Museum or University was not the field for these speculations; they were probably discountenanced and even opposed by the Fellows and Professors of that ancient and respectable seat of learning. Aristotelian science, aggrandised by many noble developments in astronomy and physics, was still the knowledge expounded by the accredited men of learning, and the last persons likely to join the Therapeutæ would have been the Dons of the Museum. The revelation, as usual, was to babes, not to the wise and prudent. And the revelation was sporadic, accepted indeed with enthusiasm by scattered sections of serious people through the world, but scorned and neglected by the majority, and by those who clung to the teaching of the schools. Such was the condition of the thinking world at the opening of that great period of rest and peace, called the Augustan age, but in the provinces rather the Imperial age, which established good order in the world for 200 years.

[1] *École d'Alexandrie*, vol. iii. p. 272.

CHAPTER IX

WESTERN HELLENISM UNDER THE EARLY ROMAN
EMPERORS—COLONISATION

WE now arrive at a period where materials of a certain kind come freely to hand, but unfortunately not the sort of materials we require. The Augustan age has a great reputation in the world as an age of peace and of culture, but rather of Roman culture than of Greek, and not only of peace, but of political and literary stagnation in the provinces. There were, of course, literary men left, and we have from them some of the longest and most important of our Greek books, but these men are isolated, generally wanderers over the world, making at Rome their principal sojourn, at Alexandria their second—in fact citizens of the world, while they still take care to name and to love their birthplace. Such are Diodorus the Sicilian, and Strabo the Cappadocian, whose encyclopædic works exhibit strongly both the merits and the defects of the prose writing of that age.

Diodorus tells us very little about himself, and his work is so strictly a compilation from older books that there is seldom any personal experience to be found in his remains, such as the anecdote already quoted.[1] Strabo is

[1] Above, p. 164.

more communicative, and tells us of his family, of their intimate relations to the kings of Pontus, of which he is proud, of his own studies and travels, and also of his opinions on various literary questions. From his book we may, therefore, draw a picture of what a learned Greek in those days could attain, and what was the world in which he moved. His life extended to at least twenty years after our era, and from several internal data in his geography, we may take him to have lived at least thirty years on either side of the birth of Christ. Diodorus was about a generation older, but so far as we can infer, lived in a world very similar in social aspects, though disturbed by the last great civil wars of the Republic. To Strabo the great feature of his world is the tranquillity and order imposed by Augustus, and the safety of the ways by sea and land. But with this blessed change the spirit of speculation and adventure had been checked, and with it any exuberance of imagination that may have lingered here and there among the irreconcilables in the Hellenistic world.

But we must not dally with generalities; let us proceed to details.

Before I enter upon this task, I must warn the reader that a great part of Strabo's accounts[1] are confessedly borrowed from much older authors, even so far back as Polybius, and not perhaps in any case more recent than three generations before his own time. Such are Apollodorus of Artemita, on Mesopotamia; Artemidorus, above all Eratosthenes, and Agatharchides on the Red Sea; on India no writer newer than Megasthenes. In other words, the outlying parts of the world as described by Strabo are in the Hellenistic, not in the Roman period. I will go

[1] I quote uniformly from the marginal pages preserved in every good edition of Strabo.

even further and say that almost the whole of his account of Greece proper is taken not from autopsy, but from older authors, and I have come to the conclusion that he never made any travels through Greece, not even to Athens, the capital of Hellenistic sentiment.

This novel conclusion is based upon the following arguments. He gives in general terms[1] the extent of his travels, from the Euxine (Pontus) to the borders of Æthiopia (Syene), and from Armenia to the west coast of Etruria, opposite Corsica. He says this was a wider range than had been traversed by almost any previous writer on geography, which I quite believe, as we know the Greeks to have been very much addicted to copying from older books, and even to passing off this second-hand knowledge as personal experience. But Strabo in this statement takes care not to specify any details, or name the order or amount of his travels within these extreme limits. Whether this vagueness has any dishonest intent I leave the reader to determine. For in contrast to it he does not fail to record carefully his personal observations whenever he had really visited any country. Thus his descriptions of Asia Minor—Comana, Tralles, Nysa etc.—are interspersed with frequent statements of what he personally saw, and for this reason his *Asia Minor* is the most valuable section of all his geography. So also his *Egypt*, as he resided at Alexandria, and as he ascended to Syene in the retinue of his friend Ælius Gallus, is full of personal reminiscences. But on the other parts of the world we find him usually repeating older writers with his φασί, and when we question his text closely we can only be sure that he sailed along the coast of Africa, on his way to Rome; that he knew Rome and some parts of Italy well; and that on the route to Asia he stopped at Corinth and at Gyaros.

[1] P. 117.

I can find no trace of his personal experience anywhere in Greece except at the places just named, and think this silence, in contrast to his constant habit of telling his reminiscences about Asia Minor and Egypt, to be conclusive that he only knew Greece from books. His account of Athens[1] in particular is that of a man encumbered with written descriptions lying before him, and with no personal observations or recollections to help him in his selection. The fact was that in these days Greece proper, with the exception of Nicopolis, Patræ, Corinth, and Athens, was really the least important part of the Hellenistic world, and in miserable decay. But even his many statements of its depopulation seem to me borrowed from older books, which date from the close of the second century B.C.

The result is this : where Strabo states his own observations, we have pictures of the Hellenistic world about the time of Christ; where he does not, we may take for granted that the evidence is of older days, and therefore rather belonging to the times described in earlier chapters, or in my previous volume on *Greek Life and Thought*.[2]

Returning from this digression, we shall take the Roman world in Strabo's order, thus beginning with Spain, of which his account is perhaps the freshest part of the book. For though he had never seen it, he corrects his authorities by constant references to its improved condition in his own day, which he evidently learned at Rome from Romans familiar with the country. Spain can, indeed, hardly be included within the limits of Hellenism in the sense now accepted

[1] P. 396.
[2] I must here call attention to the procedure of Theodor Mommsen, who generally uses the statements in the geographer not only for the Augustan, but even for the later condition of the Roman world? I cannot but think this a doubtful basis for many inferences in the famous fifth volume of his *Roman History*.

among scholars, for whatever still survived of Greek settlements and Greek culture either dated from a time long anterior to Alexander's, or was the creation of Massilia, which must be called a Hellenic rather than a Hellenistic town.

But as I noticed already the old Greek culture of the Sea of Asov, and shall return to it again, so I may say a word about Spain in relation to the settlements of Massilia down the Spanish coast from Ampurias (Emporiæ) to Carthagena, which, though not reaching outside the Straits to the strange mart of Gades, must nevertheless have had much influence even on the exclusive Phœnicians. Strabo speaks of the settlement of Emporiæ as typical of these distant colonies. 'The Greeks of Emporiæ first settled upon an outlying island, still (that is, when Artemidorus or Posidonius wrote) called the old city, but now they dwell on the mainland in a city cut in twain by a wall, having formerly some indigenous people, who, though under a separate polity, were nevertheless desirous to dwell within the same surrounding wall as the Greeks, for safety's sake ; but it was divided across the middle by the other wall already mentioned. In time they coalesced into the one city with mixed customs, Greek and barbarian, a thing which has happened in the case of other such cities.'[1] We are told elsewhere in the book that the remains of an old Phœnician settlement looked quite different, but the details are not specified.

Of the old Phœnician towns which still flourished, by far the most remarkable was Gades, which exhibits what we should call a thoroughly Phœnician character, had we not modern analogies in non-Semitic settlements. Strabo relates with wonder how a little barren island, with no territory (till the Roman conqueror Balbus ceded to it a strip of coast),

[1] P. 160.

not only covered the trading lines of the Mediterranean with ships, but maintained in them a population inferior to no city but Rome.[1] A few of them dwelt at home, many more as commercial agents in Rome, where in a census during Strabo's sojourn 500 of them were assessed at equestrian incomes, a catalogue of wealth to be matched in Patavium only. The population lived upon the sea, and made great fortunes in trade. Can any one fail to see the curious analogy between all this and the condition of Hydra before the peace of 1815, when a similar barren island owned a great and rich population, and only maintained it by keeping it on sea?[2] The Gaditani had profited chiefly by the tin trade with the Cassiterides, or tin islands, which they had kept so completely to themselves that even Strabo's authorities thought them to be situate in the high seas far north of Spain.[3] But even without the Cassiterides Gades had a splendid trade in the salt-fish of the Atlantic, which is so superior to that of the Mediterranean, and still more in commanding the mouth of the Bætis, which ran its upper course through a country rocky and barren,[4] but full of gold, silver, copper, and tin ore. Such mineral wealth was not known in any other part of the ancient world; and no sooner did the river leave this poor soil, with its auriferous and argentiferous rocks, than it entered a vale of such agricultural wealth as was equally without parallel. So careful was the breeding of sheep there, that a talent (£240) was paid for a first-rate ram.

The only plague in that blessed country—for there were hardly any noxious beasts or reptiles—was the predominance of rabbits, which did great harm to agriculture (Strabo thinks

---

[1] P. 168.   [2] Cf. my *Rambles and Studies*, p. 367.
[3] They were probably the small islands in Vigo Bay, not the Scilly Isles (cf. Elton, *Origins of Eng. Hist.* p. 24).
[4] Strabo, p. 142.

by cutting the roots of trees and crops underground), and were at that time infesting all the south-west of Europe as far as Massilia, including the islands, such as Corsica and the Balearic Isles, whose inhabitants, probably those lately imported by the Romans, besought the Senate to grant them another territory free from this plague.[1] The Spaniards had devised various remedies for this serious evil, among others the domestication of the 'African weasel,' 'which they muzzle and send into the holes, when it either pulls out the rabbit with its nails (?) or makes it bolt for the men and dogs standing ready.'[2]

The natural produce of Spain in minerals, cattle, wool, salt-fish, etc., was so enormous that Rome was supplied by this and the province of Africa in about equal shares, to judge from the relative importance of the merchant shipping of Ostia the Spanish, and Puteoli the African, marts. And this fact, though not within Hellenistic limits, must have had a considerable effect in depressing the condition of the Hellenic peninsula. What use was there in mining deep and laboriously at Laurium for a small and uncertain profit, when one Spanish mine (Carthagena) out of many could employ 40,000 hands, and could yield £1000 of our money daily?

It required 200 years of fighting and negotiating and colonising for the Romans to civilise Spain, and that not completely, for in Strabo's day (if we may trust his information as here fresh Roman and not obsolete Greek) there were still savage Cantabri, who dwelt not in cities (πόλεις),

[1] P. 144.
[2] The fact that this widely extended plague has completely disappeared from Spain, France, and the islands, suggests that in Australia too the day will come when natural causes will accomplish what seems too vast for human ingenuity. I am not aware that we hear of these rabbits in later classical authorities, so I suppose they must have been disappearing even in Strabo's time.

like civilised men, but in villages (κωμηδόν), or even in forests, and only submitted slowly and unwillingly to the Roman peace. These were the people who, when staying as allies in a Roman camp, saw the Roman officers walking up and down the main avenues for exercise, and laid hold of them to bring them to their tents, thinking they must be mad,[1] for no savage understands exercise as such without some motive, such as hunting or fighting. The language of Horace[2] proves, I think, that what Strabo says is here true of his own time. Here then the greatest contrast between barbarism and civilisation was to be found.

The region, again, on both sides of the Bætis up to Corduba, the highest navigable point of the river, above which the rugged mining country began, was full of rich homesteads, orchards, and pastures dotted with sheep and cattle. Corduba was full of Roman citizens, as well as of naturalised natives, so that Strabo concludes his account of this province[3] by saying: 'With the wealth of the country the Turdetani have naturally become tame and civilised;[4] this habit prevails also among the (Spanish) Celts, either because of their proximity, or, as Polybius says, their kinship with the others; but in a less degree, for they mostly live in villages (κωμηδόν). But the Turdetani, especially on the Bætis, are completely Romanised, and have even forgotten their old language. Most of them have become (politically) Latins, and have received Roman colonists, so that they are nearly all to be counted as Romans. The cities now established, Paxanguita (Badajos) among the Celts, Augusta Emerita (Merida) among the Turduli, Cæsar Augusta (Saragossa), and some other colonies, mark this change in the above-named people. And as many of the Spaniards as

[1] Strabo, iii. 4, 16.   [2] *Odes*, ii. 6. 1.
[3] P. 151.   [4] ἥμερον καὶ πολιτικόν.

have adopted this course are called *togati*, and among these are the Celtiberians, once thought the most savage.'

I have entered on these details about Spain, not for their intrinsic interest, great as it is, but in order to bring before the reader a large example of the Roman treatment of a conquered race, in order that I may compare it with the Hellenistic solution of the same problem. Nor can we avoid saying a word in this connection concerning the older Hellenic colonisation which preceded both. Though the subject has often been handled, and with great ability, I think I can put the facts from a fresh point of view, for most historians have only thought of contrasting the Hellenic, and not the Hellenistic, practice with that of the Romans. And yet the two former were widely different. Alexander inaugurated a policy new and unprecedented in Europe.

There can be no doubt that the Phœnicians were the teachers of the old Greeks, and that apart from the very early national migration to Asia Minor, which may perhaps be paralleled by the foundation of Carthage, most Greek colonies were trading marts, just like the Phœnician, worked upon the same principles, and producing about the same effect on the surrounding barbarians. It is commonly said that the old Greeks were more insinuating and had more talent for assimilating foreigners than the Semite traders, and this is one of those general statements for which a good deal of evidence may be adduced. But unfortunately the Phœnician side is not represented in the remains of our classical literature, and if we take the case best known to us, that of Sicily, which was occupied by both races, we shall hesitate to say that the inhabiting Greeks with all their assimilating genius laid a greater hold upon the island than the mere trading Carthaginians. So also when Hamilcar saw that to contend with success against the Romans he must procure a more numerous and a better infantry than that of Libyans and Hellenistic mercenaries, the facility with which his Carthaginians made an empire in Spain shows an ability for conciliating barbarians as remarkable as any similar case in the history of the Greeks.

There were, indeed, many deep contrasts between these colonising races, but they are not so obvious as the resemblances. Both nations brought their gods with them, and paid little honour to the local deities; neither seems to have been proficient in learning the native language of its new abodes. Both almost invariably settled on a seaboard, and trusted to the 'wet ways' to keep up their communications with one another and with the mother country. If the Greeks succeeded ultimately in ousting their rivals from most of the Mediterranean trade, it was not, I think, on account of their superior genius but on account of their superior numbers; they drew from a home population—counting all the cities and coasts and islands round the Levant—many hundred times greater than the population of Phœnicia.

As regards seamanship it is probable that the Phœnicians were always superior; Xenophon certainly alludes to a big Phœnician ship in the harbour of Corinth as a special sight to see, on account of its decided superiority in order, neatness, and marine resources.[1] But in this feature both kinds of colonies were alike, that though possessing, by means of ships, an easy communication with their mother-lands, they were expected to take care of themselves, and except in the rarest cases received from the old home no material support in their difficulties. In fact their relations with that home were oftener strained by commercial jealousies than strengthened by mutual sympathy in misfortunes.

[1] Cf. my *Social Life in Greece*, p. 419.

As regards their nearer relations with the surrounding natives it is, I think, generally assumed that the Phœnicians did not fuse by marriage with their neighbours, and that the Greeks did. The traces of old Phœnician settlements at Athens, Thebes, and Corinth, which, as the local religions of these cities show, did not always terminate with the expulsion of the Semites as enemies, appear to contradict this assumption, at least as regards very old times. It is not unlikely that the known exclusiveness of the Jews in the *diaspora*[1] has inclined historians to ascribe a similar spirit to the Phœnicians, though these latter had no capital like Jerusalem, with its unique worship of Jehovah, for their ideal rallying-point. If Strabo had told us what the difference was in the aspect of Phœnician and Greek coast settlements,[2] we might know more of their respective treatment of the natives. The case of Emporiæ, which he there describes, shows how slow and tentative was the native amalgamation with the Greeks; and the general inability of the Italiot cities, rich and old as they were, to effect any peaceable settlement with the Apulians and Samnites, speaks little for Greek colonising ability.

With Alexander the Great begins a very different system, carried out on Asiatic principles, which is very unfortunately called by the same name. Macedonia was in its essential features an inland and not a naval power, and the conqueror sought to annex provinces, not to found mere trading marts. He desired to embrace in one empire widely-scattered and various domains, and he sought to establish his power by founding many local centres of Græco-Macedonian influence along the old high roads, and on the exposed frontiers of his conquests. We must remember that he had his great thoroughfares prepared for him by the Persian monarchs.

[1] Cf. *Greek Life and Thought*, p. 469.
[2] Cf. above, p. 193, and Strabo, iii. 4, 2.

High roads and posts were an old institution through Asia, so far as he penetrated. So were military colonies in remote provinces to hold the natives in check.[1] His primary object was to secure these roads both for commerce and for administration, to protect exposed frontiers, and to impose upon his new subjects visible signs of the power and unity of the Macedonian Empire. He also desired to endow his veterans with lands, and create garrisons with a vital interest in defending their fortresses.

His foundation of Alexandria is, to my mind, quite a different thing. It was from the first intended as a capital or centre for his empire, and though it is possible that Babylon would have supplanted it, when he found himself master of all the far East, yet from first to last Alexandria was far more than a colony in any sense of the word. But the many towns of the same name founded in Upper Asia, of which Candahar[2] and Secunderabad still remain, were distinctly military colonies of the Asiatic type, in which his veterans and other Macedonian or Greek immigrants received grants of land or full civic rights, while the surrounding population remained in an inferior condition. But if these settlements were threatened from without they had, theoretically at least, the whole power of the Empire at their back, and were not thrown loose from, far less permitted to act in opposition to, the mother country, in any such sense as the old Greek or Phœnician colonies so often were.

If the Romans wanted a model for their 'occupying' colonies, it was surely there that they found it. They did

---

[1] Cf. Strabo (xiii. 4, 13), who thus explains the geographical names *Hyrcanian Plain* and *Cyrus' Plain*, close to Mount Tmolus in Asia Minor.

[2] From Iskandar, the Eastern form of Alexander, which Semitic people understood as if *al* was an article, hence the apparently divergent from. Mr. Sayce tells me the old Assyrian colonies were the model copied by all the later conquerors of Asia.

not, indeed, find roads ready as Alexander did; they had to make them for themselves; but their insistence upon this very task looks very like a servile copying of his policy. Thus they fought for eighty years to secure a high road along the Riviera to the mouth of the Rhone, whereas they had all the time ample naval power to keep up their communications by sea. They settled their outposts in some fruitful valley, like that of Corduba or Lugdunum, and so made centres for Roman settlers to promote both agriculture and commerce. The gradations by which the Romans proposed to bring the natives gradually into the Imperial system were more definite than those usual in the Hellenistic kingdoms; but the fact that we still dispute whether the Jews of Antioch and Alexandria had equal civic rights with the Greeks shows that such admissions were perfectly recognised at that time. There can be no doubt that by intermarriages and by performing public benefits the native men of importance obtained promotion to full Hellenistic rights.

But the complication which affected all the colonies of Alexander in Asia, so far as it was civilised, was the occurrence of free Greek cities in Asia Minor, whose privileges he respected, and whose communal independence he secured to them as soon as he had broken their very light Persian yoke. This condition of being a free city, managing its own affairs, and not tolerating a Macedonian governor, was the favoured stage to which all the new Græco-Macedonian colonies constantly aspired. As soon as the central power grew weak this right was demanded with no uncertain sound, and this was the so-called 'liberty of the Greeks' which makes such a figure in the politics of the great wars after Alexander.[1] The power of Macedon was too well consolidated to tolerate such cities within its proper limits; the

---

[1] Cf. my *Greek Life and Thought*, p. 79.

Ptolemies, who had Egypt thoroughly organised as a royal property, only founded Ptolemais in the Thebaid and Arsinoe in the Fayoum, which had special privileges, but in no sense autonomy.[1] It was in Syria and Palestine that the numerous Hellenistic foundations, originally controlled by Seleucid governors, asserted and received this modified independence, which they marked by distinct coinage and by commencing the era of their history from the date of their charters. Similar special privileges were continued to towns in inner Asia by the Arsacids, who, for example, gave Seleucia on the Tigris various immunities in return for its allegiance. These so-called free Greek cities were a great source of weakness to the Seleucid Empire, as may be amply verified by reading the Histories of Polybius or of Josephus.

It is remarkable that in this detail also Roman provincial administration copied its Hellenistic forerunners. There were free cities in nominal alliance with Rome wherever there were important outlying Hellenic foundations, such as Massilia, several towns in Sicily, many in Asia Minor, etc. But I need hardly add that these cities never had the same power for mischief that we find them exercising in the Seleucid Empire. Massilia indeed had for a moment distinct importance in the opposition to Cæsar,—Alexandria was then still outside the Roman dominions,—but otherwise they were quite insignificant as opponents of the Empire. Nor were

---

[1] Perhaps there were more, but their number was certainly small. We know from inscriptions the title *Hellenomemphites*; on Thebes (cf. above, p. 168). We have from Pa-khem in the Thebaid (the Greek Panopolis), a piece of leather with this inscription: ἱερὸς εἰσελευστικὸς οἰκουμενικὸς ὀλυμπικὸς ἀγῶν Πέρσεως οὐρανίου τῶν μεγάλων Πανείων, showing a Greek festival there in Roman days, and this too not a merely local festival. Maspero thinks (*Rev. des études grecques*, ii. 164) that this Perseus was probably the Egyptian deity worshipped in the place as *Pahrison*.

they the really important civilisers under Rome. The *urbes togatæ*, if I may so call them—Carthage, Narbo, Cæsar-Augusta, and the rest—were now the real leaven which brought new and as yet uncivilised races under the fascination of letters and of art. But apart from this difference, not of principle but of circumstances, all the main features of Roman colonisation had been long recognised in the Hellenistic world.

There was even one curious application of it frequent under the Seleucids and Ptolemies, of which the Romans had no need—I mean the founding of a city as an acknowledged royal foundation in territory beyond the sovran's control and the bounds of his dominion. That the Ptolemies should do this in the Troglodyte country only means that they established trading marts among the outlying savages; but what shall we say to such towns as Lysimachia and Arsinoe, founded by kings Lysimachus and Ptolemy II respectively in Ætolia, the refounding of Patara in Lycia as Arsinoe by the latter, and of Attalia in Pamphylia by Attalus Philadelphus? That these settlements were intended to extend the influence of their founders is certain, but in what manner? I will here advance a conjecture as to the Ætolian and Lycian foundations at all events. Both these territories were at the time under the political condition of free leagues, in which each city had a vote. Probably it was not considered constitutional among the free cities, or dignified for a Ptolemy or a Lysimachus, that a great king should be a formal member of such a league as the Ætolian, and yet in matters of restitution, especially of piratical spoils, such membership was very valuable.[1] Hence by the means of a special foundation these kings may have acquired a vote and voice in the league, and secured themselves against its

[1] Cf. my *Greek Life and Thought*, p. 366.

hostility. The other instance is equally in the country of a league—the Lycian—which may have extended into Pamphylia. By this device then Hellenistic kings could acquire diplomatic rights as well as personal popularity beyond the bounds of their dominions. Whether there were such cases elsewhere I do not know.

The more we recede from the West the more we come within the reach of mixed influences, old Hellenic and recent Roman, upon the inferior races. I say inferior, in the sense of development, for the inhabitants of Northern Europe have since shown that they waxed slower indeed, but not to a less perfection. The great bodies of the British youths whom Strabo saw in Rome were ungainly in his eyes; so was their mental condition; but in the words of Tacitus, *sera atque ideo inexhausta juventas*. The account given of Massilia, no longer indeed a colony, but really a metropolis with her own settlements along the Ligurian and Spanish coasts, is among the most interesting passages in Strabo.[1] When her naval power and real independence were gone she became by her ancient and pure Hellenic culture a favoured seat of higher Roman education.[2]

[1] Pp. 179-181.

[2] Since, he says, the surrounding barbarians have been tamed, and have turned to city life and husbandry owing to the Roman sway, the Massiliots no longer require to attend to their military and naval power. This their present condition proves: πάντες γὰρ οἱ χαρίεντες πρὸς τὸ λέγειν τρέπονται καὶ φιλοσοφεῖν, ὥσθ' ἡ πόλις μικρὸν μὲν πρότερον τοῖς βαρβάροις ἀνεῖτο παιδευτήριον, καὶ φιλέλληνας κατεσκεύαζε τοὺς Γαλάτας, ὥστε καὶ τὰ συμβόλαια Ἑλληνιστί γράφειν· ἐν δὲ τῷ παρόντι καὶ τοὺς γνωριμωτάτους Ῥωμαίων πέπεικεν, ἀντὶ τῆς εἰς Ἀθήνας ἀποδημίας ἰέναι ἐκεῖσε, φιλομαθεῖς ὄντας. In imitation of this the Gauls have taken to these studies not only individually, but as public affairs, for they hire 'sophists' not only privately but even as public officers, in the same way that cities hire doctors.

It is a great pity these interesting texts are so seldom read by scholars.

I think it very remarkable that this Hellenic influence was comparatively powerless till protected by Roman energy and arms. It was the foundation of Aquæ Sextiæ as a military post among the tribes threatening that coast which first freed Massilia from constant apprehensions of Gallic tumults. So also it was the eighty years' determined conflict which the Romans waged with the Ligurians, to assert and maintain the security of the Riviera coast, which relieved Massilia from the cost of protecting all her traders against the pirates of that dangerous route.

But let it be remembered, that this was one of the most perfect specimens of Hellenic, as distinguished from Hellenistic colonisation. If the truth be told, the effects it produced in six centuries, despite its excellent internal government, its thrift, its energy, were singularly small. The Massiliots could tell Scipio Æmilianus nothing about Britain, nor could they tell Strabo.[1] Even their traders therefore stuck to the Mediterranean, and seldom ventured round Spain or across the plains of Gaul to the Atlantic. What was true of Massilia must have been true in even a higher degree of the inferior trading settlements of the Hellenes. It was not till the Romans became the pupils of the Massiliots that Hellenic fashions really 'took' among the inhabitants of Gaul, but it was not merely that they copied the fashion of their new masters; their old occupations were gone, and were thus replaced.

I will cite a modern though remote parallel. No doubt the culture of the Persians has been of late so superior to that of the Turkomans of the Steppes that these barbarians adopted from them many improvements; but it is only since the strong domination of the Russians has compelled them to lay aside their ancestral habit of raiding and man-stealing

[1] P. 190.

that they are adopting the agricultural habits of their weaker southern neighbours. Whatever other ambitions Russia may foster within her secret counsels, this has been her great and very important mission in Upper Asia.

But I must leave these western lands, which are not within the scope of this inquiry. Still the separating lines which distinguish Hellendom from Hellenism are now again becoming effaced, so that the consideration of any Greek communities under the Empire can hardly be foreign to our studies.

CHAPTER X

THE REMAINING HELLENISM OF ITALY (CHIEFLY MAGNA GRÆCIA)

LET us now pass to Italy and Sicily, on which our geographer deserves a close examination. And here if anywhere we should have expected personal notes of value, seeing that he certainly lived long at Rome, and must have been in the middle of good society in that great capital. Yet apart from the general description of the splendours of the city, and its contrast to Greek towns both in the inferiority of the site, and its superiority in the building of roadways, drains, and in its splendid water supply, he really tells us nothing beyond these two facts—that he saw a Sicilian bandit torn to pieces by beasts at a gladiatorial show, the criminal being dropped into a cage full of them, and that he heard the grammarian Tyrannio. Strabo belonged to that important class of literary men who now made Rome their permanent home or their frequent residence, and to whom is mainly due the earnest attempt to revive old style and strict taste in Greek letters. I am afraid we cannot include in this worthy class the many epigrammatists whom we shall consider presently. But as regards prose we have not only such solid works as those of Strabo and Nicolaus in actual history and geography—we have a considerable literature in grammar and rhetoric, and more especially essays on æsthetic taste, such as those of the so-called Longinus, and also of Dionysius of Halicarnassus, who certainly did more than any man ever did to disseminate sound views upon the real excellences of the old Greek masters.

To him the advent of Cæsar is an age of gold, not only for the political world but for the literature of Greece. During his twenty-two years' residence he had lived to see the change coming, and heralds it in a remarkable passage,[1] where he says Rome is the active cause, in that her greatness forces every city to look to her; and her rulers, being educated and just men, have promoted the sound elements in her population and compelled folly and ignorance to hold their peace. Hence have already arisen many refined works on history and philosophy, and no doubt many more are yet to come.

Apart from Rome there were three different loci of old Greek influence still recognised in Italy—the tract round Ravenna, the southern Campanian coast, and the remains of the old Magna Græcia from Tarentum to Croton. Ravenna, which Strabo describes (from his authorities) much as we should describe Venice now—a city with more canals than streets, was once inferior to the neighbouring Spina, which enjoyed, as did the Etrurian Cære, the dignity of possessing a special treasure-house at Delphi. But all the country round had now gone into pasture land, and Cisalpine Gaul, as it was called, that is to say, Italy north of the Apennines and reaching down on the east coast to Ravenna, was now supplying Rome with beef and pork. The Greek settlements made from Sicily in the days of the tyrant Dionysius were least of all affected by the Hellenistic wave. Their trade was

[1] *De oratt. antiqq.* 2.

probably ruined by the Illyrian pirates of the opposite coast long before the Romans subdued that country, so that their greatness and influence was but a waning tradition saved from oblivion by Strabo.

As his information about Spina was from books, so he draws his account of Magna Græcia, of Sicily, and of the Liparæan islands from Antiochus, from Polybius, in fact from very old literary sources, nor can I find that he anywhere does more than verify their statements by the accounts of occasional eye-witnesses. We may likewise feel sure that when he describes the decay and desolation of Lucania and Calabria, which had gone back into wild pasture land, studded with occasional villages, he represents what was told him by some of his Roman friends who had traversed the country. The Roman rule over these once rich and thriving coasts seems to have been little better than king Bomba's management.[1] Still we should have been thankful for some personal notes, instead of being put off with long antiquarian disquisitions about the mythical founders of the Hellenic colonies in the West. Tarentum was still alive, and Brundusium, on account of its importance as a starting-point for the East, which has recently again revived; and Tarentum—as we may infer from its later history, its colossi,[2] its condottieri—did partake of Hellenistic ideas, and was, therefore, with Syracuse, perhaps the main representative of this modern kind of Greek life in the 'Two Sicilies.' But all the coast and its inner country were gone in importance, decayed in population, the cities

[1] Thus Strabo, speaking of the whole country once called Magna Græcia, says (p. 252): νυνὶ δὲ πλὴν Τάραντος καὶ 'Ρηγίου καὶ Νεαπόλεως ἐκβεβαρβαρῶσθαι συμβέβηκεν ἅπαντα, καὶ τὰ μὲν Λευκάνους καὶ Βρεττίους κατέχειν, τὰ δὲ Καμπάνους, καὶ τούτοις λόγῳ, τὸ δ'ἀληθὲς 'Ρωμαίοις· καὶ γὰρ αὐτοὶ 'Ρωμαῖοι γεγόνασιν.

[2] Cf. Strabo, vi. 3, 2, on a colossus transferred to Rome.

reduced to villages, the villages to single farmsteads, nor was there any part of the Roman Empire which showed more melancholy decay from its ancient splendour.

The one spot in Italy which still represented Greek manners and Greek feeling was the northern arm of the Bay of Naples. There had been a very ancient Greek city—Cumæ —settled near it in almost pre-historic times.[1] This city was to the north of the promontory which runs out towards Procida, and lay in an exceedingly volcanic country—evidently the centre of disturbance previous to the historic outbreak of Vesuvius. These Greeks had afterwards founded both Dicæarchia and Neapolis in the shelter of the bay. Of these Naples had in earlier times been obliged to admit Samnites (or Campanians, as Strabo calls them) to its privileges, and was so far not a purely Greek town, but had in consequence obtained immunity from the attacks which ruined Elea, Posidonia, and the other coast cities. But in the days which are now under our consideration a curious change had taken place. Naples had remained stationary, had in fact become quiet and old fashioned, and was now thought essentially Greek. Strabo agrees precisely with Cicero[2] when he says that elderly or delicate Romans liked living there in retirement, and adopting Greek dress and manners.[3] I have already quoted, in connection with the orator, the geographer's account of the Hellenic dress and customs maintained there, as well as of the feasts, both old and new, which attracted companies of Dionysiac players from Greece

---

[1] Probably in the eighth century B.C. Not of course at the ridiculous date 1050 B.C., which was set down by Ephorus (of Kyme) to glorify his native city and her colonies. Nothing has misled simple modern scholars, both German and English, more than this very common kind of mendacity, which Greek historians considered a sort of duty, or at least a very laudable patriotism.

[2] Above, p. 115; cf. also *pro Balbo*, § 55.   [3] P. 246.

and Asia Minor.[1] Strabo goes on to describe the tunnel on the road leading to Puteoli. Naples had also hot springs and arrangements for baths.

The two towns lying seaward, Puteoli and Baiæ, though still within the sheltering arm of the headland, had absorbed the business and the fashion of that part of the world. The whole coast of Campania was indeed covered with sumptuous Roman villas—palaces ($βασίλεια$) Strabo repeatedly calls them, and Persian palaces—as well as with pleasure grounds, but as a fashionable public watering-place Baiæ exceeded all the rest. This resort was, however, more distinctly Roman; the great Hellenistic port for all the eastern trade of Rome was the neighbouring Dicæarchia, renamed Puteoli (Pozzuoli). This place had long since been established as the open port for Alexandrian ships, at a time when the Romans would have been very jealous of allowing foreigners to enter the Tiber at Ostia; and so it always remained the mart of Rome with the East. If you did not land at Brundusium and come through Tarentum and Apulia, you came to Puteoli. For heavy merchandise the long and mountainous land journey was expensive and unsuitable; we may even assume that at Puteoli the more cumbrous articles were reshipped into coasting vessels and brought to the Tiber. But from Puteoli there were at least no mountains to be crossed on the way to Rome. As the railway now winds through the spurs of the Abruzzi which approach the coast about Ceprano and Gaeta, so the old high road could avoid all difficult passes; and these were days when any land journey might be safer than the perils of the sea from pirates.

Such were the reasons which made Puteoli the channel

[1] We shall hear of these players again in discussing the Hellenism of Brutus.

of that Hellenistic influence which is so manifest in the remains of Herculaneum and Pompeii. We have in these curious and affecting relics of the great catastrophe of 79 A.D., both upon the spot and in the great Museum of Naples, the clearest possible evidence of that fusion of Hellenistic taste with Roman life which was the type of the civilisation of Strabo's age. In this part, therefore, of his survey we can supplement the geographer's account by the numerous Greek inscriptions now collected in the *Corpus*, as well as by the splendid collection of art and household objects in the Museum of Naples, not to speak of the unique impression produced by walking about the deserted streets of the once gay and lively Pompeii.

As regards Naples, the evidence of the inscriptions shows clearly that it was, as Strabo and Cicero tell us, far the most distinctly Greek town remaining on the Campanian coast. For Cumæ, a purely Greek foundation, had so decayed that the body of its population had migrated to Neapolis.[1] The remainder even begged the Roman Senate (180 B.C.) to allow them *publice Latine loqui*, and so to assimilate themselves to the Roman municipia.[2] The Neapolitans, on the other hand, profited so much from their reputation among Roman fashionables as a Greek centre, especially from their right of harbouring Roman exiles of distinction,[3] that they hesitated to accept higher political privileges from Rome, and at last did so only under the condition that they were *not* to use Latin in their public acts.[4] Thus we have Roman names with Greek official titles commemorated in Greek

[1] Which, in this case, Mommsen rightly conjectures (*CIL* x. 170), implies no Palæopolis except Cumæ, there being no evidence either from inscriptions or coins of any other forerunner to Neapolis.
[2] Livy, xl. 42.—*Cumanis petentibus permissum, ut publice Latine loquerentur et præconibus Latine vendendi jus esset.*
[3] Polyb. vi. 14, 8. [4] Cf. Mommsen's account of this, *CIL* x. 172.

inscriptions. We know that the Dionysiac artists made it their favourite resort; we find a regular Greek four-years' feast with artistic and athletic contests established there under the title Ἰταλικὰ Ῥωμαῖα Σεβαστὰ Ἰσολύμπια,[1] which served as an epoch from the year 2 A.D.; and numerous bilingual inscriptions—nay, even some in a jumble of Greek and Latin[2]—attest the general knowledge and use of Greek at Naples down to the fourth century A.D.

There are many obvious reasons why the greater and more stirring port of Puteoli should not show in its inscriptions so thoroughly Greek a flavour. The trade relations with Rome, and perhaps the rivalries of many nationalities represented by guilds of trading agents, would make a closer approach to Roman municipal arrangements more convenient. It was the business place, not the fashionable resort, like Baiæ, or the refined literary retreat like Naples. And so the inscriptions show us a far more systematic use of Latin, though the absorption of all that has been found in these regions into the Museum of Naples makes it hard to pass a positive judgment in such matters. Until the locus of each inscription is carefully recorded there will

---

[1] *CIG* 5805. At these games Alexandrians frequently appear. In 5804—ἡ φιλοσέβαστος καὶ φιλορώμαιος Ἀλεξανδρέων περιπολιστικὰ εὐσεβὴς σύνοδος honour an Alexandrian Zosimus for his victories.

[2] Here is one from Sorrento (*CIG* 5870) in Greek characters, as follows:—   Δ. Ε. Μ.
ΑΥΡΗΛΙΟΥΣ ΙΝΠΕΤΡΑΤΟΥΣ Β. Κ. Μ.
ΒΕΙΞΙΤ ΑΝΟ [Σ]* ΙΙ ΜΗΖΕΣ Σ ΔΕΙ Ν ΚΟΖΟΥ ΣΙΜΒΕΙΑ
ΕΙΡΗΝΑ ΜΑΡΙΤΟ ΒΕΝΕ ΜΕΡΕΝΤΙ. ΙΝ. [ΦΗ] ΚΕΤ
As a specimen of a bilingual inscription I give No. 5876:—
ΔΕΣΠΟΙΝΗ ΝΕΜΕΣΕΙ ΚΑΙ ΣΥΝΝΑΟΙΣΙ ΘΕΟΙΣΙΝ
ΑΡΡΙΑΝΟC ΒΩΜΟΝ ΤΟΝΔΕ ΚΑΘΕΙΔΡΥΣΑΤΟ
  Justitiæ nemesi Aris quam voverat aram
  Numina sancta colens Cammarius posuit.
This is a very free translation, cf. further Nos. 5820, 5821.

always remain great difficulty in deciding such questions. Perhaps the most interesting of all those collected in Boeckh's *Corpus* is that recording the complaint of the Tyrian Company at Puteoli, who sent a formal statement to their mother city that the whole expense of keeping up the Tyrian cults at Puteoli devolved upon them, while the Tyrians settled at Rome, who made far greater profits on the goods imported through Puteoli, did not contribute to this burden. The reply from Tyre follows, ordaining that the Tyrians at Rome should bear their share in this duty.[1] The fact that these old and famous Semite traders recorded their corporate but purely national affairs in Greek gives us evidence perhaps more striking than any usually cited to prove the adoption of the Hellenistic idiom as the language of the civilised world.

When we come to Pompeii the case is again different. In the first place Pompeii was not a Greek but an Oscan foundation, though even here we find the principal temple to be a very old construction, in the Doric style of its great extant neighbour at Pæstum, and possibly dating from the sixth century B.C.[2] Then came a period of Sabellian influence, concluded by Sylla's sending a colony of veterans to settle there, to whom the older inhabitants were obliged to cede one-third of their lands. Here, then, we have a town neither in origin nor in circumstances very liable to Hellenistic influences, if we except the fact that it was the near neighbour of Hellenic and Hellenistic populations.

Accordingly we find from the numerous inscriptions

[1] *CIG* 5853, the most interesting of all the Puteolan inscriptions; but as it dates from the reign of the Emperor Marc. Aurelius (174 A.D) I forbear to quote it.

[2] It is now so completely ruined that I cannot think this inference from its remnants quite conclusive, and suspect it may possibly have been a later copy of these great models. But the art critics, such as Overbeck, who have examined it, seem to feel no doubts on the point.

yielded by its walls and monuments that Greek was not the usual or even frequent language of its people, though this language was taught in its schools, for the children have left us numerous specimens of the Greek alphabet scratched upon the walls on their way through the streets. And yet when we turn from the inscriptions to the actual houses and their contents, there is hardly any corner of the life and ways of the inhabitants which does not show clear traces of Hellenistic influence—Hellenistic, I say, and not Hellenic; for with the exception of a very few bronzes which may possibly go back to originals as early as Praxiteles—I mean the famous dancing Faun and the Narcissus—all the statues, paintings, mosaics, vases, bronze and silver ornaments, as well as the designs of the houses and public buildings, are distinctly modelled on Alexandrian ideas.[1]

A great part of the unearthed town can be referred to the work of a very few years, 63-79 A.D.; for in the former of these Vesuvius gave the first premonitory sign of the horrors that were to come by an earthquake with subterranean noises, which destroyed most of the town. So grave was the case that the Roman government even debated whether the site should not at once be abandoned, and many citizens are said to have left the place. Nevertheless the rebuilding was actively resumed, just as the people of Casamicciola are now rebuilding their town over another quasi-extinct volcano at Ischia, which may presently cause a similar tragedy. But it would be a great mistake to compare a second-rate town in the first century with a second-rate town in modern Italy. Though Pompeii was no doubt vastly inferior to Naples and Puteoli, the elegance and wealth of some of the houses show that people of large means and high culture resided there. The interior of

[1] Cf. Th. Schreiber in *Mitth. des deutsch. Inst.* (*MDI*), x. 399.

several of these mansions would satisfy the most fastidious modern magnate in everything but the size of the rooms. All this elegance was in design and probably in execution Greek work. The researches of Helbig have established what he calls an osco-Roman character in some of the rudest and worst of the paintings, but all the subjects of the better class are from Greek mythology, unless it be that Alexandrian habits have suggested a few Egyptian subjects,[1] which seem to hold the place in this epoch that Chinese designs have assumed in western decoration.

On the other hand, the decoration of this generation was not genuine Greek work, but surface imitation. The whole new town was a town of stucco. Overbeck has well explained[2] that though the use of stucco to cover rough stone surfaces for the purpose of painting them is quite legitimate and commonly found in the best Greek architecture, the enlargement of this use into the imitation of stone forms, such as architraves, mouldings, etc., thus adding sham members to the real structure, is a proof of decaying taste. This no doubt is true, though both the Saracens in their mosques and the Renaissance decorators in their ceilings have produced wonderful effects with stucco additions to the real structure. But what shall we say to the occurrence in Pompeii of a colonnade turned from the Doric into the Corinthian order by the addition of stucco capitals laid

---

[1] The temple of Isis, of which considerable portions still remain, and which was decorated throughout with Egyptian figures or in Egyptian style, must have given a model for this sort of ornament. Even a hieroglyphic tablet was set up in it, which had no reference to the temple. Cf. the full description of this building in Overbeck's *Pompeii*, p. 102 *sq*. We know from *CIG* 5793 that the statues even of Greek gods, such as Apollo, were dedicated in temples of Isis. He appears in a triad with Horus and Harpocrates.

[2] *Pompeii*, pp. 439, 467, 469.

round the original echinus? In the same style is the constant effort to imitate variegated marbles by painting, and other devices intended to suggest materials more precious than those actually employed.[1]

The recent researches of the French school at Delos have also led to the discovery of private houses, one of them not ruined beyond recognition. A comparison with the house-building of Pompeii is obviously suggested, as the houses at Delos were evidently ruined in the first century (either by Mithradates or the pirates), and because Delos then contained, like Pompeii, a Græco-Roman population. In an article[2] by M. Paris there is a plan of such a house, with many interesting details. The outcome is this: that while there was much less decoration by painting, and while the Delian householder was content with plain panels upon his wall with no ornament, the materials of his pillars and the general construction were far superior to the very shoddy building of Pompeii.

We have before us, therefore, in Pompeii a civilisation recognising a certain kind of culture, both external and internal, as so tyrannically the fashion, that those who cannot afford to live up to it in reality will rather content themselves with cheap imitations than adopt any other simpler and truer life. With these defects and drawbacks we have, nevertheless, before us in this buried town the picture of a graceful and cheery life, with much that was really beautiful and refined, and with less of grossness or immorality than would be hereafter found in most of our modern towns were they now suddenly sealed up for the inspection of future generations.

Herculaneum was covered with lava (not with ashes),

---

[1] *Pompeii*, p. 464. This too was a very old Egyptian device, as Mr. Sayce informs me.   [2] *BCH* viii. 473.

and therefore its excavation has been more troublesome and far less complete. But the library found in one of the mansions, doubtless that of a Roman noble, is curiously significant in its defects. In the first place, among the 250 rolls unravelled and deciphered there is an exceedingly small proportion of Latin. In the next place, all the Greek rolls as yet published are Epicurean tracts, and of these almost all are either documents of the master, or treatises by Philodemus, a very tenth-rate pupil whom we have already met in the course of this book. So far, not a single masterpiece of Greek literature, not a single work on history, nothing of general interest, has been discovered. I cannot but think that among the many charred rolls still lying in the Naples Museum some few may contain a text of higher interest; those, however, who have spent most time upon them seem not to have much hope. If then the only library we have yet found in this corner of Roman Hellenism, whether by accident or not, indicates but a poor attempt at culture, and shows that the owner either read nothing or was limited to one very narrow subject in his choice, it is perhaps more likely that his Greek confidant, whether it was Philodemus or not, collected his books for him, and that the studies of the host were simply dictated to him by his household professor.

This verification in sundry details of the general indications in Strabo, vague and scanty as they are, makes us long for some similar help in the case of other Hellenistic districts of Italy. But we have every reason to believe his statement that there was, except in Campania, general decay and depopulation. He does not notice the fact that Sicily was even ceasing to be the corn granary of Rome, owing to the superior productiveness and the earliness of the African soil and climate. But he does say that this country also was in his day abandoned to shepherds, neat-herds, and horse-breeders,[1] which was certainly not its condition when Cicero went there to gather evidence against Verres; and it was a Sicilian bandit who infested these wilds who was publicly executed at Rome. Strabo also gives an interesting description of Mount Ætna, derived as he tells us from the accounts of recent tourists there,[2] and implies that the town of Ætna lived on the new trade of providing for these tourists, who were now very numerous. Unfortunately he endeavours to supply his want of further information, not by an even superficial personal visit, but by antiquarian lore taken from Dionysius of Syracuse, Polybius, and other old books. The same is the case with the African coast —Carthage and Cyrene, which latter he merely saw from the sea[3] as he was sailing to and from Alexandria. He can give us no clear account of the restored Carthage, or of Cirta, both of which must have had many Hellenistic elements, for he tells us that king Micipsa, the father of Jugurtha, known to us through Sallust, settled many Greeks in the latter, and made it a great capital. Here then was an outlying centre of Greek culture. In the days now before us king Juba had married the daughter of Antony and Cleopatra, and having lived a life of literary labour, which indicates high civilisation, had left his kingdom of Mauretania to his son Ptolemy, a late survival of this royal name and line. This Juba probably reigned at Cirta, and had a seaport which he enlarged and called Cæsarea. Utica had been from the second Punic war the centre of Roman influence.

[1] τὴν οὖν ἐρημίαν κατανοήσαντες οἱ Ῥωμαῖοι, κατακτησάμενοι τά τε ὄρη καὶ τῶν πεδίων τὰ πλεῖστα ἱπποφορβοῖς καὶ βουκόλοις καὶ ποιμέσι παρέδοσαν (p. 273).
[2] P. 274 : οἱ δ᾽ οὖν νεωστὶ ἀναβάντες διηγοῦντο ἡμῖν.
[3] xvii. 3, § 20.

The extant inscriptions from the five towns of the Cyrenaica show us that there too survived a great deal of Greek life which would have been worth a visit, had Strabo taken the trouble. A very interesting text now preserved in Provence, but brought from Berenice in that district, shows us an arrangement clearly copied from Alexandria and Antioch, by which the Jews there formed a separate polity under their own officers, distinct from the ordinary citizens. This community records the virtues and gentle manners of a Roman prætor, Titius, significantly too in the Greek language, and with the intention of being set up in a conspicuous place in the amphitheatre.[1]

Unfortunately, inscriptions seldom give the kind of information of which we are in search. We get lists of victors at games, or public officers; catalogues of property or of expenses; on the tombs many records of sincere grief, no doubt also of affected lamentation—the latter in metrical epigrams of more or less grace or correctness. But these, even when heartfelt and simple, only reiterate the universal sorrows of every age and clime, the sense of bereavement, the feeling of gratitude for the kindnesses of the departed, the feeling of rebellion against death, which takes not only the old and ripe, but the young and the strong, before they have tasted the sweets of life and love, or rewarded by their success the anxious cares and hopes of their parents, who protest against this injustice with unavailing earnestness.

---

[1] *CIG* 5361.—ἐπεὶ Μ. Τιτιὸς (his public functions follow) οὐ μόνον δὲ ἐν τούτοις ἀβαρῆ ἑαυτὸν παρέσχηται, ἀλλὰ καὶ τοῖς ἐντυγχάνουσι τῶν πολιτῶν ἔτι δὲ καὶ τοῖς ἐκ τοῦ πολιτεύματος ἡμῶν Ἰουδαίοις καὶ κοινῇ καὶ κατ' ἰδίαν εὔχρηστον προστασίαν ποιούμενος οὐ διαλείπει, ἔδοξε τοῖς ἄρχουσι καὶ τῷ πολιτεύματι τῶν ἐν Βερενίκῃ Ἰουδαίων ἐπαινέσαι καὶ στεφανοῦν, etc. It was set up in the amphitheatre, and its date is probably 13 B.C. This document is very important in giving us evidence that the Jews did not count among the ordinary Greek citizens in Hellenistic towns.

This frame of mind is perhaps the chief peculiarity which these sepulchral inscriptions disclose, as compared with later texts commemorating Christian grief.

There is perhaps another peculiarity in the mention by civic authorities how hard it was to bring any consolation to bear on the afflicted, whose dead the city honours in pompous praises, or rather phrases, by way of balm to heal the gaping wounds in the hearts of the survivors.[1] These things are worth a passing mention, but give us little towards a distinctive picture of the peculiar race and age we are sketching. There remains yet another feature, which strikes me as far more characteristic. Any one who will take the trouble to wade through the Greek inscriptions in any collection, or to watch the new additions to the great *Corpus*, recorded in the current journals of epigraphy, cannot but be struck with the recurrence on almost every page of *good manners* as the quality in men and women which earns their grateful recognition during their life and affectionate remembrance from posterity. The text just cited is one of a thousand which state that 'because such an one has not only performed his duties, general or special, but also has been courteous to those whom he met in daily intercourse,'[2] —therefore he is honoured with a statue, an inscription, civic immunities, citizenship, as the case may be. Nor are these laudations confined to men of high official station, whose urbanity or the reverse was of real importance to their

---

[1] Such phrases as παραμυθεῖσθαι κοινῇ οὓς δύσχερές ἐστι παραμυθεῖσθαι (*CIG* 5838) are common. This subjectivity in *post mortem* laudations is very characteristic.

[2] Here is a charming instance (*BCH* xii. 328) : one Tyrannus, a freedman of the emperor Claudius, who returned to his native town, Magnesia (Meandri), as a fashionable physician is publicly commended for having behaved ὥστε μηδένα ὑπ' 'αὑτοῦ παρὰ τὴν ἀξίαν τοῦ καθ' ἑαυτὸν μεγέθους ἐπιβεβαρῆσθαι.

companions. They are adjudged to horse-doctors, corn-dealers, foreigners residing for pleasure in a city—in fact to people so many and so various that we wonder how these honorary inscriptions can have been regarded as an honour.[1] Nevertheless they have put it on record that in the Hellenistic world good manners were regarded as having a seriousness and an importance quite foreign to modern civilisation. Perhaps the Germanic elements in England and Prussia, with their rudeness in virtue, and their almost suspicion of good manners, have caused this change. I have indeed, in an Irish epitaph, which I have elsewhere quoted,[2] seen a man praised for being *an affable superior and a polished equal*. But this, which would have been a matter-of-course eulogy on a Hellenistic tombstone, strikes the modern observer as grotesque, if not indecent. The grave is too solemn and the question of the future life too serious to admit of superficial considerations. But in Hellenistic days they were not superficial; human society was then the great object of life, and whatever tended to improve and refine it was a real virtue, and a solid recommendation to the world. Thus we may explain this marked contrast in two conditions of the world which present so many striking resemblances.

[1] Indeed Cicero (*pro Flacco*, §§ 75, 76) ridicules them as meaningless. Domestic virtues often obtained this public recognition, and not unfrequently those of women, *e.g. CIG* 1433 on a Spartan woman whose only claim seems to have been sixty years of respectable married life. So youths of Tralles (*BCH* v. 340) are praised not only for athletic victories, but φιλοπονίας, εὐταξίας, εὐεξίας ἕνεκα.

[2] *Art of Conversation*, p. 60.

CHAPTER XI

EASTERN HELLENISM UNDER THE EARLY ROMAN EMPIRE.

In passing from West to East, from the newer acquisitions to the proper seat of the Greek life inaugurated by Alexander, we feel that we are provided with surer evidence and more details to guide us. In the first place the indications of Strabo, which were hitherto (except for Rome and some spots in Italy) based upon hearsay, or upon the books of far older authors, and which even for Greece itself seem to rest upon second-hand knowledge, are upon Asia Minor and Egypt full and personal. Our author tells us frequently what he has himself seen, not what he has copied from others. In the next place we have, for the times of Vespasian, Titus, and Domitian, not only the fabulous life and acts of Apollonius of Tyana—a most characteristic figure, but the orations of Dion Chrysostom, which give us many valuable details upon the city life of those days. The inscriptions from these parts of the Empire are also very numerous, and agree in suggesting that here rather than in Greece proper should we now look for the spiritual life of the Greeks. The prosperity of Asia remained, while that of Greece was ruined; a dozen cities in the former were richer and more populous than either of the famous old Greek capitals.

The final settlement of Roman Asia was practically that of Pompey; the great battles of the civil war were not fought out on Asiatic soil, and the considerate conduct of Augustus and Tiberius soon healed the wounds caused by the tyranny and the exactions of Brutus, Cassius, and Antony. Tiberius, indeed, was called upon to aid in a far different misfortune. The early years of his reign are marked in history as one of those periods when volcanic activity has been peculiarly mischievous. Many great cities were riven with earthquakes, and Strabo describes the whole rich region about Philadelphia as so disturbed and devastated with eruptions that the inhabitants had taken to the open country, and were afraid to trust themselves under any building. In our own day the island of Chio has been subject to like visitations. There is still preserved the copy of a monument set up by twelve great cities of Asia to Tiberius for his large and charitable subventions when they were subject to this calamity in various years from 17 to 29 A.D.[1] The copy was set up at Puteoli, and is a valuable specimen of the art notions of the period, for the cities are personified and represented in relief.[2]

But well might the cities set up memorials to Augustus and Tiberius; these rulers had saved the Hellenistic East from far worse than earthquakes—from the rapacities of the leaders in civil wars, and of the Roman nobles and knights who preyed as governors and capitalists upon the

[1] Tac. *Ann.* ii. 47; *CIL* No. 1624 (vol. x. 1, 159).
[2] From this point of view it has been reproduced and discussed by Overbeck (*Griech. Plastik*, ii. 435 *sq.*) We have now a corroborating inscription from Magnesia, dated by the thirty-third *potestas trib.* of the emperor, and so of the year 31 A.D., which calls him κτιστὴς ἐνὶ καιρῷ δώδεκα πόλεων (cf. *BCH* xi. 70).

subjects of the Empire. This was indeed the Roman peace, which, if it turned many parts of Italy and Greece into a solitude, produced in Asia a prosperity greater than had ever been attained in that most populous and prosperous home of the Hellenic race. For the old Greek civilisation east of the Ægean had been a mere fringe on the coast, not reaching inland save in a few isolated spots. Now the whole heart of the peninsula was settled in great and flourishing polities—free cities with their territories, dynasts of more or less moderation under Roman supervision, and what is perhaps more curious, religious polities, under the sovranty of a high priest either hereditary, or appointed by the local king from his immediate family.

These things remind us at once of mediæval parallels. The abbot of Monte Cassino, with his large territory and enormous wealth, was not unfrequently the brother of the Norman king of Apulia and Sicily. There were in modern Germany even in the present century prince-bishops, at Salzburg, Fulda, Würzburg, with similar secular powers, and this was so to some extent with our Bishop of Durham. Such was Pessinus, then a great mart for trade, and still ruled by priests who had been dynasts under the Attalid kings, and whose temple had been adorned by these kings in Hellenistic splendour. Such was Comana,[1] the great entrepot for Armenian goods, to which all the Asiatic world streamed together when the goddess was brought out in solemn procession. Strabo speaks of it as another Corinth, with its luxurious life, its crowds of temple slaves living ' by their bodies.' Such were to a lesser extent Zela and Mylasa, each with their high priest ruling in sacrosanct dignity. Such, as we now know, was the famous sanctuary and asylum of Hecate at Stratoniceia in Caria, which was a

[1] Strabo, xii. 3, § 36.

separate community, with its own population and precincts, under a ruling high priest, though close beside the city.[1] Strabo even mentions in his own day a certain Cleon,[2] who was a bandit chief, at first useful to Pompey, then siding with Antony and Labienus, who changed over so cleverly at the critical moment before Actium as to receive great rewards and consideration from the Octavian party; so he dropped the bandit trade and turned dynast, using as his cloak of respectability the fact that he was priest of the Abrettene Zeus, a Mysian god. At last he was promoted to the priesthood of Comana, which he had only held a month when he died, people said as a visitation for bringing swine's flesh into the priest's residence—an abomination as great there as it was to the Jews.

These sanctuaries seem all to have promoted trade and to have injured morals, even if we make some allowance for the naturalism sanctioned by many Asiatic cults. For the deities worshipped were in all cases Asiatic, even when called by Greek names, and their worship was of that orgiastic character which is called nature-worship, and is generally opposed to those civilised cults, which recoil from this conception of religion. The Romans did not interfere with such things more frequently than we do with the rites and cults of our Indian subjects, and yet they kept as much control over the dynasts, priests, and free cities as we do in India. Thus with a great deal of communal freedom, and the survival of dignities and emoluments, as well as even of titular sovranty, there was a certain solidarity attained

[1] Cf. *BCH* xi. 156. It was ravaged by Labienus and the Parthians. We have lists (*op. cit.* p. 35) of great sacerdotal families, members of whom, including women, had enjoyed one year's high priesthood, which was the culmination of a series of lesser priesthoods. Here then the title ἱερεύς ἐξ ἱερέων means *noble*.

[2] xii. 8, § 9.

under the headship of Rome which was eminently useful in obviating border wars, privateering, and the other evils of multiplied independencies.

We shall do well to verify these general statements by some of the details to be found in our two authorities. For we may now quote Dion Chrysostom as well as Strabo, seeing that there was no serious change in life or society, though Dion's life and work in Asia Minor were two generations later than those of the geographer. The volcanoes had indeed subsided, and some emperors had supervened not so wise as Tiberius, but on the whole the management of the provinces was little altered, and the evidence of Dion, so far as we can judge, may be used in our sketch of this period.[1] Dion was also a traveller, indeed a far greater traveller than Strabo, and went about not only professionally, but also to see the world and its social curiosities. Like Strabo, he was a native of northern Asia Minor, of Prusa in Bithynia, and his many orations to Asiatic cities concerning his and their affairs show an intimacy with the same lands which Strabo knew personally. The information we obtain from Dion is fortunately of a different kind from that supplied by the geographer; it concerns the inner life, the jealousies, the quarrels of such rivals as Nicæa and Nicomedia; the disturbances at Apamea; the peculiarities of life in Rhodes, Tarsus, Alexandria. It is evidence to be supplemented, not only by the invaluable letters of Pliny from Bithynia, which sometimes tell the very same facts from an official point of view, but by the allusions in the *Acts of the Apostles*, and the *Epistles* of S. Paul, which date from about the same period.

[1] In the same way we may say that, socially at least, the Greece of Plutarch had changed but little even from the Greece of Polybius, hardly at all from the Greece of the end of the first century B.C. But this inference may yet be considerably modified by further discoveries.

It is only recently that explorers such as Messrs. Ramsay, Sterrett, Hogarth, and Fabricius, have begun to go through this country, and gather what still remains of inscriptions, in addition to those of the older travellers collected in Bœckh's *Corpus* and Le Bas's *Voyage*. We may therefore expect to have our knowledge of this great and rich civilisation considerably enlarged as time goes on. The new Ilium of the Roman period, for example, was not recognised till the brilliant discoveries of Dr. Schliemann showed that the ancient and venerable site had received a new and handsome city upon the foundations of so many older settlements, and that it was even the head of a local confederation; we only knew that it was unusually favoured by the Romans for sentimental reasons, though this did not prevent Fimbria from devastating it in the Syllan time, and Agrippa from imposing upon the inhabitants an enormous fine for a misadventure to a Roman princess, which they could hardly have averted,[1] and which was remitted at the intercession of Herod the Great.

We may give some account of these important centres of Hellenistic life, beginning from the north-east, the home of our authorities, and culling from them what still has some interest for the historian of social life. But we shall not tie ourselves to geographical lines, when we can find any stronger affinities to guide us. For there were cities which affected to be old, which were strictly conservative, boasting their mythical descent from Argos or Sparta, or even from a founding by Heracles or Dionysus,[2] and again those

[1] Nicolaus Damasc. *de vita sua*, frag. 3 (in Müller's *FHG* iii. 353).

[2] So Dion, speaking at Nicæa (ii. 87), invokes 'Dionysus, ancestor of this city, and Heracles its founder, and Zeus Policus and Athene and Aphrodite,' etc., etc. It is highly characteristic that while the cities claimed this remote origin, Dion says elsewhere it is not the right thing

which were confessedly the foundations of Antigonus, Lysimachus, or the Attalids. Even these latter in many cases (notably that of Pergamum) invented some pre-existence in another condition to make themselves respectable. But all the genealogical trees of the Pergamenes could not make men believe that this upstart city was of such nobility as, for example, Miletus, where certain families still retained the name and the social dignity of royalty, owing to their descent from the Neleids, who led the first Ionic migration from Greece.[1]

It is difficult for the modern traveller who ventures into the heart of Asia Minor, and finds nothing but rude Kurds and Turkish peasants living among mountains and wild pastures, not connected even by ordinary roads, to imagine the splendour and rich cultivation of this vast country, with its brilliant cities and its teeming population. The two districts most praised by Strabo for fertility are the inner slope of the Caucasus, the present Georgia, and the slopes of Cappadocia descending to the Euxine.[2] Since the rise of Hellenism civilisation had spread into the interior, which now vies with the coast, and perhaps has more to show of peculiar and distinctive life. It was probably the greatness of Mithradates and of his predecessors that raised Pontus and Cappadocia into the first rank among the Asianic districts. Nicomedes of Bithynia[3] had founded

for the citizens to go back more than two steps in personal genealogies, for if you do, no one will be able to show that he belonged originally to any city.—ii. 102 : τὸ γὰρ ἀπωτέρω δυοῖν βαθμοῖν ζητεῖν τὸ γένος οὐδαμῶς ἐπιεικές. οὐδεὶς γὰρ οὕτω τό γε ἀληθὲς ἐξ οὐδεμιᾶς εὑρεθήσεται πόλεως.

[1] The antiquities of Ionia in this respect are given in detail in the opening chapters of Pausanias's seventh book (the *Achaica*).

[2] xii. 3, § 15.

[3] Strabo does not profess to know which Nicomedes. But it must have been the first, for Polybius implies that Prusias I., his grandson, resided there.

Nicomedia, and there was already the older foundation of Nicæa[1] in the same country. Sinope had been the capital of Mithradates's power, and no doubt an additional reason for the increased importance of the Pontic towns was the stimulus he and others gave to the Armenian and Indian trade, which came by the Caspian up the valley of the Cyrus, and so by the Black Sea to the west.

The older Cappadocian dynasty of Ariarathes had evidently pursued a different policy, for their capital Mazaca, concerning which I have elsewhere spoken,[2] was in the very heart of the country, rather nearer the Pisidian coast. Strabo tells a strange story of one of these kings, named Ariarathes, who made himself a great artificial lake by damming up in this inner country one of the affluents of the upper Euphrates. The water broke loose and flooded the Cappadocian and Galatian country, causing such devastation that the king was obliged to pay his subjects, according to the arbitration of the Romans, 300 talents for damages (£73,000). And yet when this dynasty died out, and the Romans offered Cappadocia 'freedom and autonomy,' that people, to the astonishment of all the sentimental doctrinaires, begged to be excused from accepting these great privileges, and asked for a king.[3]

The Bithynian cities, Nicæa, Nicomedia, and Apamea, the names recur often in other provinces, as if the founder desired thus to stamp his creations,—are those which Dion Chrysostom in particular exhorts to lay aside their jealous rivalries, and agree to live in harmony and

---

[1] Originally the Antigoneia of Antigonus, founded in 316 B.C., but refounded and renamed by king Lysimachus.
[2] *Greek Life and Thought*, p. 462.
[3] xii. 2, § 11.

good fellowship.[1] He tells us that these cities maintained an attitude of mutual enmity, not for any solid reason, but concerning the nominal primacy, to which each of them laid claim. In Strabo it is clearly Nicæa which is called the metropolis, but Nicomedia had been the old capital of Prusias, and therefore for a time superior.[2] Though Dion will not allow that there is anything beyond a quarrel of etiquette in this matter, he tells us elsewhere [3] that the right of having the Roman assizes held in a town gathered a great population into it, not only of lawyers and clients, but of idlers, artists, and worse people, all of whom spent money. The other attraction a city could possess was a great religious *panegyris* (the modern Kermesse), to which all the world streamed together, as they still do to such feasts in the Greek islands.[4] This was the real importance of the ecclesiastical cities with their high priests. Here is, for example, what Dion says about Celænæ in Phrygia—a town of no prominence in history, and yet at this time great, populous, and wealthy :[5]

'I see this city now second to none, and I congratulate it. For ye inhabit both the strongest and richest site on the continent, and have ample water and fertile land bearing ten-thousand fold, with many flocks too and herds. The greatest and most profitable rivers have here their source,

---

[1] These very jealousies form the leading topic of Pliny's letters to Trajan, to which I shall revert in chap. xiv.

[2] Cf. Mr. Hardy's instructive note on the relations of these two cities in his edition of *Pliny's Correspondence with Trajan*, p. 127. The term πρώτη πόλις was left to the Nicæans, but Nicomedia became the μητρόπολις, the residence of the proconsul, and the seat of the provincial council. The greater antiquity of Nicæa must have made her citizens peculiarly jealous of this.

[3] ii. 44, 98. I quote uniformly from the Teubner text, which is the only handy and critical one (ed. Dindorf, 1857).

[4] Cf. the interesting chapter on the existing festival at Tino in Mr. Theodore Bent's *Cyclades*. [5] ii. 43.

the Orbas, the Marsyas, flowing through your city, and the Mæander. You command in situation Phrygia, Lydia, and Caria. Besides this, populous nations surround you, Cappadocians, Pamphylians, and Pisidians, to all of whom you afford a market and a meeting-place. You have also as subjects many cities without name, and many rich villages. But the greatest proof of your power is the amount of your tribute.

'Besides all this the (Roman) assizes are held every second year (παρ' ἔτος) with you, and there comes together a countless crowd of people, plaintiffs, defendants, lawyers, officers, attendants, slaves, panders, jockeys, traders, courtesans, and artificers, so that whatever you have to sell obtains the highest price, and nothing lies idle in the city, neither carriages nor houses nor women. This is no small subvention. For wherever the greatest crowd collects, there necessarily most money is found, and the place is likely to prosper; and as I suppose the place where most sheep are penned is most improved for agriculture by their dung, and men request shepherds to keep sheep upon their land for this purpose, so the assizes are held to contribute most of all to a city's importance, and there is nothing sought after with such eagerness.[1] The principal cities obtain this privilege year about. But now they say the assizes will be changed at longer intervals, for that people will not tolerate being continually bustled about in all directions. You have also a share in the religious festivals of Asia, and receive as much of the outlay for them as the cities where the actual ceremonies take place.'

I cite this interesting passage, which may have been

---

[1] This picture of an assize town—either Sardis or Ephesus—is corroborated by a parallel passage at the close of Plutarch's tract comparing the passions of the soul and of the body.

written in the reign of the tyrannous Nero, or Domitian, as well as under Vespasian or Trajan, to show what the liberty and comfort of the Asiatic world was in the early Empire. Even the administration of the humane Cicero during the Republic, not to say the rule of Flaccus or of Cassius,[1] shows us very different features.

There is then no allusion at this epoch to any undue or oppressive Roman interference, such as there must have existed a generation before the Christian era; there is, on the contrary, in inscriptions, much evidence of fulsome flattery of Rome in the very names of tribes as well as in eulogistic decrees.[2] The condition of the other cities of Asia Minor —Lystra, Iconium, Derbe, Ephesus, in the *Acts of the Apostles*, composed at a date between the evidence of Strabo and that of Dion—seems to be quite similar. There is no interference with the public affairs of these towns—nay, not even with public disturbances consequent on the 'right of public meeting,' until a serious riot takes place. Then the town authorities are held responsible by the Romans, and perhaps punished or dismissed, or else the festival, which led to the disturbance, may have been suppressed for a time by the Roman governor. An interesting inscription from Ephesus contains an appeal to the proconsul L. Mestrius Florus (83-84 A.D.) to permit the celebration of the mysteries of *Demeter Thesmophorus* and *Carpophorus* and of the *Augustan gods*. It says that these feasts have been sanctioned by kings, emperors, and *yearly proconsuls*, as their letters testify. Even though fragmentary, this text is an important elucidation of the fears of the 'town-clerk' in the

[1] Above, pp. 133, 161.
[2] Cf. *MDI* xii. 176 for specimens from the inscriptions of the κοινόν of Bithynia. There are tribes called Σεβαστηνή, Γερμανική, Τιβεριανή 'Αντωνιανή, all therefore before the Flavian period, and a man is praised for being φιλοκαίσαρ, and φιλορωμαῖος.

Acts of the Apostles, who tells the people that they run the risk of being held accountable for any uproar. A strike of bakers at Magnesia (Mæandri) is met by a severe rescript forbidding all unions among these tradesmen, and ordering them to obey the convenience of the public.[1]

Tarsus stands before the rest as a remarkable centre of culture, the cradle of much of the Stoic thought, which has influenced the world from the preaching of S. Paul down to the austerities of his Puritan followers in this country.

We hear from Strabo [2] not only of its fair site, with the ice-cold Cydnus running through it, but that the inhabitants had such zeal for philosophy and education as to exceed Athens and Alexandria and every other place where such objects are pursued. 'But in this point they are peculiar, that the learners are all natives, and that hardly any strangers sojourn there; nor do the natives remain at home, but seek the completion of their education abroad, and then seldom return. In the other cities I have alluded to, excepting Alexandria, the reverse is the case, for thither many strangers come for the sake of education and dwell there, while of the natives few travel for that purpose, or indeed show a love of learning at home. The Alexandrians do both. They both receive many strangers, and go abroad themselves.' In fact, as he elsewhere says, Rome was crammed with Tarsian and Alexandrian educators.

This is the bright side of this peculiar and brilliant metropolis. The shadows are supplied by Dion Chrysostom

---

[1] Cf. *Acts* xix. 40, and *BCH* i. 209. Mytilene owed its privileges, forfeited for a while by its adherence to Mithradates, first to the influence of Pompey's *ancient* Theophanes, who is almost deified in extant inscriptions of the city; afterwards to a mission of Crinagoras and Potamon, to which I shall revert hereafter (below, p. 355). On Magnesia cf. *BCH* vi. 565.   [2] xiv. 5, 13.

in the two curious *Orations to the Tarsians*. We need hardly lay much stress on the strange lecture he gives them for their universal habit of snoring, which he says they do even when awake, 'whereas it is elsewhere exceptional even in sleepers, unless they be drunken or surfeited or lying in some awkward position.'[1] He rings the changes upon this shocking social vice through twenty pages. The really instructive picture is given in the next speech, which is an appeal to lay aside, first, their internal jealousies and discords; secondly, their hostility and contempt towards their lesser neighbours—Mallus in particular. There was discord among the various classes of citizens, the council against the assembly, the old against the young, all against the president, whose office seems to have been peculiarly thankless. Outside all these was a large number of inhabitants without franchise, though born of parents and even ancestors native in Tarsus, but apparently needy labourers, who could not produce the 500 drachmæ necessary as a franchise qualification.[2] These people were courted or contemned, according to the political exigencies of the moment. The orator shows that such conduct is unworthy of a civilised community with distinguished traditions; that the quarrels with neighbouring cities are really ridiculous. 'Whether the Ægeans quarrel with you, or the Apameans with Antioch (in Pisidia), or the Smyrnæans with Ephesus, they are all, as the proverb goes, contending for the ass's shadow. For the real power and presidency lies in other hands.'[3]

These utterances of the great lay preacher show us a population rich and prosperous, intellectual and cultivated, but with the vices of the Greek character unextinguished in their hearts. It is quite plain that were

[1] ii. 12.   [2] ii. 29.   [3] ii. 37.

there not a Jupiter in their Olympus, careless perhaps and sleepy, easily imposed upon, and slow to wrath, but yet with the thunderbolt in his hands, and unapproachable in strength, we should have had over again the civil wars and strifes which had worn out the brilliant mother country, till it passed through foreign domination to hopeless decay.

In a future chapter I shall revert to this subject in connection with the administration of Pliny under Trajan. The permanence of these features will perhaps be thus better impressed upon the reader. But before I revert to the now deserted and forlorn mother country, it will be well to give from our two authors a picture of the two greatest centres of Hellenism outside Asia Minor—Rhodes and Alexandria.

The account of Rhodes given by Strabo labours, I think, under the same disadvantage as his account of Athens. I can find no trace of any personal observations in his description, and I cannot but suspect that he never visited the island. He says that the Colossus was still lying broken upon the ground, and he mentions the pictures of Protogenes —the Ialysos and the Resting Satyr. He says that the fortifications, the harbours, the streets, and other appointments, are such that he can mention no equal, not to say superior, in the world. But there is not a word that he might not have copied from any of a dozen books, or heard from any traveller.[1] The very diffuse oration of Dion (xxxi) is a far more valuable source. The orator indeed applies himself throughout to one argument—his censure of the disgraceful habit of erasing the inscriptions on old statues, and re-dedicating them to Roman legates. But in the course of his varied reasonings on so very obvious a matter, he mentions a great many interesting particulars about this famous city.

[1] Strabo, xiv. 2, § 5 *sq.*

He tells us that it was almost the only remaining Asiatic city where any fortifications remained, those of the rest having fallen into decay by reason of the prevailing peace and slavery. He says that the Rhodian walls were indeed no longer tested by enemies, but kept up by the taste of the citizens, as a sign of former greatness as well as of present affluence.[1] This wealth he asserts to be undoubtedly greater than that of any Greek city — I suppose in Hellas or Asia Minor, and he regards it as the direct result not only of their energy and good government, but more especially of that commercial honesty for which they had long been celebrated in Greece.[2] More especially in the dreadful times of the last Roman civil war, when the city was captured by Cassius, and nothing left to the inhabitants but their houses, they showed after his plunder and exactions an example of mercantile honour unique in that part of the world. Augustus thought to relieve the excessive distress of the eastern provinces by permitting an abolition of debts.[3] While the other cities gladly accepted this supposed boon, the Rhodians steadily refused it, knowing that credit abroad was far more valuable than immediate profit at home. So they recovered their prosperity, and being now relieved of all expense as regards their navy or war preparations, possessing merely a couple of open men-of-war to bring their officials to Corinth, they had perhaps ampler resources than ever for the remaining duties of a leading Greek city—their internal administration, their public honours to distinguished friends, their philosophic

---

[1] i. 387. Let me add from Plutarch (περὶ φιλοπλουτίας, 5) : Stratonicus used to ridicule the extravagance of the Rhodians, saying that they built as if they were immortal, but ate as if they were creatures of a day.

[2] Cf. my *Greek Life and Thought*, p. 333.

[3] Dion, i. 367, ὅθεν πᾶσιν ἐδόθη τοῖς ἔξωθεν χρεῶν ἄφεσις.

schools, and their yearly feasts. This made Rhodes a favourite resort for many strangers, especially Romans, all of whom were subdued and improved in manners by the strict, chaste, cultivated tone of the citizens, the order and sobriety of the thoroughfares, the artistic beauty of the temples and public monuments.[1]

The number of these last was quite extraordinary now, at the end of the first century; for while Roman emperors and generals had long indulged in the habit of plundering Greek cities to adorn palaces and temples at Rome, by some extraordinary good fortune Rhodes had escaped. Nay, even Nero, who was so ruthless about this as not to refrain from the monuments of Olympia and Delphi—the holiest of shrines, and who even carried off most of the statues on the Acropolis of Athens, as well as many from Pergamum (which he considered his private property), not only left the Rhodians unplundered, but when his art-agent Acratus came round to that city and the citizens were naturally in dismay, this man, who had searched and plundered every village in the civilised world, astonished them by saying that he only came to see the place, from which he had no permission to remove anything.[2] But the Rhodians, whose own laws as regards the defacing of a statue or inscription, the stealing of a spear or tripod from a statue's hand, were stringent unto death, were now so degraded by the slavery of former days that they thought it necessary to honour not only every emperor but every

[1] That this was no mere rhetorical flattery appears from the fact that Dion brings it out again in his lecture to the Alexandrians, with whom he contrasts the Rhodians most favourably : ἴστε 'Ροδίους ἐγγὺς ὄντας οὕτως ὑμῶν ζῶντας ἐν ἐλευθερίᾳ καὶ μετὰ πάσης ἀδείας, ἀλλὰ παρ' ἐκείνοις οὔτε τὸ δραμεῖν ἐν τῇ πόλει δοκεῖ μέτριον, ἀλλὰ καὶ τῶν ξένων ἐπιπλήττουσι τοῖς εἰκῇ βαδίζουσι. And on this he comments at length.
[2] i. 394.

Roman prætor; and for this purpose their president (στρατηγός) would simply order the inscription under some old statue to be erased, and a new dedication to be inscribed. This latter was also done in the case of ancient statues not named, as having been set up to gods or to heroes too well known for description.[1] In such cases it was actually sacrilegious. But it was at least ridiculous in the case of mere portrait statues, when some old man was presented not only with a statue but with youth, a weak man with great muscles, when a sybarite who always went in his litter stood forth in bronze as a boxer in the Rhodian streets. And as actors successively undertook various parts, so these statues played various characters in turn, undoing the reputation of the city for gratitude and for an honourable adherence to its old decrees.

The orator's argument shows, I think, rather a disregard of very old statues than any graver vice.[2] And yet Rhodian language, Rhodian eloquence, Rhodian manners, were all redolent of antiquity, and represented the most conservative society in the Greek world at this time.

We turn to the vastly different city of Alexandria, described in the very next speech of Dion (xxxii), but also visited by Strabo, who here as usual leaves us in no doubt, when he has anything personal to tell us, of his actual visit. Still his description is but sketchy and partial, and makes us long that we had even such a traveller as Pausanias to give us his impressions. Unfortunately what is very well

---

[1] Philo (*Legat. in Caium*, § 20) describes the mob of Alexandria hurrying an old battered bronze equestrian statue from the gymnasium, and setting it up in the principal synagogue as a statue of Caligula. It had been dedicated by the first Cleopatra.

[2] P. 347. He hints very plainly that most people now thought all the various gods really modifications of the same Being, so that a change of dedication, if confined to gods, was of little import.

known is often least talked about in any book intended for contemporaries, and many interesting and important things in every age are passed over in silence by those who spend time and labour upon obscure and trifling oddities. There is not a step in our inquiry into social life where we have not this very inconvenient fact suggested by our constant perplexities. Let us turn then to the account of Strabo,[1] from which I cull various details not strictly Hellenistic, to give the reader an impression of what a cultivated tourist at this time thought worthy of notice.

There is something curiously modern about his travels in this land of wonders. There was of course a vast number of splendid buildings and tombs which have now disappeared, and there were still large and populous cities on the site of Memphis and at Ptolemais in the Thebaid. But taking Cairo now to represent the former, there was perhaps only one more large city in Egypt then than now, and the account he gives of Thebes, inhabited in separate villages (κωμηδόν), with only its ruined temples to tell of its ancient splendour, might almost be written by any of the tourists who now visit Luxor. He was in the train of Aelius Gallus, the Roman prefect, and mentions how with a large retinue they went to hear the music of the statue of Memnon. At dawn he indeed heard the sound, but will not affirm that it really proceeded from the statue; he evidently thinks it was produced by some of the many natives or priests who were crowding round the feet and had even climbed up on its knees. As is now settled by the researches of Letronne,[2] it was the earthquake of 27 B.C. which broke the statue, and exposed the heart of the stone to the air— a cause sufficient to produce a crackling sound upon sudden changes of temperature. The many inscriptions—Latin

[1] xvii. 1, § 6 *sq.* [2] *La Statue vocale de Memnon.*

and Greek—of tourists who say they did, or did not, hear the sound, reach down to the days of Septimius Severus, who repaired the broken part with rude masonry, and silenced for ever the mysterious voice.

This was the sort of thing Strabo and his Roman patron went to see. They watched the feeding of the sacred crocodiles, whose mouths were pulled open by the attendants, and their food stuffed in, and he tells of a similar exhibition of crocodiles at Rome. He notes that the Egyptian priests had forgotten all their knowledge, and ridicules one Chæremon,[1] who was with them at Heliopolis, and who pretended to interpret the hieroglyphics. He is very explicit on the labyrinth, and lake Mœris, which are now gone, but at Aswan and Philæ he saw hardly more than we see, and was most interested by the natives shooting the cataracts in their boats, which they then did, as they now do, for money. But when he says that on the drive from Aswan to Philæ he saw pieces of diorite lying about, he is hardly to be believed, for he makes the wonderful statement that the third pyramid—that of Menkara, which we still see covered with slabs of red granite from Syene, was made of black diorite! Nor does he mention the great sphinx at all, though he comments on avenues of sphinxes at Memphis, partly covered up with sand. He describes the population as we now should, a very industrious and numerous peasantry, bringing up all their children (instead of exposing them), but wholly unwarlike, inasmuch as nine cohorts of Roman infantry, with a few troops of cavalry, were perfectly able to keep the

[1] Not to be confounded with the Chæremon who was Librarian at Alexandria till 40 A.D., when he went to Rome as tutor to Nero. He was also a ἱερογραμματεύς, and really understood the hieroglyphics, as we may infer from his fragments in Müller's *FHG* vol. iii. (cf. also *BCH* i. 122).

country quiet. Of these one-third was on the southern frontier (Syene), one third was required for Alexandria alone. For the rest of Egypt, as Dion says,[1] was a mere body provided for Alexandria to use, or rather a mere appendage to it.

I have given in a former volume [2] the details known to us about this great city in earlier days; what is now to be added should be compared with what I have there said, and need not here repeat. The government of the city, as indeed of all Egypt, had hardly been altered by the Romans. The Lord-Lieutenant of Augustus controlled the old Ptolemaic officers, who in their turn controlled the native officers, found by Ptolemy in the old native system of government, which he did not change in any important principle. The city had from the outset been peopled with many races, and nevertheless preserved a very constant and peculiar character, though we are told that the Greek element had been almost exterminated by the seventh Ptolemy, and though we may be sure that the Macedonian element now gave little but its ancient and glorious name to the dominant classes. The Jews had no doubt increased in number and importance here and all through Egypt.[3] We must also never forget the strange power possessed by

---

[1] ἡ γὰρ Αἴγυπτος, τηλικοῦτον ἔθνος, σῶμα τῆς πόλεώς ἐστι, μᾶλλον δὲ προσθήκη (i. 412).

[2] *Greek Life and Thought*, p. 160 *sqq*.

[3] Strabo says that the papyrus growers of the Delta were in his day emulating the Jewish policy of limiting the culture of balm in Gilead, that the price might increase and a monopoly be created; and here he suggests the beginning of that regrettable neglect or mismanagement, which permitted the total disappearance of this precious product from the land of Egypt. The only papyrus now growing wild in any country known to me is that in the Anapus near Syracuse. But both lotus and papyrus, and the great Egyptian bean from which the natives made cups, seem gone for ever from the Delta.

every land, especially so peculiarly uniform and unchangeable a land as Egypt, of assimilating foreigners by making their children gradually conform to the national type. Of this we have signal examples in the assimilation of hordes of Slavs and Albanians into the Greek people; in the assimilation of hordes of northmen and English settlers into the Irish type. Thus though the language of Alexandria was principally Greek, though all the foundations of the Ptolemies were professedly Greek (and it is noted as remarkable in Cleopatra that she could even speak the old Egyptian language), nevertheless the city and its population became gradually less and less Hellenistic, and reverted to the Egyptian, or to an Egyptian type. There was a certain orgiastic uncontrolled love of noisy and reckless pleasure, especially in feasts and competitions, combined with fierce superstition and strong faith in the supernatural quite foreign to Greek character.[1] There was bound up with much *bonhomie*, with much love of sarcasm and ridicule, with much levity under injustice and oppression, a vein of iron determination to resist at a certain point, of horrible cruelty in wreaking revenge, which is only to be paralleled in very few cities, ancient or modern. The Alexandrian love of pleasure was not keener than their love of business; their immorality not more shocking than their superstition; their barbarism not more pronounced than their culture—a strange public, sometimes deadly to play with, sometimes easy to oppress, with a temper never safe to forecast, and at times as resolute in resistance as if they had been all Jews or Carthaginians.

[1] There seems, therefore, to be truth in the expression of Philo (*Leg.* § 18), who calls them ὁ Ἀλεξανδρέων μεγὰς καὶ συμπεφορημένος ὄχλος, and accuses them indiscriminately of beast worship (§ 20 *sub. fin.*), though this is the testimony of a bitter hater of the Greeks as enemies of his own nation.

In the myriad quarrels of their own Ptolemaic dynasty they always took a strong and even violent, though not always a consistent part; when the Romans succeeded to the dominion we find the Alexandrians in every case siding with the East against the West—with Pompey, the hero of the East, against Cæsar; with Antony, who made himself one with their fascinating queen and her interests, against Augustus. Nowhere did the great Julius meet so obstinate and dangerous a national resistance; and though Augustus encountered no such difficulties upon his arrival in pursuit of Antony, he marked his successful landing and defeat of the national party by founding another Nicopolis close to Alexandria, as he had done near the promontory of Actium. The jealous care with which the emperor excluded all important senators from Egypt, and kept it a close domain under his own immediate servants, must have arisen from what he saw of the dangers of Alexandria and its terrible mob; for everybody must have told him how completely pacific and docile was the population of the rest of Egypt. Since the ruin of Thebes, in the days of Auletes, we never hear of an internal disturbance. Nor can the modern traveller conceive such a thing possible. The Fellahs are, indeed, to use the words of Plautus, *patientissimum genus hominum*.[1] But not so the ancient Alexandrians. The great series of palaces built by successive Ptolemies which Strabo saw, the dockyards, the arsenals, were indeed empty; but the parks and colonnades, the

---

[1] Unless they were inhabitants of the three or four Greek cities in Egypt they could never attain the freedom of Alexandria. Unless they had obtained this latter privilege they were considered ineligible for Roman citizenship by the emperors. This appears from an interesting correspondence between Trajan and Pliny concerning a certain Harpocras, whom the emperor, at Pliny's instance, had ignorantly made a Roman citizen in violation of this rule (cf. Plin. *Epp*. v.-viii. *ad Trajanum*).

gymnasia and temples with their grounds, the *Sema* with its Alexander, now cased in glass instead of gold, the Museum with its Fellows meeting in the common hall—all these Hellenistic features remained intact. Its streets were full of life, of business, and pleasure, and it ranked without question as the second city of the world both to Strabo and to Dion.[1]

Dion begins his very severe lecture or sermon to the Alexandrians by describing their extraordinary frivolity, their devotion to sport and laughter, their complete want of seriousness. Yet we know that in the first trading city of the East there must have been many diligent and serious people, not to mention the professors and students at the Museum. But through the whole of the speech he never directly mentions these richly-endowed college dons either for good or evil. Naturally the itinerant preacher in his worn cloak, whose presence was mean and his speech nothing extraordinary,[2] would feel a certain jealousy or dislike for these endowed officials. The following passage[3] seems to me to do more than ignore them. He is asking his audience not to interrupt him, or call out impatiently: when will the juggler (or some other worthless amusement) begin: 'For these you have always with you, and there is no fear of their failing you, but such discourses as will profit the city, and make men wiser and better, you seldom hear —I will not say never. This indeed is not your fault, as you will show by listening to me to-day; it rather lies with the so-called philosophers; for some of them never go near the public, and will not make the venture, perhaps despair-

---

[1] Cf. Dion, *Oratt.* i. 412.

[2] ἐγὼ δὲ ἄνθρωπος οὐδεὶς οὐδαμόθεν ἐν τριβωνίῳ φαύλῳ μήτε ᾄδειν ἡδὺς μήτε μεῖζον ἑτέρου φθεγγόμενος (i. 407). Yet elsewhere he confesses that he was called *the nightingale of sophists*.

[3] P. 402.

ing of improving the crowd, while those in the so-called public lecture rooms make a mere display of voice (φωνασ-κοῦσιν), admitting only hearers bound by fixed conditions and tame to their hand. But of those called Cynics there is no small number in the city, an influx of them having taken place as of other things—men who have no knowledge, not even of the most vulgar kind, but merely seek a living; these in the crossways and lanes and gateways of temples collect and impose upon children and sailors and such like with jokes and buffoonery and answering riddles. Wherefore these people instead of good do the greatest harm, teaching the thoughtless to despise philosophers, as if one were to teach children to despise their masters. But of those who come before you as educated men, some make oratorical displays, and some compose poems which they sing to you, knowing that you love music. If these people pose as rhetors or poets it does no harm, but if they pose as philosophers, for the sake of lucre and vainglory, and not for your benefit, then they are indeed mischievous. It is as if a physician called in to see the sick were to disregard their symptoms and bring them garlands, and courtesans, and unguents.'

I suppose that at the opening of this passage he must have had the professors of the Museum in his mind. His main object is, however, to contrast himself not with these, but with those other itinerant teachers, who were, as I have elsewhere remarked, like the begging Franciscan monks in the Europe of the last century.[1] The crowd which they addressed included women and children, for these, as was remarked by observers two centuries earlier, were constantly in the streets, and added vastly to any public disturbance. The whole town lived, Dion says, for ex-

---

[1] *Greek Life and Thought*, p. 373.

citement, and when the manifestation of the god (Apis) took place all Alexandria went fairly mad with concerts and horse-races. When doing their ordinary work they were apparently sane, but the instant they entered the theatre or the race-course they appeared as if poisoned by some intoxicating drug, so that they no longer knew or cared what they said or did. And this was the case even with women and children, so that when the show was over, and the first madness past, all the streets and byways were seething with excitement for days, like the swell after a storm. The strange point is that Persians and Bactrians, who must ride for the sake of their liberty or their wars, have no such madness; but the Alexandrians, who never ride or touch a horse, go mad over races, like lame men contending about foot-races.

All this reminds us strongly of the similar mania in Byzantium when the Blues and the Greens were important factors in state revolutions and successions.[1] The same unmannerly excitement took place when they went to hear singers or actors, the whole audience hanging upon their words or notes, as if felicity were acquired through the ears, and calling some wretched professional their god and saviour because he satisfied their craving. It is curious that all this excitement was derived from singing with the cithara, not the flute, for accompaniment. What would have happened had this more exciting instrument been used it is hard to say.

For the humours of this maddened crowd often proceeded to murder, and no one who thwarted them for a moment

[1] Cf. Mr. Bury's *Later Roman Empire*, i. 338. In Suetonius (*Caligula*, 55) the *prasina factio* already appears; and (*Nero*, 22) '*querentibus dominis factionum.*' Mr. L. C. Purser gives me as even earlier instances Pliny, *H.N.* vii. 186 (perhaps 20 B.C.), and Ovid, *Am.* iii. 2, 76.

was safe. I spoke in a former chapter of the Roman who was 'lynched' because he killed a cat. The same thing would no doubt have happened a century later, for Juvenal tells of the atrocities which occurred in a local quarrel between Ombi and Tentyra (*Satir.* xv.), and the picture of that Roman Swift cannot be wholly imaginary. Dion, indeed, admits particularly (p. 404) the very religious character of the people. But he tells them plainly that while their religion consists in violent emotions, in miracles, in omens, in strange providences, in a multiplicity of gods, true religion consists in rational views, in ordinary providence, in the conduct of everyday life; not in madness and in mystery. The deeper religion of the day must be reserved for another place, and so must the opposition between the Jewish and the Hellenistic spirit, which was so prominent in Alexandria.

There is but one common feature belonging to the two cities we have contrasted—their political insignificance. To the Rhodians the orator can hold out no higher ambition than the giving of splendid feasts, which (like the Exhibitions in our capitals) would bring together visitors, and spread the popularity of the city, and thus its wealth and social influence. To the Alexandrians the highest hope he protends is a possible visit from the emperor himself, if he hears of their good conduct.[1] We know from Philo that they had been grievously disappointed by the death of Caligula, who had determined upon a state visit of this kind. Yet when Hadrian came, a generation later, the result was not mutual satisfaction, but estrangement.

[1] i. 398, 433.

CHAPTER XII

THE CONDITION OF GREECE FROM AUGUSTUS TO VESPASIAN —THE HELLENISM OF THE EARLY EMPERORS

WE come back to the true home of Greek life, the inmost hearth from which the sacred fire of Greek culture has often been carried with such copious hands as to leave scarce a spark to illumine the old country. Yet over and over again, after brilliant centuries of Asiatic or western Hellenedom or Hellenism, the old rough nurse of liberty, of art, and of refinement has reasserted her pre-eminence and proved that no other land can ever appropriate her title to be the foster-mother, if not the mother, of European culture.

Were we to trust implicitly the eloquence of Dion addressed to the Rhodians, this decadence of Greece had reached its nadir in his day. He refuses to take the example of Athens as any precedent: 'Athens, which has hailed as *Olympian* some nobody, not even a born citizen, but a Phœnician, and not even from Tyre and Sidon, but from some inland village; which has not only set up in bronze, but beside Menander, some cheap poet, who exhibited here before you. This may well be cited in pity for the condition into which the whilome leaders of the Greeks have now fallen.'[1] And again: 'Formerly the reputation of Greece

[1] i. 383.

was sustained by many—the Athenians, Spartans, Thebans, nay, Corinthians and Argives in turn. But now they are all gone—some actually destroyed, while others are disgraced by the acts you hear of, and are ruining their ancient fame, thinking this a luxury, poor souls, and a gain, if no one prevents them from degrading themselves. So far as these are concerned, there is no reason that the Greeks were not long since below the level of Phrygians and Thracians. There is nothing but the stones and the ruins of their buildings to show the old splendour of Greece, since even the Mysians would repudiate the present inhabitants and politicians as their descendants. Hence it is that I even consider the totally destroyed cities as the most fortunate, since our memories of them at least are safe and not soiled by recent events; for is it not better that the bodies of the dead should be buried out of our sight than that they should putrefy before our eyes?'[1] And with this agrees the letter of Apollonius of Tyana, in which he writes to the Museum of Alexandria: 'I have become barbarised, not by staying away from, but by staying in, Greece.'[2] In estimating these texts we must, however, make considerable allowance for the desire at the moment to extol Rhodes, and indeed Asiatic Hellenism, at the expense of the ancient capitals of Hellenic life.

For there is considerable reason to think that the days of Dion were by no means the worst which Greece had seen, but that a considerable revival had taken place since its complete exhaustion after the great civil wars with their terrible requisitions upon life and property. It is true, and very remarkable, that Asia Minor revived, and recovered her

---

[1] i. 397.
[2] *Epp.* 34. —ἐβαρβαρώθην οὐ χρόνιος ὢν ἀφ' Ἑλλάδος ἀλλὰ χρόνιος ὢν ἐν Ἑλλάδι.

commercial prosperity with promptitude and lasting success, whereas that of Greece can hardly ever be called flourishing again till the trade in silk and in currants made some stir in Justinian's time. Still there were always certain articles of export which, in other days and with other habits, would have employed much industry. Horses from the now extended pastures of the depopulated country, oil from other provinces as well as Attica, honey from the slopes of Mount Hymettus, were always prized. Far more profitable to labour was the production—no longer as a fine art, but as a trade—of statues at Athens and elsewhere for the adornment of Asiatic and Italian temples;[1] so were the famous marble quarries of the Cyclades, which seem, however, like the gold and silver mines, to have been often a monopoly of the Roman fiscus, and thus less productive than might be expected.[2]

But the effect of this trade is only seen in scattered and special localities, such as Corinth, Patræ, Tithorea, and Hypata; the last two described by Plutarch[3] and Apuleius (if we can believe him) as flourishing, evidently owing to recent and special causes. In most parts of Greece landed property had passed into the hands of large proprietors; the *Latifundia*, which had long since destroyed the yeomanry of Italy, had done the same in the Hellenic peninsula; the general influx of the pauper rural population into the towns,

[1] Cf. the curious chapter in Philostratus (*Vita Apoll.* v. 20). Plutarch tells us (*Life of Publicola*, 17) that the pillars for the restored Capitol under Domitian were made at Athens of Pentelic marble, and of admirable proportions, but were spoilt by repolishing at Rome, which made them too slight for their height.

[2] Prince Victor of Hohenlohe, who has tried several specimens of Parian marble for his statues, tells me that the old Greeks seem to have exhausted the sound parts of that quarry. All the pieces brought to him had cracks or flaws, which made them useless.

[3] *Sylla*, 15, and the opening of the *Metamorphoses* of Apuleius.

upon which I wrote in a former volume,[1] had increased the evil ; and we now find a population which appears to do nothing but assemble in sham political unions, or attend public feasts and games, to enjoy the amusements provided for them by the liberality either of the State or of wealthy individuals, to pass resolutions and decrees of gratitude and of deification to those who satisfied their sordid wants, and occasionally to riot for amusement or some trivial cause of offence.

The only serious disputes of this age seem to be about boundaries of territory, and yet each such dispute of which we hear seems to have occupied years of litigation and arbitration. Such was a dispute between the community of Daulis and one of its rich citizens as to the boundaries of an estate he had acquired, as it bordered on or invaded the public land of the commune.[2] But what was this quarrel of perhaps ten years, which we could easily match with a chancery suit, compared with the ancient feud between Sparta and Messene, which took the form of a claim of both for the *ager Dentheliates* on the west slope of Taygetus ? After many decisions and reversals of decisions the affair was apparently settled by Tiberius and the Senate, after hearing all the claims and counterclaims since the first Messenian war, in favour of Messene.[3] A very similar case between Delphi on the one hand and Amphissa and Anticyra

---

[1] *Greek Life and Thought*, p. 326 *sq.*

[2] Cf. Hertzberg, ii. 152, who gives the details from an inscription in Boeckh's *CIG* No. 1739. Other cases in S. Reinach's *Epigraphie*, p. 44.

[3] Tac. *Ann.* iv. 43. Cf. the other evidence cited by Hertzberg (ii. 31 *sq.*) Since his book appeared there have been found eight coins of Thuria in that district marked ΑΑ, which indicate that the dispute was not even then over (in Trajan's time), but had recently been again settled by reverting to the decision of Augustus in favour of Sparta, to which Pausanias (in the second century) refers—so interminable was this dispute. Cf. the article by Weil in *MDI* vii. 211 *sq.*, who also cites a dispute at Delphi settled in the same reign by Nigrinus (*CIL*. iii. No. 567).

on the other only went back some 250 years to the settlement of M. Acilius Glabrio in 191 B.C., and was decided, after careful examination of the boundaries, by a legate of Claudius.[1]

The whole impression produced by the life of Greece during the first two generations of this century is so curiously empty and vapid—idyllic is Hertzberg's strange epithet—that I can only cite as a parallel in our modern Europe the monks of Mount Athos, whom I found living the same sort of existence,—attending with care and ceremony to feasts and fasts, maintaining with rigid conservatism the old traditions of their religion, but lost to all newer and more living interests; employed in perpetual litigation about their boundaries, waiting anxiously in their retirement for some new thing as a subject of gossip; agreeable, hospitable, dignified, trivial—a fossil society feeding upon its traditions, petrified beyond the hope of renovation or healthy growth. Indeed, if I had not seen and studied this now unique society I should feel wholly at a loss to comprehend the picture of Greece which the many inscriptions and few authors of the period of Augustus have disclosed to us.

It is hard to blame the policy of the emperors for this melancholy senility, though we may safely say that the enactments of Augustus were well adapted to maintain it; they were the enactments of a narrow and pedantic mind, unable to think out any large or serious remedies for the national decay, and yet, from a certain traditional respect for Greece, anxious to do what was possible to amuse and satisfy the Greeks. The tyrannical establishment of Nicopolis to commemorate his victory, with its Actian games,[2]

---

[1] *Op. cit.* ii. 44, and *CIG* No. 1711.
[2] The temple of Apollo at Actium had been the old sanctuary of the κοινόν of Acarnania.

its amphictyony, its many privileges, was clearly an imitation of the old Hellenistic habit of copying Alexander, whom Augustus evidently considered his only rival in fame. The neighbouring Ætolia, Thessaly, and Acarnania were depopulated for this purpose, and their old κοινά abolished, just as Tigranes had depopulated tracts of Asia Minor to fill his new capital Tigranocerta.[1] For a generation or two this mushroom foundation outshone Athens, Argos, and the other venerable seats of Greek culture, and was rivalled only by the Roman Corinth and the hardly less Roman Patræ. The assembly or conclave of cities which met at Argos and passed shadowy resolutions and complimentary decrees, did perhaps less harm but no good. We cannot even imagine any serious Greeks satisfied with such a mockery of old republican institutions.

For Augustus, though well instructed, like Julius Cæsar, in Greek letters, though he interlarded his epistles and his talk with Greek phrases,[2] perhaps in imitation of Cicero, was, like Cæsar, a thorough Roman, who used the Greeks for his service and his amusements, but never dreamt of them as his social equals.[3]

[1] Above, p. 92, and *BCH* x. 166.

[2] Cf. the specimens quoted by Suetonius (*Tiberius*, 21 ; *Claudius*, 4), and the general account of his Greek education in *Octavian*, 89. *Ne Græcarum quidem disciplinarum leviore studio tenebatur. In quibus et ipsis præstabat largiter, magistro dicendi usus Apollodoro Pergameno, quem jam grandem natu Apolloniam quoque secum ab urbe juvenis ad hoc eduxerat, deinde eruditione etiam varia repletus per Arei philosophi filiorumque ejus Dionysi et Nicanoris contubernium ; non tamen ut aut loqueretur expedite aut componere aliquid auderet, nam si quid res exigeret, Latine formabat vertendumque alii dabat.*

This last was the received practice of the Roman Senate, in their decrees concerning the Greek world, as I explained above.

[3] I do not feel that this remark needs qualification from the story of Plutarch (*Reip. gub. præc*, 18), that he entered Alexandria holding the philosopher Areus by the hand, and telling the people that he spared

The same is true of Tiberius, whose very pedantic purism in rejecting every Greek word throughout all the solemn records of the Roman State shows clearly how inferior he thought his Greek associates. I do not think we need be misled in either case by such distinct *outings* in the life of each as the assumption of Greek habits by Augustus at Puteoli and Naples, in return for the compliments of Alexandrian sailors, or the life of Tiberius at Rhodes, which became more decidedly Greek the more he wished to avoid the notice and the jealousy of Augustus.[1] It is hard to say anything certain about Caligula's notions, seeing that he was little better than a raving lunatic. But he seems to have felt that the worship of his own divinity and other ceremonies were better performed by Greeks, and so imported from the province of Asia choristers for this purpose.[2]

But after the dreadful interlude of Caligula's insanity we arrive with Claudius at quite a different condition of things. Claudius had lived most of his life in a private station, and was occupied, like every private gentleman of education at Rome, with Greek letters. He was too old to change his habits on the throne, and sat there as a literary, and therefore as the first

the city for this his friend's sake. Nor do I lay the same stress that the Germans do upon the mission of Crinagoras, the Mytilenæan, and its success owing to this man's intimacy with the imperial household, for he was probably the Greek tutor of Marcellus, and apparently a person of consequence at home, perhaps because of this very position. Cf. Cichorius's tract, *Rom und Mytilene*, and Rubensohn's edition of the *Epigrams of Crinagoras*.

[1] Suetonius says (*Octav.* 98) of Augustus: *lege proposita, ut Romani Græco, Græci Romano habitu et sermone uterentur*, and that he spent days with the ephebi of Capreæ. This passage by itself would assimilate Augustus as a Hellenist with Claudius and lead to serious mistakes. So also *Tiber.* 11, 12 on Tiberius's life at Rhodes. When in great fear of Augustus's displeasure, *redegit se, deposito patrio habitu, ad pallium et crepidas*.

[2] Jos. *Antiqq.* xix. 1, § 14.

Hellenistic, emperor. The favours he heaped upon Greece itself, the public use he made of Greek in the Senate house, the elevation of his Greek freedmen to the position of state ministers and privy councillors, speak plainly of this change ; and if we remember how the fashion of the Roman court dominated the world, we shall date from this reign the first symptoms of recovery in Greece, the first steps towards that new and real fusion of Greek and Roman life which culminated in the removal of the seat of government from Rome to Byzantium.

The Hellenism of Claudius was carried still further by Nero, whose hideous crimes and follies have almost all this foreign stamp about them. His exhibitions were Greek, his Neronia *more Græco*,[1] his expedition to the Olympian and other games, his plundering of art treasures, every vagary and outrage of his almost incredible life, had this aspect. I think, therefore, the story told by Apollonius of Tyana [2] that in his day he found a Roman governor at Corinth who knew no Greek and could not be understood by the people, so that his council sold justice and did what they liked, is either false or must be referred to some other reign. The pompous declaration of the freedom of all the Greeks at the Isthmian games of 67 A.D. seems to have been purely mischievous. The actual text has recently been discovered on an inscription at Acræphiæ in Bœotia, and published by M. Holleaux in the *Bulletin de Correspondance hellénique* for 1888. I here give this curious text.

The emperor Cæsar says : 'Desiring to requite the most noble Hellas for her goodwill towards me, and her piety, I invite as many as possible from this province to be present at Corinth the 4th day before the Calends of December.'

---

[1] Cf. the whole account in Tacitus, *Ann.* xiv. 14 *sq.*
[2] In Philostratus's *Life*, v. 36.

When the multitude assembled in the *ecclesia* he addressed them at follows :

'With an unexpected gift, men of Hellas, do I favour you, even though nothing be surprising from my generosity —a gift such as ye would not even ask. Do ye now, all Greeks who inhabit Achæa and what was hitherto called Peloponnesus, receive liberty free of all tribute, a thing which not even in your most prosperous days did all of you enjoy, for ye were slaves either to foreigners or to one another. Would that I might have granted this gift when Hellas was in her strength, in order that many more might enjoy my favour; wherefore I owe Time a grudge, as it has forestalled me in taking from the greatness of this boon. But now not through pity but through goodwill do I benefit you, and requite your gods, whose good Providence I have experienced both by land and sea, in that they vouchsafed me to do so great a good work. For other rulers have freed cities : Nero has freed a whole province.'[1]

This harangue speaks plainly enough the vanity and folly of its author. There are traces, in the scanty evidence which remains, that local feuds and violences broke out immediately upon the recovery of this autonomy. Moreover it fostered even in respectable Greeks false hopes, and when the prudent Vespasian interfered, and restored the order which was necessary to sound administration, he caused unreasonable discontent. The ostentatious clemency of Nero did not prevent his ruthlessly invading the sacred *Altis* of Olympia by building a palace for himself and a new entrance to the enclosure, as has been shown by recent excavations.[2]

---

[1] Then follows an honorary decree, proposed by Epaminondas, to whom we shall presently revert. The text is quite complete, save that the name of Nero has been carefully erased in all but two places on the stone (cf. *op. cit.* p. 510 *sq.*, and Appendix A for the Greek text).

[2] Cf. Dörpfeld in *MDI* xiii. 331.

I repeat, then, that Hellenistic fashions maintained by two successive despots of the world and lasting for a whole generation—nearly thirty years—moulded all the courtiers, all the officials, all the soldiers who sought high place, into the once despised culture. Even the rude Sabine Vespasian, who had been obliged to accompany Nero to his performances, and had not been able to conceal his *ennui*, yet betrayed by his recreations, when an emperor, that he had studied Greek in a manner new and strange for a bluff Roman soldier, and his sons were distinctly of the Neronian not of the older Roman type. I say this of Vespasian's recreations, for his serious measures were of a different kind—first, his abolishing the so-called liberties of all the Greek lands round the Levant and reducing them to provinces;[1] secondly, his governmental endowment of professors.[2]

The Capitoline games, established by Domitian, show plainly how this ruler conceived the relation of Rome to Greek culture. For the whole account of Suetonius shows us the Greek complexion of the feast. It was threefold—*musicum, equestre, gymnicum*. There were prose (recitation) contests in Greek and Latin; there were *chorocitharistæ* and *psilocitharistæ*. He presided in thoroughly Greek dress—*crepidatus, purpureaque amictus toga Græcanica*. I quote this passage because the historian afterwards[3] says that he neglected higher studies at the opening of his reign, except

---

[1] Suet. *Vesp.* 8.
[2] *Ibid.* 18. *Primus e fisco Latinis Græcisque rhetoribus annua centena constituit; præstantes poetas, nec non artifices insigni congiario magnaque mercede donavit.* On his amusements, *ibid.* 23, *utebatur versibus Græcis tempestive satis*, with specimens which justify Suetonius's previous remark: *Erat enim dicacitatis plurimæ, et sic scurrilis et sordidæ, ut ne prætextatis quidem verbis abstineret.*
[3] *Domitian*, 4. 20.

that he repaired very carefully the loss of Roman libraries by fire; for he sent to Alexandria and had new copies of the lost books supplied.

This brief review justifies what I said above, that the first generation of this century was the lowest moment for Greece, the moment at which it was most neglected and despised, and that with Claudius began the period of its revival, which culminated with Hadrian. Even Trajan, who spent his life in wars, affected or felt such an admiration for the Greek Dion, that he took the rhetor publicly about in his chariot, though he naïvely declared that he could not understand one word of Dion's talk in philosophy.

But, as I have already said, we are strangely ill-supplied with Greek authors of this time, while at its close Dion, Plutarch, and in Latin Apuleius spring up to tell us many things about the social and intellectual condition of Greek-speaking people. Still the seeds were germinating which produced the phil-Hellenism of Hadrian. Not that there were wanting rich men and powerful men in Greece. We hear of the Spartan Eurycles, the intimate of Herod and, like him, a sort of dynast bequeathing his power, who was even connected with some of the direst tragedies in that tyrant's life. For if we are to credit Josephus[1] it was Eurycles who fomented the suspicions of Herod against his sons and caused their execution. At home he was not only rich and powerful, but owned the island of Cythera, and spent large sums on public buildings and on the establishment of games at Sparta.[2] We hear also of a new Epami-

[1] *Antiqq. Jud.* xvi. 10, § 1.
[2] *CIG* Nos. 1378, 1389 mention games called *Eurycleia* in Sparta, and speak of their profits to the city (cf. Hertzberg, i. 523). As these Eurycleia are coupled with 'the great Cæsarian games' at Sparta, and as another inscription (at Mistra, *CIG* No. 1299) tells us of *Agrippeastæ*, a guild in honour of Agrippa, we may conclude this Eury-

nondas, whose benefactions to his country were very different from those of his great namesake, but not, I fear, the less suited to the times in which he lived. He is lauded in extant inscriptions for having represented Bœotia in the embassy of congratulation to Caligula (37 A.D.), and also for defraying all the expenses of a great public festival at Ptoon, at which he provided feasting for the Bœotian public, in addition to prizes for artists and athletes.[1]

Such texts occur in every collection; they are found upon every site, and force upon us two questions: First, How is it that the Greeks seem never tired not only of attending the existing festivals, but of establishing new contests? There appears to have been quite a traffic in embassies going from one city to another, inviting each κοινόν to acknowledge a new or newly-organised festival in various

cles to have been a friend of the Romans and popular with them like Herod. Cf. the article on Eurycles and his son, J. Cæsar Lacon, by R. Weil, in *Mitth. deutsch. Instit.* (*MDI*) vi. 11 *sq.* It is here shown that Eurycles was a far more important man than Josephus would lead us to suspect. The author even calls Josephus's account a caricature. Eurycles was the man who pursued Antony so ostentatiously after the battle of Actium (Plut. *Ant.* 67). His public buildings are mentioned by Pausanias (ii. 3, 5; iii. 14, 6). His *Eurycleia* and their cost are referred to in Wescher, *Inscr. de Delphes*, p. 436. We hear of his having influence in Cappadocia also, so that this dynast reminds us in many ways of Herod, and his wide connections with the Hellenistic world.

[1] The details are given by Hertzberg (ii. 64) from the long inscription *CIG* No. 1625, and from Keil's studies of Bœotian inscriptions. Other similar cases of belauding citizens for undertaking showy embassies to Rome, for establishing feasts, for squandering money in presents to the idle populace, are quite common (cf. *op. cit.* ii. 202, 203). Hertzberg notes that after the pompous laudations of Epaminondas for useless squandering, his reopening of the old drains to lower the Copaic Lake, a really useful public work, is hurried over with the briefest mention. There is now a more complete copy of the inscription in *BCH* xii. 309. He brought back from Caligula ἀπόκριμα πρὸς τὸ ἔθνος πάσης φιλανθρωπίας καὶ ἐλπίδων πλῆρες.

formal ways. These often included the recognition of the
right of asylum at the temple where the festival was to be
held; always the formal mission of sacred commissioners
to attend the feast; and the promise to recognise and
reward publicly such citizens as might win garlands at
this feast.[1] Secondly, How is it that all the stones of the
country seem hardly sufficient for the laudatory inscriptions
which give formal thanks to citizens for their public benefactions, sometimes for the mere morality and general respectability of their life, sometimes even for no higher claim
than their good manners? It seems worth while to suggest
answers to both these questions, which are not asked and
certainly not answered in the histories of the time.

There seem to be two reasons for the constant multiplication of festivals—for the Actia, Cæsaria, Neronia, Capi-
tolina, which were added to the ancient list, and even for
the repeating of the ancient games in other places than their
original home.[2] Quite apart from the worship and flattery
of the emperors, which were promoted in this way, it was
in the first place the accredited occasion for ostentatious
largesses from wealthy private citizens, and where there were
many paupers every additional occasion of the kind increased the chances of a dole. Secondly, it is important to
call attention to a very neglected passage in Plutarch,[3] which

[1] Cf. M. Paris in *BCH* xi. 334.

[2] Thus the people of Antioch sought for special leave to celebrate
Olympic games at Daphne, and this leave must be obtained, and for a
high price, from the people of Elis (cf. Hertzberg, ii. 58, note).

At present there are Olympic games, which I witnessed, celebrated
every four years in the Panathenaic stadium at Athens—a curious revival.

[3] *De exilio*, 12.—'For is it not permitted even for the banished (ἔξεστι
δή που τῷ μεθεστῶτι) to spend his time at the mysteries of Eleusis, to
join in the Dionysiac festival at Argos, to go to Delphi, when the
Pythia occur, when the Isthmia to Corinth, if he be fond of shows?
But if not, he has his philosophic school, his walk, his book, his placid

tells us that the exiles relegated to desert islands in the Ægean were allowed to attend these semi-religious festivities. Now, seeing that most of these islands were at this time peopled with Roman exiles, mostly of the highest nobility, and with very wealthy connections, can we wonder that the accommodating Greeks multiplied this means of softening the rigors of banishment, of making friends among these great nobles, any of whom might come back to public influence with a turn of the wheel of fortune, all of whom in any case must have been only too delighted to escape from the rocks of Gyaros or Seriphos to a festival where they met not only all Greek society, but many Roman friends or relations, and heard news of that capital, which every Roman loved so well? The fact that this privilege, so unmistakably precious to the exiles, should only once be mentioned need not surprise us; of course it was purposely kept quiet at the time, lest the cruelty of a Nero or a Domitian might cut off this one solace of the miserable. It made these rocks, so notorious for their barrenness, far more tolerable than the remote Tomi, whither Ovid was despatched, or Pandataria, where there was no Hellenic celebration within reach. Nay, possibly the horrors of the Ægean islands were purposely magnified by the exiles to cloak this very privilege.

sleep, as Diogenes said : 'Aristotle breakfasts when Philip pleases, I do when Diogenes.' The inference, which I take from Hertzberg (ii. 50, note) is, like most of that learned man's conclusions, not quite convincing, for in this chapter Plutarch is discussing the case of his friend who was only banished *from* (not *to*) a particular place. On the whole, however, I am disposed to agree with him in his interpretation. The relations of the banished were certainly allowed to visit them (Plut. *op. cit.* 11). It is commonly supposed from the allusions in this tract that his friend, whom he carefully avoids naming, was banished from Sardis. I take this to be a disguised allusion to Rome, and think the tract was intended for some noble Roman whose name must be concealed for fear of further persecution by a jealous emperor.

I pass to the second question proposed—the extraordinary frequency of complimentary decrees. We stand before a decayed society of very rich men and paupers, the latter of whom had become accustomed to begging, and subventions from the rich, not to pay for labour, but to obviate hostility and to earn acclamation. Thus we find all the uses made of large fortunes during the period before us to be of this ostentatious and well-nigh immoral character. There is no attempt to start a new industry, to develop a new traffic, to enable the poor to help themselves by honest labour. The unfortunate precedent set to the world by Rome was indeed of fatal influence. There it had long been the custom to give huge presents to the city mob, in the way of food and amusements, formerly to secure their votes, now to secure their favour; and the same policy had been extended to the Household Troops (Prætorian Guards). This was the pattern imitated by the capitalists of Greece—the crime of distributing money to idle recipients, who had votes in their local assemblies, and could offer no return but acclamations and pompous decrees engraved on marble. We have no evidence left us how the ordinary resentment of this idle and outspoken populace was manifested; but if I understand the temper of the times, the mere non-attainment of a decree of gratitude may have meant to the rich man that he would be scowled at or hooted when he went abroad, that he would be maligned at headquarters,[1] and put in danger of confiscation by emperors seeking for any fair excuse to replenish their treasury. These decrees, then, formal and foolish as they appear, may have been a sort of title to hold wealth in security and without constant

---

[1] I shall quote in a subsequent chapter Dion's account of the treatment he received from his fellow-citizens, from which the reader will see how far my inferences are justified (cf. also below, p. 309).

molestation. Such are the considerations which explain to me the fantastic phenomena noticed by all the historians of later Greece.

I need hardly add that this distribution of money, in a country where all the capital is in a few hands, where labour emigrates, and where the circulation consists in occasional lavishing of large sums upon a populace which has not earned them, is fatal not only to all material prosperity, but to the moral dignity of the people. We know in our own day nations whose poverty and discontent arise from idleness, from the massing of wealth in the hands of a small minority, and from the extinction of a healthy middle class of farmers and traders. Here, too, we hear the cry, if not yet for confiscations, at least for royal residences, for those Exhibitions which are the modern analogue of the Greek festivals, for any occasional and transitory novelty 'which will bring money into the country,' as the phrase goes. Here, too, sudden plenty, the possibility of earning large wages for slight duties, the pleasure of an exciting stir, are regarded as if they were the return of real prosperity to an idle or decaying society. It is the old story of applying stimulants to revive depression and mistaking the excitement produced for the vigour of returning health.

The economists from Finlay onward who have speculated upon the financial life of the Roman Empire, and its passage from apparent opulence to universal penury or bankruptcy, have noticed as an active cause the great waste of precious metals in furniture and ornaments, as well as their constant exportation to the far East in payment for luxuries such as jewels, unguents, etc., without any parallel production in Europe to induce a return of gold for European industry. Silver, especially, became scarcer and scarcer, so that the reckless Nero had recourse to a debasement of the coinage to relieve his difficulties. This diminution in the circulation of precious metals had a depressing influence on trade, and especially on the condition of the poorer classes. Debt and insolvency became very frequent in Greece, and the Roman usurers who profited by these misfortunes no longer kept large and well farmed estates, as Pomponius Atticus had done, in Greece. The lands of the Greek capitalists, as has been already observed, were in pasture and managed by a few slaves. Mining, once so productive in Macedonia and Greece, had first been discouraged by the Romans, and now, when their jealousy was allayed, seems not to have been capable of revival. At least we hear that the mines of Laurium were exhausted, which we now know was false, and not a word transpires concerning the once prolific mines of Mount Pangæus and Thasos. The precious marble quarries near Carystos in Eubœa were imperial property, and so were probably most of those on the islands. In any case such work required large capital both in slaves and in ships.

The only special manufacture still thoroughly alive in Greece was the manufacture of education, and even in this matter Athens, formerly the capital of universities, and again destined to be so in later days, was now obscured by Rhodes, Alexandria, and Tarsus. We may be sure then that most of the ability in Greece migrated to Italy, where the house-stewards, the secretaries, the schoolmasters, the musicians, the painters, the actors, the dancers, were Greek, and more probably Greeks of the depressed Hellas than of the prosperous Asia Minor or its islands.

I regard the proclamation of the liberty of Greece by Nero as a mere piece of mischievous fooling.[1] Though Philostratus represents the sage Apollonius as indignant at the sensible Vespasian for withdrawing this liberty, we

[1] Cf. the text above, p. 257.

can find no revival of any good thing during this feverish moment. If the people were relieved from taxes they probably injured themselves to more than the amount by passing extravagant measures in their assemblies, and making property insecure by attacks upon the rich. The needy seem to have felt some advantage from it, probably that of voting away other people's money; the strange phenomenon of false Neros arising and drawing a multitude after them cannot otherwise be explained.

These days of Nero are synchronous with the visits of S. Paul. It is indeed almost wholly from the visits of distinguished strangers that we must draw our pictures, until we reach the gentle and patriotic Plutarch. If the history of Apollonius of Tyana had been put together in a sober and critical spirit by Philostratus, we should have had another source of insight into the Greek world of no small importance, but this long and curious book is so evidently a mere fairy tale, composed for the purpose of painting an ideal sage and wonder-worker of the neo-Pythagorean school, that all recent critics have justly rejected it as a source for history. It appears to me a counterpart, not of the life of Christ, as Baur and Zeller maintain, but of the fabulous history of Alexander, which I have elsewhere discussed, and it sets up a moral and religious conqueror of the world in contrast to the king and the man-of-arms.

But let us now return to S. Paul, whose visits to Greece, quite apart from their theological side, will afford us at least one trustworthy and independent picture of the state of things in the cities which the apostle visited. And as we are not concerned with the dogmatic side, so also we need not trouble ourselves concerning the particular years of his visits. His work was certainly under the reign of Nero, and to all appearance before the artistic visit of that eccentric personage had set all Greece into a ferment with its silly benevolences and its serious injustices.

The first entry of the apostle was into Macedonia, where three cities—Philippi, Thessalonica, and Beroea—were the scenes of his labours. Those who have followed with me the total ruin of Macedonia by the Roman conquest will be somewhat surprised when they reflect that S. Paul found at least three flourishing towns in that country. But all these towns were practically new foundations. Thessalonica, formerly Therma, from which the Thermaic Gulf received its name, had been *synœkised* by Casander from the surrounding villages into a Hellenistic town, which attained importance from its mercantile position when Macedonia had been ruined, and so was important enough to be declared a 'free city' when its inhabitants had fortunately sided with Octavian and Antony in the campaign of Philippi.

To mark the site of the great victory at this latter place a Roman colony was established, and so we find S. Paul, on his first arrival in Europe, visiting in succession a town of Roman complexion, and one of the prevalent Hellenistic type, not assimilated to Italian ideas in its internal economy. The commentators on S. Paul's life[1] have shown many interesting differences between these two places, implied by the author of the *Acts* incidentally through his narrative. At Philippi the apostle was charged with preaching a new religion not authorised, and therefore illegal to Roman citizens. He is brought by lictors before prætors, scourged with rods, and finally turns the tables upon his persecutors by claiming to be a Roman citizen, and to have been beaten and condemned without trial, contrary to the established privileges of that favoured class. When he comes to

[1] *E.g.* Conybeare and Howson, *Life, etc., of S. Paul*, i. 357 of the quarto edition.

Thessalonica he has to contend with an assembly of Greek people and their elected magistrates, whom the writer calls by a curious name, *politarchs*, since verified by an extant inscription on the Roman archway at Salonica.[1]

But the common feature in these widely contrasted societies was the presence of a large number of Jews, who naturally, since their wholesale importation by Antiochus the Great to the coast of Asia Minor,[2] had got much of the Levantine trade into their hands, and would of course seize the opportunity of settling in any new foundation made by the Romans. It is plain that the Jewish population were always the first object of the apostle's care, nor do we know of his founding a successful church among pure Greeks, such as the people of Athens or Sparta. It was always among the mixed populations—and wherever they were mixed there were plenty of Jews—that he found the proper soil for sowing his spiritual seed. It is this close combination of cosmopolitan Judæism with cosmopolitan Hellenism which gave the new religion its non-local, non-parochial character, and fitted it (humanly speaking) for the acceptance of the world.

But while this was doubtless the general character of all these new cities, we can see in the apostle's preaching and his persecutions a varying complexion. While, as I have said, at the Roman Philippi he is charged with contravening the Roman ordinances about religion, the charge against him at Thessalonica is that he joins with those who are not Cæsar's friends, and this, together with his emphatic proclamation of the coming kingdom of Christ as spiritual, and not necessarily as proximate, shows that the hope of many Thessalonians was for some new kingdom better and

---

[1] The two narratives are in Acts xvi. and xxii., and with them cf. the chapters (i. ix.) in Conybeare and Howson's excellent book.
[2] *Greek Life and Thought*, p. 487.

milder than the Roman dominion; perhaps even traditions and memories of the old Macedonian glories were still alive among these people, as well as the fresher recollections of the cruel devastations of the Roman conquest. Berœa seems to have gathered into one what remained both of Pella and Ægæ (Edessa), which were now nothing but miserable ruins. This town was some way from the sea, yet the trade of supplying the inland mountaineers was sufficient to induce Jews to settle there also.

From these Macedonian cities S. Paul came directly by sea to the far less congenial Athens, where there were indeed some Jews settled, as we know from sepulchral inscriptions,[1] but where the traditions and interests of the old religions were too strong to admit of any inroads from newer and deeper faiths. The philosophers were indeed ready to hear any new thing, but the temples and images of the gods, which attracted as many visitors as the schools, were still precious to the people, and made Athens the stronghold of paganism long after all real faith in the Greek gods had passed away. All this was consistent with plenty of scepticism in the educated classes, and with many superstitions not strictly Hellenic among the people. The fact that about this time three writers within a century mention altars to the unknown (or unknowable) gods seems to show that this worship was in some respect novel, and though we are at first disposed to set it down as a peculiar form of homage to Demeter and Cora, there may really have been some feeling, such as that suggested by the narrative of the *Acts*, that the anger of some neglected deity could be appeased by anonymous sacrifice. But I am not here going to discuss these points, which have been appropriated

[1] *CIG* iv. 585 *sq.*, where Jewish inscriptions from Athens, Ægina, etc., are quoted.

by theologians. There are controversies enough in the field before us without turning aside to join in the undying strife over New Testament history.

Passing on then from Athens, about which the *Acts* tell us nothing which we could not take or infer from other sources, we come to Corinth, where the apostle spent much time and laboured with great success. Indeed his second epistle is addressed not only to the Corinthians but to the saints throughout the whole of Achaia, a term then including northern Greece as well as the Peloponnesus. But most unfortunately for us, he does not seem to have visited the other two places, where there was a mixed population of Jews, Greeks, and Romans, such as those known to us through his letters. These remaining towns were Patræ and Nicopolis,—each owing its present prosperity to Roman favour, each in the rank of colonies, and Patræ, moreover, a great trading place like Corinth.

I do not think we are warranted in describing all the splendour of Corinth detailed in Philostratus, Lucian and Aristides as belonging to this period, though this course has been adopted by Hertzberg,[1] for we may be certain that after the earthquake in Vespasian's time (about 76 A.D.), his and other emperors' benevolences made the restored town much more magnificent than the old foundation of Julius Cæsar had been. All the descriptions to which I refer date from the days after Hadrian's astonishing display of architecture and engineering over the world. But without doubt Corinth was even in S. Paul's day, and before the visit of Nero, a thriving and beautiful city, less Greek, however, excepting Nicopolis and Patræ, than any other town in the peninsula, and no doubt the most cosmopolitan of all. People from all parts of the world came there; the costumes

[1] *Op. cit.* ii. 239 *sq.*

and the tongues of all nations might be found in its streets.
Here, if anywhere, the miraculous gift of tongues, had it been
intended for missionary purposes, would have found ample
scope for its exercise.[1] Nero's folly and ostentation prompted
him to undertake the cutting of the Isthmus—a project well-
nigh accomplished a few years ago, and suspended,
like Nero's work, from want of funds.[2] When he undertook this work, and all manner of people were pressed in
to help in the digging, there must have been a moment of
strange activity in this thoroughfare.[3] We are told that
at Corinth also, in accordance with its Roman character,
gladiatorial combats, repugnant to the good taste and
humanity of the Greeks, were first introduced, and Dion
notices with horror and disgust that these barbarities had
from thence penetrated to Athens, where a stone balustrade
round the orchestra (pit) of the theatre of Dionysus shows
too plainly the bloody nature of the exhibitions to which
that splendid palace of art was degraded. 'But now there
is nothing which happens there (in Greece) at which a man
would not be ashamed. To give an obvious example, as
regards gladiatorial combats, the Athenians have been so
anxious to rival the Corinthians, or rather have so far
exceeded both them and others in degradation, that while
the Corinthians witness these exhibitions outside their town
in a ravine able to contain a crowd, but otherwise so rough

[1] It is very remarkable that it is to this very church that S. Paul writes in a manner precluding altogether the vulgar supposition that this gift enabled men to preach in foreign languages to the nations of the world. Cf. 1 *Corinth.* cap. xvi.

[2] The project is now, or ought to be, antiquated. Steamers can double Cape Malea without danger or delay, and the railway from Patras to Athens has forestalled any possible passenger traffic.

[3] Philostratus (*vita Apoll.* v. 19), whatever his authority is worth, says that the philosopher Musonius was forced to labour, and tells anecdotes how both he and Apollonius 'improved the occasion.'

and neglected that no one would even bury a free man in it, the Athenians witness this delightful spectacle under the very acropolis, where they have set Dionysus over the orchestra, so that often a man is butchered among the very marble seats, where the hierophant and other priests have their seats.'[1] Perhaps the extant balustrade is later in date than Dion's speech, and was suggested by it. Let me add a pathetic touch from Plutarch :[2] 'I notice among gladiators, if they be not utter barbarians, but Greeks, that when the hour of the show approaches, and a splendid feast is set before them, they prefer to settle their affairs, to entrust their wives to trusty friends, and free their personal attendants.' The wilder races evidently went into the arena after a reckless feast. There is evidence of 'amphitheatre sports' in many other parts of Greece, and in some actually of gladiatorial combats, but I do not think all the instances collected by the learned are trustworthy, and am inclined to think that this non-Hellenic pastime was only adopted in special imitation of the Romans, and where either many Romans or many ostentatious philo-Romans had their homes.[3] The only actual traces of an amphitheatre are said to be at Corinth, and even there they appeared to me so faint as to be very doubtful.

We must not wonder at what may be called this illogical sentimentalism on the part of a nation who systematically

---

[1] i. 385. [2] *Non posse suaviter*, 17.

[3] Cf. Hertzberg, ii. 253, note; Friedländer, *Sittengeschichte*, ii. 383 *sq*. The latter thinks it was only the dregs of the people who liked these cruelties, because Plutarch, Demonax, Lucian, etc., condemn them as barbarous in every sense. He forgets that Romans as good as Trajan and Hadrian openly favoured them, and that probably the remaining wealthy people in Greece were far more likely to be led by the fashion of the Roman court than the philosophy of the Chæronean sage.

approved of torture in judicial proceedings, and who, moreover, for the last three centuries had been accustomed to the semi-oriental punishments inflicted by Hellenistic kings. Such inconsistencies are common in all societies, and the line drawn between the tolerable and the intolerable in public taste can be determined by no logical reason, but rather by the weight and force of a number of conflicting traditions, which together make up that curiously inconsistent thing—a national character. In no case known to me is the composition of this character so complex and therefore so difficult to estimate as in the case of the Hellenistic Greeks. I can give no better example than to turn to the simple and old fashioned life of the period as described in the works of Dion.

The first is the picture he gives[1] of life at Borysthenes, a Greek settlement at the mouth of the Dnieper on the north coast of the Euxine, whose inhabitants had long been severed from their mother country, and surrounded with Scythian barbarians far more intractable to civilisation than Parthians or even Celts. The introduction to this speech, which is really an essay on monarchy, as suggested by Monotheism, or monarchy among the gods, is like the scenery of the oration *on Poverty*, which we shall presently discuss, and therefore I cannot but suspect the former, as I suspect the latter, of being mere dramatic invention. Thus in discussing with the Borysthenites the Platonic view that the rule of one man is best, he never once alludes to the fact that the 'Bosporan kingdom,' which included the Crimea and the Greek marts on either side of it, had now been for a long time under the control of *kings*,—the last kings tolerated within the Roman sway, a nominal kingdom till the reign of Constantine. In Dion's time Pliny mentions a messenger

[1] *Or.* xxxvi.

from king Sauromates coming to Nicæa.[1] If it be, however, true that the town of Olbia (the other name for Borysthenes) was left independent, it would still be more odd that he should discuss with a 'free people' the propriety of monarchy without the smallest allusion to the practical bearing of the question. Still, as he repeats in his *Olympica* that he had visited this outlying region from curiosity, I think we may, in this case, accept the sophist's picture as historical.

He begins with a very graphic description of the city lying on a tongue of land where the great rivers Borysthenes and Tanais meet, and thence continue their course to the sea over vast shallows studded with lofty reeds, which appear like a forest of masts to approaching mariners. Here was the great factory for preparing salt which supplied all the barbarians of the interior. The city itself he found greatly shrunken away by successive stormings of the surrounding barbarians, with whom it had been for centuries at war—the last great reverse being the conquest by the Getæ of the whole coast as far as Apollonia about 120 B.C. From this the Greek cities had never recovered, some being wholly deserted, others rebuilt on a small scale, and obliged to admit barbarians as occupiers.[2] Borysthenes, however, was settled again, to serve as a mart for the Scythians with the Greeks, who would otherwise have abandoned altogether any attempt to deal with the barbarians. Yet even in its restored state the houses were mean and the area of the city contracted. It was attached, so to speak, to part of the old circuit wall, with a few towers remaining of the old size and strength.

---

[1] Ep. 63 *ad. Traj.* with Mr. Hardy's note.

[2] This statement is now corroborated by an inscription of Odessus (Varna), giving a list of priests who had officiated μετὰ τὴν κάθοδον, after the return of the Greeks to their devastated town (cf. *MDI* xi. 201).

The new wall, which joins the arc of the old circuit, is low and weak, and the area within only partially occupied by houses. There are solitary towers still standing out in the country far apart from the present town.[1] Another sign of its old disaster is that not a single statue in the shrines is intact, but all are mutilated, as are also those on the other monuments of the city.

Such was the town which Dion was observing with interest on a summer forenoon from the suburb along the river. Some of the townsmen joined him, and there comes up on horseback a fine young man, who dismounts and gives his horse to an attendant. Under his short light black Greek cloak (black in imitation of the Scythians) he had a huge sword and trousers, and in fact Scythian dress. This Callistratus was reputed equally formidable in battle and zealous in philosophy. Indeed the whole population is so devoted to Homer and to the worship of his Achilles (whose temple is on a neighbouring island), that though they talk very bad and barbarised Greek, most of them have Homer off by heart; a few go so far as to study Plato.

Dion then quotes to them a saw of Phocylides, whose name they do not know, and makes some disparaging remark on Homer and his many details of Achilles's jumping and shouting, while the Gnomic poet gathers much ethical wisdom into a couplet. They tell Dion that but for their extreme respect and liking for him, no citizen of the place would have tolerated any aspersion upon the divine Achilles and the well-nigh divine Homer. But they are ready to hear what Dion has to say, even though they run some risk in discoursing with him outside the city. 'For yesterday at noon the Scythians surprised our sentries, slaying some,

[1] This curious phenomenon may still be seen at the Messene of Epaminondas (cf. my *Rambles and Studies*, p. 391).

and taking others alive, as we did not know which way they had fled, and could not help them, and even then the gates had been shut, and the war signal was flying from the walls. Yet so keen were they that they all came down armed to hear him.' Dion then proposes not to discourse on the promenade, but to go inside the city, and they gather at the public place in front of the temple of Zeus—the magistrates and elders sitting round upon stone steps, and the crowd standing behind them. The sight was delightful to a philosopher, to see these people dressed in antique fashion with long hair and beards, one of them only being cropped and shaven, much to their disgust and contempt. For he was supposed to be obsequious to the Romans, and to have adopted their fashion accordingly.

I need not go into Dion's discourse, which is most politely interrupted by one who tells him how scarce is a decent visitor in these parts. 'For most of the Greeks who come are more barbarous than we are, traders and hucksters, bringing in worthless rags and bad wine and getting nothing better in exchange.' Starting from a query about Plato, Dion then discourses in favour of an intelligent monarchy.

Let us now turn to a very different picture—that of primitive rural life in his seventh oration.[1] 'This,' he opens, 'I am going to narrate from my own experience, not from hearsay. For perhaps loquacity and the difficulty of dropping a subject are not only features of old age—they may also be the characteristics bred by a roving life, probably because in each case there are many experiences which men recall with pleasure. I am now going to tell what men and manners I stumbled upon, I may say, in the midst of Hellas.

[1] Entitled εὐβοικὸς ἢ κυνηγὸς, and even more properly περὶ πενίας, which is the serious subject of the oration.

'I happened to be crossing from Chios with some fishermen in a very little boat, not in the summer season. A great storm rose, and with difficulty we escaped into the "hollows of Eubœa." There they smashed the boat, running her ashore on a rough shingle beach under the cliffs, and they went off to some purple-shell fishers at anchor inside the nearest claw of land, intending to work with them and remain there. So I was left behind alone, with no place of refuge, and I was wandering at random along the shore, on chance of meeting some ship at anchor or sailing by. After a long walk, during which I did not meet a soul, I came upon a buck which had just fallen from the cliff down to the very edge of the water, still gasping as it was being touched by the waves. And presently I thought I heard the baying of dogs far above me, indistinctly by reason of the roar of the sea. Proceeding therefore, and climbing up with great difficulty to the height above me, I found the dogs beating about, which I concluded had forced the game to spring over the cliff, and presently I came upon a man, whose look and dress implied a hunter, of healthy complexion, wearing his hair long behind in no unmanly fashion, but like the Eubœans whom Homer describes coming to Troy. And he hailed me: "Stranger, have you seen a buck coming this way?" to which I answered: "There he is, in the wash of the sea;" and I brought him down to his game. So he drew the buck back from the water, and skinned him with his knife, I helping as well as I could, and then he took the haunches with the skin, and proceeded to carry them away. He invited me too to follow and eat a share of the venison, as his dwelling was not far off. "When you have rested the night with us you can come back to the sea, since at present sailing is impossible; nor need you apprehend that there will be a change while you are resting, for I should be glad to think the storm would subside within the next five days, but it is not likely, so long as you see the mountain tops capped with clouds as they now are." He went on to ask whence I came, and how I got there, and whether my boat was not wrecked. "It was a very small one," I answered, "belonging to fishermen, who were crossing, and I, being pressed for time, was their only passenger, but we were wrecked upon the shore." "Very naturally—look how wild the coast is. This is what they call the 'hollows' of Eubœa, and a ship driven in here hardly ever gets out again. Even the crews are generally lost, unless they are in very light boats, like yours. But come with me, and don't fear. First get over your fatigues, and to-morrow we shall consult what to do to send you on safe, as we have now made acquaintance with you. For you seem to me some city person, not a sailor or a mechanic, and to have worn down your body by some other kind of hardship than theirs." I of course went with him gladly, for I never was afraid of being robbed, having nothing with me but a shabby cloak—so hallowed and sacrosanct a thing have I found poverty, which men violate more rarely even than they would a herald with his insignia.

'On the way he told me how he lived with his wife and children. "There are two of us living in the same place; we have married sisters, and both have sons and daughters. We live mostly by the chase, with the help of a little farming. For the land is not ours, but our fathers were poor and free like ourselves, earning their bread by herding cattle for one of the rich men of this island, who possessed many droves of horses and oxen, many flocks of sheep, many broad acres, and much other wealth; in fact, all the mountains you see around you. But when he died, and his property was confiscated—they say he was put to death by the emperor (βασιλέως) for the sake of his wealth—his herds were at once driven away, and with them some of our few poor beasts, and nobody thought of paying our wages. So we had to remain where we were with what cattle we had left, setting up some tents, and a courtyard fenced with paling, not large but secure, on account of the calves, for our summer use. For in winter we grazed the plains, where we had plenty of grass, and made hay. In the summer we go off to the mountains."' The orator proceeds to describe in detail the beautiful situation of these hunters' home, on a slope close to running water, with fruitful patches of land well manured from their stable, and fair trees giving ample shade. And as they had spare time they turned from herding to hunting with their dogs; for when the cattle were all driven away, two of the dogs who went with them, missing the herdsmen, turned back after some time to their accustomed home. These dogs followed the herdsmen, and only gradually learned to pursue game,[1] being originally mere watch-dogs to keep off wolves. 'But when winter came on, our parents had no out-of-door work, and they never went down to the city or any village; so they made their huts and courtyards water-tight and comfortable, and took into cultivation the land about them, and found hunting far easier in the winter. For tracks are clearer in the wet soil, and snow shows the game far off, and leaves tracks as clear as a high road.' So they settled there, and were content. The two original settlers were now dead, having lived out a hale and vigorous old age. One of their widows still remained. It was her son whom Dion had met. 'The other man [his cousin] has never been to the city, though now fifty years old, but I twice only—once with

[1] He adds a satirical touch: καὶ ἀπέβησαν ἀντὶ βουκόλων τοιοῦτοί τινες ὀψιμαθεῖς καὶ βραδύτεροι θηρευταί.

my father when we kept the great man's herds, and again when a man came asking us for money, as if we had any, and commanding us to follow him to the city. We swore we had none, for we would have given it to him at once if we had. So we entertained him as best we could, and gave him two buckskins, and then I went with him to the city [probably Carystos, though Dion takes care to leave it so vague that Chalcis would suit as well]. For he said one of us must go and tell all about it. So I saw again many great houses and a strong wall round them, with square towers in it, and many ships lying in the harbour, as if in an inland lake. We have nothing like it here, where you landed; that is why the ships get lost. These things I saw and a great crowd gathered together and much confusion and shouting, so that I thought there was a general fight going on.

'The man then brought me to the magistrates, and said laughing: "This is the man you sent me for, but he owns nothing except his back hair and a hut of very strong sticks." Then the magistrates went to the theatre, and I along with them.' The hunter here describes the theatre, adding, 'Perhaps you are laughing at me for telling you what you know quite well. For some time the mob was engaged at other things, at times shouting in good humour and applauding, at times the very reverse. This, their anger, was dangerous, and they terrified the men at whom they shouted, so that some went round supplicating, and some threw off their cloaks in dread, for the sound was like a sudden wave, or thunder. Indeed I myself was almost knocked down by the shout. And various people got up to address the assembly from the midst of it, or from the stage; some with few words, others with many. Some they listened to for a long time, others they would not stand from the outset, or allow them to utter a syllable.

'At last they put me forward also. And one spoke as follows: "This, gentlemen, is one of those who till the public land these many years, not only himself, but his father before him, and they graze our mountains, and farm and hunt and build them many houses, and plant vines, and have many comforts, neither paying any rent nor having a grant from this people. And why, indeed, should they? for holding our lands and becoming rich they never bear the expenses of any public service, or pay any tax on their profits, but live free and without burdens, as if they were public benefactors of our city. Indeed, I suppose they never came here before." Whereat I shook my head, and the crowd that saw me burst out laughing. Then the speaker got angry, and became abusive. "Well, then," he went on, "if you approve of this why don't we all proceed to plunder the public property, whether money or land, if you allow these brutes to own for nothing more than 1000 plethra of land, which would give you three measures of wheat per man?" And I burst out laughing as loud as I could, but the mob no longer laughed but made a noise. Then the speaking man got angry, and scowling at me, said: "Look at the dissembling and insolence of the brute—how he brazens it out and laughs, whom I can hardly refrain from having summarily executed along with his accomplice. For I understand that there are two of them, the ringleaders of the gang who have seized the whole mountain. Indeed I think they are not innocent of wrecking what is driven upon their shore, living as they do near the promontory of Caphereus. How else could they have amassed such wealth in villages and cattle? Don't be misled by his coming here in rags like a beggar. Indeed I shuddered as he seemed to me the traditional Nauplios of the myths coming from Caphereus. Like that person, I doubt not that he shows light from the cliffs in order to decoy ships upon the rocks." When all this and much more had been said the crowd was much excited, and I was in suspense, fearing they would do me some harm.

'Then there rose up another, a respectable man, to judge from his words and dress, and asked for a hearing. He argued that those who occupied and tilled idle land did no harm, but good, and that those only ought to be punished who do it harm ; for see now, he added, "how two-thirds of our territory are deserted through neglect and want of population. I too possess many acres, both in the uplands and in the plain, which if any man will till, I shall not only allow it gratis, but even pay him money to do it. For of course it will become more valuable to me, and waste land is not only useless but a miserable and pitiful sight, showing some misfortune in its owners. You should therefore encourage every occupation of such public land, both by people of means and by the poor, in order that the country may be worked and the people better disposed, when your citizens escape from two crying evils—laziness and penury. Let any of them have it free for ten years, and then pay a small tax on their produce, not on their cattle. Let even a stranger have it for five years, and then a double tax. Whoever tills 200 plethra let him be made a citizen. Since now even the land without the gates is wild and horrid like a remote wilderness, and not the suburb of a city ; and most of what is inside the walls is now in crops and grass. And yet these sycophants attack men who are working hard at our extremest bounds, while they say nothing about those who plough up the gymnasium and graze in the agora. Look yourselves, I pray you, at your gymnasium turned into a corn-field, so that Heracles and the other statues, even those of the gods, are hidden by the crops; the sheep of the last speaker graze every day in the agora round the old public offices, so that every stranger first derides and then pities this city."

'At this the mob was very angry. "Yet he proposes to punish these poor men, so that no one else shall follow their example, but either turn brigands outside or thieves within the city. Let them off, I tell you, with a small tax for the future, or let them buy their land on cheaper terms than you would give it to others." Then followed an angry altercation. At last they told me to say what I chose. "About what?" said I. "In answer to the speeches," said one of those sitting by. [I must abridge the speech that here follows.] "I say then that my accuser told a pack of lies about broad acres and villages. We have nothing of the kind, and would that we had, for we should willingly give them to you and ourselves be fortunate. But take anything we have, if you like, for we can procure other such." At this there was applause, and the magistrate asked me what we could give the people, and I said, "Four very fine buckskins." Then the crowd laughed, but the magistrate grew angry. "The bearskins," I proceeded, "are hard and the goatskins not very good; but take them if you wish." Then he told me I was an absolute boor (ἄγροικος). "Here you are, said I, talking again of fields (ἄγρους), which we don't possess." But he asked me if each of us would give an Attic talent. To which I answered: "We do not weigh out our meat, but will give what we have, dry or salted" [he understands talent to mean a weight for meat]. The magistrate then questions him in detail about wheat, wine, etc., all of which he is ready to give, such as they have, if they will send a man with a vessel to hold them; and he gives a simple inventory of their rustic goods—eight she-goats, a cow and calf, four sickles, four spades, three spears and a knife each to fight the wild beasts, earthen pots, and a wife and children each. They are ready to give up all, provided they are not treated with violence, and are given an empty house in the city, where there are many. But as it is, he suggests that they are innocent citizens, bringing up sons who will fight for the city better than the scolding politicians.

'"But I had well-nigh forgotten," he adds, "the thing I ought to have said first of all. Which of you could believe us guilty of such shocking impiety as wrecking, especially on a coast where nothing comes ashore but splinters. Indeed, the baskets I once found on the shore I pinned up to the sacred oak by the sea. May I never, O Zeus, profit by the misfortune of others![1] But many a time have I pitied the shipwrecked, and brought them home, and escorted them safely out of the wilds. But as I don't know who they were, I cannot now cite them as witnesses. May none of you ever fall into such a plight as to do me this service."

'Thereupon a man started up from the midst and exclaimed: "Long since I thought I recognised him, but was uncertain. But now that I know him, I should be an impious villain not to stand up and speak in his behalf. I, and this man beside me (who then stood up), are, as you know, citizens, and we happened to sail in the ship of Socles two years ago. We were wrecked at Caphareus, and most of us lost. We two made our way up the cliffs with great difficulty and well-nigh naked, hoping to find some shelter with a shepherd, before we died of hunger and thirst. At last we came to some huts, and shouted to those

---

[1] I fear the modern inhabitants of the wild coasts of Europe, even of Scotland and Ireland, entertain very different feelings. All of us know stories of wrecking, and Mr. Purser calls my attention to notes H and I appended to Scott's *Pirate*, as giving the attitude imputed by the demagogue to the innocent rustic.

within, whereupon this man came out and brought us in, and lit a fire, and he and his wife rubbed us with lard, for they had no oil, and then with hot water. Then they fed us and gave us wine, and kept us for three days. And as we departed they gave each of us meat and a fine skin. And seeing me still suffering he took the tunic off his daughter and put it on me, and she had to wear some other rag. This I gave back to him when he had brought us as far as the village. Thus, under providence, do we own our safety to this man." Then I remembered them and said, Hail Sotades, and went up and kissed both him and his friend, at which the crowd laughed loudly. So I discovered that in cities people don't kiss any more.'[1]

So his former defender got up and proposed that for these merits he should be asked to dine in the council house, he should get a new tunic and cloak, have his land free, and be given one hundred drachmæ to stock it, which the speaker offered to contribute himself. All this was carried by acclamation, and the clothes and money brought to the theatre. 'And I wanted not to take them, but they said: "You cannot possibly go to dinner in a leather jerkin." For he had been invited to dine with the magistrates. "Well then," said I, "I will do without dinner to-day." But they insisted on putting me into the clothes, and I wanted to put on the jerkin outside, but they would not stand that. The money I refused absolutely, and said: "Give it to the politician who attacked me, that he may bury it; for he plainly knows how to do that."'

[1] So the contemporary Plutarch says (*Conjug. præcepta*, 13): 'Cato expelled from the Senate a man who kissed his wife in presence of his daughter. This is perhaps going too far; but if it be shameful (αἰσχρόν), as it really is, to be embracing and kissing in the presence of others, how much worse is it to quarrel in their presence? All signs of affection to your wife should therefore be in secret,' etc.

Meanwhile they had approached the hut, and found about it a fair garden full of fruit-trees and vegetables. 'There we proceeded to feast for the rest of the day, sitting upon leaves and skins on a raised bench, the man's wife sitting beside him. But a grown-up daughter waited upon us, and brought us sweet red wine to drink.'[1] We pass by the reflections of the orator concerning this simple but perfect happiness. But then follows an idyllic scene too charming and exceptional in Greek prose literature to be here omitted.

'When we had now well feasted the neighbour came in, and with him his son, a comely youth, carrying a hare. He blushed as he came in, and while his father was saluting us he kissed the girl and gave her the hare. Then the girl ceased serving and sat down by her mother, and the youth attended instead. And I asked mine host: "Is this the girl whose tunic you gave to the shipwrecked man?" and he answered smiling: "No, that one has been married long since to a rich man in the village, and already has big children." "Well then," said I, "they help you when you require it." "We want nothing," said the mother, "but they get their share of our hunting or grapes or vegetables. For they have no garden. Last year we got from them some wheat for seed, but gave it back after our reaping." "And are you going," said I, "to give this girl to another rich man, that he too may lend you seed upon usury?" Whereupon I saw both the youth and the maiden blushing. "No," replied the father, "she will have a poor man, a hunter like ourselves," and he looked kindly towards the youth. "Then why don't you get her married?" said I; "are you waiting for him to come from the village?" "Indeed he is not far off, but here present, and we will have the marriage when we

---
[1] Cf. Plato, *Rep.* ii. 372.

can find a suitable day." "What do you mean by that?" "When the moon is full," said he, "for the air must be pure and the sky clear." "Is he really a good sportsman?" said I. "Well," said the youth, "I can hunt down a deer, and stand up to a boar; you may come and see yourself, stranger, to-morrow, if you like." "Did you run down this hare?" "No," said he smiling; "I took it in a net by night, for the sky is beautifully clear and the moon bigger than I ever saw it." Then the two elder men laughed, and he was ashamed and silent.

'Thereupon the girl's father said, "I am making no delay, but your father is waiting until he can go and buy a proper sacrifice. For we must offer our dues to the gods." Whereupon a young brother of the girl broke in: "But this boy has long since got his sacrifice ready, and it is being fattened to a fine size here behind the hut." And they asked the youth, "Is this so?" and he confessed it. "But where did you get it?" "When we came upon the wild sow with the young ones, all the rest escaped; indeed they were fleeter than hares; but one I knocked over with a stone, and threw my jerkin over it; this I exchanged in the village for a porker, and kept it in a sty I made for it behind the other pig-sty." "So this," said his father, "is why your mother kept laughing when I noticed the noise of pigs, and this is how you used up the grain. Let us see it." So he and the children rushed out in high glee. Meanwhile the girl went out and brought from her store winter apples and fine grapes and other dainties, wiping the table with leaves, and putting fresh ferns under the fruit. Then they brought in the pig with great laughter and jokes. And there came in with them the mother of the youth and two of his little brothers, bringing white bread and boiled eggs and vegetables. She embraced her relations, and sitting down by her husband said: "This is the victim, which he has long been preparing for his marriage: and we have everything else we want, except perhaps a little wine, which we can easily get from the village." And her son stood behind her and watched our host, who said: "Perhaps he wants to wait till he fattens his pig." The lad answered that it was ready to burst with fat.

'"Take care," said I, desirous to back him up, "that while your pig gets fat your boy doesn't get lean." "Indeed the stranger is right," said his mother; "the boy has not been at all like himself, and I noticed him the other night sleepless and walking about outside the hut." "The dogs were barking," said he, "and I went out to see." "Not you," she answered, "but you were wandering about distraught. Let us not distress him any longer;" and she put her arms about the girl's mother. So the latter said to her husband: "Let it be as they desire," and they fixed the day after the morrow for the wedding, inviting me to wait for it. This I was delighted to do, reflecting at the time how different is the life of the rich in this as well as in all else, with their intermediaries, and their inquiries into property and family, with their dowries and presents and promises and deceits, with their bonds and settlements, and often in the end their reproaches and feuds at the very wedding.'

The orator proceeds after this preamble to discuss the prevailing poverty and depopulation of Greek cities, and to recommend the wholesome country life of peasants to the indigent idlers through the towns. He notices, among other points, that at Thebes all but the Cadmea was in ruins, with but a small population, and that there too, as in his picture of the city just drawn, a votive Hermes, set up for some victory in flute-playing, still stood up out of weeds among the ruins in the ancient agora. This then is the kind of reality to be sought in his story, nor need we be duped into taking it for sober history, because he opens with the traditional falsehood of all good story-tellers, that the thing actually happened to himself. I notice that none of his ancient critics ever dreams of regarding the whole speech as anything but a clever piece of rhetoric. Yet as dramatic poetry is declared to be truer than history, so I take this remarkable sketch of the extreme contrasts of town and country to embody a general truth, though I am disposed to think that most neatherds and goatherds in the wilds of Greece were more like the rustics dressed up by Theocritus than like those of Dion. Both authors drew from their poetical imagination; both testify that in the later days of Hellenism, and in the Alexandria which had gone through all its stages in a single generation, there was a growing respect and attraction towards country life, a wholesome reaction against the opposite tendency, so prevalent in the first days of Hellenism.[1]

There were even ridiculous exaggerations of this return to nature, this living in the freedom of the woods, this contempt of athletic sports as compared with field sports and the life of a hunter. Hertzberg has cited[2] from Plutarch, Apuleius, and Philostratus cases of wild men of the woods imitating the life of Herakles, which was always an ideal with the Cynics, and even posing among the country people as the sons of deified heroes. These personages—we know of at least two—despised every form of culture. But surely the *naturalism* of such life is likely to be more prominent than its simplicity. Among the inscriptions collected at Naples is the following:[3] 'We love thickets and caves;

[1] Cf. *Greek Life and Thought*, p. 307. [2] *Gesch. Griech.* ii. 286.
[3] *CIG* No. 5814: δρυμοὺς καὶ ἄντρα φιλοῦμεν, ἄφροντις καὶ φιλοτιμίας ἄνευ ὁ ἐν ὕλαις βίος. ἐν ταῖς ὕλαις ἐλευθερία περιποιεῖται καὶ ἀνάπαυλα ἑτοιμάζεται.

without care or ambition is life in the woods. In the woods freedom is attained and rest prepared.' But the emblems on the *tessera* which contains these simple words are phallic, and it is very plain that the *unreserve* of forest life is the prominent idea in the writer's mind.

We have now come to the end of the lowest and poorest epoch to be found hitherto in the history of Greece. Let us close our chapter, and begin afresh with the gradual rise of Greece, together with all the Empire, under the reformed rule of the Flavian dynasty and their immediate successors.

CHAPTER XIII

PLUTARCH AND HIS TIMES—PUBLIC LIFE

As our principal authority in the last chapter has been Dion, whose activity reached from Greece eastward, so now we shall endeavour to extract what we can from Plutarch, whose experience is mainly from Greece westward. Dion too is plainly an Asiatic Hellenist who looks with contempt on the degradation of the mother-land, while Plutarch regards it with true affection as his home, which he will not abandon lest it may lose even a single honest citizen. In a former chapter we sought to learn the temper of the most cultivated Roman society by searching the works of Cicero, and making his personality the centre round which we grouped our details; it will be convenient to adopt the same plan now, and make the sage of Chæronea the spokesman of the better life which still survived in Greece and the Greek world, in the 'Martinmas summer' of its history. The great biographer is not without his faults. As a stylist he is inferior to Lucian, though with better opportunities, and it is only recently and timidly that modern scholarship is reintroducing his *Lives* into the Grecian studies of the young. He is garrulous too, often repeating his little anecdotes, and urging again his old arguments, wanting perhaps in that humour which is so inestimable a safeguard against twaddle and platitude. But he is very eloquent withal, and very happy in the illustrations he borrows or invents.

Thus, to cite an example or two, he calls the sun the first great prototype of nomad life, seeing that he wanders in his chariot through the pastures of the sky.[1] In the same dialogue he is comparing the relation of God to the soul with that of the soul to the body; 'for the body is the instrument of the soul, as the soul is of God, answering to His touch, as to the Scythian does his bow, or to the Greek his lyre.' He calls sleep the 'lesser mysteries' (the initiation to the great mystery) of death. Again, he says: 'The soul is as it were enclosed in the body like an oyster in its shell, because it remembers not from what honour or wealth it has been exiled—not from Sardis to Athens, not from Corinth to Lemnos or Syros, but taking this poor earth in exchange for heaven and the moon; and yet if it be moved here but a little way from place to place, it frets and feels strange, like a poor growth that will not bear transplantation without withering.'[2] There are also pathetic traits of very modern aspect, as when he describes the Thracian and Celtic gladiators preparing for the combat by eating and drinking the rich banquet given to these doomed men, while those of Greek blood spend these precious moments in taking leave of their families and giving advices to those who will hear them no more.[3] Another very touching passage is that in which he notes the fact that no infant ever smiles in the waking moments of its first few weeks, but

---

[1] This is in the mouth of the Scythian Anacharsis *Sept. Sap. Conv.* 12.
[2] *De exilio.* sub. fin.
[3] *Non posse suaviter*, etc. 17.

only when it falls asleep. This he explains by the Platonic doctrine that the transplanted soul is disturbed and terrified by the aspect of this world, which it regards with displeasure, while in sleep it recalls its happier state with God and smiles at the glorious vision.[1] Had Wordsworth known this passage we should probably now have it in a splendid poetical form.

Still more eloquent than these specimens of rhetoric is that moral dignity which he has given to great historical characters, so that the leading men of the world from that day to our own have been more influenced by the *Parallel Lives* than by any other book we could name, even from the most classical period, and of the most classical purity. We feel him, as we feel Sir Walter Scott, not only the originator[2] of an inestimably instructive form of historiography, but also essentially a gentleman—a man of honour and of kindliness, the best type of the best men of his day. He lived indeed in times very different as to taste from the times of Scott, and in a widely different society. Though far more modern and developed in many respects, the world of Plutarch, with all its art, its literature, its criticism, had features still clinging to it which we cannot but regard as revolting. These terrible stains on the polished surface of Hellenism Plutarch and his fellows censured and deplored, but not in the language of disgust and horror which would burst from the lips of any ordinary reader to whom I should dare to present the details. The *naturalism* of the Greek was not extinguished by any amount of refinement, and so we find the amiable and pure-minded sage implying as a

[1] περὶ ψυχῆς, fr. 13.
[2] There were of course previous biographers, as there were previous novelists, but neither are worth mentioning in comparison with the two great masters.

matter of course in his advices that a wife must be prepared to overlook her husband's infidelities, provided they are committed away from home; that growing boys will be shown pictures which they must be taught to regard as mere art to prevent their learning lessons in immorality. So also we find him in a discourse upon the worship of Isis, addressed to Klea, a distinguished priestess of a guild at Delphi, discussing the exhibitions of the generative principle in nature with an unreserve which we should not tolerate in conversation, not to say in a published missive to a lady.

The fact that these things occur casually in his writings persuades me to treat them as evidence far more valuable than the often rhetorical generalities with which he introduces a moral subject, as when, for example, he prefaces his tract *on Brotherly Love* with the stock-complaint that this with the other virtues is disappearing from among men, and that now its occurrence is regarded with the same surprise as its absence was in simpler days.[1] There were pure affections, strong attachments, lasting friendships then as in every epoch of extended culture.

But while every student of Hellenism during this time of Roman influence must admit certain unpleasant features, I protest against employing as historical evidence another writer, largely cited by all the German authorities who have discussed the morals of waning Greece. Both Friedländer in his monumental *Sittengeschichte* and Hertzberg in his meritorious *History*, as well as Göll and others who are mere essayists, make large use of the novel of Apuleius, called his *Metamorphoses*, as giving a fair picture of Northern Greece and its society in the generation now before us.

---

[1] Hertzberg (ii. 283) quotes this statement just as other German critics quote the famous reflections in Thucydides's third book, without any suspicion or any feeling of their exaggeration.

It tells the adventures of one *Lucius*, who narrates in the first person that his family on the father's side had its ancestors in Athens, Sparta, and Corinth, while his mother's relations are to be found in Thessaly. The father's pedigree has all the appearance of a clumsy attempt to assert respectability among the ignorant by parading a catalogue of famous city names. The mother's connection was required by the plot of the book, for Lucius must be brought to Thessaly to stumble upon the witchcraft and witches whom the poets had long since located there, and a great Thessalian lady, who is his maternal aunt, plays a prominent part for some chapters. The mother, however, of this Attico-Corintho-Spartan youth, who herself hails from Thessaly, is called in good Latin Salvia, and his aunt Byrrhæna. He says he was nurtured as a boy at Athens, and learned Latin at Rome with difficulty, and this he makes an excuse for his style. But if his style has faults, if it has a Greek and an artificial flavour, it is surely not from late or imperfect knowledge of Latin. No author of the period is richer in vocabulary, more profuse in rhetoric, more various in idiom. Exuberance is the main characteristic of his style. The danger which he felt arose from another cause. He was translating and adapting from Greek stories, and says it plainly enough in his opening words. He calls his novel a *Græcanica fabula*. He interlards it perpetually with digressive tales very like in character to those of the *Decamerone*. These were the 'Milesian Tales' which he utilised, and which we find worked up into the later Greek novels of Xenophon Ephesius, Achilles Tatius, and others.[1] He is in fact repeating Greek fairy tales or robber stories, and placing them in a geography of his own.

[1] They are collected in the *Scriptores Erotici Græci*, published in the Teubner series, and edited by Hercher.

He begins, as I have said, in Thessaly, for he desired to dilate upon witchcraft and describe the transformation of his hero by these arts into an ass. But where is the *nobilissima civitas*, the renowned city of Hypata, where his hero begins his adventures? It is not known to Strabo in his careful survey of the Thessalian towns. It never appeared prominently, except only in one long-past campaign, that of the Romans against Antiochus the Great and the Ætolians,[1] though Thessaly was so often 'Mars's orchestra.'

During most of the succeeding adventures and wanderings of the transformed hero with his various masters, the author confines himself to the formula, *devenimus in aliam quandam nobilem civitatem*, 'we come to another distinguished city,' and it is well, for when he does attempt closer precision and describes an assault of robbers upon Thebes, he regards this city as upon the sea-coast! The robbers, being beaten off with the loss of two of their leaders, think it best to bury them in the sea before retiring to the neighbouring Platæa! And here a rich citizen was preparing to give a great enter-

---

[1] The only literary occurrence of the name I can find is in Livy xxxvi. 16-30, where he copies from Polybius the details of this war, and Hypata is the usual meeting-place for negotiations between the Roman Lucius and the Ætolians. It is called there a town of Thessaly, but was really the central town of the Ænianes on the northern slopes of Mount Œta. Strabo (ix. 4, § 11) says they were completely ruined by the Ætolians and the Athamanians under king Amynander. He mentions no town on the north slope of Œta, and seems to have little information about the district. Had Hypata then been of the smallest note it could not possibly have escaped him. I will add that Hertzberg (ii. 19, note) cites from Ross an inscription mentioning the friendship of a citizen of Hypata with Germanicus, and *CIL* iii. 586 alludes to a quarrel between Hypata and Lamia. There are a few Greek inscriptions in which the name occurs, *CIG* 1717, 1774, etc., and another in *BCH* i. 120. Pliny (*H. N.* xxv. 5, 49) alludes to its hellebore. Hertzberg only expresses a faint doubt about the splendour of this Hypata (ii. 209).

tainment in the way of a gladiatorial show with numbers of wild beasts to his fellow-citizens—at Plataea! We know indeed from Pausanias that the old temples still stood there, and that yearly and five-yearly feasts were still celebrated in honour of the ancient victories over the Persian. But if every indication we have both in Pausanias and Strabo be not false, Plataea was like all its neighbours a decayed and empty village, living upon the tourists who came to see its antiquities, and only waking up annually to receive those who gathered to celebrate its venerable feasts.

The whole geography of the book is, therefore, either from ignorance or deliberate carelessness unreal, and full of such violations of fact as the author could have avoided by any superficial acquaintance with Northern Greece. His account of Corinth, on the other hand, speaks of clear personal knowledge. He knows the new and brilliant city; he knows its harbours, and the feasts celebrated there to Isis and other deities. But here it is that he portrays to us such a state of public morals that I refuse to accept his evidence for the social condition of even the Greek towns which he knew. He not only describes the most monstrous immoralities as being committed by women of wealth and position with impunity, but when they become known, preparations being actually made to repeat these hideous violations of all natural decency in the public theatre for the amusement of the populace. It is impossible for me to repeat a single detail in the story. But I am convinced that very Roman as was the complexion of New Corinth, very immoral as was the atmosphere of that city at all times, very extravagant as may have been the license of the many oriental traders who resorted thither—and we know what the sport of orientals is from the *Arabian Nights*—no such exhibition could ever have been tolerated in any civilised city of the first century save only at Rome, and at the court of Nero in Rome. Suetonius—and is he credible ?—tells us of similar bestialities performed before Nero,[1] and it is here only that our author could have found the facts, which he adapted to another scene. If such things ever were thought of at Corinth, it was in imitation of the orgies of Nero.

I suggest, therefore, that the strange book of Apuleius, with its mixture of extravagant obscenity, enthusiastic ritualism, gross naturalism culminating in the strictest piety, was written with a strong Roman flavour by a Roman, for the depraved society of Nero's court, and that the crimes piled up upon the Greeks of Thessaly and Bœotia are partly the gross inventions of the Milesian fablers, partly the depraved imaginings of that emperor's intimates. We might as well charge all society in France with being addicted to one form of vice, because recent French fiction occupies itself almost exclusively with this as the material for its plots. The society *for which such books are written* must have shown that they are to its taste ; the society *which such books portray* may be wholly different, and grossly libelled by being made to reflect the vices of the author and his readers.

The whole problem is complicated by the fact that a novel attributed to Lucian, called *The Ass*, but now rejected from his works by critical editors, gives the same story in a much briefer form, with close similarity of details, but omitting many of the irrelevant digressions of Apuleius, as well as his pious conclusion.

It is perfectly plain that either author has copied the other, unless both have copied from a common source. The now prevalent theory seems to be that Apuleius copied and enlarged Lucian's story ; but there is this grave difficulty,

---

[1] Nero, cap. 12. Cf. Tac. *Ann.* xv. 37.

that both writers were about contemporary; indeed I am not sure that we can prove Lucian the senior. Internal evidences are to me still more destructive of the theory. I ask any man of common sense, is it more likely that a superstitious and enthusiastic writer should have taken for his model a scurrilous and sceptical story and grafted his piety on this stock, or that a sceptic should have taken from a verbose and ample original, full of superstition and devotion, the substance for a more compendious satire upon such old wives' fables? The date of both authors, however, being clearly beyond the limits of this volume—for they lived under Hadrian and the Antonines—I should not have entered upon this discussion were it not that both, in my opinion, borrowed from an older Greek original, *The Metamorphoses of Lucius of Patrae*, which the patriarch Photius[1] read along with the story of Lucian, and then expresses his hesitation which of the two was the original. He decides very sensibly that Lucius is the prior, because he is much fuller and because he writes in a credulous and naïve spirit. These are the very features which distinguish the version of Apuleius from that of Lucian, so that the inference seems obvious that we have in Apuleius's work a more faithful copy of the (now lost) original which Lucian, or some brother sceptic, reduced in length, traduced in spirit, and brought out independently of the Latin version. This Lucius of Patræ then must have lived within the first century (probably under Nero), if his work became, early in the next, the model of an African and of a Syrian author, both of whom probably learned to know it during their early studies at Athens.

But the arguments above urged against the historical value of Apuleius's copy still lie against the citizen of Patræ.

[1] Cod. 129.

The introduction concerning his journey and the company on the way, with stories interlarded somewhat in Chaucer's fashion, gives us a real picture of what a citizen of the Roman colony of Patræ, a Greek with a Roman name, would know familiarly. But his deliberate intention is to be fabulous, and to assert the powers of magic and the violations of nature to be leading facts in our daily life. These are the reasons which forbid me to follow the example of Hertzberg,[1] and to entertain my readers with marvellous tales of robbers, and of the wealth and refinement of country towns in Thessaly. Such simplicity in a critic is no doubt refreshing to the reader, but only instructive as a psychological reflex of the mind which displays it. Let us return to the soberer Plutarch.

The general effect produced by the many pictures, allusions, references, illustrations he takes from the Greek world of his times shows clearly that romantic adventures, great passions, monstrous crimes were foreign to the small and shabby gentility of Roman Greece. The highest rewards he can set before the keenest ambition are no better than if we should now fire our youths' imaginations with the prospect of becoming parish beadles, vestrymen, or even town councillors. He confesses honestly that a rescript from the Roman governor brooks no delay in obedience, and that all attempts to stir up a spirit of real independence are worse than futile. This was what drove sterner and stronger spirits into the refuge of philosophy, the Cynic's cloak and beard, the Stoic's contempt of worldly goods, the Epicurean's patronising smile at the tea-cup storms of local rivalries.

But Plutarch was a man who abhorred extremes. He loved compromises. In philosophy his adherence to the Academy was loose even for that very broad and undogmatic

[1] *Gesch. Griech.* ii. 281 *sq.*

school. It would be hard to say whether the number of Stoic dogmas which he rejects exceeds that which he quotes with approval. While he inculcates submission to the powers that be, he is always advocating a spirit of dignified independence almost inconsistent with that submission. While he teaches monotheism and the spirituality of God in words of splendour, and while he feels the strength and comfort of religion pure and undefiled, he will not abandon the old temples and their sacrifices. Even the vulgar prose responses of the rustic Pythia and her proletarian priests, interpreting the advice of Apollo upon questions too trivial to deserve a literary reply—even this he defends with his conservative spirit because the oracle is old, because it was once highly honoured and is still morally useful; he also devises many subtle and plausible arguments to support his opinion. He will not adopt with Plato the equality of the sexes, or with the Stoics the injustice of slavery, or with the Pythagoreans the rights of the lower animals to justice at the hands of men, yet he goes a long way with all three—magnifying the position and the dignity of the house-mother both by example and precept, inculcating everywhere kindness and consideration to slaves, adopting even vegetarian doctrines in some of his earlier treatises, and upholding with satire and with paradox the superior insight and intelligence of the animals we patronise or oppress.

His leading feature, and he lets us see that he is both conscious and proud of it, is sympathy with all his fellows; his leading ambition is in consequence to act as adviser and director to all that need it—from the king on his throne and the councillor in his ripe old age to the giddy youth and reckless child. We have in every society instances of that amiable vanity, which is indeed not uncommon in advanced age among those who love their fellows, and think that the lapse of years has of necessity brought wisdom in the wake of ample experience.

We may notice that this general direction of consciences assumed by Plutarch is very much confined to Greek life and habits, and only applicable in a general way to Romans. He dedicates indeed many of his treatises to Sossius Senecio, and other distinguished persons at Rome, where he had delivered public lectures when a young man.[1] The atmosphere of Rome, however, seems to have been distasteful to him, and he spent all his mature life in Chæronea, perhaps as distinctly the last of the Greeks as his contemporaries Juvenal and Tacitus are 'the last of the Romans.'

Let us develop into detail some of these general statements. We must remember, when weighing Plutarch's statements concerning the politics still possible for an ambitious Greek that, whether from the influence of the great master of his school, Plato, or from a practical view of things similar to that of Polybius—indeed of all the literary classes in all ages of Greek life—he was strongly opposed to democracy in the modern sense. He regarded the lowering of the franchise to include free paupers as idle and mischievous. He thinks that monarchy is ideally the most perfect state;[2] he is perhaps alone among literary

[1] *De curios.* 15.—'Once when I was lecturing at Rome, and that Rusticus whom Domitian afterwards put to death from envy of his reputation was among the audience, an orderly came right through the room and handed him a missive from Cæsar. So when there was silence, as I paused that he might read the letter, he would not have it so, and refused to open it till my lecture was over and the audience dismissed.' An interesting glimpse into a Greek lecture-room at Rome.

[2] *De Monarch.* etc. 4. In the various definitions of a democracy put into the mouths of the seven sages, if that dialogue be genuine (*Sept. Sap. Conviv.* 11), the will of the majority is never once mentioned as a mark.

Greeks in admitting the justice and the usefulness of many tyrants;[1] he holds that the liberties still accorded to the Greek towns are as much as they can bear. What they have lost, he thinks, is counterbalanced by the peace and security afforded through Roman sway. 'For see[2] that if we enumerate the greatest blessings which polities[3] enjoy— peace, liberty, material prosperity, populousness, harmony— as far as *peace* is concerned the communities have nothing to desire from their politicians; every Greek, every barbarian war has departed from us and vanished;[4] as regards *liberty* they have as much as the rulers accord to such communities, and perhaps as much as is good for them.[5] *Good seasons* and *populousness* are blessings to be sought from the gods.'[6] But while he goes on to advise against *discord*, which can only be allayed by the skill and good temper of local leaders, it is very interesting that he feels, almost like Edmund Burke,[7] the value of parties in each state.

[1] *De sera num.* 6-8.   [2] *Reip. ger. præc.* 32.

[3] I think it best to use this old-fashioned word to describe that sort of community which is a single city and yet counts as a separate state, the Greek πόλις, of which Monaco, San Marino, and Hamburg are or were up to our own generation the only modern examples.

[4] See a parallel passage on the safety and comfort of life at this time, *de tranquill.* ii.

[5] ἐλευθερίας δέ, ὅσον οἱ κρατοῦντες νέμουσι τοῖς δήμοις, μέτεστι, καὶ τὸ πλέον ἴσως οὐκ ἄμεινον.

[6] The rest of this important passage I shall quote in the sequel (pp. 305, 306). Here is another casual piece of evidence. A friend gallops out on horseback to announce to the company talking together at Helicon (Thespiæ) that a fair widow in Thebes has just kidnapped a youth whom she desires to marry. The excited rider introduces his news thus: 'Ye Gods, what will be the end of this liberty, which is upsetting our polity? For now matters have passed through autonomy into lawlessness' (anomy—a pun).

[7] Cf. W. H. Lecky, *Hist. of Eng. in the Eighteenth Century*, iii. 196 *sqq.* for a masterly statement of the uses and abuses of party government.

His examples are indeed derived from the political days of Greece, but the passage is very interesting.[1] Since every public is ill-natured and censorious towards its politicians, and suspects that whatever is done without opposition and debate is managed by a sort of conspiracy (for which reason political clubs and brotherhoods are in such bad repute), no just cause for hatred and variance must be allowed. We should act like Onomademus, demagogue of the Chians, who when he got the upper hand in a political struggle would not allow all his opponents to be banished, 'lest we begin to quarrel with our friends when no enemies are left us.' This was perhaps silly, adds Plutarch, and then, with his usual habit of compromise: 'But when the crowd is suspicious of some great and salutary measure, it is inexpedient that all the speakers should agree about it, as if by pre-arrangement, but two or three should dissent, and oppose in a friendly way the proposal, and then give in after some persuasion. For in this way, appearing to be convinced by sound arguments, they will carry with them the populace. Also in trifling matters it is better that members of the Government should have and express real differences of opinion, so that on vital matters their harmony shall not appear pre-concerted. It is only a finer form of the old adage attributed to Jason, the famous tyrant of Pheræ: "Those who desire to do justice in great things must be unjust in small."'[2] Here we have an antique example, as is usual with Plutarch, and indeed when he does illustrate his precepts by modern cases, we find ourselves

---

[1] *Reip. ger. præc.* 16. Cf. also the remark of Melanthius (*de aud. poet.* 4), that Athens was saved by the conflicts of her politicians.

[2] *Reip. ger. præc.* 24. It is the reverse of a famous observation in Machiavelli's *Principe*, whose great injustices are prepared by strict justice in trifles.

baulked by ignorance of all the details, as is so often the case with our reading of Aristotle's *Politics*.

There is one famous figure in the older days whom we seek in vain throughout Plutarch's world—the demagogue who gained power and wealth by virulent political opposition, whose public spirit and private ends were so interwoven that the most diverse judgments upon his honesty and policy could be equally justified. Such were men of the type of Cleon, Caius Gracchus, even Julius Cæsar, to take the most brilliant examples. All scope for this kind of talent was now gone. If there was indeed a low, self-seeking person, whose ambition was the mainspring of action, he no longer courted the *demos* of his town, even were it Athens or Ephesus, but the Roman governors, or the Roman court,[1] if he could contrive to go on an embassy to the capital. We hear constantly from Plutarch of this type, which seems even to have invaded social life to a degree unknown and intolerable to us.[2] The higher class of demagogue, the man of true political ambition, had no field whatever left for his energies. 'Nothing else remains,' he tells us in the sequel of the passage above cited, 'than this, which is not less important than any of the other blessings I have enumerated, in producing harmony and goodwill

[1] It is, I think, remarkable that all through this tract *on Policy* Plutarch never alludes to the communal flattery of the towns which awarded divine honours not only to the emperors who claimed them (such as Caligula and Nero) but to those who repudiated them, nay, even to their female relations (Livia, Drusilla, etc.), and even to provincial governors like Lucullus and Censorinus. This was surely the most prominent and is to us the most disgraceful flattery of the day. The tract *Whether Vice suffices for Misery* opens with an amusing account of what we call *snobbery*, of people who thrust themselves forward uninvited, and submit to all manner of trouble, insult, and neglect in order to carry off some memento of the favour of kings.

[2] Cf. his whole tract *on The Flatterer and Friend*.

among those that dwell together, and allaying all strife and variance, as one would among personal friends ;—I mean approaching first the party that feel most aggrieved, identifying oneself with their griefs and repeating their complaints, then gradually soothing them, and teaching them that men who forego their victory in a quarrel are superior not only in gentleness, but in loftiness and greatness of soul; and that a small concession will now give them a great and substantial victory. And then one should teach them both individually and collectively the weak condition of Greek polities, fit to enjoy thorough quiet and concord, if men of sense will make the best of it, since no higher prize has been left us to win by fortune. For what glory, what dominion is left for those that prevail, what power which the brief mandate of a proconsul hath not abolished or transformed, nay, even if it remain is it worth any trouble? For as a conflagration seldom starts from temples or public buildings, but some lamp neglected in a private house, or a rubbish-heap set on fire has set up a great blaze and wrought public loss and damage, so public rivalries do not always precede a revolution, but differences starting from private affairs have often broken out into public affairs, and upset the whole polity.' He proceeds to illustrate this principle by cases notorious to his hearers, but now passed into oblivion.

Dion, in whom we can find parallel passages to most of Plutarch's pages, says very similar things in his forty-eighth oration, addressed to his countrymen at Prusa. He entreats them to settle their differences peaceably, now that the excellent Varenus, the Roman governor, has allowed them again the right of public meeting, and above all things to make no difficulties about accounting for the public money, into which Varenus will certainly inquire, whether they like it or not. The orator describes the same condition of things which Pliny gives us in his *Letters* from the Roman point of view.

It is this altered state of public life which justifies Plutarch's portrait of the ideal Greek citizen, the popular man in the true sense of the word, a portrait which we cannot but suspect to be intended for his own. For the naïve self-consciousness of the man appears through every part of his works. In this, as in so many other features, both of his inner spirit and his outward surroundings, does he remind us of Polybius, whose principles and policy, though adopted at the very outset of this decadence, were so closely analogous. Upon this resemblance I desire particularly to insist, for I know no more remarkable evidence of the persistence of the same kind of life and thinking in Greece for at least 200 years.

Here is the portrait in question : First of all let him be easy of access, and the common property of all, keeping open house, as it were a harbour of refuge to all that need it; showing his protection and his generosity not merely in cases of want and by active help, but also in sympathy with the afflicted, and rejoicing with those that rejoice ; never annoying others by bringing with him a crowd of attendants to the public baths, or by securing good places at the theatre; never notorious for his offensive luxury and lavishness, but living like the rest of his neighbours in dress and diet, in the bringing up of his children, and the appointments of his wife, as intending to be a man and a citizen on a par with the public about him. He should also be ever ready to give friendly advice and gratuitous advocacy, and offer sympathetic arbitration in differences of man and wife, of friend and friend, spending no small part of the day on the bema[1] or

---

[1] From which, as from the French *tribune*, councillors seem to have addressed the assembled people.

in the market-place, and in all his other life drawing to him, as the south wind does the clouds, wants and trusts from all sides, serving the state with his private thoughts, and not regarding politics, as many do, a troublesome business or tax upon his time, but rather a life's work. By these and all other such means he attracts and attaches to him the public, which contrasts the bastard and spurious fawning and bribing in others with this man's genuine public spirit and character.[1]

There had been days when such a man would have hoped for absolute sway in his city, nor do Plutarch's tirades against tyrants, copied from the commonplaces of the old dispossessed aristocrats, outweigh his distinct preference for the rule of one man, whose duty it once had been, if he were convinced of his own fitness, to assume the diadem. But now all that a popular politician could gain was the responsibility and burden of expensive honorary duties. In the tract *Upon Exile*, a very rhetorical performance, which rather makes a case than expresses a conviction, the main profit of exile is represented as the escape from these duties. 'You have no longer a fatherland dragging at you, bothering you, ordering you about; crying: pay taxes, go on an embassy to Rome, entertain the governor, undertake public festivals.'[2] Of these requirements I fancy the journeys to Rome must have been the most exacting. For though very young men might greatly enjoy a trip to the capital, even with the risks of dying abroad,[3] the envoys sent with formal compliments, in the hope of obtaining real benefits, were more likely to be

---

[1] *Reip. ger. praec.* 31.   [2] § 8.
[3] Like the youth lamented by Crinagoras who seems to have been one of the attendants on such an embassy (cf. Cichorius, *Rom und Mytilene*, p. 53).

elderly men; they were not certain to find the emperor at Rome, and must follow him even to the pillars of Hercules, or at least through Italy, where the inn-keepers were notorious extortioners;[1] and moreover the waiting in ante-rooms, the insolence of Roman senators and Imperial officials, must have been galling even to an obsequious Greek. We can well imagine how the public at home, who were ready to accord them statues and honorary inscriptions if they succeeded, would treat them if they returned without gaining their object—by far the most likely result. But of these failures we have not, of course, many records, and these I shall examine in due course. We have now to consider the many inscriptions which rewarded the successes of such missions.

We cannot but wonder how the extraordinary profusion of these latter, even among the scanty remains still extant, did not so detract from their value as to make them utterly contemptible, like the innumerable crowns to be gained at various local contests, which Plutarch calls mere rubbish ($\sigma\nu\rho\phi\epsilon\tau\acute{o}s$). Long since a Roman conqueror had refused the honour of a statue in Greece with the remark *turmales sibi displicere*,—'that he did not like the regiment.'[2] But the adherence of the Greeks to honours and occupations once dignified, and hallowed by long use, seems incapable of feeling the effects of wear and tear, the stress of weariness or the shafts of ridicule. All these pompous enumerations of civic virtues and benefits went on from generation to generation, and now became one of the main features in public life.

[1] *Symp.* ii. 1.—'Worse than the Italian inn-keepers, who on the eve of a battle, when the enemy are upon them, keep an accurate account how much liquor each man who dined with them has consumed.'

[2] Cic. *de Orat.* ii. 65. The argument urged above (p. 263) also applies in this more special case.

The desire of semi-Hellenistic dynasts to be thus honoured, and inscribed on stone as benefactors of the Greeks, was of course very natural, and we have already found in Herod a specimen of that type. The inscriptions afford us many more. Thus [1] Ariobarzanes Philopator, king of Cappadocia late in the first century B.C., is lauded for having restored with the help of Roman builders the Odeum at Athens, burnt in the Mithradatic war. In the next number of Bœckh's collection his son Eusebes philo-Romæus is honoured by the Athenian people. Again [2] the last descendant of king Juba, Ptolemy (who was put to death by Caligula), is commended for adorning the statue of his ancestor, the Egyptian Ptolemy. These were kings, but there are many mere Roman citizens mentioned in the succeeding numbers, all from Athens.[3] We find, moreover, constant compliments paid to citizens of other cities in Greece.

For I will add that if the centralising of the world's power at Rome had as yet failed to produce any real unity of sentiment throughout the Empire, it had at least produced, after so many abortive attempts in earlier history, a real social unity throughout Greece. Thus Plutarch lays the scenes of his entertainments and friendly conversations almost indiscriminately through Greece, at Delphi, Athens, Hyampolis, Elis, Ædepsus, Thespiæ, Corinth, without any other feeling than that Greeks are all friends and neighbours. Apuleius, if he were to be trusted, makes the wealthy society of Hypata even quite Roman in style, and describes many specially Roman luxuries at the feast of Byrrhæna, who

[1] *CIG* No. 358.
[2] *CIG* No. 360. This sort of decree is preserved in hundreds of examples.
[3] Here is a specimen (No. 367): ὁ δῆμος κ.τ.λ. Μάρκον 'Αρτώριον εὐεργεσίας καὶ εὐνοίας ἕνεκα. He was a physician of Augustus, drowned after the battle of Actium.

behaves like a very free Roman lady, not like a Greek. I think the lists of *proxeni* recently discovered, informing the citizens of each place, who intended to travel, whom they would find in each city, ready to be their official friend, are very significant. We have from Narthakion in Thessaly[1] even a list of the *proxeni* of other cities residing in that town, so that the stranger on his arrival could at once find and apply to his own official host. We have also many inscriptions telling us of arbitrations in local quarrels, referred to, and settled by Greek cities quite remote, and not connected by any but the general bond of Hellenism with the disputants.[2]

Plutarch shows us a greater conservative persistence in the second main department of public life, *religion*—ritual and festivals which were the public relaxation, as contrasted with politics, which were still the pretended business of every Greek polity. On this side of life the information our author gives us is not less explicit, and full of the same inconsistencies. It will be understood that for the present I shall omit all account of philosophy as a school of morals, a very notable part of Greek religion in one sense, but wholly dissociated from the traditional rites and ceremonies, and the traditional theologies, of the people. It is the general effect as regards public worship in the temples and at oracles, and at the established festivals, which I seek now to derive from Plutarch. Nor is the task very easy for a man of compromises, who desires to adopt reforms and yet retain the old courses, who would be a philosopher and yet a defender of tradition. I think his real attitude is best to be gathered from the following very noble passage:[3] 'For the deity is not a thing without soul or spirit under the hand of man [he has just been censuring the use of Demeter for

[1] *BCH* vi. 587. [2] *BCH* vi. 247. [3] *De Iside*, 67.

wheat, and of Dionysus for wine], but of such material gifts have we considered the gods to be the givers, who grant them to us continuously and adequately—the gods who differ not one from the other, as barbarian and Greek, as of the south or of the north; but if the sun and the moon and heaven, earth, and sea, are the same to all, though they be called by different names, so for the One Reason that sets all these things in order and the One Providence that controls them, and for the subordinate forces that direct each several department, various honours and titles have been established by law among divers nations, and men use hallowed symbols, here obscure, there clearer, which lead our thoughts to God, not without risk of failure; for some have slipped altogether from the path, and fallen into superstition, while others avoiding the slough of superstition have gone over the precipice of atheism.'

All the peculiarities of Plutarch's theology are here stated or implied. If he meant to uphold the many foreign rituals which had come into Hellenism from the old religions of Asia Minor and of Egypt, especially those of Isis and of Mithras, he must hold the identity of many local gods of various names, and this is the main purpose of his long treatise on Isis and Osiris—Isis, whose worship we find established in a special temple at Pompeii on a par with the Helleno-Roman gods; Osiris, into whose worship Klea, the high priestess of the (Dionysiac) Thyiadæ at Delphi, was initiated by right of heredity.[1] He tries to show in myriad instances that the rituals of Egyptians and Greeks were the same in idea; and as regards the myths, he has recourse to either of the explanatory processes which he strongly deprecates when their consequences are carried out boldly—rationalism and allegory. The former was the Epicurean, the

[1] *De Iside*, 35.

latter the Stoic device, adopted of course by other schools in their turn. Plutarch will only adopt them when they suit his convenience, and supplements them with another 'theory of evasion' which made a great noise in the early Christian controversies. I mean his doctrine[1] of *demons*, or beings intermediate between man and God, who are both beneficent and maleficent, in fact both angels and devils, and to whom are to be attributed all the polytheistic vagaries of popular mythology. The so-called immoralities of the gods, so great a stumbling-block to every sober critic, were all to be referred to the maleficent demons.

But there was another and a greater difficulty, which has not yet departed from theology. I mean the explanation not of the alleged immoralities committed by the gods, but of human immoralities being permitted by them without inflicting condign punishment. This difficulty was then, and has been ever since, one of the strongest stays of atheism. Nor could Plutarch appeal like the modern apologists to a firm belief in future rewards and punishments as his principal support, even though he does compose a long myth at the end of his treatise, in imitation of the close of Plato's *Republic*, wherein Nero's soul appears studded with red hot nails,[2] and wherein, along with the usual tortures of hell, the delights of the Elysian fields are also portrayed. But this is only an

[1] Mr. Purser points out to me that Plutarch rather popularised than originated this doctrine, and himself refers it (*Ibid.* 25, *Def. Orac.* 17) to various older philosophers. Diogenes L. refers it (vii. 151) to the Stoics. Mr. Sayce tells me it came from Babylonia.

[2] *de sera num. vind.* sub. fin. He adds with curious bathos, that being of a musical turn Nero was presently to be turned into a marsh-frog, for that he had expiated part of his misdoings by his conduct towards Greece, ὀφείλεσθαι δέ τι καὶ χρηστὸν αὐτῷ παρὰ θεῶν, ὅτι τῶν ὑπηκόων τὸ βέλτιστον καὶ θεοφιλέστατον γένος ἠλευθέρωσεν, τὴν Ἑλλάδα. This survival of national folly and vanity is very interesting in Plutarch.

appendix to his Apology, which takes a line analogous to that of Bishop Butler, yet with an eloquence and richness of illustration very different from the tame and unattractive logic of the good bishop. The notable instances of punishment after many years are evidences that Divine Providence is not forgetful. Hurry and precipitation are human faults and foreign to an eternal Being. And though there seems to have been delay, how can we know that we are not merely displaying our ignorance in asserting it. Who knows whether the criminal all the while has not been bearing his own cross to the scene of his final punishment;[1] who knows whether instead of being punished in old age he has not grown old in punishment.[2]

Here is one more remarkable passage:[3] 'Let us further consider this, that setting things right in human tribunals consists in requiting with evil, in making the ill-doer suffer ill, and in nothing further'—correctionary punishments seem unknown in Greek codes—'wherefore they pursue the offender barking at him like a dog, and follow up the crime hot-foot. We must rather expect God, whatever diseased soul He treats with correction, to judge its passions, whether they will give way to repentance, and to allow time for recovery to those whose wickedness is not absolute and ineradicable. For knowing what share of virtue human souls brought with them when they came from Him to their birth, and how strong in them and inextinguishable is this nobility of origin, and that they 'come out' upon the surface with wickedness when impaired by bad nurture and evil company, but when properly treated recover their

---

[1] καὶ τῷ μὲν σώματι τῶν κολαζομένων ἕκαστος κακούργων ἐκφέρει τὸν αὑτοῦ σταυρόν, *op. cit.* 9.

[2] οὐ μετὰ πλείονα χρόνον, ἀλλ' ἐν πλείον χρόνῳ, τιμωρίαν μακροτέραν οὐ βραδυτέραν τίνουσιν· οὐδὲ γηράσαντες ἐκολάσθησαν, ἀλλ' ἐγήρασαν κολαζόμενοι.   [3] *Op. cit.* 6.

natural health—knowing all this, He does not apply the same punishment to all, but extirpates what is incurable forthwith from the world, as it is offensive to the rest, and most of all to Himself, to see wickedness ever in His presence. But to those whose fault arises rather from ignorance of the right than deliberate choice of the vile, He gives time for repentance; and if they persist, them too He punishes, for with Him there is no fear lest they should escape.'

I will not apologise for bringing the opinions of the sage at this length before the reader, for as they are not revolutionary or peculiar opinions, held by a reformer or original thinker, but essentially those of a man of practical sense and common wisdom, they express to us what I will call the religious drift of the age.

It was noticed by all Roman observers, and appears clearly from the later inscriptions which form the main body of Bœckh's *Corpus*, that in religious rites and usages Greece was extraordinarily conservative. So far as this regards the celebration of festivals, which were always religious meetings, it is I think partly to be explained by the popularity of these meetings among all the wealthy Roman and other visitors, who came to Greece for this purpose, not to speak of the exiles who were allowed to attend them. The Olympic, Isthmian, and Pythian festivals seem to me to have been somewhat like the Passion Play at Ammergau in attracting crowds of strangers—a play which is perhaps still a real cult, but which will certainly be kept up for financial reasons when its religious element has passed away. To the antiquarian visitor, however, the ruder local usages, and the many local celebrations of old historic events, like the battles of Marathon and Platæa, were even more interesting, and of these there is a long catalogue.[1] Even the remaining aristo-

[1] Cf. Hertzberg, ii. 256 *sq*.

cracy of Greece was mainly an aristocracy of religion. The list of the ἐργαστῖναι, who worked the sacred peplos for Athene at Athens in 98 B.C. are all noble names, chosen from the old tribes (φύλαι).[1] I have already alluded to the priestly aristocracy of Stratoniceia.[2] We also know from inscriptions that the three ancient Doric tribes, the Hylleis, Pamphyli, and Dymanes existed in various Doric polities in Hellenistic days,[3] at Cos, Calymna, and at Nemea. There was still the bloody scourging of youths at Sparta, already mentioned, and other remains of gloomy rites, such as that of Orchomenos, at which a priest with a sword pursued certain daughters of the old Minyæ, to allay an ancient curse.[4]

But I think this natural conservatism was helped by meaner reasons, and I do not believe in the very strict adherence to old dogmas of people who were so ready to admit foreign rites. The worship of Isis seems now as extended over Greece as any other, and perhaps more popular, and yet this was distinctly a novel worship as compared with the venerable shrines and historic celebrations I have mentioned. Osiris too and Sarapis had their temples and their priests, and though there were not wanting many assertions of their real identity with some Hellenic god—Isis with Demeter and the others with Dionysus especially—such cults were really foreign, the people who conducted them were chiefly foreign, and not in harmony with the simple and unquestioning people which went on repeating the old services

[1] *MDI* viii. 61. [2] Above, p. 226, and *BCH* xi. 35.
[3] *BCH* viii. 29, ix. 351.
[4] But when, in the course of this ceremony, the priest actually performed the duty, and slew a woman, there was a commotion even greater than had the emperor abolished the custom, and the people took from the offending priest's family this hereditary dignity (Plut. *Quæst. Græca.* 38).

and consulting the old oracles.[1] In the better classes we must assume an increasing carelessness for these rites, and, where spiritual wants were indeed felt, a desire to seek satisfaction either in some new revelation or in the philosophic life. But I can see no decided break with the old and the superstitious, unless it be among the trenchant spirits who deliberately chose to violate the decencies of religious fashion.

This sort of compromise between orthodoxy and the freedom of advanced spirits was in Plutarch's day very much as it is now. The philosophers had shown endless difficulties, and had adopted a broader and more cosmopolitan conception of the Deity and His relation to the world; just as now our sceptics will not allow the exclusive claims of particular churches, or exclusive creeds, while they usually admit some general basis for them all. In respectable society and among people who read and think, but are not prepared to break with tradition, we have a public very like that of Plutarch, holding a good many of the new truths, confessing them, when pressed, to be inconsistent with the teaching of their church, and yet living on in a sort of practical compromise, gladly hearing every defence of the old, while they read with curiosity and not without approval the assertions of the new.

Perhaps the strongest objection to this comparison will be made by those who read the tract *on Superstition*, in which they will find not only that there are no future punishments threatened to the atheist, his belief being regarded as a vagary of thought rather regrettable than detestable, but that the fault of atheism is distinctly regarded as less than that of superstition. Nothing shocked

---

[1] This foreign tone was particularly strong in the religious clubs or associations in the mercantile cities, cf. above, p. 180.

the worthy divines of the Renaissance more than this unchristian attitude in a moralist otherwise very much akin to Christianity, and there were not wanting those who even accused him in consequence of being an atheist in disguise.[1]

I cannot but think that an attentive study of this tract will show it to be one of those sophistical exercises practised by every one in that age—I mean the defence of a paradox with subtlety and ingenuity, taking little account of sober truth in comparison with dialectical plausibility. Plutarch opened his career by giving such lectures at Rome, and good critics have already noticed how several of his tracts have the air of mere juvenile declamations.[2] But they have not noticed the introduction, in some of the more serious treatises, of sophistical passages intended to show the author's acuteness and education in rhetoric; as, for example, the grotesque passage on the swallow as an inhospitable and wicked bird;[3] the debate on the comparative intelligence of marine and land animals; the carefully polished argument in which one of Circe's hogs (*Gryllus*) proves to Ulysses the great moral superiority of beasts over men; the laudation of *Exile* in a man of strong patriotism and attachment to his home; and many of the silly questions proposed for discussion at his *Banquet*. The exaggerations and under-statements with which the tract *on Superstition* abounds, the brief and sketchy nature of the argument, the highly-coloured picture of the terrors of superstition compared with the calmness and ease of atheism,

[1] Cf. the citations in Oct. Gréard, *la Morale de Plutarque*, p. 288 *sq.* and notes.

[2] Gréard (*op. cit.* p. 41) cites as examples the *comparative usefulness of water and fire, the glory of Athens, the primum frigidum*, and the Pythagorean essays *on the use of meat*. All these he justly refers to the early years of Plutarch, and his declamations at Rome.

[3] *Sympos.* viii. qu. 7, § 3.

the total absence of all mention either of the special cults which promote this vice or of the special sex which has always been subject to it—these and many other details make me regard it as a picture suggested perhaps by the popular play of Menander (the *Superstitious Man*), but not as describing any prevalent type in the society of his day. Perhaps the portrait of the Flatterer, to which I have already alluded, suffers from a like exaggeration. But however that may be, all our other evidence tells us that men, at least in those days, were very free from the grovelling fears and miseries here attributed to them by Plutarch. The belief in future happiness is gravely adopted by him in spite of sceptical objections in the *Consolations* he addressed to Apollonius[1] and to his wife on the loss of their children; and as future bliss seems to imply future pain, it seems very strange that nothing of the kind is held out as a danger to the deliberate atheist, who is, moreover, frequently the superstitious man tormented out of all belief!

But enough of this. The critics who adopt Plutarch's argument as based on fact must also assert a recovery of ceremonial religion among the men of that generation, and this they support by his statement that the oracle at Delphi, of late fallen into total decay, had revived its activity, and was, in Plutarch's day, again frequently consulted. They may now also cite an inscription found by Dr. Lolling on the peninsula of Methone, and belonging to the obscure town of Korope, which possessed an oracle of Apollo Koropæus. The inscription provides in great detail for the appointment of officers to take charge of the sanctuary, to receive the inquirers and issue the responses in due order, and to plant with trees and protect from trespass the sacred

[1] The genuineness of this tract is disputed by Volkmann, but I think needlessly.

enclosure. The distinct reason given is the benefit derived from the god through the many strangers who now visit the place.[1] If Dr. Lolling has rightly fixed the date of this interesting document as the first century B.C.,[2] it is, however, but a partial corroboration; and I hesitate to adopt so strange a fact about religion generally from a solitary passage in a treatise, which is throughout an *apologia* for the decay of faith. Plutarch indeed takes personal credit for having restored and beautified Pylæa (the suburb of Delphi where the Pythian games were held), with the help of two friends and of the governor of Delphi—probably a great aid to his own popularity, but indicating no general revival of belief in oracles throughout the Greek world. Gradually the great shrine had gone down in estimation; the priests had no longer the position and wide knowledge of their predecessors; the Pythia was a common peasant, who talked in vulgar prose; the subjects of inquiry were domestic and trivial, only fit, he says, to be answered in common language—Am I to marry, to sail, to invest money, or in the case of cities, questions about their crops, their cattle, and their sanitation?[3] And yet for all these changes Plutarch ingeniously finds natural causes, which should content men with this decadence, just as he exhorts them to acquiesce in their political decay. And here I note as remarkable that the development of religion in Greece brought down the conception of providential interference to the trivial affairs of everyday life, whereas our modern tendency is exactly the reverse. We now hesitate even to pray for rain or fair weather, as our fathers did, but, as it were, restrict the domain of Providence to grave moral matters.

---

[1] *MDI* vii. 71 *sq*.
[2] This is his correction in the second article (cf. *ibid*. vii. 340).
[3] *De Pyth*. 28.

There is much that is reasonable, much that is eloquent, in the treatise; and yet what is more singular, what more melancholy, than to see the sage clinging to the sinking ship, or rather trying to stop the leak and declare her seaworthy, while in his own country, as well as through the Hellenistic East, there had lately been preached a new faith which he never took pains to understand. He can tell us how the Jewish high-priest was clothed, but as to even Jewish dogmas he manifests the grossest ignorance.[1] His collection of the *placita* of philosophers is superficial and jejune; his studies in comparative religion, though his theory asserted the equal dignity and veracity of all religions, are even more superficial and careless. He professed himself a cosmopolitan thinker; he was really a narrow and bigoted Hellene; as narrow and exclusive as the old opponents of Alexander had been in their day. This ingrained bigotry was the real secret of the decay and downfall of Greece. While the Asiatic cities had learned at least something from contact with the East, Greece had remained behind, had become poor and depopulated, stagnant in thought as well as in active life. There is no more signal instance of this stagnation than the sayings and counsels of Plutarch on politics and on religion.

The same may be said of his utterances on art. No new production of any merit is mentioned; old statues, old temples, old pictures were still prized. People went to be shown round Delphi by chattering cicerones; they frequented picture galleries; they admired the bloom on ancient bronzes,[2] the splendour of Homer or Pindar, the

---

[1] Cf. *Symp.* iv. qu. 6, *On the God of the Jews*. This ignorance seems to prove that the many Jews now at Athens, Corinth, and elsewhere through Greece never mixed in good Greek society.

[2] No setting of a dialogue was ever more appropriate or promising

music of the ancients, which was no longer understood. On these things Plutarch copies Plato or Aristoxenus. But though statues were set up in crowds to benefactors of their several cities, we hear that these monuments of liberality were kept in stock, often without the heads, which were added when the dedication was ascertained and the statue bought; and even this was more tolerable than the practice above mentioned (p. 239) of erasing old dedications and renaming the effigies of ancient gods and heroes. Let us then turn to the only life still remaining—the private and domestic doings of Plutarch's friends.

than that of Plutarch's *on the Pythian Oracle*. A party of visitors are being led round by the professional showmen, whom they ridicule while they follow them, interrupting their follies with serious talk on religion and art. As usual in Greek literature, the splendid natural features of the place are never mentioned. The openings of the first seventeen chapters contain interesting allusions to old treasure houses and the offerings they contained. The habit of visiting picture galleries is clearly implied by the opening sentence of the tract *on the Genius of Socrates*. An artist compares the visits of ignorant visitors to his gallery (οἱ θεώμενοι τοὺς γεγραμμένους πίνακας) to the confused applause of a crowd, those of the cultivated and critical to acquaintances who individually address him.

CHAPTER XIV

PLUTARCH AND HIS TIMES—PRIVATE LIFE

No generation of men ever felt more keenly than Plutarch's contemporaries that they represented the old age of their country. Not only is there no outlook before them, but when discussing the treatment and education of the child, we find Plutarch dealing with the various efforts to overcome the constitutional delicacies derived from unhealthy parents, a difficulty which earlier theorists would have met with far more trenchant remedies. Exposing of children was still perhaps as common as of old, but now they were exposed from poverty,[1] while Plutarch's wealthy friends, however unfit to be parents, never reflected upon the sin of spreading hereditary disease among their race. There were even medical courses of treatment, intended to protect children from the probable outbreak of such diseases. Plutarch uses all this as an illustration of his principle that the apparent delays of divine justice are only larger and deeper justice, and considers that the 'skipping of generations' so often noticeable in gout and other punitive diseases arises from the insight of the Deity into the virtues of those that are spared.[2]

---

[1] οἱ μὲν γὰρ πένητες οὐ τρέφουσι τέκνα κ.τ.λ. (*de amore prolis*, sub. fin.)
[2] *De sera num. vind.* 19-22. *De lib. educ.* 3.—If this tract be

In considering the treatment of children he sets himself strongly against that selfish luxury in parents which causes them to neglect personal supervision. There may be, indeed, excessive and injurious forcing of children,—a very modern vice in parents—but this is not so usual as its opposite.[1] Beginning with the duty of the mother to nurse her own child—which, by the way, his own wife did not perform—he inveighs against the crime of economising by the selection of cheap or broken-down slaves to look after the children,[2] still more against the crime of allowing private interest or the thoughtless recommendation of friends to influence the parents' choice of teachers.[3] He seems to feel all through—in this perhaps reflecting the influence of Roman habits on Greek fashion—that education is no longer a state affair, but the private duty of parents. There is hardly a word, in his instructions, upon schools and schooling. But he alludes casually to the strange scenes which boys were allowed to witness—criminals dressed up with robes and crowns, and presently stripped and publicly tortured; paintings of subjects so objectionable that we should carefully explain to the child the distinction between art as such and art as a vehicle of morals. On the other hand deportment was strictly watched: for example, not to use the left hand[4] unless it were to hold bread at dinner, while other food was taken with the right; to walk in the

genuine, he knows that drunken parents produce drunkards. In Philo (*Leg. ad Caium*, § 8) there is a remarkable argument put in Caligula's mouth that his ancestors were his educators in imperial qualities, in that they transmitted his training to him in his blood.

[1] *Op. cit.* 13.
[2] If a nurse be employed, let her be a Greek with a good accent (*op. cit.* 5); on the quality of the pædagogue slave, cap. 7.
[3] *On false shame*, 8.
[4] Cf. on the impoliteness of using the left hand, *de Tranq.* 5; Theodorus's remark, *de Fortuna*, 5; *Virt. doceri posse*, 3.

streets without looking up; to touch salt-fish with one finger, fresh-fish, bread, meat, with two; *to scratch yourself thus;* to fold your cloak thus.[1] Not only is the necessity of early education insisted upon, but even of a library of standard books for the boy to know and enjoy; and Plutarch also expresses the old Greek contempt for the man of late or of self-education. If in our day science, which can be learned in mature life, were not taken into account, we should probably hold very similar views, for literary culture is not thus attainable.[2]

If you complain that all this instruction costs more time and money than the poor can afford, Plutarch admits it, but says he is only concerned with the more refined classes. 'But some one may object that I, undertaking to give prescriptions on the training of the children of free citizens, apparently neglect the training of poor townsmen, and only think of instructing the rich—to which the obvious answer is: that I should desire the training I prescribe to be attainable alike by all; but if any, through want of private means, cannot obtain it, let them blame their fortune and not their adviser. Every effort, then, must be made, even by the poor, to train their children in the best possible way, and if this is beyond them, to do it according to their means.'[3]

This remark is more particularly applicable to bodily training, on which the age had attained to far greater wisdom and more modern common sense than we should have expected. In the first place Plutarch sets himself against any iron rules, which make a man the slave of his body, and purchase health at the cost of accepting idleness and

[1] *Op. cit.* 9.
[2] Cf. *Symp.* ix. qu. 14, § 3, where ὀψιμαθής and ἄγροικον are coupled together.
[3] *De lib. educ.* 11: cf. also *de san. præc.* 25.

stupidity along with it. Thus the rule of the trainers that men should not excite themselves with talk at meals he rejects as probably wrong, and in any case socially inexpedient. Even special diet is bad, and so are all extremes, such as the ostentation [1] of taking cold baths. Whatever is not natural he regards as unhealthy; and not only does he speak with the greatest disgust and contempt of the habit of taking emetics, but he puts purgatives in the same category, as being quite superfluous to those who live a regular and temperate life, and as being only invented to relieve excess.[2] Still he is human enough to admit, in the mouth of his leading character in the dialogue, that it is not easy to maintain strict moderation at a large and sumptuous feast, where refusing many things is perhaps not polite. 'You should prepare for such occasions by abstemiousness beforehand. But if you be really indisposed, it is a case of false shame to accept such invitations, when a properly worded excuse *with a smart point in it* will often please as much as an acceptance. A similar defence of your abstemiousness at table will often help you easily out of the difficulty.' Like all later Greek authorities he prefers field sports and general military training to athletic competitions.

There is little to be gleaned, as I have said before, concerning school life; the later education of the youth now consisted chiefly in hearing lectures and practising rhetoric or disputation, as an introduction either to practical life or that higher calling known as philosophy. He seems to attach but little importance to those *ephebic* institutions, which played so prominent a part in the Hellenistic days of Athens.[3] Plutarch is very emphatic on the proper mental

[1] ἐπιδεικτικὸν καὶ νεανικόν, *san. praec.* 15.
[2] μιαρὰ παραμύθια πλησμονῆς (the loathsome solace of surfeiting), *cp. cit.* 20.
[3] Inscriptions indeed of such bodies still abound, and we have from

attitude for the youthful hearers of lectures, readers of poets, and students of art, both as regards the matter brought before them and the person of the teacher. Great care must be taken to separate the mere art side in dramatic poetry and in painting from the ethical. If they see representations of violent or indecent passion they must only attend to the talent of the drawing. And as regards the quality of the teachers, the mere exhibiting sophist is very different from the solid philosopher, who probes our faults, and gives us serious and stern advice ; 'and you must not be like the many who delight in and applaud him so long as he talks of things indifferent ; but whenever he comes to home questions and takes men to task individually, they get angry and think him intrusive ; for they naturally assume that hearing philosophers in the schools is much the same as hearing actors in the theatre, people who differ in nowise from themselves in their private lives. Now this is true enough as regards the sophists, who, when they leave their professional chair and lay aside their books, are in the real affairs of life insignificant and on a level with the many. But as regards real philosophers, men ignore that both their earnest and their sport, their smile and their frown, and most of all their advice to each man in private, bear precious fruit to those who will accustom themselves to attend to them.'[1]

Thus we find ourselves in the presence of what may be called a parochial clergy disseminated through all the towns,

---

the opening of the second century (111, 130 A.D., etc.) onward a most interesting series of the busts of the Athenian *cosmetæ*, or controllers of the *ephebi*. The great contrasts in the appearance, and the often non-Hellenic types, of these men, who were at least socially of the highest class, are a plain indication how cosmopolitan even Attic society, with all its conservative tendencies, had now become (cf. the busts reproduced by A. Dumont in *BCH* i. and ii., with his article, i. 229).

[1] *De rect. rat. aud.* 12.

who consoled people in grief, who received confessions and
gave advice in private, and preached their gospel in public.
Nor does Plutarch, nor did his age, confine themselves to
hearing one philosophic creed. Whether Cynics, or Stoics,
or Academicians, or, what was most frequent, Eclectics—all
taught serious moral lessons and the acknowledged virtues
with no greater differences or contentions than, for example,
the various sects of Protestants exhibit in America; dis-
puting often, and sometimes angrily, on special points of
doctrine, but still agreeing on the broad general lines, and
supported in turn by serious men as all knowing and teaching practical truths. Plutarch himself derides the paradoxes
of the Stoics, and indeed his compromising temper was
constitutionally opposed to their trenchant dogmas, but
how many points does he not adopt from them? His professed master, and head of the original Academy, was Plato,
and yet all Plutarch's tracts on married life show that the
Platonic *Republic* must have appeared to him not only im-
practicable but positively inhuman. He desires no heroic
remedies; he expects no great reform in society, but
preaches personal dignity as the basis of truthfulness,
purity, charity, such as they were understood in the heathen
world. I put it in this way because there is a naturalistic
vein in him foreign to the heights of Stoic or Christian morality. If a husband lapses from his fidelity let him do it elsewhere than at home; if the wife hears of it let her ignore
it; if she feels repelled from or by her parents-in-law let
her cultivate them with peculiar affection; let her educate
herself even so far as to study geometry and Plato, but on
no account allow religious cults foreign to her husband to
creep into the house.[1] He censures the cruelties of a hot-

---

[1] This is probably pointed at Christianity, as well as at those oriental
cults which we know to have done domestic mischief in those days.

tempered house-master, the miseries of a superstitious one
—all the petty weaknesses and vices that attack every over-
ripe and decaying society are pictured in his pages.

But what remedies does he propose? Not the revelation
of any mystery, not the ardent love of a new creed, not the
uncompromising courage of a Stoic principle. He borrows
from the prosaic Aristotle the doctrine of habit, of gradual
progress in virtue, of gradual falling away into vice, and
exhorts his hearers to watch small things, to begin with
small resolves, to practise 'active habits of virtue,' and so
train themselves gradually to self-control, good temper,
liberality, calmness of mind. There is not even any trenchant denunciation of the grave immoralities which permeated
Greek society. He inveighs indeed against the new and
extravagant terms of praise uttered by the audiences in
lecture rooms, because here there is excess.[1] He cannot endure the poet Aristophanes, for in the first place, he
says: 'If you recite him at a feast, each guest must have a
grammarian beside him to explain the allusions, and then
how coarse he is, and obscene, and how little he studies the
proper diction of his various characters.' But on the splendours of the poet—his unequalled richness of humour,
his exquisite diction, his lyric sweetness,—not a word.
Every eulogy is reserved for Menander, the only poet
(beside Euripides) worth reciting in society, the most perfect
outcome of Greek literature, the most perfect mirror of
human life.[2] Let the reader turn to my *Greek Life and*

---

[1] *De rect. rat. aud.* 15.—'Those who have brought in the fashion of new exclamations at lectures, such as *Divine, Inspired, Unapproach-able* (θείως, θεοφορήτως, ἀπροσίτως), instead of the old καλῶς, σοφῶς, or ἀληθῶς, behave with great indecency, and damage the lecturer by sug-gesting that he desires such extravagant eulogy.'

[2] Even Euripides and Pindar he charges with the vulgarities of boast-fulness and conceit (*on Self-Praise*, § 1).

Thought,[1] where I have weighed the Attic New Comedy in the scale of morals. He will be persuaded that a more mesquin and frivolous society has never been brought upon the stage. But Menander and his society were polished; there was nothing raw or harsh about them; their vices were venial, or at least curable; they went through their lives without any offensive tragedy or any vulgar suicide.

This, then, is really Plutarch's mission—apart from his work as a biographer—to feel the pulse of society, to give ordinary rules and advices, to make human intercourse smoother and more agreeable. Here it is that all those qualities which make his philosophy superficial and his morals feeble aid him to direct social life with tact and give entertainments with refinement. This is, therefore, a topic worthy of special attention; for here, if anywhere, the Greeks were still acknowledged masters, and gave the tone to all the society of the civilised world.

Indeed we may pass almost naturally from the philosophic lectures, which we have just mentioned, to the question of conversation, for the whole tract *on Proper Conduct at Lectures* is partly moral, partly social in its tone. All through it he feels that the danger of his age was over-attention to words, to form, to purity and grace of diction, and neglect of the real substance. 'Wherefore we should imitate not the flower-girl, but the bee, in seeking for the essence. For the former gathers rich and scented flowers, and weaves them into garlands sweet indeed, but ephemeral and fruitless; whereas the bee, after flying through meadows of violas and roses and hyacinths, lights upon the strongest and most pungent thyme, and hence obtains what is best for its honey.' The showy flowers of the field are therefore the food of drones, just as the phrases and periods of the sophist satisfy vulgar

[1] Pp. 115-123.

hearers. 'Nay, rather as a man about to leave the barber's shop stands up before the looking-glass, and feels his head, and notes the change in the cut of his hair and beard,' so he that stands up to leave a lecture-room should examine his mind and see what he has gained.[1]

Nevertheless, *form* is a delightful thing, and young men are quite right to admire it. But remember that nothing is worse than that critical attitude, which cannot praise without some carping or detraction; here you must observe the mean[2] between the gushing and the sneering hearer. But the admiration of form should come after the serious matters, 'just as those at a feast, when their thirst is allayed, then begin to look at the plate and turn the cups in their hands, so when the hearer is well fed with dogmas, he may consider what elegance there is in the exposition. But he that from the outset does not hold to the substance, but requires the diction to be Attic and chaste,[3]

---

[1] *Op. cit.* 8.   [2] *Op. cit.* 13.

[3] Cf. also *de profect.* 8. It is remarkable that he ridicules (*de vit. pud.* 16) as pedantic the avoidance of *hiatus* in composition, a law carefully attended to by most Attic writers, *and indeed apparently by himself.* I will here say a word upon this test, so generally accepted, since the famous tract of Benseler, by critics of the Plutarchean collection. Volkmann, in the second or critical part of his exhaustive work (*Leben, Schriften und Philosophie des Plutarch*, Berlin, 1869), endeavours to show that in nearly every case internal reasons support this external test. Whenever in a tract of the *Moralia* hiatus is admitted, he finds other reasons to prove its spuriousness. But here, as elsewhere, the reader will find strongly subjective convictions taking the place of arguments. Thus the *Consolatio ad Apollonium* is judged by critics so great as Wyttenbach and Bähr to be excellent, an echo of Plato, lofty in diction to the limits of tragedy (*op. cit.* i. 130); by Volkmann (*op. cit.* 144) frigid and strained, overladen with false ornament, etc. One cannot but feel that he was led by the new test of Benseler, and that had the *Consolation* avoided hiatus it would have also escaped his censure. And what shall we say of the cases which are doubtful? Thus the tract *de Garrulitate* in general avoids hiatus, but has nevertheless so

is like the man who will not drink an antidote unless it be handed him in Attic ware, or put on a cloak in winter unless the wool be of Attic sheep, but sits idle in his thin and unsubstantial vesture of Lysian language.'[1] The curious feature in all this is that the imitators were as unable to reproduce Attic purity as our Renaissance builders to reproduce Attic architecture. These later sophists and their hearers had so completely lost the secret that, with the qualified exception of Lucian, who passed muster till he fell into the hands of Cobet, none of them even approximated to Attic purity. They were as degenerate in eloquence as were their contemporaries who affected to copy the old philosophic masters by adopting 'the lisp of Aristotle and the stoop of Plato.'[2] To repeat the fine illustration with which he closes the tract : 'As if one went to seek fire from his neighbour, and finding it bright and cheery were to sit down there and stay warming himself, so is he who comes to seek instruction from another and forgets to kindle his own flame, but in delight at what he hears sits soothed

---

many grave admissions of it as to make Benseler pause. But Volkmann gets rid of some of them by emendation, apologises for the rest, and accepts the tract.

The whole discussion, therefore, in his book, though acute and suggestive, seems to me to want finality, especially so long as we do not possess a complete *index græcitatis* to Plutarch (based on some better text than Reiske's) and ascertain what variations of vocabulary the tracts contain. I have therefore felt justified in quoting from some of the tracts under suspicion, which seem to me to represent manners and customs of Plutarch's date, though in general the reader will find my conclusions based upon the recognised and unmistakable works of our author. It seems to me very remarkable that Volkmann has taken no notice of the passage which has suggested this note.

[1] On this allusion to the clearness and transparency of the *tenue genus* of Lysias, cf. my *Greek Literature*, ii. 152.

[2] *De aud poet.* 59.—ὥσπερ οἱ τὴν Πλάτωνος ἀπομιμούμενοι κυρτότητα, καὶ τὴν Ἀριστοτέλους τραυλότητα, a phrase he repeats elsewhere.

with the ruddiness and reflected glow upon his face, and brings home no flame to dissipate the inner darkness and mildew of his soul, or to air it with philosophy.'[1]

Perhaps these things are but splendid commonplaces; what is not so is the demand of Plutarch, himself a lecturer, for the warm and even undisguised sympathy of his audience. He expects attentive watching of the lecturer, an upright sitting posture, and a countenance beaming with interest in what is said. Such conduct as sprawling on the benches, assuming a negligent attitude, whispering to one's neighbour, yawning, giggling, is censured as a social crime. 'For some think the speaker only has duties and the hearers none; that he must come well prepared and full of thoughts, but that they without any consideration are to sit down as to a feast which they enjoy at the cost of another's labour. Yet as surely as good company is necessary to the feast, so is a good hearer to the lecture; for barbarisms and solecisms are quite as possible in the audience as in the speaker.'[2]

But if Plutarch makes these demands upon the audience at a discourse, he is even more exacting when he discusses society proper and social entertainments. Then as now, dinner-parties at which ladies were sometimes present, and wine parties of men, were the prevalent occasions for such gatherings. It was the habit, he tells us, at Sybaris, to send out invitations with a year's notice, in order that the ladies might have time to prepare a splendid toilette.[3] As far as the internal preparation of the guests is concerned a year is no notice; it is the whole education of the man which comes out in his social intercourse. 'For the guest does

---

[1] *Op. cit.* sub. fin.   [2] *Op. cit.* 13, 14.
[3] They are not yet quite so extravagant in London, though I have often seen an invitation to dine six weeks later in that city.

not go in like a vessel to be filled, but with a mind to give and take in earnest and in jest, for which this is the proper opportunity. And be it remembered that it is easy to decline a dish if it be ill-cooked, or take to water if the wine be bad, but a *table-mate*[1] who gives you a headache or makes you ill destroys all the pleasure of wines or dainties or music, nor can you send away from the table this source of disgust, which often produces lifelong dislikes, as it were the after-taste[2] of the unpleasantnesses which occurred at table. Hence Chilon, invited yesterday, was quite right in saying that he would not come till he heard who were to be the company; in war or on sea voyages you must submit to an unpleasant comrade; to do so in society is folly.'[3]

The host, having taken precautions concerning this matter, which indeed was not so easy as it now is, seeing that guests often brought friends with them who were strangers to him, is next bound to see that there is ample room for all, the crowding of a table in any sense being quite inexcusable. Large dinner-parties of twenty-five or thirty were hardly ever successful, as the conversation, which ought to be general, then breaks up into private dialogues;[4] and as the dining-rooms of Greek houses were comparatively small, such feasts generally implied very tight fitting of the guests, which Plutarch condemns. 'Should by any accident the food or the wine run short it is easy to say I am very sorry, but the servants have made away with it, whereas such a polite excuse (!) is impossible in the case of room, over which the master has absolute control.' He introduces his eighth query in the eighth book of his *Table-talk*, by say-

---

[1] It is a scandalous thing that the English language has no proper word for σύνδειπνος, *convive*.

[2] *Hot-coppers*, the German *Katzenjammer*, would be even more literal for ἑωλοκρασία, as used in this connection.

[3] *Sept. Sap. Conv.* 2.   [4] v. 5.

ing that they avoided the large and mixed parties given at the Isthmian games by Sospis, when president of the feast and keeping open house for both citizens and guests, but he afterwards praises[1] the banquet given by the wealthy Ammonius, strategus of Athens, after an examination of the ephebi at the Diogenion. I may add that at the select party given by the former a schoolmaster (γραμματικός) and a cicerone (περιηγητής) figure as guests—certainly not an aristocratic pair in any modern or in a Roman sense; indeed Plutarch introduces the self-conscious vanity of the former as part of the scene;[2] the man was silent and sulky because he had not gained applause in a public display. Physicians play a leading part in Plutarch's society, and evidently enjoyed a good social position now as heretofore in Greece.[3] But the whole society at Ammonius's house is distinctly *professional*—rhetoricians, gymnastic trainers, farmers; not a single *grandee* or person living idly from his estates can be found among them. The few Romans, like Sossius Senecio, who actually take part in the discussions, may perhaps count as exceptions.

Simple appointments and a short *menu* are commended,[4] as the whole feast turns upon the mental qualities of the company. But we may note that the absence of an old and wealthy aristocracy with splendid heirlooms in plate and pictures, with princely residences of long tradition,

[1] ix. I. [2] *Symp.* ix. 5.
[3] Cf. Hertzberg's learned note, ii. 174, 175.
[4] His notions of wicked luxury are curiously subjective—snow for cooling drinks, the straining of wine, the use of wether mutton and ox-beef (instead of rams and bulls), the making fowl tender by artificial processes, the fattening of geese for their livers, and many other of the ordinary devices of civilisation are censured (*Symp.* lib. vi. *passim*). Nevertheless the art of cooking, even in Greece, had reached an advanced stage (cf. lib. iv. qu. 1, § 2).

makes Plutarch underrate the external setting of a dinner-party. The only splendour in display which he knows is that of the *nouveau riche*, the vulgar upstart, the imitator of the state of Hellenistic courts. This absence of an aristocracy, with recognised titles and precedence in society, seems to have also increased the difficulty of placing the guests at table, for the jealousies of human nature, which are universal, were not tempered, as they are with us, by grades of dignity universally recognised. Plutarch insists in many places on the truly democratic nature of social converse, where all should affect, if they do not feel, equality. He even regards it as 'oligarchical and offensive' to come late; 'democratical and polite' to be in good time.[1] But the proper placing of the guests seems to him a task in strategy, no less than to manœuvre a phalanx. He even illustrates it, not without an apology, by the instance of the Divine architect ordering the world from chaos, not adding or destroying one particle of matter, but merely putting each element in its right place.

The discussion which follows[2] is as instructive to-day as it was in the first century. If you make distinctions and fix places you are sure to cause offence. If you let things take their course you will have a random result, in which wrong people are sure to get together, and fail to enjoy themselves. Plutarch's general solution is to abandon ceremony as to rank, to hold to the democratic aspect of the feast, but to take great care about having suitable people to sit together. And this is not easy, seeing that likeness of character is sometimes a cause of conflict, as with game-cocks, sometimes a cause of friendly consorting, as with jackdaws. There are some that drink too much wine, and some water-drinkers;[3] some old men with their conceit, some

[1] *Symp.* viii. 6, § 2.   [2] *Ibid.* i. qu. 2.   [3] *Ibid.* vi. qu. 4.

young with their folly. 'I advise then not to set the rich by the rich, or the young by the young, or the magistrate beside his colleague, or two intimates together; for so the conversation will have no general activity; but rather the eager learner beside the distinguished scholar, the benign beside the peevish, the ingenuous youth beside the vain old talker, the reserved beside the boaster, the silent beside the passionate; and if you have a lavish *richard*, draw from the obscure corner some worthy poor man, on the chance of the full cup overflowing into his empty vessel. But don't put a sophist beside a sophist, or a poet beside a poet; separate also the captious and the litigious, inserting some sort of buffer between them. Whereas I should bring together athletic people and sportsmen and farmers, so also those fond of drinking and the amorous, not merely those who have fallen in love, but those given to wine and women; for men warmed at the same fire more readily consort, provided, by Jove, that they are not in pursuit of the same person.' He recognises, moreover, what we call *grouting* at a party. All the company need not be brilliant; for as we mix water with wine to temper its strength, and as consonants are necessary between the sonants (vowels), so are silent but well-disposed listeners.[1] The established custom that ladies should sit by their husbands and boys beside their parents solved that side of the difficulty.

He proceeds to discuss whether the old fashion, then exploded, of having a regular *symposiarch*, a master of the feast, was of advantage or not. There was much to be said on both sides, but here again it seems to me that Hellenistic society required more controlling than ours, seeing that display of gifts and forwardness were certainly more common than they are with us northerners. This we may infer

[1] *Symp.* i. 1, § 3.

from a passage[1] in which he apprehends that without regulation the *symposium* will become in turn a democratic assembly, a sophist's school, a gambling-house, or a scenic stage—such was the taste for display in oratory, recitation, acting.[2] A governor of the feast will have to vary the entertainment, and as they say that a walk along the sea, and a sail along the land are the pleasantest, so he must combine earnest and jest.

The *table-talk* left us by our author gives a large assortment of the topics suitable for agreeable conversation. Any one who examines them will see how easy it is to frame theories, and how hard to satisfy practical requirements in detail. Modern and sensible as are his views, there are few of the questions raised which are not either silly, trivial, or even shocking in their naturalism to modern refinement. Here are some specimens: Why are men more greedy towards the end of autumn? Which came first: a hen or an egg? Why is A the first letter of the alphabet? Why is the tear of a wild boar sweet, while that of a stag is salt?—a charming inquiry![3] Whether philosophers should wear garlands at a feast? And yet he thinks it vulgar to talk about a feast one has enjoyed, or a procession, or to tell a dream, or a personal dispute one has had.[4] Nay, he even thinks an account of one's travels rather dull and second-rate.[5]

[1] *Symp.* i. qu. 4, § 3.
[2] The habit of recitations in Greek had lately (he says) come into fashion at Rome, in his own day, and he discusses (*Symp.* vii. qu. 8) what authors are fit for this purpose. He protests against Plato's dialogues being paraded at a dinner table, but says elsewhere (*ibid.* qu. 5, § 4) that Euripides, Pindar, and Menander, especially the last, are more suitable.
[3] I can but refer to iii. 6, περὶ καιροῦ συνουσίας.
[4] *De rect. rat. aud.* 3.
[5] Nevertheless the two travellers whom he introduces at the opening

Perhaps the best of all his advices is that on the proper questions to ask so that the guests may display their knowledge, and have the pleasure of doing so; and again, what exact place jokes and sarcasms should have in a conversation; when they will amuse without doing damage, and when they will ruffle the temper of the *table-mates*. Here is an abstract of this discussion,[1] which is too long for quotation. I shall weave in many other parallel passages.

He opens his eighth book by saying that to expel philosophy from feasts is worse than putting out the light, for when ignorance and bad manners prevail not even the famous golden lamp of the Parthenon would make the gathering decent and orderly. To meet merely for the purpose of eating in silence, if it were possible, is swinish, whereas to take no care about the order and usefulness of the discourse is to serve up the victuals and the wine raw and unprepared, so that the best materials are disgusting. This reverts to the old and universal Greek principle that art has little to do with spontaneity, but is in every phase the result of careful training.[2] For example, it is very important to put such questions as may induce good temper and ready converse in the guests. Obviously people like to be asked what they think the rest of the company do not know, and what they themselves wish to make known. Thus those who have travelled widely by land and sea like

---

of the tract *on the Decay of the Oracles* are among the most interesting figures he draws.

[1] *Symp.* ii. 1.

[2] Cf. his tract *de Fortuna*, where he mentions (§ 4) the famous story of the painter producing the bloody froth on the war-horse's mouth as the only known case where chance gave a new resource to art. Yet we must not forget Aristotle's quotation, τέχνη τύχην ἔστερξε, καὶ τέχνην τύχη.

to be asked about some distant colony, or perilous sea, or barbarian customs, and dilate upon them and describe them, accepting this as a sort of consolation for all their previous toil. And more generally, whatever we are anxious to talk about without any pressure, we like to be asked to tell, thinking we are conferring a favour in doing what we can hardly be restrained from doing even when it is a bore.[1] This is a peculiar weakness in mariners; whereas refined people like to be asked what they want to tell, but are ashamed to volunteer, from regard to their company; as, for example, their own successes and achievements—such as in embassies and politics.[2] Accordingly, jealous and ill-natured people avoid such questions, and turn off the conversation so as to keep it from leading up naturally to such subjects, and rather take up what a man's adversaries would like to hear. Avoid therefore allusions to misfortunes, such as the loss of a suit at law, the death of a child, or misfortunes in trade by sea and land.

Here, on the contrary, are agreeable topics. Men delight in being repeatedly questioned about their success in a harangue, or how they were addressed by the king, or how they escaped storms or pirates, while their fellows were caught; for they seem to enjoy the thing all over again in telling it. They like also to be asked about their children's progress in learning, and about their own intercourse or intimacy with princes. The misfortunes of their

[1] In the two tracts *on Loquacity* and *on Curiosity* he adds many wise advices to those who are given to excessive talk, and those who will not refrain from prying questions. 'For it is pleasanter to associate with villains who have tact than with worthy people who are bores.' He comments too (*de Garr.* 18) on the loquacity permitted to slaves in Greece as compared with their training in Roman houses. At no time did the Greeks generally appreciate what he justly calls τὸ σεμνὸν καὶ τὸ ἅγιον καὶ τὸ μυστηριῶδες τῆς σιωπῆς.

[2] Further examples of long-winded stories are given, *de Garr.* 21, 22.

enemies too they delight in telling, when they are asked, but avoid volunteering on this subject, as it seems like spite. So you should ask a sportsman about dogs, an athlete about contests, an amorous man about beauty. But the pious man, who is given to sacrifices, and likes talking of dreams, and how he made a hit by observing omens, or victims, or by the favour of the gods, should be questioned accordingly. Old people too, though they may have nothing to say, are always pleased and set going by questions, while those who curtail their conversation, and want mere categorical answers, take away the chief pleasure which the old have in society. To sum up: If you desire to be agreeable ask questions for which the answerer will gain not blame, but approval; not dislike, but goodwill from the company. I will add that in another place [1] he comments on the gross impoliteness of answering a question addressed to another without waiting for his reply. It implies that he does not know, or that you know better, and says to the questioner: Why did you ask another, when I was present; ofttimes too the question was not intended to elicit information, but merely to draw a silent or modest man into the conversation and make him feel at home. All this the chatterbox upsets by his meddlesome forwardness. Many of these points are illustrated from Homer, whose poems were to Plutarch, as to all the literary Greeks of that age, a mine not only of philosophy and religion but of good manners.

There follows a long discussion on the expediency of wit or ridicule, and the great dangers of its indiscriminate use. This inquiry has its Latin parallel in Cicero's study of the same subject from the orator's point of view in the second book of his treatise *de Oratore*. Plutarch sees

[1] *De Garr.* 19.

clearly that ridicule is disguised censure, and that a jibe, like a barbed dart, will stick faster and hurt more than a serious reproof. Moreover, the laughter of the company is taken as assent and approval of the censure, and fills the object of it with spite against them. To joke, therefore, without hurting requires no ordinary experience and tact. If your ridicule touches a serious defect, acknowledged or even commonly suspected in its object, harm and hurt ensue. Whereas if it be ostentatiously false, and even suggests the opposite virtue, it is pleasant. You may joke a water-drinker about going home drunk, or a millionaire about his creditors, or a beauty about his plain looks, but you must not congratulate a thief on his honesty, or on having his hand in his own pocket—to use a modern phrase. The most agreeable praise is often suggested by its manifest contradiction. Thus the bitterness of a joke is removed by the joker being himself the joint object of it, as when a poor man ridicules poverty, or a low-born man low birth. In this way the harper stopped king Philip from displaying his amateur criticisms;[1] for when lectured by the king upon chords and harmonies, he replied: 'I pray heaven, O king, you may never come down so far in the world as to understand these things better than I do.'

Of all subjects that of love is here, as in all other respects, incommensurable. For some like being chaffed about it, while others get angry, so that you must study the particular case. For as a fire can be extinguished at the outset by the blast which afterwards feeds it, so a budding passion resents being made public, whereas when once declared it is fed by allusions and receives them with laughter. You may, moreover, ridicule a lover about his passion in the presence of his beloved, but about nothing

[1] τὴν ὀψιμαθίαν ἅμα καὶ περιεργίαν, *Conviv. quaest.* (ii. 1, 12).

else. So those who happen to be in love with their own wives glory in being ridiculed about it when the ladies are present. Finally, let us remember that smart and biting words are justifiable as *repartees*, when a man is attacked and on his defence, which are inexcusable if he volunteered them without provocation.[1]

In all these social advices regard must be had to the varying intimacy of the guests with the host and with one another. These conditions range from the relative or the family friend—who should talk with kindly familiarity to the trusty slaves, interest himself in the wife's troubles, offer mediation in family disputes, carry about the children like his own—to the almost a stranger, who had not even a direct invitation, but came as the companion or *umbra* of another guest.[2] There is a whole chapter on the propriety of bringing such secondary guests, or of accepting such secondary invitations from guests. Plutarch apparently decides that you must allow people to take this liberty, as it is an established fashion,[3] but that he will never go out himself on these terms. Moreover, if it prevail, you transfer your party into the hands of others, and may have your table unduly crowded with unsuitable guests.[4] On the other side it is urged that if it be grossly vulgar to inquire beforehand from the guests what they like to eat, and what wine and unguents they prefer, it is not so to secure the most pleasant company they can have by

---

[1] *Reip. ger. praec.* 7.
[2] *Conv. quaest.* vii. 6, § 1.—τὸ τῶν ἐπικλήτων ἔθος οὓς νῦν Σκιὰς καλοῦσι.
[3] διὸ καλῶν μὲν ἑτέρους ἔδωκά ποτε σκιάς, ἰσχυρὰ γὰρ ἡ τῆς πόλεως (apparently Delphi) συνήθεια καὶ δυσπαραίτητος (vii. 6, § 2).
[4] One hears nowadays that in London certain august personages send beforehand to the host a list of the persons they desire to meet, and this too without having the sense to inquire whether the guests they thus inflict upon their host are on good terms with him or with each other.

letting them bring some of their best friends. And the
conclusion is just as we should draw it; in cases of great
intimacy, and of a small party, where there are special
social reasons, such a fashion is not only harmless but
often a great help to make an evening pleasant.

I turn from these details, which are only samples of
the harvest to be gathered from Plutarch's works, to a
general estimate of the society which he represents.

It is, as I said before, strikingly modern in most respects,
even over-ripe, and tending towards decay from over-refine-
ment; and yet we are frequently pulled up by something
quite foreign to modern culture, something to us highly
indecent, or else some moral judgment singularly lax in a
very sound and religious mind, which surely reflects the
highest and purest feelings of that society and that age.
Yet there was no lack of moral dignity; no want of lofty
claims. 'Will not the good man,' he exclaims,[1] 'consider
every day a festival, and a splendid one too, if he has
reasonable aspirations? For the world is the most august
of temples, and most worthy of its Lord; into this temple
man is introduced at his birth, into the presence not of
statues made with hands and motionless, but such as the
Divine mind has manifested to our senses, copies of what
is spiritual, as Plato said, having in them the principle of
life and motion—even the sun, moon, and stars, and the
rivers ever pouring forth fresh water, and the earth producing food for plants and animals. As this life then is the
most perfect of initiations into the most exalted of mysteries,
we should ever be filled with cheerfulness and joy; not like
the crowd that frequent the Kronia and Panathenæa, or
other such feasts, that they may for a day enjoy purchased
laughter from actors and dancers. But let us rather take

[1] *De Tranq.* 20.

our places reverently and with fair words, for no man may lament at his initiation into the mysteries, nor does he weep at the Pythian games. Yet do men violate these mysteries which God has provided for them, living constantly in lamentation and dejection and wearing anxiety. And while they delight in sweet music, and singing-birds, and cattle sporting in the fields, but are annoyed at their howling and bellowing, nevertheless, seeing their own life joyless and troubled, weighed down with endless griefs and cares, they will neither seek a remedy in themselves, nor receive from the philosopher the true medicine for their souls.' The duties of charity, of gentleness, of truthfulness are rather deduced from this lofty view of the dignity of our nature, and what it demands, than from the dictates of a moral law or the obligations of duty.

Yet it might fairly have been argued by the Christian apologists, who were just about to arise in this society, that these philosophies had not shown the power of purifying the soul from its baser passions. I have above (p. 133) quoted a statement to show how little the sanctity of oaths was respected, and what shameful demands were made from friends to support friends by their testimony. What shall we say of Plutarch's sentiment as regards chastity? First of all he regards the adultery of a wife as an annoyance to be borne by the philosophic husband without losing his temper! 'How can you call anything a misfortune which does not damage either your soul or your body, as for example the low origin of your father, the adultery of your wife, the loss of a crown or seat of honour, none of which a man requires for the highest condition of body and mind!'[1] Again: 'are you childless, reflect that up to this date not a

[1] *De Tranq.* 17.

single Roman emperor has left a son to succeed him.[1] Are you poor? Who was greater than Epaminondas, and yet he was poor. Has your wife gone astray? Don't you know that Agis, one of the greatest Lacedæmonian kings, had a wife who boasted among her maids that her child was by Alcibiades;'[2] and Plutarch calls it one of the follies of prying curiosity that in addition to a man's intemperance he commits the absurdity of passing by common and public women and following after one who is rich and guarded within her husband's house. Thus he tells without any feeling of aversion how when the news reached Pergamum that Eumenes had been assassinated at Delphi, his brother Attalus II took the diadem of his brother, and cohabited with his brother's wife; when the wounded king came home, his brother with many protestations of affection handed him back diadem and wife, both of which in the end he received back again by bequest when Eumenes really died.[3] Nowhere indeed, does Plutarch manifest any deep reprobation for unchastity, even when contrary to nature, if it be not a violation of other people's rights, or an excess which injures health and activity. The open way in which such topics are discussed is not, I think, to be brought as an additional charge against that age, for it is likely that the excessive prudery of some societies has done more harm than this naturalism, which is often consistent with sound moral health.

[1] He must then have written these words before Titus succeeded in 79 A.D.   [2] *De Tranq.* 6.
[3] One of the speakers in his *Amatorius* even goes so far as to say 'that there is not a particle of Romantic Love in the marriage relation, nor will I admit that those affected by women or maidens are in love, any more than a fly is with milk, or a bee with honey, or people with the calves or birds which they fatten for their own use' (§ 4). A second adds (§ 6) that while many a man has made over his wife or his mistress to another for some large reward, such a case has never been known in the romantic affections which he describes.

But in other respects also the society of Greece does not appear to us in very fair colours, even through this most favourable medium. I repudiate, indeed, altogether the picture drawn by Hertzberg in his History[1] of the shocking features taken from the novels of the day—features rendered impossible by the virtues which he extracts from Plutarch's and Dion's society. This random setting down of every narrative now extant as equally good evidence is a proceeding only saved from ridicule by the great learning and earnestness of the writer.

But, making all due reservations, there is something vain and self-conscious not only in the general complexion of the social meetings which Plutarch so carefully describes; there is even some of it in the old man himself, who is evidently proud of his position, his virtues, his reputation, and though he often alludes to the follies, the loquacity, the conceit of old age, affords in his own person a specimen, though perhaps a very lovable one, of all these imperfections. There is to me in this, as in every other phase of Greek life which I have studied, a certain want, an absence of the calmness and dignity which we require in the perfect gentleman. Aristotle's disagreeable *grand seigneur*,[2] who ever stands upon his dignity, is as far removed from our ideal as is Plutarch, with his garrulous unreserve. Nor do I imagine that the domestic arrangements of the Greek houses, even the most wealthy, ever attained the real cleanliness which we consider the essence of refinement. The prying man, he tells us,[3] is to avoid looking in at open doors, 'For it is not right or fair to the owners, nor is the result pleasant. Within, ill-favoured sights meet the stranger's eye, pots and pans lying in disorder, and women-slaves sitting about, and

---

[1] ii. 279 *sq*.   [2] The μεγαλόψυχος (*Nic. Eth.* iv.)
[3] *De Curios.* 12.

nothing fine or delightful.' It was well if you did not hear the lash, or the outcry of the slaves being punished, or maids upon the rack;[1] an ominous passage, for he couples it with the untidinesses to be witnessed about the home of a dissolute man, the ground wet with wine, and the fragments of garlands lying about.[2] No doubt our superior notions regarding these matters are due to the influence of the women of the house.

And yet it is plain that in this age the mistress of the house had at last obtained some of her rights. It was probably in imitation of what they saw in Rome that the richer people in Bœotia and Attica adopted the freer treatment of the sex, which they had long noticed, but not copied, at Sparta. Plutarch's wife paid visits and received guests, even when her husband was absent, sat at table with him, and joined in all his public interests. But nevertheless his *conjugal precepts* make it plain that he regarded all this as a mere concession or toleration on the part of the husband, to which the wife had no claim in the nature of things, just as he enjoins kindness and mercy to slaves, without for one moment disallowing slavery. In fact the age was mending its manners little by little, by gradual improvement and gentler habits, just as its moralist is always exhorting the individual to combat his vices by daily resolves and small advances. Such a course of moral hygiene is rational, but has never been really effectual. It requires a new dogma, a great revelation, a startling reform to carry with it the weak and wavering masses of mankind, who have not the strength or the patience to work out their own salvation.

Even now 'the Word had been made flesh, and dwelt

---

[1] *De cohib. ira*, 15.
[2] Cf. on an earlier period my *Social Life in Greece*, chap. xi.

among them, full of grace and truth;' even now the Gospel had been preached in Syria, in 'all Asia,' in Macedonia, in Corinth; and yet the great contemporaries Dion, Plutarch, nay, even Josephus, seem never to have heard of it. Had Plutarch been at Athens when S. Paul came there, he would have been the first to give the apostle a respectful hearing, as he himself preached the real identity of all religions, the spirituality and unity of the Deity, and the right of all nations to name inferior gods or demons in accordance with their various traditions. But no; as Judæism was unknown to him beyond the vestments of the high priest, so Christianity, first identified everywhere as a Jewish schism, was still beyond his ken.

It is not till the first century has actually closed that Pliny is startled to find in Bithynia the temples deserted, the altars forgotten, and a new religion overrunning the province. Even then we may assume that Christianity was very little known in Greece beyond Corinth, and in all the Macedonian towns only among Jews and people of the poorest class. For the severance of Greece and Asia Minor is not less remarkable at this time than their respective unity under Roman rule. I have spoken of this already as regards the Greece of Plutarch. But even he stands aloof completely from the Hellenism of Asia Minor, and there is but one brief tract (and is it genuine?) which represents the writer as residing in the turmoil and confusion of the principal assize town of the province—Ephesus or Pergamum—which he describes as a scene of passion and of misery.[1] So Dion[2] on his side speaks with a sort of complacency of the decay and disgrace of Athens, and of its vulgar and base imitations of Roman vices—as if the jealous

---

[1] *Whether the passions of the soul or of the body are worse*, § 4.
[2] i. 383, 385.

Asiatic Hellenist felt that although the wealth and prosperity of the Asiatic towns were now vastly superior, there was still a primacy of sentiment about the name of Athens and of Greece which no *stoas*, or *exedras*, or liberalities from emperors and rich citizens could supply.

CHAPTER XV

EASTERN HELLENISM UNDER THE FLAVIAN HOUSE

LET us then pass once more through the islands to the East, where we can survey with Pliny the economic condition of the cities which Dion had so earnestly exhorted to economy and concord.

We have already noted that Plutarch was essentially a Greek of the Greeks, and so far thoroughly provincial that, despite his early sojourn at Rome, his friendship with a few noble Romans, and his studies in Roman biography, he never mastered Latin, and evidently preferred the provincial Chæronea to the imperial metropolis. His Hellenism does not even include Asia Minor, but is confined to the old Hellenic centres of culture. And yet if we had no work of his except his tract *on Exile* surviving, what a thorough cosmopolitan he would appear in the German histories of later Greece. 'Man,' he tells us (§ 5), 'is no plant of the soil, but of heavenly origin, and the bounds of the world are his present habitation, nor can any one be an exile or a stranger where there is the same fire, water, air, the same rulers and dispensers of our life, the sun, the moon, and the morning star; the same universal laws of one great system, the winter solstice and the summer, the equinox, the

Pleiads, Arcturus, the time of sowing and of growth, moreover one king and governor, God, in whom is the beginning, the centre, the end of everything, whom justice attends to punish violations of His law, which rules us all—citizens of the same polity.' 'Do you not inhabit Sardis? Neither does every Athenian or Spartan the fashionable quarter of their cities. We laugh at the man who thought there was a better moon at Athens than at Corinth, and yet though nature has started us into life free and unshackled we confine and fetter ourselves within small and shabby limits. For no sooner are we transferred elsewhere than we fret longing for the Kephissus or the Eurotas, for Taygetus or Parnassus, so making the rest of the world citiless and uninhabitable by our own discontent.'

All this is very true and fine, but when he proceeds to maintain that life on the barren islands of the Cyclades is after all free from all the burdensome duties and expenses of political life, free from all those imperial cares which pursued Tiberius even to an equally barren island, we feel that his eloquence is intended for a particular class— the Roman exiles in the Levant. He takes care indeed to address his argument formally to Greeks. 'When you enumerate to me heavy taxes, embassies to Rome, receptions of the proconsul, I prefer to live an exile in barren Gyaros or rocky Kinaros.' He goes on to compare Naxos and Hyria with Capri. 'And yet these Cyclades were once the home of Codrus's and Neleus's children, far larger than the retreat of Xenophon at Scillus or the Academy which Xenocrates never left but once a year. See, too, in what terms Homer has spoken of many of them. And now they take a man away from the risks of voyage and the tumult of the agora into a steady leisurely personal existence, circumscribing as with a compass the requirements of his life.

For which of these islands has not *a house, a promenade, a bath, fishing and hare-hunting for those who desire that relaxation;*[1] most of all repose, for which others thirst and cannot find even in the seclusion of their homes or their suburban villas and gardens, from which busybodies and sycophants drag them to the court or to the marketplace. To your island no busybody or usurer or candidate comes to trouble you, *but from friendship and longing for your society the best of your relations and friends make special voyages to see you.*' Compared with this the state of the man who is ever travelling, and spends his time in hotels and boats, is as inferior as that of a planet to a fixed star. Still more absurd is the case of a man exiled not to but from one place, with all the rest of the earth open to him.

I need not proceed. This rhetorical consolation, which I have already considered, shows us a whole society upon these islands whom it was thought disloyal and perhaps dangerous to name, but who might any day return to influence, and who were only too glad to receive visits from their friends, whom they also met at those religious festivals which exiles were permitted to attend. But upon all this there is, unfortunately for us, great reticence. It appears, however, that so long as the seas were safe from pirates, under the efficient government of the Flavians and Antonines, there was more life and society on the islands of the Cyclades than has been suspected by the historians. Let us pass on to Asia Minor.

---

[1] So Philo (*Leg. ad Caium*, § 43) speaks of those whom Caligula had exiled, τοὺς ἀρίστους καὶ εὐγενεστάτους, ἤδη ζῶντας ὡς ἐν πατρίσι ταῖς νήσοις καὶ τὴν ἀτυχίαν εὐτυχέστατα φέροντας, which, though in a rhetorical speech, must have agreed with current notions as regards this secluded life. I have already noticed this point above, p. 262.

I have already cited[1] the evidence of Strabo for the prosperity of Asia Minor in general and the fertility of its Hellenistic territories. The picture we can now draw from Dion and from Pliny is not so flattering, either because they chance to give us the reverse side of the same picture, or because the earthquakes to which I above alluded—the great national calamity of the first century— or the worse than earthquakes upon the Roman throne, had already begun to work that dissolution which was stayed by the Flavians and Antonines, but set in with unmistakable seriousness before the second century had drawn to a close. Strabo speaks as an intelligent traveller who visits these cities and sees their material prosperity, Dion as the counsellor who exhorts them to lay aside their foolish jealousies and factions, Pliny as the prudent administrator who finds them reckless and dishonest in their administration and likely to repudiate their obligations. Pliny does not condescend to notice their mutual jealousies, but to Dion it is the main feature in their life, and that which mars their prosperity. Nor is it difficult to perceive that, however culpable, it was directly induced by the Roman policy of settlement (65 B.C.) The dynasts, the ecclesiastical cities, the free cities, were co-ordinated with varying privileges and various concessions of local autonomy. There were free cities (polities) under a treaty (*liberæ et fœderatæ*), free under no treaty (*liberæ*), Roman colonies, and mere subject polities (*civitates stipendiariæ*), lastly cities with the right of being the assize towns of the province, of receiving the incoming proconsul in their port, etc. But this was not all. As if these differences made between cities which claimed equality did not cause sufficient friction, the Roman

---

[1] Above, chap. xi.

authorities even changed them frequently, and as far as we know without sufficient reason.[1]

For what strikes us as remarkable when we consider these cases is that the changes are not only ascribed to the conduct of the cities in some crisis—a reasonable cause—but to the influence of particular men. Thus in the history of Mytilene alone two men, otherwise insignificant, the philosopher Theophanes and the poet Crinagoras appear, the one worshipped as the hero-founder of his city,[2] the other thanked in honorary inscriptions.[3] There seems little doubt that, in these cases at least, personal influence with Pompey and with Augustus was regarded as the cause of the city's recovery of its privileges.

If this was the case even with such serious politicians as Augustus; if he told the Alexandrians that he pardoned

---

[1] Thus Byzantium, which always counted as an Asiatic city, was in the days of the war with Perseus made a *civitas foederata* (about 167 B.C.) In the days of Lucullus (90 B.C.) it was a *civitas libera*. In 53 A.D. it appears as a *stipendiaria*, while Suetonius says its liberty was taken away by Vespasian (75 A.D.), and Pliny a little later speaks of it as free. Thus Cyzicus was first *libera* after the Mithradatic wars, lost the title in 20 B.C., regained it in 15 B.C., and lost it again under Tiberius. (I take these facts from Mr. Hardy's note, *Pliny's Correspondence*, p. 145.) So Mytilene was *libera* (probably *foederata*) after the defeat of Antiochus (190 B.C.), captured by Lucullus and reduced to a *stipendiaria* (80 B.C.), made free again by Pompey, through the influence of Theophanes, probably reduced again by Antony, restored by treaty with Augustus (about 29 B.C.) through the intervention of Crinagoras. Chios, though not a *civitas foederata*, yet possessed the right usually confined to such cities of trying civil suits affecting Roman residents (cf. *CIG* 2222 and the commentary of Mr. Hicks's *Manual of Inscrips.* p. 356). There are no doubt many other such cases. Cf. the excellent tract of Conrad Cichorius on *Mytilene* (Leipzig, 1888).

[2] Cf. the passages from Strabo and Tacitus, the inscriptions found at Mytilene, and the coins cited by Cichorius, *Rom und Mytilene*, p. 7.

[3] Cf. the newly-discovered inscription of Fabricus and Cichorius, *op. cit.* p. 9 *sq.*

them for the sake of a personal friend; if Herod acquired a great popularity by his interventions on behalf of cities like Ilium with Agrippa,[1] what shall we say when such random rulers as Caligula or Claudius were in power, one of them led by the caprice of the moment, the other confessedly by his freedmen and women? Need we wonder that the richest and most persuasive citizens were told off to go to Rome—a great burden and a great trouble—and intercede with the emperor for some preservation or increase of privileges? Let us consider three cases, of which the first has only been made clear by recent discoveries, and which concerns Mytilene.

In or about 27 B.C. the Mytilenæans sent an embassy to Rome to pray for the renewal of an old 'treaty of alliance,' which would bring them under the class *liberæ et immunes*. They also carried with them as a present a golden crown, and announced a series of extraordinary honours conferred upon Augustus. They found that the emperor was abroad, and they were obliged to follow him to Spain. He sent a polite reply to Mytilene, and granted their request through a decree of the Senate. But not only do the people of Mytilene issue the most laudatory decrees to the principal envoys, the poet Crinagoras and the grammarian Potamon, but these persons were clearly selected because the former was (as we know from his extant epigrams) an intimate of Octavia, of Marcellus, and the rest of the imperial family, while Potamon had been the instructor and was the intimate of Tiberius, the emperor's stepson, and successor. The decree of the Mytilenæans even openly thanks Julia (Livia), Augustus's wife; Octavia, his sister; and the children and relations of the imperial house (*e.g.* Tiberius, Drusus, Marcellus) for their friendly influence. So unblushing was the assertion

[1] Above, p. 176.

that private influence, and not the urging of just arguments, obtained these favours.

In consequence of such cases as this the high-road to Rome was trodden by a constant procession of embassies, carrying crowns and copies of decrees to the emperor, seeking either to settle some local quarrel in some one's favour[1] or to obtain some privilege which a neighbour city had or ought not to have. And not only were the cities led into extravagance and the laying of heavy taxes on their wealthier citizens, for the purpose of giving and sending these honours and making these demands, but, as we shall see presently, they went into all manner of local ostentation in the way of public buildings, in order that the city of each might appear to the proconsul or the emperor, if he came there, worthy of the claims put forward for primacy or other privileges. But before we come to our evidence for this in Dion and Pliny let us consider another example of an embassy, not indeed narrated to us by the Greek side, but even more instructive

---

[1] Historians often express surprise at the insignificance of the questions referred by Pliny in Bithynia to the Emperor at Rome, but we have at least one rescript of Augustus to the authorities of Cnidos, which relates to an equally local affair. Here is his letter (*BCH* vii. 63):

'The Emperor Cæsar, son of the God, Augustus, high-priest, elected consul for the twelfth time, in the eighteenth year of his *potestas trib.* to the magistrates, council, and people of the Cnidians, greeting. Your ambassadors Dionysius [etc.] had audience with me at Rome, and handed me the decree (which they brought) accusing Anaxandridas, already deceased, and his wife Tryphera, here present, of the death of Eubulus, son of Chrysippus. But I, having directed Gallus Asinius my friend [he was proconsul of Asia] to examine by torture the slaves implicated in the affair, ascertained that Philinus, son of Chrysippus, came three successive nights to the house of Anaxandrides and Tryphera with insults, and so to speak besieged them, and on the third occasion even brought his brother Eubulus with him; that then the proprietors, A. and T., when they were unable either by reasoning with Philinus, or by barring the house against his attacks, to enjoy safety within their own dwelling, directed

in showing us the trials and troubles of missions to such miscreants as Caligula, Nero, or Domitian. I allude to the well-known *Embassy to Caligula* preserved to us in the works of the Jew Philo.

The antagonism of Jews and Greeks seems to have been peculiarly bitter; perhaps because they were the two leading subject races in character and ability, and had indeed contended for predominance even under the Ptolemaic and Seleucid monarchies; of this the reader will find ample evidence in my earlier volume on Hellenistic life. In the present case the ambassadors of the anti-Jewish Alexandrians could not aspire to secure such high influence as the relations of Caligula, if indeed those that remained could venture to approach this homicidal lunatic, but they were believed, says Philo, to have heavily bribed beforehand Helico, his favourite freedman, jester, and boon-companion. We have in Philo's very rhetorical tract on the character and policy of this emperor an account of what the writer

one of their household slaves not to kill him, as perhaps others might have done in anger, and not without justification, but to check him by emptying slops upon him, and that the slave, whether intentionally or not (he has persisted in denying all intention), let the utensil go with its contents, and Eubulus succumbed to it, who less deserved this fate than his brother. I have moreover sent you the records of my investigation.

'I should be surprised that the defendants in this case so greatly apprehended the examination of their slaves before your court, did you not seem to me very prejudiced against them, and affected with misplaced indignation, not against those who deserved whatever they suffered, coming as they did thrice by night with insults and violence to other people's houses, and violating public security, but against those who were unfortunate, but not criminal, in defending themselves. But now you will, I think, do well to attend to my decision in this matter, and see that your public records are in agreement with it. Farewell.'

This is a case of the authorities of a free town consulting the Emperor before they made their decision. But if all such local disputes came up before the Emperor, how could the Imperial Government ever get through its business? I give the Greek text in Appendix B.

and his four companions had to endure during their mission to Italy. The madness of the emperor made their audience stranger and more absurd than would otherwise have been the case; they were obliged to run about after him through various new apartments in his villas, and wait for stray observations and jokes vouchsafed to them during intervals in his inspection and direction of his appointments. The rival embassy of Alexandrian Greeks, and apparently other envoys, followed with them, for poor old Philo tells with disgust how there were cheers and clapping of hands when Caligula uttered some jibe against the Jews and their religion. Such loud expressions vexed the emperor's household, who thought a mere smile the strongest utterance of pleasure consistent with court-etiquette. However exaggerated Philo's story, and indeed his style, may be, the impression he produces is so thoroughly in harmony with other evidence that we may give him general credence.

He tells us that ambassadors must submit to any indignities for the sake of the polities they represent, and indeed what they had to expect when they returned is told us by Dion,[1] when recounting to his fellow-citizens his conduct towards them and their requital. 'But I wonder most of all at the ill-nature of some men, or rather their folly, when I remember how they began to talk about the embassy of congratulation which we sent to Rome.[2] It was said that the emperor did not receive the embassy courteously, but was rather vexed with it, as if they expected him to meet us at his hall door, and to embrace those that came, and ask after those not yet arrived by name, and make inquiries about Dick, Tom, and Harry, what they are doing, and why they did not come. Others again said that he

---

[1] περὶ ὁμονοίας, ii. 92.
[2] On either Nerva's or Trajan's accession.

was giving great gifts to Smyrna and its people, and by Jove added that if somebody had been sent to talk to him, he would have granted 10,000 councillors at this person's request, and turned a flood of gold into the city, and no end of money would have been distributed. In all of which there was not a word of truth. Why should we be vexed if other people obtained great gifts? For the emperor, being the most amiable and sensible of men, granted alike to me what I asked and to others what they petitioned for.'

Probably the answer made to all this was: Why then did you not ask for more? since Dion was rather fond of parading his intimacy with Nerva. Nothing is more disappointing to foolish people than to fail in obtaining some frivolous advantage through one who professes himself of influence among the great. And this disappointment finds vent in spite against the mediator who has excited delusive hopes.

Accordingly the orator tells us that having returned, when in favour at Rome and in power, to his native Prusa, after his long exile and wanderings under Domitian's tyranny, he desired to present his city with a new *stoa* or colonnade, which seems to have occupied the same sort of importance in these Hellenistic cities as the recent glass arcades which the Italians have built in Milan and Genoa, and for which they threaten to destroy historic buildings in Florence and Rome. It is the public lounge in bad weather for people who cannot bear rain. However, Dion proposed to build this stoa, 'seeing,' he says, 'that we were behind neighbouring cities in this respect.' Of course the proposal was received with applause, and ratified by votes of the council and the assembly in the theatre. 'I will not detail what I underwent, measuring and calculating, when the work began, how it might turn out handsome, and might not, like so many other such buildings, fall to pieces and be of no use; or what I underwent in journeys to the mountain (to the quarries) a thing in which I had no experience. But then there arose constant talk, though not among many, yet most disgusting, that I was demolishing the whole town, and was turning all the citizens out of their houses: that the whole place was tumbled upside down and destroyed, so that nothing remained. And there were some lamenting over somebody's smithy, and grieving that these memories of our ancient splendours should not be preserved, talking as if the Propylæa or Parthenon at Athens, or the Heræon at Samos were being disturbed, and not shabby and contemptible ruins, worse than the hovels in which they keep sheep, which not a shepherd or even a better class dog will enter —buildings at which you blush and look the other way when the proconsul comes to see us, while your adversaries laugh at them; in which even the mechanics could not stand up; which gaped and shook at every stroke of the hammer. And yet there were people grieved at the disappearance of this our former poverty and obscurity, who would not look at the pillars and pediments rising around them, or at the workshops built elsewhere for the dispossessed; as if they cared for nothing but to keep you down to your old level. For you know well that it is by public buildings and feasts, and having your own law courts, and not having your accounts examined elsewhere, or paying taxes in common with others, that a city attains self-respect and is honoured by the strangers who reside in it, and by the Roman governors.'

Before I comment further on this passage, let me conclude concerning Dion's grievances, which are further noticed in his forty-seventh oration, and corroborated by the eighty-first letter in Trajan and Pliny's *Correspondence*. The opposition went so far that a certain Flavius Archippus, a philosopher, a man evidently of bad character,[1] charged the orator with spending public money on his stoa without rendering account of it. Dion[2] complains bitterly of this treatment, and calls upon his townsmen to make up their minds, and either to trust him with the work or to declare against it, in which case he will leave the city, and retire to one of the many which have elected him to honorary citizenship, and will be proud to receive him.

In weighing the statements of Dion I do not feel sure that the objections to his stoa were altogether so frivolous as he represents them. There are, and always have been, in every town a minority who love the old and the dilapidated for their own sakes, and who, though unable to restrain the majority from erecting monuments of their recent and vulgar prosperity, have a great effect as grumblers, and easily persuade the jealous mob that the new plans are bad, that the contracts are jobbed, and that in fact the so-called improvements are not improvements at all, or at least nothing like what had been expected. This may have given the real backbone to the objections against Dion's liberality, not to speak of the niggard allowance made by the average man for pure patriotism and unselfish generosity in those who are his superiors, and whose motives he cannot interpret by his own.

Let me add that these suspicions must have been much fortified by the general condition of the public works undertaken by the several cities, as we find them described in Pliny's *Correspondence*.[3] While Nicomedia and Nicæa

---

[1] This appears not only from letter 58 of the series, which mentions his condemnation to the quarries for perjury, but from his conduct in this dispute when ordered to state his case.

[2] ii. 135.　　　　　　　　　　　[3] Ed. Hardy, Epp. 37, 39.

were quarrelling furiously about the title of primacy, which Nicæa still claimed though Nicomedia was the legal metropolis, Nicomedia had undertaken—for the purpose, no doubt, of *living up to* its claims—an expensive aqueduct, Nicæa a great theatre and the rebuilding of a burnt down gymnasium on an enlarged scale, both of which Pliny found unfinished, useless, and in ruins. On such undertakings the cities had lavished money which was simply thrown away. He consults Trajan whether these buildings should be finished at public cost, whether the money promised by ambitious citizens should be demanded; he adds that a rival architect had assured him (apparently on false grounds) that one of these works (the gymnasium) would require complete rebuilding.[1]

Other such cases occur in these letters, where the polities seem steeped in debt, and have evidently squandered their money on pure ostentation, and that not even of a successful kind. For it seems plain from Pliny's constant requests for an architect or surveyor to be sent from Rome (though Trajan reminds him that there are clever people of the kind among the Greeks, whom they even import to Rome) that there was scandalous jobbery, that either the architects or the contractors selected by the cities were dishonest, for the work seems always unfinished or going to pieces. Pliny, it is true, never makes this moral charge; indeed the sentence just quoted is the only one where he mentions the rivalries of the architects; but the facts he reports, and the general character of these Greeks, as disclosed to us by Dion, make the inference inevitable. The Bithynian Greeks were mixed with the aborigines[2] they were very anxious, as

[1] *Præterea architectus, sane æmulus ejus a quo opus inchoatum est, adfirmat parietes quanquam XXII. pedes latos imposita onera sustinere non posse* (*op. cit.* p. 139, with Mr. Hardy's notes).

[2] This is clearly shown by the strange list of Ilian names just found by Dr. Schliemann, and announced in the *Neue Freie Presse*, 13 Aug. 1890.

appears from various allusions in Dion, to pose as pure Hellenes; but without attaining the virtues of the old Greeks, they exhibited their defects with remarkable faithfulness.

The Greek levity had no doubt long since been contrasted strongly by the Romans with the seriousness of the only other subject race which furnished them with remarkable men, I mean the Jews. We can hardly find any Greeks of more importance in the imperial counsels than Herod and Agrippa, his grandson; and the jealousy of the two races as regards Roman favour was accentuated by many collisions in which the Greeks were by no means always the victors. Many Greek cities were thankful to invoke the mediation of Herod, and the great prominence given by Tacitus to the war of Titus against the Jews shows how clearly the strong Roman felt the opposing strength of another race with ineradicable traditions, and a more than Stoic contempt of pain and death. It is true that the Jews occupied but a small territory in Southern Syria encompassed with many Greek cities. But just as the strength of the Greeks lay not in their decaying peninsula, but in their *diaspora*—their settlements all over the world; so the Jews were an ubiquitous nation, imbued at the same time with a strong affection for the one spiritual centre of the race at Jerusalem. This gave them unity and power which the Greeks did not possess. Philo, composing a very rhetorical letter as the missive sent by king Agrippa to Caligula, speaks of the spreading of the Jews as follows:[1] 'This sacred city is the metropolis not only of the one country Judæa, but of most lands, by reason of the settlements she sent out from time to time to the bordering lands of Egypt, Phœnicia, and the rest of Syria; also into the more remote Pamphylia, Cilicia, most of Asia as far as the recesses of Pontus;

[1] *Leg. ad Caium*, § 36.

likewise to Europe, Thessaly, Bœotia, Macedonia, Ætolia, Attica, Argos, Corinth, as well as most and the best parts of the Peloponnese. And not only are the continents full of Jewish settlements, but so are the most famous of the islands, Eubœa, Cyprus, Crete. I omit the lands beyond the Euphrates. For very nearly all Babylon and whatever other satrapies have good land, have Jewish settlers. If therefore my fatherland obtain from you benefits, not one city, but tens of thousands are put under obligation, which are settled over every latitude of the habitable world—in Europe, Asia, Libya, in continents, islands, on sea-coasts and far inland.'

This then was the most important element antagonistic to Hellenism in the first century. The Greeks had the advantage in language. If the Jews desired to rival them they must submit to speak in the established *lingua franca* of the Empire. And they did so with difficulty. Josephus says that up to his time only two or three Jews (of Palestine) had learned to speak Greek with fluency and good accent, seeing that the talking of many languages was despised among his people, being the mere accomplishment of any slave that chose to learn other than high and sacred knowledge. He himself had laboured to learn Greek grammatically in order to speak to the world.[1]

What he has told most plainly is the ineradicable mutual hatred of Jews and Greeks. The main cause of revolt against the Herods was their adorning the Greek cities of Palestine and elsewhere with those public buildings which were essential to Roman Hellenism, while most of them were an abomination to the Jews—theatres, circuses, temples, votive monuments with graven images.[2] 'King Agrippa

[1] Cf. the very interesting personal epilogue, *Antiqq*, lib. xx.
[2] Cf. Josephus, *Antiqq*. xx. 9, § 4.

gave the people of Berytus at great cost a theatre for their yearly shows, and spent many myriads on distributions of corn and oil to the populace. And he adorned all the city with statues and images copied from ancient models—here we have the usual Roman copies of great Greek originals— and transferred to them well nigh all the splendour of his kingdom. Hatred therefore against him waxed strong among his people because he took away their substance to adorn a strange city.' And yet this Agrippa is represented by Philo as a most zealous and patriotic Jew, risking his life with Caligula to prevent the profanation of the temple.

How hateful this tampering with Greek fashions was to the Jews, and how increasing was the bitterness of feeling, appears still more clearly from the massacres of Jews by Greeks and of Greeks by Jews, mentioned in Josephus's *Life*. 'Those that dwelt in the cities of Syria round about, seizing the Jews that dwelt among them with their wives and children, slew them, having not a single charge against them.'[1] 'The party of (the insurgent) Jews murder all the Greeks dwelling in the king's palace (near Tiberias), even such as before the war had already been their enemies.'[2] In the opinion of Josephus it was Gessius Florus, a Greek of Clazomenæ, whose appointment by Nero over the Jews led to the downfall of Jerusalem.[3] So also in the fragments of Nicolaus,[4] which tell of the troubles after the death of Herod the Great, it appears that while both Jews and Greek cities agreed in desiring to escape from the Asmonean

---

[1] § 7.   [2] § 12.
[3] *Antiqq*. xx. 11. The first form of this great war, which broke out in April 66 A.D., was between the ἔθνος of the Jews and the Greek πόλεις, each of whom massacred such opponents as were in their power (Jos. *B. J.* ii. 18).
[4] Müller, *FHG* iii. 353.

dominion, of which the Greek cities had hitherto been the main support, the nationalities were at deadly variance. Josephus reports an insurrection or civic conflict at Cæsarea put down by Felix, Nero's governor, with military interference. It was between Greeks and Jews of this city concerning equal rights (περὶ ἰσοπολιτείας). The Jews, relying on their wealth and consequent importance, asserted their rights on the ground that their king Herod had been the founder. The Greeks retorted that it had been a city known as *Strato's Tower* long before, and that of this ancient city no Jew was among the founders. The Roman governor, of course, sided with the Greeks.[1] When, therefore, we are told in the Gospel[2] that certain Greeks desired to see Jesus, and forthwith He exclaims: 'The hour is come, that the Son of man should be glorified,' we must understand these Greeks to have been inhabitants of some of the surrounding and independent polities, established there in antagonism to the Jews, hostile intruders in race and religion, who stood aloof from them with hatred and contempt. To interest these people in the Gospel, to conquer such prejudices, was indeed the victory which overcame the world.

If the hatred of the Jews was outspoken and intense, the hatred of the Greeks was silent and contemptuous. Though thousands of Jews were settled in Greece and in Asia, neither Dion nor Plutarch mentions them except to express contempt; the great Jewish books already before the world in Greek receive no attention; and when the war in Judæa ended with the destruction of Jerusalem, it may have appeared that the battle was won by the Greek, and that his ever-present, subtile, persistent rival in the mart, in the palace, in the very household of the Roman magnate, was finally defeated. But if the Greek was pre-eminent

[1] *Antiqq.* xx. 8, § 7. [2] S. John, xii. 20.

in language, the Jew was superior in what the Greek lacked—that religious fervour which not only preached a dogma but made it a principle, and so satisfied the spiritual craving of the world for some refuge against the tempests of unbelief and superstition. These great topics are, however, not within our present subject.

CHAPTER XVI

THE LITERATURE OF THE FIRST CENTURY

IT remains for me to say something of the general character of Greek literature as we know it in the first century. So poor are, indeed, its representatives, so little was done of importance between the days of Diodorus and Strabo on the one hand, and those of Dion and Plutarch on the other, that it was not worth while interrupting our inquiries into social life to give a separate estimate of letters under the early emperors. As we progress in time, and the Hellenistic tendencies of the emperors become accentuated, there is a corresponding recovery in Greek letters, so that under Hadrian, who comes next upon the scene, a positive revival takes place. And no doubt this revival was announced in the works of Dionysius and Longinus, of Dion and Plutarch. For with the age of Hadrian comes what is called the sophistical development, to which I have so often alluded in the foregoing pages.

Every revival in literature depends upon the general conditions of the society to which it appeals, and which appeals to it, for it must be the voice of the people, or a large part of the people, even as Dion says that Homer is universally popular because he expresses the sentiments which are universal.[1] I will therefore recapitulate briefly what is scattered through the preceding chapters concerning the literary aspects of Greek life, and add some details which have not yet found place in these pages.

In the first place, the general observation holds good for this time also, that the masses of the poorer people were excluded from most of the benefits of literature. They were divided, of course, into country poor and city poor. Dion, in the sequel to the idyll which I have translated in a previous chapter, enters at length into the contrasts of these classes, and points out the miseries of the city poor, who must pay for every necessary of life, or beg for it, while the neediest country peasant can supply himself in kind. But while he urges upon his hearers to promote as much as possible country life, his own ideal picture shows that he did not conceive the pleasures of literature as forming any part of it. Even those who in his day professed to retire from society (for which the term *anachorete* (anchorite) was already in use) could in his opinion do it adequately by that mental abstraction which you may see practised in the streets of any town, 'whereas the mere search after solitude gives no more help in the long run than changing the bed of the sick. For you may see the flute-player performing or teaching his pupils on the very highway, nor does the noise or number of those that pass disturb him, and the dancer or dancing-master in the gymnasium does not mind those undressing or wrestling or idling near him, so it is also with the harpist or the painter; nay, even those that teach children to read sit with their pupils by the wayside, and in this thoroughfare there is no impediment either to teaching or to learning.

[1] Dion, *Or.* vii. (1, 130).

For not unfrequently have I seen, as I passed through the hippodrome, crowds of men at various pursuits, one piping, another dancing, another exhibiting sleight of hand, another reading out a poem, another singing, another reciting a history or a tale, and yet not a single one of these hindered the rest from pursuing his course. Philosophers, no doubt, and philologers demand seclusion and silence for themselves, and will not allow a sight or sound to disturb them, like sick people trying to go asleep. Yet men who live by the sea are not troubled by far greater noise; for they do not keep counting the waves, or noting the changes in their sound, or watching the seagulls skimming along, and floating upon the ruffled water.'[1]

I have allowed myself to run on in translating this picturesque passage, for it leads us back to the superior condition of the city poor, as regards their chances of education. The great days of political discussion, such as those in the theatre of Athens or of Megalopolis, were gone, and from such meetings as that of which Dion has given a description, cited above (p. 280 *sq.*), no good could come. But though the climate of Greek lands made the life of the country poor far pleasanter than it is with us, and though there was not, in addition to the great inducements of paved ways, and lamps, and shops, that of escaping from mud and cold, which has acted so powerfully in clearing the country people into the towns of England; yet to the lively Greek the lively aspects and sounds of the town must have been very attractive. And if he could not, any more than his country brother, buy and read books, he at least could hear what was going on, he could listen to recitations, and to the specimens from new works read out by the booksellers; and of course he could profit by those constant doles or

---

[1] *Or.* xx. (1, 292).

money and those public shows which the rich citizen felt compelled to afford him.

Even with extreme poverty there remained in these people no little pride; and Dion, in discussing what trades they should pursue, is (like Plutarch) curiously fastidious in excluding not only all professional promotion of immorality, but many skilled handicrafts, such as the ornamenting of the walls and ceilings of stately mansions, or the making of rouge or unguents, because they subserve to the luxury of the rich classes. He mentions by the way that it was habitual to cast up to people not only their actual employments but those of their parents; if, for example, a man's mother had been a reaper or a vintager, or had been a wet-nurse for hire, or if his father had taught children, or brought them to and from school. This sort of society, vain, impatient, frivolous, which must in any case have been educated by hearing and not by reading, afforded indeed a very unpromising atmosphere for literature. To such people the old masters were no doubt tedious; the old tragedies and comedies out of date. They must have something startling, new, exciting, meant not for permanent profit but for present amusement.

I think this tendency to superficiality must have been strongly promoted by the marked severance which now existed between serious philosophy and the other forms of literature—poetry and rhetoric. We can illustrate it not merely by contrasting authors, but by comparing an author with himself. Thus, for example, the philosopher Philodemus, of whom I have already spoken, has left us two kinds of work—dry prose tracts on music or on poetry, composed, as was the Epicurean fashion, with a deliberate contempt for style. The same man has left us poems on sportive or even loose subjects, filed and polished with the most minute care. He evidently regarded the two occupations as totally and radically distinct. Plutarch, indeed, and Dion endeavoured to combine moral teaching with grace of style, but the professional philosophers, especially those Cynics whom the orator describes as very numerous in Alexandria,[1] were, as the reader may see by looking back (p. 246), mere itinerant beggars, who collected crowds of children or sailors or idlers about them, and amused them with some performance partaking more of a mountebank's than a reformer's work. There are not wanting in our own day extravagant forms of open-air preaching not very unlike these performances. We find in an epitaph by Meleager, a century older, philosophy is even named as a kind of trade together with husbandry and shipping.[2]

Even more solid professors of philosophy, who corresponded in so many respects to our clergy, assumed the long hair, beard, and cloak, which were distinctly an uniform, and which were regarded with the same kind of dislike that a clerical garb encounters among the ruder and looser classes in our own day. The street boys of Asia went even further, for Dion tells us[3] that though nobody minds a country yokel or a petty trader wearing any dress he finds convenient, when they see a man with long hair, wrapped in a cloak without any tunic under it, they cannot let him pass by in peace, but provoke and worry and revile him, or even pull him about, if they think him not strong or likely to be assisted, although he merely wears the received garb of a philosopher. And not only is this so, but philosophers are not rare, like Getæ and Persians and Nasamones, with their strange

[1] i. 403.
[2] *Anth. Pal.* ed. Didot. i. p. 363, No. 470:—
ζήσας δὲ τίνα στέργων βίον ; οὐ τὸν ἀρότρου
οὐδὲ τὸν ἐκ νηῶν, τὸν δὲ σοφοῖς ἕταρον.
[3] Cf. Dion, ii. 39, 43.

clothes, but there are such crowds of them as exceed the cobblers or fullers or mountebanks or any other calling. Moreover, this is the usual dress in which men see the gods in temples, or ancient public benefactors, represented by the sculptors.

Dion attributes this unpopularity[1] to the expressed or implied assumption of superiority in the profession—an assumption not justified by the lives of many of these teachers. Here, however, I am not further concerned with this crowd of self-constituted pastors of the people more than to insist upon their severance from literature, both poetical and prose, and hence the danger to writers in that day of neglecting the solid and permanent teaching which is conveyed through letters, the most universal and effective of the fine arts, and attending to mere formal perfection. And again, even in literature, we have another deep gulf between the learned grammarians, the analysts of Epic and Attic diction, of metre, of rythm, and those who devoted themselves to *belles-lettres*. Not that the latter were wanting in even excessive learning. But serious and sportive subjects, were now incongruous; the former were monopolised by prose writers; the latter was wholly given up to that crowd of epigrammatists which is the only really prominent feature in the poetry of this long and famous epoch.

The great body of this Greek poetry, now gathered, with much that is both earlier and later, in the *Anthology*, has received but occasional and scant attention from modern scholars, so that the workmanship of the principal poets has only been disclosed by very recent researches. It now appears that to write an epigram in strict form was no easy task, and that the niceties of caesura and rythm must have been discussed at Alexandria, Cos, and Gadara with even

[1] *Or.* lxxii. *on the Philosophic Garb.*

more minuteness than the laws of the sonnet among modern poets. It is not the province of this book to go into such special questions; I shall therefore content myself with giving the results gathered by Rubensohn in his recent edition of Crinagoras, where the tracts on this special subject are named, and their essence extracted.

It appears that Callimachus was the father of this new and more precise method of writing elegiacs,[1] according to which each verse was to begin with sedateness, and hurry towards its conclusion. Thus spondees were almost the rule at the opening of each line—the second half of the pentameter being necessarily dactylic. If the former half was dactylic, this defect was to be remedied by having at least two cæsuras. The earlier and better poets adhered strictly to these rules.[2] Here is another law. The pentameter must not end with an iambus in a separate word—the only two cases occurring in Callimachus being accounted for by one being a proper name and the other a rhetorical point. Crinagoras also has but two doubtful instances. Turning back to the hexameter, of which the first four feet only are variable, we find Crinagoras, out of 137 verses, writing 90 in one of the following four forms: *dsdd* (30), *dddd* (22) *sddd* (23) and *ssdd* (15). Of the other twelve possible combinations two are not at all, the rest very sparingly, used. It appears further that a spondee is not allowed before the bucolic cæsura (where the fourth foot ends a word), neither is the second syllable of a dactyl in that position permitted to end a word, so that a line emended by Boissonade into Ἄχρι τεῦ, ἆ δείλαιε, κεναῖσιν ἐν ἐλπίσι θυμέ thus violates the laws of Crinagoras. This poet went even so far in the more polished inscriptions on votive monuments as to make all

[1] Cf. Kaibel's *Philodemus* (*Epigrams*), Greifswald, 1885.
[2] Cf. the cases cited, *op. cit.* p. 20.

his hexameters uniform in cæsura. He was however, very free in admitting hiatus, and in this latter point he differed from Meleager and the more careful of his school, who only admitted hiatus at the end of a foot, and generally at the end of the fourth. What is called trochaic hiatus—between the second and third syllables of a dactyl—was carefully eschewed.[1] But as regards cæsura the stricter epigrammatists were seldom content with that in the third foot, supplementing it with the favourite bucolic cæsura, which they regarded as almost necessary if the first cæsura did not occur till the fourth foot.

These are but some of the subtleties which have been recently discovered by the minute patience of Kaibel, Meyer, and others, and no doubt they will be increased in number as time goes on. It appears, according to the Hellenistic poetasters, that the opening line of Homer's *Iliad* contains three violations of strict metrical rules.[2]

When, therefore, we wonder at the stiffness and the obscurity of many of these short poems, we should remember that the poets put themselves under restrictions as exacting as those of the most complicated lyric poetry. Of course it did not require a poet, but a smart person, to compose these little sportive pieces, as we know from an interesting allusion in Plutarch. He tells us of a soldier who found after a long time the coins he had hidden in the half-closed hand of Demosthenes's statue at Athens, and that there was quite a competition among the *Euphuists* in composing epigrams, when so a striking subject came

---

[1] Cf. the details in Kaibel's *Philodemus*, p. 5.

[2] Cf. Rubensohn, *op. cit.* p. 33. Any word belonging to the first foot must not end in the second with a trochee, as does ἄειδε. Then the strong cæsura must not be obtained by an iambic word like θεά. Lastly the cæsuras in the third and fifth feet are not to be used in the same line!

before the public.[1] These poems are, therefore, an evidence of a certain phase of social life, though they contains few allusions to anything distinctive in manner and customs. Nor did they help any more in educating the people—which poetry ought to do—than the writing and solving of acrostics do nowadays.

To attempt any detailed review of the great group written during the period of the present book would require a volume in itself, and I think vague generalities so unfruitful, that it seems better to select two or three of the best, and say a word or two on them with some quotations. Even this task is not easy, seeing that in the wild thicket of the *Anthology* no attempt is made at chronological order, and the works of many centuries are jumbled together in inextricable confusion. Separate editions of single poets, such as the excellent ones above cited, are still rare, and not easily accessible.

Let us begin with Meleager of Gadara, one of the best of them, who was, moreover, the first collector of a large selection into what he called a *garland*.

The poet leaves us in no doubt as to his origin. He was born in *the Attic Gadara* [2] *founded among the Assyrians*, as these writers often call Syria; he was brought up at Tyre; in his old age he settled at Cos, not without travelling as far as Byzantium. All this he writes in the epitaphs he composed for his own tomb. He boasts that he combined Love, the Graces and Wisdom, in his work. I take this *wisdom* to mean poetic artifice, for of philosophy I find no trace. The reader will note that just as it was remarked of

---

[1] Plut. *Demosth.* 31.—πολλοὶ τῶν εὐφυῶν ὑπόθεσιν λαβόντες . . . διημιλλῶντο τοῖς ἐπιγράμμασι.

[2] Philodemus of Gadara, his contemporary Antipater of Sidon, and other names show that Syria was now a fruitful source of literature.

Nicolaus,[1] so here Meleager is proud of his Syrian home, for while in this and the next century it could claim more literary distinctions than belong to any other province of Hellenism —not of course including the invented myths, which gave an old Attic or Argolic origin to these really Macedonian settlements—he allows contact with Syria to tell upon his work. He twits one of his flames for being addicted to a quiet Sabbath, and says Love is feverish even on that day. He says farewell, in one of his auto-epitaphs, in Aramaic, in Phœnician, and in Greek. We may therefore regard him as the most perfect embodiment of that Hellenism which transfused the Eastern Empire. There is no allusion to Jewish troubles, to the conflict with the Greeks, to the settlement of Pompey, to any one of all the momentous events which happened during the poet's life. Were we to believe his epigrams, he spent all his passionate days among fair women and boys, of the most perfect beauty and the most abandoned character. But if I read aright this child of his age, we need no more credit his picture of the promiscuous amorousness of Helleno-Syrian society than the contrasted picture of the ideal shepherds in Dion's idyll, who knew nothing but the bond of marriage. We may even suspect this hyper-anacreontic Anacreon, with his wicked beauties and his distracting ganymedes, to have been a respectable and hardworking man, labouring out his elegant conceits, polishing his lines, and seeking by the simulation of art to produce the impression of the storm and tumult of a love-tost soul.[2]

In three directions I hold him to have attained great per-

[1] Above, p. 177.
[2] Cf. what was cited above, p. 128, from Cicero, in describing his contemporary Philodemus, whose very similar epigrams were composed to suit the taste of Roman libertines, perhaps even with disgust and contempt, by the dependent philosopher.

fection,—in pathetic exclamation, in passionate soliloquy, and in a Carlylesque richness of pictorial epithets.[1] And if he tells us nothing of the politics or home life of his day, he is both observant and picturesque upon natural phenomena, as when he beseeches the mosquitoes, 'shrill sounding, shameless siphons of human blood, two-winged monsters of the night,' to spare his beloved; or again to wake her with his love message, while they leave her husband asleep; as when he prays the cicada, 'the beguiler of his desire, the lyre of Nature, drunk with dew, to bring him mid-day sleep beneath the plane-tree's shade.'[2] His garlands of flowers too are composed of real spring flowers, and such as bloom together[3]—the narcissus, the crocus, smiling lilies that haunt the hills, the purple hyacinth, and the opening rose are entwined about his beloved's head.[4] In consonance with this is his famous hexameter poem on the spring, which has led to countless imitations, from Horace to Goethe.[5]

These features present to us a far more interesting personality than that of Crinagoras, with his stricter verse, his frequent allusions to the imperial house, his display of affectation, varied with only one single exclamation

[1] Here are specimens of each, I quote from the Didot edition of the *Anthology*:—
(vii. No. 476), Αἰαῖ, ποῦ τὸ ποθεινὸν ἐμοὶ θάλος ; ἅρπασεν ’Αίδας
ἅρπασεν· ἀκμαῖον δ’ ἄνθος ἔφυρε κόνις.
(xii. 117), Βεβλήσθω κύβος· ἅπτε· πορεύσομαι. Ἠνίδε τόλμα,
οἰνοβαρές, τίν’ ἔχεις φροντίδα ; κωμάσομαι.
Κωμάσομαι ; ποῖ, θυμὲ τρέπῃ ; τί δ’ ἔρωτι λογισμός ;
ἅπτε τάχος. Ποῦ δ’ ἡ πρόσθε λόγων μελέτη ;
(v. 177), Ἔστι δ’ ὁ παῖς γλυκύδακρυς ἀείλαλος, ὠκύς, ἀταρβὴς
σιμὰ γελῶν, πτερόεις νῶτα, φαρετροφόρος.
[2] v. 151, 152; vii. 195, 196.
[3] If we except the rose, which we know was artificially forced.
[4] v. 144, 147.
[5] ix. 73. I have printed the full text in the Appendix C.

from the heart in the midst of all his artificial politeness.[1] But as this latter poet as well as Philodemus can be easily bought and read in a good and cheap edition, I shall not further discuss them, but select another of the poets credibly assigned to the first century after Christ.

Philippus of Thessalonica was the second collector of a garland of epigrams, and tells a certain Camillus, to whom he dedicates it, that as Meleager has preserved the more ancient poets, he will gather the more modern, of whom he gives a list—Antipater, Crinagoras, Antiphilus, etc. He himself contributes about eighty pieces, but not by any means of the same merit as those of Meleager. Many of them are votive inscriptions on the tools of various tradespeople— fishermen, sailors, weavers, etc., who retire in old age and lay aside their work. There is hardly anything, however, personal to be found; he mentions Actium, and Leucadia; he is styled 'of Thessalonica'; he wonders at the great piers of Agrippa that made the harbour of Puteoli, at the elephants which, once a resource of war, now only serve to draw the car of Cæsar. This exclusive attention to Rome and Roman affairs is in fact the only personal feature of this poet (who seems to have lived till the days of Nero), of Crinagoras and the rest in the Imperial epoch, as contrasted with the earlier Meleager and his fellows. Many Romans, even Marcellus and Germanicus, appear as contributors to Philippus's volume. Unfortunately both these earlier collections are mixed up with later and worse work in a confusion

---

[1] I mean the soliloquy numbered 28 in Rubensohn's edition:—

Ἄχρι τεῦ, ἆ δείλαιε, κεναῖς ἔτ᾽ ἐπ᾽ ἐλπίσι, θυμέ,
πωτηθεὶς ψυχρῶν ἀσσοτάτω νεφέων,
ἄλλοις ἄλλ᾽ ἐπ᾽ ὄνειρα διαγράψεις; ἀφένοιο
κτητὸν γὰρ θνητοῖς οὐδὲ ἕν αὐτόματον·
Μουσέων ἀλλ᾽ ἐπὶ δῶρα μετέρχεο· ταῦτα δ᾽ ἀμυδρά
εἴδωλα ψυχῆς ἠλεμάτοισι μέθες.

perhaps impossible to unravel. We notice in Philippus sarcastic attacks on the book-worm class, in close imitation of the men of Callimachus's day, but perhaps peculiarly suitable when learned studies had become specialised and completely separated from all polite literature. I have quoted some specimens in the Appendix D.

I do not think I should add new features of interest were I to specify many other small distinctions to be found among these poets. They plainly diffused among the higher classes a taste for this sort of ingenuity, which led people into studying a kind of art, a kind of letters, a kind of artificial verse, and the learning of mythology necessary to supply them with images and allusions. It was, as I said, an amusement like that of acrostics, but more finished and more artistic in proportion as Greek letters were more polished and more artistic than those of England.[1] Let us then turn for a few moments to the prose writing, which not only on the one hand rivalled the display and conceits of poetry, but on the other sought bravely to keep up purity of diction by a careful study of the great old masters in history and in eloquence.

The critics of Cicero's time (as represented by his rhetorical tracts), as well as Dionysius of Halicarnassus and the writer *on the Sublime*, show so perfect an appreciation of what is good and great that we wonder at the total impotence of practical men to carry out the rules so admirably discussed by the theorists, nay, even of the theorists to carry out their own principles. The highest outcome of this revival of Attic purity is the writing of Lucian, which comes in the

---

[1] The collections of translations into Latin and Greek verse—*Sabrinæ corolla, Arundines Cami*, etc.—wherein the most finished scholars of our day have exhibited their ingenuity and their grace, are another similar but more slavish 'sport' in literature.

succeeding century, and yet Cobet has amply shown how far removed he is from the masters whom he emulated. The Alexandrians studied grammar with extreme care, and with the greatest models before them, and yet we find here too that no conscious labour will replace that subtle spirit which transfuses all the minds of a certain epoch, and makes it the golden age of a nation's literature. When this moment has gone by, not even the grace of Menander, the glow of Dion, the candour of Plutarch can command it to return.

We have already tasted largely of Plutarch the essayist and Dion the moral preacher; I do not feel bound to do more than mention Nicolaus the historian, whose panegyrical history of Cæsar and Augustus is extant, as well as many fragments of his historical encyclopædia. We may suppose him to have been educated in the way which Dion recommends, and which I shall presently quote, as well as by his contact with Syrian and Roman courts and with divine philosophy, on which he wrote many tracts for Herod. And yet his panegyric on Julius Cæsar and Augustus remains buried in the great forest of Müller's *Fragments of the Greek Historians*, and will never be consulted except by specialists, or edited again for the world.

There is another historian, his contemporary, nay, his model, from whom he has copied pages. I mean Dionysius of Halicarnassus, who came to Rome shortly after the battle of Actium, and lived a literary life there for twenty-two years, giving special attention to the Latin language and historical literature. We may put him with Strabo, Nicolaus, and the so-called Longinus, as the best extant specimens of that class of Romanising Hellenists to whom the spiritual reconciliation of their country and scattered people with the domination of Rome was the ideal of a literary life. He seeks consciously to carry out the work and object of Polybius; but while that

great historian had chosen with practical sense the period
of historic contact between Greece and Rome, with its long
prepared causes in the growth of the latter power beyond
the bounds of Italy, Dionysius desires to lead the student
from the earliest times to the point where Polybius begins,
and undertakes to show in the mythical history, the legends,
the old religious usages still surviving, proofs of an ever
repeated contact between Hellas and Rome. The older
Roman writers, even Cato, had asserted this connection as
then the only means of claiming a decent national pedigree.
If not Greek in origin, you must be barbarian. But when
the historic magnificence of Rome was established beyond
all doubt, there seems to have been a certain solace to the
vanquished in asserting that after all these conquerors of the
world were derived from an asylum of thieves and fugitive
slaves, as we should say, from a criminal colony or a found-
ling hospital. This had been dilated on by some Hellenistic court-historians, themselves the slaves of royal slaves,
a kind of consolation which disguises spite and detraction.[1]

It is in reply to these anonymous persons that Dionysius
writes his History of early Rome, attributing Greek manners,
rites, language, to his Romulus and Remus, and putting into
the mouth of the early kings discourses like the speeches of
the characters in Thucydides. The appreciation of historic
evidence in all this is to us grotesque, though to a classical
author of any period, not to say a close student and imitator
of Thucydides, speeches were the natural expression of a
political situation. But how even Polybius would have
laughed outright at the notion of a speech from a mythical
character! So indeed would he have laughed at the
conservative attitude in religion of this learned rhetorician,
which is truly Herodotean rather than Polybian, and men-

[1] *Antiqq. Rom.* i. 4, *sub. fin.*

tions as one of the peculiar advantages of Italy over other lands that it is suitable not only for all kinds of culture and human habits, but for the tastes of all classes of gods— mountains and glades for Pan, meadows and rich lands for nymphs, coasts and islands for marine deities, in fine, whatever suits any god or dæmon[1] is there to be found. Indeed he often declines to give any opinion on theological difficulties, or to accept or reject the doctrine we find in Plutarch of intermediate dæmons, since all this is the speciality of that class which is quite separate and peculiar, the philosophers.[2]

And yet this man, so inferior as a historian to his great models, inferior not only in his conception of history, which he regards as a careful collection and arrangement of legends and uses, but in his very style, which cannot lay aside rhetoric in the most incongruous situations — this Dionysius makes an epoch in his careful appreciation and criticism of the *style* of the old prose masters. It had been felt, ever since the days of Cicero, that Asianic flourish was no true eloquence, and that the Attic masters must be the proper models. But the Rhodian attempt to maintain this tradition was made without proper studies, and substituted the dry and jejune for the false and turgid. Under the reign of Augustus we find even the Latin poets going back from their Alexandrian models to the great masters, and the account given by Dion Chrysostom (a man far behind his

[1] *Antiqq. Rom.* i. 38. Cf. for other specimens of the author's religious views i. 67, *sub. fin.*, where he recoils from religious curiosity, in imitation, I suspect, of Herodotus; and (ii. 19, 20) his remarks on indecent Greek myths and the difficulties they cause in religion, as compared with the more staid Roman creed.

[2] ii. 21. ·'Αλλ' ὑπὲρ μὲν τούτων τοῖς αὐτὸ μόνον τὸ θεωρητικὸν τῆς φιλοσοφίας μέρος ἀποτετμημένοις ἀφείσθω σκοπεῖν, are his words in speaking of the alleged good and bad effects of the Greek myths.

age in minute learning) of what every gentleman ought to study[1] is very sound and reasonable.

'Let Homer of course be your daily spiritual bread, the beginning, middle, and end of every culture, for young and old, who gives to each as much as he can receive.[2] Lyric and elegiac poetry is all very well, if you have great leisure, otherwise you may pass it by. Thus in tragedy you may prefer Euripides, and in comedy Menander to the older *and perhaps greater*[3] masters, because they contain more practical wisdom. History is essential, but Herodotus for charm and Thucydides for excellence are far superior to Ephorus, Theopompus, and the rest.' In oratory Demosthenes is of course supreme in force and Lysias in the disguise of force, but Dion recommends Hypereides and Æschines, as it is easier to understand their art. Nor will he object to the modern rhetoricians of the previous generation being studied, especially as men approach them with a free critical spirit, and not in that slavish admiration, which they feel towards the ancients. Among Socratic thinkers none is serviceable to the man of action except Xenophon, who indeed is in history also the most perfect and excellent of masters.

Such is the training in letters recommended by the most eminent orator of his century. It is only vague and general, not going into any detailed criticism; and this generality is also the character of the tract *on the Sublime*, formerly attributed to Longinus, but now placed by general agreement at the close of the Augustan age, and in that moment of reaction

[1] He uses ἄσκησις for careful study, thus leading the way to the later meanings, which have given us the words *ascetic* and *asceticism*.

[2] *Or.* xviii. 1, 282.—"Ὅμηρος δὲ καὶ πρῶτος καὶ μέσος καὶ ὕστατος παντὶ παιδὶ καὶ ἀνδρὶ καὶ γέροντι τοσοῦτον ἀφ' αὑτοῦ διδοὺς ὅσον ἕκαστος δύναται λαβεῖν.

[3] Here we see the contrast to Plutarch's attitude (above p. 329); Dion apologises to the critics who may object to his preference of the newer masters.

from Alexandrianism and Asianism to the pure Atticism of the golden age. This essay seeks to stimulate a taste for the real masterpieces in letters rather than to give any analysis of their excellence; it is the writing of a clever *dilettante* rather than of a professor, and though very valuable in directing the public taste, can hardly be said to have contained new knowledge. And yet among all the books of this age none has received more attention than this remarkable tract. It is certainly the most modern and enlightened of all that the Greeks have left us on the theory of art. Unfortunately the text is miserably lacerated, and often breaks off in the middle of an important discussion.

The general attitude the author assumes is that though genius is distinctly heaven-born, its splendid results are attained by using the resources of art. He rightly holds fast to the great Greek principle that nothing perfect can be produced without study, that spontaneity may suggest but will never work out what is really beautiful or majestic. But at the same time he agrees perfectly with modern criticism in recognising that irregularities may be only a flaw in genius of the highest order, perhaps even a characteristic of such genius, seeing that unvarying correctness is seldom, if ever, the attribute of the highest work. Thus in criticising the rhetor Cæcilius, who was evidently the advocate of strict correctness, and who consequently placed the pellucid but thin graces of Lysias above the richness of Plato, he breaks out (cap. 35) into the following reflections: 'What was in the minds of those godlike men who aimed at the highest perfections of their art, when they despised minute accuracy of detail? This among many other considerations, that nature hath not made our species mean and ignoble creatures, but introducing us to life and all the universe around it as to a great festival and pageant, to be spectators of all its grandeur and keen competitors for its prizes, hath engrained in our souls an indelible love of everything that is great and therefore more divine than ourselves. Hence it is that to the speculation of man and the reach of his imagination not all the universe sufficeth, but our thoughts are ever passing its furthest bounds, so that if any one will consider in his own life how far the great exceeds the beautiful, he will know forthwith whereunto we were created. It is nature which tells us not to admire the rivulet, though it be pellucid and fit for use, but the Nile, the Ister, the Rhine, and above all the ocean; nor are we struck by the fire upon the hearth, however clear be its flame, but rather by the celestial fires, oft though they be obscured, or again by the crater of Ætna, whose eruptions cast from its abysses great rocks and vast masses, and send forth rushing torrents of essential fire.'

On these grounds he worships the capricious and variable Plato, and appreciates the splendours of the rugged Thucydides. If there be a flaw in his judgment it is in his coldness towards Aristophanes.

Far more precise were the studies of Dionysius on the great prose writers of his people, especially on the orators; and had all his work been preserved we might well say that ancient criticism had nothing more to add to his researches. And yet even he does not seem to have led a school, but to have been an independent thinker. His extant studies upon Demosthenes and upon Thucydides make us regret deeply the loss of most of his parallel studies on the other orators.[1]

---

[1] Cf. on the list of his remains, Nicolai, *Griech. Lit. Gesch.* ii. 146-149; and also the constant references to him in Blass's volume on Demosthenes in his *Attische Beredsamkeit*. Dionysius, like Cæcilius, is too strictly the professor as regards Plato and Thucydides, and can-

I will not dilate further upon these interesting features of the Augustan and Claudian literary renaissance, for they are all simply forms of erudition and do not touch the social aspects of the Greek world either intimately or directly. So also I pass in silence the many collections of letters, almost all spurious, which may be found in the *Epistolographi Græci*, and of which readers of Latin will find poetical paraphrases in Ovid's *Heroides*. They, like the speeches in Greek histories, are what, in small people's judgment, great people ought to have said, not what they did say. Nor do any of the 'elegant epistles' of this century approach in value those attributed to Plato and to Demosthenes, which, if they are spurious, are so well composed as to maintain their claim for genuineness among some first-rate critics.

The whole of this literature was a literature of erudition, knowing no other excellence than to copy great ancient models, and rightly basing the perfection of this imitation on close and protracted study. No hint reaches us of popular poetry, no echo of popular stories, no fresh source in this barren land from which some new genius might, like Theocritus, draw a new 'draught of Hippocrene' and attempt the rejuvenescence of Greek literature. The so-called revival of Hadrian's day, the sophistic literature of the next three centuries, as it appears in Lucian, Aristides, Libanius, what is it? What effect did it exercise upon any large mass of the people? What model did this second-hand brilliancy show to the men of other ages and of inferior culture?

There was indeed one literary work going on during this century of the first magnitude, as the result has amply proved, but it was in a remote corner of Hellenism, unknown,

not enjoy their greatness without feeling constantly shocked at their irregularities. In this respect, therefore, we should rank our Longinus higher.

moreover, to the most learned and curious of the Greeks, to Dion and to Plutarch. For there, where Hellenism had to struggle with the force and ability of Judaism, teaching and learning with the interest of hate and the relish of antagonism, there, among the common people, were springing up those books on the life of Christ which touch the hearts of men with a directness and force very foreign to the flowery and rhetorical arguments of a Philo or a Josephus. The simplicity, the natural vigour, the unconscious picturesqueness in these narratives is so remarkable, that even had they never laid claim to any inspiration, sound judges must have condoned their faulty grammar and poor vocabulary, and acknowledged in them at least the voice of honest men speaking from the heart. Whether these writers were indeed Israelites or not, they were, as writers, without guile, and the fact that they all chose Greek for their medium has been the main cause of the persistence of Greek studies to this day.

The slow recognition of these books—for their influence is first recognised in the correspondence of Pliny, if indeed the movement he reports did not result from mere preaching —is a feature well worthy of our notice. Whether they were kept secret from the cavils of the Greeks we know not; but considering the principles openly asserted in those days, considering the slavish adherence to the great Attic models, what was more obvious, what more certain, than that such pictures as the opening scenes of S. Luke's Gospel or the Sermon on the Mount would be despised by the critics as the work of late-learning and self-taught people, who knew nothing of the art of expression, or of the laws of composition? And yet the world has judged differently; the idyll of Bethlehem lives, while the idyll of Euboea lies buried in Dion; Herod as the tyrant lives, while as the polished Hellenist he is forgotten; the metaphors on the mount, the parables by the way, have outlived the paradoxes of the Stoic, the moralities of the lecture-room.

Yet as the vehicle of this new doctrine, this new exposition, was Greek, so it borrowed from Hellenism much of its tone, of its terminology, of its subtler thinking. Let no man imagine that the Christian faith owes nothing, or even little, to the Greeks. 'The fulness of time' for the Gospel came when Greek conquered Jew and Jew conquered Greek, and the world inherited the legacy of their struggle through Roman hands. For it was through Rome that the Greek spirit must be subdued—I mean the wordliness, the triviality, the slavishness which had infected the Hellenistic world. Though all men used Greek and professed Greek culture, the influence of the Roman master was everywhere seen. Roman villas in their splendour have left their traces in many parts of Greece and Asia Minor; Roman luxuries are the natural form which wealth adopts in the Hypata of Apuleius, the Corinth of Aristides. There is hardly a treatise we have quoted which is not addressed to a Roman patron, and Roman names were everywhere being assumed as a distinction by Greeks.

Nor is it easy to estimate, as a feature in this Roman domination over the world, the effects of that apotheosis which was so often claimed by the emperors and so often thrust upon them by their Hellenistic subjects. As is well known, the gods of popular belief were so familiarised by the treatment of poets and painters, that the gulf between an exalted man and a god could hardly seem insuperable. And perhaps it was rather the gods who were further assimilated to the emperor than the emperor to the gods. From one point indeed he was greater than any of them. Not only was his will law, but any one who violated it was promptly and visibly punished. Indeed, according as the imperial system became more completely regulated, the hand of the emperor reached more and more directly into the affairs of every province and controlled the life of every citizen. It is of course dangerous to draw inferences from individual cases, but the decree of the proconsul in Nero's day which has been preserved,[1] and dating a generation earlier than Pliny's commission to Bithynia, shows either a very different kind of man or a far more reasonable system. This officer expresses it as his principle to adhere to the decisions made by his predecessor, but when old documents bearing on the question and properly attested are produced, he settles (in the first person) a very knotty point, and reserves an exceptional privilege for the Christians by reversing the previous decree.

We cannot imagine Pliny doing such a thing. On every question, however trivial, he sends for Trajan's decision, and in no case does the emperor, though at times a little impatient, ever direct him to depend generally upon his own judgment.[2] And if the proconsuls and legates made themselves, or were made, mere ciphers by this centralisation, there are already occasional signs of what becomes so painfully prominent in later days—the transformation of provincial honours into provincial burdens. Pliny proposes to make wealthy men take up public loans in order that he may secure interest on the provincial funds, as there was some difficulty in investing them profitably. When the state cannot find men ready to invest for the security it offers, or when it insists upon higher than the current interest, we may be sure that there is something radically unsound in the economic situation.

[1] Cf. Hicks, *Man. of Inscrips.* p. 355.
[2] It is perhaps to be urged in defence of this, that Pliny was not a regular governor, with officially-defined powers, such as a proconsul, but a special commissioner sent to act for the emperor in a special inquiry.

Perhaps the wonder is that things lasted so well and that the crisis did not come for so many generations. Long before the days of Pliny thoughtful men had seen that the imperial system, destructive to local politics, had silenced the voice of eloquence and changed the historian and the poet into the chronicler and panegyrist of imperial splendour. There is no more striking passage in the striking tract *on the Sublime*, which I have already noticed, than the passage in which he discusses the alleged effects of this organised submission to Rome, this just slavery, as he very properly calls it. The decadence of Greek literature was openly assigned by many to the embrace of this political boa-constrictor. Here is what Longinus says (§ 46):

'One thing however remains, which, my dear and valued friend, because of your desire for learning, I shall not hesitate to add and explain clearly. It is that difficulty which one of the philosophers very recently propounded. "I wonder," said he, "as doubtless do many others, how it is that in our age there is plenty of rhetorical power and forensic ability, pungency and readiness, fluency and charm of style, but none now, or almost none, of the true Sublime, the really majestic order of genius. Such a dearth is there over all the world of oratory proper! Can it be," said he, "that we are to believe the common murmur, that democracy is the fostering nurse of genius, with which, almost exclusively, the race of orators flourished and with which it died away? For the province, they say, of freedom is to encourage the thoughts of the lofty-minded and to cheer them on, to promote the eagerness of emulous rivalry and the generous ambition to excel. Moreover by the prizes proposed under free constitutions the intellectual advantages of the orators are exercised and sharpened time after time; they have as it were their edges whetted; they shine forth, as might be expected, free with the freedom whose cause they serve. But we of the present day," said he, "seem to learn from childhood the discipline of a moderate slavery, having been from our tenderest years well-nigh swathed in its manners and customs, never tasting oratory's noblest and purest fountain, viz. liberty, for which reason we turn out nothing but magnificent flatterers." For this cause he held that any other profession was tenable even by the menial class, but that a slave could never be an orator; for, on the first effort, a long familiarity with enforced reticence and dungeon-cells and continual thrashings bubbles up and leaves the orator tongue-tied, even as Homer says,—

"The half of valour goes when slavery comes."[1]

"Precisely then," saith he, "if the thing may be credited, as the boxes, in which the so-called Pygmies or dwarfs are brought up, not only hinder the growth of the prisoners, but even by the bands surrounding their bodies contract their original dimensions; so might one represent all slavery, be it ever so moderate, as an encasing of the soul and neither more nor less than a general prison."[2]

'I however, taking him up, said: It is easy, my good friend, and quite natural for every generation to find fault with its own position; but may it not be that while the development of fine genius is indeed hindered by the peaceable state of the world, it is far more so by this boundless war that moves our lusts at its will, and further by these inflictions which hold this our age at their mercy, harrying and spoiling it without restraint? For the love of

[1] *Odyssey*, xvii, 322.
[2] See the comment upon this passage in Gibbon, *Decline and Fall*, ii. 195, ed. Milman. (Tr.)

gain for which we are all now-a-days morbidly insatiable, and the love of pleasure, bring us into bondage, or rather, so to phrase it, cause a foundering of our lives, in which all hands are lost. Devotion to money is a degrading infirmity, devotion to pleasure a most degraded one. I cannot imagine, after the extravagant honouring, or, more truly, deifying of vast wealth, how it is possible when its attendant evils invade our souls, to deny them entrance. For, hard upon enormous and excessive wealth, and, so to speak, keeping step with it, follows lavish expenditure, and when the one throws open the gateways of cities and mansions, into which the former enters, there also the other makes its home. Then, having established their footing in men's lives, both build themselves nests, as philosophers tell us, and soon falling to procreation, they engender haughtiness and pride and luxury, not falsely fathered upon them, but their very and legitimate offspring. But if one also suffers these descendants of wealth to attain maturity, speedily do they breed in the souls they occupy tyrants inexorable, insolence and licence and shamelessness. For such results must needs follow, and no more can men gaze upward, no more can reputation be of account, but the ruin of such a life must step by step be gathering to its close, while all nobility and grandeur of soul must decline and wither and waste away, whenever men unduly exalt the perishable and sensual parts of their nature, and fail to cherish those which are immortal. For a man cannot, when he has taken a bribe for his decision,—he cannot, I say, be an impartial and upright judge in the cause of right and honour. One so corrupted can see no honour or right but in what advantages himself. But where we all give over our lives, now without intermission, to the control of bribery and legacy-hunting and seeking for dead men's places, while we sell for gain, no matter whence, our very souls being enslaved without exception by the love of money, do we still, I ask, expect to find, amid all this pestilential corruption of life, judges of the sublime or the immortal, free and uncorrupted, uninfluenced in their votes by the passion for gain? But perhaps in such a state of society, and that state is our's, subjection is better than freedom; since otherwise the covetous feelings of men, discharged in a mass upon their neighbours, like beasts let loose from a den, might even set the whole world on fire with the miseries that would follow. In short, the present standard of mind and talent, I observed, was largely due to that indifference in which we all, with few exceptions, pass our lives, never labouring, never learning, except with the single view to applause or pleasure, but doing nothing for the just ambition and the merited renown of general usefulness.'[1]

There is nothing more difficult than to determine priority in the case of those reciprocal causes and effects which act upon large societies. No doubt the loss of political liberty draws with it many grave consequences to national character, but on the other hand political liberty will not be lost so long as the holders of it maintain their dignity and practise self-sacrifice for the public weal. All the vices which invade decaying states are inter-connected, and none of them produces its fellow without being reproduced in its turn. It is more than probable therefore that both our author and the philosophers whom he criticises were right, and that a complication of disorders had already begun to affect the Roman empire.

If these thinkers had gone back to Plato they might have found another consideration, which, if it had not

[1] I cite from Mr. Stebbing's translation (London 1867).

brought them consolation, would have vindicated partly at least the decay which they deplored. By them, as by modern political theorists, the life of states is presumed to be permanent, never to pass away unless some active cause from without disturbs the equilibrium of things and produces a convulsion or a stagnation in the political cosmos. To them the Roman Empire was everlasting, as to us the permanence of our respective modern states is a sort of axiom which no one seems to question. But to the older political philosophers among the Greeks, to Plato, to Aristotle, who had collected 250 different constitutions, the survey of this crowd of smaller polities, passing in and out of the atmosphere like meteors, suggested that even the larger and remoter bodies were not destined to be permanent, and each philosopher had accordingly set down in the natural history, even of an ideal constitution, those inherent causes which lead to the old age and the decay of the body politic, apart from all accidents or attacks from without. We can now see that such causes were at work even in the early Roman Empire ; and no enumeration of defects or vices, no exhortations to reform, could possibly have averted the destiny of the ancient world.

It is probable that the same considerations apply to literature. Not all the education, all the analysis, all the criticism in the world can preserve or even prolong a golden age of letters which has arisen almost suddenly, spontaneously, the reflex of other greatness, the fruit of some marvellous summer, whose colour and flavour has a richness which no cultivation can reproduce. Such splendid seasons do not recur except at long and uncertain intervals. One of them was come and gone for Greek literature. Yet never were Greek letters more favoured and flattered than under the Flavian and

Antonine emperors. Never was the world more happy and prosperous. Never were the conditions of society in the old world more humane and civilised. But in letters this age only produced a Renascence, the bloom of sophistical prose, which dazzled indeed its contemporaries, but laid no hold upon the world. What was paraded as gold we now recognise as pinchbeck and tinsel. This is the period reserved, if my years fail me not, for another volume.

APPENDIX A. (cf. p. 257)

THE INSCRIPTION OF ACRÆPHIÆ CONTAINING NERO'S SPEECH

Αὐτοκράτωρ Καῖσαρ λέγει· " Τῆς εἰς με εὐνοίας τε καὶ εὐσεβείας ἀ[μ]είψασθαι θέλων τὴν εὐγε-
νεστάτην Ἑλλάδα, κελεύω, πλείστους καθ' ὅ[σ]ο[ν]
ἐνδέχεται ἐκ ταύτης τῆς ἐπαρχείας παρῖναι
ἰς Κόρινθον τῇ πρὸ τεσσάρων καλανδῶν δε-
κεμβρίων."

Συνελθόντων τῶν ὄχλων ἐν ἐκκλησίᾳ προσεφώ-
νησεν τὰ ὑπογεγραμμένα·

"'Απροσδόκητον ὑμεῖν, ἄνδρες Ἕλληνες, δωρεάν,
εἰ καὶ μηδὲν παρὰ τῆς ἐμῆς μεγαλοφροσύνης
ἀνέλπιστον, χαρίζομαι, τοσαύτην ὅσην οὐκ ἐχωρή-
σατε αἰτεῖσθαι. Πάντες οἱ τὴν Ἀχαΐαν καὶ τὴν ἕως
νῦν Πελοπόννησον κατοικοῦντες Ἕλληνες
λάβετ(ε) ἐλευθερίαν ἀνισφορίαν ἣν οὐδ' ἐν τοῖς εὐτυ-
χεστάτοις ὑμῶν πάντες χρόνοις ἔσχετε,
ἢ γὰρ ἀλλοτρίοις ἢ ἀλλήλοις ἐδουλεύσατε.
Εἴθε μὲν οὖν ἀκμαζούσης τῆς Ἑλλάδος παρειχό-
μην ταύτην τὴν δωρεὰν ἵνα μου πλείονες ἀπο-
λα[ύ]ωσι τῆς χάριτος, διὸ καὶ μέμφομαι τὸν αἰῶνα
προδαπανήσαντά μου τὸ μέγεθος τῆς χάριτος.
Καὶ νῦν δὲ οὐ δι' ἔλεον ὑμᾶς ἀλλὰ δι' εὔνοιαν εὐερ-

γετῶ, ἀμείβομαι δὲ τοὺς θεοὺς ὑμῶν ὧν καὶ διὰ
γῆς καί διὰ θαλάττης αἰεί μου προνοουμένων πε-
πείραμαι ὅτι μοι τηλικαῦτα εὐεργετεῖν παρέσχον.
Πόλεις μὲν γὰρ καὶ ἄλλοι ἠλευθέρωσαν ἡγεμόνες,
[Νέρων δὲ ὅλην τὴν] ἐπαρχείαν."

Ὁ ἀρχιερεὺς τῶν Σεβαστῶν διὰ βίου καὶ Νέρωνος
Κλαυδίου Καίσαρος Σεβαστοῦ Ἐπαμεινώνδας
Ἐπαμεινώνδου εἶπεν· προβεβουλευμένον ἑαυ-
τῷ εἶναι πρός τε τὴν βουλὴν καὶ τὸν δῆμον·
ἐπιδὴ ὁ τοῦ παντὸς κόσμου κύριος Νέρων αὐτοκράτωρ μέγιστος, δημαρχικῆς ἐξουσίας τὸ τρὶς
καὶ δέκατον ἀποδεδειγμένος, πατὴρ πατρίδος,
νέος Ἥλιος ἐπιλάμψας τοῖς Ἕλλησιν, προειρεμέ-
νος εὐεργετεῖν τὴν Ἑλλάδα, ἀμειβόμενος δὲ
καὶ εὐσεβῶν τοῖς θεοῖς ἡμῶν παριστανομένοις
αὐτῷ πάντοτε ἐπὶ προνοίᾳ καὶ σωτηρίᾳ, τὴν ἀπὸ
παντὸς τοῦ αἰῶνος αὐθιγενῆ καὶ αὐτόχθονα ἐλευθερίαν πρότερον ἀφαιρεθεῖσαν τῶν Ἑλλήνων εἷς
καὶ μόνος τῶν ἀπ' αἰῶνος αὐτοκράτωρ μέγιστος
φιλέλλην γενόμενος [Νέρων] Ζεὺς Ἐλευθέριος ἔδω-
κεν, ἐχαρίσατο, ἀποκατέστησεν εἰς τὴν ἀρχαιό-
τητα τῆς αὐτονομίας καὶ ἐλευθερίας προσθεὶς
τῇ μεγάλῃ καὶ ἀπροσδοκήτῳ δωρεᾷ καὶ ἀνεισφο-
ρίαν, ἣν οὐδεὶς τῶν πρότερον Σεβαστῶν ὁλοτελῆ
ἔδωκεν· δι' ἃ δὴ πάντα δεδογμένον εἶναι τοῖς τε ἄρχουσι καὶ συνέδροις καὶ τῷ δήμῳ καθιερῶσαι μὲν κατὰ τὸ παρὸν τὸν πρὸς τῷ Διὶ τῷ Σωτῆρι βωμόν, ἐπι-
γράφοτας· Διὶ Ἐλευθερίῳ [Νέρωνι] εἰς αἰῶνα, καὶ ἀλάγμα-
τα ἐν τῷ ναῷ τοῦ Ἀπόλλωνος τοῦ Πτωΐου συνκαθει-
δρύοντας τοῖς [ἡμῖν] πατρίοις θεοῖς [Νέρωνός τε] Διὸς
Ἐλευθερίου καὶ θεᾶς Σεβαστῆς [Μεσσαλίνης?], ἵνα
τούτων οὕτως τελεσθέντων καὶ ἡ ἡμετέρα πόλις
φαίνηται πᾶσαν τειμὴν καὶ εὐσέβειαν ἐκπεπληρω-

κυΐα εἰς τὸν τοῦ κυρίου Σεβαστοῦ [Νέρωνος . . . ?],
εἶναι δὲ ἐν ἀναγραφῆι τὸ ψήφισμα παρά τε τῷ Διί τῷ Σωτῆρι ἐν τῇ ἀγορᾷ ἐν στήλῃ καὶ ἐν τῷ ἱερῷ τοῦ Ἀπόλλωνος τοῦ Πτωίου.

APPENDIX B

Augustus's Letter to the Cnidians (p. 357)

Αὐτοκράτωρ Καῖσαρ θεοῦ υἱὸς Σεβαστὸς ἀρχιερεύς
ὕπατος τὸ δωδέκατον ἀποδεδειγμένος
καὶ δημαρχικῆς ἐξουσίας τὸ ὀκτωικαιδέκατον
Κνιδίων ἄρχουσι βουλῆι δήμωι χαίρειν. οἱ πρεσ-
-βεις ὑμῶν Διονυσιος β̄ καὶ Διονυσιος β̄ τοῦ Διονυ-
-σίου ἐνέτυχον ἐν Ῥώμηι μοι καὶ τὸ ψήφισμα ἀποδόντες
κατηγόρησαν Εὐβούλου μὲν τοῦ Ἀναξανδρίδα τεθνε-
-ῶτος ἤδη, Τρυφέρας δὲ τῆς γύναικος αὐτοῦ παρούσης
περὶ τοῦ θανάτου τοῦ Εὐβούλου τοῦ Χρυσίππου· ἐγὼ
δὲ ἐξετάσαι προστάξας Γάλλωι Ἀσινίωι τῶι ἐμῶι φίλωι
τῶν οἰκετῶν τοὺς ἐνφερομένους τῆι αἰτία διὰ βα-
σάνων, ἔγνων Φιλεῖνον τὸν Χρυσίππου τρεῖς νύ-
-κτας συνεχῶς ἐπεληλυθότα τῆι οἰκία τῆι Εὐβου-
-λου καὶ Τρυφέρας μεθ᾽ ὕβρεως καὶ τρόπωι τινὶ πολ-
-ιορκίας, τῆι τρίτηι δὲ συνεπηιγμένον καὶ τὸν ἀδελ-
φὸν Εὔβουλον, τοὺς δὲ τῆς οἰκίας δεσπότας Εὔβου-
-λον καὶ Τρυφέραν, ὡς οὔτε χρηματίζοντες πρὸς
τὸν Φαλεῖνον οὔτε ἀντιφραττόμενοι ταῖς προσ-
βολαῖς ἀσφαλείας ἐν τῆι ἑαυτῶν οἰκίαι τυχεῖν ἠδυνάν-
το, προστεταχότας ἑνὶ τῶν οἰκέτων οὐκ ἀποκτεῖ-
ναι, ὥ[ς ἴ]σως ἄν τις ὑπ᾽ ὀργῆς οὐκ ἀδίκου προήχθηι, ἀλ-
-λὰ ἀνεῖρξαι ἀνασκεδάσαντα τὰ κόπρια αὐτῶν, τὸν
δὲ οἰκέτην σὺν τοῖς καταχεομένοις εἴτε ἑκόντα
εἴτε ἄκοντα, αὐτὸς γὰρ ἐνέμεινεν ἀρνούμενο[ς],
ἀφεῖναι τὴν γάστραν [καὶ] Εὔβουλον ὑποπεσεῖν, δικαιό

2 D

τερον ἄν σωθέντα [τοῦ ἀ]δελφοῦ·πέπονφα δὲ ὑμεῖν καὶ α[ὐ
τ]ὰς τὰς ἀνακρίσεις. ἐθαύμαζον δ' ἄν, πῶς εἰς τόσον
ἔδεισαν τὴν παρ' ὑμεῖν ἐξετασίαν τῶν δούλων οἱ φ[εύ-]
γοντες τὴν δίκην, εἰ μή μοι σφόδρα ἐδόξ[ατε]
χαλεποὶ γεγονέναι καὶ πρὸς τὰ ἐναντία μισοπόνη[ροι],
μὴ κατὰ τῶν ἀξίων πᾶν ὁτιοῦν παθεῖν ἐπ' ἀλλο[τρίων]
οἰκίων νύκτωρ μεθ' ὕβρεως καὶ βίας τρὶς ἐπεληλ[υθό-]
των, καὶ τὴν κοινὴν ἁπάντων ὑμῶν ἀσφάλει[αν ἀναι-]
ρούντων ἀγανακτοῦντες, ἀλλὰ κατὰ τῶν καὶ [ὅτε ἠ-]
μύνοντο ἠτυχηκότων, ἠδικηκότων δὲ οὐδέ[ν].
ἀλλὰ νῦν ὀρθῶς μοι δοκεῖτε ποιῆσαι τῆι ἐμῆι π[ερὶ τού-]
των γνώμηι προνοήσαντες καὶ τὰ ἐν τοῖς δημ[οσίοις]
ὑμῶν ὁμολογεῖν γράμματα. ἔρρωσθε.

APPENDIX C. (Cf. p. 379)

(MELEAGER ON SPRING)

Χείματος ἠνεμόεντος ἀπ' αἰθέρος οἰχομένοιο,
πορφυρέη μείδησε φερανθέος εἴαρος ὥρη·
Γαῖα δὲ κυανέη χλοερὴν ἐστέψατο ποίην,
καὶ φυτὰ θηλήσαντα νέοις ἐκόμησε πετήλοις.
Οἱ δ' ἁπαλὴν πίνοντες ἀεξιφύτου δρόσον Ἠοῦς
λειμῶνες γελόωσιν, ἀνοιγομένοιο ῥόδοιο.
Χαίρει καὶ σύριγγι νομεὺς ἐν ὄρεσσι λιγαίνων,
καὶ πολιοῖς ἐρίφοις ἐπιτέρπεται αἰπόλος αἰγῶν.
Ἤδη δὲ πλώοισιν ἐπ' εὐρέα κύματα ναῦται
πνοίῃ ἀπημάντῳ Ζεφύρου λίνα κολπώσαντος.
Ἤδη δ' εὐάζουσι φερεσταφύλῳ Διονύσῳ,
ἄνθει βοτρυόεντος ἐρεψάμενοι τρίχα κισσοῦ.
Ἔργα δὲ τεχνήεντα βοηγενέεσσι μελίσσαις
καλὰ μέλει, καὶ σίμβλῳ ἐφήμεναι ἐργάζονται

λευκὰ πολυτρήτοιο νεύρρυτα κάλλεα κηροῦ.
Πάντη δ' ὀρνίθων γενεὴ λιγύφωνον ἀείδει,
ἀλκυόνες περὶ κῦμα, χελιδόνες ἀμφὶ μέλαθρα.
κύκνος ἐπ' ὄχθαισιν ποταμοῦ, καὶ ὑπ' ἄλσος ἀηδών.
Εἰ δὲ φυτῶν χαίρουσι κόμαι, καὶ γαῖα τέθηλεν,
συρίζει δὲ νομεύς, καὶ τέρπεται εὔκομα μῆλα,
καὶ ναῦται πλώουσι, Διώνυσος δὲ χορεύει,
καὶ μέλπει πετεεινά, καὶ ὠδίνουσι μέλισσαι,
πῶς οὐ χρὴ καὶ ἀοιδὸν ἐν εἴαρι καλὸν ἀεῖσαι;

Anthology, ix. No. 363.

APPENDIX D. (Cf. p. 381)

(ON THE DOMESTICATED ELEPHANTS OF ROME)

Specimens from Philip of Thessalonica's Epigrams

Οὐκέτι πυργωθεὶς ὁ φαλαγγομάχας ἐπὶ δῆριν
ἄσχετος ὁρμαίνει μυριόδους ἐλέφας.
ἀλλὰ φόβῳ στείλας βαθὺν αὐχένα πρὸς ζυγοδέσμους,
ἄντυγα διφρουλκεῖ Καίσαρος οὐρανίου.
Ἔγνω δ' εἰρήνης καὶ θὴρ χάριν· ὄργανα ῥίψας
Ἄρεος, εὐνομίης ἀντανάγει πατέρα.

Anthol. ix. No. 285.

(ON AGRIPPA'S MOLE AT PUTEOLI)

Ἔζευξ' Ἑλλήσποντον ὁ βάρβαρος ἄφρονι τόλμῃ,
τοὺς δὲ τόσους καμάτους πάντας ἔλυσε χρόνος·
ἀλλὰ Δικαιάρχεια διηπείρωσε θάλασσαν,
καὶ βυθὸν εἰς χέρσον σχῆμα μετεπλάσατο·

λᾶα, βαθὺ στήριγμα, κατερρίζωσε πέλωρον,
χερσὶ Γιγαντείαις δ' ἔστασε νέρθεν ὕδωρ.
Ἢν ἄλ' ἀεὶ πλώειν· διοδευομένη δ' ὑπὸ ναύταις
ἄστατος, εἰς πεζοὺς ὡμολόγησε μένειν.

Anthol. ix. No. 708.

(RIDICULE OF PEDANTS)

Γραμματικοὶ Μώμου στυγίου τέκνα, σῆτες ἀκανθῶν,
τελχῖνες βίβλων, Ζηνοδότου σκύλακες,
Καλλιμάχου στρατιῶται, ὃν ὡς ὅπλον ἐκτανύσαντες,
οὐδ' αὐτοῦ κείνου γλῶσσαν ἀποστρέφετε,
συνδέσμων λυγρῶν θηρήτορες, οἷς τὸ "μὶν" ἢ "σφὶν"
εὔαδε, καὶ, ζητεῖν εἰ κύνας εἶχε Κύκλωψ,
τρίβοισθ' εἰς αἰῶνα κατατρύζοντες ἀλιτροὶ
ἄλλων· ἐς δ' ἡμᾶς ἰὸν ἀποσβέσατε.

Anthol. xi. No. 321.

(RIDICULE OF PEDANTS)

Χαίροιθ' οἱ περὶ κόσμον ἀεὶ πεπλανηκότες ὄμμα,
οἵ τ' ἀπ' Ἀριστάρχου σῆτες ἀκανθολόγοι.
Ποῖ γὰρ ἐμοὶ ζητεῖν τίνας ἔδραπεν ἥλιος οἴμους,
καὶ τίνος ἦν Πρωτεύς, καὶ τίς ὁ Πυγμαλίων;
Γινώσκοιμ' ὅσα λευκὸν ἔχει στίχον· ἡ δὲ μέλαινα
ἱστορίη τήκοι τοὺς Περικαλλιμάχους.

Anthol. xi. No. 347.

(ON HERAS THE ATHLETE)

Ἴσως με λεύσσων, ξεῖνε, ταυρογάστορα
καὶ στερρόγυιον, ὡς Ἄτλαντα δεύτερον,

θαμβεῖς, ἀπιστῶν εἰ βρότειος ἡ φύσις.
Ἀλλ' ἴσθι μ' Ἡρᾶν Λαδικῆα πάμμαχον,
ὃν Σμύρνα καὶ δρῦς Περγάμου κατέστεφεν,
Δελφοί, Κόρινθος, Ἦλις, Ἄργος, Ἄκτιον·
λοιπῶν δ' ἀέθλων ἢν ἐρευνήσῃς κράτος,
καὶ τὴν Λίβυσσαν ἐξαριθμήσεις κόνιν.

Anthol. xiii. No. 321.

INDEX

Academy, the new, 73
Achaea, province of, 257
Achaeus, a slave leader, 7
Açoka, 20 *sq.*; his inscriptions, 21
Acratus, Nero's agent, 238
Actium, games at, 253
Acts of the Apostles, 227, 234
Ægean, the, 225
Ælius Gallus, 240
Ænianes, 296
Ætna, Mount, 219
Ætolia, cities founded by kings in, 203
Agatharchides, on the Red Sea, 54; on mining, *ibid.*
Agrippa, M. V., 259
Agrippa, king, 364, 366
Alcibiades, 346
Alexander the Great, his prospects of a world Empire, 1; his new idea in colonisation, 108
Alexander Bala, 40
Alexander Zebinas, 43
Alexandria, 200; character of, 243 *sq.*
Amafinius, C. (Epicurean), 74
Amitrochates (Vindusara), 20
Ammonius, scholarch at Athens, 335
Ammonius, successor to Aristarchus, 47
Amphiaraus, a doubtful God, 147
Amphicrates, sophist, 95
Analogies, modern, to Greeks and Romans, 134
Anchorite, 370
Anoekism, of the Chians, 92
Anthology, the, 129, 374 *sq.*
Antiochus, assumed as a royal title by slave leaders, 7
Antiochus Cyzicenus and Grypus, 43
Antiochus Eusebes, 39
Antiochus Sidetes, 40, 43
Antiquarianism, 321-2
Antonius, the orator, 84, 117
Antony, M., his character and style, 162-3
Apellicon of Teos, 98
Apollodorus, *Tyrant of the Garden*, 71
Apollodorus of Artemita (historian), 25
Apollonius of Tyana, 183, 250, 256, 266
Apotheosis, effects of, 390-1
Appian, 86, 93-4
Appius, porch of, at Eleusis, 123
Arabs, rise in importance of, 45
Archelaus, 176
Archias, the poet, 125-6
Architect, the, in Indian theatres, 35; Greek, 363
Ariarathes, 230
Aristion (Athenion), tyrant of Athens, 94 *sq.*
Aristobulus the Maccabee, 44
Aristocracy, want of, in Greece, 335
Aristomenes, tutor to Ptolemy V., 54
Aristonicus, his war with Rome, 9, 77, 117

Aristophanes, 329
Aristotle, 329, 332, 347
Arsaces, rise of, 22
Arsacids, 202
Arsinoe (the Fayoum district), Preface xi, 203
Art, alleged Indo-Greek, 27
Art, Pompeian, 215
Artillery, field, 90
Arts, the, of Greece, at Rome, 80, 104 *sq.*
Asceticism, Pythagorean, 182 *sq.*, 187-8, 385
Asia, Greek cities in, 201, 223, 354
Asia Minor acquiesces in Roman rule, 101; richness of, 229
Assimilation, national, 243
Assizes, the right of, 231-2
Associations, religious, 180
Assyrian colonisation, model for Persians, etc., 200
Aswan (*see* Syene)
Asylum, right of, 91
Athenæus, on Alexander Bala, 40; on Antiochus Sidetes, 40; on Epicureans, 66
Athenodorus ravages Delos, 111
Athens, stops Sylla, 93, 98; its treatment by Rome, 97; recovers Delos, 109; visited by Antonius and Crassus, 118; not appreciated by Cicero, 122-3; and Brutus, 157; naval weakness, 161; Strabo's account of, 192; degradation of, 249; S. Paul at Athens, 269
Athos, Mount, 253
Attalus III, 9
Atticus buys pictures, 142
Augustus, 355, 357; his Greek policy, 253; his education, 254-5; and Cnidos, 357
Aulus Postumius, 70
Autodidact, despised in Greece, 81
Azas, coins of king, 29

BABYLON, 200
Bacchæ of Euripides (in Parthia), 33
Bacchanalia, panic about the, 66
Bactria, revolt of, and kingdom, 20 *sq.*

Bædeker's *Greece*, 123
Bætis, the river, 194, 196
Balbus conquers Spain, 193
Balearic islands plagued with rabbits, 195
Bandits in Sicily, 219
BCH (*Bulletin de correspondance hellénique*), 89, 90, 91, 102, 107, 112, 145, 171, 181, 221, 222, 226, 234, 241, 256, etc., etc.
Beaudouin, M., in *BCH*, cited, 102
Benseler, his law of hiatus, 331
Berœa, 269
Bishops, prince, 225
Bithynia, Christianity in, 349; Hellenism of, 363
Bithynians, 363
Blossius of Cumæ, 77, 117
Boethus of Sidon, 75
Bogos, king of Morocco, 50
Bomba, king, 209
Borysthenes, the Greeks of, 273 *sq.*
Bosphorus, the Cimmerian, 87 *sq.*
Brundusium, 209
Brutus, and Athens, 157-8; sentimentality of, 158-9
Buddha Gaya, remains at, 27
Buddhism spread by Açoka, 21 *sq.*; in Syria, 186
Bury, Mr. J. B., cited, 247 and Preface
Byzantium, 355

CÆSAR, JULIUS, a true Roman, 156; a demagogue, 305
Cæsarea, 176, 367
Caligula, 255, 358, 260, 324
Callimachus, his metric, 375
Caphereus, 281
Capital, distribution of, 264
Capitals, Greek, of pillars, copied in India, 28
Cappadocia, 95, 229
Caria, the League of, 91
Carneades, 62 *sq.*; his mission to Rome, 68 *sq.*
Carthage, fertility of, 4-5
Carystos, 265, 280
Casamicciola, 215
Cassino, Monte, compared to religious foundations in Asia Minor, 225

INDEX 409

Cassiterides, the, 194
Cassius, and Brutus, 160; his character, 161-2, 237
Cassius Dionysius, translator of Mago, 5
Cato the elder, and Carthage, 5; and philosophers, 67, 70; and Rutilius, 77
Cato the younger, and Dejotarus, 120; and Brutus, 159-60; his character, 160
Celænæ, described, 231-2
Chæremon, 241
Chandragupta (*see* Sandracottus)
Chastity, 345-6; Plutarch on, 345
Chautauqua, 72
Cheerfulness, duty of, 344-5
Chersonnesus, town of, 90
Children, exposing of, 323; treatment of infant, 324; education of, 324 *sq.*
Chios, 355; ill-treated by Mithradates, 92; adorned by Herod, 176
Christianity, 328, 345, 349
Cicero on Dejotarus, 6; on Sardinia, 15; on Carneades, 63; on art, 139 *sq.*; on Greek philosophy at Rome, 68, 70, 74; *de officiis*, 76; on literary servants, 82; on Delos, 111; his Hellenism, 113 *sq.*; speaks Greek in Sicily, 116; his consolations, 124; his Greek friends, 135-6; his name on an inscription, 145
Cicero, junior, letter of, 121
Cicerones, 335
Cichorius, cited, 255, 355
CIG (corpus inscriptionum Græcarum), 221, 228, 252, 259, 310, 355, etc.
CIL (corpus inscriptionum Latinarum), cited, 90, 224, 225, etc.
Cimbric invasion, crisis of the, 8
Cirta, 219
Cities, Greek, in inner Asia, 38; in Syria and Palestine, 39; of the Syrian coast, 41, 201; names of, 46; in Egypt, 202; old and new, 228-9
Citizenship, Roman and Greek, contrasted by Cicero, 148; conditions of, 244
City, contrasted with village, 15, 195, 280; with country, 370-1
Civa, worship of, 34
Civil wars, Roman, their effect on Greece, 155 *sq.*
Claudius, 259; Hellenism of, 255
Cleon, a bandit-priest, 226
Cleopatra, and Antony, 163; and Herod, 165-7; and Octavian, 167; a linguist, 243
Clitomachus of Carthage, 73
Cnidus, brawl at, 357
Cocce, Cleopatra, 44, 49
Coins, Bactrian and Indian, 23 *sq.*, 30; of Aristion at Athens, 94
Collectors of art at Rome, 106
Colonies, Roman, their influence in later days, 42; date of, given by Scymnus, 57; the, of Cæsar, 157
Colonisation, Hellenic and Phœnician, 197-8; Hellenistic and Roman, 199, 202
Colonnades, 216, 360
Columella, cited on Mago, 5
Comana, 225
Comedy, Greek, at Rome, 71
Company, the placing of, 337
Confiscation, 263
Conversation, the art of, 338 *sq.*
Cooking, Greek, 335
Corduba, 196
Corinth, 256; S. Paul at, 270-2; Apuleius on, 297
Corinthian capitals, found in Media, 29; used by Herod, 176
Cornelia, letters of, 84
Corporations at Delos, 110
Correspondents, war, 125
Cosmetæ, portraits of, 327
Crassus the orator, 84, 117
Crimea, the kingdom of, 87 *sq.*; its products, 88
Crinagoras (*see* Krinagoras)
Critolaus, philosopher, 69
Crocodiles, exhibited, 241
Crocodilopolis, Preface x
Ctesiphon, the Parthian Royal Residence, 38
Cumæ, 210, 212

Cunningham, General, cited, 27 *sq.*
Cyclades, exiles on the, 352-3
Cynics, the, 246
Cyrenaica, Greek life in, 220 ; Jews at, *ibid.*
Cythera, 259
Cyzicus, 355

DAMASCUS, Nicolaus of, 176-7
Damon of Chæronea, 151 *sq.*
Daulis, dispute concerning land at, 252
Decay of nations, inevitable, 396
Deities, Asiatic, worshipped under Greek names, 226
Dejotarus, king, an agriculturist, 6 ; visited by Romans, 120
Delos, discoveries and inscriptions at, 107; history under the Romans, 109 *sq.*
Delphi, 107, 252, 321
Delta, the 243
Demagogues, extinct, 305
Demetrius, Soter (of Syria), 39
Demons, Plutarch's theory of 313
Demosthenes cited, 87
Dentheliates ager, dispute about, 252
Depopulation, 101-2, 192
Deputations, modern and ancient compared, 72
Diadochi, their common ambition, 2
Diaspora, the Jewish, 199, 364
Dicæarchia (*see* Puteoli)
Dignity, human, in Plutarch, 344
Dinner parties, Plutarch on, 325 *sq.*, 333 *sq.* ; places at, 336
Diodorus, on Roman luxury, 3 ; on Eunus's state, 7 ; on mining, 54-5 ; on Alexandria, 164
Diodotus, first Greek king of Bactria, 21
Diogenes, an Epicurean philosopher at Antioch, 40
Diogenes, the Stoic, at Rome, 69
Diogenes Laertius, cited, 61, 72
Dionysiac artists, 213
Dionysius, Cicero's clerk, 82
Dionysius of Halicarnassus, 207, 382 *sq.*, 387
Dionysius Thrax, 84
Dionysus, guilds of, 33, 96

Diophanes, translator of Mago, 5
Diophantus, Mithradates' general, 89
Dion Chrysostom, 223 ; compared with Strabo, 227 ; on Nicæa, 228 ; on genealogies, 229 ; on Celænæ, 231-2 ; on Tarsus, 235-6 ; on Rhodes, 237-8 ; on Alexandria, 245 *sq.* ; on gladiatorial combats, 271-2 ; on Borysthenes (Olbia), 274 *sq.* ; on Eubœa, 277 *sq.* ; on Prusa, 359 *sq.* ; on poverty, 288, 370 ; on a course of reading, 385
Discipline, its power in war, 89
Dittenberger, his *Sylloge* cited, 89
Divine honours, 305
Dogs, 279
Doric pillars, alleged copies in India and in Egypt, 28
Dörpfeld, W., on arsenal of Philon, 99
Dorylaos, friend of Mithradates, 92
Drama, Indian, how related to Greek, 31 *sq.* ; its peculiarities, 32 ; number of plays, 34
Dress, Greek, worn by Romans, 115
Dublin, Italian art in, 106
Dyme, revolt at, 100 ; pirates settled at, 153

EARTHQUAKES in first century, 215, 224, 271
Eastern Hellenism, 18 *sq.*
Eclecticism, in philosophy, 63, 183, 328
Education, Roman, 82 ; of Cicero, 118-9 ; cost of, 325 ; Dion on, 385
Egypt refuses Lucullus help, 90 ; religion in, 164
Egypt, Roman Government of, 242-4
Elephants, capture of, 55
Elton, cited, 194
Embassies to Rome, 357 *sq.*
Empires of the world compared, 15, 396
Emporiæ, 193
Encyclopædias, of Diodorus and Strabo, 189
Endurance of Greeks, 132
England, after peace of 1815, com-

INDEX

pared to Rome, 81 ; poverty in compared to Greek, 371
Epaminondas, 257, 260
Ephebic institutions, 326-7
Ephesus appeals to Florus for permission to celebrate a feast, 233-4
Ephorus, criticised, 210
Epicureans, unpopular, 41 ; at Herculaneum, 218 ; expelled from Rome, 66 ; not politicians, 71 ; Piso and Philodemus, as, 127 *sq.*; Vatinius, as, 148-9
Epicurus, libelled, 72 ; his school at Rome, 64, 74
Eras, local, of Greek cities, 41
Essenes, sect of the, 185 *sq.*
Euboea, Dion's idyll in, 277-88
Eucrates, Græco-Indian king, 23
Eucratidcia, his capital, 23
Eudoxus the explorer, adventures of, 48 *sq.*
Euemerus of Messene, 64
Eunus, a slave leader, 7
Eupatoria, 95
Euphuists, 376
Euripides, the poet of society, 329-85
Eurycles, 259-60
Euthydemus, king, 24
Ezekiel, on Tyre, quoted, 47

FABRICIUS, M., cited, 355
Factions, the, of the Circus, 247
Feasts, Antigoneia, Euergesia, Ptolemæa, at Delos, 108 ; at Jerusalem, 175 ; in Asia, 232-3
Fellahs, the Egyptian, 244
Fergusson (architect), on the age of stone-building in India, 25
Ferrets, early use of, in Spain, 195
Festivals, Greek, 260
FHG (Fragmenta Historicorum Græcorum, ed. C. Müller), 177, 228, 241, etc.
Fidelity, conjugal, 328
Figulus, P. Nigidius, 79, 184
Financial crisis at Rome, 93
Flaccus, Cicero's defence of, 133
Flavian dynasty, the, and Hellenism, 351 *sq.*
Foucart, M., cited, 181

Franciscans, the, compared to Cynics, 246
Freedom of cities, granted, 87 ; under the Romans, 226 ; of Hellas declared by Nero, 257
French culture in England, 81
Fulvius, patron of Ennius, 64

GADARA, 377
Gades, ships of, 49 ; Eudoxus at, 50 ; wealth of, 193-4
Gallus, Ælius, 340, 357
Garrison, the Roman, of Egypt, 241-2
Gaza, destruction of, 45 ; Stark on, 46
Gellius, L., and the schools of Athens, 149
Genealogies, in Asiatic cities, not real or long, 229
Gentlemen, deficiences of the Greek, 847
Geography, study of in second cent. B.C., 48 *sq.*
Gessius Florus, 366
Gladiators, war of the, 10 ; in Greece, 271-2
Godhead, unity of the, 181
Gods, strange, at Delos, 110
Gospel, the, 367 ; greatness of the, 389 ; long ignored, *ibid.*
Government, centralisation in, 391
Gracchus, C., his speeches, 84
Gracchus, Ti., 77 ; and Blossius, 117
Gravitas, the Roman, 70
Greece, decadence of, described by Dion, 249 *sq.*
Greek character, Cicero on, 133-4
Greek citizenship, 148 ; prose 148 ; its colonising powers, 197 ; against Jews, 364 *sq.*
Guide books, old Greek, 53 *sq.*

HADRIAN, 248, 369
Hair, dyeing of, by Herod, 165
Hamilcar, 197
Hardy, Mr., ed. of Pliny's correspondence, cited, 231, 355, 363
Harpocras, the case of, 244
Hecate, temple of, at Stratoniceia, 91, 225

Hcius, of Messina, 14
Heliopolis, the proposed city of Arsitonicus, 9
Hellenic life in the Crimea, 36
Hellenism, its despair under Rome, 11; its form that of cities, 14; Roman, 16, 46; Maccabean, 43; reaction against, 16, 156; sentimental, 15 *sq.*; of Herod, 174 *sq.*; at Naples, Pompeii, etc., 212; of emperors, 254 *sq.*; Syrian, 378
Hellenomemphites, 202
Heraclea founds Chersonnesus, 89
Herculaneum, the papyri of, 129, 218
Hermathena, cited, 4 *sq.*
Herod the Great and Cleopatra, 165-6; character of, 171 *sq.*; his Memoirs, 172; and Eurycles, 259
Hertzberg, *Geschichte Griechenland's*, cited, 252, 262, 272, 289, 296, 347
Hiatus, the law of, as a test of genuineness, 331
Hicks, E. L., his *Manual of inscrips.*, cited, 91, 391
Hieroglyphics, 241
History as conceived by Dionysius Halicarn., 383
Holiness the source of wisdom, 183
Holleaux, M., in *BCH.*, on Nero, 256
Hollows of Euboea, 277-8
Homer, at Olbia, 275; in Plutarch, 341; in Dion, 385
Honesty, commercial, of Rhodians, 237
Horse races at Alexandria, 247-8
Hospitality, rustic, 286; Dion on, 385
House architecture at Pompeii, 215-6; at Delos, 217
Hungary, climate of, 88
Hunter's life, Euboean, 277 *sq.*
Hydra, modern analogy to Gades, 194
Hypata, 296
Hyrcanian Plain, the, 200
Hyrcanus, the Maccabee, 43-4,

IALYSOS, the, of Protogenes, 236

Ice, battle on the, 88
Ideals, philosophic, in first century, 183
Ilium sacked by Fimbria, 99, 228
Images honoured by Herod, 177
Improvements, architectural, unpopular, 360-2
Indian trade, 230
Innkeepers, Italian, 309
Inscriptions, cited on Diophantus, 89; on Delos, 107 *sq.*; Graeco-Latin, 213; cited on M. Titius, by Jews of Cyrenaica, 220; funeral, 220-2; cited on Tiberius, 224 (see *BCH, MDI, CIG, CIL*).
Invitations, long, 333
Ionia, antiquities of, in Pausanias, 228
Ionic capitals, to be found in India, 28
Iris, temple of, at Pompeii, 216
Irish epitaph cited, 222
Ischia, 215
Iskanderovnah (Scanderoon), 200
Islands, the Aegean, 262, 352-3
Isthmia, games of, 67 B.C., 256
Italians, massacre of, in Asia, 92
Italy, theological advantages of, 383-4

JASON (tyrant), 304
Jerusalem adorned by Herod, 175 *sq.*; Philo on, 364-5
Jews, influence in Egypt, 47; in Greece, 268, 321, 349; ignorance concerning, in Plutarch, 321; oppose Hellenism, 16, 42, 358 *sq.*, 564 *sq.*; and their *diaspora*, 199
Jobbing in Greek cities, 363
Jokes, Plutarch on, 342
Josephus, on discontent of Greek cities under the Parthians, 38; on policy of the Maccabees, 42; on Hyrcanus, 45; on Antony, 163; on Herod, 171 *sq.*; on the Essenes, 185; on free Greek cities in Syria, 202; on Eurycles, 259; autobiography, 365
Juba, 219
Jugurtha, 7, 219

Juvenal on Egyptian cruelty, 248

KAIBEL, on Philodemus, 129, 375-6
Kermesse, the modern, analogous to Greek *panegyris*, 231
Kertch, Museum of, 87
Kings in the Crimea, 273; titular, in free Greek cities, 89
Kissing out of fashion, 285
Κοινά, various, in Greece, 102, 253-4
Krinagoras, 157, 255, 355, 379
Kurds, the, 229

LABERIUS, on Cicero, 113
Labienus, ravages Caria, 226
Lagina, inscription of, 91
Land question in Euboea, 282
Lassen, *Indische Alterthumskunde*, cited, 19; on evidence of coins, 24; on the Indian drama, 31, 36
Latifundia in Greece, 251
Latinisms in Greek decrees of the Senate, 147
Laudations of private people in inscriptions, 112, 261; their meaning, 263
Lecky, W. H. cited, 303
Lectures, Greek, at Rome, 70; proper conduct at, 330-1, 333
Letronne cited, 240
Letter of Augustus, 357-8
Leucon, tyrant in the Crimea, 87
Levity, Greek, 132 *sq.*, 364
Liberty of Greeks, 257, 265; variations in the terms of, in Asiatic cities, 354-5
Libraries, 325
Liguria, struggle of Rome with, 201, 205
Lions at Megara, 158
Litigations, land, in Greece, 252
Livy, cited, 65, 296
Longinus, 385, 392 *sq.*
Loquacity, Plutarch on, 340 *sq.*
Love, Plutarch on, 346
Lovers, in society, 337, 342
Lucian, 332, 381
Lucilius (poet), 73, 82, 83
Lucius of Patrae, 295 *sq.*
Lucretius, his poem, 78

Lucullus raises a fleet, 90; protects Asia, 93; saves Chaeronea, 152-3
Luxury, Plutarch on, 335
Lycia, league of, 203
Lysias, his style, 332
Lysimachus founds a city in Ætolia, 203

MACCABEES, rise of the, 41; policy of the, 43
Macchiavelli, cited, 304
Macedonia, 199; S. Paul in, 267
Macedonian, a title in Egypt, 165, 242
Mago on agriculture, 5 *sq.*
Manius Aquillius, 97
Manners, Plutarch on, 324 *sq.*; lauded in inscriptions, 221; in epitaphs, 112
Marble, Greek trade in, 251
Mariamne, 167, 172-4
Marriages, rich and poor compared, 288
Massanassa, named at Delos, 112
Massilia, Greek centre in the West, 85; Hellenic not Hellenistic, 193; opposes Caesar, 202, 205
Mathematics, Greek, 48
Matter, on Alexandria, 188
Mauretania explored, 50
MDI (*Mittheilungen des deutschen Instituts in Athen*), 94, 98, 233, 252, 257, 260, 274, 316, etc.
Medeon amalgamates with Stiris, 102
Mediation in philosophy objected to by Cicero, 150
Megara, kings at, 89
Megasthenes, his *Indica*, 19 *sq.*, 26
Melanthius, 340
Meleager (poet), 373, 377, and Appendix C
Memmius and the Epicureans at Athens, 123
Memnon, the statue of, 240
Memphis, 241
Menander, Indo-Greek king, 23
Menander, the poet, in Terence's versions, 71, 249; praised by Plutarch, 329
Messene, 252

Military colonies of Alexander and of Romans, 200
Mining in Pontus, 10 ; in Egypt, 10; in Nubia, 54 ; unproductive, 265
Mithradates, 86, 90, 92 *sq.*
Mob, the city, 263, 280
Mommsen, Th., his authority cited, 60, 82, 146, 192, 212
Monarch, a magisterial title, 89
Monarchical rule preferred by Asiatics, 101
Monopoly in papyrus, 242
Monotheism, 273
Morality, Plutarch's, 328, 344
Müller, C., *Fragmenta Historicorum Græcorum*, cited, 177
Munk, quoted, 48
Museum, the Alexandrian, and Aristotle, 188 ; and Dion, 245-6, and Apollonius, 250
Music, Philodemus on, 130
Musonius, 271
Mylasa, the city, 225
Mystagogi = cicerones, 140
Mytilene, 355-6

NÆVIUS, 83
Naples, a Greek town, 115, 210, 212 ; Museum of, 218
Nasamones, the, 373
Νεκροκορίνθια, 157
Nero spares Rhodian art, 238 ; Hellenism of, 256 *sq.*; speech of, preserved, 256-7, 271, and Appendix A ; and isthmus of Corinth, 271 ; court of, 298 ; soul of, 313
Nicæa, 228, 231, 363
Nicolaus Damascenus (historian), cited on an Indian embassy, 30 ; on Herod, 176-7, 228, 377; criticised, 382
Nicomedes of Bithynia, his answer to the Senate, 8, 229
Nicomedes III, addressed by Scymnus, 57-8, 60
Nicomedia, 230, 231, 363
Nicopolis, 253
Nigidius Figulus, Pub. (philosopher), 79
Northern barbarians civilised, by Massilia, 204

Numa, the books of, 64 *sq.*
OATHS, not respected by Greeks, 133
Obscurity in *Anthology*, 129
Octavia, 356
Octavian party in the civil war, 226
Oeta, Mount, 296
Olbia, 274
Olympia, treasures of, stolen by Nero, 238 ; *Altis* of, 257
Olympia, games at, 256 ; transferred, 261
Ombi, 248
Onomademus, 304
Opposition to city improvement, 361-2
Oppression, Roman, gone under the Empire, 233
Opsimathes despised in Greece, 81
Oracle, the Pythian, 321 ; decay of, 329
Oratore, de, Cicero, 118, 341
Oratory, Roman school of, 84 ; Longinus on, 392 *sq.*
Oriental religions, their effects on Hellenism, 180
Oscan art at Pompeii, 214
Ostia, 195, 211
Overbeck on Pompeii, 214-16 ; on use of stucco, 216 ; on Puteolan relief, 224
Ovid copies Philodemus, 129; exiled, 262 ; *Heroides,* 388
Oxford, inscription at, 91

PALIMBOTHRA (Pataliputra), the capital of Sandracottus, 19 ; described, 26
Panætius (at Rome), 75 *sq.*
Panopolis, festival at, 203
Papyrus, the growth of, 242, 243
Paris, M., on Delos, 217
Parisades, king of Tauric Chersonnese, 89
Parthia, revolt of, 22 *sq.*
Parthians invade Asia Minor, 169-70 ; Hellenism of, 170
Paul, *Epistles* of, 227 ; in Greece, 266-8
Pausanias, 252
Peace, the Roman, 225

INDEX 415

Pergamum, kings of, praised, 57
Petilius, L., finds Pythagorean books, 65
Petrie, Mr. F., his discovery of Greek papyri, Preface ix *sq.*
Phanias, 40
Philip of Thessalonica (poet), 380-1, and Appendix D
Philippi, 267
Philo (Judaeus) on Augustus, 171 ; on Therapeutæ, 184 ; on Alexandria, 243 ; on exile, 353 ; mission to Caligula, 358 *sq.*; on Caligula, 359 *sq.*
Philodemus of Gadara, 127 *sq.*, 218
Philosophers expelled by Antiochus Sidetes, 40 ; sent on missions, 68-9 ; household, at Rome, 100 ; accompany Roman generals, 102 ; compared with sophists, 327
Philosophy, Greek, at Rome, 60 *sq.* ; in Latin, 114 ; ascetic, in first century, 178 *sq.*, 370
Philostratus, his *Life of Apollonius* cited, 29, 266
Phocylides, 275
Phœnician settlements differ from Greek, 193 ; at Athens, etc., 199
Phœnicians, their seamanship, 198
Photius, 299
Picture galleries, 322
Περιηγητής (Cicerone), 53
Piræus dismantled by Sylla, 98
Pirates, the, 153
Piso, Cicero's picture of, 127
Places at dinner, 336
Platæa, 297
Plate, old silver, its value at Rome, 80
Plato, 332, 338, 386
Plays, Indian (*see* Drama)
Pliny, the elder, cited, 5 ; on Metrodorus, 68
Pliny, the younger, cited, 227
Plotius, L., teaches Latin rhetoric, 118
Plutarch, on king Menander's death and popularity, 23 ; on Æm. Paullus, 68 ; on the days of Mithradates, 86 ; on Marius, 104 ; on Damon Peripoltas, 151-3 ; on Antony, 162 ; on exile, 261-2 ; on gladiators, 272 ; on the Jews, 321 ; on manners and education, 323 *sq.* ; and law of *hiatus*, 331
Poets thanked for praising Delos, 112
Politarchs at Thessalonica, 268
Polity, 303
Polybius, the crisis of his time, 1, 4 ; his position, 67 ; on Roman luxury, 3 ; on Roman education, 81 ; compared with Dionysius Hal., 383
Pompeii, 214 *sq.*
Pompey, settlement of the East by, 46, 224 ; character, 143 ; and the pirates, 154-5
Porus, title of Indian kings, 30
Posidonius quoted on luxury of Syrian cities, 46 ; on Aristion, 96 ; and Pompey, 103
Priesthoods, title of nobility, 226
Probability, doctrine of, in Carneades' teaching, 63
Prose, Latin, created by Cicero, 114
Provinces, Cicero's picture of the, 144
Provincialism derided, 138
Psephisma, the Greek, its defects, 134
Ptolemæa at Delos, 108
Ptolemy Lathyrus, 44, 54
Publicani, oppression of the, 8, 146
Punctuality at dinner, 336
Purser, Mr. L. C., quoted, 55, 313 and Preface
Puteoli replaces Delos, 112, 211 *sq.*
Pyramids, Strabo on the, 241
Pyrrho, school of, 62
Pyrrhus, his successes against Rome, 1
Pythagoras, alleged books of, 65 ; new school of, 79, 179 *sq.* ; mythical portrait of, 181

QUEEN-MOTHERS, their importance in Seleucid and Ptolemaic history, 39, 44
Quintus Cicero, letters to, 136, 138

RABBITS, plague of, 194-5
Rabirius at the Alexandrian court 115

Rajendralala Mitra opposes Fergusson on age of Indian stone building, 25 *sq.*
Ravenna, 208
Reinach, Th., cited, 98
Religion in Greek and Phœnician colonies, 198
Renaissance, the, and stucco, 216
Revolutions, Roman, injure Hellenism, 85
Rhetoric, Greek, as opposed to Roman, 84
Rhodes, Strabo on, 236 *sq.* ; Dion on, 237, 248
Rhodians, control Delos, 109 ; conquered by Cassius, 161 ; poverty of, 237-8
Rhone, the, 201
Riviera, the, 201
Roads, Roman, essential to their colonies, 201
Roman governor, rapacity of, 14, 143 *sq.*
Roman *gravitas* compared to English, 11
Rome, and Alexander, 1; not educated for undertaking an empire, 2-4 ; asserts superiority to Greece, 131 ; mission of, in the East, 37 ; the only capital of the world, 12 ; enforces Hellenism, 205 ; Strabo on, 206; policy in Asia Minor, 354
Rubensohn on Crinagoras, 376
Rudeness, Germanic, 222
Rufus, Rutilius, 76, 78, 97
Rules of verse, strict, 375
Rural life in Greece, Dion on, 276 *sq.*, 370-2

SAMARIA, destroyed by Maccabees, 43
Samnites occupy Naples, 210
Sandracottus, his alliance with Seleucus, 19
Sanskrit, the language of the Indian drama, 32
Sardinia, low condition of, 15
Saviour, expected by the slaves, 9
Sayce, Prof., cited, 200, 313, and Preface

Scaptius, 158
Scepsis, MSS. of Aristotle at, 99
Scepticism, failure of, 180
Schliemann, Dr., on Novum Ilium, 228, 363
Scholarchs, Athenian, 61 ; character of, in second century, 62
Schools, philosophic, and their policy, 94
Schürer, his *History of Israel* quoted, 46
Scipio and Polybius, 67 ; and Panætius, 76
Scipionic circle, 3
Scymnus of Chios, his geography, 56, 59
Scythians, 90, 274-5
Sea, the Red, 54-5
Sebaste, 176
Seleucia on the Tigris, 38
Seleucus I., his Eastern policy, 18
Senart (in *Journal Asiatique* for 1885) on the inscription of Açoka, 22
Senate, the Roman, missions to the, from the Maccabees, 43 ; decree on the books of Numa, 66 ; on Stratoniceia, 91 ; on Oropus, 145 ; on Narthakion, 146
Senatus-consulta, 145 *sq.*
Senatus-consultum, of Lagina, 91 ; about Sparta and Messene, 252
Sicily, slaves in, 7 ; the Greeks of, according to Cicero, 131-2 ; Phœnicians and Greeks in, 197 ; decay of, 218-9
Silanus, D., translator of Mago, 5
Simon, the Maccabee, 42
Sinope, 95
Slaves, Carthaginian, 6 ; their first revolt in Sicily, 7 ; its Hellenistic character, 7 ; their second revolt, 7-9 ; combine with gladiators, 10
Snake, caught for Ptolemy II, 56
Snoring of the Tarsians, 235
Sophist, the, compared with the philosopher, 327
Spain, Hellenism of, 192 *sq.* ; effect of, on the East, 195
Sparta, games at, 259
Spartacus, 10

Stark, Professor B., quoted on Philistia and Palestine, 41 sq.
Statues, renaming of, 239
Stilo, L. Ælius, teaches Latin, 84
Stiris, 102, 152
Stoas, 360 sq.
Stoics, Roman, 75-6, 85, 159, 160; antiquated, 180; affected by the East, 187
Strabo, on mining and its hardships, 10; quotes Megasthenes, 19; on king Menander, 23; cites Apollodorus, 25; Nicolaus, 30; criticises story of Eudoxus, 51; on the tyrants of the Crimean Bosphorus, 87; on Mithradates, 92; on Aristotle's books, 99; on the Corinthian pottery, 157; general estimate of, 189-92; travels, 191; on Spain, 192 sq.; Emporiæ, 193; on rabbits, 195; on the Celts, 204; on Rome, 206; his mission, 206-7; on Asia, 232 sq.; on Comana, 225-6; on Rhodes, 236-7; on Egypt, 240 sq.; on papyrus and balm of Gilead, 242
Strategus, military, at Athens, 98
Stratonicea, in Caria, 91, 146
Stucco, use of, 216
Style, 384, 386; decay of, 392 sq.
Sublime, Longinus on the, 385 sq.
Suetonius, on Augustus, 162; on Vespasian, 258; on Domitian, 258-9
Superstition of Sylla, 103
Sybaris, 333
Syene (Aswân) 241
Sylla turns back the stream of history, 13; in Caria, 91; his memoirs, 93-4; his associates, 103; sends veterans to Pompeii, 214
Symposiarch, the, 337-8
Syria, its vicissitudes in the second century B.C., 39; rich in producing philosophers, 61; under Tigranes, 90, 168; its Greek cities restored, 169

TABLE-TALK of Plutarch, 338 sq.
Tacitus, 256, 284

Tact, want of, in great personages, 343
Tarentum, 209
Tarsus, description of, 234 sq.
Taxila, Hellenistic temple at, 28-9
Tenos, festival at, 231
Terence, translates Menander, 83
Theatres, Indian, 33
Thebes, Egyptian, revolt and destruction of, 168
Thebes, Bœotian, deserted, 288
Theorists on style, 381
Therapeutæ, sect of the, 184
Thessalonica, 267-8
Tiberius, the Emperor, restores cities in Asia, 224; Hellenism of, 255
Tigranes, 90, 92; monarch of Syria, 168
Tigranocerta, 92
Tiro and Cicero, 135
Toparchs, 46
Tory dreams, realisation of, 11
Toy-cart, the, 35
Trade, in Greece, 250-1
Training, bodily, Plutarch on, 325-6
Trajan, 259, 263, 391
Treasures of art carried to Rome, 104 sq.; in Sicily, 142
Troglodytes, in Nubia, 55
Trophies, set up by Herod at Jerusalem, 175
Tryphon, a slave leader, 9
Tubero, a Stoic, 149
Turcomans, the, 205
Turdetani, the, 196
Tyrannicide, why popular, 160
Tyrannio, heard by Strabo, 206
Tyrants, in Babylon, etc., 38; on Syrian coast, 41; in the Crimea, 87
Tyrian companies at Puteoli, 214

Umbræ at dinner, 343
Unhealthiness, hereditary, common, 323
Unity of the Deity preached by Pythagoreans, 181; by Dion, 239; by Plutarch, 311-2
Universities, 265
Unknown gods, the, 269
Unpopularity of philosophers, 374
Urbes togatæ, 203

Utica, 219
VALERIUS ANTIAS (historian), cited by Livy, 65
Varenus, 306
Ventidius conquers the Parthians, 170
Verres, Cicero against, 139 *sq.* ; his outrages, 141
Vespasian, cancels Nero's edict, 257-8, 355 ; his Hellenism, 258
Vesuvius, its eruption, 215
Vices of Longinus's age, 393-4
Viereck, on the Greek of the Senate, 147
Vigo bay, 194
Villages, 15, 195, 240
Violence, Greek, in accusation, 138
Virtues, domestic, lauded on Epitaphs, 222
Volkmann, on Plutarch, 319 ; criticised, 331

WEIL, R., in *MDI*, 94
Wilson, Prof. H. H., on the Indian drama, 31 *sq.*
Wills, Græco-Egyptian, Preface x, xi

Windisch, Prof., on the Indian drama, 34-6
Wise man, the Stoic, 183
Wit in conversation, 342
Women, the rights of, 358
World-empire, the idea of its growth, 2
Wrecking, 281, 284
Wyttenbach on Plutarch, 331

XENOCRATES, 352
Xenophon cited on οἰκουμένη, 15 ; on Phœnician ship, 178 ; at Scillus, 352

Yavanikâ, the stage curtain, 35
Yokel, the country, 373

ZELA, a religious foundation in Asia Minor, 225
Zeller, his *Philosophie der Griechen* cited, 61, 67, 183, 185, 187, 266
Zeno, of Tarsus, 75
Zeus, Abrettene, 226 ; temple of, at Olbia, 276
Zumpt on the succession of Athenian scholarchs, 61

WORKS BY J. P. MAHAFFY,

FELLOW, ETC., OF TRINITY COLLEGE, DUBLIN;
HON. FELLOW OF QUEEN'S COLLEGE, OXFORD, ETC.

Social Life in Greece, from Homer to Menander. Sixth Edition, enlarged. Crown 8vo. 9s.

The *Athenæum* says:—"Mr. Mahaffy has, in this little volume, given us the results of considerable reading, and has given them in a form which is both pleasant and interesting... No omission greatly detracts from the merits of a book so fresh in its thought and so independent in its criticism.... One feels that the author is no mere compiler, but an original thinker; and whether we agree with his conclusions or not, we at least respect the boldness and straightforwardness with which he holds his own."

Greek Life and Thought, from the Age of Alexander to the Roman Conquest. Crown 8vo. 12s. 6d.

The *Academy* says:—"These studies of Greek life and thought may be regarded as complementary to more than one of Professor Mahaffy's other volumes upon Greek affairs. They carry further the account of *Social Life in Greece*; they take note of authors later than the point at which the *History of Greek Literature* ends; and they supply the domestic and literary features necessary to body-out the brilliant sketch of *Alexander's Empire*. Mr. Mahaffy vindicates, in an eloquent introduction, the importance of his subject.... The subject is a grand one, and the author's opportunity is the better because the subject has been comparatively neglected. The political and social experiments of the time; the spread of Greek culture necessary for the future of humanity; the actual achievements in architecture and sculpture, in poetry and in painting—these things arouse instantly the interest of the historian and the artist, while the philosopher will be curious to see how Mr. Mahaffy justifies his favourable opinion of the morality and the daily life. This splendid subject has now found an English historian competent to do it justice."

The *Guardian* says:—"... At his own immediate subject Mr. Mahaffy has worked with much skill and care. It is pleasant to visit Alexandria, Antioch, and Pergamon in his company, and to make acquaintance with their kings, their poets, and their philosophers. We see what kind of literature, what kind of philosophy grew up in a very artificial and conscious age, an age which, as Mr. Mahaffy does not fail often to remind us, has so very much in common with modern Europe."

The Greek World under Roman Sway, from Polybius to Plutarch. Crown 8vo. 10s. 6d.

Rambles and Studies in Greece. With Illustrations. Third Edition, Revised and Enlarged. Crown 8vo. 10s. 6d.

The *St. James's Gazette* says:—"It is unnecessary to praise this book, which the public has already decided to be one of the best of its kind. The present edition is enriched with a good deal of additional information."

MACMILLAN AND CO., LONDON.

WORKS BY J. P. MAHAFFY—Continued.

A History of Classical Greek Literature. In two Volumes. Crown 8vo. Vol. I.—The Poets, with an Appendix on Homer by Professor SAYCE. Second Edition. Revised throughout. 9s. Vol. II.—New Issue in Two Parts. (Third Edition. Revised throughout.) Part 1.—Herodotus to Plato. Part II.— Isocrates to Aristotle. 4s. 6d. each.

The *Athenæum* says:—"An excellent scholar, a practised litterateur, a traveller, and a man of very large general culture, Professor Mahaffy writes with full knowledge of his subject, and with enthusiasm still untainted by the pedantry that too often clings to the collegiate cap and gown. His book, in fact, apart from its intrinsic value as a history, is excessively entertaining.... It is manifestly impossible within the limits of our space to do anything like justice to Professor Mahaffy's learning, or to the ability with which he has compressed his facts into a narrow and convenient compass. Of his merits his book itself is the best and only possible advertisement. Were the criticism as bad as could be, the paragraphs on bibliography would redeem it, and make the work valuable; but the criticism is good and honest and happily expressed, and may be recommended with the heartiest approbation. In conclusion it should be added that the first volume is enriched by Mr. Sayce with a remarkably neat essay on Homeric diction, where the intermixture of various dialects and of real and spurious archaisms is admirably dissected."

The *Educational Times* says:—"Professor Mahaffy, moreover, is always instructive and generally interesting. Taking his book as a whole we may fairly claim for it an absolute pre-eminence in the subject of which it treats. It is a real necessity for every scholar's library."

Euripides. 18mo. 1s. 6d. [*Classical Writers.*

The *Academy* says:—"No better book on the subject has previously been written in English. Mr. Mahaffy is scholarly and not pedantic, appreciative, and yet just."

Greek Antiquities. Illustrated. 18mo. 1s.
[*Literature Primers.*

The *Saturday Review* says:—"We can conceive no handbook of a hundred pages which furnishes readers with so much light upon the civil and domestic life of the Greeks."

The Decay of Modern Preaching. An Essay. Crown 8vo. 3s. 6d.

The *Saturday Review* says:—"The work is clever and sensible in most of its criticisms and suggestions."
The *Church of England Pulpit* says:—"It is an excellent little book."

The Principles of the Art of Conversation. Second Edition. Crown 8vo. 4s. 6d.

The *Saturday Review* says:—"The book is full of shrewd observations.... Most of his rules and recommendations are aimed at promoting conversation and directing it into the right channel."

Euripides. Hippolytus. Edited, with Introduction and Notes, by J. P. MAHAFFY and J. B. BURY. Fcap. 8vo. 3s. 6d.
[*Classical Series.*

MACMILLAN AND CO., LONDON.

Catalogue of Books

PUBLISHED BY

MACMILLAN AND CO.

BEDFORD STREET, COVENT GARDEN, LONDON

September, 1890.

ABBOT (Francis). SCIENTIFIC THEISM. Crown 8vo. 7s. 6d.
—— THE WAY OUT OF AGNOSTICISM; or, The Philosophy of Free Religion. Cr. 8vo. 4s. 6d.
ABBOTT (Rev. E. A.).—A SHAKESPEARIAN GRAMMAR. Extra fcp. 8vo. 6s.
—— CAMBRIDGE SERMONS. 8vo. 6s.
—— OXFORD SERMONS. 8vo. 7s. 6d.
—— FRANCIS BACON: AN ACCOUNT OF HIS LIFE AND WORKS. 8vo. 14s.
—— BIBLE LESSONS. Crown 8vo. 4s. 6d.
ABBOTT (Rev. E. A.) and RUSHBROOKE (W. G.).—THE COMMON TRADITION OF THE SYNOPTIC GOSPELS, IN THE TEXT OF THE REVISED VERSION. Crown 8vo. 3s. 6d.
ACLAND (Sir H. W.).—THE ARMY MEDICAL SCHOOL. Address at Netley Hospital. 1s.
ACTS OF THE APOSTLES. The Greek Text of Bp. Westcott and Dr. Hort. With Notes by T. E. PAGE, M.A. Fcp. 8vo. 4s. 6d.
ADAMS (Sir F. O.) and CUNNINGHAM (C.)—THE SWISS CONFEDERATION. 8vo. 14s.
ADDISON. By W. J. COURTHOPE. Crown 8vo. 1s. 6d.; sewed, 1s.
ADDISON, SELECTIONS FROM. Chosen and Edited by J. R. GREEN. 18mo. 4s. 6d.
ÆSCHYLUS.—PERSÆ. Edited by A. O. PRICKARD, M.A. Fcp. 8vo. 3s. 6d.
—— EUMENIDES. With Notes and Introduction, by BERNARD DRAKE, M.A. 8vo. 5s.
—— PROMETHEUS VINCTUS. With Introduction, Notes, and Vocabulary, by Rev. H. M. STEPHENSON, M.A. 18mo. 1s. 6d.
—— THE "SEVEN AGAINST THEBES." With Introduction, Commentary, and Translation, by A. W. VERRALL, Litt.D. 8vo. 7s. 6d.
—— THE "SEVEN AGAINST THEBES." With Introduction and Notes, by A. W. VERRALL and M. A. BAYFIELD. Fcp. 8vo. 3s. 6d.
—— AGAMEMNON. With Introduction, Commentary, and Translation, by A. W. VERRALL, Litt.D. 8vo. 12s.
—— THE SUPPLICES. Text, Introduction, Notes, Commentary, and Translation, by Prof. T. G. TUCKER. 8vo. 10s. 6d.
ÆSOP—CALDECOTT.—SOME OF ÆSOP'S FABLES, with Modern Instances, shown in Designs by RANDOLPH CALDECOTT. 4to. 5s.
AGASSIZ (Louis): HIS LIFE AND CORRESPONDENCE. Edited by ELIZABETH CARY AGASSIZ. 2 vols. Crown 8vo. 18s.

AINGER (Rev. Alfred).—SERMONS PREACHED IN THE TEMPLE CHURCH. Extra fcp. 8vo. 6s.
—— CHARLES LAMB. Globe 8vo. (Library Edition). 5s.—Crn. 8vo. 1s. 6d.; swd. 1s.
AIRY (Sir G. B.).—TREATISE ON THE ALGEBRAICAL AND NUMERICAL THEORY OF ERRORS OF OBSERVATION AND THE COMBINATION OF OBSERVATIONS. Crown 8vo. 6s. 6d.
—— POPULAR ASTRONOMY. With Illustrations. Fcp. 8vo. 4s. 6d.
—— AN ELEMENTARY TREATISE ON PARTIAL DIFFERENTIAL EQUATIONS. Cr. 8vo. 5s. 6d.
—— ON SOUND AND ATMOSPHERIC VIBRATIONS. With the Mathematical Elements of Music. 2nd Edition. Crown 8vo. 9s.
—— GRAVITATION. An Elementary Explanation of the Principal Perturbations in the Solar System. 2nd Edition. Crown 8vo. 7s. 6d.
AITKEN (Mary Carlyle).—SCOTTISH SONG. A Selection of the Choicest Lyrics of Scotland. 18mo. 4s. 6d.
AITKEN (Sir W.)—THE GROWTH OF THE RECRUIT AND YOUNG SOLDIER. With a view to the selection of "Growing Lads" for the Army, and a Regulated System of Training for Recruits. Crown 8vo. 8s. 6d.
ALBEMARLE (Earl of).—FIFTY YEARS OF MY LIFE. 3rd Ed., revised. Cr. 8vo. 7s. 6d.
ALDIS (Mary Steadman).—THE GREAT GIANT ARITHMOS. A MOST ELEMENTARY ARITHMETIC. Illustrated. Globe 8vo. 2s. 6d.
ALEXANDER (C. F.).—THE SUNDAY BOOK OF POETRY FOR THE YOUNG. 18mo. 4s. 6d.
ALEXANDER (T.) and THOMSON (A.). —ELEMENTARY APPLIED MECHANICS. Part II. Transverse Stress; upwards of 150 Diagrams, and 200 Examples carefully worked out. Crown 8vo. 10s. 6d.
ALLBUTT (Dr. T. Clifford).—ON THE USE OF THE OPHTHALMOSCOPE. 8vo. 15s.
ALLEN (Grant).—ON THE COLOURS OF FLOWERS, as Illustrated in the British Flora. With Illustrations. Crown 8vo. 3s. 6d.
ALLINGHAM (William).—THE BALLAD BOOK. 18mo. 4s. 6d.
AMIEL (Henri Frederic).—THE JOURNAL INTIME. Translated by Mrs. HUMPHRY WARD. 2nd Edition. Crown 8vo. 6s.
AN ANCIENT CITY, AND OTHER POEMS. Extra fcp. 8vo. 6s.

AN AUTHOR'S LOVE. Being the Unpublished Letters of PROSPER MÉRIMÉE'S "Inconnue." 2 vols. Ex. cr. 8vo. 12s.

ANDERSON (A.).—BALLADS AND SONNETS. Crown 8vo. 5s.

ANDERSON (Dr. McCall).—LECTURES ON CLINICAL MEDICINE. Illustrated. 8vo. 10s. 6d.

ANDERSON (L.).—LINEAR PERSPECTIVE AND MODEL DRAWING. Royal 8vo. 2s.

ANDOCIDES.—DE MYSTERIIS. Edited by W. J. HICKIE, M.A. Fcp. 8vo. 2s. 6d.

ANDREWS (Dr. Thomas): THE SCIENTIFIC PAPERS OF THE LATE. With a Memoir by Profs. TAIT and CRUM BROWN. 8vo. 18s.

ANGLO-SAXON LAW: ESSAYS ON. Med. 8vo. 18s.

ANTONINUS, MARCUS AURELIUS.— BOOK IV. OF THE MEDITATIONS. The Greek Text Revised. With Translation and Commentary, by HASTINGS CROSSLEY, M.A. 8vo. 6s.

APPLETON (T. G.).—A NILE JOURNAL. Illustrated by EUGENE BENSON. Cr. 8vo. 6s.

ARATUS.—THE SKIES AND WEATHER FORECASTS OF ARATUS. Translated by E. POSTE, M.A. Crown 8vo. 3s. 6d.

ARIOSTO.—PALADIN AND SARACEN. Stories from Ariosto. By H. C. HOLLWAY-CALTHROP. Illustrated. Crown 8vo. 6s.

ARISTOPHANES.—THE BIRDS. Translated into English Verse, with Introduction, Notes, and Appendices. By Prof. B. H. KENNEDY, D.D. Crown 8vo. 6s.

—— HELP NOTES FOR THE USE OF STUDENTS. Crown 8vo. 1s. 6d.

ARISTOTLE ON FALLACIES; OR, THE SOPHISTICI ELENCHI. With Translation and Notes by E. POSTE, M.A. 8vo. 8s. 6d.

ARISTOTLE.—THE FIRST BOOK OF THE METAPHYSICS OF ARISTOTLE. Translated into English Prose, with marginal Analysis and Summary of each Chapter. By a Cambridge Graduate. 8vo. 5s.

—— THE POLITICS. Translated with an Analysis and Critical Notes by J. E. C. WELLDON, M.A. 2nd Edition. 10s. 6d.

—— THE RHETORIC. By the same Translator. Crown 8vo. 7s. 6d.

ARMY PRELIMINARY EXAMINATION, Specimens of Papers set at the, 1882-89. With Answers to the Mathematical Questions. Crown 8vo. 3s. 6d.

ARNAULD, ANGELIQUE. By FRANCES MARTIN. Crown 8vo. 4s. 6d.

ARNOLD (Matthew).—THE COMPLETE POETICAL WORKS. New Edition. 3 vols. Crown 8vo. 7s. 6d. each.—Vol. I. Early Poems, Narrative Poems, and Sonnets. —Vol. II. Lyric and Elegiac Poems.— Vol. III. Dramatic and Later Poems.

—— COMPLETE POETICAL WORKS. 1 vol. Crown 8vo. 7s. 6d.

—— ESSAYS IN CRITICISM. 6th Edition. Crown 8vo. 9s.

—— ESSAYS IN CRITICISM. Second Series. With an Introductory Note by LORD COLERIDGE. Crown 8vo. 7s. 6d.

ARNOLD (Matthew). ISAIAH XL.—LXVI. WITH THE SHORTER PROPHECIES ALLIED TO IT. With Notes. Crown 8vo. 5s.

—— ISAIAH OF JERUSALEM. In the Authorised English Version, with Introduction, Corrections, and Notes. Crown 8vo. 4s. 6d.

—— A BIBLE-READING FOR SCHOOLS. The Great Prophecy of Israel's Restoration (Isaiah xl.-lxvi.) Arranged and Edited for Young Learners. 4th Edition. 18mo. 1s.

—— HIGHER SCHOOLS AND UNIVERSITIES IN GERMANY. Crown 8vo. 6s.

—— SELECTED POEMS. 18mo. 4s. 6d.

—— POEMS OF WORDSWORTH. Chosen and Edited by MATTHEW ARNOLD. With Portrait. 18mo. 4s. 6d.
Large Paper Edition. 9s.

—— POETRY OF BYRON. Chosen and arranged by MATTHEW ARNOLD. With Vignette. 18mo. 4s. 6d.
Large Paper Edition. 9s.

—— DISCOURSES IN AMERICA. Cr. 8vo. 4s. 6d.

—— JOHNSON'S LIVES OF THE POETS, THE SIX CHIEF LIVES FROM. With Macaulay's "Life of Johnson." With Preface and Notes by MATTHEW ARNOLD. Crown 8vo. 4s. 6d.

—— EDMUND BURKE'S LETTERS, TRACTS AND SPEECHES ON IRISH AFFAIRS. Edited by MATTHEW ARNOLD. Crown 8vo. 6s.

—— REPORTS ON ELEMENTARY SCHOOLS, 1852-82. Edited by the Right Hon. Sir FRANCIS SANDFORD, K.C.B. Cr. 8vo. 3s. 6d.

ARNOLD (T.).—THE SECOND PUNIC WAR. By the late THOMAS ARNOLD, D.D. Edited by WILLIAM T. ARNOLD, M.A. With Eight Maps. Crown 8vo. 8s. 6d.

ARNOLD (W. T.).—THE ROMAN SYSTEM OF PROVINCIAL ADMINISTRATION. Crn. 8vo. 6s.

ARRIAN.—SELECTIONS. Edited by J. BOND, M.A., and A. S. WALPOLE, M.A. 18mo. 1s. 6d.

ART AT HOME SERIES. Edited by W. J. LOFTIE, B.A.

MUSIC IN THE HOUSE. By JOHN HULLAH. Fourth Edition. Crown 8vo. 2s. 6d.

THE DINING-ROOM. By Mrs. LOFTIE. With Illustrations. 2nd Edition. Crown 8vo. 2s. 6d.

THE BEDROOM AND BOUDOIR. By Lady BARKER. Crown 8vo. 2s. 6d.

AMATEUR THEATRICALS. By WALTER H. POLLOCK and LADY POLLOCK. Illustrated by KATE GREENAWAY. Crown 8vo. 2s. 6d.

NEEDLEWORK. By ELIZABETH GLAISTER. Illustrated. Crown 8vo. 2s. 6d.

THE LIBRARY. By ANDREW LANG, with a Chapter on English Illustrated Books, by AUSTIN DOBSON. Crown 8vo. 3s. 6d.

ARTEVELDE. JAMES AND PHILIP VAN ARTEVELDE. By W. J. ASHLEY. Crown 8vo. 6s.

ATKINSON (J. B.). — AN ART TOUR TO NORTHERN CAPITALS OF EUROPE. 8vo. 12s.

ATTIC ORATORS, SELECTIONS FROM THE. Antiphon, Andocides, Lysias, Isocrates, and Isaeus. Edited, with Notes, by Prof. R. C. JEBB, Litt.D. 2nd Edition. Fcp. 8vo. 6s

ATTWELL (H.)—A BOOK OF GOLDEN THOUGHTS. 18mo. 4s. 6d.

AULUS GELLIUS (STORIES FROM). Edited by Rev. G. H. NALL, M.A. 18mo. 1s. 6d.

AUSTIN (Alfred).—SAVONAROLA: A TRAGEDY. Crown 8vo. 7s. 6d.

—— SOLILOQUIES IN SONG. Crown 8vo. 6s.

—— AT THE GATE OF THE CONVENT; AND OTHER POEMS. Crown 8vo. 6s.

—— PRINCE LUCIFER. Crown 8vo. 6s.

—— MADONNA'S CHILD. Crown 4to. 3s. 6d.

—— THE TOWER OF BABEL. Crown 4to. 9s.

—— ROME OR DEATH. Crown 4to. 9s.

—— THE GOLDEN AGE. Crown 8vo. 5s.

—— THE SEASON. Crown 8vo. 5s.

—— LOVE'S WIDOWHOOD: AND OTHER POEMS. Crown 8vo. 6s.

—— THE HUMAN TRAGEDY. Cr. 8vo. 7s. 6d.

—— ENGLISH LYRICS. Crown 8vo. 3s. 6d.

AUTENRIETH (Dr. G.).—AN HOMERIC DICTIONARY. Translated from the German, by R. P. KEEP, Ph.D. Crown 8vo. 6s.

AWDRY (Frances). THE STORY OF A FELLOW SOLDIER. (A Life of Bishop Patteson for the Young.) With a Preface by CHARLOTTE M. YONGE. Globe 8vo. 2s. 6d.

BABRIUS. With Introductory Dissertations, Critical Notes, Commentary, and Lexicon, by W. G. RUTHERFORD, LL.D. 8vo. 12s. 6d.

"BACCHANTE." THE CRUISE OF H.M.S. "BACCHANTE," 1879-1882. Compiled from the private Journals, Letters and Note-books of PRINCE ALBERT VICTOR and PRINCE GEORGE OF WALES. By the Rev. Canon DALTON. 2 vols. Medium 8vo. 52s. 6d.

BACON. By the Very Rev. Dean CHURCH, Globe 8vo. 5s.; Crn. 8vo. 1s. 6d.; swd., 1s.

BACON'S ESSAYS AND COLOURS OF GOOD AND EVIL. With Notes and Glossarial Index, by W. ALDIS WRIGHT, M.A. With Vignette. 18mo. 4s. 6d.

—— ESSAYS. Edited by Prof. F. G. SELBY, M.A. Globe 8vo. 3s. 6d.

BACON (FRANCIS): ACCOUNT OF HIS LIFE AND WORKS. By E. A. ABBOTT. 8vo. 14s.

BAINES (Rev. Edward).—SERMONS. With a Preface and Memoir, by ALFRED BARRY, D.D., late Bishop of Sydney. Crn. 8vo. 6s.

BAKER (Sir Samuel White).—ISMAILIA. A Narrative of the Expedition to Central Africa for the Suppression of the Slave Trade, organised by ISMAIL, Khedive of Egypt. Crown 8vo. 6s.

—— THE NILE TRIBUTARIES OF ABYSSINIA, AND THE SWORD HUNTERS OF THE HAMRAN ARABS. Crown 8vo. 6s.

—— THE ALBERT N'YANZA GREAT BASIN OF THE NILE AND EXPLORATION OF THE NILE SOURCES. Crown 8vo. 6s.

—— CYPRUS AS I SAW IT IN 1879. 8vo. 12s. 6d.

—— CAST UP BY THE SEA: OR, THE ADVENTURES OF NED GRAY. With Illustrations by HUARD. Crown 8vo. 6s.

—— THE EGYPTIAN QUESTION. Letters to the Times and the Pall Mall Gazette. 8vo. 2s.

BAKER (Sir Samuel White). TRUE TALES FOR MY GRANDSONS. Illustrated by W. J. HENNESSY. Crown 8vo. 7s. 6d.

—— WILD BEASTS AND THEIR WAYS IN ASIA, AFRICA, AMERICA, FROM 1845—1888. Illustrated. 2 vols. 8vo.

BALFOUR (The Right Hon. A. J.) A DEFENCE OF PHILOSOPHIC DOUBT. Being an Essay on the Foundations of Belief. 8vo. 12s.

BALFOUR (Prof. F. M.).—ELASMOBRANCH FISHES. With Plates. 8vo. 21s.

—— COMPARATIVE EMBRYOLOGY. With Illustrations. 2 vols. 2nd Edition. 8vo.—Vol. I. 18s.—Vol. II. 21s.

—— THE COLLECTED WORKS. Memorial Edition. Edited by M. FOSTER, F.R.S., and ADAM SEDGWICK, M.A. 4 vols. 8vo. 6l. 6s. Vols. I. and IV. Special Memoirs. May be had separately. Price 73s. 6d.

BALL (Sir R. S.).—EXPERIMENTAL MECHANICS. Illustrated. New Edit. Cr. 8vo. 6s.

BALL (W. W. R.). THE STUDENT'S GUIDE TO THE BAR. 5th Edition, revised. Crown 8vo. 2s. 6d.

—— A SHORT ACCOUNT OF THE HISTORY OF MATHEMATICS. Crown 8vo. 10s. 6d.

BALLIOL COLLEGE. PSALMS AND HYMNS FOR BALLIOL COLLEGE. 18mo. 2s. 6d.

BARKER (Lady).—FIRST LESSONS IN THE PRINCIPLES OF COOKING. 3rd Ed. 18mo. 1s.

—— A YEAR'S HOUSEKEEPING IN SOUTH AFRICA. Illustrated. Crown 8vo. 3s. 6d.

—— STATION LIFE IN NEW ZEALAND. Crown 8vo. 3s. 6d.

—— LETTERS TO GUY. Crown 8vo. 5s.

—— THE BED ROOM AND BOUDOIR. With numerous Illustrations. Crown 8vo. 2s. 6d.

BARNES. LIFE OF WILLIAM BARNES, POET AND PHILOLOGIST. By his Daughter, LUCY BAXTER ("Leader Scott"). Cr. 8vo. 7s. 6d.

BARRY (Bishop). FIRST WORDS IN AUSTRALIA: Sermons. Crown 8vo. 5s.

BARTHOLOMEW (J. G.).—ELEMENTARY SCHOOL ATLAS. 4to. 1s.

—— LIBRARY REFERENCE ATLAS OF THE WORLD. With Index to 100,000 places. Folio. 2l. 12s. 6d. net.

—— PHYSICAL AND POLITICAL SCHOOL ATLAS. Royal 4to.

BARWELL (Richard, F.R.C.S.).—THE CAUSES AND TREATMENT OF LATERAL CURVATURE OF THE SPINE. Crown 8vo. 5s.

—— ON ANEURISM, ESPECIALLY OF THE THORAX AND ROOT OF THE NECK. 3s. 6d.

BASTIAN (H. Charlton).—THE BEGINNINGS OF LIFE. 2 vols. Crown 8vo. 28s.

—— EVOLUTION AND THE ORIGIN OF LIFE. Crown 8vo. 6s. 6d.

—— ON PARALYSIS FROM BRAIN DISEASE IN ITS COMMON FORMS. Crown 8vo. 10s. 6d.

BATHER (Archdeacon).—ON SOME MINISTERIAL DUTIES, CATECHIZING, PREACHING, &c. Edited, with a Preface, by C. J. VAUGHAN, D.D. Fcp. 8vo. 4s. 6d.

BATH (Marquis of).—OBSERVATIONS ON BULGARIAN AFFAIRS. Crown 8vo. 3s. 6d.

BEASLEY (R. D.)—AN ELEMENTARY TREATISE ON PLANE TRIGONOMETRY. With numerous Examples. 9th Ed. Cr. 8vo. 3s. 6d.

BEAUMARCHAIS. LE BARBIER DE SEVILLE, OU LE PRÉCAUTION INUTILE. Comedie en Quatre Actes. Edited by L. P. BLOUET, B.A., Univ. Gallic. Fcp. 8vo. 3s. 6d.

BECKER (B. H.)—DISTURBED IRELAND. Letters written during 1880–81. Crn. 8vo. 6s.

BEESLY (Mrs.)—STORIES FROM THE HISTORY OF ROME. Fcp. 8vo. 2s. 6d.

BELCHER (Rev. H.)—SHORT EXERCISES IN LATIN PROSE COMPOSITION, AND EXAMINATION PAPERS IN LATIN GRAMMAR; WITH A CHAPTER ON ANALYSIS OF SENTENCES. 18mo. 1s. 6d.

KEY (for Teachers only). 3s. 6d.

—— SHORT EXERCISES IN LATIN PROSE COMPOSITION. Part II. On the Syntax of Sentences. With an Appendix. 18mo. 2s.

KEY (for Teachers only). 18mo. 3s.

BENHAM (Rev. W.)—A COMPANION TO THE LECTIONARY. Crown 8vo. 4s. 6d.

BENTLEY. By Professor JEBB. Crown 8vo. 1s. 6d. ; sewed, 1s.

BERLIOZ (Hector). AUTOBIOGRAPHY OF. Transl. by RACHEL and ELEANOR HOLMES. 2 vols. Crown 8vo. 21s.

BERNARD (M.)—FOUR LECTURES ON SUBJECTS CONNECTED WITH DIPLOMACY. 8vo. 9s.

BERNARD (St.) THE LIFE AND TIMES OF ST. BERNARD, ABBOT OF CLAIRVAUX. By J. C. MORISON, M.A. Crown 8vo. 6s.

BERNERS (J.)—FIRST LESSONS ON HEALTH. 18mo. 1s.

BESANT (Walter).—CAPTAIN COOK. With Portrait. Crown 8vo. 2s. 6d.

BETHUNE-BAKER (J. F.)—THE INFLUENCE OF CHRISTIANITY ON WAR. 8vo. 5s.

—— THE STERNNESS OF CHRIST'S TEACHING, AND ITS RELATION TO THE LAW OF FORGIVENESS. Crown 8vo. 2s. 6d.

BETSY LEE: A FO'C'S'LE YARN. Extra fcp. 8vo. 3s. 6d.

BETTANY (G. T.)—FIRST LESSONS IN PRACTICAL BOTANY. 18mo. 1s.

BIGELOW (M. M.)—HISTORY OF PROCEDURE IN ENGLAND FROM THE NORMAN CONQUEST. The Norman Period, 1066–1204. 8vo. 16s.

BIKÉLAS (D.).—LOUKIS LARAS; OR, THE REMINISCENCES OF A CHIOTE MERCHANT DURING THE GREEK WAR OF INDEPENDENCE. Translated by J. GENNADIUS, Greek Minister in London. Crown 8vo. 7s. 6d.

BINNIE (the late Rev. William).—SERMONS. Crown 8vo. 6s.

BIRKBECK (William Lloyd).—HISTORICAL SKETCH OF THE DISTRIBUTION OF LAND IN ENGLAND. Crown 8vo. 4s. 6d.

BIRKS (Thomas Rawson, M.A.).—FIRST PRINCIPLES OF MORAL SCIENCE; OR, FIRST COURSE OF LECTURES DELIVERED IN THE UNIVERSITY OF CAMBRIDGE. Cr. 8vo. 8s. 6d.

—— MODERN UTILITARIANISM; OR, THE SYSTEMS OF PALEY, BENTHAM, AND MILL EXAMINED AND COMPARED. Crn. 8vo. 6s. 6d.

BIRKS (Thomas Rawson).—THE DIFFICULTIES OF BELIEF IN CONNECTION WITH THE CREATION AND THE FALL, REDEMPTION AND JUDGMENT. 2nd Edit. Crn. 8vo. 5s.

—— COMMENTARY ON THE BOOK OF ISAIAH, CRITICAL, HISTORICAL, AND PROPHETICAL; INCLUDING A REVISED ENGLISH TRANSLATION. 2nd Edition. 8vo. 12s. 6d.

—— THE NEW TESTAMENT. Essay on the Right Estimation of MS. Evidence in the Text of the New Testament. Cr. 8vo. 3s. 6d.

—— SUPERNATURAL REVELATION; OR, FIRST PRINCIPLES OF MORAL THEOLOGY. 8vo. 8s.

—— MODERN PHYSICAL FATALISM, AND THE DOCTRINE OF EVOLUTION. Including an Examination of Mr. Herbert Spencer's "First Principles." Crown 8vo. 6s.

—— JUSTIFICATION AND IMPUTED RIGHTEOUSNESS. Being a Review of Ten Sermons on the Nature and Effects of Faith by JAMES THOMAS O'BRIEN, D.D., late Bishop of Ossory, Ferns, and Leighlin. Cr. 8vo. 6s.

BJÖRNSON (B.).—SYNNÖVE SOLBAKKEN. Translated by JULIE SUTTER. Cr. 8vo. 6s.

BLACK (William).—THE STRANGE ADVENTURES OF A PHAETON. Illustrated. Cr. 8vo. 6s.

—— A PRINCESS OF THULE. Crown 8vo. 6s.

—— THE MAID OF KILLEENA, AND OTHER TALES. Crown 8vo. 6s.

—— MADCAP VIOLET. Crown 8vo. 6s.

—— GREEN PASTURES AND PICCADILLY. Crown 8vo. 6s.

—— MACLEOD OF DARE. With Illustrations by eminent Artists. Crown 8vo. 6s.

—— WHITE WINGS: A YACHTING ROMANCE. Crown 8vo. 6s.

—— THE BEAUTIFUL WRETCH: THE FOUR MACNICOLS: THE PUPIL OF AURELIUS. Crown 8vo. 6s.

—— SHANDON BELLS. Crown 8vo. 6s.

—— YOLANDE. Crown 8vo. 6s.

—— JUDITH SHAKESPEARE. Crown 8vo. 6s.

—— GOLDSMITH. Cr. 8vo. 1s. 6d.; sewed, 1s.

—— THE WISE WOMEN OF INVERNESS: A TALE. AND OTHER MISCELLANIES. Cr. 8vo. 6s.

—— WHITE HEATHER. Crown 8vo. 6s.

—— SABINA ZEMBRA. Crown 8vo. 6s.

BLACKBURNE. LIFE OF THE RIGHT HON. FRANCIS BLACKBURNE, late Lord Chancellor of Ireland, by his son, EDWARD BLACKBURNE. With Portrait. 8vo. 12s.

BLACKIE (Prof. John Stuart).—GREEK AND ENGLISH DIALOGUES FOR USE IN SCHOOLS AND COLLEGES. 3rd Edition. Fcp. 8vo. 2s. 6d.

—— HORÆ HELLENICÆ. 8vo. 12s.

—— THE WISE MEN OF GREECE: IN A SERIES OF DRAMATIC DIALOGUES. Cr. 8vo. 9s.

—— GOETHE'S FAUST. Translated into English Verse. 2nd Edition. Crown 8vo. 9s.

—— LAY SERMONS. Crown 8vo. 6s.

—— MESSIS VITAE: Gleanings of Song from a Happy Life. Crown 8vo. 4s. 6d.

—— WHAT DOES HISTORY TEACH? Two Edinburgh Lectures. Globe 8vo. 2s. 6d.

LIST OF PUBLICATIONS. 5

BLAKE (J. F.) ASTRONOMICAL MYTHS. With Illustrations. Crown 8vo. 9s.

BLAKE. LIFE OF WILLIAM BLAKE. With Selections from his Poems and other Writings. Illustrated from Blake's own Works. By ALEXANDER GILCHRIST. New and Enlarged Edition. 2 vols. cloth gilt. Medium 8vo. 2l. 2s.

BLAKISTON (J. R.).—THE TEACHER: HINTS ON SCHOOL MANAGEMENT. Cr. 8vo. 2s. 6d.

BLANFORD (H. F.).—THE RUDIMENTS OF PHYSICAL GEOGRAPHY FOR THE USE OF INDIAN SCHOOLS. 12th Edition. Illustrated. Globe 8vo. 2s. 6d.

—— A PRACTICAL GUIDE TO THE CLIMATES AND WEATHER OF INDIA, CEYLON AND BURMAH, AND THE STORMS OF INDIAN SEAS. 8vo. 12s. 6d.

—— A GEOGRAPHY OF INDIA. Illustrated. Globe 8vo. 2s. 6d.

BLANFORD (W. T.).—GEOLOGY AND ZOOLOGY OF ABYSSINIA. 8vo. 21s.

BLYTH (A. Wynter).—A MANUAL OF PUBLIC HEALTH. 8vo.

BÖHM-BAWERK (Prof.).—CAPITAL AND INTEREST. Translated by W. SMART, M.A. 8vo. 14s.

BOLDREWOOD (Rolf).—ROBBERY UNDER ARMS: A STORY OF LIFE AND ADVENTURE IN THE BUSH AND IN THE GOLDFIELDS OF AUSTRALIA. Crown 8vo. 3s. 6d.

—— THE MINER'S RIGHT. 3 vols. 31s. 6d.

—— THE SQUATTER'S DREAM. Cr.8vo. 3s.6d.

—— THE COLONIAL REFORMER. 3 vols. Cr. 8vo. [*In the Press.*

BOLEYN (ANNE): A Chapter of English History, 1527-1536. By PAUL FRIEDMANN. 2 vols. 8vo. 28s.

BONAR (James).—MALTHUS AND HIS WORK. 8vo. 12s. 6d.

BOOK OF GOLDEN DEEDS OF ALL TIMES AND ALL LANDS. By CHARLOTTE M. YONGE. 18mo. 4s. 6d. Edition for Schools. Globe 8vo. 2s. Abridged Edition. 18mo. 1s.

BOOLE (George).—A TREATISE ON THE CALCULUS OF FINITE DIFFERENCES. Edited by J. F. MOULTON. 3rd Edition. Cr. 8vo. 10s. 6d.

—— THE MATHEMATICAL ANALYSIS OF LOGIC. 8vo. Sewed, 5s.

BOTTOMLEY (J. T.).—FOUR-FIGURE MATHEMATICAL TABLES. Comprising Logarithmic and Trigonometrical Tables, and Tables of Squares, Square Roots and Reciprocals. 8vo. 2s. 6d.

BOUGHTON (G. H.) and ABBEY (E. A.).—SKETCHING RAMBLES IN HOLLAND. With Illustrations. Fcp. 4to. 21s.

BOWEN (H. Courthope).—FIRST LESSONS IN FRENCH. 18mo. 1s.

BOWER (Prof. F. O.).—A COURSE OF PRACTICAL INSTRUCTION IN BOTANY. Cr. 8vo. 10s. 6d.

BRADSHAW (J. G.).—A COURSE OF EASY ARITHMETICAL EXAMPLES FOR BEGINNERS. Globe 8vo. 2s. With Answers. 2s. 6d.

BRAIN. A JOURNAL OF NEUROLOGY. Edited for the Neurological Society of London, by A. DE WATTEVILLE. Published Quarterly. 8vo. 3s. 6d. (Part I. in January, 1878.) Yearly Vols. I. to XII. 8vo, cloth. 15s. each. [Cloth covers for binding, 1s. each.]

BREYMANN (Prof. H.).—A FRENCH GRAMMAR BASED ON PHILOLOGICAL PRINCIPLES. 3rd Edition. Extra fcp. 8vo. 4s. 6d.

—— FIRST FRENCH EXERCISE BOOK. 2nd Edition. Extra fcp. 8vo. 4s. 6d.

—— SECOND FRENCH EXERCISE BOOK. Extra fcp. 8vo. 2s. 6d.

BRIDGES (John A.). IDYLLS OF A LOST VILLAGE. Crown 8vo. 7s. 6d.

BRIGHT (John).- SPEECHES ON QUESTIONS OF PUBLIC POLICY. Edited by Professor THOROLD ROGERS. 2nd Edition. 2 vols. 8vo. 25s. With Portrait. *Author's Popular Edition.* Extra fcp. 8vo. 3s. 6d.

—— PUBLIC ADDRESSES. Edited by J. E. T. ROGERS. 8vo. 14s.

BRIGHT (H. A.)—THE ENGLISH FLOWER GARDEN. Crown 8vo. 3s. 6d.

BRIMLEY (George).—ESSAYS. Globe 8vo. 5s.

BRODIE (Sir Benjamin).—IDEAL CHEMISTRY. Crown 8vo. 2s.

BROOKE, Sir JAS., THE RAJA OF SARAWAK (Life of). By GERTRUDE L. JACOB. 2 vols. 8vo. 25s.

BROOKE (Stopford A.).—PRIMER OF ENGLISH LITERATURE. 18mo. 1s. Large Paper Edition. 8vo. 7s. 6d.

—— RIQUET OF THE TUFT: A LOVE DRAMA. Extra crown 8vo. 6s.

—— POEMS. Globe 8vo. 6s.

—— MILTON. Fcp. 8vo. 1s. 6d. Large Paper Edition. 8vo. 21s. net.

—— POEMS OF SHELLEY. Edited by STOPFORD A. BROOKE, M.A. With Vignette. 18mo. 4s. 6d. Large Paper Edition. 12s. 6d.

—— DOVE COTTAGE, WORDSWORTH'S HOME, FROM 1800—1808. Globe 8vo. 1s.

—— EARLY ENGLISH LITERATURE. 2 vols. 8vo. [*Vol. I. in the Press.*

BROOKS (Rev. Phillips).—THE CANDLE OF THE LORD, AND OTHER SERMONS. Crown 8vo. 6s.

—— SERMONS PREACHED IN ENGLISH CHURCHES. Crown 8vo. 6s.

—— TWENTY SERMONS. Crown 8vo. 6s.

—— TOLERANCE. Crown 8vo. 2s. 6d.

BROOKSMITH (J.).——ARITHMETIC IN THEORY AND PRACTICE. Crown 8vo. 4s. 6d.

BROOKSMITH (J. and E. J.).—ARITHMETIC FOR BEGINNERS. Globe 8vo. 1s. 6d.

BROOKSMITH (E. J.).—WOOLWICH MATHEMATICAL PAPERS, for Admission in the Royal Military Academy for the years 1880—1888. Edited by E. J. BROOKSMITH, B.A. Crown 8vo. 6s.

—— SANDHURST MATHEMATICAL PAPERS, for Admission into the Royal Military College, 1881—89. Edited by E. J. BROOKSMITH, B.A. Crown 8vo. 3s. 6d.

BROWN (J. Allen).—PALÆOLITHIC MAN IN NORTH-WEST MIDDLESEX. 8vo. 7s. 6d.

BROWN (T. E.).—THE MANX WITCH; AND OTHER POEMS. Crown 8vo. 7s. 6d.

BROWNE (J. H. Balfour).—WATER SUPPLY. Crown 8vo. 2s. 6d.

BROWNE (Sir Thomas).—RELIGIO MEDICI; LETTER TO A FRIEND, &c., AND CHRISTIAN MORALS. Edited by W. A. GREENHILL, M.D. With Portrait. 18mo. 4s. 6d.

BRUNTON (Dr. T. Lauder).—A TEXT-BOOK OF PHARMACOLOGY, THERAPEUTICS, AND MATERIA MEDICA. 3rd Edition. Medium 8vo. 21s.

—— DISORDERS OF DIGESTION: THEIR CONSEQUENCES AND TREATMENT. 8vo. 10s. 6d.

—— PHARMACOLOGY AND THERAPEUTICS; OR, MEDICINE PAST AND PRESENT. Cr. 8vo. 6s.

—— TABLES OF MATERIA MEDICA: A COMPANION TO THE MATERIA MEDICA MUSEUM. 8vo. 5s.

—— THE BIBLE AND SCIENCE. With Illustrations. Crown 8vo. 10s. 6d.

—— CROONIAN LECTURES ON THE CONNECTION BETWEEN CHEMICAL CONSTITUTION AND PHYSIOLOGICAL ACTION. Being an Introduction to Modern Therapeutics. 8vo.

BRYANS (Clement).—LATIN PROSE EXERCISES BASED UPON CAESAR'S "GALLIC WAR." With a Classification of Caesar's Phrases, and Grammatical Notes on Caesar's Chief Usages. Pott 8vo. 2s. 6d.
KEY for Teachers only. 4s. 6d.

BRYCE (James, M.P., D.C.L.).—THE HOLY ROMAN EMPIRE. 8th Edition. Crown 8vo. 7s. 6d.—*Library Edition.* 8vo. 14s.

—— TRANSCAUCASIA AND ARARAT. 3rd Edition. Crown 8vo. 9s.

—— THE AMERICAN COMMONWEALTH. 2nd Edition. 2 vols. Extra Crown 8vo. 25s.

BUCHHEIM (Dr.).—DEUTSCHE LYRIK. 18mo. 4s. 6d.

—— DEUTSCHE BALLADEN. 18mo. [*In the Press.*

BUCKLAND (Anna).—OUR NATIONAL INSTITUTIONS. 18mo. 1s.

BUCKLEY (Arabella).—HISTORY OF ENGLAND FOR BEGINNERS. With Coloured Maps and Chronological and Genealogical Tables. Globe 8vo. 3s.

BUCKNILL (Dr.).—THE CARE OF THE [I]NSANE. Crown 8vo. 3s. 6d.

BUCKTON (G. B.).—MONOGRAPH OF THE BRITISH CICADÆ, OR TETTIGIDÆ. In 8 parts, Quarterly. Part 1. January, 1890. 8vo. Parts I. II. and III. ready. 8s. each.

BUMBLEBEE BOGO'S BUDGET. By a RETIRED JUDGE. Illustrations by ALICE HAVERS. Crown 8vo. 2s. 6d.

BUNYAN (John).—THE PILGRIM'S PROGRESS FROM THIS WORLD TO THAT WHICH IS TO COME. 18mo. 4s. 6d.

BUNYAN. By J. A. FROUDE. Crown 8vo. 1s. 6d.; sewed, 1s.

BURGON (Dean).—POEMS. Ex. fcp. 8vo. 4s. 6d.

BURKE (Edmund).—LETTERS, TRACTS, AND SPEECHES ON IRISH AFFAIRS. Edited by MATTHEW ARNOLD, with Preface. Cr. 8vo. 6s.

BURKE. By JOHN MORLEY. Globe 8vo. 5s. Crown 8vo. 1s. 6d.; sewed, 1s.

—— REFLECTIONS ON THE FRENCH REVOLUTION. Ed. by F. G. SELBY, M.A. Gl. 8vo.

BURN (Robert).—ROMAN LITERATURE IN RELATION TO ROMAN ART. With Illustrations. Extra Crown 8vo. 14s.

BURNETT (F. Hodgson).—"HAWORTH'S." Globe 8vo. 2s.

—— LOUISIANA; AND THAT LASS O' LOWRIE'S. Two Stories. Illustrated. Cr. 8vo. 3s. 6d. Cheap Edition. Globe 8vo. 2s.

BURNS, THE COMPLETE WORKS OF. Edited by ALEXANDER SMITH. Globe 8vo. 3s. 6d.

—— THE POETICAL WORKS. With a Biographical Memoir by ALEXANDER SMITH. In 2 vols. fcp. 8vo. 10s.

BURNS. By Principal SHAIRP. Crown 8vo. 1s. 6d.; sewed, 1s.

BURY (J. B.).—A HISTORY OF THE LATER ROMAN EMPIRE FROM ARCADIUS TO IRENE, A.D. 390—800. 2 vols. 8vo. 32s.

BUTCHER (Prof. S. H.).—DEMOSTHENES. Fcp. 8vo. 1s. 6d.

BUTLER (Archer).—SERMONS, DOCTRINAL AND PRACTICAL. 11th Edition. 8vo. 8s.

—— SECOND SERIES OF SERMONS. 8vo. 7s.

—— LETTERS ON ROMANISM. 8vo. 10s. 6d.

BUTLER (George).—SERMONS PREACHED IN CHELTENHAM COLLEGE CHAPEL. 8vo. 7s. 6d.

BUTLER (Col. Sir W.).—GENERAL GORDON. With Portrait. Crown 8vo. 2s. 0d.

—— SIR CHARLES NAPIER. With Portrait. Crown 8vo. 2s. 6d.

BUTLER'S HUDIBRAS. Edited by ALFRED MILNES. Fcp. 8vo. Part I. 3s. 6d. Part II. and III. 4s. 6d.

BYRON.—POETRY OF BYRON, chosen and arranged by MATTHEW ARNOLD. 18mo. 4s. 6d. Large Paper Edition. Crown 8vo. 9s.

BYRON. By Prof. NICHOL. Crown 8vo. 1s. 6d.; sewed, 1s.

CAESAR.—THE HELVETIAN WAR. Selected from Book I. of The Gallic War, with Notes, Vocabulary, and Exercises, by W. WELCH and C. G. DUFFIELD. 18mo. 1s. 6d.

—— THE INVASION OF BRITAIN. Being Selections from Books IV. and V. of the Gallic War. With Notes, Vocabulary, and Exercises, by W. WELCH, M.A., and C. G. DUFFIELD, M.A. 18mo. 1s. 6d.

—— SCENES FROM THE FIFTH AND SIXTH BOOKS OF THE GALLIC WAR. Selected and Ed. by C. COLBECK, M.A. 18mo. 1s. 6d.

—— THE GALLIC WAR. Edited by the Rev. J. BOND, M.A., and Rev. A. S. WALPOLE, M.A. Fcp. 8vo. 6s.

—— THE GALLIC WAR. Book I. Edited, with Notes and Vocabulary by Rev. A. S. WALPOLE, M.A. 18mo. 1s. 6d.

—— THE GALLIC WAR.—Books II. and III. Edited by W. G. RUTHERFORD, LL.D. 18mo. 1s. 6d.

—— THE GALLIC WAR.—Book IV. Edited, with Introduction, Notes, and Vocabulary, by CLEMENT BRYANS, M.A. 18mo. 1s. 6d.

LIST OF PUBLICATIONS. 7

CAESAR.—THE GALLIC WAR.—Book V. Edited with Notes and Vocabulary, by C. COLBECK, M.A. 18mo. 1s. 6d.
—— THE GALLIC WAR. Book VI. By the same Editor. With Notes and Vocabulary. 18mo. 1s. 6d.
—— THE GALLIC WAR—Book VII. Edited by the Rev. J. BOND, M.A., and Rev. A. S. WALPOLE, M.A. With Notes and Vocabulary. 18mo. 1s. 6d.
CAIRNES (Prof. J. E.).—POLITICAL ESSAYS. 8vo. 10s. 6d.
—— SOME LEADING PRINCIPLES OF POLITICAL ECONOMY NEWLY EXPOUNDED. 8vo. 14s.
—— THE SLAVE POWER. 8vo. 10s. 6d.
—— THE CHARACTER AND LOGICAL METHOD OF POLITICAL ECONOMY. Crown 8vo. 6s.
CALDERON.—SELECT PLAYS OF CALDERON. Edited by NORMAN MACCOLL, M.A. Crown 8vo. 14s.
CALDERWOOD (Prof.) HANDBOOK OF MORAL PHILOSOPHY. Crown 8vo. 6s.
—— THE RELATIONS OF MIND AND BRAIN. 2nd Edition. 8vo. 12s.
—— THE PARABLES OF OUR LORD. Crown 8vo. 6s.
—— THE RELATIONS OF SCIENCE AND RELIGION. Crown 8vo. 5s.
—— ON TEACHING. 4th Edition. Extra fcp. 8vo. 2s. 6d.
CALVERT (A.).—SCHOOL-READINGS IN THE GREEK TESTAMENT. With Notes and Vocabulary, by A. CALVERT. Fcp. 8vo. 4s. 6d.
CAMBRIDGE. COOPER'S LE KEUX'S MEMORIALS OF CAMBRIDGE. Illustrated with 90 Woodcuts in the Text, 154 Plates on Steel and Copper by LE KEUX, STORER, &c., including 20 Etchings by R. FARREN. 3 vols. 4to, half levant morocco. 10l. 10s.
CAMBRIDGE SENATE-HOUSE PROBLEMS AND RIDERS, WITH SOLUTIONS:
1848—51. RIDERS. By JAMESON. 8vo. 7s. 6d.
1875. PROBLEMS AND RIDERS. Edited by Prof. A. G. GREENHILL. Cr. 8vo. 8s. 6d.
1878. SOLUTIONS BY THE MATHEMATICAL MODERATORS AND EXAMINERS. Edited by J. W. L. GLAISHER, M.A. 8vo. 12s.
CAMEOS FROM ENGLISH HISTORY. By the Author of "The Heir of Redclyffe." Extra fcp. 8vo. 5s. each volume.
Vol. I. Rollo to Edward II. II. The Wars in France. III. The Wars of the Roses. IV. Reformation Times. V. England and Spain. VI Forty Years of Stuart Rule (1603—43). VII. The Rebellion and Restoration (1642-78).
CAMERON (V. L.).—OUR FUTURE HIGHWAY TO INDIA. 2 vols. Crown 8vo. 21s.
CAMPBELL (Dr. John M'Leod).—THE NATURE OF THE ATONEMENT. 6th Edition. Crown 8vo. 6s.
—— REMINISCENCES AND REFLECTIONS. Ed., with an Introductory Narrative, by his Son, DONALD CAMPBELL, M.A. Cr. 8vo. 7s. 6d.
—— RESPONSIBILITY FOR THE GIFT OF ETERNAL LIFE. Compiled from Sermons preached at Row, in the years 1829—31. Cr. 8vo. 5s.

CAMPBELL.(Dr. John M'Leod).—THOUGHTS ON REVELATION. 2nd Edition. Cr. 8vo. 5s.
CAMPBELL (J. F.).—MY CIRCULAR NOTES. Cheaper issue. Crown 8vo. 6s.
CAMPBELL (Lord George).—LOG-LETTERS FROM THE "CHALLENGER." Crown 8vo. 6s.
CAMPBELL (Prof. Lewis.—SOPHOCLES. Fcp. 8vo. 1s. 6d.
CANDLER (H.).—HELP TO ARITHMETIC. 2nd Edition. Globe 8vo. 2s. 6d.
CANTERBURY (His Grace Edward White, Archbishop of).—BOY-LIFE: ITS TRIAL, ITS STRENGTH, ITS FULNESS. Sundays in Wellington College, 1859—73. 4th Edition. Crown 8vo. 6s.
—— THE SEVEN GIFTS. Addressed to the Diocese of Canterbury in his Primary Visitation. 2nd Edition. Crown 8vo. 6s.
—— CHRIST AND HIS TIMES. Addressed to the Diocese of Canterbury in his Second Visitation. Crown 8vo. 6s.
CAPES (Rev. W. W.)—LIVY. Fcp. 8vo. 1s. 6d.
CARLES (W. R.).—LIFE IN COREA. 8vo. 12s. 6d.
CARLYLE (Thomas).—REMINISCENCES. Ed. by CHARLES ELIOT NORTON. 2 vols. Crown 8vo. 12s.
—— EARLY LETTERS OF THOMAS CARLYLE. Edited by C. E. NORTON. 2 vols. 1814—26. Crown 8vo. 18s.
—— LETTERS OF THOMAS CARLYLE. Edited by C. E. NORTON. 2 vols. 1826—36. Crown 8vo. 18s.
—— GOETHE AND CARLYLE, CORRESPONDENCE BETWEEN. Edited by C. E. NORTON. Crown 8vo. 9s.
CARMARTHEN (Marchioness of). — A LOVER OF THE BEAUTIFUL. Crn. 8vo. 6s.
CARNOT--THURSTON.—REFLECTIONS ON THE MOTIVE POWER OF HEAT, AND ON MACHINES FITTED TO DEVELOP THAT POWER. From the French of N. L. S. CARNOT. Edited by R. H. THURSTON, LL.D. Crown 8vo. 7s. 6d.
CARPENTER 'Bishop W. Boyd.—TRUTH IN TALE. Addresses, chiefly to Children. Cr. 8vo. 4s. 6d.
—— THE PERMANENT ELEMENTS OF RELIGION: Bampton Lectures, 1887. 8vo. 14s.
CARR (J. Comyns).—PAPERS ON ART. Cr. 8vo. 8s. 6d.
CARROLL (Lewis).—ALICE'S ADVENTURES IN WONDERLAND. With 42 Illustrations by TENNIEL. Crown 8vo. 6s.
People's Edition. With all the original Illustrations. Crown 8vo. 2s. 6d.
A GERMAN TRANSLATION OF THE SAME. Crown 8vo, gilt. 6s.
A FRENCH TRANSLATION OF THE SAME. Crown 8vo, gilt. 6s.
AN ITALIAN TRANSLATION OF THE SAME. Crown 8vo, gilt. 6s.
—— ALICE'S ADVENTURES UNDER-GROUND. Being a Facsimile of the Original MS. Book, afterwards developed into "Alice's Adventures in Wonderland." With 27 Illustrations by the Author. Crown 8vo. 4s.

CARROLL (Lewis).—THROUGH THE LOOKING-GLASS AND WHAT ALICE FOUND THERE. With 50 Illustrations by TENNIEL. Crown 8vo, gilt. 6s.
— *People's Edition*. With all the original Illustrations. Crown 8vo. 2s. 6d.
— *People's Edition* of "Alice's Adventures in Wonderland," and "Through the Looking-Glass." 1 vol. Crown 8vo. 4s. 6d.
— THE GAME OF LOGIC. Crown 8vo. 3s.
— RHYME? AND REASON? With 65 Illustrations by ARTHUR B. FROST, and 9 by HENRY HOLIDAY. Crown 8vo. 6s.
— A TANGLED TALE. Reprinted from the "Monthly Packet." With 6 Illustrations by ARTHUR B. FROST. Crown 8vo. 4s. 6d.
— SYLVIE AND BRUNO. With 46 Illustrations by HARRY FURNISS. Cr. 8vo. 7s. 6d.
— THE NURSERY "ALICE." Twenty Coloured Enlargements from TENNIEL'S Illustrations to "Alice's Adventures in Wonderland," with Text adapted to Nursery Readers. 4to. 4s.
— THE HUNTING OF THE SNARK, AN AGONY IN EIGHT FITS. With 9 Illustrations by HENRY HOLIDAY. Crown 8vo. 4s. 6d.

CARSTARES (WM.): A Character and Career of the Revolutionary Epoch (1649—1715). By R. H. STORY. 8vo. 12s.

CARTER (R. Brudenell, F.C.S.).—A PRACTICAL TREATISE ON DISEASES OF THE EYE. 8vo. 16s.

CARTER (R. Brudenell).—EYESIGHT, GOOD AND BAD. Cr. 8vo. 6s.
— MODERN OPERATIONS FOR CATARACT. 8vo. 6s.

CASSEL (Dr. D.).—MANUAL OF JEWISH HISTORY AND LITERATURE. Translated by Mrs. HENRY LUCAS. Fcp. 8vo. 2s. 6d.

CATULLUS.—SELECT POEMS. Edited by F. P. SIMPSON, B.A. Fcp. 8vo. 5s.

CAUCASUS: NOTES ON THE. By "Wanderer." 8vo. 9s.

CAUTLEY G. S.).—A CENTURY OF EMBLEMS. With Illustrations by the Lady MARIAN ALFORD. Small 4to. 10s. 6d.

CAZENOVE (J. Gibson).—CONCERNING THE BEING AND ATTRIBUTES OF GOD. 8vo. 5s.

CHALMERS (J. B.).—GRAPHICAL DETERMINATION OF FORCES IN ENGINEERING STRUCTURES. 8vo. 24s.

CHALMERS (M.D.).—LOCAL GOVERNMENT. Crown 8vo. 3s. 6d.

CHASSERESSE (D.).—SPORTING SKETCHES. Illustrated. Crown 8vo. 3s. 6d.

CHATTERTON: A BIOGRAPHICAL STUDY. By Sir DANIEL WILSON, LL.D. Crown 8vo. 6s. 6d.

CHAUCER. By Prof. A. W. WARD. Crown 8vo. 1s. 6d.; sewed, 1s.

CHEYNE (C. H. H.).—AN ELEMENTARY TREATISE ON THE PLANETARY THEORY. Crown 8vo. 7s. 6d.

CHEYNE (T. K.).—THE BOOK OF ISAIAH CHRONOLOGICALLY ARRANGED. Crown 8vo. 7s. 6d.

CHILDREN'S GARLAND FROM THE BEST POETS. Selected and arranged by COVENTRY PATMORE. 18mo. 4s. 6d.
Globe Readings Edition for Schools. 2s.

CHOICE NOTES ON THE FOUR GOSPELS, drawn from Old and New Sources. Crown 8vo. 4 vols. 4s. 6d. each. (St. Matthew and St. Mark in 1 vol. 9s.)

CHRISTIE (J.). CHOLERA EPIDEMICS IN EAST AFRICA. 8vo. 15s.

CHRISTIE (J. R.). ELEMENTARY TEST QUESTIONS IN PURE AND MIXED MATHEMATICS. Crown 8vo. 8s. 6d.

CHRISTMAS CAROL, A. Printed in Colours, with Illuminated Borders from MSS. of the Fourteenth and Fifteenth Centuries. 4to. 21s.

CHRISTY CAREW. By the Author of "Hogan, M.P." Globe 8vo. 2s.

CHURCH Very Rev. R. W.).—THE SACRED POETRY OF EARLY RELIGIONS. 2nd Edition. 18mo. 1s.
— ST. ANSELM. Globe 8vo. 5s.
— HUMAN LIFE AND ITS CONDITIONS. Cr. 8vo. 6s.
— THE GIFTS OF CIVILISATION, and other Sermons and Lectures. Crown 8vo. 7s. 6d.
— DISCIPLINE OF THE CHRISTIAN CHARACTER, and other Sermons. Crown 8vo. 4s. 6d.
— ADVENT SERMONS. 1885. Cr. 8vo. 4s. 6d.
— MISCELLANEOUS WRITINGS. Collected Edition. 5 vols. Globe 8vo. 5s. each.
Vol. I. MISCELLANEOUS ESSAYS. II. ST. ANSELM. III. DANTE: AND OTHER ESSAYS. IV. SPENSER. V. BACON.
— SPENSER. Globe 8vo. *Library Edition*. 5s.—Crown 8vo. 1s. 6d.; sewed, 1s.
— BACON. Globe 8vo. *Library Edition*. 5s.—Crown 8vo. 1s. 6d.; sewed, 1s.

CHURCH (Rev. A. J.).—LATIN VERSION OF SELECTIONS FROM TENNYSON. By Prof. CONINGTON, Prof. SEELEY, Dr. HESSEY, T. E. KEBBEL, &c. Edited by A. J. CHURCH, M.A. Extra fcp. 8vo. 6s.
— HENRY V. With Portrait. Cr. 8vo. 2s. 6d.
— STORIES FROM THE BIBLE. Illustrated. Crown 8vo.

CHURCH (A. J.) and BRODRIBB (W. J.).—TACITUS. Fcp. 8vo. 1s. 6d.

CICERO. THE LIFE AND LETTERS OF MARCUS TULLIUS CICERO. By the Rev. G. E. JEANS, M.A. 2nd Edition. Crown 8vo. 10s. 6d.
— THE ACADEMICA. The Text revised and explained by J. S. REID, M.L. 8vo. 15s.
— THE ACADEMICS. Translated by J. S. REID, M.L. 8vo. 5s. 6d.
— DE AMICITIA. Edited by E. S. SHUCKBURGH, M.A. With Notes, Vocabulary, and Biographical Index. 18mo. 1s. 6d.
— DE SENECTUTE. Edited, with Notes, Vocabulary, and Biographical Index, by E. S. SHUCKBURGH, M.A. 18mo. 1s. 6d.
— SELECT LETTERS. Edited by Rev. G. E. JEANS, M.A. 18mo. 1s. 6d.
— SELECT LETTERS. Edit. by Prof. R. Y. TYRRELL, M.A. Fcp. 8vo.

LIST OF PUBLICATIONS.

CICERO. THE SECOND PHILIPPIC ORATION. Edited by Prof. JOHN E. B. MAYOR. New Edition, revised. Fcp. 8vo. 5s.
—— PRO PUBLIO SESTIO. Edited by Rev. H. A. HOLDEN, M.A., LL.D. Fcp. 8vo. 5s.
—— THE CATILINE ORATIONS. Edited by Prof. A. S. WILKINS, Litt.D. New Edition. Fcp. 8vo. 3s. 6d.
—— PRO LEGE MANILIA. Edited by Prof. A. S. WILKINS, Litt.D. Fcp. 8vo. 2s. 6d.
—— PRO ROSCIO AMERINO. Edited by E. H. DONKIN, M.A. Fcp. 8vo. 4s. 6d.
—— STORIES OF ROMAN HISTORY. With Notes, Vocabulary, and Exercises by G. E. JEANS, M.A., and A. V. JONES. 18mo. 1s. 6d.
CLARK. MEMORIALS FROM JOURNALS AND LETTERS OF SAMUEL CLARK, M.A. Edited by his Wife. Crown 8vo. 7s. 6d.
CLARK (L.) and SADLER (H.).—THE STAR GUIDE. Roy. 8vo. 5s.
CLARKE (C. B.).—A GEOGRAPHICAL READER AND COMPANION TO THE ATLAS. Cr. 8vo. 2s.
—— A CLASS-BOOK OF GEOGRAPHY. With 18 Coloured Maps. Fcp. 8vo. 3s. 6d.; swd., 3s.
—— SPECULATIONS FROM POLITICAL ECONOMY. Crown 8vo. 3s. 6d.
CLARKE (F. W.).— A TABLE OF SPECIFIC GRAVITY FOR SOLIDS AND LIQUIDS. (Constants of Nature, Part I.) 8vo. 12s. 6d.
CLASSICAL WRITERS. Edited by JOHN RICHARD GREEN. Fcp. 8vo. 1s. 6d. each.
EURIPIDES. By Prof. MAHAFFY.
MILTON. By the Rev. STOPFORD A. BROOKE.
LIVY. By the Rev. W. W. CAPES, M.A.
VERGIL. By Prof. NETTLESHIP, M.A.
SOPHOCLES. By Prof. L. CAMPBELL, M.A.
DEMOSTHENES. By Prof. BUTCHER, M.A.
TACITUS. By CHURCH and BRODRIBB.
CLAUSIUS(R.).—THE MECHANICAL THEORY OF HEAT. Translated by WALTER R. BROWNE. Crown 8vo. 10s. 6d.
CLERGYMAN'S SELF-EXAMINATION CONCERNING THE APOSTLES' CREED. Extra fcp. 8vo. 1s. 6d.
CLIFFORD (Prof. W. K.).—ELEMENTS OF DYNAMIC. An Introduction to the Study of Motion and Rest in Solid and Fluid Bodies. Crown 8vo. Part I. Kinematic. Books I.—III. 7s. 6d. Book IV. and Appendix, 6s.
—— LECTURES AND ESSAYS. Ed. by LESLIE STEPHEN and Sir F. POLLOCK. Cr. 8vo. 8s. 6d.
—— SEEING AND THINKING. With Diagrams. Crown 8vo. 3s. 6d.
—— MATHEMATICAL PAPERS. Edited by R. TUCKER. With an Introduction by H. J. STEPHEN SMITH, M.A. 8vo. 30s.
CLIFFORD(Mrs.W.K.).—ANYHOW STORIES. With Illustrations by DOROTHY TENNANT. Crown 8vo. 1s. 6d.; paper covers, 1s.
CLIVE. By Col. Sir CHARLES WILSON. With Portrait. Crown 8vo. 2s. 6d.
CLOUGH (A. H.).—POEMS. New Edition. Crown 8vo. 7s. 6d.
—— PROSE REMAINS. With a Selection from his Letters, and a Memoir by his Wife. Crown 8vo. 7s. 6d.

COAL: ITS HISTORY AND ITS USES. By Profs. GREEN, MIALL, THORPE, RUCKER, and MARSHALL. 8vo. 12s. 6d.
COBDEN (Richard.).—SPEECHES ON QUESTIONS OF PUBLIC POLICY. Ed. by J. BRIGHT and J. E. THOROLD ROGERS. Gl. 8vo. 3s. 6d.
COCKSHOTT (A. and WALTERS (F. B.). —A TREATISE ON GEOMETRICAL CONICS. Crown 8vo. 5s.
COHEN (Dr. Julius B.).—THE OWENS COLLEGE COURSE OF PRACTICAL ORGANIC CHEMISTRY. Fcp. 8vo. 2s. 6d.
COLBECK (C.).—FRENCH READINGS FROM ROMAN HISTORY. Selected from various Authors, with Notes. 18mo. 4s. 6d.
COLENSO(Bp.). THE COMMUNION SERVICE FROM THE BOOK OF COMMON PRAYER, WITH SELECT READINGS FROM THE WRITINGS OF THE REV. F. D. MAURICE. Edited by the late BISHOP COLENSO. 6th Ed. 16mo. 2s. 6d.
COLERIDGE.—THE POETICAL AND DRAMATIC WORKS OF SAMUEL TAYLOR COLERIDGE. 4 vols. Fcp. 8vo. 31s. 6d. Also an Edition on Large Paper, 2l. 12s. 6d.
COLERIDGE. By H. D. TRAILL. Crown 8vo. 1s. 6d.; sewed, 1s.
COLLECTS OF THE CHURCH OF ENGLAND. With a Coloured Floral Design to each Collect. Crown 8vo. 12s.
COLLIER (John).— A PRIMER OF ART. 18mo. 1s.
COLQUHOUN.—RHYMES AND CHIMES. By F. S. COLQUHOUN (née F. S. FULLER MAITLAND). Extra fcp. 8vo. 2s. 6d.
COLSON (F. H.).—FIRST GREEK READER. Stories and Legends. With Notes, Vocabulary, and Exercises. Globe 8vo. 3s.
COLVIN (S.). LANDOR. Crown 8vo. 1s. 6d.; sewed, 1s.
COLVIN (S.).—SELECTIONS FROM THE WRITINGS OF W. S. LANDOR. 18mo. 4s. 6d.
—— KEATS. Crown 8vo. 1s. 6d.; sewed, 1s.
COMBE. LIFE OF GEORGE COMBE. By CHARLES GIBBON. 2 vols. 8vo. 32s.
—— EDUCATION: ITS PRINCIPLES AND PRACTICE AS DEVELOPED BY GEORGE COMBE. Edited by WILLIAM JOLLY. 8vo. 15s.
CONGREVE (Rev. John).—HIGH HOPES AND PLEADINGS FOR A REASONABLE FAITH, NOBLER THOUGHTS, LARGER CHARITY. Crown 8vo. 5s.
CONSTABLE (Samuel).—GEOMETRICAL EXERCISES FOR BEGINNERS. Cr. 8vo. 3s. 6d.
CONWAY (Hugh). — A FAMILY AFFAIR. Globe 8vo. 2s.
—— LIVING OR DEAD. Globe 8vo. 2s.
COOK (CAPTAIN). By WALTER BESANT. With Portrait. Crown 8vo. 2s. 6d.
COOK (E. T.). — A POPULAR HANDBOOK TO THE NATIONAL GALLERY. Including, by special permission, Notes collected from the Works of Mr. RUSKIN. 3rd Edition. Crown 8vo, half morocco. 14s. Also an Edition on Large Paper, limited to 250 copies. 2 vols. 8vo.
COOKE (Josiah P., jun.).—PRINCIPLES OF CHEMICAL PHILOSOPHY. New Ed. 8vo. 16s.

COOKE (Josiah P., jun.).—RELIGION AND CHEMISTRY. Crown 8vo. 7s. 6d.
—— ELEMENTS OF CHEMICAL PHYSICS. 4th Edition. Royal 8vo. 21s.
COOKERY. MIDDLE CLASS BOOK. Compiled for the Manchester School of Cookery. Fcp. 8vo. 1s. 6d.
CO-OPERATION IN THE UNITED STATES: HISTORY OF. Edited by H. B. ADAMS. 8vo. 15s.
COPE (E. M.).—AN INTRODUCTION TO ARISTOTLE'S RHETORIC. 8vo. 14s.
COPE (E. D.).—THE ORIGIN OF THE FITTEST. Essays on Evolution. 8vo. 12s. 6d.
CORBETT (Julian).—THE FALL OF ASGARD: A Tale of St. Olaf's Day. 2 vols. 12s.
—— FOR GOD AND GOLD. Crown 8vo. 6s.
—— KOPHETUA THE THIRTEENTH. 2 vols. Globe 8vo. 12s.
—— MONK. With Portrait. Cr. 8vo. 2s. 6d.
—— DRAKE. With Portrait. Cr. 8vo.
CORE (T. H.).—QUESTIONS ON BALFOUR STEWART'S "LESSONS IN ELEMENTARY PHYSICS." Fcp. 8vo. 2s.
CORFIELD Dr. W. H.'.—THE TREATMENT AND UTILISATION OF SEWAGE. 3rd Edition, Revised by the Author, and by LOUIS C. PARKES, M.D. 8vo. 16s.
CORNAZ (S.).—NOS ENFANTS ET LEURS AMIS. Ed. by EDITH HARVEY. Gl. 8vo. 1s. 6d.
CORNELL UNIVERSITY STUDIES IN CLASSICAL PHILOLOGY. Edited by I. FLAGG, W. G. HALE, and B. I. WHEELER. I. The CUM-Constructions: their History and Functions. Part I. Critical. 1s. 8d. net. Part II. Constructive. By W. G. HALE. 3s. 4d. net. II. Analogy and the Scope of its Application in Language. By B. I. WHEELER. 1s. 3d. net.
CORNEILLE.—LE CID. Ed. by G. EUGÈNE FASNACHT. 18mo. 1s.
COSSA.—GUIDE TO THE STUDY OF POLITICAL ECONOMY. From the Italian of Dr. LUIGI COSSA. Crown 8vo. 4s. 6d.
COTTERILL (Prof. James H.).—APPLIED MECHANICS: An Introduction to the Theory of Structures and Machines. 2nd Edition. Med. 8vo. 18s.
COTTERILL (Prof. J. H.) and SLADE (J. H.). — ELEMENTARY APPLIED MECHANICS. Crown 8vo.
COTTON (Bishop).—SERMONS PREACHED TO ENGLISH CONGREGATIONS IN INDIA. Crown 8vo. 7s. 6d.
COTTON and PAYNE.—COLONIES AND DEPENDENCIES. Part I. INDIA. By J. S. COTTON. Part II. THE COLONIES. By E. J. PAYNE. Crown 8vo. 3s. 6d.
COUES (Elliott).—KEY TO NORTH AMERICAN BIRDS. Illustrated. 8vo. 2l. 2s.
—— HANDBOOK OF FIELD AND GENERAL ORNITHOLOGY. Illustrated. 8vo. 10s. net.
COURTHOPE (W. J.).—ADDISON. Crown 8vo. 1s. 6d.; sewed, 1s.
COWELL (George). LECTURES ON CATARACT; ITS CAUSES, VARIETIES, AND TREATMENT. Crown 8vo. 4s. 6d.

COWPER.—COWPER'S POETICAL WORKS. Edited by Rev. W. BENHAM. Globe 8vo. 3s. 6d.
—— THE TASK: An Epistle to Joseph Hill, Esq.; TIROCINIUM, or a Review of the Schools; and the HISTORY OF JOHN GILPIN. Edited by WILLIAM BENHAM. Globe 8vo. 1s.
—— LETTERS OF WILLIAM COWPER. Edited by the Rev. W. BENHAM. 18mo. 4s. 6d.
—— SELECTIONS FROM COWPER'S POEMS. Introduction by Mrs. OLIPHANT. 18mo. 4s. 6d.
COWPER. By GOLDWIN SMITH. Crown 8vo. 1s. 6d.; sewed, 1s.
COX (G. V.).—RECOLLECTIONS OF OXFORD. 2nd Edition. Crown 8vo. 6s.
CRAIK (Mrs.).—OLIVE. Illustrated. Crown 8vo. 3s. 6d.
—— THE OGILVIES. Illustrated. Crown 8vo. 3s. 6d.—Cheap Edition. Globe 8vo. 2s.
—— AGATHA'S HUSBAND. Illustrated. Crown 8vo. 3s. 6d.—Cheap Edition. Globe 8vo. 2s.
—— THE HEAD OF THE FAMILY. Illustrated. Crown 8vo. 3s. 6d.
—— TWO MARRIAGES. Crown 8vo. 3s. 6d.— Globe 8vo. 2s.
—— THE LAUREL BUSH. Crown 8vo. 3s. 6d.
—— MY MOTHER AND I. Illustrated. Crown 8vo. 3s. 6d.
—— MISS TOMMY: A MEDIÆVAL ROMANCE. Illustrated. Crown 8vo. 3s. 6d.
—— KING ARTHUR: NOT A LOVE STORY. Crown 8vo. 3s. 6d. [Nov. 1890.
—— POEMS. New and Enlarged Edition. Extra fcp. 8vo. 6s.
—— CHILDREN'S POETRY. Ex. fcp. 8vo. 4s. 6d.
—— SONGS OF OUR YOUTH. Small 4to. 6s.
—— CONCERNING MEN: AND OTHER PAPERS. Crown 8vo. 4s. 6d.
—— ABOUT MONEY: AND OTHER THINGS. Crown 8vo. 6s.
—— SERMONS OUT OF CHURCH. Cr. 8vo. 6s.
—— AN UNKNOWN COUNTRY. Illustrated by F. NOEL PATON. Royal 8vo. 7s. 6d.
—— ALICE LEARMONT: A FAIRY TALE. With Illustrations. 4s. 6d.
—— AN UNSENTIMENTAL JOURNEY THROUGH CORNWALL. Illustrated. 4to. 12s. 6d.
—— OUR YEAR: A CHILD'S BOOK IN PROSE AND VERSE. Illustrated. 2s. 6d.
—— LITTLE SUNSHINE'S HOLIDAY. Globe 8vo. 2s. 6d.
—— THE ADVENTURES OF A BROWNIE. Illustrated by Mrs. ALLINGHAM. 4s. 6d.
—— THE LITTLE LAME PRINCE AND HIS TRAVELLING CLOAK. A Parable for Old and Young. With 24 Illustrations by J. McL. RALSTON. Crown 8vo. 4s. 6d.
—— THE FAIRY BOOK: THE BEST POPULAR FAIRY STORIES. Selected and rendered anew. With a Vignette by Sir NOEL PATON. 18mo. 4s. 6d.
CRAIK (Henry).—THE STATE IN ITS RELATION TO EDUCATION. Crown 8vo. 3s. 6d.
CRANE (Lucy).—LECTURES ON ART AND THE FORMATION OF TASTE. Cr. 8vo. 6s.

LIST OF PUBLICATIONS.

CRANE (Walter).—THE SIRENS THREE. A Poem. Written and Illustrated by WALTER CRANE. Royal 8vo. 10s. 6d.

CRAVEN (Mrs. Dacre).—A GUIDE TO DISTRICT NURSES. Crown 8vo. 2s. 6d.

CRAWFORD (F. Marion).—MR. ISAACS: A TALE OF MODERN INDIA. Cr. 8vo. 3s. 6d.

—— DOCTOR CLAUDIUS: A TRUE STORY. Crown 8vo. 3s. 6d.

—— A ROMAN SINGER. Crown 8vo. 3s. 6d.

—— ZOROASTER. Crown 8vo. 3s. 6d.

—— A TALE OF A LONELY PARISH. Crown 8vo. 3s. 6d.

—— MARZIO'S CRUCIFIX. Crown 8vo. 3s. 6d.

—— PAUL PATOFF. Crown 8vo. 3s. 6d.

—— WITH THE IMMORTALS. Cr. 8vo. 3s. 6d.

—— GREIFENSTEIN. Crown 8vo. 6s.

—— SANT ILARIO. Crown 8vo. 6s.

—— A CIGARETTE MAKER'S ROMANCE. 2 vols. Globe 8vo.

CREIGHTON (M.).—ROME. 18mo. 1s.

—— CARDINAL WOLSEY. Crown 8vo. 2s. 6d.

CROMWELL (OLIVER). By FREDERIC HARRISON. Crown 8vo. 2s. 6d.

CROSS (Rev. J. A.).—BIBLE READINGS SELECTED FROM THE PENTATEUCH AND THE BOOK OF JOSHUA. 2nd Ed. Globe 8vo. 2s. 6d.

CROSSLEY (E.), GLEDHILL (J.), and WILSON (J. M.).—A HANDBOOK OF DOUBLE STARS. 8vo. 21s.

CORRECTIONS TO THE HANDBOOK OF DOUBLE STARS. 8vo. 1s.

CUMMING (Linnæus').—ELECTRICITY. An Introduction to the Theory of Electricity. With numerous Examples. Cr. 8vo. 8s. 6d.

CUNNINGHAM (Sir H. S.).—THE CŒRULEANS: A VACATION IDYLL. Cr. 8vo. 3s. 6d.

—— THE HERIOTS. 3 vols. Cr. 8vo. 31s. 6d.

—— WHEAT AND TARES. Crn. 8vo. 3s. 6d.

CUNNINGHAM (Rev. W.).—THE EPISTLE OF ST. BARNABAS. A Dissertation, including a Discussion of its Date and Authorship. Together with the Greek Text, the Latin Version, and a New English Translation and Commentary. Crown 8vo. 7s. 6d.

CUNNINGHAM (Rev. W.).—CHRISTIAN CIVILISATION, WITH SPECIAL REFERENCE TO INDIA. Crown 8vo. 5s.

—— THE CHURCHES OF ASIA: A METHODICAL SKETCH OF THE SECOND CENTURY. Crown 8vo. 6s.

CUNNINGHAM (Rev. John).—THE GROWTH OF THE CHURCH IN ITS ORGANISATION AND INSTITUTIONS. Being the Croall Lectures for 1886. 8vo. 9s.

CUNYNGHAME (Gen. Sir A. T.).—MY COMMAND IN SOUTH AFRICA, 1874—78. 8vo. 12s. 6d.

CURTEIS (Rev. G. H.).—DISSENT IN ITS RELATION TO THE CHURCH OF ENGLAND. Bampton Lectures for 1871. Cr. 8vo. 7s. 6d.

—— THE SCIENTIFIC OBSTACLES TO CHRISTIAN BELIEF. The Boyle Lectures, 1884. Cr. 8vo. 6s.

CUTHBERTSON (Francis). — EUCLIDIAN GEOMETRY. Extra fcp. 8vo. 4s. 6d.

DAGONET THE JESTER. Cr. 8vo. 4s. 6d.

DAHN (Felix). FELICITAS. Translated by M. A. C. E. Crown 8vo. 4s. 6d.

"DAILY NEWS."—CORRESPONDENCE OF THE WAR BETWEEN RUSSIA AND TURKEY, 1877. TO THE FALL OF KARS. Cr. 8vo. 6s.

—— CORRESPONDENCE OF THE RUSSO-TURKISH WAR. FROM THE FALL OF KARS TO THE CONCLUSION OF PEACE. Crown 8vo. 6s.

DALE (A. W. W.).—THE SYNOD OF ELVIRA, AND CHRISTIAN LIFE IN THE FOURTH CENTURY. Crown 8vo. 10s. 6d.

DALTON (Rev. T.).—RULES AND EXAMPLES IN ARITHMETIC. New Edition. 18mo. 2s. 6d.

—— RULES AND EXAMPLES IN ALGEBRA. Part I. New Ed. 18mo. 2s. Part II. 2s. 6d. KEY TO ALGEBRA. Part I. Cr. 8vo. 7s. 6d.

DAMIEN (Father): A JOURNEY FROM CASHMERE TO HIS HOME IN HAWAII. By EDWARD CLIFFORD. Portrait. Crown 8vo. 2s. 6d.

DAMPIER. By W. CLARK RUSSELL. With Portrait. Crown 8vo. 2s. 6d.

DANIELL (Alfred).—A TEXT-BOOK OF THE PRINCIPLES OF PHYSICS. With Illustrations. 2nd Edition. Medium 8vo. 21s.

DANTE.—THE PURGATORY OF DANTE ALIGHIERI. Edited, with Translations and Notes, by A. J. BUTLER. Cr. 8vo. 12s. 6d.

—— THE PARADISO OF DANTE. Edited, with a Prose Translation and Notes, by A. J. BUTLER. Crown 8vo. 12s. 6d.

—— DE MONARCHIA. Translated by F. J. CHURCH. 8vo. 4s. 6d.

—— DANTE: AND OTHER ESSAYS. By the DEAN OF ST. PAUL'S. Globe 8vo. 5s.

—— READINGS ON THE PURGATORIO OF DANTE. Chiefly based on the Commentary of Benvenuto Da Imola. By the Hon. W. W. VERNON, M.A. With an Introduction by the Very Rev. the DEAN OF ST. PAUL'S. 2 vols. Crown 8vo. 24s.

DARWIN (Charles).—MEMORIAL NOTICES, reprinted from Nature. By T. H. HUXLEY, G. J. ROMANES, ARCHIBALD GEIKIE, and W. T. THISELTON DYER. With a Portrait. Crown 8vo. 2s. 6d.

DAVIES (Rev. J. Llewelyn).—THE GOSPEL AND MODERN LIFE. 2nd Edition, to which is added MORALITY ACCORDING TO THE SACRAMENT OF THE LORD'S SUPPER. Extra fcp. 8vo. 6s.

—— WARNINGS AGAINST SUPERSTITION. Ex. fcp. 8vo. 6s.

—— THE CHRISTIAN CALLING. Ex. fcp. 8vo. 6s.

—— THE EPISTLES OF ST. PAUL TO THE EPHESIANS, THE COLOSSIANS, AND PHILEMON. With Introductions and Notes. 2nd Edition. 8vo. 7s. 6d.

—— SOCIAL QUESTIONS FROM THE POINT OF VIEW OF CHRISTIAN THEOLOGY. 2nd Ed. Crown 8vo. 6s.

DAVIES (J. Ll.) and VAUGHAN (D. J.).— THE REPUBLIC OF PLATO. Translated into English. 18mo. 4s. 6d.

DAWKINS (Prof. W. Boyd).—EARLY MAN IN BRITAIN AND HIS PLACE IN THE TERTIARY PERIOD. Medium 8vo. 25s.

DAWSON (Sir J. W.).—ACADIAN GEOLOGY, THE GEOLOGICAL STRUCTURE, ORGANIC REMAINS, AND MINERAL RESOURCES OF NOVA SCOTIA, NEW BRUNSWICK, AND PRINCE EDWARD ISLAND. 3rd Ed. 8vo. 21s.

DAWSON (James).—AUSTRALIAN ABORIGINES. Small 4to. 14s.

DAY (Rev. Lal Behari).—BENGAL PEASANT LIFE. Crown 8vo. 6s.
—— FOLK TALES OF BENGAL. Cr. 8vo. 4s. 6d.

DAY (R. E.).—ELECTRIC LIGHT ARITHMETIC. Pott 8vo. 2s.

DAY (H. G.).—PROPERTIES OF CONIC SECTIONS PROVED GEOMETRICALLY. Crown 8vo. 3s. 6d.

DAYS WITH SIR ROGER DE COVERLEY. From the *Spectator*. With Illustrations by HUGH THOMSON. Fcp. 4to. 6s.

DEÁK (FRANCIS): HUNGARIAN STATESMAN. A Memoir. 8vo. 12s. 6d.

DEFOE (Daniel).—THE ADVENTURES OF ROBINSON CRUSOE. Ed. by HENRY KINGSLEY. Globe 8vo. 3s. 6d.
Golden Treasury Series Edition. Edited by J. W. CLARK, M.A. 18mo. 4s. 6d.

DEFOE. By W. MINTO. Crown 8vo. 1s. 6d.; sewed, 1s.

DELAMOTTE (Prof. P. H.).—A BEGINNER'S DRAWING-BOOK. Progressively arranged. With Plates. 3rd Edit. Crn. 8vo. 3s. 6d.

DEMOCRACY: AN AMERICAN NOVEL. Crown 8vo. 4s. 6d.

DEMOSTHENES.—ADVERSUS LEPTINEM. Ed. Rev. J. R. KING, M.A. Fcp. 8vo. 4s. 6d.
—— THE ORATION ON THE CROWN. Edited by B. DRAKE, M.A. 7th Ed. Fcp. 8vo. 4s. 6d.
—— THE FIRST PHILIPPIC. Edited by Rev. T. GWATKIN, M.A. Fcp. 8vo. 2s. 6d.

DEMOSTHENES. By Prof. S. H. BUTCHER, M.A. Fcp. 8vo. 1s. 6d.

DE MAISTRE.—LA JEUNE SIBÉRIENNE ET LE LÉPREUX DE LA CITÉ D'AOSTE. Edited, with Notes and Vocabulary, by S. BARLET, B.Sc. Globe 8vo. 1s. 6d.

DE MORGAN (Mary).—THE NECKLACE OF PRINCESS FIORIMONDE, AND OTHER STORIES. Illustrated by WALTER CRANE. Extra fcp. 8vo. 3s. 6d. Also a Large Paper Edition, with the Illustrations on India Paper. 100 copies only printed.

DE QUINCEY. By Prof. MASSON. Crown 8vo. 1s. 6d.; sewed, 1s.

DEUTSCHE LYRIK. THE GOLDEN TREASURY OF THE BEST GERMAN LYRICAL POEMS. Selected and arranged by Dr. BUCHHEIM. 18mo. 4s. 6d.

DEUTSCHE BALLADEN.—THE GOLDEN TREASURY OF THE BEST GERMAN BALLADS. Selected and arranged by the same Editor. 18mo. [*In the Press.*

DE VERE (Aubrey).—ESSAYS CHIEFLY ON POETRY. 2 vols. Globe 8vo. 12s.
—— ESSAYS, CHIEFLY LITERARY AND ETHICAL. Globe 8vo. 6s.

DE WINT.—MEMOIR OF PETER DE WINT. By WALTER ARMSTRONG, B.A. Oxon. Illustrated by 24 Photogravures from the Artist's pictures. Super-Royal 4to. 31s. 6d.

DICEY (Prof. A. V.).—LECTURES INTRODUCTORY TO THE STUDY OF THE LAW OF THE CONSTITUTION. 3rd Edition. 8vo. 12s. 6d.
—— LETTERS ON UNIONIST DELUSIONS. Crown 8vo. 2s. 6d.
—— THE PRIVY COUNCIL. Crown 8vo. 3s. 6d.

DICKENS (Charles).—THE POSTHUMOUS PAPERS OF THE PICKWICK CLUB. With Notes and numerous Illustrations. Edited by CHARLES DICKENS the younger. 2 vols. Extra crown 8vo. 21s.

DICKENS. By A. W. WARD. Crown 8vo. 1s. 6d.; sewed, 1s.

DICKSON (R.) and EDMOND (J. P.).—ANNALS OF SCOTTISH PRINTING, FROM THE INTRODUCTION OF THE ART IN 1507 TO THE BEGINNING OF THE SEVENTEENTH CENTURY. Dutch hand-made paper. Demy 4to, buckram, 2l. 2s. net.—Royal 4to, 2 vols. half Japanese vellum, 4l. 4s. net.

DIDEROT AND THE ENCYCLOPÆDISTS. By JOHN MORLEY. 2 vols. Globe 8vo. 10s.

DIGGLE (Rev. J. W.).—GODLINESS AND MANLINESS. A Miscellany of Brief Papers touching the Relation of Religion to Life. Crown 8vo. 6s.

DILETTANTI SOCIETY'S PUBLICATIONS.—ANTIQUITIES OF IONIA. Vols. I. II. and III. 2l. 2s. each, or 5l. 5s. the set. Vol. IV., folio, half morocco, 3l. 13s. 6d.
—— PENROSE (Francis C.). An Investigation of the Principles of Athenian Architecture. Illustrated by numerous engravings. New Edition. Enlarged. Folio. 7l. 7s.
—— SPECIMENS OF ANCIENT SCULPTURE: EGYPTIAN, ETRUSCAN, GREEK, AND ROMAN. Selected from different Collections in Great Britain by the Society of Dilettanti. Vol. II. Folio. 5l. 5s.

DILKE (Sir C. W.).—GREATER BRITAIN. A RECORD OF TRAVEL IN ENGLISH-SPEAKING COUNTRIES DURING 1866-67. (America, Australia, India.) 9th Edition. Crown 8vo. 6s.
—— PROBLEMS OF GREATER BRITAIN. Maps. 2 vols. 2nd Edition. 8vo. 36s.

DILLWYN (E. A.).—JILL. Crown 8vo. 6s.
—— JILL AND JACK. 2 vols. Globe 8vo. 12s.

DOBSON (Austin).—FIELDING. Crown 8vo. 1s. 6d.; sewed, 1s.

DODGSON (C. L.).—EUCLID. Books I. and II. With Words substituted for the Algebraical Symbols used in the first edition. 4th Edition. Crown 8vo. 2s.
—— EUCLID AND HIS MODERN RIVALS. 2nd Edition. Cr. 8vo. 6s.
—— SUPPLEMENT TO FIRST EDITION "EUCLID AND HIS MODERN RIVALS." Crown 8vo. Sewed, 1s.
—— CURIOSA MATHEMATICA. Part I. A New Theory of Parallels. 2nd Ed. Cr. 8vo. 2s.

DONALDSON (Prof. James).—THE APOSTOLICAL FATHERS. A CRITICAL ACCOUNT OF THEIR GENUINE WRITINGS, AND OF THEIR DOCTRINES. 2nd Ed. Cr. 8vo. 7s. 6d.

DONISTHORPE (Wordsworth).—INDIVIDUALISM: A SYSTEM OF POLITICS. 8vo. 14s.

LIST OF PUBLICATIONS. 13

DOWDEN (Prof. E.).—SHAKSPERE. 18mo. 1s.
—— SOUTHEY. Crown 8vo. 1s. 6d.; sewed, 1s.
DOYLE (J. A.).—HISTORY OF AMERICA. With Maps. 18mo. 4s. 6d.
DOYLE (Sir F. H.).—THE RETURN OF THE GUARDS: AND OTHER POEMS. Cr. 8vo. 7s. 6d.
DRAKE. By JULIAN CORBETT. With Portrait. Crown 8vo.
DREW (W. H.).—A GEOMETRICAL TREATISE ON CONIC SECTIONS. 8th Ed. Cr. 8vo. 5s.
DRUMMOND (Prof. James).—INTRODUCTION TO THE STUDY OF THEOLOGY. Crown 8vo. 5s.
DRYDEN : ESSAYS OF. Edited by Prof. C. D. YONGE. Fcp. 8vo. 2s. 6d.
—— POETICAL WORKS. Edited, with Memoir, Revised Text, and Notes, by W. D. CHRISTIE, C.B. Globe 8vo. 3s. 6d. [Globe Edition.
DRYDEN. By G. SAINTSBURY. Crown 8vo. 1s. 6d.; sewed, 1s.
DU CANE (Col. Sir E. F.). THE PUNISHMENT AND PREVENTION OF CRIME. Crown 8vo. 3s. 6d.
DUFF (Right Hon. Sir M. E. Grant).—NOTES OF AN INDIAN JOURNEY. 8vo. 10s. 6d.
—— MISCELLANIES, POLITICAL AND LITERARY. 8vo. 10s. 6d.
DUMAS.—LES DEMOISELLES DE ST. CYR. Comédie par ALEXANDRE DUMAS. Edited by VICTOR OGER. 18mo. 1s. 6d.
DÜNTZER (H.).—LIFE OF GOETHE. Translated by T. W. LYSTER. With Illustrations. 2 vols. Crown 8vo. 21s.
—— LIFE OF SCHILLER. Translated by P. E. PINKERTON. Illustrations. Cr. 8vo. 10s. 6d.
DUPUIS (Prof. N. F.).—ELEMENTARY SYNTHETIC GEOMETRY OF THE POINT, LINE, AND CIRCLE IN THE PLANE. Gl. 8vo. 4s. 6d.
DYER (J. M.).—EXERCISES IN ANALYTICAL GEOMETRY. Crown 8vo. 4s. 6d.
DYNAMICS, SYLLABUS OF ELEMENTARY. Part I. LINEAR DYNAMICS. With an Appendix on the Meanings of the Symbols in Physical Equations. Prepared by the Association for the Improvement of Geometrical Teaching. 4to. 1s.
EADIE (Prof. John).—THE ENGLISH BIBLE: AN EXTERNAL AND CRITICAL HISTORY OF THE VARIOUS ENGLISH TRANSLATIONS OF SCRIPTURE. 2 vols. 8vo. 28s.
—— ST. PAUL'S EPISTLES TO THE THESSALONIANS, COMMENTARY ON THE GREEK TEXT. 8vo. 12s.
—— LIFE OF JOHN EADIE, D.D., LL.D. By JAMES BROWN, D.D. 2nd Ed. Cr. 8vo. 7s. 6d.
EAGLES (T. H.).—CONSTRUCTIVE GEOMETRY OF PLANE CURVES. Crown 8vo. 12s.
EASTLAKE (Lady).—FELLOWSHIP : LETTERS ADDRESSED TO MY SISTER-MOURNERS. Cr. 8vo. 2s. 6d.
EBERS (Dr. George).—THE BURGOMASTER'S WIFE. Translated by CLARA BELL. Crown 8vo. 4s. 6d.
—— ONLY A WORD. Translated by CLARA BELL. Crown 8vo. 4s. 6d.
ECCE HOMO. A SURVEY OF THE LIFE AND WORK OF JESUS CHRIST. 20th Ed. Cr. 8vo. 6s.

ECONOMICS, THE QUARTERLY JOURNAL OF. Vol. II. Parts II. III. IV. 2s. 6d. each; Vol. III. 4 parts, 2s. 6d. each; Vol. IV. 4 parts, 2s. 6d. each.
EDGAR (J. H.) and PRITCHARD (G. S.).—NOTE-BOOK ON PRACTICAL SOLID OR DESCRIPTIVE GEOMETRY, CONTAINING PROBLEMS WITH HELP FOR SOLUTION. 4th Edition, Enlarged. By ARTHUR G. MEEZE. Globe 8vo. 4s. 6d.
EDWARDS (Joseph).—AN ELEMENTARY TREATISE ON THE DIFFERENTIAL CALCULUS. Crown 8vo. 10s. 6d.
EDWARDS-MOSS (J. E.). A SEASON IN SUTHERLAND. Crown 8vo. 1s. 6d.
EICKE (K. M.).—FIRST LESSONS IN LATIN. Extra fcp. 8vo. 2s.
EIMER (G. H. T.).—ORGANIC EVOLUTION AS THE RESULT OF THE INHERITANCE OF ACQUIRED CHARACTERS ACCORDING TO THE LAWS OF ORGANIC GROWTH. Translated by J. T. CUNNINGHAM, M.A. 8vo. 12s. 6d.
ELDERTON (W. A.).—MAP DRAWING AND MAP MAKING. Pott 8vo.
ELLERTON (Rev. John).—THE HOLIEST MANHOOD, AND ITS LESSONS FOR BUSY LIVES. Crown 8vo. 6s.
ELLIOT (Hon. A.).—THE STATE AND THE CHURCH. Crown 8vo. 3s. 6d.
ELLIOTT. LIFE OF HENRY VENN ELLIOTT, OF BRIGHTON. By JOSIAH BATEMAN, M.A. 3rd Edition. Extra fcp. 8vo. 6s.
ELLIS (A. J.).—PRACTICAL HINTS ON THE QUANTITATIVE PRONUNCIATION OF LATIN. Extra fcp. 8vo. 4s. 6d.
ELLIS (Tristram).—SKETCHING FROM NATURE. Illustr. by H. STACY MARKS, R.A., and the Author. 2nd Edition. Cr. 8vo. 3s. 6d.
EMERSON.—THE LIFE OF RALPH WALDO EMERSON. By J. L. CABOT. 2 vols. Crown 8vo. 18s.
—— THE COLLECTED WORKS OF RALPH WALDO EMERSON. 6 vols. (1) MISCELLANIES. With an Introductory Essay by JOHN MORLEY. (2) ESSAYS. (3) POEMS. (4) ENGLISH TRAITS; AND REPRESENTATIVE MEN. (5) CONDUCT OF LIFE; AND SOCIETY AND SOLITUDE. (6) LETTERS; AND SOCIAL AIMS, &c. Globe 8vo. 5s. each.
ENGLAND (E. B.).—EXERCISES IN LATIN SYNTAX AND IDIOM. Arranged with reference to Roby's School Latin Grammar. Crown 8vo. 2s. 6d.
KEY. Crown 8vo. 2s. 6d.
ENGLISH CITIZEN, THE.—A Series of Short Books on his Rights and Responsibilities. Edited by HENRY CRAIK, C.B. Crown 8vo. 3s. 6d. each.
CENTRAL GOVERNMENT. By H. D. TRAILL, D.C.L.
THE ELECTORATE AND THE LEGISLATURE. By SPENCER WALPOLE.
THE POOR LAW. By the Rev. T. W. FOWLE.
THE NATIONAL BUDGET; THE NATIONAL DEBT; TAXES AND RATES. By A. J. WILSON.
THE STATE IN RELATION TO LABOUR. By W. STANLEY JEVONS, LL.D., F.R.S.

ENGLISH CITIZEN, THE—*continued.*
THE STATE AND THE CHURCH. By the Hon. ARTHUR ELLIOTT, M.P.
FOREIGN RELATIONS. By SPENCER WALPOLE.
THE STATE IN ITS RELATION TO TRADE. By Sir T. H. FARRER, Bart.
LOCAL GOVERNMENT. By M. D. CHALMERS.
THE STATE IN ITS RELATION TO EDUCATION. By HENRY CRAIK, C.B.
THE LAND LAWS. By Sir F. POLLOCK, Bart. 2nd Edition.
COLONIES AND DEPENDENCIES. Part I. INDIA. By J. S. COTTON, M.A. II. THE COLONIES. By E. J. PAYNE.
JUSTICE AND POLICE. By F. W. MAITLAND.
THE PUNISHMENT AND PREVENTION OF CRIME. By Colonel Sir EDMUND DU CANE.
THE NATIONAL DEFENCES. By Colonel MAURICE, R.A. [*In the Press.*

ENGLISH HISTORY, READINGS IN.—Selected and Edited by JOHN RICHARD GREEN. 3 Parts. Fcp. 8vo. 1s. 6d. each. Part I. Hengist to Cressy. II. Cressy to Cromwell. III. Cromwell to Balaklava.

ENGLISH ILLUSTRATED MAGAZINE, THE. Profusely Illustrated. Published Monthly. Number I. October, 1883. 6d. Vol. I. 1884. 7s. 6d. Vols. II.—VII. Super royal 8vo, extra cloth, coloured edges. 8s. each. [Cloth Covers for binding Volumes, 1s. 6d. each.]

—— Proof Impressions of Engravings originally published in *The English Illustrated Magazine.* 1884. In Portfolio 4to. 21s.

ENGLISH MEN OF ACTION.—Crown 8vo. With Portraits. 2s. 6d. each.
The following Volumes are Ready:
GENERAL GORDON. By Col. Sir W. BUTLER.
HENRY V. By the Rev. A. J. CHURCH.
LIVINGSTONE. By THOMAS HUGHES.
LORD LAWRENCE. By Sir RICHARD TEMPLE.
WELLINGTON. By GEORGE HOOPER.
DAMPIER. By W. CLARK RUSSELL.
MONK. By JULIAN CORBETT.
STRAFFORD. By H. D. TRAILL.
WARREN HASTINGS. By Sir ALFRED LYALL.
PETERBOROUGH. By W. STEBBING.
CAPTAIN COOK. By WALTER BESANT
SIR HENRY HAVELOCK. By A. FORBES.
CLIVE. By Colonel Sir CHARLES WILSON.
SIR CHARLES NAPIER. By Col. Sir WM. BUTLER.
The undermentioned are in the Press or in Preparation:
WARWICK, THE KING-MAKER. By C. W. OMAN.
DRAKE. By JULIAN CORBETT.
MONTROSE. By MOWBRAY MORRIS.
MARLBOROUGH. By Col. Sir WM. BUTLER.
RODNEY. By DAVID HANNAY.
SIR JOHN MOORE. By Colonel MAURICE.

ENGLISH MEN OF LETTERS.— Edited by JOHN MORLEY. Crown 8vo. 2s. 6d. each. Cheap Edition. 1s. 6d.; sewed, 1s.
JOHNSON. By LESLIE STEPHEN.
SCOTT. By R. H. HUTTON.
GIBBON. By J. COTTER MORISON.
HUME. By T. H. HUXLEY.
GOLDSMITH. By WILLIAM BLACK.
SHELLEY. By J. A. SYMONDS.
DEFOE. By W. MINTO.

ENGLISH MEN OF LETTERS—*contd.*
BURNS. By Principal SHAIRP.
SPENSER. By the DEAN OF ST. PAUL'S.
THACKERAY. By ANTHONY TROLLOPE.
MILTON. By MARK PATTISON.
BURKE. By JOHN MORLEY.
HAWTHORNE. By HENRY JAMES.
SOUTHEY. By Prof. DOWDEN.
BUNYAN. By J. A. FROUDE.
CHAUCER. By Prof. A. W. WARD.
COWPER. By GOLDWIN SMITH.
POPE. By LESLIE STEPHEN.
BYRON. By Prof. NICHOL.
DRYDEN. By G. SAINTSBURY.
LOCKE. By Prof. FOWLER.
WORDSWORTH. By F. W. H. MYERS.
LANDOR. By SIDNEY COLVIN.
DE QUINCEY. By Prof. MASSON.
CHARLES LAMB. By Rev. ALFRED AINGER.
BENTLEY. By Prof. JEBB.
DICKENS. By A. W. WARD.
GRAY. By EDMUND GOSSE.
SWIFT. By LESLIE STEPHEN.
STERNE. By H. D. TRAILL.
MACAULAY. By J. COTTER MORISON.
FIELDING. By AUSTIN DOBSON.
SHERIDAN. By Mrs OLIPHANT.
ADDISON. By W. J. COURTHOPE.
BACON. By the DEAN OF ST. PAUL'S.
COLERIDGE. By H. D. TRAILL.
SIR PHILIP SIDNEY. By J. A. SYMONDS.
KEATS. By SIDNEY COLVIN.

ENGLISH POETS. Selections, with Critical Introductions by various Writers, and a General Introduction by MATTHEW ARNOLD. Edited by T. H. WARD, M.A. 2nd Edition. 4 vols. Crown 8vo. 7s. 6d. each.
Vol. I. CHAUCER TO DONNE. II. BEN JONSON TO DRYDEN. III. ADDISON TO BLAKE. IV. WORDSWORTH TO ROSSETTI.

ENGLISH STATESMEN (TWELVE). Crown 8vo. 2s. 6d. each.
WILLIAM THE CONQUEROR. By EDWARD A. FREEMAN, D.C.L., LL.D. [*Ready.*
HENRY II. By Mrs. J. R. GREEN. [*Ready.*
EDWARD I. By F. YORK POWELL.
HENRY VII. By JAMES GAIRDNER. [*Ready.*
CARDINAL WOLSEY. By Prof. M. CREIGHTON. [*Ready.*
ELIZABETH. By E. S. BEESLY.
OLIVER CROMWELL. By FREDERIC HARRISON. [*Ready.*
WILLIAM III. By H. D. TRAILL. [*Ready.*
WALPOLE. By JOHN MORLEY. [*Ready.*
CHATHAM. By JOHN MORLEY.
PITT. By JOHN MORLEY.
PEEL. By J. R. THURSFIELD.

ESSEX FIELD CLUB MEMOIRS. Vol. I. REPORT ON THE EAST ANGLIAN EARTHQUAKE OF 22ND APRIL, 1884. By RAPHAEL MELDOLA, F.R.S., and WILLIAM WHITE, F.E.S. Maps and Illustrations. 8vo. 3s. 6d.

ETON COLLEGE, HISTORY OF, 1440-1884. By H. C. MAXWELL LYTE, C.B. Illustrations. 2nd Edition. Med. 8vo. 21s.

EURIPIDES. MEDEA. Edited by A. W. VERRALL, Litt.D. 8vo. 7s. 6d.

—— HIPPOLYTUS. Edited by J. P. MAHAFFY. M.A., and J. B. BURY. Fcp. 8vo. 3s. 6d.

—— HECUBA. Edit. by Rev. J. BOND, M.A., and A. S. WALPOLE, M.A. 18mo. 1s. 6d.

LIST OF PUBLICATIONS. 15

EURIPIDES.- IPHIGENIA IN TAURIS. Edit. by E. B. ENGLAND, M.A. Fcp. 8vo. 4s. 6d.
—— MEDEA. Edited by A. W. VERRALL, Litt.D. Fcp. 8vo. 3s. 6d.
—— MEDEA. Edited by A. W. VERRALL, Litt.D., and Rev. M. A. BAYFIELD, M.A. 18mo. 1s. 6d.
—— ION. Edited by Rev. M. A. BAYFIELD, M.A. Fcp. 8vo. 3s. 6d.
—— ALCESTIS. Edited by Rev. M. A. BAYFIELD, M.A. 18mo. 1s. 6d.
EURIPIDES. By Prof. MAHAFFY. Fcp. 8vo. 1s. 6d.
EUROPEAN HISTORY, NARRATED IN A SERIES OF HISTORICAL SELECTIONS FROM THE BEST AUTHORITIES. Edited and arranged by E. M. SEWELL and C. M. YONGE. 2 vols. 3rd Edition. Crown 8vo. 6s. each.
EUTROPIUS. Adapted for the Use of Beginners. With Notes, Exercises, and Vocabularies. By W. WELCH, M.A., and C. G. DUFFIELD, M.A. 18mo. 1s. 6d.
EVANS (Sebastian). BROTHER FABIAN'S MANUSCRIPT, AND OTHER POEMS. Fcp. 8vo, cloth. 6s.
—— IN THE STUDIO: A DECADE OF POEMS. Extra fcp. 8vo. 5s.
EVERETT (Prof. J. D.).—UNITS AND PHYSICAL CONSTANTS. 2nd Ed. Globe 8vo. 5s.
FAIRFAX. LIFE OF ROBERT FAIRFAX OF STEETON, Vice-Admiral, Alderman, and Member for York, A.D. 1666—1725. By CLEMENTS R. MARKHAM, C.B. 8vo. 12s. 6d.
FAITH AND CONDUCT: AN ESSAY ON VERIFIABLE RELIGION. Crown 8vo. 7s. 6d.
FARRAR (Archdeacon).—THE FALL OF MAN, AND OTHER SERMONS. 5th Ed. Cr. 8vo. 6s.
—— THE WITNESS OF HISTORY TO CHRIST. Being the Hulsean Lectures for 1870. 7th Edition. Crown 8vo. 5s.
—— SEEKERS AFTER GOD. THE LIVES OF SENECA, EPICTETUS, AND MARCUS AURELIUS. 12th Edition. Crown 8vo. 6s.
—— THE SILENCE AND VOICES OF GOD. University and other Sermons. 7th Ed. Cr. 8vo. 6s.
—— IN THE DAYS OF THY YOUTH. Sermons on Practical Subjects, preached at Marlborough College. 9th Edition. Cr. 8vo. 9s.
—— ETERNAL HOPE. Five Sermons, preached in Westminster Abbey. 28th Thousand. Crown 8vo. 6s.
—— SAINTLY WORKERS. Five Lenten Lectures. 3rd Edition. Crown 8vo. 6s.
—— EPHPHATHA; OR, THE AMELIORATION OF THE WORLD. Sermons preached at Westminster Abbey. Crown 8vo. 6s.
—— MERCY AND JUDGMENT. A few Last Words on Christian Eschatology. 2nd Ed. Crown 8vo. 10s. 6d.
—— THE MESSAGES OF THE BOOKS. Being Discourses and Notes on the Books of the New Testament. 8vo. 14s.
—— SERMONS AND ADDRESSES DELIVERED IN AMERICA. Crown 8vo. 7s. 6d.
—— THE HISTORY OF INTERPRETATION. Being the Bampton Lectures, 1885. 8vo. 16s.

FARREN (Robert). THE GRANTA AND THE CAM, FROM BYRON'S POOL TO ELY. Thirty-six Etchings. Large Imperial 4to, cloth gilt. 52s. 6d. net.
A few Copies, Proofs, Large Paper, of which but 50 were printed, half morocco. 8l. 8s. net.
—— CAMBRIDGE AND ITS NEIGHBOURHOOD. A Series of Etchings. With an Introduction by JOHN WILLIS CLARK, M.A. Imp. 4to. 52s. 6d. net.—Proofs, half mor., 7l. 7s. net.
—— A ROUND OF MELODIES. A Series of Etched Designs. Oblong folio, half morocco. 52s. 6d. net.
—— THE BIRDS OF ARISTOPHANES. 13s. net. Proofs. 47s. net.
—— CATHEDRAL CITIES: ELY AND NORWICH. With Introduction by E.A. FREEMAN, D.C.L. Col. 4to. 3l. 3s. net.
Proofs on Japanese paper. 6l. 6s. net.
—— —— PETERBOROUGH. WITH THE ABBEYS OF CROWLAND AND THORNEY. With Introduction by EDMUND VENABLES, M.A. Col. 4to. 2l. 2s. net. Proofs, folio, 5l. 5s. net.
The Edition is limited to 125 Small Paper and 45 Large.
—— THE EUMENIDES OF ÆSCHYLUS. As performed by Members of the University at the Theatre Royal, Cambridge. Oblong 4to. Small size, 10s. 6d. net. Large size, India Proofs, 21s. net. On Whatman paper, 27s. net.
—— THE OEDIPUS TYRANNUS OF SOPHOCLES. As performed at Cambridge. Oblong 4to. Prints, 10s. 6d. net. Proofs, 21s. net.
FARRER (Sir T. H.).—THE STATE IN ITS RELATION TO TRADE. Crown 8vo. 3s. 6d.
FASNACHT (G. Eugène).—THE ORGANIC METHOD OF STUDYING LANGUAGES. I. FRENCH. Extra fcp. 8vo. 3s. 6d.
—— A SYNTHETIC FRENCH GRAMMAR FOR SCHOOLS. Crown 8vo. 3s. 6d.
FAWCETT (Rt. Hon. Henry).- MANUAL OF POLITICAL ECONOMY. 7th Edition, revised. Crown 8vo. 12s.
—— AN EXPLANATORY DIGEST OF PROFESSOR FAWCETT'S MANUAL OF POLITICAL ECONOMY. By CYRIL A. WATERS. Cr. 8vo. 2s. 6d.
—— SPEECHES ON SOME CURRENT POLITICAL QUESTIONS. 8vo. 10s. 6d.
—— FREE TRADE AND PROTECTION. 6th Edition. Crown 8vo. 3s. 6d.
FAWCETT (Mrs. H.).—POLITICAL ECONOMY FOR BEGINNERS, WITH QUESTIONS. 7th Edition. 18mo. 2s. 6d.
—— SOME EMINENT WOMEN OF OUR TIMES. Short Biographical Sketches. Cr. 8vo. 2s. 6d.
FAWCETT (Rt. Hon. Henry and Mrs. H.).— ESSAYS AND LECTURES ON POLITICAL AND SOCIAL SUBJECTS. 8vo. 10s. 6d.
FAY (Amy.)— MUSIC-STUDY IN GERMANY. With a Preface by Sir GEORGE GROVE, D.C.L. Crown 8vo. 4s. 6d.
FEARNLEY (W.).—A MANUAL OF ELEMENTARY PRACTICAL HISTOLOGY. Cr. 8vo. 7s. 6d.
FEARON (D. R.).—SCHOOL INSPECTION. 6th Edition. Crown 8vo. 2s. 6d.
FERREL (Prof. W.).—A POPULAR TREATISE ON THE WINDS. 8vo. 18s.

FERRERS (Rev. N. M.).—A TREATISE ON TRILINEAR CO-ORDINATES, THE METHOD OF RECIPROCAL POLARS, AND THE THEORY OF PROJECTIONS. 4th Ed. Cr. 8vo. 6s. 6d.

—— SPHERICAL HARMONICS AND SUBJECTS CONNECTED WITH THEM. Crown 8vo. 7s. 6d.

FESSENDEN (C.).—PHYSICS FOR PUBLIC SCHOOLS. Globe 8vo.

FIELDING. By AUSTIN DOBSON. Crown 8vo. 1s. 6d.; sewed, 1s.

FINCK (Henry T.).—ROMANTIC LOVE AND PERSONAL BEAUTY. 2 vols. Cr. 8vo. 18s.

FIRST LESSONS IN BUSINESS MATTERS. By A BANKER'S DAUGHTER. 2nd Edition. 18mo. 1s.

FISHER (Rev. Osmond).—PHYSICS OF THE EARTH'S CRUST. 2nd Edition. 8vo. 12s.

FISKE (John).—OUTLINES OF COSMIC PHILOSOPHY, BASED ON THE DOCTRINE OF EVOLUTION. 2 vols. 8vo. 25s.

—— DARWINISM, AND OTHER ESSAYS. Crown 8vo. 7s. 6d.

—— MAN'S DESTINY VIEWED IN THE LIGHT OF HIS ORIGIN. Crown 8vo. 3s. 6d.

—— AMERICAN POLITICAL IDEAS VIEWED FROM THE STAND-POINT OF UNIVERSAL HISTORY. Crown 8vo. 4s.

—— THE CRITICAL PERIOD IN AMERICAN HISTORY, 1783—89. Ex. Cr. 8vo. 10s. 6d.

—— THE BEGINNINGS OF NEW ENGLAND; OR, THE PURITAN THEOCRACY IN ITS RELATIONS TO CIVIL AND RELIGIOUS LIBERTY. Crown 8vo. 7s. 6d.

FISON (L.) and HOWITT (A. W.).—KAMILAROI AND KURNAI GROUP. Group-Marriage and Relationship and Marriage by Elopement, drawn chiefly from the usage of the Australian Aborigines, also the Kurnai Tribe, their Customs in Peace and War. With an Introduction by LEWIS H. MORGAN, LL.D. 8vo. 15s.

FITCH (J. G.).—NOTES ON AMERICAN SCHOOLS AND TRAINING COLLEGES. Reprinted by permission from the Report of the English Education Department for 1888—89. Globe 8vo. 2s. 6d.

FITZGERALD (Edward): LETTERS AND LITERARY REMAINS OF. Ed. by W. ALDIS WRIGHT, M.A. 3 vols. Crown 8vo. 31s. 6d.

—— THE RUBÁIYÁT OF OMAR KHÁYYÁM. Extra Crown 8vo. 10s. 6d.

FITZ GERALD (Caroline).—VENETIA VICTRIX, AND OTHER POEMS. Ex. fcp. 8vo. 3s. 6d.

FLEAY (Rev. F. G.).—A SHAKESPEARE MANUAL. Extra fcp. 8vo. 4s. 6d.

FLEISCHER (Dr. Emil).—A SYSTEM OF VOLUMETRIC ANALYSIS. Translated by M. M. PATTISON MUIR, F.R.S.E. Cr. 8vo. 7s. 6d.

FLEMING (George).—A NILE NOVEL. Gl. 8vo. 2s.

—— MIRAGE. A Novel. Globe 8vo. 2s.

—— THE HEAD OF MEDUSA. Globe 8vo. 2s.

—— VESTIGIA. Globe 8vo. 2s.

FLITTERS, TATTERS, AND THE COUNSELLOR; WEEDS; AND OTHER SKETCHES. By the Author of "Hogan, M.P." Globe 8vo. 2s.

FLORIAN'S FABLES. Selected and Edited by Rev. CHARLES YELD, M.A. Illustrated. Globe 8vo. 1s. 6d.

FLOWER (Prof. W. H.).—AN INTRODUCTION TO THE OSTEOLOGY OF THE MAMMALIA. With numerous Illustrations. 3rd Edition, revised with the assistance of HANS GADOW, Ph.D., M.A. Crown 8vo. 10s. 6d.

FLÜCKIGER (F. A.) and HANBURY (D.).—PHARMACOGRAPHIA. A History of the principal Drugs of Vegetable Origin met with in Great Britain and India. 2nd Edition, revised. 8vo. 21s.

FO'C'SLE YARNS, including "Betsy Lee," and other Poems. Crown 8vo. 7s. 6d.

FORBES (Archibald).—SOUVENIRS OF SOME CONTINENTS. Crown 8vo. 6s.

—— SIR HENRY HAVELOCK. With Portrait. Crown 8vo. 2s. 6d.

FORBES (Edward): MEMOIR OF. By GEORGE WILSON, M.D., and ARCHIBALD GEIKIE, F.R.S., &c. Demy 8vo. 14s.

FORBES (Rev. Granville).—THE VOICE OF GOD IN THE PSALMS. Crown 8vo. 6s. 6d.

FORBES (George).—THE TRANSIT OF VENUS. Crown 8vo. 3s. 6d.

FORSYTH (A. R.).—A TREATISE ON DIFFERENTIAL EQUATIONS. Demy 8vo. 14s.

FOSTER (Prof. Michael).—A TEXT-BOOK OF PHYSIOLOGY. Illustrated. 5th Edition. 3 Parts. 8vo. Part I., Book I. Blood—The Tissues of Movement, the Vascular Mechanism. 10s. 6d.—Part II., Book II. The Tissues of Chemical Action, with their Respective Mechanisms—Nutrition. 10s. 6d. Part III., Book III. The Central Nervous System and its Instruments. Book IV. The Tissues and Mechanisms of Reproduction.

—— PRIMER OF PHYSIOLOGY. 18mo. 1s.

FOSTER (Prof. Michael) and BALFOUR (F. M.) (the late).—THE ELEMENTS OF EMBRYOLOGY. Edited by ADAM SEDGWICK, M.A., and WALTER HEAPE. Illustrated. 3rd Ed., revised and enlarged. Cr. 8vo. 10s. 6d.

FOSTER (Michael) and LANGLEY (J. N.).—A COURSE OF ELEMENTARY PRACTICAL PHYSIOLOGY AND HISTOLOGY. 6th Edition, enlarged. Crown 8vo. 7s. 6d.

FOTHERGILL (Dr. J. Milner).—THE PRACTITIONER'S HANDBOOK OF TREATMENT; OR, THE PRINCIPLES OF THERAPEUTICS. 3rd Edition, enlarged. 8vo. 16s.

—— THE ANTAGONISM OF THERAPEUTIC AGENTS, AND WHAT IT TEACHES. Cr. 8vo. 6s.

—— FOOD FOR THE INVALID, THE CONVALESCENT, THE DYSPEPTIC, AND THE GOUTY. 2nd Edition. Crown 8vo. 3s. 6d.

FOWLE (Rev. T. W.).—THE POOR LAW. Cr. 8vo. 3s. 6d. [English Citizen Series.

—— A NEW ANALOGY BETWEEN REVEALED RELIGION AND THE COURSE AND CONSTITUTION OF NATURE. Crown 8vo. 6s.

FOWLER (Rev. Thomas).—LOCKE. Crown 8vo. 1s. 6d.; sewed, 1s.

—— PROGRESSIVE MORALITY: AN ESSAY IN ETHICS. Crown 8vo. 5s.

FOWLER (W. W.).—TALES OF THE BIRDS. Illustrated. Crown 8vo. 3s. 6d.

FOWLER (W. W.).—A Year with the Birds. Illustrated. Crown 8vo. 3s. 6d.

FOX (Dr. Wilson). On the Artificial Production of Tubercle in the Lower Animals. With Plates. 4to. 5s. 6d.

—— On the Treatment of Hyperpyrexia, as Illustrated in Acute Articular Rheumatism by means of the External Application of Cold. 8vo. 2s. 6d.

FRAMJI (Dosabhai). — History of the Parsis: including their Manners, Customs, Religion, and Present Position. With Illustrations. 2 vols. Medium 8vo. 36s.

FRANKLAND (Prof. Percy).—A Handbook of Agricultural Chemical Analysis. Founded upon "Leitfaden für die Agricultur-Chemische Analyse," von Dr. F. Krocker. Crown 8vo. 7s. 6d.

FRASER — HUGHES. — James Fraser, Second Bishop of Manchester: A Memoir. By T. Hughes. Crown 8vo. 6s.

FRASER-TYTLER. — Songs in Minor Keys. By C. C. Fraser-Tytler (Mrs. Edward Liddell). 2nd Ed. 18mo. 6s.

FRASER.—Sermons. By the Right Rev. James Fraser, D.D., Second Bishop of Manchester. Edited by Rev. John W. Diggle. 2 vols. Crown 8vo. 6s. each.

FRATERNITY: A Romance. 2 vols. Cr. 8vo. 21s.

FRAZER (J. G.).—The Golden Bough : A Study in Comparative Religion. 2 vols. 8vo. 28s.

FREDERICK (Mrs.).—Hints to Housewives on Several Points, particularly on the Preparation of Economical and Tasteful Dishes. Crown 8vo. 1s.

FREEMAN (Prof. E. A.).—History of the Cathedral Church of Wells. Crown 8vo. 3s. 6d.

—— Old English History. With 5 Col. Maps. 9th Edition, revised. Extra fcp. 8vo. 6s.

—— Historical Essays. First Series. 4th Edition. 8vo. 10s. 6d.

—— Historical Essays. Second Series. 3rd Edition. With Additional Essays. 8vo. 10s. 6d.

—— —— Third Series. 8vo. 12s.

—— The Growth of the English Constitution from the Earliest Times. 5th Edition. Crown 8vo. 5s.

—— General Sketch of European History. With Maps, &c. 18mo. 3s. 6d.

—— Europe. 18mo. 1s. [Literature Primers.

—— Comparative Politics. Lectures at the Royal Institution. To which is added "The Unity of History." 8vo. 14s.

—— Historical and Architectural Sketches: Chiefly Italian. Illustrated by the Author. Crown 8vo. 10s. 6d.

—— Subject and Neighbour Lands of Venice. Illustrated. Crown 8vo. 10s. 6d.

—— English Towns and Districts. A Series of Addresses and Essays. 8vo. 14s.

FREEMAN (Prof. E. A.).—The Office of the Historical Professor. Inaugural Lecture at Oxford. Crown 8vo. 2s.

—— Disestablishment and Disendowment. What are they? 4th Edition. Crown 8vo. 1s.

—— Greater Greece and Greater Britain: George Washington the Expander of England. With an Appendix on Imperial Federation. Cr. 8vo. 3s. 6d.

—— The Methods of Historical Study. Eight Lectures at Oxford. 8vo. 10s. 6d.

—— The Chief Periods of European History. Six Lectures read in the University of Oxford, with an Essay on Greek Cities under Roman Rule. 8vo. 10s. 6d.

—— Four Oxford Lectures, 1887. Fifty Years of European History—Teutonic Conquest in Gaul and Britain. 8vo. 5s.

—— William the Conqueror. Crown 8vo. 2s. 6d. [Twelve English Statesmen.

FRENCH COURSE.—See p. 37.

FRENCH READINGS FROM ROMAN HISTORY. Selected from various Authors. With Notes by C. Colbeck. 18mo. 4s. 6d.

FRIEDMANN (Paul).—Anne Boleyn. A Chapter of English History, 1527—36. 2 vols. 8vo. 28s.

FROST (Percival).—An Elementary Treatise on Curve Tracing. 8vo. 12s.

—— The First Three Sections of Newton's Principia. 3rd Edition. 8vo. 12s.

—— Solid Geometry. 3rd Edition. 8vo. 16s.

—— Hints for the Solution of Problems in the Third Edition of Solid Geometry. 8vo. 8s. 6d.

FROUDE (J. A.).—Bunyan. Crown 8vo. 1s. 6d. ; sewed, 1s.

FURNIVALL (F. J.).—Le Morte Arthur. Edited from the Harleian MS. 2252, in the British Museum. Fcp. 8vo. 7s. 6d.

FYFFE (C. A.).—Greece. 18mo. 1s.

GAIRDNER (Jas.).—Henry VII. Crown 8vo. 2s. 6d.

GALTON (Francis). — Meteorographica; or, Methods of Mapping the Weather. 4to. 9s.

—— English Men of Science: their Nature and Nurture. 8vo. 8s. 6d.

—— Inquiries into Human Faculty and its Development. 8vo. 16s.

—— Record of Family Faculties. Consisting of Tabular Forms and Directions for Entering Data. 4to. 2s. 6d.

—— Life History Album: Being a Personal Note-book, combining the chief advantages of a Diary, Photograph Album, a Register of Height, Weight, and other Anthropometrical Observations, and a Record of Illnesses. 4to. 3s. 6d.—Or, with Cards of Wools for Testing Colour Vision. 4s. 6d.

—— Natural Inheritance. 8vo. 9s.

GAMGEE (Prof. Arthur).—A Text-book of the Physiological Chemistry of the Animal Body, including an account of the Chemical Changes occurring in Disease. Vol. I. Med. 8vo. 18s.

2

GANGUILLET (E.) and KUTTER (W. R.).—A GENERAL FORMULA FOR THE UNIFORM FLOW OF WATER IN RIVERS AND OTHER CHANNELS. Translated by RUDOLPH HERING and JOHN C. TRAUTWINE, Jun. 8vo. 17s.

GARDNER (Percy).—SAMOS AND SAMIAN COINS. An Essay. 8vo. 7s. 6d.

GARNETT (R.).—IDYLLS AND EPIGRAMS. Chiefly from the Greek Anthology. Fcp. 8vo. 2s. 6d.

GASKOIN (Mrs. Herman). — CHILDREN'S TREASURY OF BIBLE STORIES. 18mo. 1s. each.—Part I. Old Testament ; II. New Testament ; III. Three Apostles.

GEDDES (Prof. William D.).—THE PROBLEM OF THE HOMERIC POEMS. 8vo. 14s.

—— FLOSCULI GRÆCI BOREALES, SIVE ANTHOLOGIA GRÆCA ABERDONENSIS CONTEXUIT GULIELMUS D. GEDDES. Cr. 8vo. 6s.

—— THE PHAEDO OF PLATO. Edited with Introduction and Notes. 2nd Ed. 8vo. 8s. 6d.

GEIKIE (Archibald).—PRIMER OF PHYSICAL GEOGRAPHY. With Illustrations. 18mo. 1s.

—— PRIMER OF GEOLOGY. Illust. 18mo. 1s.

—— ELEMENTARY LESSONS IN PHYSICAL GEOGRAPHY. With Illustrations. Fcp. 8vo. 4s. 6d.—QUESTIONS ON THE SAME. 1s. 6d.

—— OUTLINES OF FIELD GEOLOGY. With numerous Illustrations. Crown 8vo. 3s. 6d.

—— TEXT-BOOK OF GEOLOGY. Illustrated. 2nd Edition. 7th Thousand. Med. 8vo. 28s.

—— CLASS-BOOK OF GEOLOGY. Illustrated. 2nd Edition. Crown 8vo 4s. 6d.

—— GEOLOGICAL SKETCHES AT HOME AND ABROAD. With Illustrations. 8vo. 10s. 6d.

—— THE SCENERY OF SCOTLAND. Viewed in connection with its Physical Geology. 2nd Edition. Crown 8vo. 12s. 6d.

—— THE TEACHING OF GEOGRAPHY. A Practical Handbook for the use of Teachers. Globe 8vo. 2s.

—— GEOGRAPHY OF THE BRITISH ISLES. 18mo. 1s.

GEOMETRY, SYLLABUS OF PLANE. Corresponding to Euclid I.--VI. Prepared by the Association for the Improvement of Geometrical Teaching. New Edition. Crown 8vo. 1s.

GEOMETRY, SYLLABUS OF MODERN PLANE. Association for the Improvement of Geometrical Teaching. Crown 8vo, sewed. 1s.

GIBBON. By J. C. MORISON. Crown 8vo. 1s. 6d. ; sewed, 1s.

GILES (P.). — MANUAL OF GREEK AND LATIN PHILOLOGY. Cr. 8vo. [In the Press.

GILMAN (N. P.). — PROFIT-SHARING BETWEEN EMPLOYER AND EMPLOYÉ. A Study in the Evolution of the Wages System. Crown 8vo. 7s. 6d.

GILMORE (Rev. John).—STORM WARRIORS ; OR, LIFEBOAT WORK ON THE GOODWIN SANDS. Crown 8vo. 3s. 6d.

GLADSTONE (Rt. Hon. W. E.).—HOMERIC SYNCHRONISM. An Inquiry into the Time and Place of Homer. Crown 8vo. 6s.

—— PRIMER OF HOMER. 18mo. 1s.

GLADSTONE (J. H.).— SPELLING REFORM FROM AN EDUCATIONAL POINT OF VIEW. 3rd Edition. Crown 8vo. 1s. 6d.

GLADSTONE (J. H.) and TRIBE (A.).—THE CHEMISTRY OF THE SECONDARY BATTERIES OF PLANTÉ AND FAURE. Crown 8vo. 2s. 6d.

GLAISTER (Elizabeth). — NEEDLEWORK. Crown 8vo. 2s. 6d.

GLOBE EDITIONS. Gl. 8vo. 3s. 6d. each.

THE COMPLETE WORKS OF WILLIAM SHAKESPEARE. Edited by W. G. CLARK and W. ALDIS WRIGHT.

MORTE D'ARTHUR. Sir Thomas Malory's Book of King Arthur and of his Noble Knights of the Round Table. The Edition of Caxton, revised for modern use. By Sir E. STRACHEY, Bart.

THE POETICAL WORKS OF SIR WALTER SCOTT. With Essay by Prof. PALGRAVE.

THE POETICAL WORKS AND LETTERS OF ROBERT BURNS. Edited, with Life and Glossarial Index, by ALEXANDER SMITH.

THE ADVENTURES OF ROBINSON CRUSOE. With Introduction by HENRY KINGSLEY.

GOLDSMITH'S MISCELLANEOUS WORKS. Edited by Prof. MASSON.

POPE'S POETICAL WORKS. Edited, with Memoir and Notes, by Prof. WARD.

SPENSER'S COMPLETE WORKS. Edited by R. MORRIS. Memoir by J. W. HALES.

DRYDEN'S POETICAL WORKS. A revised Text and Notes. By W. D. CHRISTIE.

COWPER'S POETICAL WORKS. Edited by the Rev. W. BENHAM, B.D.

VIRGIL'S WORKS. Rendered into English by JAMES LONSDALE and S. LEE.

HORACE'S WORKS. Rendered into English by JAMES LONSDALE and S. LEE.

MILTON'S POETICAL WORKS. Edited, with Introduction, &c., by Prof. MASSON.

GLOBE READERS, THE.—A New Series of Reading Books for Standards I.—VI. Selected, arranged, and Edited by A. F. MURISON, sometime English Master at Aberdeen Grammar School. With Original Illustrations. Globe 8vo.

Primer I.	...	...	(48 pp.)	3d.
Primer II.	...	...	(48 pp.)	3d.
Book I.	...	...	(96 pp.)	6d.
Book II.	...	...	(136 pp.)	9d.
Book III.	...	...	(232 pp.)	1s. 3d.
Book IV.	...	...	(328 pp.)	1s. 9d.
Book V.	...	...	(416 pp.)	2s.
Book VI.	...	...	(448 pp.)	2s. 6d.

GLOBE READERS, THE SHORTER. — A New Series of Reading Books for Standards I.—VI. Edited by A. F. MURISON. Gl. 8vo.

Primer I.	...	...	(48 pp.)	3d.
Primer II.	...	...	(48 pp.)	3d.
Standard I.	...	...	(92 pp.)	6d.
Standard II.	...	...	(124 pp.)	9d.
Standard III.	...	...	(178 pp.)	1s.
Standard IV.	...	...	(182 pp.)	1s.
Standard V.	...	...	(216 pp.)	1s. 3d.
Standard VI.	...	...	(228 pp.)	1s. 6d.

*** This Series has been abridged from the "Globe Readers" to meet the demand for smaller reading books.

LIST OF PUBLICATIONS.

GLOBE READINGS FROM STANDARD AUTHORS. Globe 8vo.

COWPER'S TASK: An Epistle to Joseph Hill, Esq.; TIROCINIUM, or a Review of the Schools; and the HISTORY OF JOHN GILPIN. Edited, with Notes, by Rev. WILLIAM BENHAM, B.D. 1s.

GOLDSMITH'S VICAR OF WAKEFIELD. With a Memoir of Goldsmith by Prof. MASSON. 1s.

LAMB'S (CHARLES) TALES FROM SHAKSPEARE. Edited, with Preface, by Rev. ALFRED AINGER, M.A. 2s.

SCOTT'S (SIR WALTER) LAY OF THE LAST MINSTREL; and the LADY OF THE LAKE. Edited by Prof. F. T. PALGRAVE. 1s.

MARMION; and THE LORD OF THE ISLES. By the same Editor. 1s.

THE CHILDREN'S GARLAND FROM THE BEST POETS. Selected and arranged by COVENTRY PATMORE. 2s.

A BOOK OF GOLDEN DEEDS OF ALL TIMES AND ALL COUNTRIES. Gathered and narrated anew by CHARLOTTE M. YONGE. 2s.

GODFRAY (Hugh). — AN ELEMENTARY TREATISE ON LUNAR THEORY. 2nd Edition. Crown 8vo. 5s. 6d.

—— A TREATISE ON ASTRONOMY, FOR THE USE OF COLLEGES AND SCHOOLS. 8vo. 12s. 6d.

GOETHE — CARLYLE. — CORRESPONDENCE BETWEEN GOETHE AND CARLYLE. Edited by C. E. NORTON. Crown 8vo. 9s.

GOETHE'S LIFE. By Prof. HEINRICH DÜNTZER. Translated by T. W. LYSTER. 2 vols. Crown 8vo. 21s.

GOETHE. — FAUST. Translated into English Verse by JOHN STUART BLACKIE. 2nd Edition. Crown 8vo. 9s.

—— Part I. Edited, with Introduction and Notes; followed by an Appendix on Part II., by JANE LEE. 18mo. 4s. 6d.

—— REYNARD THE FOX. Trans. into English Verse by A. D. AINSLIE. Crn. 8vo. 7s. 6d.

—— GÖTZ VON BERLICHINGEN. Edited by H. A. BULL, M.A. 18mo. 2s.

GOLDEN TREASURY SERIES. — Uniformly printed in 18mo, with Vignette Titles by Sir J. E. MILLAIS, Sir NOEL PATON, T. WOOLNER, W. HOLMAN HUNT, ARTHUR HUGHES, &c. Engraved on Steel. Bound in extra cloth. 4s. 6d. each.

THE GOLDEN TREASURY OF THE BEST SONGS AND LYRICAL POEMS IN THE ENGLISH LANGUAGE. Selected and arranged, with Notes, by Prof. F. T. PALGRAVE.

THE CHILDREN'S GARLAND FROM THE BEST POETS. Selected by COVENTRY PATMORE.

THE BOOK OF PRAISE. From the best English Hymn Writers. Selected by ROUNDELL, EARL OF SELBORNE.

THE FAIRY BOOK: THE BEST POPULAR FAIRY STORIES. Selected by the Author of "John Halifax, Gentleman."

THE BALLAD BOOK. A Selection of the Choicest British Ballads. Edited by WILLIAM ALLINGHAM.

THE JEST BOOK. The Choicest Anecdotes and Sayings. Arranged by MARK LEMON.

BACON'S ESSAYS AND COLOURS OF GOOD AND EVIL. With Notes and Glossarial Index by W. ALDIS WRIGHT, M.A.

GOLDEN TREASURY SERIES—contd.

THE PILGRIM'S PROGRESS FROM THIS WORLD TO THAT WHICH IS TO COME. By JOHN BUNYAN.

THE SUNDAY BOOK OF POETRY FOR THE YOUNG. Selected by C. F. ALEXANDER.

A BOOK OF GOLDEN DEEDS OF ALL TIMES AND ALL COUNTRIES. By the Author of "The Heir of Redclyffe."

THE ADVENTURES OF ROBINSON CRUSOE. Edited by J. W. CLARK, M.A.

THE REPUBLIC OF PLATO. Translated by J. LL. DAVIES, M.A., and D. J. VAUGHAN.

THE SONG BOOK. Words and Tunes Selected and arranged by JOHN HULLAH.

LA LYRE FRANÇAISE. Selected and arranged, with Notes, by G. MASSON.

TOM BROWN'S SCHOOL DAYS. By AN OLD BOY.

A BOOK OF WORTHIES. By the Author of "The Heir of Redclyffe."

GUESSES AT TRUTH. By TWO BROTHERS.

THE CAVALIER AND HIS LADY. Selections from the Works of the First Duke and Duchess of Newcastle. With an Introductory Essay by EDWARD JENKINS.

SCOTTISH SONG. Compiled by MARY CARLYLE AITKEN.

DEUTSCHE LYRIK. The Golden Treasury of the best German Lyrical Poems. Selected by Dr. BUCHHEIM.

CHRYSOMELA. A Selection from the Lyrical Poems of Robert Herrick. By Prof. F. T. PALGRAVE.

POEMS OF PLACES—ENGLAND AND WALES. Edited by H. W. LONGFELLOW. 2 vols.

SELECTED POEMS OF MATTHEW ARNOLD.

THE STORY OF THE CHRISTIANS AND MOORS IN SPAIN. By CHARLOTTE M. YONGE.

LAMB'S TALES FROM SHAKSPEARE. Edited by Rev. ALFRED AINGER, M.A.

SHAKESPEARE'S SONGS AND SONNETS. Ed. with Notes, by Prof. F. T. PALGRAVE.

POEMS OF WORDSWORTH. Chosen and Edited by MATTHEW ARNOLD.
Large Paper Edition. 9s.

POEMS OF SHELLEY. Ed. by S. A. BROOKE.
Large Paper Edition. 12s. 6d.

THE ESSAYS OF JOSEPH ADDISON. Chosen and Edited by JOHN RICHARD GREEN.

POETRY OF BYRON. Chosen and arranged by MATTHEW ARNOLD.
Large Paper Edition. 9s.

SIR THOMAS BROWNE'S RELIGIO MEDICI; LETTER TO A FRIEND, &c., AND CHRISTIAN MORALS. Ed. by W. A. GREENHILL, M.D.

THE SPEECHES AND TABLE-TALK OF THE PROPHET MOHAMMAD. Translated by STANLEY LANE-POOLE.

SELECTIONS FROM WALTER SAVAGE LANDOR. Edited by SIDNEY COLVIN.

SELECTIONS FROM COWPER'S POEMS. With an Introduction by Mrs. OLIPHANT.

LETTERS OF WILLIAM COWPER. Edited, With Introduction, by Rev. W. BENHAM.

THE POETICAL WORKS OF JOHN KEATS. Edited by Prof. F. T. PALGRAVE.

LYRICAL POEMS OF LORD TENNYSON. Selected and Annotated by Prof. FRANCIS T. PALGRAVE.
Large Paper Edition. 9s.

IN MEMORIAM. By LORD TENNYSON, Poet Laureate.
Large Paper Edition. 9s.

GOLDEN TREASURY SERIES—*contd.*
THE TRIAL AND DEATH OF SOCRATES Being the Euthyphron, Apology, Crito and Phaedo of Plato. Translated by F. J. CHURCH.
A BOOK OF GOLDEN THOUGHTS. By HENRY ATTWELL.
PLATO.—PHAEDRUS, LYSIS, AND PROTAGORAS. A New Translation, by J. WRIGHT.
THEOCRITUS, BION, AND MOSCHUS. Rendered into English Prose by ANDREW LANG. Large Paper Edition. 9s.
BALLADS, LYRICS, AND SONNETS. From the Works of HENRY W. LONGFELLOW.
DEUTSCHE BALLADEN. The Golden Treasury of the Best German Ballads. Selected and arranged by Dr. BUCHHEIM. [*In the Press.*
GOLDEN TREASURY PSALTER. THE STUDENT'S EDITION. Being an Edition with briefer Notes of "The Psalms Chronologically Arranged by Four Friends." 18mo. 3s. 6d.
GOLDSMITH. By WILLIAM BLACK. Crown 8vo. 1s. 6d.; sewed, 1s.
GOLDSMITH.— MISCELLANEOUS WORKS. With Biographical Essay by Prof. MASSON. Globe 8vo. 3s. 6d.
—— ESSAYS OF OLIVER GOLDSMITH. Edited by C. D. YONGE, M.A. Fcp. 8vo. 2s. 6d.
—— THE TRAVELLER AND THE DESERTED VILLAGE. With Notes by J. W. HALES, M.A. Crown 8vo. 6d.
—— THE TRAVELLER AND THE DESERTED VILLAGE. Edited, with Introduction and Notes, by Prof. A. BARRETT, M.A. Gl. 8vo. 1s. 6d.
—— THE VICAR OF WAKEFIELD. With a Memoir of Goldsmith by Prof. MASSON. Globe 8vo. 1s.
GONE TO TEXAS. LETTERS FROM OUR BOYS. Edited, with Preface, by THOMAS HUGHES, Q.C. Crown 8vo. 4s. 6d.
GOODALE (G. L.).—PHYSIOLOGICAL BOTANY. Part I. OUTLINES OF THE HISTORY OF PHÆNOGAMOUS PLANTS; II. VEGETABLE PHYSIOLOGY. 6th Edition. 8vo. 10s. 6d.
GOODWIN (Prof. W. W.).—SYNTAX OF THE GREEK MOODS AND TENSES. 8vo. 14s.
—— A GREEK GRAMMAR. Crown 8vo. 6s.
—— A SCHOOL GREEK GRAMMAR. Crown 8vo. 3s. 6d.
GORDON (General). A SKETCH. By REGINALD H. BARNES. Crown 8vo. 1s.
—— LETTERS OF GENERAL C. G. GORDON TO HIS SISTER, M. A. GORDON. 4th Edition. Crown 8vo. 3s. 6d.
GORDON. By Colonel Sir WILLIAM BUTLER. With Portrait. Crown 8vo. 2s. 6d.
GORDON (Lady Duff).— LAST LETTERS FROM EGYPT, TO WHICH ARE ADDED LETTERS FROM THE CAPE. 2nd Edition. Cr. 8vo. 9s.
GOSCHEN (Rt. Hon. George J.).—REPORTS AND SPEECHES ON LOCAL TAXATION. 8vo. 5s.
GOSSE (E.).—GRAY. Cr. 8vo. 1s. 6d.; swd., 1s.
GOW (Dr. James).—A COMPANION TO SCHOOL CLASSICS. Illustrated. 2nd Ed. Cr. 8vo. 6s.
GOYEN (P.).- HIGHER ARITHMETIC AND ELEMENTARY MENSURATION, for the Senior Classes of Schools and Candidates preparing for Public Examinations. Globe 8vo. 5s.

GRAHAM (David).—KING JAMES I. An Historical Tragedy. Globe 8vo. 7s.
GRAHAM (John W.). NEÆRA: A TALE OF ANCIENT ROME. Crown 8vo. 6s.
GRAND'HOMME. — CUTTING OUT AND DRESSMAKING. From the French of Mdlle. E. GRAND'HOMME. 18mo. 1s.
GRAY (Prof. Andrew).—THE THEORY AND PRACTICE OF ABSOLUTE MEASUREMENTS IN ELECTRICITY AND MAGNETISM. 2 vols. Crown 8vo. Vol. I. 12s. 6d.
—— ABSOLUTE MEASUREMENTS IN ELECTRICITY AND MAGNETISM. 2nd Edition, revised. Fcp. 8vo. 5s. 6d.
GRAY (Prof. Asa).—STRUCTURAL BOTANY; OR, ORGANOGRAPHY ON THE BASIS OF MORPHOLOGY. 8vo. 10s. 6d.
—— THE SCIENTIFIC PAPERS OF ASA GRAY. Selected by CHARLES S. SARGENT. 2 vols. 8vo. 21s.
GRAY (Thomas).—Edited by EDMUND GOSSE. In 4 vols. Globe 8vo. 20s.—Vol. I. POEMS, JOURNALS, AND ESSAYS.—II. LETTERS.—III. LETTERS. — IV. NOTES ON ARISTOPHANES; AND PLATO.
GRAY. By EDMUND GOSSE. Crown 8vo. 1s. 6d.; sewed, 1s.
GREAVES (John).—A TREATISE ON ELEMENTARY STATICS. 2nd Ed. Cr. 8vo. 6s. 6d.
—— STATICS FOR BEGINNERS. Gl. 8vo. 3s. 6d.
GREEK ELEGIAC POETS. FROM CALLINUS TO CALLIMACHUS. Selected and Edited by Rev. H. KYNASTON. 18mo. 1s. 6d.
GREEK TESTAMENT. THE NEW TESTAMENT IN THE ORIGINAL GREEK. The Text revised by Bishop WESTCOTT, D.D., and Prof. F. J. A. HORT, D.D. 2 vols. Crn. 8vo. 10s. 6d. each.—Vol. I. Text; II. Introduction and Appendix.
—— THE NEW TESTAMENT IN THE ORIGINAL GREEK, FOR SCHOOLS. The Text revised by Bishop WESTCOTT, D.D., and F. J. A. HORT, D.D. 12mo. cloth. 4s. 6d.—18mo. roan, red edges. 5s. 6d.; morocco, 6s. 6d.
—— SCHOOL READINGS IN THE GREEK TESTAMENT. Being the Outlines of the Life of our Lord as given by St. Mark, with additions from the Text of the other Evangelists. Edited, with Notes and Vocabulary, by A. CALVERT, M.A. Fcp. 8vo. 4s. 6d.
—— THE GREEK TESTAMENT AND THE ENGLISH VERSION, A COMPANION TO. By PHILIP SCHAFF, D.D. Crown 8vo. 12s.
—— THE GOSPEL ACCORDING TO ST. MATTHEW. Greek Text as Revised by Bishop WESTCOTT and Dr. HORT. With Introduction and Notes by Rev. A. SLOMAN, M.A. Fcp. 8vo. 2s. 6d.
—— THE GOSPEL ACCORDING TO ST. LUKE. The Greek Text as revised by Bp. WESTCOTT and Dr. HORT. With Introduction and Notes by Rev. J. BOND, M.A. Fcp. 8vo.
—— THE ACTS OF THE APOSTLES. Being the Greek Text as Revised by Bishop WESTCOTT and Dr. HORT. With Explanatory Notes by T. E. PAGE, M.A. Fcp. 8vo. 4s. 6d.

LIST OF PUBLICATIONS. 21

GREEN (John Richard).—A SHORT HISTORY OF THE ENGLISH PEOPLE. With Coloured Maps, Genealogical Tables, and Chronological Annals. New Edition, thoroughly revised. Cr. 8vo, 8s. 6d. 150th Thousand. Also the same in Four Parts. With the corresponding portion of Mr. Tait's "Analysis." 3s. each. Part I. 607 1265. II. 1204 1553. III. 1540—1689. IV. 1660—1873.

—— HISTORY OF THE ENGLISH PEOPLE. In 4 vols. 8vo. Vol. I. With 8 Coloured Maps. 16s.— II. 16s.—III. With 4 Maps. 16s.— IV. With Maps and Index. 16s.

—— THE MAKING OF ENGLAND. With Maps. 8vo. 16s.

—— THE CONQUEST OF ENGLAND. With Maps and Portrait. 8vo. 18s.

—— READINGS IN ENGLISH HISTORY. In 3 Parts. Fcp. 8vo. 1s. 6d. each.

—— ESSAYS OF JOSEPH ADDISON. 18mo. 4s. 6d.

GREEN (J. R.) and GREEN (Alice S.).— A SHORT GEOGRAPHY OF THE BRITISH ISLANDS. With 28 Maps. Fcp. 8vo. 3s. 6d.

GREEN (Mrs. J. R.).—HENRY II. Crown 8vo. 2s. 6d.

GREEN (W. S.).—AMONG THE SELKIRK GLACIERS. Crown 8vo. 7s. 6d.

GREENHILL (Prof. A. G.).—DIFFERENTIAL AND INTEGRAL CALCULUS. Cr. 8vo. 7s. 6d.

GREENWOOD (Jessy E.). — THE MOON MAIDEN: AND OTHER STORIES. Crown 8vo. 3s. 6d.

GREENWOOD (J. G.).—THE ELEMENTS OF GREEK GRAMMAR. Crown 8vo. 5s. 6d.

GRIFFITHS (W. H.).—LESSONS ON PRESCRIPTIONS AND THE ART OF PRESCRIBING. New Edition. 18mo. 3s. 6d.

GRIMM'S FAIRY TALES. A Selection from the Household Stories. Translated from the German by LUCY CRANE, and done into Pictures by WALTER CRANE. Crown 8vo. 6s.

GRIMM.—KINDER-UND-HAUSMÄRCHEN. Selected and Edited, with Notes and Vocabulary, by G. E. FASNACHT. Gl. 8vo. 2s. 6d.

GUEST (M. J.).—LECTURES ON THE HISTORY OF ENGLAND. Crown 8vo. 6s.

GUEST (Dr. E.).—ORIGINES CELTICÆ (A Fragment) and other Contributions to the History of Britain. Maps. 2 vols. 8vo. 32s.

GROVE (Sir George).—A DICTIONARY OF MUSIC AND MUSICIANS, A.D. 1450—1889. Edited by Sir GEORGE GROVE, D.C.L. In 4 vols. 8vo, 21s. each. With Illustrations in Music Type and Woodcut.— Also published in Parts. Parts I.—XIV., XIX.—XXII. 3s. 6d. each; XV. XVI. 7s.; XVII. XVIII. 7s.; XXIII.—XXV., Appendix, Edited by J. A. FULLER MAITLAND, M.A. 9s. [Cloth cases for binding the volumes, 1s. each.]

— — A COMPLETE INDEX TO THE ABOVE. By Mrs. E. WODEHOUSE. 8vo. 7s. 6d.

—— PRIMER OF GEOGRAPHY. Maps. 18mo. 1s.

GUILLEMIN (Amédée).—THE FORCES OF NATURE. A Popular Introduction to the Study of Physical Phenomena. 455 Woodcuts. Royal 8vo. 21s.

GUILLEMIN (A.). THE APPLICATIONS OF PHYSICAL FORCES. With Coloured Plates and Illustrations. Royal 8vo. 21s.

—— ELECTRICITY AND MAGNETISM. A Popular Treatise. Translated and Edited, with Additions and Notes, by Prof. SYLVANUS P. THOMPSON. Royal 8vo. [In the Press.

GUIDE TO THE UNPROTECTED, In Every-day Matters relating to Property and Income. 5th Ed. Extra fcp. 8vo. 3s. 6d.

GUIZOT.—GREAT CHRISTIANS OF FRANCE. ST. LOUIS AND CALVIN. Crown 8vo. 6s.

GUNTON (George).—WEALTH AND PROGRESS. Crown 8vo. 6s.

HADLEY (Prof. James).—ESSAYS, PHILOLOGICAL AND CRITICAL. 8vo. 14s.

HADLEY—ALLEN.—A GREEK GRAMMAR FOR SCHOOLS AND COLLEGES. By Prof. JAMES HADLEY. Revised and in part Rewritten by Prof. FREDERIC DE FOREST ALLEN. Crown 8vo. 6s.

HAILSTONE (H.). - NOVAE ARUNDINES; OR, NEW MARSH MELODIES. Fcap. 8vo. 3s. 6d.

HALES (Prof. J. W.). - LONGER ENGLISH POEMS, with Notes, Philological and Explanatory, and an Introduction on the Teaching of English. 12th Edition. Extra fcp. 8vo. 4s. 6d.

HALL (H. S.) and KNIGHT (S. R.).—ELEMENTARY ALGEBRA FOR SCHOOLS. 5th Ed., revised. Gl. 8vo. 3s. 6d. With Answers, 4s. 6d.

—— ALGEBRAICAL EXERCISES AND EXAMINATION PAPERS to accompany "Elementary Algebra." 2nd Edition. Globe 8vo. 2s. 6d.

—— HIGHER ALGEBRA. A Sequel to "Elementary Algebra for Schools." 3rd Edition. Crown 8vo. 7s. 6d.

—— SOLUTIONS OF THE EXAMPLES IN "HIGHER ALGEBRA." Crown 8vo. 10s. 6d.

—— ARITHMETICAL EXERCISES AND EXAMINATION PAPERS. Globe 8vo. 2s. 6d.

HALL (H. S.) and STEVENS (F. H.).— A TEXT-BOOK OF EUCLID'S ELEMENTS. Globe 8vo. Book I. 1s.; I. II. 1s. 6d.; I.— IV. 3s.; III.—VI. 3s.; V. VI. and XI. 2s. 6d.; I.—VI. and XI. 4s. 6d.; XI. 1s.

HALLWARD (R. F.).—FLOWERS OF PARADISE. Music, Verse, Design, Illustration. Royal 4to. 6s.

HALSTED (G. B.).—THE ELEMENTS OF GEOMETRY. 8vo. 12s. 6d.

HAMERTON (P. G.).—THE INTELLECTUAL LIFE. 4th Edition. Crown 8vo. 10s. 6d.

—— ETCHING AND ETCHERS. 3rd Edition, revised. With 48 Plates. Colombier 8vo.

—— THOUGHTS ABOUT ART. New Edition. Crown 8vo. 8s. 6d.

—— HUMAN INTERCOURSE. 4th Edition. Crown 8vo. 8s. 6d.

—— FRENCH AND ENGLISH: A COMPARISON. Crown 8vo. 10s. 6d.

HAMILTON (John). — ON TRUTH AND ERROR. Crown 8vo. 5s.

—— ARTHUR'S SEAT; OR, THE CHURCH OF THE BANNED. Crown 8vo. 6s.

—— ABOVE AND AROUND: THOUGHTS ON GOD AND MAN. 12mo. 2s. 6d.

HAMILTON (Prof. D. J.).—ON THE PATHOLOGY OF BRONCHITIS, CATARRHAL PNEUMONIA, TUBERCLE, AND ALLIED LESIONS OF THE HUMAN LUNG. 8vo. 8s. 6d.
—— A TEXT-BOOK OF PATHOLOGY, SYSTEMATIC AND PRACTICAL. Illustrated. Vol. I. 8vo. 25s.

HANBURY (Daniel). — SCIENCE PAPERS, CHIEFLY PHARMACOLOGICAL AND BOTANICAL. Medium 8vo. 14s.

HANDEL. LIFE OF GEORGE FREDERICK HANDEL. By W. S. ROCKSTRO. Crown 8vo. 10s. 6d.

HARDWICK (Ven. Archdeacon). — CHRIST AND OTHER MASTERS. 6th Edition. Crown 8vo. 10s. 6d.
—— A HISTORY OF THE CHRISTIAN CHURCH. Middle Age. 6th Edition. Edit. by Bishop STUBBS. Crown 8vo. 10s. 6d.
—— A HISTORY OF THE CHRISTIAN CHURCH DURING THE REFORMATION. 9th Edition. Revised by Bishop STUBBS. Cr. 8vo. 10s. 6d.

HARDY (Arthur Sherburne).-- BUT YET A WOMAN. A Novel. Crown 8vo. 4s. 6d.
—— THE WIND OF DESTINY. 2 vols. Globe 8vo. 12s.

HARDY (H. J.). — A LATIN READER FOR THE LOWER FORMS IN SCHOOLS. Globe 8vo. 2s. 6d.

HARDY (Thomas). — THE WOODLANDERS. Crown 8vo. 3s. 6d.
—— WESSEX TALES: STRANGE, LIVELY, AND COMMONPLACE. Crown 8vo. 3s. 6d.

HARE (Julius Charles).—THE MISSION OF THE COMFORTER. New Edition. Edited by Prof. E. H. PLUMPTRE. Crown 8vo. 7s. 6d.
—— THE VICTORY OF FAITH. Edited by Prof. PLUMPTRE, with Introductory Notices by the late Prof. MAURICE and by the late Dean STANLEY. Crown 8vo. 6s. 6d.
—— GUESSES AT TRUTH. By Two Brothers, AUGUSTUS WILLIAM HARE and JULIUS CHARLES HARE. With a Memoir and Two Portraits. 18mo. 4s. 6d.

HARMONIA. By the Author of "Estelle Russell." 3 vols. Crown 8vo. 31s. 6d.

HARPER (Father Thomas). — THE METAPHYSICS OF THE SCHOOL. In 5 vols. Vols. I. and II. 8vo. 18s. each; Vol. III., Part I. 12s.

HARRIS (Rev. G. C.).—SERMONS. With a Memoir by CHARLOTTE M. YONGE, and Portrait. Extra fcp. 8vo. 6s.

HARRISON (Frederic).—THE CHOICE OF BOOKS. Globe 8vo. 6s.
Large Paper Edition. Printed on handmade paper. 15s.
—— OLIVER CROMWELL. Crown 8vo. 2s. 6d.

HARRISON (Miss Jane) and VERRALL (Mrs.).—MYTHOLOGY AND MONUMENTS OF ANCIENT ATHENS. Illustrated. Cr. 8vo. 16s.

HARTE (Bret).—CRESSY: A Novel. Crown 8vo. 3s. 6d.
—— THE HERITAGE OF DEDLOW MARSH: AND OTHER TALES. Crown 8vo. 3s. 6d.

HARTLEY (Prof. W. Noel).—A COURSE OF QUANTITATIVE ANALYSIS FOR STUDENTS. Globe 8vo. 5s.

HARWOOD (George).—DISESTABLISHMENT; OR, A DEFENCE OF THE PRINCIPLE OF A NATIONAL CHURCH. 8vo. 12s.
—— THE COMING DEMOCRACY. Cr. 8vo. 6s.
—— FROM WITHIN. Crown 8vo. 6s.

HASTINGS (WARREN). By Sir ALFRED LYALL. With Portrait. Crown 8vo. 2s. 6d.

HAUFF.—DIE KARAVANE. Edited, with Notes and Vocabulary, by HERMAN HAGER, Ph. D. Globe 8vo. 3s.

HAVELOCK (SIR HENRY). By ARCHIBALD FORBES. Portrait. Crn. 8vo. 2s. 6d.

HAWTHORNE (Nathaniel). By HENRY JAMES. Crown 8vo. 1s. 6d.; sewed, 1s.

HAYWARD (R. B.).—THE ELEMENTS OF SOLID GEOMETRY. Globe 8vo. 3s.

HEARD (Rev. W. A.).—A SECOND GREEK EXERCISE BOOK. Globe 8vo. 2s. 6d.

HEINE. SELECTIONS FROM THE REISEBILDER AND OTHER PROSE WORKS. Edited by C. COLBECK, M.A. 18mo. 2s. 6d.

HELLENIC STUDIES, THE JOURNAL OF.—Vol. I. 8vo. With Plates of Illustrations. 30s.— Vol. II. 8vo. 30s. With Plates of Illustrations. Or in 2 Parts, 15s. each.— Vol. III. 2 Parts. 8vo. With Plates of Illustrations. 15s. each.—Vol. IV. 2 Parts. With Plates. Part I. 15s. Part II. 21s. Or complete, 30s.—Vol. V. With Plates. 30s.—Vol. VI. With Plates. Part I. 15s. Part II. 15s. Or complete, 30s.—Vol. VII. Part I. 15s. Part II. 15s. Or complete, 30s.—Vol. VIII. Part I. 15s. Part II. 15s.— Vol. IX. 2 Parts. 15s. each.—Vol. X. 30s.—Vol. XI. Pt. I. 15s.
The Journal will be sold at a reduced price to Libraries wishing to subscribe, but official application must in each case be made to the Council. Information on this point, and upon the conditions of Membership, may be obtained on application to the Hon. Sec., Mr. George Macmillan, 29, Bedford Street, Covent Garden.

HELPS.—ESSAYS WRITTEN IN THE INTERVALS OF BUSINESS. Edited by F. J. ROWE, M.A., and W. T. WEBB, M.A. Globe 8vo. 2s. 6d.

HENRY II. By Mrs. J. R. GREEN. Crown 8vo. 2s. 6d.

HENRY V. By the Rev. A. J. CHURCH. With Portrait. Crown 8vo. 2s. 6d.

HENRY VII. By J. GAIRDNER. Cr. 8vo. 2s. 6d.

HENSLOW (Rev. G.).—THE THEORY OF EVOLUTION OF LIVING THINGS, AND THE APPLICATION OF THE PRINCIPLES OF EVOLUTION TO RELIGION. Crown 8vo. 6s.

HERODOTUS.—Books I.—III. Edited by A. H. SAYCE, M.A. 8vo. 16s.
—— BOOK III. Edited by G. C. MACAULAY, M.A. Fcp. 8vo.
—— BOOK VI. Edit. by Prof. J. STRACHAN, M.A. Fcp. 8vo.
—— BOOK VII. Edited by Mrs. MONTAGU BUTLER. Fcp. 8vo.
—— SELECTIONS FROM BOOKS VII. and VIII. THE EXPEDITION OF XERXES. Edited by A. H. COOKE, M.A. 18mo. 1s. 6d.
—— THE HISTORY. Translated into English, with Notes and Indices, by G. C. MACAULAY, M.A. 2 vols. Crown 8vo. 18s.

LIST OF PUBLICATIONS.

HERRICK. — CHRYSOMELA. A Selection from the Lyrical Poems of ROBERT HERRICK. Arranged, with Notes, by Prof. F. T. PALGRAVE. 18mo. 4s. 6d.

HERTEL (Dr.).—OVERPRESSURE IN HIGH SCHOOLS IN DENMARK. With Introduction by Sir J. CRICHTON-BROWNE. Cr. 8vo. 3s. 6d.

HERVEY (Rt. Rev. Lord Arthur).—THE GENEALOGIES OF OUR LORD AND SAVIOUR JESUS CHRIST. 8vo. 10s. 6d.

HICKS (W. M.).—ELEMENTARY DYNAMICS OF PARTICLES AND SOLIDS. Cr. 8vo. 6s. 6d.

HILL (Florence D.).—CHILDREN OF THE STATE. Ed. by FANNY FOWKE. Cr. 8vo. 6s.

HILL (Octavia).—OUR COMMON LAND, AND OTHER ESSAYS. Extra fcp. 8vo. 3s. 6d.

—— HOMES OF THE LONDON POOR. Sewed. Crown 8vo. 1s.

HIORNS (Arthur H.). PRACTICAL METALLURGY AND ASSAYING. A Text-Book for the use of Teachers, Students, and Assayers. With Illustrations. Globe 8vo. 6s.

—— A TEXT-BOOK OF ELEMENTARY METALLURGY FOR THE USE OF STUDENTS. Gl. 8vo 4s.

—— IRON AND STEEL MANUFACTURE. A Text-Book for Beginners. Illustr. Gl. 8vo. 3s. 6d.

—— MIXED METALS AND METALLIC ALLOYS. Globe 8vo.

HISTORICAL COURSE FOR SCHOOLS. Ed. by EDW. A. FREEMAN, D.C.L. 18mo.
Vol. I. GENERAL SKETCH OF EUROPEAN HISTORY. By E. A. FREEMAN. With Maps, &c. 3s. 6d.
II. HISTORY OF ENGLAND. By EDITH THOMPSON. Coloured Maps. 2s. 6d.
III. HISTORY OF SCOTLAND. By MARGARET MACARTHUR. 2s.
IV. HISTORY OF ITALY. By the Rev. W. HUNT, M.A. With Coloured Maps. 3s. 6d.
V. HISTORY OF GERMANY. By JAMES SIME, M.A. 3s.
VI. HISTORY OF AMERICA. By J. A. DOYLE. With Maps. 4s. 6d.
VII. HISTORY OF EUROPEAN COLONIES. By E. J. PAYNE, M.A. Maps. 4s. 6d.
VIII. HISTORY OF FRANCE. By CHARLOTTE M. YONGE. Maps. 3s. 6d.

HOBART. — ESSAYS AND MISCELLANEOUS WRITINGS OF VERE HENRY, LORD HOBART. With a Biographical Sketch. Edited by MARY, LADY HOBART. 2 vols. 8vo. 25s.

HOBDAY (E.). — VILLA GARDENING. A Handbook for Amateur and Practical Gardeners. Extra crown 8vo. 6s.

HODGSON (F.).—MYTHOLOGY FOR LATIN VERSIFICATION. 6th Edition. Revised by F. C. HODGSON, M.A. 18mo. 3s.

HODGSON. — MEMOIR OF REV. FRANCIS HODGSON, B.D., SCHOLAR, POET, AND DIVINE. By his Son, the Rev. JAMES T. HODGSON, M.A. 2 vols. Crown 8vo. 18s.

HÖFFDING (Prof.).— OUTLINES OF PSYCHOLOGY. Translated by M. E. LOWNDES. Crown 8vo. [In the Press.

HOFMANN (Prof. A. W.).—THE LIFE WORK OF LIEBIG IN EXPERIMENTAL AND PHILOSOPHIC CHEMISTRY. 8vo. 5s.

HOGAN, M.P. Globe 8vo. 2s.

HOLE (Rev. C.).—GENEALOGICAL STEMMA OF THE KINGS OF ENGLAND AND FRANCE. On a Sheet. 1s.

—— A BRIEF BIOGRAPHICAL DICTIONARY. 2nd Edition. 18mo. 4s. 6d.

HOLLAND (Prof. T. E.).—THE TREATY RELATIONS OF RUSSIA AND TURKEY, FROM 1774 TO 1853. Crown 8vo. 2s.

HOLMES (O. W., Jun.).—THE COMMON LAW. 8vo. 12s.

HOMER.—THE ODYSSEY OF HOMER DONE INTO ENGLISH PROSE. By S. H. BUTCHER, M.A., and A. LANG, M.A. 7th Edition. Crown 8vo. 6s.

—— ODYSSEY. Book I. Edited, with Notes and Vocabulary, by Rev. J. BOND, M.A., and Rev. A. S. WALPOLE, M.A. 18mo. 1s. 6d.

—— ODYSSEY. Book IX. Edited by JOHN E. B. MAYOR, M.A. Fcp. 8vo. 2s. 6d.

—— ODYSSEY. THE TRIUMPH OF ODYSSEUS. Books XXI.—XXIV. Edited by S. G. HAMILTON, B.A. Fcp. 8vo. 3s. 6d.

—— THE ODYSSEY OF HOMER. Books I.—XII. Translated into English Verse by the EARL OF CARNARVON. Crown 8vo. 7s. 6d.

—— THE ILIAD. Edited, with English Notes and Introduction, by WALTER LEAF, Litt.D. 2 vols. 8vo. 14s. each.—Vol. I. Bks. I.—XII; Vol. II. Bks. XIII.—XXIV.

—— ILIAD. THE STORY OF ACHILLES. Edited by J. H. PRATT, M.A., and WALTER LEAF, Litt.D. Fcap. 8vo. 6s.

—— ILIAD. Book I. Edited by Rev. J. BOND, M.A., and Rev. A. S. WALPOLE, M.A. With Notes and Vocabulary. 18mo. 1s. 6d.

—— ILIAD. Book XVIII. THE ARMS OF ACHILLES. Edited by Rev. S. R. JAMES, M.A., with Notes and Vocabulary. 18mo. 1s. 6d.

—— ILIAD. Translated into English Prose. By ANDREW LANG, WALTER LEAF, and ERNEST MYERS. Crown 8vo. 12s. 6d.

HON. MISS FERRARD, THE. By the Author of "Hogan, M.P." Globe 8vo. 2s.

HOOKER (Sir J. D.). — THE STUDENT'S FLORA OF THE BRITISH ISLANDS. 3rd Edition. Globe 8vo. 10s. 6d.

—— PRIMER OF BOTANY. 18mo. 1s.

HOOKER (Sir Joseph D.) and BALL (J.).— JOURNAL OF A TOUR IN MAROCCO AND THE GREAT ATLAS. 8vo. 21s.

HOOLE (C. H.).—THE CLASSICAL ELEMENT IN THE NEW TESTAMENT. Considered as a Proof of its Genuineness, with an Appendix on the Oldest Authorities used in the Formation of the Canon. 8vo. 10s. 6d.

HOOPER (G.).—WELLINGTON. With Portrait. Crown 8vo. 2s. 6d.

HOOPER (W. H.) and PHILLIPS (W. C.).— A MANUAL OF MARKS ON POTTERY AND PORCELAIN. 16mo. 4s. 6d.

HOPE (Frances J.).—NOTES AND THOUGHTS ON GARDENS AND WOODLANDS. Cr. 8vo. 6s.

HOPKINS (Ellice).—AUTUMN SWALLOWS: A Book of Lyrics. Extra fcp. 8vo. 6s.

HOPPUS (Mary).—A GREAT TREASON: A Story of the War of Independence. 2 vols. Crown 8vo. 9s.

HORACE.—THE WORKS OF HORACE RENDERED INTO ENGLISH PROSE. By J. LONSDALE and S. LEE. Globe 8vo. 3s. 6d.
—— STUDIES, LITERARY AND HISTORICAL, IN THE ODES OF HORACE. By A. W. VERRALL, Litt.D. 8vo. 8s. 6d.
—— THE ODES OF HORACE IN A METRICAL PARAPHRASE. By R. M. HOVENDEN, B.A. Extra fcap. 8vo. 4s. 6d.
—— LIFE AND CHARACTER: AN EPITOME OF HIS SATIRES AND EPISTLES. By R. M. HOVENDEN, B.A. Extra fcp. 8vo. 4s. 6d.
—— WORD FOR WORD FROM HORACE: The Odes Literally Versified. By W. T. THORNTON, C.B. Crown 8vo. 7s. 6d.
—— ODES. Books I. II. III. and IV. Edited by T. E. PAGE, M.A. With Vocabularies. 18mo. 1s. 6d. each.
—— ODES. Books I.—IV. and CARMEN SECULARE. Edited by T. E. PAGE, M.A. Fcap. 8vo. 6s.; or separately, 2s. each.
—— THE SATIRES. Edited by ARTHUR PALMER, M.A. Fcap. 8vo. 6s.
—— THE EPISTLES AND ARS POETICA. Edited by A. S. WILKINS, Litt.D. Fcp. 8vo. 6s.
—— SELECTIONS FROM THE EPISTLES AND SATIRES. Edited by Rev. W. J. F. V. BAKER, B.A. 18mo. 1s. 6d.
—— SELECT EPODES AND ARS POETICA. Edited by Rev. H. A. DALTON, M.A. 16mo. 1s. 6d.
HORT.—TWO DISSERTATIONS. I. On ΜΟΝΟΓΕΝΗΣ ΘΕΟΣ in Scripture and Tradition. II. On the "Constantinopolitan" Creed and other Eastern Creeds of the Fourth Century. By FENTON JOHN ANTHONY HORT, D.D. 8vo. 7s. 6d.
HORTON (Hon. S. Dana).—THE SILVER POUND AND ENGLAND'S MONETARY POLICY SINCE THE RESTORATION. With a History of the Guinea. 8vo. 14s.
HOWELL (George).—THE CONFLICTS OF CAPITAL AND LABOUR. 2nd Edition. Crown 8vo. 7s. 6d.
HOWES (Prof. G. B.).—AN ATLAS OF PRACTICAL ELEMENTARY BIOLOGY. With a Preface by Prof. HUXLEY. 4to. 14s.
HOWSON (Very Rev. J. S.).—BEFORE THE TABLE: AN INQUIRY, HISTORICAL AND THEOLOGICAL, INTO THE MEANING OF THE CONSECRATION RUBRIC IN THE COMMUNION SERVICE OF THE CHURCH OF ENGLAND. 8vo. 7s. 6d.
HOZIER (Lieut.-Colonel H. M.).—THE SEVEN WEEKS' WAR. 3rd Edition. Crown 8vo. 6s.
—— THE INVASIONS OF ENGLAND. 2 vols. 8vo. 28s.
HÜBNER (Baron von).—A RAMBLE ROUND THE WORLD. Crown 8vo. 6s.
HUGHES (Thomas).—ALFRED THE GREAT. Crown 8vo. 6s.
—— TOM BROWN'S SCHOOL DAYS. By AN OLD BOY. Illustrated Edition. Crown 8vo. 6s.—Golden Treasury Edition. 4s. 6d.—Uniform Edition. 3s. 6d.—People's Edition. 2s.—People's Sixpenny Edition, Illustrated. Med. 4to. 6d. Uniform with Sixpenny Kingsley. Medium 8vo. 6d.

HUGHES (Thomas).—TOM BROWN AT OXFORD. Crown 8vo. 6s.—Uniform Edition. 3s. 6d.
—— MEMOIR OF DANIEL MACMILLAN. With Portrait. Cr. 8vo. 4s. 6d.—Popular Edition. Sewed. Crown 8vo. 1s.
—— RUGBY, TENNESSEE. Crown 8vo. 4s. 6d.
—— GONE TO TEXAS. Edited by THOMAS HUGHES, Q.C. Crown 8vo. 4s. 6d.
—— JAMES FRASER, Second Bishop of Manchester. A Memoir, 1818—85. Cr. 8vo. 6s.
—— THE SCOURING OF THE WHITE HORSE, AND THE ASHEN FAGGOT. Uniform Ed. 3s. 6d.
—— LIVINGSTONE. With Portrait and Map. Cr. 8vo. 2s. 6d. [*English Men of Action*.
HULL (E.).—A TREATISE ON ORNAMENTAL AND BUILDING STONES OF GREAT BRITAIN AND FOREIGN COUNTRIES. 8vo. 12s.
HULLAH (John).—THE SONG BOOK. Words and Tunes from the best Poets and Musicians. With Vignette. 18mo. 4s. 6d.
—— MUSIC IN THE HOUSE. 4th Edition. Crown 8vo. 2s. 6d.
HULLAH (M. E.).—HANNAH TARNE. A Story for Girls. Globe 8vo. 2s. 6d.
HUME. By THOMAS H. HUXLEY. Crown 8vo. 1s. 6d.; sewed, 1s.
HUMPHRY (Prof. G. M.).—THE HUMAN SKELETON (INCLUDING THE JOINTS). With 260 Illustrations drawn from Nature. Med. 8vo. 14s.
—— THE HUMAN FOOT AND THE HUMAN HAND. With Illustrations. Fcp. 8vo. 4s. 6d.
—— OBSERVATIONS IN MYOLOGY. 8vo. 6s.
—— OLD AGE. The Results of Information received respecting nearly nine hundred persons who had attained the age of eighty years, including seventy-four centenarians. Crown 8vo. 4s. 6d.
HUNT (Rev. W.).—HISTORY OF ITALY. Maps. 3rd Edition. 18mo. 3s. 6d.
HUNT (W.).—TALKS ABOUT ART. With a Letter from Sir J. E. MILLAIS, Bart., R.A. Crown 8vo. 3s. 6d.
HUSS (Hermann).—A SYSTEM OF ORAL INSTRUCTION IN GERMAN. Crown 8vo. 5s.
HUTTON (R. H.).—ESSAYS ON SOME OF THE MODERN GUIDES OF ENGLISH THOUGHT IN MATTERS OF FAITH. Globe 8vo. 6s.
—— SCOTT. Crown 8vo. 1s. 6d.; sewed, 1s.
—— ESSAYS. 2 vols. Globe 8vo. 6s. each. —Vol. I. Literary Essays; II. Theological Essays.
HUXLEY (Thomas Henry).—LESSONS IN ELEMENTARY PHYSIOLOGY. With numerous Illustrations. New Edit. Fcp. 8vo. 4s. 6d.
—— LAY SERMONS, ADDRESSES, AND REVIEWS. 9th Edition. 8vo. 7s. 6d.
—— ESSAYS SELECTED FROM LAY SERMONS, ADDRESSES, AND REVIEWS. 3rd Edition. Crown 8vo. 1s.
—— CRITIQUES AND ADDRESSES. 8vo. 10s. 6d.
—— PHYSIOGRAPHY. AN INTRODUCTION TO THE STUDY OF NATURE. 13th Ed. Cr.8vo. 6s.

LIST OF PUBLICATIONS. 25

HUXLEY (T. H.).—AMERICAN ADDRESSES, WITH A LECTURE ON THE STUDY OF BIOLOGY. 8vo. 6s. 6d.
—— SCIENCE AND CULTURE, AND OTHER ESSAYS. 8vo. 10s. 6d.
—— INTRODUCTORY PRIMER. 18mo. 1s.
—— HUME. Crown 8vo. 1s. 6d.; sewed, 1s.
HUXLEY'S PHYSIOLOGY, QUESTIONS ON, FOR SCHOOLS. By T. ALCOCK, M.D. 5th Edition. 18mo. 1s. 6d.
HUXLEY (T. H.) and MARTIN (H. N.).— A COURSE OF PRACTICAL INSTRUCTION IN ELEMENTARY BIOLOGY. New Edition, Revised and Extended by Prof. G. B. HOWES and D. H SCOTT, M.A., Ph.D. With Preface by T. H. HUXLEY, F.R.S. Cr. 8vo. 10s. 6d.
IBBETSON (W. J.). AN ELEMENTARY TREATISE ON THE MATHEMATICAL THEORY OF PERFECTLY ELASTIC SOLIDS. 8vo. 21s.
ILLINGWORTH (Rev. J. R.).- SERMONS PREACHED IN A COLLEGE CHAPEL. Crown 8vo. 5s.
IMITATIO CHRISTI, LIBRI IV. Printed in Borders after Holbein, Dürer, and other old Masters, containing Dances of Death, Acts of Mercy, Emblems, &c. Cr. 8vo. 7s. 6d.
INDIAN TEXT-BOOKS.—PRIMER OF ENGLISH GRAMMAR. By R. MORRIS, LL.D. 18mo. 1s.; sewed, 10d.
PRIMER OF ASTRONOMY. By J. N. LOCKYER. 18mo. 1s.; sewed, 10d.
EASY SELECTIONS FROM MODERN ENGLISH LITERATURE. For the use of the Middle Classes in Indian Schools. With Notes. By Sir ROPER LETHBRIDGE. Cr. 8vo. 1s. 6d.
SELECTIONS FROM MODERN ENGLISH LITERATURE. For the use of the Higher Classes in Indian Schools. By Sir ROPER LETHBRIDGE, M.A. Crown 8vo. 3s. 6d.
SERIES OF SIX ENGLISH READING BOOKS FOR INDIAN CHILDREN. By P. C. SIRCAR. Revised by Sir ROPER LETHBRIDGE. Cr. 8vo. Book I. 5d.; Nagari Characters, 5d.; Persian Characters, 5d.; Book II. 6d.; Book III. 8d.; Book IV. 1s.; Book V. 1s. 2d.; Book VI. 1s. 3d.
HIGH SCHOOL READER. By ERIC ROBERTSON. Crown 8vo. 2s.
A GEOGRAPHICAL READER AND COMPANION TO THE ATLAS. By C. B. CLARKE, F.R.S. Crown 8vo. 2s.
A CLASS-BOOK OF GEOGRAPHY. By the same. Fcap. 8vo. 3s. 6d.; sewed, 3s.
THE WORLD'S HISTORY. Compiled under direction of Sir ROPER LETHBRIDGE. Crown 8vo. 1s.
EASY INTRODUCTION TO THE HISTORY OF INDIA. By Sir ROPER LETHBRIDGE. Crown 8vo. 1s. 6d.
HISTORY OF ENGLAND. Compiled under direction of Sir ROPER LETHBRIDGE. Crown 8vo. 1s. 6d.
EASY INTRODUCTION TO THE HISTORY AND GEOGRAPHY OF BENGAL. By Sir ROPER LETHBRIDGE. Crown 8vo. 1s. 6d.
ARITHMETIC. With Answers. By BARNARD SMITH. 18mo. 2s.
ALGEBRA. By I. TODHUNTER. 18mo. 2s. 3d.

INDIAN TEXT-BOOKS -continued.
EUCLID. First Four Books. With Notes, &c. By I. TODHUNTER. 18mo. 2s.
ELEMENTARY MENSURATION AND LAND SURVEYING. By the same Author. 18mo. 2s.
EUCLID. Books I.—IV. By H. S. HALL and F. H. STEVENS. Gl. 8vo. 3s.; sewed, 2s. 6d.
PHYSICAL GEOGRAPHY. By H. F. BLANFORD. Crown 8vo. 2s. 6d.
ELEMENTARY GEOMETRY AND CONIC SECTIONS. By J. M. WILSON. Ex. fcp. 8vo. 6s.
INGRAM (T. Dunbar).—A HISTORY OF THE LEGISLATIVE UNION OF GREAT BRITAIN AND IRELAND. 8vo. 10s. 6d.
—— TWO CHAPTERS OF IRISH HISTORY: I. The Irish Parliament of James II.; II. The Alleged Violation of the Treaty of Limerick. 8vo. 6s.
IONIA.—ANTIQUITIES OF IONIA. Folio. Vols. I. II. and III. 2l. 2s. each, or 5l. 5s. the set.—Vol. IV. 3l. 13s. 6d.
IRVING (Joseph).—ANNALS OF OUR TIME. A Diurnal of Events, Social and Political, Home and Foreign. From the Accession of Queen Victoria to Jubilee Day, being the First Fifty Years of Her Majesty's Reign. In 2 vols. 8vo.—Vol. I. June 20th, 1837, to February 28th, 1871. Vol. II. February 24th, 1871, to June 24th, 1887. 18s. each. The Second Volume may also be had in Three Parts: Part I. February 24th, 1871, to March 19th, 1874, 4s. 6d. Part II. March 20th, 1874, to July 22nd, 1878, 4s. 6d. Part III. July 23rd, 1878, to June 24th, 1887, 9s.
IRVING (Washington).—OLD CHRISTMAS. From the Sketch Book. With upwards of 100 Illustrations by RANDOLPH CALDECOTT. Cloth elegant, gilt edges. Crown 8vo. 6s. Also with uncut edges, paper label. 6s. People's Edition. Medium 4to. 6d.
—— BRACEBRIDGE HALL. With 120 Illustrations by RANDOLPH CALDECOTT. Cloth elegant, gilt edges. Crown 8vo. 6s. Also with uncut edges, paper label. 6s. People's Edition. Medium 4to. 6d.
—— OLD CHRISTMAS AND BRACEBRIDGE HALL. Illustrations by RANDOLPH CALDECOTT. Edition de Luxe. Royal 8vo. 21s.
ISMAY'S CHILDREN. By the Author of "Hogan, M.P." Globe 8vo. 2s.
JACK AND THE BEAN-STALK. English Hexameters by the Honourable HALLAM TENNYSON. With 40 Illustrations by RANDOLPH CALDECOTT. Fcp. 4to. 3s. 6d.
JACKSON (Rev. Blomfield).—FIRST STEPS TO GREEK PROSE COMPOSITION. 12th Edit. 18mo. 1s. 6d.
—— KEY (supplied to Teachers only). 3s. 6d.
—— SECOND STEPS TO GREEK PROSE COMPOSITION. 18mo. 2s. 6d.
—— KEY (supplied to Teachers only). 3s. 6d.
JACKSON (Helen).—RAMONA: A Story. Globe 8vo. 2s.
JACOB (Rev. J. A.).—BUILDING IN SILENCE, AND OTHER SERMONS. Extra fcp. 8vo. 6s.
JAMES (Henry).—THE EUROPEANS: A Novel. Crown 8vo. 6s.
—— DAISY MILLER, AND OTHER STORIES. Crown 8vo. 6s.—Globe 8vo. 2s.

JAMES (Henry).—THE AMERICAN. Crown 8vo. 6s.
— RODERICK HUDSON. Crown 8vo. 6s.—Globe 8vo. 2s.
— THE MADONNA OF THE FUTURE, AND OTHER TALES. Crown 8vo. 6s.—Globe 8vo. 2s.
— WASHINGTON SQUARE; THE PENSION BEAUREPAS. Crn. 8vo. 6s.—Globe 8vo. 2s.
— THE PORTRAIT OF A LADY. Cr. 8vo. 6s.
— STORIES REVIVED. In Two Series. Crown 8vo. 6s. each.
— THE BOSTONIANS. Crown 8vo. 6s.
— NOVELS AND TALES. Pocket Edition. 18mo. 14 vols. 2s. each volume: THE PORTRAIT OF A LADY. 3 vols.—RODERICK HUDSON. 2 vols.—THE AMERICAN. 2 vols.—WASHINGTON SQUARE. 1 vol.—THE EUROPEANS. 1 vol.—CONFIDENCE. 1 vol.—THE SIEGE OF LONDON; MADAME DE MAUVES. 1 vol.—AN INTERNATIONAL EPISODE; THE PENSION BEAUREPAS; THE POINT OF VIEW. 1 vol.—DAISY MILLER, A STUDY; FOUR MEETINGS; LONGSTAFF'S MARRIAGE; BENVOLIO. 1 vol.—THE MADONNA OF THE FUTURE; A BUNDLE OF LETTERS; THE DIARY OF A MAN OF FIFTY; EUGENE PICKERING. 1 vol.
— HAWTHORNE. Cr. 8vo. 1s. 6d.; swd. 1s.
— FRENCH POETS AND NOVELISTS. New Edition. Crown 8vo. 4s. 6d.
— TALES OF THREE CITIES. Cr. 8vo. 4s. 6d.
— PORTRAITS OF PLACES. Cr. 8vo. 7s. 6d.
— THE PRINCESS CASAMASSIMA. Crown 8vo. 6s.—Globe 8vo. 2s.
— PARTIAL PORTRAITS. Crown 8vo. 6s.
— THE REVERBERATOR. Crown 8vo. 6s.
— THE ASPERN PAPERS; LOUISA PALLANT; THE MODERN WARNING. 2 vols. Globe 8vo. 1s.
— A LONDON LIFE. Crown 8vo. 3s. 6d.
— THE TRAGIC MUSE. 3 vols. Crown 8vo. 31s. 6d.

JAMES Rev. Herbert). — THE COUNTRY CLERGYMAN AND HIS WORK. Cr. 8vo. 6s.

JAMES (Right Hon. Sir William Milbourne). —THE BRITISH IN INDIA. 8vo. 12s. 6d.

JARDINE (Rev. Robert).—THE ELEMENTS OF THE PSYCHOLOGY OF COGNITION. Third Edition. Crown 8vo. 6s. 6d.

JEANS (Rev. G. E.).— HAILEYBURY CHAPEL, AND OTHER SERMONS. Fcp. 8vo. 3s. 6d.
— THE LIFE AND LETTERS OF MARCUS TULLIUS CICERO. Being a Translation of the Letters included in Mr. Watson's Selection. Crown 8vo. 10s. 6d.

JEBB (Prof. R. C.).—THE ATTIC ORATORS, FROM ANTIPHON TO ISAEOS. 2 vols. 8vo. 25s.
— THE ATTIC ORATORS. Selections from Antiphon, Andocides, Lysias, Isocrates, and Isaeos. Ed., with Notes. 2nd Ed. Fcp. 8vo. 6s.
— MODERN GREECE. Two Lectures. Crown 8vo. 5s.
— PRIMER OF GREEK LITERATURE. 18mo. 1s.
— BENTLEY. Crown 8vo. 1s. 6d.; sewed, 1s.

JELLETT (Rev. Dr.).—THE ELDER SON, AND OTHER SERMONS. Crown 8vo. 6s.
— THE EFFICACY OF PRAYER. 3rd Edition. Crown 8vo. 5s.

JENNINGS (A. C.).—CHRONOLOGICAL TABLES OF ANCIENT HISTORY. With Index. 8vo. 5s.

JENNINGS (A. C.) and LOWE (W. H.).—THE PSALMS, WITH INTRODUCTIONS AND CRITICAL NOTES. 2 vols. 2nd Edition. Crown 8vo. 10s. 6d. each.

JEVONS (W. Stanley).—THE PRINCIPLES OF SCIENCE: A TREATISE ON LOGIC AND SCIENTIFIC METHOD. Crown 8vo. 12s. 6d.
— ELEMENTARY LESSONS IN LOGIC: DEDUCTIVE AND INDUCTIVE. 18mo. 3s. 6d.
— PRIMER OF LOGIC. 18mo. 1s.
— THE THEORY OF POLITICAL ECONOMY. 3rd Edition. 8vo. 10s. 6d.
— PRIMER OF POLITICAL ECONOMY. 18mo. 1s.
— STUDIES IN DEDUCTIVE LOGIC. 2nd Edition. Crown 8vo. 6s.
— INVESTIGATIONS IN CURRENCY AND FINANCE. Edited, with an Introduction, by H. S. FOXWELL, M.A. Illustrated by 20 Diagrams. 8vo. 21s.
— METHODS OF SOCIAL REFORM. 8vo. 10s. 6d.
— THE STATE IN RELATION TO LABOUR. Crown 8vo. 3s. 6d.
— LETTERS AND JOURNAL. Edited by HIS WIFE. 8vo. 14s.
— PURE LOGIC, AND OTHER MINOR WORKS. Edited by R. ADAMSON, M.A., and HARRIET A. JEVONS. With a Preface by Prof. ADAMSON. 8vo. 10s. 6d.

JEX-BLAKE (Dr. Sophia).—THE CARE OF INFANTS: A Manual for Mothers and Nurses. 18mo. 1s.

JOHNSON (W. E.).—A TREATISE ON TRIGONOMETRY. Crown 8vo. 8s. 6d.

JOHNSON (Prof. W. Woolsey).—CURVE TRACING IN CARTESIAN CO-ORDINATES. Crown 8vo. 4s. 6d.
— A TREATISE ON ORDINARY AND DIFFERENTIAL EQUATIONS. Crown 8vo. 15s.
— AN ELEMENTARY TREATISE ON THE INTEGRAL CALCULUS. Crown 8vo. 9s.

JOHNSON'S LIVES OF THE POETS. The Six Chief Lives, with Macaulay's "Life of Johnson." Edited by MATTHEW ARNOLD. Crown 8vo. 4s. 6d.

JOHNSON. By LESLIE STEPHEN. Crown 8vo. 1s. 6d.; sewed, 1s.

JONES (D. E.).—EXAMPLES IN PHYSICS. Fcp. 8vo. 3s. 6d.
— SOUND, LIGHT, AND HEAT. An Elementary Text-Book. Fcp. 8vo.

JONES (F.).—THE OWENS COLLEGE JUNIOR COURSE OF PRACTICAL CHEMISTRY. With Preface by Sir HENRY E. ROSCOE. New Edition. 18mo. 2s. 6d.
— QUESTIONS ON CHEMISTRY. A Series of Problems and Exercises in Inorganic and Organic Chemistry. 18mo. 3s.

JONES (Rev. C. A.) and CHEYNE (C. H.).—ALGEBRAICAL EXERCISES. Progressively arranged. 18mo. 2s. 6d.

JONES (Rev. C. A.) and CHEYNE (C. H.). —SOLUTIONS OF SOME OF THE EXAMPLES IN THE ALGEBRAICAL EXERCISES OF MESSRS. JONES AND CHEYNE. By the Rev. W. FAILES. Crown 8vo. 7s. 6d.

JUVENAL. THIRTEEN SATIRES OF JUVENAL. With a Commentary by Prof. J. E. B. MAYOR, M.A. 4th Edition. Vol. I. Crown 8vo. 10s. 6d.—Vol. II. Crown 8vo. 10s. 6d. SUPPLEMENT to Third Edition, containing the Principal Changes made in the Fourth Edition. 5s.

—— THIRTEEN SATIRES. Edited, for the Use of Schools, with Notes, Introduction, and Appendices, by E. G. HARDY, M.A. Fcp. 8vo. 5s.

—— SELECT SATIRES. Edited by Prof. JOHN E. B. MAYOR. Satires X. and XI. 3s. 6d.— Satires XII. and XVI. Fcp. 8vo. 4s. 6d.

—— THIRTEEN SATIRES. Translated into English after the Text of J. E. B. MAYOR by ALEX. LEEPER, M.A. Cr. 8vo. 3s. 6d.

KANT.—KANT'S CRITICAL PHILOSOPHY FOR ENGLISH READERS. By JOHN P. MAHAFFY, D.D., and JOHN H. BERNARD, B.D. New Edition. 2 vols. Crown 8vo. Vol. I. THE KRITIK OF PURE REASON EXPLAINED AND DEFENDED. 7s. 6d.—Vol. II. THE "PROLEGOMENA." Translated, with Notes and Appendices. 6s.

KANT—MAX MÜLLER.— CRITIQUE OF PURE REASON BY IMMANUEL KANT. Translated by F. MAX MÜLLER. With Introduction by LUDWIG NOIRÉ. 2 vols. 8vo. 16s. each.—Sold separately Vol. I. HISTORICAL INTRODUCTION, by LUDWIG NOIRÉ, etc., etc.; Vol. II. CRITIQUE OF PURE REASON.

KAY (Rev. W.).—A COMMENTARY ON ST. PAUL'S TWO EPISTLES TO THE CORINTHIANS. Greek Text, with Commentary. 8vo. 9s.

KEARY (Annie).—JANET'S HOME. Globe 8vo. 2s.

—— CLEMENCY FRANKLYN. Globe 8vo. 2s.

—— OLDBURY. Globe 8vo. 2s.

—— A YORK AND A LANCASTER ROSE. Crn. 8vo. 3s. 6d.

—— CASTLE DALY: THE STORY OF AN IRISH HOME THIRTY YEARS AGO. Cr. 8vo. 3s.6d.

—— A DOUBTING HEART. Crown 8vo. 6s.

—— NATIONS AROUND. Crown 8vo. 4s. 6d.

KEARY (Eliza).—THE MAGIC VALLEY; OR, PATIENT ANTOINE. With Illustrations by "E.V.B." Globe 8vo. 4s. 6d.

KEARY (A. and E.).—THE HEROES OF ASGARD. Tales from Scandinavian Mythology. Globe 8vo. 2s. 6d.

KEATS.—THE POETICAL WORKS OF JOHN KEATS. With Notes, by Prof. F. T. PALGRAVE. 18mo. 4s. 6d.

KEATS. By SIDNEY COLVIN. Crown 8vo. 1s. 6d.; sewed, 1s.

KELLAND (P.) and TAIT (P. G.).—INTRODUCTION TO QUATERNIONS, WITH NUMEROUS EXAMPLES. 2nd Edition. Cr. 8vo. 7s. 6d.

KELLOGG (Rev. S. H.).—THE LIGHT OF ASIA AND THE LIGHT OF THE WORLD. Cr. 8vo. 7s. 6d.

KEMPE.(A. B.). HOW TO DRAW A STRAIGHT LINE. A Lecture on Linkages. Cr. 8vo. 1s.6d.

KENNEDY (Prof. Alex. W. B.).—THE MECHANICS OF MACHINERY. With Illustrations. Crown 8vo. 12s. 6d.

KERNEL AND THE HUSK (THE): LETTERS ON SPIRITUAL CHRISTIANITY. By the Author of "Philochristus." Crown 8vo. 5s.

KEYNES (J. N.). STUDIES AND EXERCISES IN FORMAL LOGIC. 2nd Ed. Cr. 8vo. 10s.6d.

KIEPERT (H.).—MANUAL OF ANCIENT GEOGRAPHY. Crown 8vo. 5s.

KILLEN (W. D.).—ECCLESIASTICAL HISTORY OF IRELAND, FROM THE EARLIEST DATE TO THE PRESENT TIME. 2 vols. 8vo. 25s.

KINGSLEY (Charles).—NOVELS AND POEMS. Eversley Edition. 13 vols. Gl. 8vo. 5s. each. WESTWARD HO! 2 vols.—TWO YEARS AGO. 2 vols.—HYPATIA. 2 vols.—YEAST. 1 vol. —ALTON LOCKE. 2 vols.— HEREWARD THE WAKE. 2 vols.—POEMS. 2 vols.

—— Complete Edition OF THE WORKS OF CHARLES KINGSLEY. Cr. 8vo. 3s. 6d. each. WESTWARD HO! With a Portrait. HYPATIA. YEAST. ALTON LOCKE. TWO YEARS AGO. HEREWARD THE WAKE. POEMS. THE HEROES; OR, GREEK FAIRY TALES FOR MY CHILDREN. THE WATER BABIES: A FAIRY TALE FOR A LAND-BABY. MADAM HOW AND LADY WHY; OR, FIRST LESSONS IN EARTH-LORE FOR CHILDREN. AT LAST: A CHRISTMAS IN THE WEST INDIES. PROSE IDYLLS. PLAYS AND PURITANS. THE ROMAN AND THE TEUTON. With Preface by Professor MAX MÜLLER. SANITARY AND SOCIAL LECTURES. HISTORICAL LECTURES AND ESSAYS. SCIENTIFIC LECTURES AND ESSAYS. LITERARY AND GENERAL LECTURES. THE HERMITS. GLAUCUS; OR, THE WONDERS OF THE SEA-SHORE. With Coloured Illustrations. VILLAGE AND TOWN AND COUNTRY SERMONS. THE WATER OF LIFE, AND OTHER SERMONS. SERMONS ON NATIONAL SUBJECTS, AND THE KING OF THE EARTH. SERMONS FOR THE TIMES. GOOD NEWS OF GOD. THE GOSPEL OF THE PENTATEUCH, AND DAVID. [Nov. DISCIPLINE, AND OTHER SERMONS. [Dec. WESTMINSTER SERMONS. [Jan. 1891. ALL SAINTS' DAY, & OTHER SERMONS. [Feb.

—— A Sixpenny Edition OF CHARLES KINGSLEY'S NOVELS. Med. 8vo. 6d. each. WESTWARD HO! HYPATIA. YEAST.— ALTON LOCKE. — TWO YEARS AGO. — HEREWARD THE WAKE.

KINGSLEY (Charles).—THE WATER BABIES: A FAIRY TALE FOR A LAND BABY. New Edition, with a Hundred New Pictures by LINLEY SAMBOURNE; engraved by J. SWAIN. Fcp. 4to. 12s. 6d.

KINGSLEY (Charles).—HEALTH AND EDUCATION. Cr. 8vo. 6s.
—— POEMS. Pocket Edition. 18mo. 1s. 6d.
—— SELECTIONS FROM SOME OF THE WRITINGS OF CHARLES KINGSLEY. Cr. 8vo. 6s.
—— OUT OF THE DEEP: WORDS FOR THE SORROWFUL. From the Writings of CHARLES KINGSLEY. Extra fcp. 8vo. 3s. 6d.
—— DAILY THOUGHTS. Selected from the Writings of CHARLES KINGSLEY. By HIS WIFE. Crown 8vo. 6s.
—— THE HEROES; OR, GREEK FAIRY TALES FOR MY CHILDREN. Extra cloth, gilt edges. *Presentation Edition.* Crown 8vo. 7s. 6d.
—— GLAUCUS; OR, THE WONDERS OF THE SEA SHORE. With Coloured Illustrations, extra cloth, gilt edges. *Presentation Edition.* Crown 8vo. 7s. 6d.
—— FROM DEATH TO LIFE. Fragments of Teaching to a Village Congregation. With Letters on the "Life after Death." Edited by HIS WIFE. Fcp. 8vo. 2s. 6d.
—— CHARLES KINGSLEY: HIS LETTERS, AND MEMORIES OF HIS LIFE. Ed. by HIS WIFE. 2 vols. Crn. 8vo. 12s.—*Cheap Edition*, 6s.
—— TRUE WORDS FOR BRAVE MEN. Crown 8vo. 2s. 6d.
KINGSLEY (Henry). — TALES OF OLD TRAVEL. Crown 8vo. 5s.
KIPLING (Rudyard).—PLAIN TALES FROM THE HILLS. Crown 8vo. 6s.
KITCHENER (F. E.). — GEOMETRICAL NOTE-BOOK. Containing Easy Problems in Geometrical Drawing, preparatory to the Study of Geometry. 4to. 2s.
KLEIN (Dr. E.).—MICRO-ORGANISMS AND DISEASE. An Introduction into the Study of Specific Micro-Organisms. With 121 Engravings. 3rd Edition. Crown 8vo. 6s.
—— THE BACTERIA IN ASIATIC CHOLERA. Crown 8vo. 5s.
KNOX (A.).—DIFFERENTIAL CALCULUS FOR BEGINNERS. Fcp. 8vo. 3s. 6d.
KTESIAS.—THE FRAGMENTS OF THE PERSIKA OF KTESIAS. Edited, with Introduction and Notes, by J. GILMORE, M.A. 8vo. 8s. 6d.
KUENEN (Prof. A.). — AN HISTORICOCRITICAL INQUIRY INTO THE ORIGIN AND COMPOSITION OF THE HEXATEUCH (PENTATEUCH AND BOOK OF JOSHUA). Translated by PHILIP H. WICKSTEED, M.A. 8vo. 14s.
KYNASTON (Herbert, D.D.). — SERMONS PREACHED IN THE COLLEGE CHAPEL, CHELTENHAM. Crown 8vo. 6s.
—— PROGRESSIVE EXERCISES IN THE COMPOSITION OF GREEK IAMBIC VERSE. Extra fcp. 8vo. 5s.
KEY (supplied to Teachers only). 4s. 6d.
—— EXEMPLARIA CHELTONIENSIA. Sive quae discipulis suis Carmina identidem Latine reddenda proposuit ipse reddidit ex cathedra dictavit HERBERT KYNASTON, M.A. Extra fcp. 8vo. 5s.
LABBERTON (R. H.).—NEW HISTORICAL ATLAS AND GENERAL HISTORY. 4to. 15s.
LAFARGUE (Philip).—THE NEW JUDGMENT OF PARIS: A Novel. 2 vols. Gl. 8vo. 12s.

LA FONTAINE'S FABLES. A Selection, with Introduction, Notes, and Vocabulary, by L. M. MORIARTY, B.A. Illustrations by RANDOLPH CALDECOTT. Globe 8vo. 2s. 6d.
LAMB.—COLLECTED WORKS. Edited, with Introduction and Notes, by the Rev. ALFRED AINGER, M.A. Globe 8vo. 5s. each volume.
I. ESSAYS OF ELIA.—II. PLAYS, POEMS, AND MISCELLANEOUS ESSAYS.—III. MRS. LEICESTER'S SCHOOL; THE ADVENTURES OF ULYSSES; AND OTHER ESSAYS.—IV. TALES FROM SHAKSPEARE.—V. and VI. LETTERS. Newly arranged, with additions.
—— THE LIFE OF CHARLES LAMB. By Rev. ALFRED AINGER, M.A. Uniform with above. Globe 8vo. 5s.
TALES FROM SHAKSPEARE. 18mo. 4s. 6d. *Globe Readings Edition.* For Schools. Globe 8vo. 2s.
LAMB. By Rev. ALFRED AINGER, M.A. Crown 8vo. 1s. 6d.; sewed, 1s.
LANCIANI (Prof. R.).-ANCIENT ROME IN THE LIGHT OF RECENT DISCOVERIES. 4to. 24s.
LAND OF DARKNESS (THE). Along with some further Chapters in the Experiences of The Little Pilgrim. By the Author of "A Little Pilgrim in the Unseen." Crown 8vo. 5s.
LANDAUER (J.) — BLOWPIPE ANALYSIS. Authorised English Edition by JAMES TAYLOR and WM. E. KAY. Ext. fcp. 8vo. 4s. 6d.
LANDOR. — SELECTIONS FROM THE WRITINGS OF WALTER SAVAGE LANDOR. Arranged and Edited by SIDNEY COLVIN. 18mo. 4s. 6d.
LANDOR. By SIDNEY COLVIN. Crown 8vo, 1s. 6d.; sewed, 1s.
LANE-POOLE. — SELECTIONS FROM THE SPEECHES AND TABLE-TALK OF MOHAMMAD. By S. LANE-POOLE. 18mo. 4s. 6d.
LANG (Andrew).—THE LIBRARY. With a Chapter on Modern Illustrated Books, by AUSTIN DOBSON. Crown 8vo. 3s. 6d.
LANKESTER (Prof. E. Ray).—THE ADVANCEMENT OF SCIENCE: OCCASIONAL ESSAYS AND ADDRESSES. 8vo. 10s. 6d.
—— COMPARATIVE LONGEVITY IN MAN AND THE LOWER ANIMALS. Crn. 8vo. 4s. 6d.
LASLETT (Thomas).—TIMBER AND TIMBER TREES, NATIVE AND FOREIGN. Cr. 8vo. 8s. 6d.
LATIN ACCIDENCE AND EXERCISES ARRANGED FOR BEGINNERS. By WILLIAM WELCH, M.A., and C. G. DUFFIELD, M.A. 18mo. 1s. 6d.
LAWRENCE (LORD). By Sir RICHARD TEMPLE. With Portrait. Crown 8vo. 2s. 6d.
LEAHY (Sergeant).—THE ART OF SWIMMING IN THE ETON STYLE. With Preface by Mrs. OLIPHANT. Crown 8vo. 2s.
LECTURES ON ART. By REGD. STUART POOLE, Professor W. B. RICHMOND, E. J. POYNTER, R.A., J. T. MICKLETHWAITE, and WILLIAM MORRIS. Crown 8vo. 4s. 6d.
LEE (Margaret).- FAITHFUL AND UNFAITHFUL. Crown 8vo. 3s. 6d.
LEGGE (Alfred O.).—THE GROWTH OF THE TEMPORAL POWER OF THE PAPACY. Crown 8vo. 8s. 6d.

LIST OF PUBLICATIONS. 29

LEMON.—THE JEST BOOK. The Choicest Anecdotes and Sayings. Selected by MARK LEMON. 18mo. 4s. 6d.

LEPROSY INVESTIGATION COMMITTEE, JOURNAL OF THE. Ed. by P. S. ABRAHAM, M.A. No. I. Aug. 1890. 2s. 6d. net.

LETHBRIDGE (Sir Roper).—A SHORT MANUAL OF THE HISTORY OF INDIA. With Maps. Crown 8vo. 5s.
For other Works by this Author, see *Indian Text-Books Series*, p. 25.

LEVY (Amy).—REUBEN SACHS: A SKETCH. Crown 8vo. 3s. 6d.

LEWIS (Richard). - HISTORY OF THE LIFEBOAT AND ITS WORK. Crown 8vo. 5s.

LIECHTENSTEIN (Princess Marie).—HOLLAND HOUSE. With Steel Engravings, Woodcuts, and nearly 40 Illustrations by the Woodburytype Permanent Process. 2 vols. Medium 4to. Half mor., elegant. 4l. 4s.

LIGHTFOOT (The Right Rev. Bishop).—ST. PAUL'S EPISTLE TO THE GALATIANS. A Revised Text, with Introduction, Notes, and Dissertations. 10th Edition. 8vo. 12s.

—— ST. PAUL'S EPISTLE TO THE PHILIPPIANS. A Revised Text, with Introduction, Notes and Dissertations. 9th Edition. 8vo. 12s.

—— ST. PAUL'S EPISTLES TO THE COLOSSIANS AND TO PHILEMON. A Revised Text, with Introductions, etc. 9th Edition. 8vo. 12s.

—— PRIMARY CHARGE. Two Addresses delivered to the Clergy of the Diocese of Durham, 1882. 8vo. 2s.

—— THE APOSTOLIC FATHERS. Part II. S. IGNATIUS to St. POLYCARP. Revised Texts, with Introductions, Notes, Dissertations, and Translations. 3 vols. 2nd Ed. Demy 8vo. 48s.

—— APOSTOLIC FATHERS. Abridged Edition. With Short Introductions, Greek Text, and English Translation. 8vo.

—— ST. CLEMENT OF ROME: THE TWO EPISTLES TO THE CORINTHIANS. A Revised Text, with Introduction and Notes. New Edition. 2 vols. 8vo.

—— A CHARGE DELIVERED TO THE CLERGY OF THE DIOCESE OF DURHAM, NOV. 25TH, 1886. Demy 8vo. 2s.

—— ESSAYS ON THE WORK ENTITLED "SUPERNATURAL RELIGION." 8vo. 10s. 6d.

—— LEADERS IN THE NORTHERN CHURCH: A Series of Sermons. Crown 8vo.

—— ORDINATION ADDRESSES. Crown 8vo.

—— CAMBRIDGE SERMONS. Crown 8vo.

—— ST. PAULS' SERMONS. Crown 8vo.

LIGHTWOOD (J. M.)—THE NATURE OF POSITIVE LAW. 8vo. 12s. 6d.

LINDSAY (Dr. J. A.).—THE CLIMATIC TREATMENT OF CONSUMPTION. Cr. 8vo. 5s.

LITTLE PILGRIM IN THE UNSEEN. 24th Thousand. Crown 8vo. 2s. 6d.

LIVINGSTONE. By THOMAS HUGHES. With Portrait and Map. Crown 8vo. 2s. 6d.

LIVY. By Rev. W. W. CAPES, Fcp. 8vo. 1s. 6d.
—— THE HANNIBALIAN WAR. Being part of the 21st and 22nd Books of Livy, adapted for the Use of Beginners. By G. C. MACAULAY, M.A. 18mo. 1s. 6d.

LIVY.—THE SIEGE OF SYRACUSE. Being part of Books XXIV. and XXV. of Livy. Adapted for the Use of Beginners, with Notes, Exercises, and Vocabulary, by G. RICHARDS, M.A., and A. S. WALPOLE, M.A. 18mo. 1s. 6d.

—— THE LAST TWO KINGS OF MACEDON. Extracts from the fourth and fifth Decades of Livy. Selected and Edited, with Introduction and Notes, by F. H. RAWLINS, M.A. With Maps. Fcp. 8vo. 3s. 6d.

—— LEGENDS OF ANCIENT ROME, FROM LIVY. Adapted and Edited, with Notes, Exercises, and Vocabularies, by H. WILKINSON, M.A. 18mo. 1s. 6d.

—— BOOK I. Edited, with Notes and Vocabulary, by H. M. STEPHENSON. 18mo. 1s. 6d.

—— BOOKS II. AND III. Edited by H. M. STEPHENSON, M.A. Fcp. 8vo. 5s.

—— BOOK XXI. Adapted from Mr. Capes' Edition. With Notes and Vocabulary by W. W. CAPES, M.A., and J. E. MELHUISH, M.A. 18mo. 1s. 6d.

—— HANNIBAL'S FIRST CAMPAIGN IN ITALY. Books XXI. and XXII. Edited by Rev. W. W. CAPES, M.A. Fcp. 8vo. 5s.

—— BOOKS XXI.-XXV. THE SECOND PUNIC WAR. Translated by A. J. CHURCH, M.A., and W. J. BRODRIBB, M.A. With Maps. Crown 8vo. 7s. 6d.

—— BOOKS XXIII. AND XXIV. Edited by G. C. MACAULAY. Maps. Fcp. 8vo. 5s.

LOCK (Rev. J. B.)—ARITHMETIC FOR SCHOOLS. 4th Edition, revised. Globe 8vo. Complete with Answers, 4s. 6d. Without Answers, 4s. 6d.—Part I., with Answers, 2s. Part II., with Answers, 3s.

—— KEY TO "ARITHMETIC FOR SCHOOLS." By the Rev. R. G. WATSON. Cr. 8vo. 10s. 6d.

—— ARITHMETIC FOR BEGINNERS. A School Class-Book of COMMERCIAL ARITHMETIC. Globe 8vo. 2s. 6d.

—— KEY TO "ARITHMETIC FOR BEGINNERS." By Rev. R. G. WATSON. Crown 8vo. 8s. 6d.

—— A SHILLING CLASS-BOOK OF ARITHMETIC ADAPTED FOR USE IN ELEMENTARY SCHOOLS. 18mo. 1s.—With Answers, 1s. 6d.

—— TRIGONOMETRY. Globe 8vo. Part I. ELEMENTARY TRIGONOMETRY. 4s. 6d.—Part II. HIGHER TRIGONOMETRY. 4s. 6d. Complete, 7s. 6d.

—— KEY TO "ELEMENTARY TRIGONOMETRY." By H. CARR, B.A. Crown 8vo. 8s. 6d.

—— TRIGONOMETRY FOR BEGINNERS. As far as the Solution of Triangles. Gl. 8vo. 2s. 6d.

—— KEY TO "TRIGONOMETRY FOR BEGINNERS." Crown 8vo. 6s. 6d.

—— ELEMENTARY STATICS. Gl. 8vo. 4s. 6d.

—— DYNAMICS FOR BEGINNERS. 3rd Edit. Globe 8vo. 4s. 6d.

LOCKE. By Prof. FOWLER. Crown 8vo. 1s. 6d.; sewed, 1s.

LOCKYER (J. Norman, F.R.S.).—ELEMENTARY LESSONS IN ASTRONOMY. Illustrations and Diagram. New Edit. 18mo. 5s. 6d.

—— CONTRIBUTIONS TO SOLAR PHYSICS. With Illustrations. Royal 8vo. 31s. 6d.

—— PRIMER OF ASTRONOMY. Illustrated. New Edition. 18mo. 1s.

LOCKYER (J. N.).—OUTLINES OF PHYSIO-
GRAPHY: THE MOVEMENTS OF THE EARTH.
Crown 8vo. 1s. 6d.
—— THE CHEMISTRY OF THE SUN. 8vo. 14s.
LOCKYER'S ASTRONOMY, QUESTIONS
ON. By J. FORBES-ROBERTSON. 18mo.
1s. 6d.
LOCKYER—SEABROKE.—STAR-GAZING
PAST AND PRESENT. By J. NORMAN
LOCKYER, F.R.S. Expanded from Short-
hand Notes with the assistance of G. M.
SEABROKE, F.R.A.S. Royal 8vo. 21s.
LODGE (Prof. Oliver J.).—MODERN VIEWS
OF ELECTRICITY. Crown 8vo. 6s. 6d.
LOEWY (B.).—QUESTIONS AND EXAMPLES
IN EXPERIMENTAL PHYSICS, SOUND, LIGHT,
HEAT, ELECTRICITY, AND MAGNETISM.
Fcp. 8vo. 2s.
—— A GRADUATED COURSE OF NATURAL
SCIENCE, EXPERIMENTAL AND THEORETI-
CAL, FOR SCHOOLS AND COLLEGES. Part I.
FIRST YEAR'S COURSE FOR ELEMENTARY
SCHOOLS AND THE JUNIOR CLASSES OF
TECHNICAL SCHOOLS AND COLLEGES. Globe
8vo. 2s.
LOFTIE (Mrs.).—THE DINING-ROOM. With
Illustrations. Crown 8vo. 2s. 6d.
LONGFELLOW.—POEMS OF PLACES: ENG-
LAND AND WALES. Edited by H. W.
LONGFELLOW. 2 vols. 18mo. 9s.
—— BALLADS, LYRICS, AND SONNETS. From
the Poetic Works of HENRY WADSWORTH
LONGFELLOW. 18mo. 4s. 6d.
LONGINUS.—ON THE SUBLIME. Translated
by H. L. HAVELL, B.A. With Introduction
by ANDREW LANG. Crown 8vo.
LOWE (W. H.).—THE HEBREW STUDENT'S
COMMENTARY ON ZECHARIAH, HEBREW AND
LXX. 8vo. 10s. 6d.
LOWELL (James Russell).—COMPLETE
POETICAL WORKS. 18mo. 4s. 6d.
—— DEMOCRACY, AND OTHER ADDRESSES.
Crown 8vo. 5s.
—— HEARTSEASE AND RUE. Crown 8vo. 5s.
—— POLITICAL ESSAYS. Ext. cr. 8vo. 7s. 6d.
—— COMPLETE WORKS. 10 vols. Crn. 8vo.
6s. each. Monthly vols. from October, 1890.
Vol. I. LITERARY ESSAYS, Vol. I.
,, II. ,, ,, Vol. II.
,, III. ,, ,, Vol. III.
,, IV. ,, ,, Vol. IV.
,, V. POLITICAL ESSAYS.
,, VI. LITERARY AND POLITICAL AD-
DRESSES.
,, VII. POETICAL WORKS, Vol. I.
,, VIII. ,, ,, Vol. II.
,, IX. ,, ,, Vol. III.
,, X. ,, ,, Vol. IV.
LUBBOCK (Sir John, Bart.).—THE ORIGIN
AND METAMORPHOSES OF INSECTS. With
Illustrations. Crown 8vo. 3s. 6d.
—— ON BRITISH WILD FLOWERS CONSIDERED
IN THEIR RELATION TO INSECTS. With
Illustrations. Crown 8vo. 4s. 6d.
—— FLOWERS, FRUITS, AND LEAVES. With
Illustrations. Crown 8vo. 4s. 6d.
—— SCIENTIFIC LECTURES. With Illustra-
tions. 2nd Edition, revised. 8vo. 8s. 6d.

LUBBOCK (Sir John, Bart.).—POLITICAL AND
EDUCATIONAL ADDRESSES. 8vo. 8s. 6d.
—— THE PLEASURES OF LIFE. New Edition.
Gl. 8vo. 1s. 6d.; swd., 1s. 60th Thousand.
Library Edition. Globe 8vo. 3s. 6d.
Part II. Globe 8vo. 1s. 6d.; sewed, 1s.
Library Edition. Globe 8vo. 3s. 6d.
—— FIFTY YEARS OF SCIENCE: Address to
the British Association, 1881. 5th Edition.
Crown 8vo. 2s. 6d.
LUCAS (F.).—SKETCHES OF RURAL LIFE.
Poems. Globe 8vo. 5s.
LUCIAN.—EXTRACTS FROM LUCIAN. Edited,
with Introduction, Exercises, Notes, and
Vocabulary, by the Rev. J. BOND, M.A.,
and Rev. A. S. WALPOLE, M.A. 18mo. 1s. 6d.
LUCRETIUS.—BOOKS I.—III. Edited by
J. H. WARBURTON LEE. Fcp. 8vo. 4s. 6d.
LUPTON (J. H.).—AN INTRODUCTION TO
LATIN ELEGIAC VERSE COMPOSITION.
Globe 8vo. 2s. 6d.
—— LATIN RENDERING OF THE EXERCISES
IN PART II. (XXV.-C.) TO LUPTON'S "INTRO-
DUCTION TO LATIN ELEGIAC VERSE COMPO-
SITION." Globe 8vo. 3s. 6d.
—— AN INTRODUCTION TO LATIN LYRIC
VERSE COMPOSITION. Gl. 8vo. 3s.—Key, 4s. 6d.
LUPTON (Sydney).—CHEMICAL ARITHME-
TIC. With 1200 Examples. Fcp. 8vo. 4s. 6d.
—— NUMERICAL TABLES AND CONSTANTS IN
ELEMENTARY SCIENCE. Ex. fcp. 8vo. 2s. 6d.
LYALL (Sir Alfred).—WARREN HASTINGS.
With Portrait. 2s. 6d.
LYSIAS.—SELECT ORATIONS. Edited by
E. S. SHUCKBURGH, M.A. Fcp. 8vo. 6s.
LYRE FRANÇAISE (LA). Selected and
arranged by G. MASSON. 18mo. 4s. 6d.
LYTE (H. C. Maxwell).—ETON COLLEGE,
HISTORY OF, 1440—1884. With Illustrations.
2nd Edition. 8vo. 21s.
—— THE UNIVERSITY OF OXFORD, A HISTORY
OF, FROM THE EARLIEST TIMES TO THE
YEAR 1530. 8vo. 16s.
LYTTON (Rt. Hon. Earl of).—THE RING OF
AMASIS: A ROMANCE. Crown 8vo. 3s. 6d.
MACARTHUR (Margaret).—HISTORY OF
SCOTLAND. 18mo. 2s.
MACAULAY. By J. C. MORISON. Crown
8vo. 1s. 6d.; sewed, 1s.
M'CLELLAND (W. J.) and PRESTON (T.).
—A TREATISE ON SPHERICAL TRIGONOME-
TRY. With numerous Examples. Crown
8vo. 8s. 6d.—Or Part I. 4s. 6d.; Part II. 5s.
McCOSH (Rev. Dr. James).—THE METHOD
OF THE DIVINE GOVERNMENT, PHYSICAL
AND MORAL. 8vo. 10s. 6d.
—— THE SUPERNATURAL IN RELATION TO
THE NATURAL. Crown 8vo. 7s. 6d.
—— THE INTUITIONS OF THE MIND. New
Edition. 8vo. 10s. 6d.
—— AN EXAMINATION OF MR. J. S. MILL'S
PHILOSOPHY. 8vo. 10s. 6d.
—— THE LAWS OF DISCURSIVE THOUGHT.
A Text-Book of Formal Logic. Crn. 8vo. 5s.
—— CHRISTIANITY AND POSITIVISM. Lec-
tures on Natural Theology and Apologetics.
Crown 8vo. 7s. 6d.

LIST OF PUBLICATIONS. 31

McCOSH (Rev. Dr. James).—THE SCOTTISH PHILOSOPHY, FROM HUTCHESON TO HAMILTON, BIOGRAPHICAL, EXPOSITORY, CRITICAL. Royal 8vo. 16s.
—— THE EMOTIONS. 8vo. 9s.
—— REALISTIC PHILOSOPHY DEFENDED IN A PHILOSOPHIC SERIES. 2 vols. Vol. I. EXPOSITORY. Vol. II. HISTORICAL AND CRITICAL. Crown 8vo. 14s.
—— PSYCHOLOGY. Crown 8vo. I. THE COGNITIVE POWERS. 6s. 6d.—II. THE MOTIVE POWERS. 6s. 6d.
—— FIRST AND FUNDAMENTAL TRUTHS. Being a Treatise on Metaphysics. 8vo. 9s.

MACDONALD (George). ENGLAND'S ANTIPHON. Crown 8vo. 4s. 6d.

MACDONELL (John). THE LAND QUESTION. 8vo. 10s. 6d.

MACFARLANE (Alexander). - PHYSICAL ARITHMETIC. Crown 8vo. 7s. 6d.

MACGREGOR (James Gordon).—AN ELEMENTARY TREATISE ON KINEMATICS AND DYNAMICS. Crown 8vo. 10s. 6d.

MACKENZIE (Sir Morell).—THE HYGIENE OF THE VOCAL ORGANS. 6th Ed. Crn. 8vo. 6s.

MACKIE (Rev. Ellis).—PARALLEL PASSAGES FOR TRANSLATION INTO GREEK AND ENGLISH. Globe 8vo. 4s. 6d.

MACLAGAN (Dr. T.).—THE GERM THEORY. 8vo. 10s. 6d.

MACLAREN (Rev. Alexander).—SERMONS PREACHED AT MANCHESTER. 11th Edition. Fcp. 8vo. 4s. 6d.
—— A SECOND SERIES OF SERMONS. 7th Edition. Fcp. 8vo. 4s. 6d.
—— A THIRD SERIES. 6th Edition. Fcp. 8vo. 4s. 6d.
—— WEEK-DAY EVENING ADDRESSES. 4th Edition. Fcp. 8vo. 2s. 6d.
—— THE SECRET OF POWER, AND OTHER SERMONS. Fcp. 8vo. 4s. 6d.

MACLAREN (Arch.). THE FAIRY FAMILY. A Series of Ballads and Metrical Tales. Crown 8vo, gilt. 5s.

MACLEAN (Surgeon-General W. C.).—DISEASES OF TROPICAL CLIMATES. Crown 8vo. 10s. 6d.

MACLEAR (Rev. Canon).—A CLASS-BOOK OF OLD TESTAMENT HISTORY. With Four Maps. 18mo. 4s. 6d.
—— A CLASS-BOOK OF NEW TESTAMENT HISTORY. Including the connection of the Old and New Testament. 18mo. 5s. 6d.
—— A SHILLING BOOK OF OLD TESTAMENT HISTORY. 18mo. 1s.
—— A SHILLING BOOK OF NEW TESTAMENT HISTORY. 18mo. 1s.
—— A CLASS-BOOK OF THE CATECHISM OF THE CHURCH OF ENGLAND. 18mo. 1s. 6d.
—— A FIRST CLASS-BOOK OF THE CATECHISM OF THE CHURCH OF ENGLAND, WITH SCRIPTURE PROOFS FOR JUNIOR CLASSES AND SCHOOLS. 18mo. 6d.
—— A MANUAL OF INSTRUCTION FOR CONFIRMATION AND FIRST COMMUNION, WITH PRAYERS AND DEVOTIONS. 32mo. 2s.

MACLEAR (Rev. Dr.).—FIRST COMMUNION, WITH PRAYERS AND DEVOTIONS FOR THE NEWLY CONFIRMED. 32mo. 6d.
—— THE ORDER OF CONFIRMATION, WITH PRAYERS AND DEVOTIONS. 32mo. 6d.
—— THE HOUR OF SORROW; OR, THE OFFICE FOR THE BURIAL OF THE DEAD. 32mo. 2s.
—— APOSTLES OF MEDIÆVAL EUROPE. Crn. 8vo. 4s. 6d.
—— AN INTRODUCTION TO THE CREEDS. 18mo. 2s. 6d.
—— AN INTRODUCTION TO THE THIRTY-NINE ARTICLES. 18mo.

M'LENNAN (J. F.).—THE PATRIARCHAL THEORY. Edited and completed by DONALD M'LENNAN, M.A. 8vo. 14s.
—— STUDIES IN ANCIENT HISTORY. Comprising a Reprint of "Primitive Marriage." New Edition. 8vo. 16s.

MACMILLAN (D.). MEMOIR OF DANIEL MACMILLAN. By THOMAS HUGHES, Q.C. Crown 8vo. 4s. 6d.
Popular Edition. Crown 8vo, sewed. 1s.

MACMILLAN (Rev. Hugh).—BIBLE TEACHINGS IN NATURE. 15th Ed. Gl. 8vo. 6s.
—— HOLIDAYS ON HIGH LANDS; OR, RAMBLES AND INCIDENTS IN SEARCH OF ALPINE PLANTS. 2nd Edition. Globe 8vo. 6s.
—— THE TRUE VINE; OR, THE ANALOGIES OF OUR LORD'S ALLEGORY. 5th Edition. Globe 8vo. 6s.
—— THE MINISTRY OF NATURE. 8th Edition. Globe 8vo. 6s.
—— THE SABBATH OF THE FIELDS. 6th Edition. Globe 8vo. 6s.
—— THE MARRIAGE IN CANA. Globe 8vo. 6s.
—— TWO WORLDS ARE OURS. 3rd Edition. Globe 8vo. 6s.
—— THE OLIVE LEAF. Globe 8vo. 6s.
—— ROMAN MOSAICS; OR, STUDIES IN ROME AND ITS NEIGHBOURHOOD. Globe 8vo. 6s.

MACMILLAN (M. C.)—FIRST LATIN GRAMMAR. Extra fcp. 8vo. 1s. 6d.

MACMILLAN'S MAGAZINE. Published Monthly. 1s.—Vols. I.—LXI. 7s. 6d. each. [Cloth covers for binding, 1s. each.]

MACMILLAN'S SIX-SHILLING NOVELS. 6s. each vol. Crown 8vo, cloth.
By the Rev. Charles Kingsley.
WESTWARD HO! | HYPATIA.
HEREWARD THE WAKE.
TWO YEARS AGO. | YEAST.
ALTON LOCKE. With Portrait.
By William Black.
A PRINCESS OF THULE.
STRANGE ADVENTURES OF A PHAETON. Illustrated.
THE MAID OF KILLEENA, AND OTHER TALES.
MADCAP VIOLET.
GREEN PASTURES AND PICCADILLY.
THE BEAUTIFUL WRETCH; THE FOUR MACNICOLS; THE PUPIL OF AURELIUS.
MACLEOD OF DARE. Illustrated.
WHITE WINGS: A YACHTING ROMANCE.
SHANDON BELLS. | YOLANDE.

MACMILLAN'S SIX-SHILLING NOVELS—continued.

By William Black.

JUDITH SHAKESPEARE.
THE WISE WOMEN OF INVERNESS, A TALE: AND OTHER MISCELLANIES.
WHITE HEATHER. | SABINA ZEMBRA.

By Mrs. Craik, Author of "John Halifax, Gentleman."

THE OGILVIES. Illustrated.
THE HEAD OF THE FAMILY. Illustrated.
OLIVE. Illustrated.
AGATHA'S HUSBAND. Illustrated.
MY MOTHER AND I. Illustrated.
MISS TOMMY: A MEDIÆVAL ROMANCE. Illustrated.
KING ARTHUR: NOT A LOVE STORY.

By J. H. Shorthouse.

JOHN INGLESANT. | SIR PERCIVAL.
A TEACHER OF THE VIOLIN, AND OTHER TALES.
THE COUNTESS EVE.

By Annie Keary.

A DOUBTING HEART.

By Henry James.

THE AMERICAN. | THE EUROPEANS.
DAISY MILLER; AN INTERNATIONAL EPISODE; FOUR MEETINGS.
THE MADONNA OF THE FUTURE, AND OTHER TALES.
RODERICK HUDSON.
WASHINGTON SQUARE; THE PENSION BEAUREPAS; A BUNDLE OF LETTERS.
THE PORTRAIT OF A LADY.
STORIES REVIVED. Two Series. 6s. each.
THE BOSTONIANS. | THE REVERBERATOR.

By F. Marion Crawford.

SANT' ILARIO. | GREIFENSTEIN.

REALMAH. By the Author of "Friends in Council."
OLD SIR DOUGLAS. By the Hon. Mrs. NORTON.
VIRGIN SOIL. By TOURGENIEF.
THE HARBOUR BAR.
BENGAL PEASANT LIFE. By LAL BEHARI DAY.
VIDA: STUDY OF A GIRL. By AMY DUNSMUIR.
JILL. By E. A. DILLWYN.
NEÆRA: A TALE OF ANCIENT ROME. By J. W. GRAHAM.
THE NEW ANTIGONE: A ROMANCE.
A LOVER OF THE BEAUTIFUL. By the MARCHIONESS OF CARMARTHEN.
PLAIN TALES FROM THE HILLS. By RUDYARD KIPLING.
A SOUTH SEA LOVER. By ALFRED ST. JOHNSTON.

MACMILLAN'S THREE-AND-SIXPENNY NOVELS. Crown 8vo. 3s. 6d.

ROBBERY UNDER ARMS: A Story of Life and Adventure in the Bush and in the Goldfields of Australia. By ROLF BOLDREWOOD.
SCHWARTZ. By D. CHRISTIE MURRAY.
NEIGHBOURS ON THE GREEN. By Mrs. OLIPHANT.
THE WEAKER VESSEL. By D. C. MURRAY.
JOYCE. By Mrs. OLIPHANT.

MACMILLAN'S THREE-AND-SIXPENNY NOVELS—continued.

CRESSY. By BRET HARTE.
FAITHFUL AND UNFAITHFUL. By MARGARET LEE.
REUBEN SACHS. By AMY LEVY.
WESSEX TALES: STRANGE, LIVELY, AND COMMONPLACE. By THOMAS HARDY.
MISS BRETHERTON. By Mrs. HUMPHRY WARD.
A LONDON LIFE. By HENRY JAMES.
A BELEAGUERED CITY. By Mrs. OLIPHANT.
CASTLE DALY. By ANNIE KEARY.
THE WOODLANDERS. By THOMAS HARDY.
AUNT RACHEL. By D. CHRISTIE MURRAY.
LOUISIANA, AND THAT LASS O' LOWRIE'S. By FRANCES HODGSON BURNETT.
THE CŒRULEANS. By Sir H. CUNNINGHAM.
THE RING OF AMASIS. By Lord LYTTON.
MAROONED. By W. CLARK RUSSELL.
WHEAT AND TARES. By Sir H. CUNNINGHAM.
THE SQUATTER'S DREAM. By ROLF BOLDREWOOD.
A YORK AND A LANCASTER ROSE. By ANNIE KEARY.
THE HERITAGE OF DEDLOW MARSH. By BRET HARTE.
JOHN VALES' GUARDIAN. By D. C. MURRAY.
THE MINER'S RIGHT. By R. BOLDREWOOD.
THE HERIOTS. By Sir H. CUNNINGHAM.
JANET'S HOME. By ANNIE KEARY.
THE ASPERN PAPERS. By HENRY JAMES.

Uniform with the above.

STORM WARRIORS; OR, LIFEBOAT WORK ON THE GOODWIN SANDS. By the Rev. JOHN GILMORE.
TALES OF OLD JAPAN. By A. B. MITFORD.
A YEAR WITH THE BIRDS. By W. WARDE FOWLER. Illustrated by BRYAN HOOK.
TALES OF THE BIRDS. By the same. Illustrated by BRYAN HOOK.
LEAVES OF A LIFE. By MONTAGU WILLIAMS, Q.C.
TRUE TALES FOR MY GRANDSONS. By Sir SAMUEL W. BAKER, F.R.S.
TALES OF OLD TRAVEL. By HENRY KINGSLEY.

MACMILLAN'S TWO SHILLING NOVELS. Globe 8vo. 2s. each.

By Mrs. Craik, Author of "John Halifax, Gentleman."

TWO MARRIAGES.
AGATHA'S HUSBAND. | THE OGILVIES.

By Mrs. Oliphant.

THE CURATE IN CHARGE.
A SON OF THE SOIL. | YOUNG MUSGRAVE.
HE THAT WILL NOT WHEN HE MAY.
A COUNTRY GENTLEMAN.
HESTER. | SIR TOM.
THE SECOND SON. | THE WIZARD'S SON.

By the Author of "Hogan, M.P."

HOGAN, M.P.
THE HONOURABLE MISS FERRARD.
FLITTERS, TATTERS, AND THE COUNSELLOR, WEEDS, AND OTHER SKETCHES.
CHRISTY CAREW. | ISMAY'S CHILDREN.

By George Fleming.

A NILE NOVEL. | MIRAGE.
THE HEAD OF MEDUSA. | VESTIGIA.

LIST OF PUBLICATIONS.

MACMILLAN'S TWO-SHILLING NOVELS—*continued*.

By Mrs. Macquoid.
PATTY.

By Annie Keary.
JANET'S HOME. | OLDBURY.
CLEMENCY FRANKLYN.
A YORK AND A LANCASTER ROSE.

By W. E. Norris.
MY FRIEND JIM. | CHRIS.

By Henry James.
DAISY MILLER; AN INTERNATIONAL EPISODE; FOUR MEETINGS.
RODERICK HUDSON.
THE MADONNA OF THE FUTURE, AND OTHER TALES.
WASHINGTON SQUARE.
PRINCESS CASAMASSIMA.

By Frances Hodgson Burnett.
LOUISIANA, AND THAT LASS O' LOWRIE'S. Two Stories.
HAWORTH'S.

By Hugh Conway.
A FAMILY AFFAIR. | LIVING OR DEAD.

By D. Christie Murray.
AUNT RACHEL.

By Helen Jackson.
RAMONA: A STORY.

A SLIP IN THE FENS.

MACMILLAN'S HALF-CROWN SERIES OF JUVENILE BOOKS. Globe 8vo, cloth, extra. 2s. 6d.

OUR YEAR. By the Author of "John Halifax, Gentleman."
LITTLE SUNSHINE'S HOLIDAY. By the Author of "John Halifax, Gentleman."
WHEN I WAS A LITTLE GIRL. By the Author of "St. Olave's."
NINE YEARS OLD. By the Author of "When I was a Little Girl," etc.
A STOREHOUSE OF STORIES. Edited by CHARLOTTE M. YONGE. 2 vols.
AGNES HOPETOUN'S SCHOOLS AND HOLIDAYS. By Mrs. OLIPHANT.
THE STORY OF A FELLOW SOLDIER. By FRANCES AWDRY. (A Life of Bishop Patteson for the Young.)
RUTH AND HER FRIENDS: A STORY FOR GIRLS.
THE HEROES OF ASGARD: TALES FROM SCANDINAVIAN MYTHOLOGY. By A. and E. KEARY.
THE RUNAWAY. By the Author of "Mrs. Jerningham's Journal."
WANDERING WILLIE. By the Author of "Conrad the Squirrel."
PANSIE'S FLOUR BIN. Illustrated by ADRIAN STOKES.
MILLY AND OLLY. By Mrs. T. H. WARD. Illustrated by Mrs. ALMA TADEMA.
THE POPULATION OF AN OLD PEAR TREE; OR, STORIES OF INSECT LIFE. From the French of E. VAN BRUYSSEL. Edited by CHARLOTTE M. YONGE. Illustrated.
HANNAH TARNE. By MARY E. HULLAH. Illustrated by W. J. HENNESSY.

MACMILLAN'S HALF-CROWN SERIES OF JUVENILE BOOKS—*continued*.

By Mrs. Molesworth. Illustrated by *Walter Crane*.
"CARROTS," JUST A LITTLE BOY.
TELL ME A STORY.
THE CUCKOO CLOCK.
A CHRISTMAS CHILD.
ROSY.
THE TAPESTRY ROOM.
GRANDMOTHER DEAR.
HERR BABY.
"US": AN OLD-FASHIONED STORY.
LITTLE MISS PEGGY.
TWO LITTLE WAIFS.
CHRISTMAS-TREE LAND.
FOUR WINDS FARM.
THE RECTORY CHILDREN.

MACMILLAN'S READING BOOKS. Adapted to the English and Scotch Codes.
Primer . . . . (48 pp.) 18mo, 2d.
Book I. for Standard I. (96 pp.) 18mo, 4d.
Book II. for Standard II. (144 pp.) 18mo, 5d.
Book III. for Standard III. (160 pp.) 18mo, 6d.
Book IV. for Standard IV. (176 pp.) 18mo, 8d.
Book V. for Standard V. (380 pp.) 18mo, 1s.
Book VI. for Standard VI. (430 pp.) Cr. 8vo, 2s.

MACMILLAN'S COPY-BOOKS.
*1. Initiatory Exercises and Short Letters.
*2. Words consisting of Short Letters.
*3. Long Letters, with words containing Long Letters. Figures.
*4. Words containing Long Letters.
4A. Practising and Revising Copybook for Nos. 1 to 4.
*5. Capitals, and Short Half-text Words beginning with a Capital.
*6. Half-text Words beginning with a Capital. Figures.
*7. Small-hand and Half-text, with Capitals and Figures.
*8. Small-hand and Half-text, with Capitals and Figures.
8A. Practising and Revising Copybook for Nos. 5 to 8.
*9. Small-hand Single Head Lines. Figures.
10. Small-hand Single Head Lines. Figures.
*11. Small-hand Double Head Lines. Figures.
12. Commercial and Arithmetical Examples, etc.
12A. Practising and Revising Copybook for Nos. 8 to 12.

The Copybooks may be had in two sizes:
(1) Large Post 4to, 4d. each;
(2) Post oblong, 2d. each.

The numbers marked * may also be had in Large Post 4to, with GOODMAN'S PATENT SLIDING COPIES. 6d. each.

MACMILLAN'S LATIN COURSE. Part I. By A. M. COOK, M.A. 2nd Edition, enlarged. Globe 8vo. 3s. 6d.
Part II. By the same. Gl. 8vo. 2s. 6d.

MACMILLAN'S SHORTER LATIN COURSE. By A. M. COOK, M.A. Being an Abridgment of "Macmillan's Latin Course, Part I." Globe 8vo. 1s. 6d.

MACMILLAN'S LATIN READER. A Latin Reader for the Lower Forms in Schools. By H. J. HARDY. Gl. 8vo. 2s. 6d.

MACMILLAN'S GREEK COURSE. Edit. by Rev. W. G. RUTHERFORD, M.A. Gl. 8vo.
I. FIRST GREEK GRAMMAR. By the Rev. W. G. RUTHERFORD, M.A. Gl.8vo. Part I. Accidence, 2s.; Part II. Syntax, 2s.; or in 1 vol. 3s. 6d.
II. EASY EXERCISES IN GREEK ACCIDENCE. By H. G. UNDERHILL, M.A. 2s.
III. SECOND GREEK EXERCISE BOOK. By Rev. W. A. HEARD, M.A.

MACMILLAN'S GREEK READER. Stories and Legends. A First Greek Reader, with Notes, Vocabulary, and Exercises, by F. H. COLSON, M.A. Globe 8vo. 3s.

MACMILLAN'S ELEMENTARY CLASSICS. 18mo. 1s. 6d. each.

This Series falls into two classes:—
(1) First Reading Books for Beginners, provided not only with *Introductions and Notes*, but with *Vocabularies*, and in some cases with *Exercises* based upon the Text.
(2) Stepping-stones to the study of particular authors, intended for more advanced students, who are beginning to read such authors as Terence, Plato, the Attic Dramatists, and the harder parts of Cicero, Horace, Virgil, and Thucydides.

These are provided with Introductions and Notes, but no *Vocabulary*. The Publishers have been led to provide the more strictly Elementary Books with Vocabularies by the representations of many teachers, who hold that beginners do not understand the use of a Dictionary, and of others who, in the case of middle-class schools where the cost of books is a serious consideration, advocate the Vocabulary system on grounds of economy. It is hoped that the two parts of the Series, fitting into one another, may together fulfil all the requirements of Elementary and Preparatory Schools, and the Lower Forms of Public Schools.

The following Elementary Books, *with Introductions, Notes, and Vocabularies*, and in some cases with *Exercises*, are either ready or in preparation:

LATIN ACCIDENCE AND EXERCISES ARRANGED FOR BEGINNERS. By WILLIAM WELCH, M.A., and C. G. DUFFIELD, M.A.

ÆSCHYLUS.—PROMETHEUS VINCTUS. Edit. by Rev. H. M. STEPHENSON, M.A.

ARRIAN.—SELECTIONS. Edited by JOHN BOND, M.A., and A. S. WALPOLE, M.A.

AULUS GELLIUS, STORIES FROM. By Rev. G. H. NALL, M.A.

CÆSAR. — THE INVASION OF BRITAIN. Being Selections from Books IV. and V. of the "De Bello Gallico." Adapted for Beginners by W. WELCH, and C. G. DUFFIELD.

— THE HELVETIAN WAR. Selected from Book I. of "The Gallic War," arranged for the use of Beginners by W. WELCH, M.A., and C. G. DUFFIELD, M.A.

— THE GALLIC WAR. Scenes from Books V. and VI. Edited by C. COLBECK, M.A.

— THE GALLIC WAR. Book I. Edited by Rev. A. S. WALPOLE, M.A.

— THE GALLIC WAR. Books II. and III. Ed. by Rev. W. G. RUTHERFORD, M.A.

MACMILLAN'S ELEMENTARY CLASSICS—*continued*.

CÆSAR.—THE GALLIC WAR. Book IV. Edited by C. BRYANS, M.A.

— THE GALLIC WAR. Books V. and VI. (separately). By the same Editor.

— THE GALLIC WAR. Book VII. Ed. by J. BOND, M.A., and A. S. WALPOLE, M.A.

CICERO.—DE SENECTUTE. Edited by E. S. SHUCKBURGH, M.A.

— DE AMICITIA. Edited by E. S. SHUCKBURGH, M.A.

— STORIES OF ROMAN HISTORY. Edited by Rev. G. E. JEANS, M.A., and A. V. JONES, M.A.

EURIPIDES.—ALCESTIS. By the Rev. M. A. BAYFIELD, M.A.

— HECUBA. Edited by Rev. J. BOND, M.A., and A. S. WALPOLE, M.A.

— MEDEA. Edited by A. W. VERRALL, Litt.D., and Rev. M. A. BAYFIELD, M.A.

EUTROPIUS. Adapted for the use of Beginners by W. WELCH, M.A., and C. G. DUFFIELD, M.A.

HOMER.—ILIAD. Book I. Ed. by Rev. J. BOND, M.A., and A. S. WALPOLE, M.A.

— ILIAD. Book XVIII. THE ARMS OF ACHILLES. Edited by S. R. JAMES, M.A.

— ODYSSEY. Book I. Edited by Rev. J. BOND, M.A., and A. S. WALPOLE, M.A.

HORACE.—ODES. Books I.—IV. Edited by T. E. PAGE, M.A. 1s. 6d. each.

LIVY. Book I. Edited by H. M. STEPHENSON, M.A.

— THE HANNIBALIAN WAR. Being part of the 21st and 22nd Books of Livy. Adapted for Beginners by G. C. MACAULAY, M.A.

— THE SIEGE OF SYRACUSE. Being part of the 24th and 25th Books of Livy. Adapted for the use of Beginners by G RICHARDS, M.A., and Rev. A. S. WALPOLE, M.A.

— Book XXI. With Notes adapted from Mr. Capes' Edition for the Use of Junior Students, by Rev. W. W. CAPES, M.A., and J. E. MELHUISH, M.A.

— LEGENDS OF ANCIENT ROME, FROM LIVY. Adapted for the Use of Beginners. With Notes, Exercises, and Vocabulary, by H. WILKINSON, M.A.

LUCIAN, EXTRACTS FROM. Edited by J. BOND, M.A., and A. S. WALPOLE, M.A.

NEPOS.—SELECTIONS ILLUSTRATIVE OF GREEK AND ROMAN HISTORY. Edited by G. S. FARNELL, B.A.

OVID.—SELECTIONS. Edited by E. S. SHUCKBURGH, M.A.

— EASY SELECTIONS FROM OVID IN ELEGIAC VERSE. Arranged for the use of Beginners by H. WILKINSON, M.A.

— STORIES FROM THE METAMORPHOSES. Arranged for the use of Beginners by J. BOND, M.A., and A. S. WALPOLE, M.A.

PHÆDRUS.—SELECT FABLES. Adapted for use of Beginners by Rev. A. S. WALPOLE, M.A.

LIST OF PUBLICATIONS. 35

MACMILLAN'S ELEMENTARY CLASSICS—*continued.*

THUCYDIDES.—THE RISE OF THE ATHENIAN EMPIRE. Book I. Chaps. lxxxix.—cxvii. and cxxviii.—cxxxviii. Edited by F. H. COLSON, M.A.

VIRGIL.—GEORGICS. Book I. Edited by T. E. PAGE, M.A.

— GEORGICS. Book II. Edited by Rev. J. H. SKRINE, M.A.

— ÆNEID. Book I. Edited by A. S. WALPOLE, M.A.

— ÆNEID. Book II. Ed. by T. E. PAGE.

— ÆNEID. Book III. Edited by T. E. PAGE, M.A.

— ÆNEID. Book IV. Edit. by Rev. H. M. STEPHENSON, M.A.

— ÆNEID. Book V. Edited by Rev. A. CALVERT, M.A.

— ÆNEID. Book VI. Ed. by T. E. PAGE.

— ÆNEID. Book VII. THE WRATH OF TURNUS. Edited by A. CALVERT, M.A.

— ÆNEID. Book IX. Edited by Rev. H. M. STEPHENSON, M.A.

— ÆNEID. Book X. Ed.byS.G.OWEN,M.A.

— SELECTIONS. Edited by E. S. SHUCKBURGH, M.A.

XENOPHON.—ANABASIS. Book I., Chaps. i.—viii. Edited by E. A. WELLS, M.A.

— ANABASIS. Book I. Edited by Rev. A. S. WALPOLE, M.A.

— ANABASIS. Book II. Edited by Rev. A. S. WALPOLE, M.A.

— ANABASIS. Book III. Edited by Rev. G. H. NALL, M.A.

— ANABASIS. Book IV. Edited by Rev. E. D. STONE, M.A.

— SELECTIONS FROM BOOK IV. OF "THE ANABASIS." Edit. by Rev. E. D. STONE.

— SELECTIONS FROM THE CYROPAEDIA. Edited by Rev. A. H. COOKE, M.A.

The following more advanced books have *Introductions, Notes,* but no *Vocabularies* :

CICERO.—SELECT LETTERS. Edit. by Rev. G. E. JEANS, M.A.

HERODOTUS.—SELECTIONS FROM BOOKS VII. AND VIII. THE EXPEDITION OF XERXES. Edited by A. H. COOKE, M.A.

HORACE.—SELECTIONS FROM THE SATIRES AND EPISTLES. Edited by Rev. W. J. V. BAKER, M.A.

— SELECT EPODES AND ARS POETICA. Edited by H. A. DALTON, M.A.

PLATO.—EUTHYPHRO AND MENEXENUS. Edited by C. E. GRAVES, M.A.

TERENCE.—SCENES FROM THE ANDRIA. Edited by F. W. CORNISH, M.A.

THE GREEK ELEGIAC POETS, FROM CALLINUS TO CALLIMACHUS. Selected and Edited by Rev. H. KYNASTON.

THUCYDIDES. Book IV., Chaps. i.—lxi. THE CAPTURE OF SPHACTERIA. Edited by C. E. GRAVES, M.A.

Other Volumes to follow.

MACMILLAN'S CLASSICAL SERIES FOR COLLEGES AND SCHOOLS.
Fcp. 8vo. Being select portions of Greek and Latin authors, edited, with Introductions and Notes, for the use of Middle and Upper Forms of Schools, or of Candidates for Public Examinations at the Universities and elsewhere.

ÆSCHINES. IN CTESIPHONTEM. Edited by Rev. T. GWATKIN, M.A., and E. S. SHUCKBURGH, M.A. [*In the Press.*

ÆSCHYLUS. PERSÆ. Edited by A. O. PRICKARD, M.A. With Map. 3*s.* 6*d.*

— THE "SEVEN AGAINST THEBES." Edit. by A. W. VERRALL, Litt.D., and M. A. BAYFIELD, M.A. 3*s.* 6*d.*

ANDOCIDES.—DE MYSTERIIS. Edited by W. J. HICKIE, M.A. 2*s.* 6*d.*

ATTIC ORATORS, SELECTIONS FROM THE. Antiphon, Andocides, Lysias, Isocrates, and Isæus. Ed. by R. C. JEBB, Litt.D. 6*s.*

CÆSAR.—THE GALLIC WAR. Edited after Kraner by Rev. J. BOND, M.A., and Rev. A. S. WALPOLE, M.A. With Maps. 6*s.*

CATULLUS. SELECT POEMS. Edited by F. P. SIMPSON, B.A. 5*s.* [The Text of this Edition is carefully adapted to School use.]

CICERO.—THE CATILINE ORATIONS. From the German of Karl Halm. Edited by A. S. WILKINS, Litt.D. 3*s.* 6*d.*

— PRO LEGE MANILIA. Edited, after Halm, by Prof. A. S. WILKINS, Litt.D. 2*s.* 6*d.*

— THE SECOND PHILIPPIC ORATION. From the German of Karl Halm. Edited, with Corrections and Additions, by Prof. J. E. B. MAYOR. 5*s.*

— PRO ROSCIO AMERINO. Edited, after Halm, by E. H. DONKIN, M.A. 4*s.* 6*d.*

— PRO P. SESTIO. Edited by Rev. H. A. HOLDEN, M.A. 5*s.*

— SELECT LETTERS. Edited by Prof. R. Y. TYRRELL, M.A.

DEMOSTHENES.—DE CORONA. Edited by B. DRAKE, M.A. New and revised edit. 4*s.*6*d.*

— ADVERSUS LEPTINEM. Edited by Rev. J. R. KING, M.A. 4*s.* 6*d.*

— THE FIRST PHILIPPIC. Edited, after C. Rehdantz, by Rev. T. GWATKIN. 2*s.* 6*d.*

EURIPIDES.—HIPPOLYTUS. Edited by Prof. J. P. MAHAFFY and J. B. BURY. 3*s.* 6*d.*

— MEDEA. Edited by A. W. VERRALL, Litt.D. 3*s.* 6*d.*

— IPHIGENIA IN TAURIS. Edited by E. B. ENGLAND, M.A. 4*s.* 6*d.*

— ION. Ed. by M. A. BAYFIELD, M.A. 3*s.*6*d.*

HERODOTUS. Book III. Edited by G. C. MACAULAY, M.A.

— Book VI. Ed. by Prof. J. STRACHAN, M.A.

— Book VII. Ed.by Mrs. MONTAGU BUTLER.

HOMER.—ILIAD. Books I. IX. XI. XVI.—XXIV. THE STORY OF ACHILLES. Ed. by J. H. PRATT, M.A., and W. LEAF, Litt.D. 6*s.*

— ODYSSEY. Book IX. Edited by Prof. J. E. B. MAYOR, M.A. 2*s.* 6*d.*

— ODYSSEY. Books XXI.—XXIV. THE TRIUMPH OF ODYSSEUS. Edited by S. G. HAMILTON, B.A. 3*s.* 6*d.*

MACMILLAN'S CLASSICAL SERIES—continued.

HORACE.—THE ODES. Edited by T. E. PAGE, M.A. 6s. (Books I. II. III. and IV. separately, 2s. each.)
— THE SATIRES. Edited by Prof. A. PALMER, M.A. 6s.
— THE EPISTLES AND ARS POETICA. Edit. by Prof. A. S. WILKINS, Litt.D. 6s.

JUVENAL.- THIRTEEN SATIRES. Edited, for the use of Schools, by E. G. HARDY, M.A. 5s. [The Text of this Edition is carefully adapted to School use.]
— SELECT SATIRES. Edited by Prof. JOHN E. B. MAYOR. X. and XI. 3s. 6d.; XII.—XVI. 4s. 6d.

LIVY. Books II. and III. Edited by Rev. H. M. STEPHENSON, M.A. 5s.
— Books XXI. and XXII. Edited by Rev. W. W. CAPES, M.A. 5s.
— Books XXIII. and XXIV. Ed. by G. C. MACAULAY. With Maps. 5s.
— THE LAST TWO KINGS OF MACEDON. Extracts from the Fourth and Fifth Decades of Livy. Selected and Edit. by F. H. RAWLINS, M.A. With Maps. 3s. 6d.

LUCRETIUS. Books I.—III. Edited by J. H. WARBURTON LEE, M.A. 4s. 6d.

LYSIAS.—SELECT ORATIONS. Edited by E. S. SHUCKBURGH, M.A. 6s.

MARTIAL. SELECT EPIGRAMS. Edited by Rev. H. M. STEPHENSON, M.A. 6s. 6d.

OVID.—FASTI. Edited by G. H. HALLAM, M.A. With Maps. 5s.
— HEROIDUM EPISTULÆ XIII. Edited by E. S. SHUCKBURGH, M.A. 4s. 6d.
— METAMORPHOSES. Books XIII. and XIV. Edited by C. SIMMONS, M.A. 4s. 6d.

PLATO.—THE REPUBLIC. Books I.—V. Edited by T. H. WARREN, M.A. 6s.
— LACHES. Edited by M. T. TATHAM, M.A. 2s. 6d.

PLAUTUS.—MILES GLORIOSUS. Edited by Prof. R. Y. TYRRELL, M.A. 5s.
— AMPHITRUO. Ed. by A. PALMER, M.A. 5s.

PLINY.—LETTERS. Books I. and II. Edited by J. COWAN, M.A. 5s.

PLINY.—LETTERS. Book III. Edited by Prof. J. E. B. MAYOR. With Life of Pliny by G. H. RENDALL. 5s.

PLUTARCH.—LIFE OF THEMISTOKLES. Ed. by Rev. H. A. HOLDEN, M.A., LL.D. 5s.
— LIVES OF GALBA AND OTHO. Edited by E. G. HARDY, M.A. 6s.

POLYBIUS. The History of the Achæan League as contained in the remains of Polybius. Edited by W. W. CAPES. 6s. 6d.

PROPERTIUS. SELECT POEMS. Edited by Prof. J. P. POSTGATE, M.A. 6s.

SALLUST. CATILINE AND JUGURTHA. Ed. by C. MERIVALE, D.D. 4s. 6d.— Or separately, 2s. 6d. each.
— BELLUM CATULINAE. Edited by A. M. COOK, M.A. 4s. 6d.

MACMILLAN'S CLASSICAL SERIES—continued.

TACITUS.—AGRICOLA AND GERMANIA. Ed. by A. J. CHURCH, M.A., and W. J. BRODRIBB, M.A. 3s. 6d.—Or separately, 2s. each.
— THE ANNALS. Book VI. By the same Editors. 2s. 6d.
— THE HISTORIES. Books I. and II. Edited by A. D. GODLEY, M.A. 5s.
— THE HISTORIES. Books III.—V. By the same Editor. 5s.

TERENCE.—HAUTON TIMORUMENOS. Edit. by E. S. SHUCKBURGH, M.A. 3s.—With Translation, 4s. 6d.
— PHORMIO. Ed. by Rev. J. BOND, M.A., and Rev. A. S. WALPOLE, M.A. 4s. 6d.

THUCYDIDES. Book IV. Edited by C. E. GRAVES, M.A. 5s.
— Book V. By the same Editor.
— Books VI. and VII. THE SICILIAN EXPEDITION. Edited by Rev. P. FROST, M.A. With Map. 5s.

VIRGIL.—ÆNEID. Books II. and III. THE NARRATIVE OF ÆNEAS. Edited by E. W. HOWSON, M.A. 3s.

XENOPHON.—HELLENICA. Books I. and II. Edited by H. HAILSTONE, M.A. 4s. 6d.
— CYROPÆDIA. Books VII. and VIII. Ed. by Prof. A. GOODWIN, M.A. 5s.
— MEMORABILIA SOCRATIS. Edited by A. R. CLUER, B.A. 6s.
— THE ANABASIS. Books I.—IV. Edited by Professors W. W. GOODWIN and J. W. WHITE. Adapted to Goodwin's Greek Grammar. With a Map. 5s.
— HIERO. Edited by Rev. H. A. HOLDEN, M.A., LL.D. 3s. 6d.
— OECONOMICUS. By the same Editor. With Introduction, Explanatory Notes, Critical Appendix, and Lexicon. 6s.

The following are in preparation:

DEMOSTHENES.—IN MIDIAM. Edited by Prof. A. S. WILKINS, Litt.D., and HERMAN HAGER, Ph.D.

EURIPIDES.—BACCHAE. Edited by Prof. R. Y. TYRRELL, M.A.

HERODOTUS. Book V. Edited by Prof. J. STRACHAN, M.A.

ISÆOS.—THE ORATIONS. Edited by Prof. WM. RIDGEWAY, M.A.

OVID.—METAMORPHOSES. Books I.—III. Edited by C. SIMMONS, M.A.

SALLUST.—JUGURTHA. Edited by A. M. COOK, M.A.

TACITUS.—THE ANNALS. Books I. and II. Edited by J. REID, Litt.D.

Other Volumes will follow.

MACMILLAN'S GEOGRAPHICAL SERIES. Edited by ARCHIBALD GEIKIE, F.R.S., Director-General of the Geological Survey of the United Kingdom.

THE TEACHING OF GEOGRAPHY. A Practical Handbook for the use of Teachers. Globe 8vo. 2s.

LIST OF PUBLICATIONS.

MACMILLAN'S GEOGRAPHICAL SERIES—*continued.*

GEOGRAPHY OF THE BRITISH ISLES. By ARCHIBALD GEIKIE, F.R.S. 18mo. 1s.

THE ELEMENTARY SCHOOL ATLAS. 24 Maps in Colours. By JOHN BARTHOLOMEW, F.R.G.S. 4to. 1s.

AN ELEMENTARY CLASS-BOOK OF GENERAL GEOGRAPHY. By HUGH ROBERT MILL, D.Sc. Edin. Illustrated. Cr. 8vo. 3s. 6d.

MAP DRAWING AND MAP MAKING. By W. A. ELDERTON. Pott 8vo.

GEOGRAPHY OF THE BRITISH COLONIES. By G. M. DAWSON and ALEX. SUTHERLAND.

GEOGRAPHY OF EUROPE. By JAMES SIME, M.A. With Illustrations. Gl. 8vo. 3s.

GEOGRAPHY OF NORTH AMERICA. By Prof. N. S. SHALER.

GEOGRAPHY OF INDIA. By H. F. BLANFORD, F.G.S. Globe 8vo. 2s. 6d.

MACMILLAN'S SCIENCE CLASS-BOOKS. Fcp. 8vo.

LESSONS IN ELEMENTARY PHYSICS. By Prof. BALFOUR STEWART, F.R.S. New Edition. 4s. 6d. (Questions on, 2s.)

EXAMPLES IN PHYSICS. By Prof. D. E. JONES, B.Sc. 3s. 6d.

QUESTIONS AND EXAMPLES ON EXPERIMENTAL PHYSICS: Sound, Light, Heat, Electricity, and Magnetism. By B. LOEWY, F.R.A.S. Fcp. 8vo. 2s.

A GRADUATED COURSE OF NATURAL SCIENCE FOR ELEMENTARY AND TECHNICAL SCHOOLS AND COLLEGES. Part I. First Year's Course. By the same. Gl. 8vo. 2s.

SOUND, ELEMENTARY LESSONS ON. By Dr. W. H. STONE. 3s. 6d.

ELECTRIC LIGHT ARITHMETIC. By R. E. DAY, M.A. 2s.

A COLLECTION OF EXAMPLES ON HEAT AND ELECTRICITY. By H. H. TURNER. 2s. 6d.

AN ELEMENTARY TREATISE ON STEAM. By Prof. J. PERRY, C.E. 4s. 6d.

ELECTRICITY AND MAGNETISM. By Prof. SILVANUS THOMPSON. 4s. 6d.

POPULAR ASTRONOMY. By Sir G. B. AIRY, K.C.B., late Astronomer-Royal. 4s. 6d.

ELEMENTARY LESSONS ON ASTRONOMY. By J. N. LOCKYER, F.R.S. New Edition. 5s. 6d. (Questions on, 1s. 6d.)

LESSONS IN ELEMENTARY CHEMISTRY. By Sir H. ROSCOE, F.R.S. 4s. 6d.—Problems adapted to the same, by Prof. THORPE. With Key. 2s.

OWENS COLLEGE JUNIOR COURSE OF PRACTICAL CHEMISTRY. By F. JONES. With Preface by Sir H. ROSCOE, F.R.S. 2s. 6d.

QUESTIONS ON CHEMISTRY. A Series of Problems and Exercises in Inorganic and Organic Chemistry. By F. JONES. 3s.

OWENS COLLEGE COURSE OF PRACTICAL ORGANIC CHEMISTRY. By JULIUS B. COHEN, Ph.D. With Preface by Sir H. ROSCOE and Prof. SCHORLEMMER. 2s. 6d.

ELEMENTS OF CHEMISTRY. By Prof. IRA REMSEN. 2s. 6d.

MACMILLAN'S SCIENCE CLASS-BOOKS *continued.*

EXPERIMENTAL PROOFS OF CHEMICAL THEORY FOR BEGINNERS. By WILLIAM RAMSAY, Ph.D. 2s. 6d.

NUMERICAL TABLES AND CONSTANTS IN ELEMENTARY SCIENCE. By SYDNEY LUPTON, M.A. 2s. 6d.

PHYSICAL GEOGRAPHY, ELEMENTARY LESSONS IN. By ARCHIBALD GEIKIE, F.R.S. 4s. 6d. (Questions on, 1s. 6d.)

ELEMENTARY LESSONS IN PHYSIOLOGY. By T. H. HUXLEY, F.R.S. 4s. 6d. (Questions on, 1s. 6d.)

LESSONS IN ELEMENTARY ANATOMY. By ST. G. MIVART, F.R.S. 6s. 6d.

LESSONS IN ELEMENTARY BOTANY. By Prof. D. OLIVER, F.R.S. 4s. 6d.

DISEASES OF FIELD AND GARDEN CROPS. By W. G. SMITH. 4s. 6d.

LESSONS IN LOGIC, INDUCTIVE AND DEDUCTIVE. By W. S. JEVONS, LL.D. 3s. 6d.

POLITICAL ECONOMY FOR BEGINNERS. By Mrs. FAWCETT. With Questions. 2s. 6d.

THE ECONOMICS OF INDUSTRY. By Prof. A. MARSHALL and M. P. MARSHALL. 2s. 6d.

ELEMENTARY LESSONS IN THE SCIENCE OF AGRICULTURAL PRACTICE. By Prof. H. TANNER. 3s. 6d.

CLASS-BOOK OF GEOGRAPHY. By C. B. CLARKE, F.R.S. 3s. 6d.; sewed. 3s.

SHORT GEOGRAPHY OF THE BRITISH ISLANDS. By J. R. GREEN and ALICE S. GREEN. With Maps. 3s. 6d.

MACMILLAN'S PROGRESSIVE FRENCH COURSE. By G. EUGÈNE FASNACHT. Extra fcp. 8vo.

I. FIRST YEAR, CONTAINING EASY LESSONS IN THE REGULAR ACCIDENCE. Thoroughly revised Edition. 1s.

II. SECOND YEAR, CONTAINING AN ELEMENTARY GRAMMAR. With copious Exercises, Notes, and Vocabularies. New Edition, enlarged. 2s.

III. THIRD YEAR, CONTAINING A SYSTEMATIC SYNTAX AND LESSONS IN COMPOSITION. 2s. 6d.

THE TEACHER'S COMPANION TO THE SAME. With copious Notes, Hints for different renderings, Synonyms, Philological Remarks, etc. 1st Year, 4s. 6d. 2nd Year, 4s. 6d. 3rd Year, 4s. 6d.

MACMILLAN'S PROGRESSIVE FRENCH READERS. By G. EUGÈNE FASNACHT. Extra fcp. 8vo.

I. FIRST YEAR, CONTAINING TALES, HISTORICAL EXTRACTS, LETTERS, DIALOGUES, FABLES, BALLADS, NURSERY SONGS, etc. With Two Vocabularies: (1) In the Order of Subjects; (2) In Alphabetical Order. 2s. 6d.

II. SECOND YEAR, CONTAINING FICTION IN PROSE AND VERSE, HISTORICAL AND DESCRIPTIVE EXTRACTS, ESSAYS, LETTERS, etc. 2s. 6d.

MACMILLAN'S FRENCH COMPOSITION. By G. EUGÈNE FASNACHT. Extra fcp. 8vo.
Part I. ELEMENTARY. 2s. 6d. — Part II. ADVANCED.
THE TEACHER'S COMPANION TO THE SAME. Part I. 4s. 6d.

MACMILLAN'S PROGRESSIVE GERMAN COURSE. By G. EUGÈNE FASNACHT. Extra fcp. 8vo.
I. FIRST YEAR, CONTAINING EASY LESSONS ON THE REGULAR ACCIDENCE. 1s. 6d.
II. SECOND YEAR, CONTAINING CONVERSATIONAL LESSONS ON SYSTEMATIC ACCIDENCE AND ELEMENTARY SYNTAX, WITH PHILOLOGICAL ILLUSTRATIONS AND ETYMOLOGICAL VOCABULARY. New Edition, enlarged. 3s. 6d.
THE TEACHER'S COMPANION TO THE SAME. 1st Year, 4s. 6d. ; 2nd Year, 4s. 6d.

MACMILLAN'S PROGRESSIVE GERMAN READERS. By G. EUGÈNE FASNACHT. Extra fcap. 8vo.
I. FIRST YEAR, CONTAINING AN INTRODUCTION TO THE GERMAN ORDER OF WORDS, WITH COPIOUS EXAMPLES, EXTRACTS FROM GERMAN AUTHORS IN PROSE AND POETRY, NOTES, VOCABULARIES. 2s. 6d.

MACMILLAN'S SERIES OF FOREIGN SCHOOL CLASSICS. Edited by G. E. FASNACHT. 18mo.
Select works of the best foreign Authors, with suitable Notes and Introductions based on the latest researches of French and German Scholars by practical masters and teachers.

FRENCH.
CORNEILLE.—LE CID. Edited by G. E. FASNACHT. 1s.
DUMAS. LES DEMOISELLES DE ST. CYR. Edited by VICTOR OGER. 1s. 6d.
FRENCH READINGS FROM ROMAN HISTORY. Selected from various Authors. Edited by C. COLBECK, M.A. 4s. 6d.
LA FONTAINE'S FABLES. Books I.—VI. Ed. by L. M. MORIARTY. [In preparation.
MOLIÈRE.— LES FEMMES SAVANTES. By G. E. FASNACHT. 1s.
— LE MISANTHROPE. By the same. 1s.
— LE MÉDECIN MALGRÉ LUI. By the same. 1s.
— L'AVARE. Edited by L. M. MORIARTY. 1s.
— LE BOURGEOIS GENTILHOMME. By the same. 1s. 6d.
RACINE.—BRITANNICUS. Edited by EUGÈNE PELLISSIER. 2s.
SAND (George).— LA MARE AU DIABLE. Edited by W. E. RUSSELL, M.A. 1s. 6d.
SANDEAU (Jules).—MADEMOISELLE DE LA SEIGLIÈRE. Edit. by H. C. STEEL. 1s. 6d.
THIERS'S HISTORY OF THE EGYPTIAN EXPEDITION. Edited by Rev. H. A. BULL, M.A.
VOLTAIRE. CHARLES XII. Edited by G. E. FASNACHT. 3s. 6d.

MACMILLAN'S FOREIGN SCHOOL CLASSICS—continued.

GERMAN.
FREYTAG.—DOKTOR LUTHER. Edited by FRANCIS STORR, M.A. [In preparation.
GOETHE.— GÖTZ VON BERLICHINGEN. Edit. by H. A. BULL, M.A. 2s.
— FAUST. Part I. Ed. by Miss J. LEE. 4s. 6d.
HEINE.—SELECTIONS FROM THE REISEBILDER AND OTHER PROSE WORKS. Edit. by C. COLBECK, M.A. 2s. 6d.
LESSING.—MINNA VON BARNHELM. Edited by J. SIME, M.A. [In preparation.
SCHILLER.- DIE JUNGFRAU VON ORLEANS. Edited by JOSEPH GOSTWICK. 2s. 6d.
— MARIA STUART. Edited by C. SHELDON, M.A., D.Lit. 2s. 6d.
— WALLENSTEIN. Part I. DAS LÄGER. Edited by H. B. COTTERILL, M.A. 2s.
— WILHELM TELL. Edited by G. E. FASNACHT. 2s. 6d.
— SELECTIONS FROM SCHILLER'S LYRICAL POEMS. Edited by E. J. TURNER, M.A., and E. D. A. MORSHEAD, M.A. 2s. 6d.
UHLAND.—SELECT BALLADS. Adapted as a First Easy Reading Book for Beginners. Edited by G. E. FASNACHT. 1s.

MACMILLAN'S PRIMARY SERIES OF FRENCH AND GERMAN READING BOOKS. Edited by G. EUGÈNE FASNACHT. With Illustrations. Globe 8vo.
CORNAZ.—NOS ENFANTS ET LEURS AMIS. Edited by EDITH HARVEY. 1s. 6d.
DE MAISTRE.—LA JEUNE SIBÉRIENNE ET LE LÉPREUX DE LA CITÉ D'AOSTE. Edit. by S. BARLET, B.Sc. 1s. 6d.
FLORIAN. SELECT FABLES. Edited by CHARLES YELD, M.A. 1s. 6d.
GRIMM.- KINDER- UND HAUSMÄRCHEN. Selected and Edited by G. E. FASNACHT. Illustrated. 2s. 6d.
HAUFF.—DIE KARAVANE. Edited by HERMAN HAGER, Ph.D. With Exercises by G. E. FASNACHT. 3s.
LA FONTAINE. FABLES. A Selection, by L. M. MORIARTY, M.A. With Illustrations by RANDOLPH CALDECOTT. 2s. 6d.
MOLESWORTH.— FRENCH LIFE IN LETTERS. By Mrs. MOLESWORTH. 1s. 6d.
PERRAULT.—CONTES DE FÉES. Edited by G. E. FASNACHT. 1s. 6d.
SCHMID.—HEINRICH VON EICHENFELS. Ed. by G. E. FASNACHT. 2s. 6d.

MACNAMARA (C.). A HISTORY OF ASIATIC CHOLERA. Crown 8vo. 10s. 6d.

MACQUOID (K. S.). PATTY. Globe 8vo. 2s.

MADAGASCAR : AN HISTORICAL AND DESCRIPTIVE ACCOUNT OF THE ISLAND AND ITS FORMER DEPENDENCIES. By Captain S. OLIVER, F.S.A. 2 vols. Med. 8vo. 2l. 12s. 6d.

MADAME TABBY'S ESTABLISHMENT. By KARI. Illustrated by L. WAIN. Crown 8vo. 4s. 6d.

MADOC (Fayr).--THE STORY OF MELICENT. Crown 8vo. 4s. 6d.

MADOC (Fayr).—MARGARET JERMINE. 3 vols. Crown 8vo. 31s. 6d.

MAGUIRE (J. F.). YOUNG PRINCE MARIGOLD. Illustrated. Globe 8vo. 4s. 6d.

MAHAFFY (Rev. Prof. J. P.). -SOCIAL LIFE IN GREECE, FROM HOMER TO MENANDER. 6th Edition. Crown 8vo. 9s.

—— GREEK LIFE AND THOUGHT FROM THE AGE OF ALEXANDER TO THE ROMAN CONQUEST. Crown 8vo. 12s. 6d.

—— RAMBLES AND STUDIES IN GREECE. Illustrated. 3rd Edition. Crown 8vo. 10s. 6d.

—— THE GREEK WORLD UNDER ROMAN SWAY. Crown 8vo. [*In the Press.*

—— A HISTORY OF CLASSICAL GREEK LITERATURE. 2 vols. Crown 8vo. Vol. I. The Poets. With an Appendix on Homer by Prof. SAYCE. 9s.—Vol. II. The Prose Writers. In 2 Parts, 4s. 6d. each.

—— GREEK ANTIQUITIES. Illust. 18mo. 1s.

—— EURIPIDES. 18mo. 1s. 6d.

—— THE DECAY OF MODERN PREACHING: AN ESSAY. Crown 8vo. 3s. 6d.

—— THE PRINCIPLES OF THE ART OF CONVERSATION. 2nd Ed. Crown 8vo. 4s. 6d.

MAHAFFY (Rev. Prof. J. P.) and ROGERS (J. E.).—SKETCHES FROM A TOUR THROUGH HOLLAND AND GERMANY. Illustrated by J. E. ROGERS. Extra crown 8vo. 10s. 6d.

MAHAFFY (Prof. J. P.) and BERNARD (J. H.).—KANT'S CRITICAL PHILOSOPHY FOR ENGLISH READERS. A new and completed Edition in 2 vols. Crown 8vo. Vol. I. THE KRITIK OF PURE REASON EXPLAINED AND DEFENDED. 7s. 6d. Vol. II. THE "PROLEGOMENA." Translated, with Notes and Appendices. 6s.

MAITLAND(F. W.). PLEAS OF THE CROWN FOR THE COUNTY OF GLOUCESTER, A.D. 1221. Edited by F. W. MAITLAND. 8vo. 7s. 6d.

—— JUSTICE AND POLICE. Cr. 8vo. 3s. 6d.

MALET (Lucas). MRS. LORIMER: A SKETCH IN BLACK AND WHITE. Cr. 8vo. 4s. 6d.

MANCHESTER SCIENCE LECTURES FOR THE PEOPLE. Eighth Series, 1876—77. With Illustrations. Cr. 8vo. 2s.

MANSFIELD (C. B.).—A THEORY OF SALTS. Crown 8vo. 14s.

—— AERIAL NAVIGATION. Cr. 8vo. 10s. 6d.

MARKHAM (C. R.).—LIFE OF ROBERT FAIRFAX, OF STEETON. 8vo. 12s. 6d.

MARRIOTT (J. A. R.).—THE MAKERS OF MODERN ITALY: MAZZINI, CAVOUR, GARIBALDI. Three Oxford Lectures. Crown 8vo. 1s. 6d.

MARSHALL (Prof. Alfred).- PRINCIPLES OF ECONOMICS. 2 vols. 8vo. Vol. 1. 12s.6d. net.

MARSHALL (Prof. A. and Mary P.).—THE ECONOMICS OF INDUSTRY. Ex.fcp.8vo. 2s.5d.

MARSHALL (J. M.).—A TABLE OF IRREGULAR GREEK VERBS. 8vo. 1s.

MARTEL (Chas.). MILITARY ITALY. With Map. 8vo. 12s. 6d.

MARTIAL.—SELECT EPIGRAMS FOR ENGLISH READERS. Translated by W. T. WEBB, M.A. Extra fcp. 8vo. 4s. 6d.

MARTIAL. SELECT EPIGRAMS. Ed. by Rev. H. M. STEPHENSON, M.A. Fcp. 8vo. 6s.6d.

MARTIN (Frances).—THE POET'S HOUR. Poetry Selected and Arranged for Children. 12mo. 2s. 6d.

—— SPRING-TIME WITH THE POETS. 18mo. 3s. 6d.

—— ANGELIQUE ARNAULD, Abbess of Port Royal. Crown 8vo. 4s. 6d.

MARTIN (Frederick).—THE HISTORY OF LLOYD'S, AND OF MARINE INSURANCE IN GREAT BRITAIN. 8vo. 14s.

MARTINEAU (Harriet). BIOGRAPHICAL SKETCHES, 1852—75. Crown 8vo. 6s.

MARTINEAU (Dr. James). SPINOZA. 2nd Edition. Crown 8vo. 6s.

MARTINEAU (Miss C. A.).—EASY LESSONS ON HEAT. Globe 8vo. 2s. 6d.

MASSON (Prof. David).—RECENT BRITISH PHILOSOPHY. 3rd Edition. Cr. 8vo. 6s.

—— DRUMMOND OF HAWTHORNDEN. Crown 8vo. 10s. 6d.

—— WORDSWORTH, SHELLEY, KEATS, AND OTHER ESSAYS. Crown 8vo. 5s.

—— CHATTERTON: A STORY OF THE YEAR 1770. Crown 8vo. 5s.

—— LIFE OF MILTON. See "Milton."

—— MILTON'S POEMS. See "Milton."

—— DE QUINCEY. Cr. 8vo. 1s. 6d. ; sewed, 1s.

MASSON (Gustave).—A COMPENDIOUS DICTIONARY OF THE FRENCH LANGUAGE (FRENCH-ENGLISH AND ENGLISH-FRENCH). Crown 8vo. 6s.

—— LA LYRE FRANÇAISE. Selected and arranged, with Notes. Vignette. 18mo. 4s. 6d.

MASSON (Mrs.).—THREE CENTURIES OF ENGLISH POETRY. Being Selections from Chaucer to Herrick. Globe 8vo. 3s. 6d.

MATHEWS.—THE LIFE OF CHARLES J. MATHEWS. Edited by CHARLES DICKENS. With Portraits. 2 vols. 8vo. 25s.

MATTHEWS (G. F.).—A MANUAL OF LOGARITHMS. 8vo. [*In the Press.*

MATURIN (Rev. W.).—THE BLESSEDNESS OF THE DEAD IN CHRIST. Cr. 8vo. 7s. 6d.

MAUDSLEY (Dr. Henry).—THE PHYSIOLOGY OF MIND. Crown 8vo. 10s. 6d.

—— THE PATHOLOGY OF MIND. 8vo. 18s.

—— BODY AND MIND. Crown 8vo. 6s. 6d.

MAURICE.—LIFE OF FREDERICK DENISON MAURICE. By his Son, FREDERICK MAURICE, Two Portraits. 3rd Ed. 2 vols. Demy 8vo. 36s. Popular Edition (4th Thousand) 2 vols. Crown 8vo. 16s.

MAURICE (Frederick Denison).—THE KINGDOM OF CHRIST. 3rd Ed. 2 vols. Cr. 8vo. 12s.

—— LECTURES ON THE APOCALYPSE. 2nd Edition. Crown 8vo. 6s.

—— SOCIAL MORALITY. 3rd Ed. Cr. 8vo. 6s.

—— THE CONSCIENCE. Lectures on Casuistry. 3rd Edition. Crown 8vo. 4s. 6d.

—— DIALOGUES ON FAMILY WORSHIP. Crown 8vo. 4s. 6d.

—— THE PATRIARCHS AND LAWGIVERS OF THE OLD TESTAMENT. 7th Ed. Cr. 8vo. 4s. 6d.

MAURICE (F. D.).—THE PROPHETS AND KINGS OF THE OLD TESTAMENT. 5th Edit. Crown 8vo. 6s.
—— THE GOSPEL OF THE KINGDOM OF HEAVEN. 3rd Edition. Crown 8vo. 6s.
—— THE GOSPEL OF ST. JOHN. 8th Edition. Crown 8vo. 6s.
—— THE EPISTLES OF ST. JOHN. 4th Edition. Crown 8vo. 6s.
—— EXPOSITORY SERMONS ON THE PRAYER-BOOK; AND ON THE LORD'S PRAYER. New Edition. Crown 8vo. 6s.
—— THEOLOGICAL ESSAYS. 4th Edition. Crn. 8vo. 6s.
—— THE DOCTRINE OF SACRIFICE DEDUCED FROM THE SCRIPTURES. 2nd Edition. Crown 8vo. 6s.
—— MORAL AND METAPHYSICAL PHILOSOPHY. 4th Edition. 2 vols. 8vo. 16s.
—— THE RELIGIONS OF THE WORLD. 6th Edition. Crown 8vo. 4s. 6d.
—— ON THE SABBATH DAY; THE CHARACTER OF THE WARRIOR; AND ON THE INTERPRETATION OF HISTORY. Fcp. 8vo. 2s. 6d.
—— LEARNING AND WORKING. Cr. 8vo. 4s. 6d.
—— THE LORD'S PRAYER, THE CREED, AND THE COMMANDMENTS. 18mo. 1s.
—— SERMONS PREACHED IN COUNTRY CHURCHES. 2nd Edition. Crown 8vo. 6s.
—— THE FRIENDSHIP OF BOOKS, AND OTHER LECTURES. 3rd Edition. Cr. 8vo. 4s. 6d.
—— THE UNITY OF THE NEW TESTAMENT. 2nd Edition. 2 vols. Crown 8vo. 12s.
—— LESSONS OF HOPE. Readings from the Works of F. D. MAURICE. Selected by Rev. J. Ll. DAVIES, M.A. Crown 8vo. 5s.
—— THE COMMUNION SERVICE FROM THE BOOK OF COMMON PRAYER, WITH SELECT READINGS FROM THE WRITINGS OF THE REV. F. D. MAURICE. Edited by the Right Rev. Bishop COLENSO. 16mo. 2s. 6d.

MAXWELL.—PROFESSOR CLERK MAXWELL, A LIFE OF. By Prof. L. CAMPBELL, M.A., and W. GARNETT, M.A. 2nd Edition. Crown 8vo. 7s. 6d.

MAYER (Prof. A. M.).—SOUND. A Series of Simple, Entertaining, and Inexpensive Experiments in the Phenomena of Sound. With Illustrations. Crown 8vo. 3s. 6d.

MAYER (Prof. A. M.) and BARNARD (C.)—LIGHT A Series of Simple, Entertaining, and Useful Experiments in the Phenomena of Light. Illustrated. Crown 8vo. 2s. 6d.

MAYOR (Prof. John E. B.).—A FIRST GREEK READER. New Edition. Fcp. 8vo. 4s. 6d.
—— AUTOBIOGRAPHY OF MATTHEW ROBINSON. Fcp. 8vo. 5s.
—— A BIBLIOGRAPHICAL CLUE TO LATIN LITERATURE. Crown 8vo. 10s. 6d. [See also under "Juvenal."]

MAYOR (Prof. Joseph B.).—GREEK FOR BEGINNERS. Fcp. 8vo. Part I. 1s. 6d.—Parts II. and III. 3s. 6d.—Complete. 4s. 6d.

MAZINI (Linda).—IN THE GOLDEN SHELL. With Illustrations. Globe 8vo. 4s. 6d.

MELEAGER. Translated into English Verse by WALTER HEADLAM. Fcp. 4to.

MELBOURNE.—MEMOIRS OF VISCOUNT MELBOURNE. By W. M. TORRENS. With Portrait. 2nd Edition. 2 vols. 8vo. 32s.

MELDOLA (Prof. R.)—THE CHEMISTRY OF PHOTOGRAPHY. Crown 8vo. 6s.

MELDOLA (Prof. R.) and WHITE (Wm.).—REPORT ON THE EAST ANGLIAN EARTHQUAKE OF 22ND APRIL, 1884. 8vo. 3s. 6d.

MENDENHALL (T. C.).—A CENTURY OF ELECTRICITY. Crown 8vo. 4s. 6d.

MERCIER (Dr. C.).—THE NERVOUS SYSTEM AND THE MIND. 8vo. 12s. 6d.

MERCUR (Prof. J.).—ELEMENTS OF THE ART OF WAR. 8vo. 17s.

MEREDITH (George).—A READING OF EARTH. Extra fcp. 8vo. 5s.
—— POEMS AND LYRICS OF THE JOY OF EARTH. Extra fcp. 8vo. 6s.
—— BALLADS AND POEMS OF TRAGIC LIFE. Crown 8vo. 6s.

MEYER (Ernst von).—HISTORY OF CHEMISTRY. Trans. by G. MACGOWAN, M.A. 8vo.

MIALL.—LIFE OF EDWARD MIALL. By his Son, ARTHUR MIALL. 8vo. 10s. 6d.

MILL (H. R.).—ELEMENTARY CLASS-BOOK OF GENERAL GEOGRAPHY. Cr. 8vo. 3s. 6d.

MILLAR (J. B.)—ELEMENTS OF DESCRIPTIVE GEOMETRY. 2nd Edition. Crown 8vo. 6s.

MILLER (R. Kalley).—THE ROMANCE OF ASTRONOMY. 2nd Ed. Cr. 8vo. 4s. 6d.

MILLIGAN (Rev. Prof. W.).—THE RESURRECTION OF OUR LORD. 2nd Ed. Cr. 8vo. 5s.
—— THE REVELATION OF ST. JOHN. 2nd Edition. Crown 8vo. 7s. 6d.

MILNE (Rev. John J.).—WEEKLY PROBLEM PAPERS. Fcp. 8vo. 4s. 6d.
—— COMPANION TO WEEKLY PROBLEMS. Cr. 8vo. 10s. 6d.
—— SOLUTIONS OF WEEKLY PROBLEM PAPERS. Crown 8vo. 10s. 6d.

MILNE (Rev. J. J.) and DAVIS (R. F.).—GEOMETRICAL CONICS. Part I. THE PARABOLA. Crown 8vo. 2s.

MILTON.—THE LIFE OF JOHN MILTON. By Prof. DAVID MASSON. Vol. I., 21s.; Vol. III., 18s.; Vols. IV. and V., 32s.; Vol. VI., with Portrait, 21s.
—— POETICAL WORKS. Edited, with Introductions and Notes, by Prof. DAVID MASSON, M.A. 3 vols. 8vo. (Uniform with the Cambridge Shakespeare.)
—— POETICAL WORKS. Ed. by Prof. MASSON. 3 vols. Fcp. 8vo. 15s.
—— POETICAL WORKS. (Globe Edition.) Ed. by Prof. MASSON. Globe 8vo. 3s. 6d.
—— PARADISE LOST. Books I. and II. Ed., with Introduction and Notes, by Prof. M. MACMILLAN. Globe 8vo. 2s. 6d. (Or separately, 1s. 6d. each Book.)
—— L'ALLEGRO, IL PENSEROSO, LYCIDAS, ARCADES, SONNETS, ETC. Edited by Prof. WM. BELL, M.A. Globe 8vo. 2s.
—— COMUS. Edited by Prof. WM. BELL, M.A. Globe 8vo. 1s. 6d.
—— SAMSON AGONISTES. By H. M. PERCIVAL, M.A. Globe 8vo. 2s. 6d.

LIST OF PUBLICATIONS.

MILTON. By Mark Pattison. Cr. 8vo. 1s. 6d.; sewed, 1s.

MILTON. By Rev. Stopford A. Brooke, M.A. Fcp. 8vo. 1s. 6d.
Large Paper Edition. 21s. net.

MINCHIN (Rev. Prof. G. M.).—Naturæ Veritas. Fcp. 8vo. 2s. 6d.

MINTO (W.).—The Mediation of Ralph Hardelot. 3 vols. Crown 8vo. 31s. 6d.
—— Defoe. Crown 8vo. 1s. 6d.; sewed, 1s.

MITFORD (A. B.). Tales of Old Japan. With Illustrations. Crown 8vo. 3s. 6d.

MIVART (St. George). Lessons in Elementary Anatomy. 18mo. 6s. 5d.

MIXTER (Prof. W. G.).—An Elementary Text-Book of Chemistry. 2nd Edition. Crown 8vo. 7s. 6d.

MIZ MAZE (THE); or, The Winkworth Puzzle. A Story in Letters by Nine Authors. Crown 8vo. 4s. 6d.

MOHAMMAD.—The Speeches and Table-Talk of the Prophet. Translated by Stanley Lane-Poole. 18mo. 4s. 6d.

MOLESWORTH (Mrs.). Illustrated by Walter Crane.
Herr Baby. Globe 8vo. 2s. 6d.
Grandmother Dear. Globe 8vo. 2s. 6d.
The Tapestry Room. Globe 8vo. 2s. 6d.
A Christmas Child. Globe 8vo. 2s. 6d.
Rosy. Globe 8vo. 2s. 6d.
Two Little Waifs. Globe 8vo. 2s. 6d.
Christmas Tree Land. Gl. 8vo. 2s. 6d.
"Us": An Old-Fashioned Story. Globe 8vo. 2s. 6d.
"Carrots," Just a Little Boy. Globe 8vo. 2s. 6d.
Tell Me a Story. Globe 8vo. 2s. 6d.
The Cuckoo Clock. Globe 8vo. 2s. 6d.
Four Winds Farm. Globe 8vo. 2s. 6d.
Little Miss Peggy. Globe 8vo. 2s. 6d.
A Christmas Posy. Crown 8vo. 4s. 6d.
The Rectory Children. Cr. 8vo. 4s. 6d.
Summer Stories. Crown 8vo. 4s. 6d.
Four Ghost Stories. Crown 8vo. 6s.
French Life in Letters. With Notes on Idioms, etc. Globe 8vo. 1s. 6d.

MOLIERE. Le Malade Imaginaire. Edit. by F. Tarver, M.A. Fcp. 8vo. 2s. 6d.
—— Les Femmes Savantes. Edited by G. E. Fasnacht. 18mo. 1s.
—— Le Médecin Malgré Lui. By the same Editor. 18mo. 1s.
—— Le Misanthrope. By the same Editor. 18mo. 1s.
—— L'Avare. Edited by L. M. Moriarty, M.A. 18mo. 1s.
—— Le Bourgeois Gentilhomme. By the same Editor. 18mo. 1s. 6d.

MOLLOY (Rev. G.). Gleanings in Science: A Series of Popular Lectures on Scientific Subjects. 8vo. 7s. 6d.

MONAHAN (James H.).—The Method of Law. Crown 8vo. 6s.

MONK. By Julian Corbett. With Portrait. Crown 8vo. 2s. 6d.

MONTELIUS—WOODS. The Civilisation of Sweden in Heathen Times. By Prof. Oscar Montelius. Translated by Rev. F. H. Woods, B.D. With Illustrations. 8vo. 14s.

MOORE (Prof. C. H.).—The Development and Character of Gothic Architecture. Illustrated. Medium 8vo. 18s.

MOORHOUSE (Rt. Rev. Bishop).—Jacob: Three Sermons. Extra fcp. 8vo. 3s. 6d.

MORISON (J. C.).—The Life and Times of Saint Bernard. 4th Edition. Crown 8vo. 6s.
—— Gibbon. Cr. 8vo. 1s. 6d.; sewed, 1s.
—— Macaulay. Cr. 8vo. 1s. 6d.; sewed, 1s.

MORISON (Jeanie).—The Purpose of the Ages. Crown 8vo. 9s.

MORLEY (John).—Works. Collected Edit. In 10 vols. Globe 8vo. 5s. each.
Voltaire. 1 vol.—Rousseau. 2 vols.—Diderot and the Encyclopædists. 2 vols.—On Compromise. 1 vol.—Miscellanies. 3 vols.—Burke. 1 vol.
—— On the Study of Literature. Crown 8vo. 1s. 6d.
Also a Popular Edition for distribution, 2d.
—— Burke. Crown 8vo. 1s. 6d.; sewed, 1s.
—— Walpole. Crown 8vo. 2s. 6d.
—— Aphorisms. An Address before the Philosophical Society of Edinburgh. Globe 8vo. 1s. 6d.

MORRIS (Rev. Richard, LL.D.).—Historical Outlines of English Accidence. Fcp. 8vo. 6s.
—— Elementary Lessons in Historical English Grammar. 18mo. 2s. 6d.
—— Primer of English Grammar. 18mo, cloth. 1s.

MORRIS (R.) and BOWEN (H. C.)—English Grammar Exercises. 18mo. 1s.

MORTE D'ARTHUR. The Edition of Caxton revised for Modern Use. By Sir Edward Strachey. Gl. 8vo. 3s. 6d.

MOULTON (Louise Chandler).—Swallow-Flights. Extra fcp. 8vo. 4s. 6d.
—— In the Garden of Dreams: Lyrics and Sonnets. Crown 8vo. 6s.

MOULTRIE(J.).—Poems. Complete Edition. 2 vols. Crown 8vo. 7s. each.

MUDIE (C. E.).—Stray Leaves: Poems. 4th Edition. Extra fcp. 8vo. 3s. 6d.

MUIR (Thomas).—A Treatise on the Theory of Determinants. Cr. 8vo. 7s. 6d.
—— The Theory of Determinants in the Historical Order of its Development. Part I. Determinants in General. Leibnitz (1693) to Cayley (1841). 8vo. 10s. 6d.

MUIR (M. M. Pattison).—Practical Chemistry for Medical Students. Fcp. 8vo. 1s. 6d.

MUIR (M. M. P.) and WILSON (D. M.).—The Elements of Thermal Chemistry. 8vo. 12s. 6d.

MÜLLER—THOMPSON.—THE FERTILISATION OF FLOWERS. By Prof. HERMANN MÜLLER. Translated by D'ARCY W. THOMPSON. With a Preface by CHARLES DARWIN, F.R.S. Medium 8vo. 21s.

MULLINGER (J. B.).—CAMBRIDGE CHARACTERISTICS IN THE SEVENTEENTH CENTURY. Crown 8vo. 4s. 6d.

MURPHY (J. J.).—HABIT AND INTELLIGENCE. 2nd Ed. Illustrated. 8vo. 16s.

MURRAY (E. C. Grenville).—ROUND ABOUT FRANCE. Crown 8vo. 7s. 6d.

MURRAY (D. Christie).—AUNT RACHEL. Crown 8vo. 3s. 6d.
—— SCHWARTZ. Crown 8vo. 3s. 6d.
—— THE WEAKER VESSEL. Cr. 8vo. 3s. 6d.
—— JOHN VALE'S GUARDIAN. Cr. 8vo. 3s. 6d.

MUSIC.—A DICTIONARY OF MUSIC AND MUSICIANS, A.D. 1450–1889. Edited by Sir GEORGE GROVE, D.C.L. In 4 vols. 8vo. 21s. each.—Parts I.—XIV., XIX.—XXII. 3s. 6d. each.- Parts XV. XVI. 7s.- Parts XVII. XVIII. 7s.—Parts XXIII.—XXV. APPENDIX. Edited by J. A. FULLER MAITLAND, M.A. 9s. [Cloth cases for binding, 1s. each.]
—— A COMPLETE INDEX TO THE ABOVE. By Mrs. E. WODEHOUSE. 8vo. 7s. 6d.

MYERS (F. W. H.).—THE RENEWAL OF YOUTH, AND OTHER POEMS. Crown 8vo. 7s. 6d.
—— ST. PAUL: A POEM. Ex. fcp. 8vo. 2s. 6d.
—— WORDSWORTH. Crown 8vo. 1s. 6d.; sewed, 1s.
—— ESSAYS. 2 vols.- I. Classical. II. Modern. Crown 8vo. 4s. 6d. each.

MYERS (E.).—THE PURITANS: A POEM. Extra fcap. 8vo. 2s. 6d.
—— PINDAR'S ODES. Translated, with Introduction and Notes. Crown 8vo. 5s.
—— POEMS. Extra fcap. 8vo. 4s. 6d.
—— THE DEFENCE OF ROME, AND OTHER POEMS. Extra fcp. 8vo. 5s.
—— THE JUDGMENT OF PROMETHEUS, AND OTHER POEMS. Extra fcp. 8vo. 3s. 6d.

MYLNE (The Rt. Rev. Bishop).—SERMONS PREACHED IN ST. THOMAS'S CATHEDRAL, BOMBAY. Crown 8vo. 6s.

NADAL (E. S.).—ESSAYS AT HOME AND ELSEWHERE. Crown 8vo. 6s.

NAPIER (SIR CHARLES). By Col. Sir W. BUTLER. With Portrait. Cr. 8vo. 2s. 6d.

NAPOLEON I., HISTORY OF. By P. LANFREY. 4 vols. Crown 8vo. 30s.

NATURAL RELIGION. By the Author of "Ecce Homo." 2nd Edition. 8vo. 9s.

NATURE: A WEEKLY ILLUSTRATED JOURNAL OF SCIENCE. Published every Thursday. Price 6d. Monthly Parts, 2s. and 2s. 6d.; Current Half-yearly vols., 15s. each. Vols. I.—XLI. [Cases for binding vols. 1s. 6d. each.]

NATURE PORTRAITS. A Series of Portraits of Scientific Worthies engraved by JEENS and others in Portfolio. India Proofs, 5s. each. [Portfolio separately, 6s.]

NATURE SERIES. Crown 8vo:
THE ORIGIN AND METAMORPHOSES OF INSECTS. By Sir JOHN LUBBOCK, M.P., F.R.S. With Illustrations. 3s. 6d.
THE TRANSIT OF VENUS. By Prof. G. FORBES. With Illustrations. 3s. 6d.
POLARISATION OF LIGHT. By W. SPOTTISWOODE, LL.D. Illustrated. 3s. 6d.
ON BRITISH WILD FLOWERS CONSIDERED IN RELATION TO INSECTS. By Sir JOHN LUBBOCK, M.P., F.R.S. Illustrated. 4s. 6d.
FLOWERS, FRUITS, AND LEAVES. By Sir JOHN LUBBOCK. Illustrated. 4s. 6d.
HOW TO DRAW A STRAIGHT LINE: A LECTURE ON LINKAGES. By A. B. KEMPE, B.A. Illustrated. 1s. 6d.
LIGHT: A SERIES OF SIMPLE, ENTERTAINING, AND USEFUL EXPERIMENTS. By A. M. MAYER and C. BARNARD. Illustrated. 2s. 6d.
SOUND: A SERIES OF SIMPLE, ENTERTAINING, AND INEXPENSIVE EXPERIMENTS. By A. M. MAYER. 3s. 6d.
SEEING AND THINKING. By Prof. W. K. CLIFFORD, F.R.S. Diagrams. 3s. 6d.
CHARLES DARWIN. Memorial Notices reprinted from "Nature." By THOMAS H. HUXLEY, F.R.S., G. J. ROMANES, F.R.S., ARCHIBALD GEIKIE, F.R.S., and W. T. DYER, F.R.S. 2s. 6d.
ON THE COLOURS OF FLOWERS. By GRANT ALLEN. Illustrated. 3s. 6d.
THE CHEMISTRY OF THE SECONDARY BATTERIES OF PLANTÉ AND FAURE. By J. H. GLADSTONE and A. TRIBE. 2s. 6d.
A CENTURY OF ELECTRICITY. By T. C. MENDENHALL. 4s. 6d.
ON LIGHT. The Burnett Lectures. By Sir GEORGE GABRIEL STOKES, M.P., P.R.S. Three Courses: I. On the Nature of Light. II. On Light as a Means of Investigation. III. On Beneficial Effects of Light. 7s. 6d.
THE SCIENTIFIC EVIDENCES OF ORGANIC EVOLUTION. By GEORGE J. ROMANES, M.A., LL.D. 2s. 6d.
POPULAR LECTURES AND ADDRESSES. By Sir WM. THOMSON. In 3 vols. Vol. I. Constitution of Matter. Illustrated. 6s.—Vol. II. Navigation.
THE CHEMISTRY OF PHOTOGRAPHY. By Prof. R. MELDOLA, F.R.S. Illustrated. 6s.
MODERN VIEWS OF ELECTRICITY. By Prof. O. J. LODGE, LL.D. Illustrated. 6s. 6d.
TIMBER AND SOME OF ITS DISEASES. By Prof. H. M. WARD, M.A. Illustrated. 6s.

NEPOS. SELECTIONS ILLUSTRATIVE OF GREEK AND ROMAN HISTORY, FROM CORNELIUS NEPOS. Edited by G. S. FARNELL, M.A. 18mo. 1s. 6d.

NETTLESHIP.—VIRGIL. By Prof. NETTLESHIP, M.A. Fcap. 8vo. 1s. 6d.

NEW ANTIGONE, THE; A ROMANCE. Crown 8vo. 6s.

NEWCOMB (Prof. Simon).—POPULAR ASTRONOMY. With 112 Engravings and Maps of the Stars. 2nd Edition. 8vo. 18s.

LIST OF PUBLICATIONS. 43

NEWMAN (F. W.). MATHEMATICAL TRACTS. Part I. 8vo. 5s.—Part II. 4s.
— ELLIPTIC INTEGRALS. 8vo. 9s.
NEWTON (Sir C. T.).—ESSAYS ON ART AND ARCHÆOLOGY. 8vo. 12s. 6d.
NEWTON'S PRINCIPIA. Edited by Prof. Sir W. THOMSON and Prof. BLACKBURN. 4to. 31s. 6d.
— FIRST BOOK. Sections I. II. III. With Notes, Illustrations, and Problems. By P. FROST, M.A. 3rd Edition. 8vo. 12s.
NICHOL (Prof. John).—PRIMER OF ENGLISH COMPOSITION. 18mo. 1s.
— BYRON. Crown 8vo. 1s. 6d.; sewed, 1s.
NICHOL (Prof. John) and M'CORMICK (W. S.). QUESTIONS AND EXERCISES IN ENGLISH COMPOSITION. 18mo. 1s.
NINE YEARS OLD. By the Author of "St. Olave's." Illustrated by FRÖLICH. New Edition. Globe 8vo. 2s. 6d.
NIXON (J. E.). PARALLEL EXTRACTS. Arranged for Translation into English and Latin, with Notes on Idioms. Part I. Historical and Epistolary. 2nd Edition. Crown 8vo. 3s. 6d.
— PROSE EXTRACTS. Arranged for Translation into English and Latin, with General and Special Prefaces on Style and Idiom. I. Oratorical. II. Historical. III. Philosophical. IV. Anecdotes and Letters. 2nd Edition, enlarged to 280 pages. Crown 8vo. 4s. 6d.
— SELECTIONS FROM PROSE EXTRACTS. Including Anecdotes and Letters, with Notes and Hints, pp. 120. Globe 8vo. 3s.
NOEL (Lady Augusta).—WANDERING WILLIE. Globe 8vo. 2s. 6d.
— — HITHERSEA MERE. 3 vols. Cr.8vo. 31s.6d.
NORDENSKIÖLD. VOYAGE OF THE "VEGA" ROUND ASIA AND EUROPE. By Baron A. E. VON NORDENSKIÖLD. Translated by ALEXANDER LESLIE. 400 Illustrations, Maps, etc. 2 vols. Medium 8vo. 45s. *Popular Edition.* With Portrait, Maps, and Illustrations. Crown 8vo. 6s.
— THE ARCTIC VOYAGES OF ADOLPH ERIC NORDENSKIÖLD, 1858—79. By ALEXANDER LESLIE. 8vo. 16s.
NORGATE (Kate). ENGLAND UNDER THE ANGEVIN KINGS. In 2 vols. With Maps and Plans. 8vo. 32s.
NORRIS (W. E.).—MY FRIEND JIM. Globe 8vo. 2s.
— CHRIS. Globe 8vo. 2s.
NORTON (the Hon. Mrs.).—THE LADY OF LA GARAYE. 9th Ed. Fcp. 8vo. 4s. 6d.
— OLD SIR DOUGLAS. Crown 8vo. 6s.
O'BRIEN (Bishop J. T.).- PRAYER. Five Sermons. 8vo. 6s.
OLD SONGS. With Drawings by E. A. ABBEY and A. PARSONS. 4to. Morocco gilt. 1l. 11s. 6d.
OLIPHANT (Mrs. M. O. W.).—A SON OF THE SOIL. Globe 8vo. 2s.
— THE CURATE IN CHARGE. Globe 8vo. 2s.
— FRANCIS OF ASSISI. Crown 8vo. 6s.

OLIPHANT (Mrs. M. O. W.). YOUNG MUSGRAVE. Globe 8vo. 2s.
— HE THAT WILL NOT WHEN HE MAY. Globe 8vo. 2s.
— SIR TOM. Globe 8vo. 2s.
— HESTER. Globe 8vo. 2s.
— THE WIZARD'S SON. Globe 8vo. 2s.
— A COUNTRY GENTLEMAN AND HIS FAMILY. Globe 8vo. 2s.
— THE SECOND SON. Globe 8vo. 2s.
— NEIGHBOURS ON THE GREEN. Crown 8vo. 3s. 6d.
— JOYCE. Crown 8vo. 3s. 6d.
— A BELEAGUERED CITY. Cr. 8vo. 3s. 6d.
— THE MAKERS OF VENICE. With numerous Illustrations. Crown 8vo. 10s. 6d.
— THE MAKERS OF FLORENCE: DANTE, GIOTTO, SAVONAROLA, AND THEIR CITY. With Illustrations. Cr. 8vo, cloth. 10s. 6d.
— ROYAL EDINBURGH. Illustr. by GEORGE REID, R.S.A. Medium 8vo. *Edition de Luxe.* Super royal 8vo.
— AGNES HOPETOUN'S SCHOOLS AND HOLIDAYS. Illustrated. Globe 8vo. 2s. 6d.
— THE LITERARY HISTORY OF ENGLAND IN THE END OF THE XVIII. AND BEGINNING OF THE XIX. CENTURY. 3 vols. 8vo. 21s.
— — SHERIDAN. Cr. 8vo. 1s. 6d.; sewed, 1s.
— SELECTIONS FROM COWPER'S POEMS. 18mo. 4s. 6d.
OLIPHANT (T. L. Kington).—THE OLD AND MIDDLE ENGLISH. Globe 8vo. 9s.
— THE DUKE AND THE SCHOLAR, AND OTHER ESSAYS. 8vo. 7s. 6d.
— THE NEW ENGLISH. 2 vols. Cr. 8vo. 21s.
OLIVER (Prof. Daniel). LESSONS IN ELEMENTARY BOTANY. Illustr. Fcp. 8vo. 4s. 6d.
— FIRST BOOK OF INDIAN BOTANY. Illustrated. Extra fcp. 8vo. 6s. 6d.
OLIVER (Capt. S. P.).—MADAGASCAR: AN HISTORICAL AND DESCRIPTIVE ACCOUNT OF THE ISLAND AND ITS FORMER DEPENDENCIES. 2 vols. Medium 8vo. 2l. 12s. 6d.
ORCHIDS: BEING THE REPORT ON THE ORCHID CONFERENCE HELD AT SOUTH KENSINGTON, 1885. 8vo. 2s. 6d.
OSTWALD (Prof. W.). — OUTLINES OF GENERAL CHEMISTRY. Translated by Dr. J. WALKER. 8vo. 10s. net.
OTTÉ (E. C.).—SCANDINAVIAN HISTORY. With Maps. Globe 8vo. 6s.
OVID. — SELECTIONS. Edited by E. S. SHUCKBURGH, M.A. 18mo. 1s. 6d.
— FASTI. Edited by G. H. HALLAM, M.A. Fcp. 8vo. 5s.
— — HEROIDUM EPISTULÆ XIII. Edited by E. S. SHUCKBURGH, M.A. Fcp. 8vo. 4s.6d.
— METAMORPHOSES. Books I.--III. Edited by C. SIMMONS, M.A.
— STORIES FROM THE METAMORPHOSES. Edited by the Rev. J. BOND, M.A., and A. S. WALPOLE, M.A. With Notes, Exercises, and Vocabulary. 18mo. 1s. 6d.
— — METAMORPHOSES. Books XIII. and XIV. Ed. by C. SIMMONS. Fcp. 8vo. 4s.6d.

OVID.—EASY SELECTIONS FROM OVID IN ELEGIAC VERSE. Arranged and Edited by H. WILKINSON. M.A. 18mo. 1s. 6d.

OWENS COLLEGE CALENDAR, 1889—90. Crown 8vo. 3s.

OWENS COLLEGE ESSAYS AND ADDRESSES. By Professors and Lecturers of the College. 8vo. 14s.

OXFORD, A HISTORY OF THE UNIVERSITY OF. From the Earliest Times to the Year 1530. By H. C. MAXWELL LYTE, M.A. 8vo. 16s.

PALGRAVE (Sir Francis). — HISTORY OF NORMANDY AND OF ENGLAND. 4 vols. 8vo. 4l. 4s.

PALGRAVE (William Gifford).—A NARRATIVE OF A YEAR'S JOURNEY THROUGH CENTRAL AND EASTERN ARABIA, 1862—63. 9th Edition. Crown 8vo. 6s.

—— ESSAYS ON EASTERN QUESTIONS. 8vo. 10s. 6d.

—— DUTCH GUIANA. 8vo. 9s.

—— ULYSSES ; OR, SCENES AND STUDIES IN MANY LANDS. 8vo. 12s. 6d.

PALGRAVE (Prof. Francis Turner).—THE FIVE DAYS' ENTERTAINMENTS AT WENTWORTH GRANGE. A Book for Children. Small 4to. 6s.

—— ESSAYS ON ART. Extra fcp. 8vo. 6s.

—— ORIGINAL HYMNS. 3rd Ed. 16mo. 1s.6d.

—— LYRICAL POEMS. Extra fcp. 8vo. 6s.

—— VISIONS OF ENGLAND : A SERIES OF LYRICAL POEMS ON LEADING EVENTS AND PERSONS IN ENGLISH HISTORY. Crown 8vo. 7s. 6d.

—— THE GOLDEN TREASURY OF THE BEST SONGS AND LYRICAL POEMS IN THE ENGLISH LANGUAGE. 18mo. 4s. 6d.

—— SONNETS AND SONGS OF SHAKESPEARE. 18mo. 4s. 6d.

—— THE CHILDREN'S TREASURY OF LYRICAL POETRY. 18mo. 2s. 6d.—Or in Two Parts, 1s. each.

—— HERRICK : SELECTIONS FROM THE LYRICAL POEMS. 18mo. 4s. 6d.

—— THE POETICAL WORKS OF JOHN KEATS. With Notes. 18mo. 4s. 6d.

—— LYRICAL POEMS OF LORD TENNYSON. Selected and Annotated. 18mo. 4s. 6d. Large Paper Edition. 8vo. 9s.

PALGRAVE (Reginald F. D.).—THE HOUSE OF COMMONS : ILLUSTRATIONS OF ITS HISTORY AND PRACTICE. Crown 8vo. 2s. 6d.

PALMER (Lady Sophia).—MRS. PENICOTT'S LODGER, AND OTHER STORIES. Cr.8vo. 2s.6d.

PALMER (J. H.).—TEXT-BOOK OF PRACTICAL LOGARITHMS AND TRIGONOMETRY. Crown 8vo. 4s. 6d.

PANSIE'S FLOUR BIN. By the Author of "When I was a Little Girl," etc. Illustrated. Globe 8vo. 2s. 6d.

PANTIN (W. E. P.).—A FIRST LATIN VERSE BOOK. Globe 8vo. 1s. 6d.

PARADOXICAL PHILOSOPHY : A SEQUEL TO " THE UNSEEN UNIVERSE." Cr. 8vo. 7s. 6d.

PARKER (H). -THE NATURE OF THE FINE ARTS. Crown 8vo. 10s. 6d.

PARKER (Prof. W. K.) and BETTANY (G. T.).—THE MORPHOLOGY OF THE SKULL. Crown 8vo. 10s. 6d.

PARKER (Prof. T. Jeffery).—A COURSE OF INSTRUCTION IN ZOOTOMY (VERTEBRATA). With 74 Illustrations. Crown 8vo. 8s. 6d.

—— ELEMENTARY LESSONS IN BIOLOGY. Illustrated. Crown 8vo. [In the Press.

PARKINSON (S.).—A TREATISE ON ELEMENTARY MECHANICS. Crown 8vo. 9s. 6d.

—— A TREATISE ON OPTICS. 4th Edition, revised. Crown 8vo. 10s. 6d.

PARKMAN (Francis). — MONTCALM AND WOLFE. Library Edition. Illustrated with Portraits and Maps. 2 vols. 8vo. 12s.6d. each.

—— THE COLLECTED WORKS OF FRANCIS PARKMAN. Popular Edition. In 10 vols. Crown 8vo. 7s. 6d. each ; or complete, 3l. 13s. 6d.—PIONEERS OF FRANCE IN THE NEW WORLD. 1 vol.—THE JESUITS IN NORTH AMERICA. 1 vol.—LA SALLE AND THE DISCOVERY OF THE GREAT WEST. 1 vol.—THE OREGON TRAIL. 1 vol.—THE OLD RÉGIME IN CANADA UNDER LOUIS XIV. 1 vol.—COUNT FRONTENAC AND NEW FRANCE UNDER LOUIS XIV. 1 vol.—MONTCALM AND WOLFE. 2 vols.—THE CONSPIRACY OF PONTIAC. 2 vols.

PASTEUR — FAULKNER. — STUDIES ON FERMENTATION : THE DISEASES OF BEER, THEIR CAUSES, AND THE MEANS OF PREVENTING THEM. By L. PASTEUR. Translated by FRANK FAULKNER. 8vo. 21s.

PATER (W.).—THE RENAISSANCE : STUDIES IN ART AND POETRY. 4th Ed. Cr.8vo. 10s.6d.

—— MARIUS THE EPICUREAN : HIS SENSATIONS AND IDEAS. 3rd Edition. 2 vols. 8vo. 12s.

—— IMAGINARY PORTRAITS. Crown 8vo. 6s.

—— APPRECIATIONS. With an Essay on Style. 2nd Edition. Crown 8vo. 8s. 6d.

PATERSON (James).—COMMENTARIES ON THE LIBERTY OF THE SUBJECT, AND THE LAWS OF ENGLAND RELATING TO THE SECURITY OF THE PERSON. 2 vols. Cr.8vo. 21s.

—— THE LIBERTY OF THE PRESS, SPEECH, AND PUBLIC WORSHIP. Crown 8vo. 12s.

PATMORE (C.).—THE CHILDREN'S GARLAND FROM THE BEST POETS. With a Vignette. 18mo. 4s. 6d.
Globe Readings Edition. For Schools. Globe 8vo. 2s.

PATTESON.—LIFE AND LETTERS OF JOHN COLERIDGE PATTESON, D.D., MISSIONARY BISHOP. By CHARLOTTE M. YONGE. 8th Edition. 2 vols. Crown 8vo. 12s.

PATTISON (Mark).—MILTON. Crown 8vo. 1s. 6d. ; sewed, 1s.

—— MEMOIRS. Crown 8vo. 8s. 6d.

—— SERMONS. Crown 8vo. 6s.

PAUL OF TARSUS. 8vo. 10s. 6d.

PAYNE (E. J.).—HISTORY OF EUROPEAN COLONIES. 18mo. 4s. 6d.

PEABODY (Prof. C. H.).—THERMODYNAMICS OF THE STEAM ENGINE AND OTHER HEATENGINES. 8vo. 21s.

LIST OF PUBLICATIONS. 45

PEDLEY (S.). - EXERCISES IN ARITHMETIC. With upwards of 7000 Examples and Answers. Crown 8vo. 5s.— Also in Two Parts. 2s. 6d. each.

PEEL (Edmund).—ECHOES FROM HOREB, AND OTHER POEMS. Crown 8vo. 3s. 6d.

PEILE (John).—PHILOLOGY. 18mo. 1s.

PELLISSIER (Eugène)—FRENCH ROOTS AND THEIR FAMILIES. Globe 8vo. 6s.

PENNELL (Joseph)—PEN DRAWING AND PEN DRAUGHTSMEN: Their Work and Methods, a Study of the Art to-day, with Technical Suggestions. With 158 Illustrations. 4to. 3l. 13s. 6d. net.

PENNINGTON (Rooke).—NOTES ON THE BARROWS AND BONE CAVES OF DERBYSHIRE. 8vo. 6s.

PENROSE (Francis).—ON A METHOD OF PREDICTING, BY GRAPHICAL CONSTRUCTION, OCCULTATIONS OF STARS BY THE MOON AND SOLAR ECLIPSES FOR ANY GIVEN PLACE. 4to. 12s.

—— AN INVESTIGATION OF THE PRINCIPLES OF ATHENIAN ARCHITECTURE. Illustrated. Folio. 7l. 7s.

PERRAULT.—CONTES DE FÉES. Edited by G. EUGÈNE FASNACHT. Globe 8vo. 1s. 6d.

PERRY (Prof. John).—AN ELEMENTARY TREATISE ON STEAM. 18mo. 4s. 6d.

PERSIA, EASTERN. AN ACCOUNT OF THE JOURNEYS OF THE PERSIAN BOUNDARY COMMISSION, 1870—71—72. 2 vols. 8vo. 42s.

PETERBOROUGH. By W. STEBBING. With Portrait. Crown 8vo. 2s. 6d.

PETTIGREW (J. Bell).—THE PHYSIOLOGY OF THE CIRCULATION. 8vo. 12s.

PHAEDRUS.—SELECT FABLES. Edited by A. S. WALPOLE, M.A. With Notes, Exercises, and Vocabularies. 18mo. 1s. 6d.

PHILLIMORE (John G.).—PRIVATE LAW AMONG THE ROMANS. 8vo. 16s.

PHILLIPS (J. A.).—A TREATISE ON ORE DEPOSITS. Illustrated. Medium 8vo. 25s.

PHILOCHRISTUS.—MEMOIRS OF A DISCIPLE OF THE LORD. 3rd Ed. 8vo 12s.

PHILOLOGY.—THE JOURNAL OF SACRED AND CLASSICAL PHILOLOGY. 4 vols. 8vo. 12s. 6d. each.

—— THE JOURNAL OF PHILOLOGY. New Series. Edited by W. A. WRIGHT, M.A., I. BYWATER, M.A., and H. JACKSON, M.A. 4s. 6d. each number (half-yearly).

—— THE AMERICAN JOURNAL OF PHILOLOGY. Edited by Prof. BASIL L. GILDERSLEEVE. 4s. 6d. each (quarterly).

—— TRANSACTIONS OF THE AMERICAN PHILOLOGICAL ASSOCIATION. Vols. I.—XX. 8s. 6d. per vol. net, except Vols. XV. and XX., which are 10s. 6d. net.

PHRYNICHUS. THE NEW PHRYNICHUS. A revised text of "The Ecloga" of the Grammarian PHRYNICHUS. With Introductions and Commentary. By W. GUNION RUTHERFORD, M.A. 8vo. 18s.

PICKERING (Prof. Edward C.). - ELEMENTS OF PHYSICAL MANIPULATION. Medium 8vo. Part I., 12s. 6d.; Part II., 14s.

PICTON (J. A.).—THE MYSTERY OF MATTER, AND OTHER ESSAYS. Crown 8vo. 6s.

PIFFARD (H. G.).—AN ELEMENTARY TREATISE ON DISEASES OF THE SKIN. 8vo. 16s.

PINDAR'S EXTANT ODES. Translated by ERNEST MYERS. Crown 8vo. 5s.

—— THE OLYMPIAN AND PYTHIAN ODES. Edited, with Notes, by Prof. BASIL GILDERSLEEVE. Crown 8vo. 7s. 6d.

—— THE NEMEAN ODES. Edited by J. B. BURY, M.A. 8vo. [In the Press.

PIRIE (Prof. G.).—LESSONS ON RIGID DYNAMICS. Crown 8vo. 6s.

PLATO.—PHÆDO. Edited by R. D. ARCHERHIND, M.A. 8vo. 8s. 6d.

—— TIMÆUS. With Introduction, Notes, and Translation, by the same Editor. 8vo. 16s.

—— PHÆDO. Ed. by Principal W. D. GEDDES, LL.D. 2nd Edition. 8vo. 8s. 6d.

—— THE TRIAL AND DEATH OF SOCRATES: BEING THE EUTHYPHRON, APOLOGY, CRITO, AND PHÆDO OF PLATO. Translated by F. J. CHURCH. 18mo. 4s. 6d.

—— EUTHYPHRO AND MENEXENUS. Ed. by C. E. GRAVES, M.A. 18mo. 1s. 6d.

—— THE REPUBLIC. Books I.—V. Edited by T. H. WARREN, M.A. Fcp. 8vo. 6s.

—— THE REPUBLIC OF PLATO. Translated by J. Ll. DAVIES, M.A., and D. J. VAUGHAN, M.A. 18mo. 4s. 6d.

—— LACHES. Edited by M. T. TATHAM, M.A. Fcap. 8vo. 2s. 6d.

—— PHAEDRUS, LYSIS, AND PROTAGORAS. A New Translation, by J. WRIGHT, M.A. 18mo. 4s. 6d.

PLAUTUS. — THE MOSTELLARIA. With Notes, Prolegomena, and Excursus. By the late Prof. RAMSAY. Ed. by G. G. RAMSAY, M.A. 8vo. 14s.

—— MILES GLORIOSUS. Edit. by Prof. R. Y. TYRRELL, M.A. 2nd Ed. Fcp. 8vo. 5s.

—— AMPHITRUO. Edited by Prof. A. PALMER, M.A. Fcp. 8vo. 5s.

PLINY.—LETTERS. Books I. and II. Edit. by JAMES COWAN, M.A. Fcp. 8vo. 5s.

—— LETTERS. Book III. Edited by Prof. JOHN E. B. MAYOR. Fcp. 8vo. 5s.

—— CORRESPONDENCE WITH TRAJAN. Ed., with Notes and Introductory Essays, by E. G. HARDY, M.A. 8vo. 10s. 6d.

PLUMPTRE (Prof. E. H.).—MOVEMENTS IN RELIGIOUS THOUGHT. Fcp. 8vo. 3s. 6d.

PLUTARCH. Being a Selection from the Lives in North's Plutarch which illustrate Shakespeare's Plays. Edited by Rev. W. W. SKEAT, M.A. Crown 8vo. 6s.

—— LIFE OF THEMISTOKLES. Edited by Rev. H. A. HOLDEN, M.A. Fcp. 8vo. 5s.

—— LIVES OF GALBA AND OTHO. Edited by E. G. HARDY, M.A. Fcp. 8vo. 6s.

POLLOCK (Prof. Sir F., Bart.).—ESSAYS IN JURISPRUDENCE AND ETHICS. 8vo. 10s. 6d.

—— THE LAND LAWS. 2nd Edition. Crown 8vo. 3s. 6d.

—— INTRODUCTION TO THE HISTORY OF THE SCIENCE OF POLITICS. Crown 8vo. 2s. 6d.

POLLOCK (W. H. and Lady).—AMATEUR THEATRICALS. Crown 8vo. 2s. 6d.

POLLOCK (Sir Frederick).—PERSONAL REMEMBRANCES. 2 vols. Crown 8vo. 16s.

POLYBIUS.—THE HISTORY OF THE ACHÆAN LEAGUE. As contained in the "Remains of Polybius." Edited by Rev. W. W. CAPES. Fcp. 8vo. 6s. 6d.

—— THE HISTORIES OF POLYBIUS. Transl. by E. S. SHUCKBURGH. 2 vols. Cr. 8vo. 24s.

POOLE (M. E.).—PICTURES OF COTTAGE LIFE IN THE WEST OF ENGLAND. 2nd Ed. Crown 8vo. 3s. 6d.

POOLE (Reginald Lane).—A HISTORY OF THE HUGUENOTS OF THE DISPERSION AT THE RECALL OF THE EDICT OF NANTES. Crown 8vo. 6s.

POOLE, THOMAS, AND HIS FRIENDS. By Mrs. SANDFORD. 2 vols. Crn. 8vo. 15s.

POPE.—THE POETICAL WORKS OF ALEX. POPE. Edited by Prof. WARD. Globe 8vo. 3s. 6d.

—— POPE. By LESLIE STEPHEN. Crown 8vo. 1s. 6d.; sewed, 1s.

POPULATION OF AN OLD PEAR TREE; OR, STORIES OF INSECT LIFE. From the French of E. VAN BRUYSSEL. Ed. by C. M. YONGE. Illustrated. Globe 8vo. 2s. 6d.

POSTGATE (Prof. J. P.).—SERMO LATINUS. A Short Guide to Latin Prose Composition. Part I. Introduction. Part II. Selected Passages for Translation. Gl. 8vo. 2s. 6d.—Key to "Selected Passages." Crown 8vo. 3s. 6d.

POTTER (Louisa).—LANCASHIRE MEMORIES. Crown 8vo. 6s.

POTTER (R.).—THE RELATION OF ETHICS TO RELIGION. Crown 8vo. 2s. 6d.

POTTS (A. W.).—HINTS TOWARDS LATIN PROSE COMPOSITION. Globe 8vo 3s.

—— PASSAGES FOR TRANSLATION INTO LATIN PROSE. 4th Ed. Extra fcp. 8vo. 2s. 6d.

—— LATIN VERSIONS OF PASSAGES FOR TRANSLATION INTO LATIN PROSE. Extra fcp. 8vo. 2s. 6d. (For Teachers only.)

PRACTICAL POLITICS. Published under the auspices of the National Liberal Federation. 8vo. 6s.

PRACTITIONER (THE): A MONTHLY JOURNAL OF THERAPEUTICS AND PUBLIC HEALTH. Edited by T. LAUDER BRUNTON, M.D., F.R.C.P., F.R.S., Assistant Physician to St. Bartholomew's Hospital, etc., etc.; DONALD MACALISTER, M.A., M.D., B.Sc., F.R.C.P., Fellow and Medical Lecturer, St. John's College, Cambridge, Physician to Addenbrooke's Hospital and University Lecturer in Medicine; and J. MITCHELL BRUCE, M.A., M.D., F.R.C.P., Physician and Lecturer on Therapeutics at Charing Cross Hospital. 1s. 6d. monthly. Vols. I.—XLIII. Half-yearly vols. 10s. 6d. [Cloth covers for binding, 1s. each.]

PRESTON (Rev. G.).—EXERCISES IN LATIN VERSE OF VARIOUS KINDS. Globe 8vo. 2s. 6d.—Key. Globe 8vo. 5s.

PRESTON (T.).—THE THEORY OF LIGHT. Illustrated. 8vo. 12s. 6d.

PRICE (L. L. F. R.).—INDUSTRIAL PEACE: ITS ADVANTAGES, METHODS, AND DIFFICULTIES. Medium 8vo. 6s.

PRIMERS.—HISTORY. Edited by JOHN R. GREEN, Author of "A Short History of the English People," etc. 18mo. 1s. each:

EUROPE. By E. A. FREEMAN, M.A.

GREECE. By C. A. FYFFE, M.A.

ROME. By Prof. CREIGHTON.

GREEK ANTIQUITIES. By Prof. MAHAFFY.

ROMAN ANTIQUITIES. By Prof. WILKINS.

CLASSICAL GEOGRAPHY. By H. F. TOZER.

FRANCE. By CHARLOTTE M. YONGE.

GEOGRAPHY. By Sir GEO. GROVE, D.C.L.

INDIAN HISTORY, ASIATIC AND EUROPEAN. By J. TALBOYS WHEELER.

PRIMERS.—LITERATURE. Edited by JOHN R. GREEN, M.A., LL.D. 18mo. 1s. each:

ENGLISH GRAMMAR. By Rev. R. MORRIS.

ENGLISH GRAMMAR EXERCISES. By Rev. R. MORRIS and H. C. BOWEN.

EXERCISES ON MORRIS'S PRIMER OF ENGLISH GRAMMAR. By J. WETHERELL, M.A.

ENGLISH COMPOSITION. By Prof. NICHOL.

QUESTIONS AND EXERCISES IN ENGLISH COMPOSITION. By Prof. NICHOL and W. S. M'CORMICK.

PHILOLOGY. By J. PEILE, M.A.

ENGLISH LITERATURE. By Rev. STOPFORD BROOKE, M.A.

CHILDREN'S TREASURY OF LYRICAL POETRY. Selected by Prof. F. T. PALGRAVE. In 2 parts. 1s. each.

SHAKSPERE. By Prof. DOWDEN.

GREEK LITERATURE. By Prof. JEBB.

HOMER. By Right Hon. W. E. GLADSTONE.

ROMAN LITERATURE. By A. S. WILKINS.

PRIMERS.—SCIENCE. Under the joint Editorship of Prof. HUXLEY, Sir H. E. ROSCOE, and Prof. BALFOUR STEWART. 18mo. 1s. each:

INTRODUCTORY. By Prof. HUXLEY.

CHEMISTRY. By Sir HENRY ROSCOE, F.R.S. With Illustrations, and Questions.

PHYSICS. By BALFOUR STEWART, F.R.S. With Illustrations, and Questions.

PHYSICAL GEOGRAPHY. By A. GEIKIE, F.R.S. With Illustrations, and Questions.

GEOLOGY. By ARCHIBALD GEIKIE, F.R.S.

PHYSIOLOGY. By MICHAEL FOSTER, F.R.S.

ASTRONOMY. By J. N. LOCKYER, F.R.S.

BOTANY. By Sir J. D. HOOKER, C.B.

LOGIC. By W. STANLEY JEVONS, F.R.S.

POLITICAL ECONOMY. By W. STANLEY JEVONS, LL.D., M.A., F.R.S.

PROCTER (Rev. F.).—A HISTORY OF THE BOOK OF COMMON PRAYER. 18th Edition. Crown 8vo. 10s. 6d.

PROCTER (Rev. F.) and MACLEAR (Rev. Canon).—AN ELEMENTARY INTRODUCTION TO THE BOOK OF COMMON PRAYER. 18mo. 2s. 6d.

LIST OF PUBLICATIONS. 47

PROPERT (J. Lumsden). A HISTORY OF MINIATURE ART. With Illustrations. Super royal 4to. 3*l.* 13*s.* 6*d.* Also bound in vellum. 4*l.* 14*s.* 6*d.*

PROPERTIUS. SELECT POEMS. Edited by J. P. POSTGATE, M.A. Fcp. 8vo. 6*s.*

PSALMS (THE). With Introductions and Critical Notes. By A. C. JENNINGS, M.A., and W. H. LOWE, M.A. In 2 vols. 2nd Edition. Crown 8vo. 10*s.* 6*d.* each.

PUCKLE (G. H.).—AN ELEMENTARY TREATISE ON CONIC SECTIONS AND ALGEBRAIC GEOMETRY. 6th Edit. Crn. 8vo. 7*s.* 6*d.*

PYLODET (L.).—NEW GUIDE TO GERMAN CONVERSATION. 18mo. 2*s.* 6*d.*

RACINE.—BRITANNICUS. Ed. by EUGÈNE PELLISSIER, M.A. 18mo. 2*s.*

RADCLIFFE (Charles B.).—BEHIND THE TIDES. 8vo. 6*s.*

RAMSAY (Prof. William).—EXPERIMENTAL PROOFS OF CHEMICAL THEORY. 18mo. 2*s.* 6*d.*

RANSOME (Prof. Cyril).—SHORT STUDIES OF SHAKESPEARE'S PLOTS. Cr.8vo. 3*s.* 6*d.*

RATHBONE (Wm.). THE HISTORY AND PROGRESS OF DISTRICT NURSING, FROM ITS COMMENCEMENT IN THE YEAR 1859 TO THE PRESENT DATE. Crown 8vo. 2*s.* 6*d.*

RAY (Prof. P. K.).—A TEXT-BOOK OF DEDUCTIVE LOGIC. 4th Ed. Globe 8vo. 4*s.* 6*d.*

RAYLEIGH (Lord).—THEORY OF SOUND. 8vo. Vol. I. 12*s.* 6*d.*—Vol. II. 12*s.* 6*d.*—Vol. III. *in preparation.*)

RAYS OF SUNLIGHT FOR DARK DAYS. With a Preface by C. J. VAUGHAN, D.D. New Edition. 18mo. 3*s.* 6*d.*

REALMAH. By the Author of " Friends in Council." Crown 8vo. 6*s.*

REASONABLE FAITH: A SHORT RELIGIOUS ESSAY FOR THE TIMES. By "THREE FRIENDS." Crown 8vo. 1*s.*

RECOLLECTIONS OF A NURSE. By E. D. Crown 8vo. 2*s.*

REED.—MEMOIR OF SIR CHARLES REED. By his Son, CHARLES E. B. REED, M.A. With Portrait. Crown 8vo. 4*s.* 6*d.*

REMSEN (Prof. Ira). AN INTRODUCTION TO THE STUDY OF ORGANIC CHEMISTRY. Crown 8vo. 6*s.* 6*d.*

—— AN INTRODUCTION TO THE STUDY OF CHEMISTRY (INORGANIC CHEMISTRY). Cr. 8vo. 6*s.* 6*d.*

—— THE ELEMENTS OF CHEMISTRY. A Text-Book for Beginners. Fcp. 8vo. 2*s.* 6*d.*

—— TEXT-BOOK OF INORGANIC CHEMISTRY. 8vo. 16*s.*

RENDALL (Rev. Frederic).—THE EPISTLE TO THE HEBREWS IN GREEK AND ENGLISH. With Notes. Crown 8vo. 6*s.*

—— THE THEOLOGY OF THE HEBREW CHRISTIANS. Crown 8vo. 5*s.*

—— THE EPISTLE TO THE HEBREWS. English Text, with Commentary. Cr. 8vo. 7*s.* 6*d.*

RENDALL (Prof. G. H.).—THE CRADLE OF THE ARYANS. 8vo. 3*s.*

RENDU—WILLS. THE THEORY OF THE GLACIERS OF SAVOY. By M. LE CHANOINE RENDU. Trans. by A. WILLS, Q.C. 8vo. 7*s.* 6*d.*

REULEAUX KENNEDY. THE KINEMATICS OF MACHINERY. By Prof. F. REULEAUX. Translated by Prof. A. B. W. KENNEDY, F.R.S., C.E. Medium 8vo. 21*s.*

REYNOLDS (J. R.). A SYSTEM OF MEDICINE. Edited by J. RUSSELL REYNOLDS, M.D., F.R.C.P. London. In 5 vols. Vols. I. II. III. and V. 8vo. 25*s.* each.—Vol. IV. 21*s.*

REYNOLDS (H. R.).— NOTES OF THE CHRISTIAN LIFE. Crown 8vo. 7*s.* 6*d.*

REYNOLDS (Prof. Osborne).—SEWER GAS, AND HOW TO KEEP IT OUT OF HOUSES. 3rd Edition. Crown 8vo. 1*s.* 6*d.*

RICE (Prof. J. M.) and JOHNSON (W. W.).— AN ELEMENTARY TREATISE ON THE DIFFERENTIAL CALCULUS. New Edition. 8vo. 18*s.* Abridged Edition. 9*s.*

RICHARDSON (Dr. B. W.).—ON ALCOHOL. Crown 8vo. 1*s.*

— — DISEASES OF MODERN LIFE. Crown 8vo. 6*s.*

—— HYGEIA: A CITY OF HEALTH. Crown 8vo. 1*s.*

—— THE FUTURE OF SANITARY SCIENCE. Crown 8vo. 1*s.*

—— THE FIELD OF DISEASE. A Book of Preventive Medicine. 8vo. 25*s.*

RICHEY (Alex. G.).—THE IRISH LAND LAWS. Crown 8vo. 3*s.* 6*d.*

ROBINSON CRUSOE. Edited by HENRY KINGSLEY. *Globe Edition.* 3*s.* 6*d.*—*Golden Treasury Edition.* Edit. by J. W. CLARK, M.A. 18mo. 4*s.* 6*d.*

ROBINSON (Prebendary H. G.).—MAN IN THE IMAGE OF GOD, AND OTHER SERMONS. Crown 8vo. 7*s.* 6*d.*

ROBINSON (Rev. J. L.).—MARINE SURVEYING: AN ELEMENTARY TREATISE ON. Prepared for the Use of Younger Naval Officers. With Illustrations. Crown 8vo. 7*s.* 6*d.*

ROBY (H. J.).—A GRAMMAR OF THE LATIN LANGUAGE FROM PLAUTUS TO SUETONIUS. In Two Parts.--Part I. containing Sounds, Inflexions, Word Formation, Appendices, etc. 5th Edition. Crown 8vo. 9*s.*—Part II. Syntax, Prepositions, etc. 6th Edition. Crown 8vo. 10*s.* 6*d.*

—— A LATIN GRAMMAR FOR SCHOOLS. Cr. 8vo. 5*s.*

—— AN ELEMENTARY LATIN GRAMMAR. Globe 8vo.

—— EXERCISES IN LATIN SYNTAX AND IDIOM. Arranged with reference to Roby's School Latin Grammar. By E. B. ENGLAND, M.A. Crown 8vo. 2*s.* 6*d.*—Key, 2*s.* 6*d.*

ROCKSTRO (W. S.).-- LIFE OF GEORGE FREDERICK HANDEL. Crown 8vo. 10*s.* 6*d.*

ROGERS (Prof. J. E. T.) — HISTORICAL GLEANINGS.--First Series. Cr. 8vo. 4*s.* 6*d.* —Second Series. Crown 8vo. 6*s.*

—— COBDEN AND POLITICAL OPINION. 8vo. 10*s.* 6*d.*

ROMANES (George J.).—THE SCIENTIFIC EVIDENCES OF ORGANIC EVOLUTION. Cr. 8vo. 2*s.* 6*d.*

ROSCOE (Sir Henry E., M.P., F.R.S.).—LESSONS IN ELEMENTARY CHEMISTRY. With Illustrations. Fcp. 8vo. 4s. 6d.
—— PRIMER OF CHEMISTRY. With Illustrations. 18mo, cloth. With Questions. 1s.
ROSCOE (Sir H. E.) and SCHORLEMMER (C.).—A TREATISE ON CHEMISTRY. With Illustrations. 8vo.—Vols. I. and II. INORGANIC CHEMISTRY: Vol. I. THE NON-METALLIC ELEMENTS. With a Portrait of DALTON. 21s.—Vol. II. Part I. METALS. 18s.; Part II. METALS. 18s.—Vol. III. ORGANIC CHEMISTRY: Parts I. II. and IV. 21s. each; Parts III. and V. 18s. each.
ROSCOE—SCHUSTER.—SPECTRUM ANALYSIS. By Sir HENRY E. ROSCOE, LL.D., F.R.S. 4th Edition, revised by the Author and A. SCHUSTER, Ph.D., F.R.S. Medium 8vo. 21s.
ROSENBUSCH—IDDINGS.—MICROSCOPICAL PHYSIOGRAPHY OF THE ROCK-MAKING MINERALS. By Prof. H. ROSENBUSCH. Translated by J. P. IDDINGS. Illustrated. 8vo. 24s.
ROSS (Percy).—A MISGUIDIT LASSIE. Crown 8vo. 4s. 6d.
ROSSETTI (Dante Gabriel).— A RECORD AND A STUDY. By W. SHARP. Crown 8vo. 10s. 6d.
ROSSETTI (Christina).—POEMS. Complete Edition. Extra fcp. 8vo. 6s.
—— A PAGEANT, AND OTHER POEMS. Extra fcp. 8vo. 6s.
—— SPEAKING LIKENESSES. Illustrated by ARTHUR HUGHES. Crown 8vo. 4s. 6d.
ROUSSEAU. By JOHN MORLEY. 2 vols. Globe 8vo. 10s.
ROUTH E. J.).—A TREATISE ON THE DYNAMICS OF A SYSTEM OF RIGID BODIES. 4th Edition, revised and enlarged. 8vo. In Two Parts.—Part I. ELEMENTARY. 14s.—Part II. ADVANCED. 14s.
—— STABILITY OF A GIVEN STATE OF MOTION, PARTICULARLY STEADY MOTION. 8vo. 8s. 6d.
ROUTLEDGE (James).—POPULAR PROGRESS IN ENGLAND. 8vo. 16s.
RUMFORD Count).—COMPLETE WORKS OF COUNT RUMFORD. With Memoir by GEORGE ELLIS, and Portrait. 5 vols. 8vo. 4l. 14s. 6d.
RUNAWAY (THE). By the Author of "Mrs. Jerningham's Journal." Gl. 8vo. 2s. 6d.
RUSH (Edward).—THE SYNTHETIC LATIN DELECTUS. A First Latin Construing Book. Extra fcp. 8vo. 2s. 6d.
RUSHBROOKE (W. G.).—SYNOPTICON: AN EXPOSITION OF THE COMMON MATTER OF THE SYNOPTIC GOSPELS. Printed in Colours. In Six Parts, and Appendix. 4to.—Part I. 3s. 6d.—Parts II. and III. 7s.—Parts IV. V. and VI., with Indices. 10s. 6d.—Appendices. 10s. 6d.—Complete in 1 vol. 35s.
RUSSELL (W. Clark).—MAROONED. Crown 8vo. 3s. 6d.
—— DAMPIER. Portrait. Cr. 8vo. 2s. 6d.
RUSSELL (Sir Charles).—NEW VIEWS ON IRELAND. Crown 8vo. 2s. 6d.

RUSSELL (Sir C.).—THE PARNELL COMMISSION: THE OPENING SPEECH FOR THE DEFENCE. 8vo. 10s. 6d.
Popular Edition. Sewed. 2s.
RUSSELL (Dean). — THE LIGHT THAT LIGHTETH EVERY MAN: Sermons. With an Introduction by the Very Rev. E. H. PLUMPTRE. D.D. Crown 8vo. 6s.
RUST (Rev. George).—FIRST STEPS TO LATIN PROSE COMPOSITION. 18mo. 1s. 6d.
—— A KEY TO RUST'S FIRST STEPS TO LATIN PROSE COMPOSITION. By W. YATES. 18mo. 3s. 6d.
RUTH AND HER FRIENDS: A STORY FOR GIRLS. Illustrated. Gl. 8vo. 2s. 6d.
RUTHERFORD (W. Gunion, M.A., LL.D.). —FIRST GREEK GRAMMAR. Part I. Accidence, 2s.; Part II. Syntax, 2s.; or in 1 vol. 3s. 6d.
—— THE NEW PHRYNICHUS. Being a revised Text of the Ecloga of the Grammarian Phrynichus, with Introduction and Commentary. 8vo. 18s.
—— BABRIUS. With Introductory Dissertations, Critical Notes, Commentary, and Lexicon. 8vo. 12s. 6d.
—— THUCYDIDES. Book IV. A Revision of the Text, illustrating the Principal Causes of Corruption in the Manuscripts of this Author. 8vo. 7s. 6d.
RYLAND (F.).—CHRONOLOGICAL OUTLINES OF ENGLISH LITERATURE. Crn. 8vo. 6s.
ST. JOHNSTON (A.).— CAMPING AMONG CANNIBALS. Crown 8vo. 4s. 6d.
—— A SOUTH SEA LOVER: A Romance. Cr. 8vo. 6s.
—— CHARLIE ASGARDE: THE STORY OF A FRIENDSHIP. Crown 8vo. 5s.
SAINTSBURY (George).—A HISTORY OF ELIZABETHAN LITERATURE. Cr. 8vo. 7s. 6d.
—— DRYDEN. Crown 8vo. 1s. 6d.; sewed, 1s.
SALLUST.—CAII SALLUSTII CRISPI CATILINA ET JUGURTHA. For Use in Schools. By C. MERIVALE, D.D. Fcp. 8vo. 4s. 6d. The JUGURTHA and the CATILINE may be had separately, 2s. 6d. each.
—— THE CONSPIRACY OF CATILINE AND THE JUGURTHINE WAR. Translated into English by A. W. POLLARD, B.A. Crown 8vo. 6s. CATILINE separately. Crown 8vo. 3s.
—— BELLUM CATULINAE. Edited, with Introduction and Notes, by A. M. COOK, M.A. Fcp. 8vo. 4s. 6d.
SALMON (Rev. Prof. George). — NON-MIRACULOUS CHRISTIANITY, AND OTHER SERMONS. 2nd Edition. Crown 8vo. 6s.
—— GNOSTICISM AND AGNOSTICISM, AND OTHER SERMONS. Crown 8vo. 7s. 6d.
SAND (G.).—LA MARE AU DIABLE. Edited by W. E. RUSSELL, M.A. 18mo. 1s.
SANDEAU (Jules).—MADEMOISELLE DE LA SEIGLIÈRE. Ed. H. C. STEEL. 18mo. 1s. 6d.
SANDERSON (F. W.).—HYDROSTATICS FOR BEGINNERS. Globe 8vo. 4s. 6d.
SANDHURST MATHEMATICAL PAPERS, FOR ADMISSION INTO THE ROYAL MILITARY COLLEGE, 1881–89. Edited by E. J. BROOKSMITH, B.A. Cr. 8vo. 3s. 6d.

LIST OF PUBLICATIONS.

SANDYS (J. E.).—AN EASTER VACATION IN GREECE. Crown 8vo. 3s. 6d.

SAYCE (Prof. A. H.).—THE ANCIENT EMPIRES OF THE EAST. Crown 8vo. 6s.

—— HERODOTOS. Books I.—III. The Ancient Empires of the East. Edited, with Notes, and Introduction. 8vo. 16s.

SCHILLER.—DIE JUNGFRAU VON ORLEANS. Edited by JOSEPH GOSTWICK. 18mo. 2s. 6d.

—— MARIA STUART. Edited, with Introduction and Notes, by C. SHELDON. 18mo. 2s. 6d.

—— SELECTIONS FROM SCHILLER'S LYRICAL POEMS. Edit. E. J. TURNER and E. D. A. MORSHEAD. 18mo. 2s. 6d.

—— WALLENSTEIN. Part I. DAS LÄGER. Edit. by H. B. COTTERILL, M.A. 18mo. 2s.

—— WILHELM TELL. Edited by G. E. FASNACHT. 18mo. 2s. 6d.

SCHILLER'S LIFE. By Prof. HEINRICH DÜNTZER. Translated by PERCY E. PINKERTON. Crown 8vo. 10s. 6d.

SCHMID.—HEINRICH VON EICHENFELS. Edited by G. E. FASNACHT. 2s. 6d.

SCHMIDT—WHITE.—AN INTRODUCTION TO THE RHYTHMIC AND METRIC OF THE CLASSICAL LANGUAGES. By Dr. J. H. HEINRICH SCHMIDT. Translated by JOHN WILLIAMS WHITE, Ph.D. 8vo. 10s. 6d.

SCIENCE LECTURES AT SOUTH KENSINGTON. With Illustrations.—Vol. I. Containing Lectures by Capt. ABNEY, R.E., F.R.S.; Prof. STOKES; Prof. A. B. W. KENNEDY, F.R.S., C.E.; F. J. BRAMWELL, C.E., F.R.S.; Prof. F. FORBES; H. C. SORBY, F.R.S.; J. T. BOTTOMLEY, F.R.S.E.; S. H. VINES, D.Sc.; Prof. CAREY FORSTER. Crown 8vo. 6s.
Vol. II. Containing Lectures by W. SPOTTISWOODE, F.R.S.; Prof. FORBES; H. W. CHISHOLM; Prof. T. F. PIGOT; W. FROUDE, LL.D., F.R.S.; Dr. SIEMENS; Prof. BARRETT; Dr. BURDON-SANDERSON; Dr. LAUDER BRUNTON, F.R.S.; Prof. MCLEOD; Sir H. E. ROSCOE, F.R.S. Illust. Cr. 8vo. 6s.

SCOTCH SERMONS, 1880. By Principal CAIRD and others. 3rd Edit. 8vo. 10s. 6d.

SCOTT.—THE POETICAL WORKS OF SIR WALTER SCOTT. Edited by Prof. F. T. PALGRAVE. Globe 8vo. 3s. 6d.

—— THE LAY OF THE LAST MINSTREL, and THE LADY OF THE LAKE. Edited, with Introductions and Notes, by Prof. F. T. PALGRAVE. Globe 8vo. 1s.

—— MARMION, and THE LORD OF THE ISLES. By the same Editor. Globe 8vo. 1s.

—— MARMION. A Tale of Flodden Field in Six Cantos. Edited, with Introduction and Notes, by Prof. M. MACMILLAN, B.A. Globe 8vo. 3s. 6d.

—— ROKEBY. By the same. Gl. 8vo. 3s. 6d.

—— THE LAY OF THE LAST MINSTREL. Cantos I.—III. Edited, with Introduction and Notes, by Prof. G. H. STUART, M.A. Globe 8vo. 1s. 6d.—Introduction and Canto I., sewed, 9d.

—— THE LADY OF THE LAKE. By the same Editor. Globe 8vo.

SCOTT. By R. H. HUTTON. Crown 8vo. 1s. 6d.; sewed, 1s.

SCOTTISH SONG: A SELECTION OF THE LYRICS OF SCOTLAND. Compiled by MARY CARLYLE AITKEN. 18mo. 4s. 6d.

SCRATCHLEY — KINLOCH COOKE.—AUSTRALIAN DEFENCES AND NEW GUINEA. Compiled from the Papers of the late Major-General Sir PETER SCRATCHLEY, R.E., by C. KINLOCH COOKE. 8vo. 14s.

SCULPTURE, SPECIMENS OF ANCIENT. Egyptian, Etruscan, Greek, and Roman. Selected from different Collections in Great Britain by the SOCIETY OF DILETTANTI. Vol. II. 5l. 5s.

SEATON (Dr. Edward C.).—A HANDBOOK OF VACCINATION. Extra fcp. 8vo. 8s. 6d.

SEELEY (Prof. J. R.).—LECTURES AND ESSAYS. 8vo. 10s. 6d.

—— THE EXPANSION OF ENGLAND. Two Courses of Lectures. Crown 8vo. 4s. 6d.

—— OUR COLONIAL EXPANSION. Extracts from "The Expansion of England." Crown 8vo. 1s.

SEILER (Carl, M.D.)—MICRO-PHOTOGRAPHS IN HISTOLOGY, NORMAL AND PATHOLOGICAL. 4to. 31s. 6d.

SELBORNE (Roundell, Earl of).—A DEFENCE OF THE CHURCH OF ENGLAND AGAINST DISESTABLISHMENT. Crown 8vo. 2s. 6d.

—— ANCIENT FACTS AND FICTIONS CONCERNING CHURCHES AND TITHES. Cr. 8vo. 7s. 6d.

—— THE BOOK OF PRAISE. From the Best English Hymn Writers. 18mo. 4s. 6d.

—— A HYMNAL. Chiefly from "The Book of Praise." In various sizes.—A. In Royal 32mo, cloth limp. 6d.—B. Small 18mo, larger type, cloth limp. 1s.—C. Same Edition, fine paper, cloth. 1s. 6d.—An Edition with Music, Selected, Harmonised, and Composed by JOHN HULLAH. Square 18mo. 3s. 6d.

SERVICE (Rev. John).—SERMONS. With Portrait. Crown 8vo. 6s.

—— PRAYERS FOR PUBLIC WORSHIP. Crown 8vo. 4s. 6d.

SHAIRP (John Campbell).—GLEN DESSERAY, AND OTHER POEMS, LYRICAL AND ELEGIAC. Ed. by F. T. PALGRAVE. Crown 8vo. 6s.

—— BURNS. Crown 8vo. 1s. 6d.; sewed, 1s.

SHAKESPEARE. THE WORKS OF WILLIAM SHAKESPEARE. Cambridge Edition. Edit. by WM. GEORGE CLARK, M.A., and W. ALDIS WRIGHT, M.A. 9 vols. 8vo. 10s. 6d. each.

—— SHAKESPEARE. By the same Editors. Globe Edition. Globe 8vo. 3s. 6d.

—— THE WORKS OF WILLIAM SHAKESPEARE. Victoria Edition.—Vol. I. Comedies.—Vol. II. Histories.—Vol. III. Tragedies. In Three Vols. Crown 8vo. 6s. each.

—— SHAKESPEARE'S SONGS AND SONNETS. Edited, with Notes, by F. T. PALGRAVE. 18mo. 4s. 6d.

SHAKESPEARE.—CHARLES LAMB'S TALES FROM SHAKSPEARE. Edited, with Preface, by the Rev. A. AINGER, M.A. 18mo. 4s.6d. *Globe Readings Edition.* For Schools. Globe 8vo. 2s.—*Library Edition.* Globe 8vo. 5s.
—— MUCH ADO ABOUT NOTHING. Edited by K. DEIGHTON. Globe 8vo. 2s.
—— RICHARD III. Edited by Prof. C. H. TAWNEY, M.A. Globe 8vo. 2s. 6d.
—— THE WINTER'S TALE. Edited by K. DEIGHTON. Globe 8vo. 2s. 6d.
—— HENRY V. By the same Editor. Globe 8vo. 2s.
—— OTHELLO. By the same Editor. Globe 8vo. 2s. 6d.
—— CYMBELINE. By the same Editor. Globe 8vo. 2s. 6d.
—— THE TEMPEST. By the same Editor. Globe 8vo. 1s. 6d.
—— TWELFTH NIGHT; OR, WHAT YOU WILL. By the same Editor. Globe 8vo. 1s. 6d.
—— MACBETH. By the same Editor. Globe 8vo. 1s.6d.
—— JULIUS CAESAR. By the same Editor. Globe 8vo. 2s.
—— THE MERCHANT OF VENICE. By the same Editor. Globe 8vo. 1s. 6d.
SHAKSPERE. By Prof. DOWDEN. 18mo. 1s.
SHANN (G.).—AN ELEMENTARY TREATISE ON HEAT IN RELATION TO STEAM AND THE STEAM-ENGINE. Illustrated. Crown 8vo. 4s. 6d.
SHARP (W.).—DANTE GABRIEL ROSSETTI. Crown 8vo. 10s. 6d.
SHELBURNE. LIFE OF WILLIAM, EARL OF SHELBURNE. By Lord EDMOND FITZMAURICE. In 3 vols.—Vol. I. 8vo. 12s.—Vol. II. 8vo. 12s.—Vol. III. 8vo. 16s.
SHELLEY. SELECTIONS. Edited by STOPFORD A. BROOKE. 18mo. 4s. 6d. Large Paper Edition. 12s. 6d.
—— COMPLETE POETICAL WORKS. Edited by Prof. DOWDEN. 1 vol. Crown 8vo.
SHELLEY. By J. A. SYMONDS, M.A. Crown 8vo. 1s. 6d.; sewed, 1s.
SHERIDAN. By Mrs. OLIPHANT. Crown 8vo. 1s. 6d.; sewed, 1s.
SHIRLEY (W. N.).—ELIJAH: FOUR UNIVERSITY SERMONS. Fcp. 8vo. 2s. 6d.
SHORTHOUSE (J. H.).—JOHN INGLESANT: A ROMANCE. Crown 8vo. 6s.
—— THE LITTLE SCHOOLMASTER MARK: A SPIRITUAL ROMANCE. Two Parts. Crown 8vo. 2s. 6d. each: complete, 4s. 6d.
—— SIR PERCIVAL: A STORY OF THE PAST AND OF THE PRESENT. Crown 8vo. 6s.
—— A TEACHER OF THE VIOLIN, AND OTHER TALES. Crown 8vo. 6s.
—— THE COUNTESS EVE. Crown 8vo. 6s.
SHORTLAND (Admiral).—NAUTICAL SURVEYING. 8vo. 21s.
SHUCKBURGH (E. S.).—PASSAGES FROM LATIN AUTHORS FOR TRANSLATION INTO ENGLISH. Crown 8vo. 2s.

SHUCHHARDT (Carl).—DR. SCHLIEMANN'S EXCAVATIONS AT TROY, TIRYNS, MYCENAE, ITHACA IN THE LIGHT OF RECENT KNOWLEDGE. Translated by EUGENIE SELLERS. With a Preface by WALTER LEAF. Litt.D. Illustrated. 8vo. [*In the Press.*
SHUFELDT (R. W.).—THE MYOLOGY OF THE RAVEN (*Corvus corax Sinuatus*). A Guide to the Study of the Muscular System in Birds. Illustrated. 8vo.
SIBSON.—DR. FRANCIS SIBSON'S COLLECTED WORKS. Edited by W. M. ORD, M.D. Illustrated. 4 vols. 8vo. 3l. 3s.
SIDGWICK (Prof. Henry).—THE METHODS OF ETHICS. 4th Edit., revised. 8vo. 14s.
—— A SUPPLEMENT TO THE SECOND EDITION. Containing all the important Additions and Alterations in the 4th Edit. 8vo. 6s.
—— THE PRINCIPLES OF POLITICAL ECONOMY. 2nd Edition. 8vo. 16s.
—— OUTLINES OF THE HISTORY OF ETHICS FOR ENGLISH READERS. Cr. 8vo. 3s. 6d.
—— THE ELEMENTS OF POLITICS. 8vo.
SIDNEY (SIR PHILIP). By JOHN ADDINGTON SYMONDS. Cr. 8vo. 1s.6d.; sewed, 1s.
SIME (James).—HISTORY OF GERMANY. 2nd Edition. Maps. 18mo. 3s.
—— GEOGRAPHY OF EUROPE. Globe 8vo. 3s.
SIMPSON (F. P.).—LATIN PROSE AFTER THE BEST AUTHORS.—Part I. CÆSARIAN PROSE. Extra fcp. 8vo. 2s. 6d.
KEY (for Teachers only). Ex. fcp. 8vo. 5s.
SIMPSON (W.).—AN EPITOME OF THE HISTORY OF THE CHRISTIAN CHURCH. Fcp. 8vo. 3s. 6d.
SKRINE (J. H.).—UNDER TWO QUEENS. Crown 8vo. 3s.
—— A MEMORY OF EDWARD THRING. Crown 8vo. 6s.
SLIP IN THE FENS (A). Globe 8vo. 2s.
SMITH (Barnard).—ARITHMETIC AND ALGEBRA. New Edition. Crown 8vo. 10s. 6d.
—— ARITHMETIC FOR THE USE OF SCHOOLS. New Edition. Crown 8vo. 4s. 6d.
—— KEY TO ARITHMETIC FOR SCHOOLS. New Edition. Crown 8vo. 8s. 6d.
—— EXERCISES IN ARITHMETIC. Crown 8vo, 2 Parts, 1s. each, or complete, 2s.—With Answers, 2s. 6d.—Answers separately, 6d.
—— SCHOOL CLASS-BOOK OF ARITHMETIC. 18mo. 3s.—Or, sold separately, in Three Parts. 1s. each.
—— KEY TO SCHOOL CLASS-BOOK OF ARITHMETIC. In Parts I. II. and III. 2s. 6d. each.
—— SHILLING BOOK OF ARITHMETIC FOR NATIONAL AND ELEMENTARY SCHOOLS. 18mo, cloth.—Or separately, Part I. 2d.; II. 3d.; III. 7d.—With Answers, 1s. 6d.
—— ANSWERS TO THE SHILLING BOOK OF ARITHMETIC. 18mo. 6d.
—— KEY TO THE SHILLING BOOK OF ARITHMETIC. 18mo. 4s. 6d.
—— EXAMINATION PAPERS IN ARITHMETIC. In Four Parts. 18mo. 1s. 6d.—With Answers, 2s.—Answers, 6d.

LIST OF PUBLICATIONS. 51

SMITH (Barnard). KEY TO EXAMINATION PAPERS IN ARITHMETIC. 18mo. 4s. 6d.
—— THE METRIC SYSTEM OF ARITHMETIC. 3d.
—— A CHART OF THE METRIC SYSTEM OF ARITHMETIC. On a Sheet, size 42 by 34 in., on Roller mounted and varnished. 3s. 6d.
—— EASY LESSONS IN ARITHMETIC. Combining Exercises in Reading, Writing, Spelling, and Dictation. Part I. for Standard I. in National Schools. Crown 8vo. 9d.
—— EXAMINATION CARDS IN ARITHMETIC. With Answers and Hints. Standards I. and II. In box. 1s.—Standards III. IV. and V. In boxes. 1s. each.—Standard VI. in Two Parts. In boxes. 1s. each.

SMITH (Catherine Barnard).—POEMS. Fcp. 8vo. 5s.

SMITH (Charles).—AN ELEMENTARY TREATISE ON CONIC SECTIONS. 7th Edition. Crown 8vo. 7s. 6d.
—— SOLUTIONS OF THE EXAMPLES IN "AN ELEMENTARY TREATISE ON CONIC SECTIONS." Crown 8vo. 10s. 6d.
—— AN ELEMENTARY TREATISE ON SOLID GEOMETRY. 2nd Edition. Cr. 8vo. 9s. 6d.
—— ELEMENTARY ALGEBRA. 2nd Edition. Globe 8vo. 4s. 6d.
—— A TREATISE ON ALGEBRA. Cr.8vo. 7s.6d.
—— SOLUTIONS OF THE EXAMPLES IN "A TREATISE ON ALGEBRA." Cr. 8vo. 10s. 6d.

SMITH (Goldwin).—THREE ENGLISH STATESMEN. New Edition. Crown 8vo. 5s.
—— COWPER. Crown 8vo. 1s. 6d.; sewed, 1s.
—— PROHIBITIONISM IN CANADA AND THE UNITED STATES. 8vo, sewed. 6d.

SMITH (Horace).- POEMS. Globe 8vo. 5s.

SMITH (J.).—ECONOMIC PLANTS, DICTIONARY OF POPULAR NAMES OF: THEIR HISTORY, PRODUCTS, AND USES. 8vo. 14s.

SMITH (W. Saumarez).—THE BLOOD OF THE NEW COVENANT: A THEOLOGICAL ESSAY. Crown 8vo. 2s. 6d.

SMITH (Rev. Travers).—MAN'S KNOWLEDGE OF MAN AND OF GOD. Crown 8vo. 6s.

SMITH (W. G.).- DISEASES OF FIELD AND GARDEN CROPS, CHIEFLY SUCH AS ARE CAUSED BY FUNGI. With 143 new Illustrations. Fcp. 8vo. 4s. 6d.

SNOWBALL (J. C.).—THE ELEMENTS OF PLANE AND SPHERICAL TRIGONOMETRY. 14th Edition. Crown 8vo. 7s. 6d.

SONNENSCHEIN (A.) and MEIKLEJOHN (J. M. D.).—THE ENGLISH METHOD OF TEACHING TO READ. Fcp. 8vo. Comprising—
THE NURSERY BOOK, containing all the Two Letter Words in the Language. 1d.— Also in Large Type on Four Sheets, with Roller. 5s.
THE FIRST COURSE, consisting of Short Vowels with Single Consonants. 7d.
THE SECOND COURSE, with Combinations and Bridges, consisting of Short Vowels with Double Consonants. 7d.
THE THIRD AND FOURTH COURSES, consisting of Long Vowels and all the Double Vowels in the Language. 7d.

SOPHOCLES.- (EDIPUS THE KING. Translated from the Greek into English Verse by E. D. A. MORSHEAD, M.A. Fcp. 8vo. 3s.6d.
—— (EDIPUS TYRANNUS. A Record by L. SPEED and F. R. PRYOR of the performance at Cambridge. Illustr. Small folio. 12s. 6d.
—— By Prof. L. CAMPBELL. Fcp. 8vo. 1s. 6d.

SOUTHEY. By Prof. DOWDEN. Crown 8vo. 1s. 6d.; sewed, 1s.

SOUTHEY.—LIFE OF NELSON. Edit., with Introduction and Notes, by Prof. MICHAEL MACMILLAN, B.A. Globe 8vo. 3s. 6d.

SPENDER (J. Kent).—THERAPEUTIC MEANS FOR THE RELIEF OF PAIN. 8vo. 8s. 6d.

SPENSER.—COMPLETE WORKS OF EDMUND SPENSER. Ed. by R. MORRIS, with Memoir by J. W. HALES. Globe 8vo. 3s. 6d.

SPENSER. By the Very Rev. Dean CHURCH. Cr. 8vo. 1s. 6d.; swd., 1s.—Library Ed., 5s.

SPINOZA: A STUDY OF. By JAMES MARTINEAU, LL.D. 2nd Ed. Cr. 8vo. 6s.

SPOTTISWOODE (W.).—POLARISATION OF LIGHT. Illustrated. Crown 8vo. 3s. 6d.

STANLEY (Very Rev. A. P.).—THE ATHANASIAN CREED. Crown 8vo. 2s.
—— THE NATIONAL THANKSGIVING. Sermons preached in Westminster Abbey. 2nd Ed. Crown 8vo. 2s. 6d.
—— ADDRESSES AND SERMONS DELIVERED AT ST. ANDREWS IN 1872-75 and 1877. Cr.8vo. 5s.
—— ADDRESSES AND SERMONS DELIVERED DURING A VISIT TO THE UNITED STATES AND CANADA IN 1878. Crown 8vo. 6s.

STANLEY (Hon. Maude).—CLUBS FOR WORKING GIRLS. Crown 8vo. 6s.

STATESMAN'S YEAR-BOOK (THE). A Statistical and Historical Annual of the States of the Civilised World for the year 1890. Twenty-seventh Annual Publication. Revised after Official Returns. Edited by J. SCOTT KELTIE. Crown 8vo. 10s. 6d.

STATHAM (R.).—BLACKS, BOERS, AND BRITISH. Crown 8vo. 6s.

STEBBING (W.)- PETERBOROUGH. Portrait. Crown 8vo. 2s. 6d.

STEPHEN (Sir J. Fitzjames, Q.C., K.C.S.I.). —A DIGEST OF THE LAW OF EVIDENCE. 5th Edition. Crown 8vo. 6s.
—— A DIGEST OF THE CRIMINAL LAW: CRIMES AND PUNISHMENTS. 4th Ed. 8vo. 16s.
—— A DIGEST OF THE LAW OF CRIMINAL PROCEDURE IN INDICTABLE OFFENCES. By Sir JAMES F. STEPHEN, K.C.S.I., etc., and HERBERT STEPHEN, LL.M. 8vo. 12s. 6d.
—— A HISTORY OF THE CRIMINAL LAW OF ENGLAND. 3 vols. 8vo. 48s.
—— THE STORY OF NUNCOMAR AND THE IMPEACHMENT OF SIR ELIJAH IMPEY. 2 vols. Crown 8vo. 15s.
—— A GENERAL VIEW OF THE CRIMINAL LAW OF ENGLAND. 2nd Edition. 8vo. 14s.

STEPHEN (J. K.).—INTERNATIONAL LAW AND INTERNATIONAL RELATIONS. Cr. 8vo.6s.

STEPHEN (Leslie).—JOHNSON. Crown 8vo. 1s. 6d.; sewed, 1s.
—— SWIFT. Crown 8vo. 1s. 6d.; sewed, 1s.
—— POPE. Crown 8vo. 1s. 6d.; sewed, 1s.

STEPHEN (Caroline E.).—THE SERVICE OF THE POOR. Crown 8vo. 6s. 6d.

STEPHENS (J. B.).—CONVICT ONCE, AND OTHER POEMS. Crown 8vo. 7s. 6d.

STERNE. By H. D. TRAILL. Crown 8vo. 1s. 6d. ; sewed, 1s.

STEVENSON (J. J.).—HOUSE ARCHITECTURE. With Illustrations. 2 vols. Royal 8vo. 18s. each. Vol. I. ARCHITECTURE. Vol. II. HOUSE PLANNING.

STEWART (Aubrey).—THE TALE OF TROY. Done into English. Globe 8vo. 3s. 6d.

STEWART (Prof. Balfour).—LESSONS IN ELEMENTARY PHYSICS. With Illustrations and Coloured Diagram. Fcp. 8vo. 4s. 6d.

—— PRIMER OF PHYSICS. Illustrated. New Edition, with Questions. 18mo. 1s.

—— QUESTIONS ON STEWART'S LESSONS ON ELEMENTARY PHYSICS. By T. H. CORE. 12mo. 2s.

STEWART (Prof. Balfour) and GEE (W. W. Haldane).—LESSONS IN ELEMENTARY PRACTICAL PHYSICS. Crown 8vo. Illustrated. Vol. I. GENERAL PHYSICAL PROCESSES. 6s. —Vol. II. ELECTRICITY AND MAGNETISM. Cr. 8vo. 7s. 6d.—Vol. III. OPTICS, HEAT, AND SOUND.

—— PRACTICAL PHYSICS FOR SCHOOLS AND THE JUNIOR STUDENTS OF COLLEGES. Globe 8vo. Vol. I. ELECTRICITY AND MAGNETISM. 2s. 6d.—Vol. II. HEAT, LIGHT, AND SOUND.

STEWART (Prof. Balfour) and TAIT (P. G.).—THE UNSEEN UNIVERSE; OR, PHYSICAL SPECULATIONS ON A FUTURE STATE. 15th Edition. Crown 8vo. 6s.

STEWART (S. A.) and CORRY (T. H.).—A FLORA OF THE NORTH-EAST OF IRELAND. Crown 8vo. 5s. 6d.

STOKES (Sir George G.).—ON LIGHT. The Burnett Lectures. Crown 8vo. 7s. 6d.

STONE (W. H.).—ELEMENTARY LESSONS ON SOUND. Illustrated. Fcap. 8vo. 3s. 6d.

STRACHAN (J. S.) and WILKINS (A. S.).—ANALECTA. Passages for Translation. Cr. 8vo. 5s.

STRACHEY (Lieut.-Gen. R.).—LECTURES ON GEOGRAPHY. Crown 8vo. 4s. 6d.

STRAFFORD. By H. D. TRAILL. With Portrait. Crown 8vo. 2s. 6d.

STRANGFORD (Viscountess). — EGYPTIAN SEPULCHRES AND SYRIAN SHRINES. New Edition. Crown 8vo. 7s. 6d.

STRETTELL (Alma).—SPANISH AND ITALIAN FOLK SONGS. Illustrated. Royal 16mo. 12s. 6d.

STUBBS (Rev. C. W.).—FOR CHRIST AND CITY. Sermons and Addresses. Cr. 8vo. 6s.

SURGERY, THE INTERNATIONAL ENCYCLOPAEDIA OF. A Systematic Treatise on the Theory and Practice of Surgery by Authors of Various Nations. Edited by JOHN ASHHURST, Jun., M.D., Professor of Clinical Surgery in the University of Pennsylvania. 6 vols. Royal 8vo. 31s. 6d. each.

SWIFT. By LESLIE STEPHEN. Crown 8vo. 1s. 6d. ; sewed, 1s.

SYMONS (Arthur).—DAYS AND NIGHTS: POEMS. Globe 8vo. 6s.

SYMONDS (J. A.).—SHELLEY. Crown 8vo. 1s. 6d. ; sewed, 1s.

—— SIR PHILIP SIDNEY. 1s. 6d. ; sewed, 1s.

TACITUS, THE WORKS OF. Transl. by A. J. CHURCH, M.A., and W. J. BRODRIBB, M.A.

THE HISTORY OF TACITUS. 4th Edition. Crown 8vo. 6s.

THE AGRICOLA AND GERMANIA. A Revised Text. With Notes. Fcp. 8vo. 3s. 6d. The AGRICOLA and GERMANIA may be had separately. 2s. each.

THE ANNALS. Book VI. With Introduction and Notes. Fcp. 8vo. 2s. 6d.

THE AGRICOLA AND GERMANIA. With the Dialogue on Oratory. Trans. Cr.8vo. 4s.6d.

ANNALS OF TACITUS. Translated. 5th Ed. Crown 8vo. 7s. 6d.

—— THE ANNALS. Edited by Prof. G. O. HOLBROOKE, M.A. 8vo. 16s.

—— THE HISTORIES. Books I. and II. Ed. by A. D. GODLEY, M.A. Fcp. 8vo. 5s.

—— THE HISTORIES. Books III.–V. Edited by A. D. GODLEY, M.A. Fcp. 8vo. 5s.

TACITUS. By A. J. CHURCH, M.A., and W. J. BRODRIBB, M.A. Fcp. 8vo. 1s. 6d.

TAIT (Archbishop).—THE PRESENT POSITION OF THE CHURCH OF ENGLAND. Being the Charge delivered at his Primary Visitation. 3rd Edition. 8vo. 3s. 6d.

—— DUTIES OF THE CHURCH OF ENGLAND. Being Seven Addresses delivered at his Second Visitation. 8vo. 4s. 6d.

—— THE CHURCH OF THE FUTURE. Charges delivered at his Third Quadrennial Visitation. 2nd Edition. Crown 8vo. 3s. 6d.

TAIT.—THE LIFE OF ARCHIBALD CAMPBELL TAIT, ARCHBISHOP OF CANTERBURY. By the Very Rev. the DEAN OF WINDSOR and Rev. W. BENHAM, B.D. 2 vols. 8vo.

TAIT.—CATHARINE AND CRAWFURD TAIT, WIFE AND SON OF ARCHIBALD CAMPBELL, ARCHBISHOP OF CANTERBURY: A MEMOIR. Edited by the Rev. W. BENHAM, B.D. Crown 8vo. 6s.

Popular Edition, abridged. Cr. 8vo. 2s.6d.

TAIT (C. W. A.).—ANALYSIS OF ENGLISH HISTORY, BASED ON GREEN'S "SHORT HISTORY OF THE ENGLISH PEOPLE." Revised and Enlarged Edition. Crown 8vo. 4s. 6d.

TAIT (Prof. P. G.).—LECTURES ON SOME RECENT ADVANCES IN PHYSICAL SCIENCE. 3rd Edition. Crown 8vo. 9s.

—— HEAT. With Illustrations. Cr. 8vo. 6s.

TAIT (P. G.) and STEELE (W. J.).—A TREATISE ON DYNAMICS OF A PARTICLE. 6th Edition. Crown 8vo. 12s.

TANNER (Prof. Henry).—FIRST PRINCIPLES OF AGRICULTURE. 18mo. 1s.

—— THE ABBOTT'S FARM ; OR, PRACTICE WITH SCIENCE. Crown 8vo. 3s. 6d.

—— THE ALPHABET OF THE PRINCIPLES OF AGRICULTURE. Extra fcp. 8vo. 6d.

—— FURTHER STEPS IN THE PRINCIPLES OF AGRICULTURE. Extra fcp. 8vo. 1s.

—— ELEMENTARY SCHOOL READINGS IN THE PRINCIPLES OF AGRICULTURE FOR THE THIRD STAGE. Extra fcp. 8vo. 1s.

LIST OF PUBLICATIONS. 53

TANNER (Prof. Henry).—ELEMENTARY LESSONS IN THE SCIENCE OF AGRICULTURAL PRACTICE. Fcp. 8vo. 3s. 6d.
TAVERNIER (Baron): TRAVELS IN INDIA OF JEAN BAPTISTE TAVERNIER, BARON OF AUBONNE. Translated by V. BALL, LL.D. Illustrated. 2 vols. 8vo. 2l. 2s.
TAYLOR (Franklin). — PRIMER OF PIANOFORTE PLAYING. 18mo. 1s.
TAYLOR (Isaac).—THE RESTORATION OF BELIEF. Crown 8vo. 8s. 6d.
TAYLOR (Isaac). — WORDS AND PLACES. 9th Edition. Maps. Globe 8vo. 6s.
—— ETRUSCAN RESEARCHES. With Woodcuts. 8vo. 14s.
—— GREEKS AND GOTHS: A STUDY OF THE RUNES. 8vo. 9s.
TAYLOR (Sedley).—SOUND AND MUSIC. 2nd Edition. Extra Crown 8vo. 8s. 6d.
—— A SYSTEM OF SIGHT-SINGING FROM THE ESTABLISHED MUSICAL NOTATION. 8vo.
TEBAY (S.).—ELEMENTARY MENSURATION FOR SCHOOLS. Extra fcp. 8vo. 3s. 6d.
TEGETMEIER (W. B.).—HOUSEHOLD MANAGEMENT AND COOKERY. 18mo. 1s.
TEMPLE (Right Rev. Frederick, D.D., Bishop of London).—SERMONS PREACHED IN THE CHAPEL OF RUGBY SCHOOL. 3rd and Cheaper Edition. Extra fcp. 8vo. 4s. 6d.
—— SECOND SERIES. 3rd Ed. Ex. fcp. 8vo. 6s.
—— THIRD SERIES. 4th Ed. Ex. fcp. 8vo. 6s.
—— THE RELATIONS BETWEEN RELIGION AND SCIENCE. Bampton Lectures, 1884. 7th and Cheaper Edition. Crown 8vo. 6s.
TEMPLE (Sir Rd.).—LORD LAWRENCE. Portrait. Crown 8vo. 2s. 6d.
TENNYSON (Lord). — COMPLETE WORKS. New and enlarged Edition, with Portrait. Crown 8vo. 7s. 6d.
School Edition. In Four Parts. Crown 8vo. 2s. 6d. each.
—— POETICAL WORKS. *Pocket Edition.* 18mo, morocco, gilt edges.
—— WORKS. *Library Edition.* In 8 vols. Globe 8vo. 5s. each. Each volume may be had separately.—POEMS. 2 vols.—IDYLLS OF THE KING.—THE PRINCESS, AND MAUD. —ENOCH ARDEN, AND IN MEMORIAM.— BALLADS, AND OTHER POEMS. — QUEEN MARY, AND HAROLD.—BECKET, AND OTHER PLAYS.
—— WORKS. *Extra Fcp. 8vo. Edition,* on Hand-made Paper. In 7 volumes (supplied in sets only). 3l. 13s. 6d. — Vol. I. EARLY POEMS; II. LUCRETIUS, AND OTHER POEMS; III. IDYLLS OF THE KING; IV. THE PRINCESS, AND MAUD; V. ENOCH ARDEN, AND IN MEMORIAM; VI. QUEEN MARY, AND HAROLD; VII. BALLADS, & OTHER POEMS.
—— THE COLLECTED WORKS. Miniature Edition, in 14 vols., viz. THE POETICAL WORKS, 10 vols. in a box. 21s.—THE DRAMATIC WORKS, 4 vols. in a box. 10s. 6d.
—— LYRICAL POEMS. Selected and Annotated by Prof. F. T. PALGRAVE. 18mo. 4s.6d. Large Paper Edition. 8vo. 9s.
—— IN MEMORIAM. 18mo. 4s. 6d. Large Paper Edition. 8vo. 9s.

TENNYSON (Lord). — THE TENNYSON BIRTHDAY BOOK. Edit. by EMILY SHAKESPEAR. 18mo. 2s. 6d.
—— THE BROOK. With 20 Illustrations by A. WOODRUFF. 32mo. 2s. 6d.
—— SELECTIONS FROM TENNYSON. With Introduction and Notes, by F. J. ROWE, M.A., and W. T. WEBB, M.A. Globe 8vo. 3s. 6d.
—— A COMPANION TO "IN MEMORIAM." By ELIZABETH R. CHAPMAN. Globe 8vo. 2s.
—— *The Original Editions.* Fcp. 8vo.
POEMS. 6s.
MAUD, AND OTHER POEMS. 3s. 6d.
THE PRINCESS. 3s. 6d.
IDYLLS OF THE KING. (Collected.) 6s.
ENOCH ARDEN, etc. 3s. 6d.
THE HOLY GRAIL, AND OTHER POEMS. 4s.6d.
BALLADS, AND OTHER POEMS. 5s.
HAROLD: A DRAMA. 6s.
QUEEN MARY: A DRAMA. 6s.
THE CUP, AND THE FALCON. 5s.
BECKET. 6s.
TIRESIAS, AND OTHER POEMS. 6s.
LOCKSLEY HALL SIXTY YEARS AFTER, etc. 6s.
DEMETER, AND OTHER POEMS. 6s.
—— *The Royal Edition.* 1 vol. 8vo. 16s.
—— SELECTIONS FROM TENNYSON'S WORKS. Square 8vo. 3s. 6d.
—— SONGS FROM TENNYSON'S WRITINGS. Square 8vo. 2s. 6d.
TENNYSON (Hallam). — JACK AND THE BEAN-STALK. With 40 Illustrations by RANDOLPH CALDECOTT. Fcp. 4to. 3s. 6d.
TERENCE.—HAUTON TIMORUMENOS. Edit. by E. S. SHUCKBURGH, M.A. Fcp. 8vo. 3s.—With Translation, 4s. 6d.
—— PHORMIO. Edited by Rev. JOHN BOND, and A. S. WALPOLE. Fcp. 8vo. 4s. 6d.
—— SCENES FROM THE ANDRIA. Edited by F. W. CORNISH, M.A. 18mo. 1s. 6d.
TERESA (ST.): LIFE OF. By the Author of "Devotions before and after Holy Communion." Crown 8vo. 8s. 6d.
THACKERAY. By ANTHONY TROLLOPE. Crown 8vo. 1s. 6d.; sewed, 1s.
THEOCRITUS, BION, AND MOSCHUS. Rendered into English Prose, with Introductory Essay, by A. LANG, M.A. 18mo. 4s.6d. Large Paper Edition. 8vo. 9s.
THOMPSON (Edith).—HISTORY OF ENGLAND. New Edit., with Maps. 18mo. 2s.6d.
THOMPSON (Prof. Silvanus P.).—ELECTRICITY AND MAGNETISM, ELEMENTARY. Illustrated. New Edition. Fcp. 8vo. 4s. 6d.
THOMPSON (G. Carslake).—PUBLIC OPINION AND LORD BEACONSFIELD, 1875—80. 2 vols. 8vo. 36s.
THOMSON (Hugh).—DAYS WITH SIR ROGER DE COVERLEY. Illustrated. Fcp. 4to. 6s.
THOMSON (J. J.).—A TREATISE ON THE MOTION OF VORTEX RINGS. 8vo. 6s.
—— APPLICATIONS OF DYNAMICS TO PHYSICS AND CHEMISTRY. Crown 8vo. 7s. 6d.

THOMSON (Sir Wm.).—REPRINT OF PAPERS ON ELECTROSTATICS AND MAGNETISM. 2nd Edition. 8vo. 18s.
—— POPULAR LECTURES AND ADDRESSES. In 3 vols.—Vol. I. CONSTITUTION OF MATTER. Illustrated. Crown 8vo. 6s.
THOMSON (Sir C. Wyville).—THE DEPTHS OF THE SEA. An Account of the General Results of the Dredging Cruises of H.M.SS. "Lightning" and "Porcupine" during the Summers of 1868-69-70. With Illustrations, Maps, and Plans. 2nd Edit. 8vo. 31s. 6d.
—— THE VOYAGE OF THE "CHALLENGER": THE ATLANTIC. With Illustrations, Coloured Maps, Charts, etc. 2 vols. 8vo. 45s.
THORNTON (W. T.).--A PLEA FOR PEASANT PROPRIETORS. New Edit. Cr. 8vo. 7s. 6d.
—— OLD-FASHIONED ETHICS AND COMMON-SENSE METAPHYSICS. 8vo. 10s. 6d.
—— INDIAN PUBLIC WORKS, AND COGNATE INDIAN TOPICS. Crown 8vo. 8s. 6d.
—— WORD FOR WORD FROM HORACE: THE ODES LITERALLY VERSIFIED. Cr.8vo. 7s.6d.
THORNTON (J.).—FIRST LESSONS IN BOOK-KEEPING. New Edition. Crown 8vo. 2s. 6d.
—— KEY. Containing all the Exercises fully worked out, with brief Notes. Oblong 4to. 10s. 6d.
—— PRIMER OF BOOK-KEEPING. 18mo. 1s.
—— KEY. Demy 8vo. 2s. 6d.
THORPE (Prof. T. E.).—A SERIES OF PROBLEMS, FOR USE IN COLLEGES AND SCHOOLS. New Edition, with Key. 18mo. 2s.
THRING (Rev. Edward).—A CONSTRUING BOOK. Fcp. 8vo. 2s. 6d.
—— A LATIN GRADUAL. 2nd Ed. 18mo. 2s.6d.
—— THE ELEMENTS OF GRAMMAR TAUGHT IN ENGLISH. 5th Edition. 18mo. 2s.
—— EDUCATION AND SCHOOL. 2nd Edition. Crown 8vo. 6s.
—— A MANUAL OF MOOD CONSTRUCTIONS. Extra fcp. 8vo. 1s. 6d.
—— THOUGHTS ON LIFE SCIENCE. 2nd Edit. Crown 8vo. 7s. 6d.
—— A MEMORY OF EDWARD THRING. By J. H. SKRINE. Portrait. Crown 8vo. 6s.
THROUGH THE RANKS TO A COMMISSION. New Edit. Cr. 8vo. 2s. 6d.
THRUPP (Rev. J. F.).—INTRODUCTION TO THE STUDY AND USE OF THE PSALMS. 2nd Edition. 2 vols. 8vo. 21s.
THUCYDIDES.--THE SICILIAN EXPEDITION. Books VI. and VII. Edited by the Rev. PERCIVAL FROST, M.A. Fcp. 8vo. 5s.
—— THE RISE OF THE ATHENIAN EMPIRE. Being Selections from Book I. Edited by F. H. COLSON, M.A. 18mo. 1s. 6d.
—— THE CAPTURE OF SPHACTERIA. Book IV. Chaps. 1—41. Edit. by C. E. GRAVES, M.A. 18mo. 1s. 6d.
—— BOOK II. Ed. by E. C. MARCHANT, M.A.
—— BOOK IV. By the same. Fcp. 8vo. 5s.
—— BOOK IV. A Revision of the Text, illustrating the Principal Causes of Corruption in the Manuscripts of this Author. By WILLIAM G. RUTHERFORD, M.A., LL.D. 8vo. 7s.6d.

THUDICHUM (J. L. W.) and DUPRÉ (A.).—TREATISE ON THE ORIGIN, NATURE, AND VARIETIES OF WINE. Medium 8vo. 25s.
TODHUNTER (Isaac). -EUCLID FOR COLLEGES AND SCHOOLS. 18mo. 3s. 6d.
—— KEY TO EXERCISES IN EUCLID. Crown 8vo. 6s. 6d.
—— MENSURATION FOR BEGINNERS. With Examples. 18mo. 2s. 6d.
—— KEY TO MENSURATION FOR BEGINNERS. By Rev. FR. L. MCCARTHY. Cr. 8vo. 7s. 6d.
—— ALGEBRA FOR BEGINNERS. With numerous Examples. 18mo. 2s. 6d.
—— KEY TO ALGEBRA FOR BEGINNERS. Cr. 8vo. 6s. 6d.
—— ALGEBRA FOR THE USE OF COLLEGES AND SCHOOLS. Crown 8vo. 7s. 6d.
—— KEY TO ALGEBRA FOR COLLEGES AND SCHOOLS. Crown 8vo. 10s. 6d.
—— TRIGONOMETRY FOR BEGINNERS. With numerous Examples. 18mo. 2s. 6d.
—— KEY TO TRIGONOMETRY FOR BEGINNERS. Crown 8vo. 8s. 6d.
—— PLANE TRIGONOMETRY FOR COLLEGES AND SCHOOLS. Crown 8vo. 5s.
—— KEY TO PLANE TRIGONOMETRY. Crown 8vo. 10s. 6d.
—— A TREATISE ON SPHERICAL TRIGONOMETRY FOR THE USE OF COLLEGES AND SCHOOLS. Crown 8vo. 4s. 6d.
—— MECHANICS FOR BEGINNERS. With numerous Examples. 18mo. 4s. 6d.
—— KEY TO MECHANICS FOR BEGINNERS. 6s. 6d.
—— A TREATISE ON THE THEORY OF EQUATIONS. Crown 8vo. 7s. 6d.
—— A TREATISE ON PLANE CO-ORDINATE GEOMETRY. Crown 8vo. 7s. 6d.
—— SOLUTIONS AND PROBLEMS CONTAINED IN A TREATISE ON PLANE CO-ORDINATE GEOMETRY. By C. W. BOURNE, M.A. Crown 8vo. 10s. 6d.
—— A TREATISE ON THE DIFFERENTIAL CALCULUS. Crown 8vo. 10s. 6d.
—— KEY TO TREATISE ON THE DIFFERENTIAL CALCULUS. By H. ST. J. HUNTER, M.A. Crown 8vo. 10s. 6d.
—— A TREATISE ON THE INTEGRAL CALCULUS. Crown 8vo. 10s. 6d.
—— KEY TO TREATISE ON THE INTEGRAL CALCULUS AND ITS APPLICATIONS. By H. ST. J. HUNTER, M.A. Cr. 8vo. 10s. 6d.
—— EXAMPLES OF ANALYTICAL GEOMETRY OF THREE DIMENSIONS. Crown 8vo. 4s.
—— THE CONFLICT OF STUDIES. 8vo. 10s. 6d.
—— AN ELEMENTARY TREATISE ON LAPLACE'S, LAMÉ'S, AND BESSEL'S FUNCTIONS. Crown 8vo. 10s. 6d.
—— A TREATISE ON ANALYTICAL STATICS. Edited by J. D. EVERETT, M.A., F.R.S. 5th Edition. Crown 8vo. 10s. 6d.

LIST OF PUBLICATIONS. 55

TOM BROWN'S SCHOOL DAYS. By An Old Boy.
  Golden Treasury Edition. 18mo. 4s. 6d.
  Illustrated Edition. Crown 8vo. 6s.
  Uniform Edition. Crown 8vo. 3s. 6d.
  People's Edition. 18mo. 2s.
  People's Sixpenny Edition. With Illustrations. Medium 4to. 6d.—Also uniform with the Sixpenny Edition of Charles Kingsley's Novels. Medium 8vo. 6d.

TOM BROWN AT OXFORD. By the Author of "Tom Brown's School Days." Illustrated. Crown 8vo. 6s.
  Uniform Edition. Crown 8vo. 3s. 6d.

TOURGÉNIEF.—VIRGIN SOIL. Translated by ASHTON W. DILKE. Crown 8vo. 6s.

TOZER (H. F.).—CLASSICAL GEOGRAPHY. 18mo. 1s.

TRAILL (H. D.).—STERNE. Crown 8vo. 1s. 6d.; sewed, 1s.
  —— CENTRAL GOVERNMENT. Cr. 8vo. 3s. 6d.
  —— WILLIAM III. Crown 8vo. 2s. 6d.
  —— STRAFFORD. Portrait. Cr. 8vo. 2s. 6d.
  —— COLERIDGE. Cr. 8vo. 1s. 6d.; sewed, 1s.

TRENCH (R. Chenevix).—HULSEAN LECTURES. 8vo. 7s. 6d.

TRENCH (Capt. F.).—THE RUSSO-INDIAN QUESTION. Crown 8vo. 7s. 6d.

TREVELYAN (Sir Geo. Otto).—CAWNPORE. Crown 8vo. 6s.

TRISTRAM (W. Outram).—COACHING DAYS AND COACHING WAYS. Illustrated by HERBERT RAILTON and HUGH THOMSON. Extra Crown 4to. 21s.

TROLLOPE (Anthony).—THACKERAY. Cr. 8vo. 1s. 6d.; sewed, 1s.

TRUMAN(Jos.).—AFTER-THOUGHTS: POEMS. Crown 8vo. 3s. 6d.

TULLOCH (Principal).—THE CHRIST OF THE GOSPELS AND THE CHRIST OF MODERN CRITICISM. Extra fcp. 8vo. 4s. 6d.

TURNER'S LIBER STUDIORUM. A Description and a Catalogue. By W. G. RAWLINSON. Medium 8vo. 12s. 6d.

TURNER (Charles Tennyson).—COLLECTED SONNETS, OLD AND NEW. Ex. fcp. 8vo. 7s. 6d.

TURNER (Rev. Geo.).—SAMOA, A HUNDRED YEARS AGO AND LONG BEFORE. Preface by E. B. TYLOR, F.R.S. Crown 8vo. 9s.

TURNER (H. H.).—A COLLECTION OF EXAMPLES ON HEAT AND ELECTRICITY. Cr. 8vo. 2s. 6d.

TYLOR (E. B.).—ANTHROPOLOGY. With Illustrations. Crown 8vo. 7s. 6d.

TYRWHITT (Rev. R. St. John).—OUR SKETCHING CLUB. 4th Ed. Cr. 8vo. 7s. 6d.
  —— FREE FIELD. Lyrics, chiefly Descriptive. Globe 8vo. 3s. 6d.
  —— BATTLE AND AFTER: Concerning Sergt. Thomas Atkins, Grenadier Guards; and other Verses. Globe 8vo. 3s. 6d.

UHLAND.—SELECT BALLADS. Edited by G. E. FASNACHT. 18mo. 1s.

UNDERHILL (H. G.).—EASY EXERCISES IN GREEK ACCIDENCE. Globe 8vo. 2s.

UPPINGHAM BY THE SEA. By J. H. S. Crown 8vo. 3s. 6d.

VAUGHAN (Very Rev. Charles J.).—NOTES FOR LECTURES ON CONFIRMATION. 14th Edition. Fcp. 8vo. 1s. 6d.
  —— MEMORIALS OF HARROW SUNDAYS. 5th Edition. Crown 8vo. 10s. 6d.
  —— LECTURES ON THE EPISTLE TO THE PHILIPPIANS. 4th Edition. Cr. 8vo. 7s. 6d.
  —— LECTURES ON THE REVELATION OF ST. JOHN. 5th Edition. Crown 8vo. 10s. 6d.
  —— EPIPHANY, LENT, AND EASTER. 3rd Edition. Crown 8vo. 10s. 6d.
  —— HEROES OF FAITH. 2nd Ed. Cr. 8vo. 6s.
  —— THE BOOK AND THE LIFE, AND OTHER SERMONS. 3rd Edition. Fcp. 8vo. 4s. 6d.
  —— ST. PAUL'S EPISTLE TO THE ROMANS. The Greek Text with English Notes. 7th Edition. Crown 8vo. 7s. 6d.
  —— TWELVE DISCOURSES ON SUBJECTS CONNECTED WITH THE LITURGY AND WORSHIP OF THE CHURCH OF ENGLAND. 4th Edition Fcp. 8vo. 6s.
  —— WORDS FROM THE GOSPELS. 3rd Edition. Fcp. 8vo. 4s. 6d.
  —— THE EPISTLES OF ST. PAUL. For English Readers. Part I. containing the First Epistle to the Thessalonians. 2nd Ed. 8vo. 1s. 6d.
  —— THE CHURCH OF THE FIRST DAYS. Series I. THE CHURCH OF JERUSALEM. 3rd Edition. 4s. 6d.—II. THE CHURCH OF THE GENTILES. 4s. 6d.—III. THE CHURCH OF THE WORLD. Fcp. 8vo. 4s. 6d.
  —— LIFE'S WORK AND GOD'S DISCIPLINE. 3rd Edition. Extra fcp. 8vo. 2s. 6d.
  —— THE WHOLESOME WORDS OF JESUS CHRIST. 2nd Edition. Fcp. 8vo. 3s. 6d.
  —— FOES OF FAITH. 2nd Ed. Fcp. 8vo. 3s. 6d.
  —— CHRIST SATISFYING THE INSTINCTS OF HUMANITY. 2nd Edit. Ext. fcp. 8vo. 3s. 6d.
  —— COUNSELS FOR YOUNG STUDENTS. Fcp. 8vo. 2s. 6d.
  —— THE TWO GREAT TEMPTATIONS. 2nd Edition. Fcp. 8vo. 3s. 6d.
  —— ADDRESSES FOR YOUNG CLERGYMEN. Extra fcp. 8vo. 4s. 6d.
  —— "MY SON, GIVE ME THINE HEART." Extra fcp. 8vo. 5s.
  —— REST AWHILE. Addresses to Toilers in the Ministry. Extra fcp. 8vo. 5s.
  —— TEMPLE SERMONS. Crown 8vo. 10s. 6d.
  —— AUTHORISED OR REVISED? Sermons on some of the Texts in which the Revised Version differs from the Authorised. Crown 8vo. 7s. 6d.
  —— ST. PAUL'S EPISTLE TO THE PHILIPPIANS. With Translation, Paraphrase, and Notes for English Readers. Crown 8vo. 5s.
  —— LESSONS OF THE CROSS AND PASSION. WORDS FROM THE CROSS. THE REIGN OF SIN. THE LORD'S PRAYER. Four Courses of Lent Lectures. Crown 8vo. 10s. 6d.
  —— UNIVERSITY SERMONS, NEW AND OLD. Crown 8vo. 10s. 6d.
  —— THE EPISTLE TO THE HEBREWS. With Notes. Crown 8vo. 7s. 6d.

VAUGHAN (D. J.).—THE PRESENT TRIAL OF FAITH. Crown 8vo. 9s.
VAUGHAN (E. T.).—SOME REASONS OF OUR CHRISTIAN HOPE. Hulsean Lectures for 1875. Crown 8vo. 6s. 6d.
VAUGHAN (Robert).—STONES FROM THE QUARRY: Sermons. Crown 8vo. 5s.
VELEY (Marg.).—A GARDEN OF MEMORIES; MRS. AUSTIN; LIZZIE'S BARGAIN. Three Stories. 2 vols. Globe 8vo. 12s.
VENN (John). — ON SOME CHARACTERISTICS OF BELIEF, SCIENTIFIC AND RELIGIOUS. Hulsean Lectures, 1869. 8vo. 7s. 6d.
—— THE LOGIC OF CHANCE. 2nd Edition. Crown 8vo. 10s. 6d.
—— SYMBOLIC LOGIC. Crown 8vo. 10s. 6d.
—— THE PRINCIPLES OF EMPIRICAL OR INDUCTIVE LOGIC. 8vo. 18s.
VERNEY (Lady).—HOW THE PEASANT OWNER LIVES IN PARTS OF FRANCE, GERMANY, ITALY, AND RUSSIA. Cr. 8vo. 3s. 6d.
VERRALL (A. W.).—STUDIES, LITERARY AND HISTORICAL, IN THE ODES OF HORACE. 8vo. 8s. 6d.
VERRALL (Mrs. M. de G.) and HARRISON (Miss Jane E.).—MYTHOLOGY AND MONUMENTS OF ANCIENT ATHENS. Illustrated. Crown 8vo. 16s.
VICTORIA UNIVERSITY CALENDAR, 1890. Crown 8vo. 1s.
VICTOR EMMANUEL II., FIRST KING OF ITALY. By G. S. GODKIN. 2nd Edition. Crown 8vo. 6s.
VIDA: STUDY OF A GIRL. By AMY DUNSMUIR. 3rd Edition. Crown 8vo. 6s.
VINCENT (Sir E.) and DICKSON (T. G.).— HANDBOOK TO MODERN GREEK. 3rd Ed. Crown 8vo. 6s.
VIRGIL.—THE WORKS OF VIRGIL RENDERED INTO ENGLISH PROSE. By JAS. LONSDALE, M.A., and S. LEE, M.A. Globe 8vo. 3s. 6d.
—— THE ÆNEID. Transl. into English Prose by J. W. MACKAIL, M.A. Cr. 8vo. 7s. 6d.
—— GEORGICS, I. Edited by T. E. PAGE, M.A. 18mo. 1s. 6d.
—— GEORGICS II. Edited by Rev. J. H. SKRINE, M.A. 18mo. 1s. 6d.
—— ÆNEID, I. Edited by A. S. WALPOLE, M.A. 18mo. 1s. 6d.
—— ÆNEID, II. Ed. by T. E. PAGE. 18mo. 1s. 6d.
—— ÆNEID, II. and III.: THE NARRATIVE OF ÆNEAS. Edit. by E. W. HOWSON, M.A. Fcp. 8vo. 3s.
—— ÆNEID, III. Edited by T. E. PAGE, M.A. 18mo. 1s. 6d.
—— ÆNEID, IV. Edited by Rev. H. M. STEPHENSON, M.A. 18mo. 1s. 6d.
—— ÆNEID, V.: THE FUNERAL GAMES. Ed. by Rev. A. CALVERT, M.A. 18mo. 1s. 6d.
—— ÆNEID, VI. Edit. by T. E. PAGE, M.A. 18mo. 1s. 6d.
—— ÆNEID, VII.: THE WRATH OF TURNUS. Ed. by Rev. A. CALVERT, M.A. 18mo. 1s. 6d.
—— ÆNEID, VIII. Ed. by Rev. A. CALVERT.
—— ÆNEID, IX. Edited by Rev. H. M. STEPHENSON, M.A. 18mo. 1s. 6d.

VIRGIL.—ÆNEID X. Edited by S. G OWEN, M.A.
—— SELECTIONS. Edited by E. S. SHUCKBURGH, M.A. 18mo. 1s. 6d.
VIRGIL. By Prof. NETTLESHIP. 8vo. 1s. 6d.
VITA.—LINKS AND CLUES. By VITA (the Hon. Lady WELBY-GREGORY). 2nd Edition. Crown 8vo. 6s.
VOICES CRYING IN THE WILDERNESS. A Novel. Crown 8vo. 7s. 6d.
VOLTAIRE.—HISTOIRE DE CHARLES XII., ROI DE SUÉDE. Edited by G. EUGÈNE FASNACHT. 18mo. 3s. 6d.
VOLTAIRE. By JOHN MORLEY. Gl. 8vo. 5s.
WALDSTEIN (C.).—CATALOGUE OF CASTS IN THE MUSEUM OF CLASSICAL ARCHÆOLOGY, CAMBRIDGE. Crown 8vo. 1s. 6d. Large Paper Edition. Small 4to. 5s.
WALKER (Prof. Francis A.).—THE WAGES QUESTION. 8vo. 14s.
—— MONEY. 8vo. 16s.
—— MONEY IN ITS RELATION TO TRADE AND INDUSTRY. Crown 8vo. 7s. 6d.
—— POLITICAL ECONOMY. 2nd Ed. 8vo. 12s. 6d.
—— A BRIEF TEXT-BOOK OF POLITICAL ECONOMY. Crown 8vo. 6s. 6d.
—— LAND AND ITS RENT. Fcp. 8vo. 3s. 6d.
—— FIRST LESSONS IN POLITICAL ECONOMY. Crown 8vo. 5s.
WALLACE (Alfred Russel).—THE MALAY ARCHIPELAGO: THE LAND OF THE ORANG UTANG AND THE BIRD OF PARADISE. Maps and Illustrations. 9th Ed. Cr. 8vo. 7s. 6d.
—— THE GEOGRAPHICAL DISTRIBUTION OF ANIMALS. With Illustrations and Maps. 2 vols. Medium 8vo. 42s.
—— ISLAND LIFE. With Illustrations and Maps. Demy 8vo. 18s.
—— BAD TIMES. An Essay on the present Depression of Trade. Crown 8vo. 2s. 6d.
—— DARWINISM. An Exposition of the Theory of Natural Selection, with some of its Applications. Illustrated. 3rd Ed. Cr. 8vo. 9s.
WALLACE (Sir D. Mackenzie).—EGYPT AND THE EGYPTIAN QUESTION. 8vo. 14s.
WALPOLE (Spencer).—FOREIGN RELATIONS. Crown 8vo. 3s. 6d.
—— THE ELECTORATE AND LEGISLATURE. Crown 8vo. 3s. 6d.
WALPOLE. By JOHN MORLEY. Cr. 8vo. 2s. 6d.
WALTON and COTTON—LOWELL.—THE COMPLETE ANGLER; OR, THE CONTEMPLATIVE MAN'S RECREATION OF IZAAK WALTON AND THOMAS COTTON. With an Introduction by JAS. RUSSELL LOWELL. Illustrated. Extra crown 8vo. 2l. 12s. 6d. net.
Also an Edition on large paper, Proofs on Japanese paper. 3l. 13s. 6d. net.
WANDERING WILLIE. By the Author of "Conrad the Squirrel." Globe 8vo. 5s.
WARD (Prof. A. W.).—A HISTORY OF ENGLISH DRAMATIC LITERATURE, TO THE DEATH OF QUEEN ANNE. 2 vols. 8vo. 32s.
—— CHAUCER. Cr. 8vo. 1s. 6d.; sewed, 1s.
—— DICKENS. Cr. 8vo. 1s. 6d.; sewed, 1s.

LIST OF PUBLICATIONS. 57

WARD (Prof. H. M.).—TIMBER AND SOME OF ITS DISEASES. Illustrated. Cr. 8vo. 6s.

WARD (John).—EXPERIENCES OF A DIPLOMATIST. 8vo. 10s. 6d.

WARD (T. H.).—ENGLISH POETS. Selections, with Critical Introductions by various Writers, and a General Introduction by MATTHEW ARNOLD. Edited by T. H. WARD, M.A. 4 vols. 2nd Ed. Crown 8vo. 7s. 6d. each.—Vol. I. CHAUCER TO DONNE.—II. BEN JONSON TO DRYDEN.—III. ADDISON TO BLAKE.—IV. WORDSWORTH TO ROSSETTI.

WARD (Mrs. T. Humphry).—MILLY AND OLLY. With Illustrations by Mrs. ALMA TADEMA. Globe 8vo. 2s. 6d.

—— MISS BRETHERTON. Crown 8vo. 3s. 6d.

—— THE JOURNAL INTIME OF HENRI-FRÉDÉRIC AMIEL. Translated, with an Introduction and Notes. 2nd Ed. Cr. 8vo. 6s.

WARD (Samuel).—LYRICAL RECREATIONS. Fcp. 8vo. 6s.

WARD (W.).—WILLIAM GEORGE WARD AND THE OXFORD MOVEMENT. Portrait. 8vo. 14s.

WARINGTON (G.).—THE WEEK OF CREATION. Crown 8vo. 4s. 6d.

WARREN HASTINGS. By Sir ALFRED LYALL. With Portrait. Cr. 8vo. 2s. 6d.

WATERTON (Charles).—WANDERINGS IN SOUTH AMERICA, THE NORTH-WEST OF THE UNITED STATES, AND THE ANTILLES. Edited by Rev. J. G. WOOD. With 100 Illustrations. Crown 8vo. 6s.
People's Edition. With 100 Illustrations. Medium 4to. 6d.

WATSON. A RECORD OF ELLEN WATSON. By ANNA BUCKLAND. Crown 8vo. 6s.

WATSON (R. Spence).—A VISIT TO WAZAN, THE SACRED CITY OF MOROCCO. 8vo. 10s.6d.

WEBSTER (Augusta).—DAFFODIL AND THE CROAXAXICANS. Crown 8vo. 6s.

WELBY-GREGORY (The Hon. Lady).—LINKS AND CLUES. 2nd Edition. Crown 8vo. 6s.

WELCH (Wm.) and DUFFIELD (C. G.).—LATIN ACCIDENCE AND EXERCISES ARRANGED FOR BEGINNERS. 18mo. 1s. 6d.

WELLDON (Rev. J. E. C.).—THE SPIRITUAL LIFE, AND OTHER SERMONS. Cr. 8vo. 6s.

WELLINGTON. By Geo. HOOPER. With Portrait. Crown 8vo. 2s. 6d.

WESTBURY (Hugh).—FREDERICK HAZZLEDEN. 3 vols. Crown 8vo. 31s. 6d.

WESTCOTT (The Rt. Rev. Bishop.)—A GENERAL SURVEY OF THE HISTORY OF THE CANON OF THE NEW TESTAMENT DURING THE FIRST FOUR CENTURIES. 6th Edition. Crown 8vo. 10s. 6d.

—— INTRODUCTION TO THE STUDY OF THE FOUR GOSPELS. 7th Ed. Cr. 8vo. 10s. 6d.

—— THE GOSPEL OF THE RESURRECTION. 6th Edition. Crown 8vo. 6s.

—— THE BIBLE IN THE CHURCH. 10th Edit. 18mo. 4s. 6d.

—— THE CHRISTIAN LIFE, MANIFOLD AND ONE. Crown 8vo. 2s. 6d.

—— ON THE RELIGIOUS OFFICE OF THE UNIVERSITIES. Sermons. Cr. 8vo. 4s. 6d.

WESTCOTT (Bishop).—THE REVELATION OF THE RISEN LORD. 4th Edition. Crown 8vo. 6s.

—— THE HISTORIC FAITH. 3rd Edition. Cr. 8vo. 6s.

—— THE EPISTLES OF ST. JOHN. The Greek Text, with Notes. 2nd Edition. 8vo. 12s. 6d.

—— THE REVELATION OF THE FATHER. Cr. 8vo. 6s.

—— CHRISTUS CONSUMMATOR. 2nd Edition. Crown 8vo. 6s.

—— SOME THOUGHTS FROM THE ORDINAL. Crown 8vo. 1s. 6d.

—— SOCIAL ASPECTS OF CHRISTIANITY. Cr. 8vo. 6s.

—— GIFTS FOR MINISTRY. Addresses to Candidates for Ordination. Crown 8vo. 1s. 6d.

—— THE EPISTLE TO THE HEBREWS. The Greek Text, with Notes and Essays. 8vo. 14s.

—— THE VICTORY OF THE CROSS. Sermons preached during Holy Week, 1888, in Hereford Cathedral. Crown 8vo. 3s. 6d.

—— FROM STRENGTH TO STRENGTH. Three Sermons (In Memoriam J. B. D.) Cr. 8vo. 2s.

—— THOUGHTS ON REVELATION AND LIFE. Selections from the Writings of Canon WESTCOTT. Edited by Rev. S. PHILLIPS. Crown 8vo. 6s.

WESTCOTT (Bishop) and HORT (Prof.).—THE NEW TESTAMENT IN THE ORIGINAL GREEK. Revised Text. 2 vols. Crown 8vo. 10s. 6d. each.—Vol. I. Text.—Vol. II. The Introduction and Appendix.

—— THE NEW TESTAMENT IN THE ORIGINAL GREEK. An Edition for Schools. The Text revised by Bp. WESTCOTT and Dr. HORT. 18mo, 4s.6d.; roan, 5s. 6d.; morocco, 6s. 6d.

WETHERELL (J.).—EXERCISES ON MORRIS' PRIMER OF ENGLISH GRAMMAR. 18mo. 1s.

WHEELER (J. Talboys).—A SHORT HISTORY OF INDIA. With Maps. Crown 8vo. 12s.

—— INDIA UNDER BRITISH RULE. 8vo. 12s.6d.

—— COLLEGE HISTORY OF INDIA. Asiatic and European. Crown 8vo. 3s. 6d.

—— PRIMER OF INDIAN HISTORY, ASIATIC AND EUROPEAN. 18mo. 1s.

WHEN I WAS A LITTLE GIRL. By the Author of "St. Olave's." With Illustrations. Globe 8vo. 2s. 6d.

WHEN PAPA COMES HOME. By the Author of "When I was a Little Girl." With Illustrations. Globe 8vo. 4s. 6d.

WHEWELL. DR. WILLIAM WHEWELL, late Master of Trinity College, Cambridge. An Account of his Writings, with Selections from his Literary and Scientific Correspondence. By I. TODHUNTER, M.A. 2 vols. 8vo. 25s.

WHITE (Gilbert).—NATURAL HISTORY AND ANTIQUITIES OF SELBORNE. Edited by FRANK BUCKLAND. With a Chapter on Antiquities by Lord SELBORNE. Cr.8vo. 6s.

WHITE (John Williams).—A SERIES OF FIRST LESSONS IN GREEK. Adapted to GOODWIN'S Greek Grammar. Crown 8vo. 3s. 6d.

WHITE (Dr. W. Hale).—A TEXT-BOOK OF GENERAL THERAPEUTICS. Illustrated. Cr. 8vo. 8s. 6d.

WHITHAM (Prof. J. M.).—STEAM ENGINE DESIGN. Illustrated. 8vo. 25s.

WHITNEY (Prof. W. D.).—A COMPENDIOUS GERMAN GRAMMAR. Crown 8vo. 4s. 6d.

—— A GERMAN READER IN PROSE AND VERSE. With Notes and Vocabulary. Cr. 8vo. 5s.

—— A COMPENDIOUS GERMAN AND ENGLISH DICTIONARY. Crown 8vo. 7s. 6d.—German-English Part separately. 5s.

WHITTIER.—COMPLETE POETICAL WORKS OF JOHN GREENLEAF WHITTIER. With Portrait. 18mo. 4s. 6d.

—— THE COMPLETE WORKS OF JOHN GREENLEAF WHITTIER. 7 vols. Crown 8vo. 6s. each.—Vol. I. NARRATIVE AND LEGENDARY POEMS.—II. POEMS OF NATURE; POEMS SUBJECTIVE AND REMINISCENT; RELIGIOUS POEMS.—III. ANTI-SLAVERY POEMS; SONGS OF LABOUR AND REFORM.—IV. PERSONAL POEMS; OCCASIONAL POEMS; THE TENT ON THE BEACH; with the Poems of ELIZABETH H. WHITTIER, and an Appendix containing Early and Uncollected Verses.—V. MARGARET SMITH'S JOURNAL; TALES AND SKETCHES. — VI. OLD PORTRAITS AND MODERN SKETCHES; PERSONAL SKETCHES AND TRIBUTES; HISTORICAL PAPERS.—VII. THE CONFLICT WITH SLAVERY, POLITICS AND REFORM; THE INNER LIFE, CRITICISM.

WICKHAM (Rev. E. C.)—WELLINGTON COLLEGE SERMONS. Crown 8vo. 6s.

WICKSTEED (Philip H.).—ALPHABET OF ECONOMIC SCIENCE.—I. ELEMENTS OF THE THEORY OF VALUE OR WORTH. Globe 8vo. 2s. 6d.

WIEDERSHEIM—PARKER.—ELEMENTS OF THE COMPARATIVE ANATOMY OF VERTEBRATES. Adapted from the German of Prof. ROBERT WIEDERSHEIM, by Prof. W. NEWTON PARKER. Illustrated. Medium 8vo. 12s. 6d.

WILBRAHAM (Frances M.).—IN THE SERE AND YELLOW LEAF: THOUGHTS AND RECOLLECTIONS FOR OLD AND YOUNG. Globe 8vo. 3s. 6d.

WILKINS (Prof. A. S.).—THE LIGHT OF THE WORLD: AN ESSAY. 2nd Ed. Cr.8vo. 3s. 6d.

—— ROMAN ANTIQUITIES. Illustr. 18mo. 1s.

—— ROMAN LITERATURE. 18mo. 1s.

WILKINSON (S.). — THE BRAIN OF AN ARMY. A Popular Account of the German General Staff. Crown 8vo. 2s. 6d.

WILLIAM THE CONQUEROR. By EDWARD A. FREEMAN, D.C.L., LL.D. Crown 8vo. 2s. 6d.

WILLIAM III. By H. D. TRAILL. Crown 8vo. 2s. 6d.

WILLIAMS (Montagu).—LEAVES OF A LIFE. 15th Thousand. Crown 8vo. 3s. 6d.; sewed, 2s. 6d.

WILLIAMS (S. E.).—FORENSIC FACTS AND FALLACIES. Globe 8vo. 4s. 6d.

WILLOUGHBY (F.).—FAIRY GUARDIANS. Illustr. by TOWNLEV GREEN. Cr. 8vo. 5s.

WILLS (W. G.).—MELCHIOR: A POEM. Cr. 8vo. 9s.

WILSON (A. J.). THE NATIONAL BUDGET; THE NATIONAL DEBT; RATES AND TAXES. Crown 8vo. 3s. 6d.

WILSON (Dr. George).- RELIGIO CHEMICI. Crown 8vo. 8s. 6d.

—— THE FIVE GATEWAYS OF KNOWLEDGE. 9th Edition. Extra fcp. 8vo. 2s. 6d.

WILSON. MEMOIR OF PROF. GEORGE WILSON, M.D. By HIS SISTER. With Portrait. 2nd Edition. Crown 8vo. 6s.

WILSON (Rev. Canon).—THE BIBLE STUDENT'S GUIDE. 2nd Edition. 4to. 25s.

WILSON (Sir Chas.).—CLIVE. With Portrait. Crown 8vo. 2s. 6d.

WILSON (Sir Daniel, LL.D.).—PREHISTORIC ANNALS OF SCOTLAND. With Illustrations. 2 vols. Demy 8vo. 36s.

—— PREHISTORIC MAN: RESEARCHES INTO THE ORIGIN OF CIVILISATION IN THE OLD AND NEW WORLD. 3rd Edition. With Illustrations. 2 vols. Medium 8vo. 36s.

—— CHATTERTON: A BIOGRAPHICAL STUDY. Crown 8vo. 6s. 6d.

—— CALIBAN: A CRITIQUE ON SHAKESPEARE'S "TEMPEST" AND " A MIDSUMMER NIGHT'S DREAM." 8vo. 10s. 6d.

WILSON (Rev. J. M.).—SERMONS PREACHED IN CLIFTON COLLEGE CHAPEL, 1879—83. Crown 8vo. 6s.

—— ESSAYS AND ADDRESSES. Cr. 8vo. 4s.6d.

—— SOME CONTRIBUTIONS TO THE RELIGIOUS THOUGHT OF OUR TIME. Crown 8vo. 6s.

—— ELEMENTARY GEOMETRY. Books I.—V. Containing the Subjects of Euclid's First Six Books, following the Syllabus of Geometry prepared by the Geometrical Association. Extra fcp. 8vo. 4s. 6d.

—— SOLID GEOMETRY AND CONIC SECTIONS. Extra fcp. 8vo. 3s. 6d.

WINKWORTH (Catherine). — CHRISTIAN SINGERS OF GERMANY. Crown 8vo. 4s. 6d.

WOLSELEY (General Viscount).—THE SOLDIER'S POCKET-BOOK FOR FIELD SERVICE. 5th Edition. 16mo, roan. 5s.

—— FIELD POCKET-BOOK FOR THE AUXILIARY FORCES. 16mo. 1s. 6d.

WOLSEY (CARDINAL). By Prof. M. CREIGHTON. Crown 8vo. 2s. 6d.

WOLSTENHOLME (Joseph). — MATHEMATICAL PROBLEMS ON SUBJECTS INCLUDED IN THE FIRST AND SECOND DIVISION OF THE SCHEDULE OF SUBJECTS FOR THE CAMBRIDGE MATHEMATICAL TRIPOS EXAMINATION. 2nd Edition. 8vo. 18s.

—— EXAMPLES FOR PRACTICE IN THE USE OF SEVEN-FIGURE LOGARITHMS. 8vo. 5s.

WOOD (Andrew Goldie).—THE ISLES OF THE BLEST, AND OTHER POEMS. Globe 8vo. 5s.

WOOD (Rev. E. G.).—THE REGAL POWER OF THE CHURCH. 8vo. 4s. 6d.

WOODS (Miss M. A.).—A FIRST POETRY BOOK. Fcp. 8vo. 2s. 6d.

—— A SECOND POETRY BOOK. 2 Parts. Fcp. 8vo. 2s. 6d. each.

—— A THIRD POETRY BOOK. Fcp. 8vo. 4s. 6d.

LIST OF PUBLICATIONS. 59

WOOLNER (Thomas). MY BEAUTIFUL LADY. 3rd Edition. Fcp. 8vo. 5s.
—— PYGMALION: A POEM. Cr. 8vo. 7s. 6d.
—— SILENUS: A POEM. Crown 8vo. 6s.
WOOLWICH MATHEMATICAL PAPERS. For Admission in the Royal Military Academy for the Years 1880—88. Edit. by E. J. BROOKSMITH, B.A. Cr. 8vo. 6s.
WORDS FROM THE POETS. With a Vignette and Frontispiece. 12th Ed. 18mo. 1s.
WORDSWORTH. By F. W. H. MYERS. Crown 8vo. 1s. 6d.; sewed, 1s.
—— SELECT POEMS. Edited by MATTHEW ARNOLD. 18mo. 4s. 6d.
Large Paper Edition. 8vo. 9s.
—— THE RECLUSE: A POEM. Fcp. 8vo. 2s. 6d.
—— THE COMPLETE POETICAL WORKS. Copyright Edition. With an Introduction by JOHN MORLEY, and Portrait. Cr. 8vo. 7s. 6d.
WORDSWORTHIANA: A SELECTION OF PAPERS READ TO THE WORDSWORTH SOCIETY. Ed. by W. KNIGHT. Cr. 8vo. 7s. 6d.
WORSHIP (THE) OF GOD, AND FELLOWSHIP AMONG MEN. By the late Prof. MAURICE and others. Fcp. 8vo. 3s. 6d.
WORTHEY (Mrs.).—THE NEW CONTINENT: A NOVEL. 2 vols. Globe 8vo. 12s.
WRIGHT (Rev. Arthur).—THE COMPOSITION OF THE FOUR GOSPELS. Crown 8vo. 5s.
WRIGHT (Miss Guthrie).—THE SCHOOL COOKERY-BOOK. 18mo. 1s.
WRIGHT (Rev. Josiah).—THE SEVEN KINGS OF ROME. Abridged from the First Book of Livy. 8th Edition. Fcp. 8vo. 3s. 6d.
—— FIRST LATIN STEPS. Crown 8vo. 3s.
—— ATTIC PRIMER. Crown 8vo. 2s. 6d.
—— A COMPLETE LATIN COURSE. Crown 8vo. 2s. 6d.
WRIGHT (Dr. Alder). METALS AND THEIR CHIEF INDUSTRIAL APPLICATIONS. Extra fcp. 8vo. 3s. 6d.
WRIGHT (Lewis). LIGHT. A Course of Experimental Optics, chiefly with the Lantern. With Illustrations and Coloured Plates. Crown 8vo. 7s. 6d.
WRIGHT (W. Aldis). -THE BIBLE WORDBOOK. 2nd Edition. Crown 8vo. 7s. 6d.
WURTZ.—A HISTORY OF CHEMICAL THEORY. By AD. WURTZ. Translated by HENRY WATTS, F.R.S. Crown 8vo. 6s.
WYATT (Sir M. Digby).—FINE ART: A Sketch of its History, Theory, Practice, and Application to Industry. 8vo. 5s.
XENOPHON.—THE COMPLETE WORKS. Translated by H. G. DAKYNS, M.A. 4 vols. Crown 8vo.—Vol. I. "THE ANABASIS" AND BOOKS I. AND II. OF "THE HELLENICA." 10s. 6d.
—— ANABASIS. Book I. chaps. 1—8. For the Use of Beginners. Edited by E. A. WELLS. M.A. 18mo. 1s. 6d.
—— ANABASIS. Book I. With Notes and Vocabulary, by A. S. WALPOLE. 18mo. 1s. 6d.
—— ANABASIS. Book II. Edited by A. S. WALPOLE, M.A. 18mo. 1s. 6d.

XENOPHON.—ANABASIS. Book III. Ed. by Rev. G. H. NALL, M.A. 18mo. 1s. 6d.
—— ANABASIS. Book IV. Edited by Rev. E. D. STONE, M.A. 18mo. 1s. 6d.
—— ANABASIS. Books I. IV. Edited, with Notes, by Professors W. W. GOODWIN and J. W. WHITE. Fcp. 8vo. 5s.
—— SELECTIONS FROM BOOK IV. OF THE ANABASIS. Edited by Rev. E. D. STONE, M.A. 18mo. 1s. 6d.
—— CYROPÆDIA. Books VII. and VIII. Edited by Prof. ALFRED GOODWIN, M.A. Fcp. 8vo. 5s.
—— SELECTIONS FROM THE CYROPÆDIA. Edit. by Rev. A. H. COOKE. 18mo. 1s. 6d.
—— HELLENICA. Books I. and II. Edited by H. HAILSTONE, M.A. With Map. Fcp. 8vo. 4s. 6d.
—— HIERO. Edited by Rev. H. A. HOLDEN, LL.D. Fcp. 8vo. 3s. 6d.
—— MEMORABILIA SOCRATIS. Edited by A. R. CLUER, B.A. Fcp. 8vo. 6s.
—— OECONOMICUS. Edited by Rev. H. A. HOLDEN, LL.D. Fcp. 8vo. 6s.
YONGE (Charlotte M.).—NOVELS AND TALES. Crown 8vo. 3s. 6d. each.
 1. THE HEIR OF REDCLYFFE.
 2. HEARTSEASE.
 3. HOPES AND FEARS.
 4. DYNEVOR TERRACE.
 5. THE DAISY CHAIN.
 6. THE TRIAL: MORE LINKS OF THE DAISY CHAIN.
 7. PILLARS OF THE HOUSE. Vol. I.
 8. PILLARS OF THE HOUSE. Vol. II.
 9. THE YOUNG STEPMOTHER.
10. CLEVER WOMAN OF THE FAMILY.
11. THE THREE BRIDES.
12. MY YOUNG ALCIDES.
13. THE CAGED LION.
14. THE DOVE IN THE EAGLE'S NEST.
15. THE CHAPLET OF PEARLS.
16. LADY HESTER: AND THE DANVERS PAPERS.
17. MAGNUM BONUM.
18. LOVE AND LIFE.
19. UNKNOWN TO HISTORY.
20. STRAY PEARLS.
21. THE ARMOURER'S PRENTICES.
22. THE TWO SIDES OF THE SHIELD.
23. NUTTIE'S FATHER.
24. SCENES AND CHARACTERS.
25. CHANTRY HOUSE.
26. A MODERN TELEMACHUS.
27. BYE WORDS.
28. BEECHCROFT AT ROCKSTONE.
—— THE POPULATION OF AN OLD PEARTREE; OR, STORIES OF INSECT LIFE. From the French of E. VAN BRUYSSEL. Illustrated. Globe 8vo. 2s. 6d.
—— A REPUTED CHANGELING; OR, THREE SEVENTH YEARS TWO CENTURIES AGO. 2 vols. Crown 8vo. 12s.
—— THE PRINCE AND THE PAGE. Gl. 8vo. 4s. 6d.
—— A BOOK OF GOLDEN DEEDS. 18mo. 4s. 6d.
 Cheap Edition. 18mo. 1s.
 Globe Readings Edition. Globe 8vo. 2s.
—— P'S AND Q'S; OR, THE QUESTION OF PUTTING UPON. Illustrated. Gl. 8vo. 4s. 6d.

YONGE (Charlotte M.).—THE LANCES OF LYNWOOD. Illustrated. Globe 8vo. 2s. 6d.
—— LITTLE LUCY'S WONDERFUL GLOBE. Illustrated. Globe 8vo. 4s. 6d.
—— THE LITTLE DUKE. Illustrated. Globe 8vo. 2s. 6d.
—— A BOOK OF WORTHIES: GATHERED FROM THE OLD HISTORIES AND WRITTEN ANEW. 18mo. 4s. 6d.
—— CAMEOS FROM ENGLISH HISTORY. Extra fcp. 8vo. 5s. each.—Vol. I. FROM ROLLO TO EDWARD II.—Vol. II. THE WARS IN FRANCE. —Vol. III. THE WARS OF THE ROSES. —Vol. IV. REFORMATION TIMES.—Vol. V. ENGLAND AND SPAIN. — Vol. VI. FORTY YEARS OF STUART RULE (1603—1643).— Vol. VII. THE REBELLION AND RESTORATION (1642—78).
—— SCRIPTURE READINGS FOR SCHOOLS AND FAMILIES. Globe 8vo. 1s. 6d. each; also with Comments, 3s. 6d. each.—GENESIS TO DEUTERONOMY.—Second Series: JOSHUA TO SOLOMON.—Third Series: KINGS AND THE PROPHETS.—Fourth Series: THE GOSPEL TIMES.—Fifth Series: APOSTOLIC TIMES.
—— FRANCE. 18mo. 1s.
—— HISTORY OF FRANCE. Maps. 18mo. 3s. 6d.
—— THE LIFE OF JOHN COLERIDGE PATTESON. 2 vols. Crown 8vo. 12s.

YONGE (Charlotte M.).—THE PUPILS OF ST. JOHN. Illustrated. Crown 8vo. 6s.
—— PIONEERS AND FOUNDERS; OR, RECENT WORKERS IN THE MISSION FIELD. Crown 8vo. 6s.
—— THE STORY OF THE CHRISTIANS AND MOORS IN SPAIN. 18mo. 4s. 6d.
—— HISTORY OF CHRISTIAN NAMES. New Edition, revised. Crown 8vo. 7s. 6d.
—— THE HERB OF THE FIELD. A New Edition, revised. Crown 8vo. 5s.
—— THE VICTORIAN HALF-CENTURY. Crown 8vo. 1s. 6d.; sewed, 1s.
—— MORE BYE WORDS. 1 vol. Crn. 8vo. 6s.
YOUNG (E. W.).—SIMPLE PRACTICAL METHODS OF CALCULATING STRAINS ON GIRDERS, ARCHES, AND TRUSSES. 8vo. 7s. 6d.
ZECHARIAH. THE HEBREW STUDENT'S COMMENTARY ON ZECHARIAH, HEBREW AND LXX. By W. H. LOWE, M.A. 8vo. 10s. 6d.
ZIEGLER.—A TEXT-BOOK OF PATHOLOGICAL ANATOMY AND PATHOGENESIS. By ERNST ZIEGLER. Translated and Edited for English Students by DONALD MACALISTER, M.A., M.D. With Illustrations. 8vo.—Part I. GENERAL PATHOLOGICAL ANATOMY. 2nd Edition. 12s. 6d.—Part II. SPECIAL PATHOLOGICAL ANATOMY. Sections I.—VIII. 2nd Edition. 12s. 6d. Sections IX.—XII. 8vo. 12s. 6d.

MACMILLAN AND CO., LONDON.

J. PALMER, PRINTER, ALEXANDRA STREET, CAMBRIDGE.

30/9/90

www.ingramcontent.com/pod-product-compliance
Lightning Source LLC
Chambersburg PA
CBHW021419300426
44114CB00010B/567